CHARLES R. SWINDOLL

SWINDOLL'S LIVING INSIGHTS

NEW TESTAMENT COMMENTARY

LUKE

Tyndale House Publishers, Inc.
Carol Stream, Illinois

Swindoll's Living Insights New Testament Commentary, Volume 3

Visit Tyndale online at www.tyndale.com.

Designed by Nicole Grimes

Published in association with Yates & Yates, LLP (www.yates2.com).

Library of Congress Cataloging-in-Publication Data
Names: Swindoll, Charles R., author.
Title: Luke / Charles R Swindoll.
Other titles: Insights on Luke
Description: Carol Stream, Illinois : Tyndale House Publishers, Inc., 2017. |
   Series: Swindoll's living insights New Testament commentary ; Volume 3 |
   Originally published under title: Insights on Luke : Grand Rapids, Mich. :
   Zondervan, c2011. | Includes bibliographical references.
Identifiers: LCCN 2017012255 | ISBN 9781414393803 (hc)
Subjects: LCSH: Bible. Luke—Commentaries.
Classification: LCC BS2595.53 .S95 2017 | DDC 226.4/07—dc23 LC record available at
   https://lccn.loc.gov/2017012255

Printed in China

23   22   21   20   19   18   17
7   6   5   4   3   2   1

CONTENTS

AUTHOR'S PREFACE

For more than sixty years I have loved the Bible. It was that love for the Scriptures, mixed with a clear call into the gospel ministry during my tour of duty in the Marine Corps, that resulted in my going to Dallas Theological Seminary to prepare for a lifetime of ministry. During those four great years I had the privilege of studying under outstanding men of God, who also loved God's Word. They not only held the inerrant Word of God in high esteem, they taught it carefully, preached it passionately, and modeled it consistently. A week never passes without my giving thanks to God for the grand heritage that has been mine to claim! I am forever indebted to those fine theologians and mentors, who cultivated in me a strong commitment to the understanding, exposition, and application of God's truth.

For more than fifty years I have been engaged in doing just that—*and how I love it!* I confess without hesitation that I am addicted to the examination and the proclamation of the Scriptures. Because of this, books have played a major role in my life for as long as I have been in ministry—especially those volumes that explain the truths and enhance my understanding of what God has written. Through these many years I have collected a large personal library, which has proven invaluable as I have sought to remain a faithful student of the Bible. To the end of my days, my major goal in life is to communicate the Word with accuracy, insight, clarity, and practicality. Without informative and reliable books to turn to, I would have "run dry" decades ago.

Among my favorite and most well-worn volumes are those that have enabled me to get a better grasp of the biblical text. Like most expositors, I am forever searching for literary tools that I can use to hone my gifts and sharpen my skills. For me, that means finding resources that make the complicated simple and easy to understand, that offer insightful comments and word pictures that enable me to see the relevance of sacred truth in light of my twenty-first-century world, and that drive those truths home to my heart in ways I do not easily forget. When I come across such books, they wind up in my hands as I devour them and then place them in my library for further reference . . . and, believe me, I often return to them. What a relief it is to have these resources to turn to when I lack fresh insight, or when I need just the right story or illustration, or when I get stuck in the tangled text and cannot find my way out. For the serious expositor, a library is essential. As a mentor of mine once said, "Where else can you have ten thousand professors at your fingertips?"

In recent years I have discovered there are not nearly enough resources like those I just described. It was such a discovery that prompted me to consider becoming a part of the answer instead of lamenting the problem. But the solution would result in a huge undertaking. A writing project that covers all of the books and letters of the New Testament seemed overwhelming and intimidating. A rush of relief came when I realized that during the past fifty-plus years I've taught and preached through most of the New Testament. In my files were folders filled with notes from those messages that were just lying there, waiting to be brought out of hiding, given a fresh and relevant touch in light of today's needs, and applied to fit into the lives of men and women who long for a fresh word from the Lord. *That did it!* I began to work on plans to turn all of those notes into this commentary on the New Testament.

I must express my gratitude to both Mark Gaither and Mike Svigel for their tireless and devoted efforts, serving as my hands-on, day-to-day editors. They have done superb work as we have walked our way through the verses and chapters of all twenty-seven New Testament books. It has been a pleasure to see how they have taken my original material and helped me shape it into a style that remains true to the text of the Scriptures, at the same time interestingly and creatively developed, and all the while allowing my voice to come through in a natural and easy-to-read manner.

I need to add sincere words of appreciation to the congregations I have served in various parts of these United States for more than five decades. It has been my good fortune to be the recipient of their love, support, encouragement, patience, and frequent words of affirmation as I have fulfilled my calling to stand and deliver God's message year after year. The sheep from all those flocks have endeared themselves to this shepherd in more ways than I can put into words . . . and none more than those I currently serve with delight at Stonebriar Community Church in Frisco, Texas.

Finally, I must thank my wife, Cynthia, for her understanding of my addiction to studying, to preaching, and to writing. Never has she discouraged me from staying at it. Never has she failed to urge me in the pursuit of doing my very best. On the contrary, her affectionate support personally, and her own commitment to excellence in leading Insight for Living for more than three and a half decades, have combined to keep me faithful to my calling "in season and out of season." Without her devotion to me and apart from our mutual partnership throughout our lifetime of ministry together, Swindoll's Living Insights would never have been undertaken.

I am grateful that it has now found its way into your hands and, ultimately, onto the shelves of your library. My continued hope and prayer is that you will find these volumes helpful in your own study and personal application of the Bible. May they help you come to realize, as I have over these many years, that God's Word is as timeless as it is true.

> The grass withers, the flower fades,
> But the word of our God stands forever. (Isa. 40:8, NASB)

Chuck Swindoll
Frisco, Texas

THE STRONG'S NUMBERING SYSTEM

Swindoll's Living Insights New Testament Commentary uses the Strong's word-study numbering system to give both newer and more advanced Bible students alike quicker, more convenient access to helpful original-language tools (e.g., concordances, lexicons, and theological dictionaries). The Strong's numbering system, made popular by the *Strong's Exhaustive Concordance of the Bible,* is used with the majority of biblical Greek and Hebrew reference works. Those who are unfamiliar with the ancient Hebrew, Aramaic, and Greek alphabets can quickly find information on a given word by looking up the appropriate index number. Advanced students will find the system helpful because it allows them to quickly find the lexical form of obscure conjugations and inflections.

When a Greek word is mentioned in the text, the Strong's number is included in square brackets after the Greek word. So in the example of the Greek word *agapē* [26], "love," the number is used with Greek tools keyed to the Strong's system.

On occasion, a Hebrew word is mentioned in the text. The Strong's Hebrew numbers are completely separate from the Greek numbers, so Hebrew numbers are prefixed with a letter "H." So, for example, the Hebrew word *kapporet* [H3727], "mercy seat," comes from *kopher* [H3722], "to ransom," "to secure favor through a gift."

INSIGHTS ON LUKE

Throughout Luke's Gospel, we discover why
a mere man should become the object of our
faith, hope, and worship: His confrontation of
evil. His welcoming of sinners. His obedience
to the Father. His willingness to suffer on
our behalf. His conquest over death. And His
open invitation to His adopted brothers and
sisters to become a new race of humanity. Luke
painstakingly presents Jesus as a human, but
one who is extraordinary, not only because of
his divinity, but also because of his character.

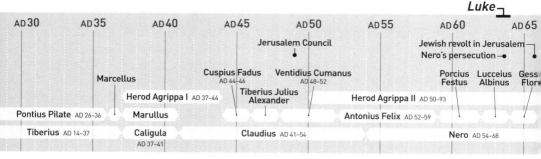

AD 30　　AD 35　　AD 40　　AD 45　　AD 50　　AD 55　　AD 60　　AD 65

Jerusalem Council

Jewish revolt in Jerusalem
Nero's persecution →

Marcellus

Cuspius Fadus
AD 44–46

Ventidius Cumanus
AD 48–52

Porcius
Festus

Lucceius
Albinus

Gess
Flor

Herod Agrippa I　AD 37–44

Tiberius Julius
Alexander

Herod Agrippa II　AD 50–93

Pontius Pilate　AD 26–36

Marullus

Antonius Felix　AD 52–59

Tiberius　AD 14–37

Caligula
AD 37–41

Claudius　AD 41–54

Nero　AD 54–68

Luke begins his story of Jesus' life in the hill country of Judea, with John the Baptizer's birth and Jesus' birth in Bethlehem. Jesus would spend much of his ministry in and around Galilee, preaching and healing. Eventually, the story returns to Judea, portraying Jesus traveling to Jerusalem and ministering in the area of the city before his death there.

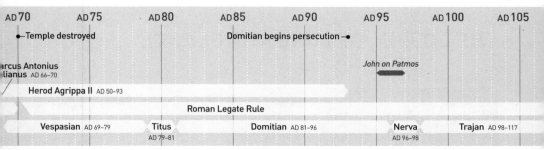

| AD 70 | AD 75 | AD 80 | AD 85 | AD 90 | AD 95 | AD 100 | AD 105 |

●—Temple destroyed

Domitian begins persecution—●

rcus Antonius
lianus AD 66–70

John on Patmos

Herod Agrippa II AD 50–93

Roman Legate Rule

Vespasian AD 69–79

Titus AD 79–81

Domitian AD 81–96

Nerva AD 96–98

Trajan AD 98–117

LUKE

INTRODUCTION

THE DOCTOR GIVES A SECOND OPINION

L uke was a people person. You can tell by the way he described the people he knew. You can also tell by the way he presented Jesus in his Gospel. He offers a perspective distinct from that of the other Gospel writers—a second opinion, if you will. Matthew established Jesus as the legitimate heir to David's throne, the King of the Jews, and the long-awaited Messiah. Mark described Him as the no-nonsense God-man who came from heaven "to serve, and to give His life a ransom for many" (Mark 10:45). John emphasized the mystery of Jesus' deity and presented Him as the tangible embodiment of divine truth. But Luke, a physician, shows how Jesus compassionately identified with the neediness of humanity. Luke marvels that God, moved by love for us, would make Himself so vulnerable.

Luke shows us an all-powerful creator taking on the fragile frame of a mortal. His Gospel presents a messiah who is never so deified as to be distant or uncaring. On the contrary, the man, Jesus, climbs down from the heavenly realms to enter the clutter and chaos of our fallen world and to subject Himself to our faults and frailties, pains and passions, sorrows and sicknesses. Only in Luke's account do we see the Almighty wrapped in swaddling clothes, a helpless infant laid in a manger. We see the Christ child match wits with the greatest theological minds of His day and become fully aware of His dual nature—His divine origin, divine purpose, and divine destiny born in human flesh. We see Jesus as a minister, healing throngs of diseased and disfigured people for no reason other than love.

Luke's carefully researched and sensitively written account of Jesus' life highlights the God-man's humanity more keenly than the other

3

THE GOSPEL OF LUKE AT A GLANCE

SECTION	LUKE'S PREFACE	ANNOUNCED AND APPEARII
PASSAGE	1:1-4	1:5–4:13
THEMES	Luke's purpose: Accuracy Excellence	The humanity of the God-man The astonishment of witnesses The fulfillment of God's promise Jesus as the promised Messiah
KEY TERMS		Amazed Tell good news Lord Immediately Christ/Messiah

MINISTERING AND SERVING	INSTRUCTING AND SUBMITTING	CONQUERING AND COMMISSIONING
4:14–9:50	9:51–19:27	19:28–24:53
Christ's authority over evil and the world it has corrupted	The Lord's intention to confront Jerusalem	The Messiah's right to rule Israel and the temple
The kingdom of God	The differences between the present world order and the kingdom of God	Israel's rejection of their Messiah
The meaning of discipleship		
The Lord's shocking agenda	The failure of Israel (as a nation) to fulfill its divine purpose	The future of Israel and the world
		Christ's atonement for sin
"Son of Man"	The cost of discipleship and its future reward	The Lord's resurrection

Disciples	Send out	Hand over
Authority	Generation	Suffer
Kingdom	Repent	Pray
Parable	Crowds	Receive
Faith	Save	
Follow		

three Gospels, implicitly placing its emphasis on the Messiah's prophetic name: Immanuel, "God with us" (Isa. 7:14). Luke shows us that this very humanity was the vehicle God chose to manifest His character and confront the sickly darkness of the world order with the wholeness and righteousness of His kingdom.

"IT SEEMED FITTING FOR ME AS WELL TO WRITE"

The Bible doesn't tell us much about Luke. We know for certain he was a Gentile by birth. When Paul listed the members of his team in a letter to the Colossians, he counted Luke among those who did not bear the outward sign of God's covenant with Abraham (Col. 4:10-14). The early church father Origen (ca. 185–254) identified Luke as the "Lucius" mentioned by Paul in Romans 16:21,[1] and this is a possibility, given the relatively late date of the letter in Paul's career. Later scholars have suggested that Luke was Lucius of Cyrene (Acts 13:1), one of the leaders in Antioch who commissioned Paul and Barnabas for the first missionary journey. Church tradition lends some assent to this theory, placing Luke in Antioch very early in church history, but the evidence is very weak. On the contrary, in Acts, Luke appears to be a junior member of Paul's evangelistic team rather than a leading member of the most influential Gentile church at that time.

If we take Scripture on its own, a more plausible theory of Luke's identity emerges. Our best evidence comes from three clear references in Paul's letters and three extended passages in Acts where Luke writes in the first person "we," indicating his own personal involvement in the narrative. It's not a lot to go on, but there are enough clues to tell us what we need to know about the man who chronicled the Lord's life and the immediate impact of the gospel in the first century.

LUKE IN THE NEW TESTAMENT
Acts 16:10-17
Acts 20:5–21:18
Acts 27:1–28:16
Colossians 4:14
Philemon 1:24
2 Timothy 4:11

According to the first of three "we" passages in Acts, it seems that Luke first encountered Paul in Troas during the apostle's second missionary journey. Paul and Silas's team had been trying to penetrate the Roman provinces of Bithynia, Asia, and Mysia with the gospel, but "the Spirit of Jesus did not permit them" (Acts 16:7). So they settled in the seaport city of Troas to consider their next move. During their stay, Paul had a night vision that convinced the men to plot a new course through Macedonia and Greece. Luke traveled with the team from Troas to Philippi, where he witnessed the beating and imprisonment of Paul and Silas (Acts 16:22-40), and as a physician (Col. 4:14), he may have been helpful in treating the men's wounds. When the team continued on to Thessalonica and then Greece, they did so without Luke, leaving him in Philippi. No negative circumstance is mentioned for his staying, and this may be an indication that Philippi had been his home before he met Paul in Troas.

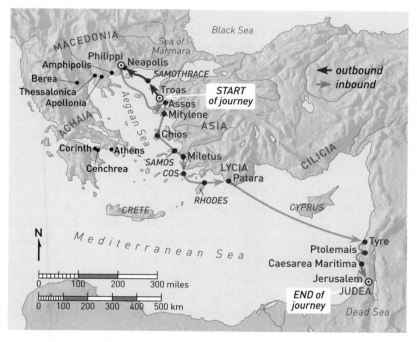

Luke Travels with Paul. Luke met Paul during the course of Paul's second missionary journey (Acts 15:36–18:22). Paul left him to work in Philippi, and then Luke rejoined him for the journey back to Jerusalem.

We do not know whether Luke was a believer before encountering Paul. Other than using the plural pronoun "we," he appears to have deliberately omitted direct reference to himself in the story of Christ (The Gospel of Luke) and the rise of the church (The Acts of the Apostles). He does not reveal when, where, or how he became a Christian, but there are two strong possibilities.

First, it is possible Luke became a believer as a direct result of Paul's ministry in Troas, where he first includes himself ("we") in the narrative (Acts 16:10-11). He may have heard about the Hebrew God from Jews living in and around Philippi, which prepared him to hear the gospel from Paul and accept Jesus as the Messiah. Or he may have been one of the many pagans living in the region, where the profiteers of pagan mystery religions held the political strings (Acts 16:16, 19-21). At least one biographer identified Luke as the "man of Macedonia" in Paul's vision (Acts 16:9), but this is mere speculation.[2] Regardless, Luke's conversion may have added extra weight to Paul's vision.

Second, Luke may have heard about Christ from a Jewish convert returning from Pentecost (Acts 2). Although Lydia (Acts 16:14) is often noted as Paul's first convert in Europe, there is evidence that Christianity preceded Paul in cities all across the empire. Paul wrote to the believers in Rome without having ever visited them, and Paul's letter to Titus indicates that the gospel had even reached the remote island of Crete before the apostle's visit. Christians undoubtedly existed in Macedonia but remained isolated and unorganized, and Luke may have been one of them. This would explain his readiness to go with Paul, which seems evident as he writes, "When he [Paul] had seen the vision, immediately we sought to go into Macedonia" (Acts 16:10).

Paul referred to Luke as a "physician" (Col. 4:14), a term that, in the ancient world, said more about a person's calling and character than his expertise or training. Although surgeries were sometimes performed, medical practice in the first century generally involved herbal remedies and traditional therapies, and there were no accrediting boards or standardized curriculums. Those who called themselves physicians had devoted themselves to helping the sick. Most had studied under another, more experienced practitioner to learn the field. This suggests that Luke had received a good education.[3] Moreover, his literary style compares favorably with classical Greek historians, demonstrating his ability to gather research, arrange facts well, and then prepare a very readable history.

Luke's chosen profession may have prompted Paul to add him to his evangelistic team, although he does not appear to have become a permanent member of the group until the end of the third missionary journey. On that last tour, Paul and his entourage passed through Philippi on their way to Greece, again without adding Luke to their numbers. After several months of ministry in Greece, Paul intended to sail directly home from Cenchrea (a port city near Corinth), but a plot to kill him changed his plans. To distract any would-be assassins, he instructed his team to board a ship in Cenchrea as originally planned, but to sail for Troas, where he would rendezvous with them. Meanwhile, he retraced his steps through Philippi (Acts 20:2-5), where evidently he invited Luke to join him. It seems clear from the second "we" passage (Acts 20:5–21:18) that Luke accompanied Paul to Troas, and it is implied that he remained Paul's traveling companion for the rest of the apostle's life.

The third "we" passage (Acts 27:1–28:16) follows Paul from his arrest in Jerusalem to confinement in the palace of Herod Agrippa, then along the journey to Rome, and on through his two years of house arrest awaiting trial. No one knows for certain where Paul traveled after his release, but within a couple of years, he was back in Rome and again in prison. As he penned his final letter to Timothy and prepared for the end, he mentioned that only Luke remained at his side (2 Tim. 4:11).

"AN ORDERLY ACCOUNT"

Luke acknowledged that "many" had undertaken to write an account of Jesus' life (Luke 1:1), which probably refers to what Darrell Bock calls "a fluid pool of traditions from which both Luke and Matthew drew."[4] Mark had written his account to spur early saints into action, but it was not a "history," per se. Consequently, believers eager for more information about the Lord started collecting and circulating their own stories and sayings of Jesus. The evidence strongly suggests Luke drew some information from Mark's Gospel and then, as he traveled with Paul, gathered scraps of various stories and source materials. These various accounts, according to Luke, prompted him to write a more excellent account. In this way, you could say the doctor offered a second opinion.

Luke, having considered the story of Jesus as a whole, settled on a perspective that he—prompted and superintended by the Holy Spirit—felt compelled to share. He then arranged and organized the data he had meticulously gathered and verified in order to craft the story of Christ, not only for the sake of fact-telling, but also to convey a heavenly, cosmic message. The latest revision of the NASB uses the phrase "in consecutive order" in Luke 1:3, but I believe the rendering "an orderly account" (NIV, ESV) or "an accurate account" (NLT) is better. The Greek word means "orderly" or "in sequence according to time, space, or *logic*." Ancient cultures did not see chronology as the most obvious means of relating history. Luke shaped his Gospel narrative geographically. While he didn't hide the fact that Jesus traversed Israel freely between Galilee and Jerusalem throughout His ministry, he nevertheless structured the narrative as a journey from north to south, from Nazareth to the temple.

After relaying the stories surrounding Jesus' birth, childhood, and preparation for ministry (1:1–4:13), Luke portrays the ministry of Jesus as based in or near Galilee (4:14–9:50). He then places several episodes within the framework of a journey south after the Lord "determined to go to Jerusalem" (9:51–19:27). Finally, Luke describes the culmination of Jesus' mission in Jerusalem (19:29–24:53).[5]

While Luke's narrative takes place entirely in Israel, moving from Galilee toward Jerusalem, it nevertheless highlights the global implications of the Jewish Messiah's mission on earth. From the outset, Jesus is recognized as a "light of revelation to the Gentiles" (2:32). As Jesus proceeds from Galilee to Jerusalem, His conflict with the spiritual darkness of this world and the Jewish religious authorities grows more intense.

Luke's story of Jesus is a sizable work—the longest book in the New Testament—written with extreme care. Perfectionists will love Luke. He has the mind of a scientist, the pen of a poet, and the heart of an artist. Through his exquisite vocabulary he gives his reader a front-row seat. Of course, Luke didn't write merely to entertain. He wrote to accomplish two specific goals: first, to provide a concrete, factual foundation for the faith of his patron, Theophilus—and for the church at large; and second, to present Jesus to unbelievers, proving Him to be the perfect God-man who came to save all of humanity, Jew and Gentile alike.

"FOR YOU, MOST EXCELLENT THEOPHILUS"

Luke dedicated his work to "most excellent Theophilus," whose identity remains a subject of debate. The name means "one who loves God," which might be Luke's subtle way of addressing a generic, believing reader. This is unlikely, however. The style of address is more typical of other histories written during this time, in which a chronicler gives homage to his patron. Therefore, Theophilus was probably the nickname of a specific person, such as a noteworthy Christian official who preferred to remain anonymous, either for the sake of humility or the need for safety.

Theophilus may have been among those described by Luke as "God-fearers," Gentiles who expressed a desire to know more about the God of Scripture and who perhaps turned to their local synagogue for instruction. Accordingly, Luke's point of view seems to be that of a Gentile walking through the doors of Jewish tradition to enter the church. He references the secular world while explaining Judaism, all the while using common Semitic expressions. He explains the geography, history, and culture of Israel without overburdening the story with details. He quotes from the Septuagint, the Greek translation of the Hebrew Scriptures. And he views all of humankind as united by a common, desperate need for a Savior.

In ancient times, some chroniclers were commissioned by wealthy patrons to research and write a history in support of a specific objective. It might be to establish one's legitimacy or suitability for leadership, or to prepare the populace for a large undertaking. In this case, it is quite possible Luke's patron cried out with the man in Mark's Gospel, "I do believe; help my unbelief" (Mark 9:24), and wanted to gain assurance for himself and other believers. Consequently, we find in Luke's account (including Acts) many references to faithfulness, assurance of God's love for all of humanity, the reality of Jesus' divine identity, the perseverance of faith over adversity, the triumph of truth over evil, and the inevitable expansion of the gospel throughout the world.

For the Christian, Luke's details do not lead to faith; they undergird the faith that already exists within the individual's heart. His history says, in effect, "Your faith is reasonable; here's why."

"THE EXACT TRUTH ABOUT THE THINGS YOU HAVE BEEN TAUGHT"

Luke clearly understood the power of stories about "beginnings." Today, an entire television channel is dedicated to telling the stories of famous people and their humble, pre-fame, pre-success circumstances. These stories offer comfort and inspiration to those who continue to struggle, subtly suggesting that, one day, victory will come to those who do not abandon hope. These stories of humble beginnings also invite us to share in the story of success and invite us to become part of a grander future.

To tell the story of the Savior, Luke reaches far back into the prehistory of the Christ. On the surface, his prologue features an obscure priest fulfilling his duties in the temple (1:5-12); but we soon discover that the story of the Christ begins with the story of the forerunner, John the Baptizer, a story which is itself a continuation of the overarching narrative of the Old Testament. For Luke, the story of Jesus continues the story of salvation, which began in Genesis. For that reason, he provides a genealogy of the Savior just as Jesus steps into the public arena—and that family tree extends all the way back to our universal common ancestor, Adam (3:23-38).

Throughout Luke's Gospel, we discover why a mere man should become the object of our faith, hope, and worship: His miraculous, divine conception. His humble identity with the lowest of the low. His righteousness displayed throughout His life, including His triumph over temptation and His compassion for infirmity. His intolerance of hypocrisy. His confrontation of evil. His welcoming of sinners. His obedience to the Father. His willingness to suffer on our behalf. His conquest over death. And His open invitation to His adopted brothers and sisters to become a new race of humanity. Luke painstakingly presents Jesus as a human, but one who is extraordinary, not only because of his divinity, but also because of his character.

Without diminishing the Lord's divine identity, Luke presents Jesus as the embodiment of God's concern for helpless humanity. Thanks to Luke, we know of the good Samaritan (10:25-37), the woman healed of her eighteen-year infirmity (13:10-17), the healing of a man with dropsy (14:1-6), the parables of the lost sheep and lost coin (15:1-10), the prodigal son (15:11-32), the greedy rich man and godly Lazarus (16:19-31), the healing of the ten lepers (17:11-19), Zaccheus (19:1-10), the penitent thief on the cross (23:39-43), and the faith of disillusioned believers restored on the road to Emmaus (24:13-35). He presumes his readers know only too well the realities of living in a sin-sick world, so he presents the Son of God as the Great Physician.

Luke also portrays the Son of Man as perfect, ideal humanity. The first man succumbed to temptation while surrounded by abundance. The Second Man overcame temptation in the deprivation of the wilderness (4:1-13). The first man plunged all of humanity into sin, despair, death, and decay; the Second Man, through obedience, offers all of humanity new life—abundant life, everlasting life, far beyond the reach of evil's horrific consequences. The first man—the first "son of God" (3:38)—fell from his place of honor as the bearer of God's image. The Second Man is God himself, in flesh and bone, sent to restore the former glory of humanity. His resurrection body foreshadows the image of redeemed men and women.

By the end of his work, Luke has accomplished something remarkable. By virtue of his faithful handling of eyewitness accounts and his divinely inspired writing skills, the Gospel of Luke transforms the passive reader into an impassioned eyewitness. Luke describes the man

Jesus and His ministry in vivid detail. You will crisscross the country-side with Him, meeting the people He came to save. You'll climb to the summit of Jerusalem to face down the enemies of grace. You'll endure the leather straps during His scourging and suffer the puncture of the nails at His crucifixion. You'll feel the weight of the sagging body as He slumps on the cross. You'll gasp your last breaths with Him. You'll walk with His followers into despair during the three days after His death and experience their confusion during the pandemonium of that first Easter. And you'll stand alongside them in worship as He ascends to heaven to sit by the Father.

Luke's history is no mere chronicle of a dead hero. This is His Story! The story of Christ not only continues today; it invites you to join the narrative and to help write the conclusion.

LUKE'S PREFACE (LUKE 1:1-4)

Each of the four inspired Gospels—Matthew, Mark, Luke, and John—begins in a unique way. Matthew starts with a genealogy tracing the legal descent of Jesus from Abraham to Joseph, highlighting His place as heir of the Abrahamic promise and the Davidic kingship (Matt. 1:1-17). After a brief quote of an Old Testament prophecy, the Gospel of Mark drops the reader right in the middle of the action of John the Baptizer's ministry . . . leading to Jesus' baptism . . . flashing through His temptation in the wilderness . . . and cutting straight to His preaching in Galilee (Mark 1:1-14). John's Gospel begins with a theologically rich "Christology from above"—a kind of hymn to the eternal Word of God, Himself God, who became man for us. Reminiscent of the powerful opening of Genesis 1, John's bold confession of the person of Christ booms and echoes like a thundering voice from on high: "In the beginning was the Word, and the Word was with God, and the Word was God" (John 1:1-18).

Unlike the other three accounts of Jesus' life and ministry, the Gospel of Luke kicks off not with a genealogy, an action sequence, or a piece of powerful prose; it begins instead with something like a sticky note. The opening verses read like a "transmittal letter," dedicating the following account to "most excellent Theophilus" (Luke 1:3). In this very brief preface, however, we not only learn the name of the first reader of the Gospel, but we also catch a glimpse of the standards of excellence for which the writer, Luke, strived in his research and writing of the account. Before stepping into the narrative in 1:5, let's take time to explore the kind of excellence Luke sought in His presentation of Jesus Christ in all His splendor.

Only the Best
LUKE 1:1-4

NASB

[1] Inasmuch as many have undertaken to compile an account of the things [a] accomplished among us, [2] just as

NLT

[1] Many people have set out to write accounts about the events that have been fulfilled among us. [2] They used

NASB

they were handed down to us by those who from the beginning [a]were eyewitnesses and [b]servants of the [c]word, 3 it seemed fitting for me as well, having [a]investigated everything carefully from the beginning, to write *it* out for you in consecutive order, most excellent Theophilus; 4 so that you may know the exact truth about the things you have been [a]taught.

1:1 [a]Or *on which there is full conviction* 1:2 [a]Lit *became* [b]Or *ministers* [c]I.e. gospel 1:3 [a]Or *followed* 1:4 [a]Or *orally instructed in*

NLT

the eyewitness reports circulating among us from the early disciples.* 3 Having carefully investigated everything from the beginning, I also have decided to write an accurate account for you, most honorable Theophilus, 4 so you can be certain of the truth of everything you were taught.

1:2 Greek *from those who from the beginning were servants of the word.*

How seldom we find true excellence. We live in an increasingly hurried and hassled society in which fewer people must generate greater output with fewer resources. The constant push for quick turnaround and instant gratification has dulled our senses and lowered our expectations. We have come to accept—and even expect—mediocrity on the job, in the marketplace, and in government. "First-rate" used to be our minimum standard; now, it is considered rude or unreasonable to ask for excellence.

Quality can't be rushed. Unfortunately, we're all in a hurry. And the consequences of slouching standards and slipshod work can be disastrous, even with seemingly insignificant tasks. As John Gardner wisely stated in his book *Excellence*, "The society that scorns excellence in plumbing because plumbing is a humble activity and tolerates shoddiness in philosophy because it is an exalted activity will have neither good plumbing nor good philosophy. Neither its pipes nor its theories will hold water."[1] Tragically, his words have proven prophetic: the cancer of mediocrity has invaded Christendom. Fewer seminaries now expect anything beyond a cursory familiarity with the original languages, and more students preparing for ministry opt for degrees with no Greek or Hebrew required. Most graduate programs compress systematic theology to fit into one or two semesters; so, with neither comprehension of orthodox doctrine nor the skills to think through the issues, we shouldn't be surprised when Christian seminaries cease to be distinctly Christian. In recent years, a prominent Methodist seminary has added clerical training for Muslims and Jews to its curriculum to become "the first truly multi-faith American seminary."[2] They also plan to add clerical training for Buddhists and Hindus.

This formerly Christian seminary did not change its stripes suddenly. The decision to abandon the "things [they] had been taught" (1:4) began with a small yet momentous compromise in their view of divine truth and its source. This undoubtedly followed a host of tiny compromises in both hermeneutics and theology. The journey toward irrelevance began with a decision to give mediocrity a passing grade.

The downward drag of mediocrity is not a new phenomenon. While traveling with Paul, Luke saw communities of believers scattered across the Roman Empire like a great number of pearls, each growing around its own core of oral tradition. As an educated man, Luke foresaw a particular danger looming on the horizon. As first-generation witnesses began to pass away, leaving fewer firsthand accounts of the Lord and His teaching, myths and fables would take the place of authentic stories. If the churches were to survive this erosion, they would need a unified, comprehensive story of Christ to bind them together. They needed a copiously researched and ruthlessly verified account that would equip them to separate truth from fiction and to remain distinctly Christian. They needed an excellent Gospel.

When the Holy Spirit compelled Luke to write, He drew upon Luke's affinity for meticulous accuracy. Luke's extraordinary devotion to excellence took four distinct forms:

Excellence in Research
Excellence in Organization
Excellence in Expression
Excellence in Discipline

— 1:1-2 —

Excellence in research. During Luke's travels with Paul, he encountered a patchwork of oral traditions preserved in the memories of aging saints who knew Jesus personally. Many had likely written informal memories on scraps of parchment and papyrus. As he traveled with Paul, gathering these scraps of written tradition and perhaps recording his own interviews with eyewitnesses, Luke felt the Holy Spirit's prompting to write a more excellent account.

He did not merely paste the pieces together to form a composite document. Luke scrupulously checked his facts. The Greek term translated "eyewitnesses" (1:2) derives from the term we transliterate "autopsy" and is not found anywhere else in the Bible—neither the Greek translation of the Old Testament nor the New Testament. It is a term used often, however, by historians such as Josephus, Herodotus, and Polybius. In ancient cultures, no evidence carried more weight than the testimony of a reputable eyewitness.

Luke interviewed the people who knew Jesus best. He spent time with the people who saw Him eat, heard Him snore, and inhaled His odor on a hot afternoon. They had been present when His ministry unfolded. A few had marveled at His transfiguration. They had witnessed His agony in Gethsemane, His writhing under the torturous scourge, and His torment on the cross. And they thrilled to see Him alive again. Luke diligently scrutinized his sources to weed out specious material, fill in missing details, correct errors, and even disclose previously unknown events. And only then, when he had assembled and vetted all the material he could find, did he begin to write.

— 1:3 —

Excellence in organization. A good historian does not merely assemble facts and then string them together. A good historian tells a story, usually for a specific purpose. He or she must choose which information to include and what data to leave out. Then the historian must organize and arrange the facts to paint an accurate, compelling, memorable, and useful picture of what occurred.

The term rendered "investigated" literally means "to follow along" or "to accompany." In addition to the important task of checking the details, Luke traced the story of Jesus from the beginning to its conclusion to see the mission and work of Christ as a whole. Only when viewing the total can one begin to appreciate the wonder of it all.

The phrase rendered "in consecutive order" (NASB) could be misleading. Luke did not do away with chronological order altogether in his history of Jesus, but he didn't use it as his main organizing principle either. A better translation might be "in an orderly sequence" (cf. the renderings in the NLT, NIV, and ESV). Ancient people did not obsess over time like we do today. Luke's overarching arrangement of the individual episodes of the Lord's life follows a geographical sequence, which ancient readers would have accepted without question.

Excellence in expression. Throughout the narrative, Luke's grammar and syntax compares very favorably with the best examples of Greek literature in his day. Moreover, his storytelling ability is nothing short of genius. He employed several marvelously sophisticated literary devices, not only to inform his reading (and listening) audiences, but also to occasionally entertain them.

Luke could have presented the facts—and only the tedious facts—in chronological order; instead, he crafted a compelling narrative that conveys the beauty, irony, complexity, excitement, and pathos of God coming to earth to save the world from sin. And it's a good thing he did. As my mentor, Howard Hendricks, often said to his teachers-in-training: "It's a *sin* to make the Bible seem boring!"

— 1:4 —

Excellence in discipline. Despite Luke's careful attention to detail and his artful use of language, he never lost sight of his primary purpose: "so that you (Theophilus [and those for whom this history was commissioned]) may know the exact truth about the things you have been taught." Luke's travels with Paul impressed upon him the perilous future that Christianity would face without an excellent record—an infallible, inerrant, wholly trustworthy account—of the Lord's life, teachings, and work. He understood that sound theology, like a house, must stand upon the solid rock of truth (cf. 6:46-49). Without an accurate and reliable account of what Jesus taught and what He did on our behalf, believers have no basis for their beliefs. After all, faith separated from divine truth will shift with the prevailing winds of popular opinion and collapse when battered by the storms of adversity.

To make matters worse, Theophilus and all these "God-lovers" lived during a time when the beginnings of a movement known as Gnosticism threatened to warp Christian doctrine just as it had begun to distort Judaism, pagan religions, and even Greek philosophy. Those who knew Christ personally and had witnessed His resurrection would soon die, and with them, firsthand knowledge of Christian truth would cease. Any vacuum of information left after their passing would soon be filled with myths and fables.

Sure enough, it was not long after the production of John, the last of our four Gospels, that Gnostic writings telling bizarre stories about Jesus began to circulate. This occurred as early as the second century. Fortunately, Luke had prepared an excellent history of Jesus and the church He commissioned. Luke saw the random collections of unverified anecdotes about Jesus as building materials—useless until assembled to build a house—and he erected a house large enough for all believers, Jew and Gentile alike, and sturdy enough to endure through the ages.

Truth has become a slippery subject in these latter days. Postmodernism denies the existence of truth, so it is not surprising that postmodern Christians see no difference between disagreement and hostility. Consequently, they quickly set aside truth to avoid disharmony, particularly with people of different belief systems. I find this attitude confusing and appalling. I can think of few gifts more precious or costly than the gift of truth, especially when knowing the truth will help someone avoid unnecessary difficulty, illness, sorrow, grief—or worse, eternal separation from God! I agree with Martin Luther, who wrote,

> Elegant and true is the sentiment which Aristotle expresses in the First Book of his *Ethics* (chapter 4): that it is better to stand by the truth than to show too much favor to those who are our close friends or even our relatives. And to do this is distinctly becoming to a philosopher. For while both the truth and our friends are dear to us, truth should enjoy the preferred place. If, then, a man [like Aristotle] who is a heathen holds that this should be done in civil disputes, how much more should it be done in matters which have the clear testimony of Scripture in their favor, so that we do not place the authority of men before Scripture! For men can be deceived, but the Word of God is itself the wisdom of God and the most certain truth. It will be the truth as I understand it, even at the risk of hurting a relationship.[3]

To set aside excellence in the pursuit of what is factual and real might make things easier in the short run. But to set aside truth for the sake of harmony with people means sacrificing something of far greater importance: harmony with God, the Author of truth. Luke pursued the truth with excellence, and the Holy Spirit kept him from error. And for nearly two millennia, the Lord has preserved this excellent, orderly account for us, so that we may have certainty about our trust in God's Son—what He taught and what He did on our behalf. With this long history of excellence behind us, let's not settle for mediocrity now! Let us, instead, boldly and lovingly proclaim what we know to be factual and true. After all, real and lasting harmony between people depends upon our acknowledging and embracing truth together.

APPLICATION: LUKE 1:1-4

Excellence as unto the Lord

Luke set a wonderful example of excellence when writing his orderly history of the Christ (The Gospel of Luke) and His church (The Acts of the Apostles). He explains his motivation in the opening lines of his dedication to "most excellent Theophilus," from which we can glean a few principles.

Excellence honors God. Be careful not to turn that statement into a battle cry for perfectionism, which merely gratifies self. But pursue excellence in everything.

Excellence stands the test of time. Luke wanted to create something that would serve the needs of endless generations to come and withstand intense scrutiny. Others had attempted to document the Lord's life, but none except the Gospel of Mark had endured (1:1).[4] Two thousand years later, Luke's Gospel hasn't lost its original beauty.

Excellence today honors the legacy it has inherited. Luke recognized his responsibility to steward what had been handed down to him by "those who from the beginning were eyewitnesses and servants of the word" (1:2). By their excellent handling of the truth, he became a child of God, and with their passing, others would look to him.

Excellence recognizes what is valuable and takes care to preserve it. Luke accepted that he had a responsibility to handle the "exact truth" with utmost care (1:4). He treated the story of Christ like a priceless heirloom and preserved it for those who would come after him.

Excellence pays attention to details. Luke "investigated everything carefully from the beginning" and then arranged the facts in orderly sequence (1:3). He scrupulously and meticulously verified every scrap of information by tracing each detail to its original, eyewitness source. His travels with Paul gave him unprecedented access to the who's who of Christian prehistory. Still, it was a significant undertaking that would have required painstaking organization to catalog and organize the data.

Excellence recognizes its duty to the welfare of others. Luke appreciated the fact that Theophilus (and the church at large) looked to his work for greater stability in their faith (1:4). While it is the Holy Spirit who draws people to the Father through Christ and who preserves their faith, the excellent work of His servants often becomes His means.

While His use of Luke's work is special,[5] He nonetheless uses the excellent work of all His servants to build and strengthen His church.

Each day, as you fight traffic, when you put in overtime, while you dutifully grind out the tasks that have been assigned to you—no matter how obscure or thankless—let excellence guide your every effort. If you are a plumber, plumb with excellence. If you are an attorney, don't merely fill out forms; approach every case with ingenuity and integrity. Regardless of your profession, let your professionalism attract others to Christ. If you are a musician, practice, even if you have it down. If you are a homemaker, make hospitality, economy, efficiency, kindness, and orderliness your profession.

Let excellence become your trademark.

For daily inspiration, here are some key passages you might consider posting near your workspace:

Whatever your hand finds to do, do it with all your might. (Eccl. 9:10)

Whether, then, you eat or drink or whatever you do, do all to the glory of God. (1 Cor. 10:31)

We have regard for what is honorable, not only in the sight of the Lord, but also in the sight of men. (2 Cor. 8:21)

With good will render service, as to the Lord, and not to men, knowing that whatever good thing each one does, this he will receive back from the Lord, whether slave or free. (Eph. 6:7-8)

Do all things without grumbling or disputing; so that you will prove yourselves to be blameless and innocent, children of God above reproach in the midst of a crooked and perverse generation, among whom you appear as lights in the world. (Phil. 2:14-15)

Whatever you do in word or deed, do all in the name of the Lord Jesus, giving thanks through Him to God the Father. (Col. 3:17)

Whatever you do, do your work heartily, as for the Lord rather than for men, knowing that from the Lord you will receive the reward of the inheritance. It is the Lord Christ whom you serve. (Col. 3:23-24)

Keep your behavior excellent among the Gentiles, so that in the thing in which they slander you as evildoers, they may because of your good deeds, as they observe them, glorify God in the day of visitation. (1 Pet. 2:12)

Whoever speaks, is to do so as one who is speaking the utterances of God; whoever serves is to do so as one who is serving by the strength which God supplies; so that in all things God may be glorified through Jesus Christ, to whom belongs the glory and dominion forever and ever. Amen. (1 Pet. 4:11)

ANNOUNCED AND APPEARING
(LUKE 1:5-4:13)

Some of the very best novels begin with a prologue. This is especially true for epic novels. A prologue is a short story that paints a grand backdrop. It establishes the setting and provides background information necessary to understand why people behave as they do, and how the main characters differ from the norm. Luke, as an educated man, understood the use of a prologue, as every good Greek play since Euripides began with a character "setting the stage."

The first section of Luke's narrative (1:5–4:13) forms an extended prologue. He first recounts events surrounding Jesus' birth that bear witness to His divine origin and mission. From this strand of vignettes, we also discover that the story of Jesus didn't begin in Nazareth, or even Bethlehem. The story of redemption is, in fact, the second act of a three-act drama. The first act began in Genesis with the creation and fall of man, continued with God's calling the nation of Israel to become the means of His redemptive plan and concluded with the nation's failure to fulfill their divine purpose. This background effectively highlights the problem of the sin-ridden world order and the evil influences that hold sway in it, setting the stage for the confrontation between that world system and the kingdom of the Messiah. In fact, the promise of a Messiah is woven throughout this dark tale, even from Genesis 3:15. And just before a four-hundred-year intermission (between the Old and New Testaments), the Lord had again offered the world hope. He promised that a forerunner would call the audience to attention and announce the arrival of the Hero (Mal. 4:5-6). Luke's prologue connects the Lord's promises in Malachi to the birth of a remarkable man of God, John, whose sole purpose in life was to prepare the way for the Christ and then step aside.

existēmi **(ἐξίστημι)** [1839] "to be astonished," "to be
  separated from something," "to be beside oneself," "to be
  out of one's senses"
This word literally means to be displaced. Figuratively, it refers to a psy-
chological state of mind in which one no longer has control over oneself.
By the time of Jesus, this had become hyperbole, in the same way we
might say someone "lost his mind" with excitement. Another, milder term
used often by Luke is *thaumazō* (see below), which simply means "astonished" or "filled with wonder." *Existēmi* is decidedly more colorful, used
to characterize someone as animated in his or her astonishment.

thaumazō **(θαυμάζω)** [2296] "to be amazed," "to marvel,"
  "to be in awe"
This term means to be extraordinarily impressed, awed, or even disturbed,
by something, especially when confronted with some form of divine
revelation. In the Septuagint it indicates worship, honor, and admiration, generally referring to "religious experience face to face with what
transcends human possibilities."[1] The three times in Luke that the word
ekplēssō [1605] appears, it is used with a sense very similar to *thaumazō*.

euangelizō **(εὐαγγελίζω)** [2097] "tell good news,"
  "announce," "proclaim," "evangelize"
In the secular sphere, this verb was used of an official messenger bringing
news—usually good—concerning notable events such as the progress of a
battle, the birth of a royal, or the pending arrival of the king. The New Testament carries over the ideas of liberation and victory, applying this word
specifically to proclaiming salvation in Jesus Christ. Of the fifty-four times
this verb appears in the New Testament, almost half occur in Luke and Acts
(ten times in Luke and fifteen in Acts). The majority of the other instances
can be found in the letters of Luke's mentor, Paul (twenty-one times).

kyrios **(κύριος)** [2962] "lord," "ruler," "owner"
This term generally denotes a person having power and authority. A subordinate may use *kyrios* as a form of address when appealing to someone
of higher social standing (Luke 13:8; 14:22). In addition to this common
use, the Septuagint translators used *kyrios* thousands of times to represent the divine name, YHWH (e.g. Deut. 6:4), a convention picked up by
the New Testament writers.

parachrēma **(παραχρῆμα)** [3916] "suddenly,"
  "immediately," "at once"
Except for one notable exception (Matt. 21:19-20), this adverb appears only
in Luke (ten times) and Acts (six times). Luke uses the term to establish a

clear cause-and-effect connection between one event and the next, usually in the context of a supernatural event. In Luke, the majority of cases refer to the immediate results of Jesus' miracles.

***Christos* (Χριστός)** [5547] "Messiah," "anointed one"

The term itself derives from *chriō*, which means "to rub," "to smear on," or "to anoint [with oil]." Prior to the New Testament, it was never used of a person except in Greek translations of Hebrew literature. The Septuagint used *christos* to translate the Hebrew word *mashiach* [H4899] (from which we get "messiah" in English), a term reserved for the king and referring to the custom of anointing a man's head with olive oil to designate him as Israel's ruler. While Israel had many "christs" (i.e. kings), the nation anticipated an ultimate "Christ," *the* Messiah, a larger-than-life consummate king.

"A Baby? At Our Age? Get Serious!"
LUKE 1:5-25

NASB

⁵In the days of Herod, king of Judea, there was a priest named ᵃZacharias, of the division of ᵇAbijah; and he had a wife ᶜfrom the daughters of Aaron, and her name was Elizabeth. ⁶They were both righteous in the sight of God, walking blamelessly in all the commandments and requirements of the Lord. ⁷But they had no child, because Elizabeth was barren, and they were both advanced in ᵃyears.

⁸Now it happened *that* while he was performing his priestly service before God in the *appointed* order of his division, ⁹according to the custom of the priestly office, he was chosen by lot to enter the temple of the Lord and burn incense. ¹⁰And the whole multitude of the people were in prayer outside at the hour of the incense offering. ¹¹And an angel of the Lord appeared to him, standing to the right of the altar of incense. ¹²Zacharias was troubled when he saw *the angel*, and fear ᵃgripped him.

NLT

⁵When Herod was king of Judea, there was a Jewish priest named Zechariah. He was a member of the priestly order of Abijah, and his wife, Elizabeth, was also from the priestly line of Aaron. ⁶Zechariah and Elizabeth were righteous in God's eyes, careful to obey all of the Lord's commandments and regulations. ⁷They had no children because Elizabeth was unable to conceive, and they were both very old.

⁸One day Zechariah was serving God in the Temple, for his order was on duty that week. ⁹As was the custom of the priests, he was chosen by lot to enter the sanctuary of the Lord and burn incense. ¹⁰While the incense was being burned, a great crowd stood outside, praying. ¹¹While Zechariah was in the sanctuary, an angel of the Lord appeared to him, standing to the right of the incense altar. ¹²Zechariah was shaken and overwhelmed with fear

13 But the angel said to him, "Do not be afraid, Zacharias, for your petition has been heard, and your wife Elizabeth will bear you a son, and you will ᵃgive him the name John. 14 You will have joy and gladness, and many will rejoice at his birth. 15 For he will be great in the sight of the Lord; and he will drink no wine or liquor, and he will be filled with the Holy Spirit ᵃwhile yet in his mother's womb. 16 And he will turn many of the sons of Israel back to the Lord their God. 17 It is he who will go *as a forerunner* before Him in the spirit and power of Elijah, TO TURN THE HEARTS OF THE FATHERS BACK TO THE CHILDREN, and the disobedient to the attitude of the righteous, so as to make ready a people prepared for the Lord."

18 Zacharias said to the angel, "How will I know this *for certain?* For I am an old man and my wife is advanced in ᵃyears." 19 The angel answered and said to him, "I am Gabriel, who ᵃstands in the presence of God, and I have been sent to speak to you and to bring you this good news. 20 And behold, you shall be silent and unable to speak until the day when these things take place, because you did not believe my words, which will be fulfilled in their proper time."

21 The people were waiting for Zacharias, and were wondering at his delay in the temple. 22 But when he came out, he was unable to speak to them; and they realized that he had seen a vision in the temple; and he kept ᵃmaking signs to them, and remained mute. 23 When the days of his priestly service were ended, he went back home.

24 After these days Elizabeth his wife became pregnant, and she ᵃkept herself in seclusion for five months, saying, 25 "This is the way the Lord has dealt with me in the days when

when he saw him. 13 But the angel said, "Don't be afraid, Zechariah! God has heard your prayer. Your wife, Elizabeth, will give you a son, and you are to name him John. 14 You will have great joy and gladness, and many will rejoice at his birth, 15 for he will be great in the eyes of the Lord. He must never touch wine or other alcoholic drinks. He will be filled with the Holy Spirit, even before his birth.* 16 And he will turn many Israelites to the Lord their God. 17 He will be a man with the spirit and power of Elijah. He will prepare the people for the coming of the Lord. He will turn the hearts of the fathers to their children,* and he will cause those who are rebellious to accept the wisdom of the godly."

18 Zechariah said to the angel, "How can I be sure this will happen? I'm an old man now, and my wife is also well along in years."

19 Then the angel said, "I am Gabriel! I stand in the very presence of God. It was he who sent me to bring you this good news! 20 But now, since you didn't believe what I said, you will be silent and unable to speak until the child is born. For my words will certainly be fulfilled at the proper time."

21 Meanwhile, the people were waiting for Zechariah to come out of the sanctuary, wondering why he was taking so long. 22 When he finally did come out, he couldn't speak to them. Then they realized from his gestures and his silence that he must have seen a vision in the sanctuary.

23 When Zechariah's week of service in the Temple was over, he returned home. 24 Soon afterward his wife, Elizabeth, became pregnant and went into seclusion for five months. 25 "How kind the Lord is!"

NASB

He looked *with favor* upon *me,* to take away my disgrace among men."

1:5 ªI.e. Zechariah ᵇGr *Abia* ᶜI.e. of priestly descent   1:7 ªLit *days*   1:12 ªOr *fell upon*   1:13 ªLit *call his name*   1:15 ªLit *from*   1:18 ªLit *days*   1:19 ªLit *stand beside*   1:22 ªOr *beckoning to* or *nodding to*   1:24 ªLit *was hidden*

she exclaimed. "He has taken away my disgrace of having no children."

1:15 Or *even from birth.*   1:17 See Mal 4:5-6.

NLT

God is full of surprises. He delights in turning impossible situations into opportunities to show His steadfast love for people. He fulfills His promises in His own way and according to His own timetable, which can be frustrating at times, but He never goes back on His word. He is always faithful to do as He has said. And when He fulfills His promises, He always exceeds our expectations.

Luke's story of Christ actually begins before the singing of angels and the arrival of shepherds, before innkeepers, or manger beds, or "peace among men." In fact, it begins more than four hundred years earlier with a mostly forgotten promise:

> Behold, I am going to send you Elijah the prophet before the coming of the great and terrible day of the LORD. He will restore the hearts of the fathers to their children and the hearts of the children to their fathers, so that I will not come and smite the land with a curse. (Mal. 4:5-6)

These are the final words of the Hebrew prophets. Four hundred years passed without another word from heaven. God's official spokesmen laid down their pens and ceased their prophetic utterance, for they had no message to report.

That's not to say the Lord turned His back on the world. He did not forsake His people. He continued to safeguard His promises to Abraham (Gen. 12:1-3), to David (2 Sam. 7:16), to Israel (Deut. 30:1, 5), and to all people (Gen. 3:15). Still, nothing was ever quite the same after Israel had returned to the Land of Promise from her exile in Babylon. The blazing light of God's presence, His shekinah, had left the temple before foreign invaders sacked Jerusalem and carried the people away (Ezek. 10:18). And though God's people had returned, His shekinah had not. Subsequently, the Hebrews rebuilt the city against all hope and despite constant opposition (Ezra–Nehemiah). Mighty men, raised up and empowered by God, led Israel to expel foreign invaders and to rededicate His desecrated temple (1 Macc. 4:36-61).

Soon they were replaced by lesser men, however, and these compromising leaders held onto the Land of Promise, not by trusting God to protect and provide for them, but through political maneuvering and backroom deals. They accepted the help of Rome to keep other invaders out. Unfortunately, their politicking left them with the mere illusion of autonomy. Like accepting favors from the mafia, the help of Rome came with strings attached. Those strings became ropes, which the Romans replaced with chains.

After the Lord had restored the Hebrews to their Promised Land and reaffirmed His commitment to protect them and to provide for their every need, they had again turned away from Him (Mal. 3:14-15). Like a vineyard of sour grapes, choked with weeds (Isa. 5:1-6), Israel produced nothing good. So it was that despite prophecies like Malachi 1:2-3, Rome had come to rule Jerusalem through a puppet leader, a descendant of Esau, who sat on the throne God had promised to the descendants of Jacob. This usurper, Herod, jealously guarded his ill-gotten title, "King of the Jews," and killed anyone who threatened to take it away, including members of his own family. Meanwhile, the priesthood had become a corrupt crime syndicate and the temple a funnel for their money.

Those who loved God and cherished His Law lacked the power to change Israel's future. The rich and powerful saw no reason to trust God for anything. Understandably, those who hoped for the coming of the Messiah and the restoration of Israel finally lost all hope. Theirs had become an impossible situation.

Against this dreary backdrop, Luke zeroes in on the personal tragedy of one priest and his wife—they were childless. They sincerely served God and sought to live blameless lives, yet this hope had remained un-fulfilled for decades, and with increasing age came the abandonment of any aspiration for a child.

Fortunately, God is full of surprises, and his surprise for them would impact their entire nation.

— 1:5-7 —

Luke begins the story of Christ with what appears at first glance to be a mundane historical reference. His original readers, however, under-stood the gravity of the phrase "in the days of Herod, king of Judea." It referred to none other than Herod the Great and the dark times he brought upon Israel. In the same way, if a present-day author were to begin his narrative with "In the days of Al Capone . . ." we would brace ourselves for a grim story.

The qualifier "king of Judea" distinguishes this Herod from his sons, who ruled smaller regions and never received the official title of "king" from Rome. Herod's family had converted to Judaism before he was born, and though he dressed like a Jew and observed many Jewish dietary laws, he didn't possess a single cell of Jewish blood. He was an Idumean who married into the Hasmonean "royal family" in order to legitimize his wearing the crown. Ironically, though, the Hasmoneans descended from the priestly line of Levi, not the kingly line of Judah. Therefore, none of the men in the "royal family" could legitimately call themselves "King of the Jews."

While this convoluted, impossible set of circumstances kept Israel on edge, it seemed to many that God had forsaken Israel. But as He often does, the Lord began working with a single individual, one

HEROD THE GREAT

LUKE 1:5

Herod the Great stopped at nothing to gain the title "King of the Jews," and he would sacrifice anything to keep it, even his own sons. Macrobius, a fifth-century historian, wrote, "When [Caesar Augustus] heard that Herod king of the Jews had ordered boys in Syria under the age of two years to be put to death and that the king's son was among those killed, he said, 'I'd rather be Herod's pig than Herod's son!'"[2]

Ironically, Herod was not of Jewish blood. His family was Idumean and had converted to Judaism sometime in the decades before his birth. His father, Antipater II, had been appointed by Rome to a high position in Judea. He was a wealthy Idumean, according to Josephus[3] and other historians. Idumeans descended from Esau, who "despised his birthright" (Gen. 25:33-34) and lost it to his scheming brother, Jacob. Herod apparently decided to turn the tables on history and snatch back what his forebear had bargained away: the right to rule Israel. Political support from Rome and a strategic marriage to a Jewish royal gave him the crown around 40 BC, and he kept it through bloody intrigue for more than forty years.

Herod pretended to be "a good Jew" by eliminating pork from his diet, but he indulged an insatiable appetite for murder—a heinous violation of the sixth commandment. He built a magnificent temple for the God of Israel—an architectural wonder in its day—yet appointed one corrupt high priest after another. He taxed Jews through the temple in keeping with the Old Testament Law but then used the proceeds to break the first commandment, building cities and temples in honor of the Roman emperor and his pantheon of Roman deities. The "days of Herod, king of Judea" were prosperous for the powerful, but horrific for everyone else.

Herod the Great was well known for his architectural feats. He rebuilt the temple and a number of structures in Jerusalem, but he also built a massive palace-fortress for himself in Bethlehem, called Herodium.

ordinary person among the many Jews of his day. God broke His four-hundred-year silence with an aging priest who had no special political or social significance. His name was Zacharias, which means "YHWH has remembered again."

Luke gives us several details about Zacharias:

1. *"of the division of Abijah"* (1:5). One of twenty-four divisions of priests, each of which ministered in the temple, performing routine duties for one week every six months, the division of Abijah was eighth in the rotation (1 Chr. 24:10).
2. *"he had a wife from the daughters of Aaron"* (Luke 1:5). He married within the priestly line of Aaron, a choice that was considered especially honorable.
3. *"They were both righteous in the sight of God"* (1:6). Their priestly pedigree was matched by their devout worship of God and their obedience to His commandments. The phrase "in the sight of God" becomes significant with the next fact about the couple.
4. *"But they had no child"* (1:7). Jewish theology at the time taught that childlessness indicated God's displeasure. To be barren was a source of incredible cultural shame, in addition to the sorrow of infertility.

5. *"They were both advanced in years"* (1:7). We don't know how old they were, but Luke's description strongly suggests Elizabeth had experienced menopause, leaving them no hope of ever having a child.

The details provided in this short introduction paint a dreary picture of hopelessness.

— 1:8-10 —

Some experts estimate the number of active priests at around twenty thousand. The twenty-four divisions (1 Chr. 24:7-18) were subdivided into four to nine "houses," each serving a daily rotation during their particular week of service. On average, each "house" may have consisted of 150 priests—far too many to serve in the confines of the inner temple. To determine which priests would fulfill each role, they drew lots.[4]

On this occasion, Zacharias received the great honor of offering incense in the holy place (Exod. 30:7-8). Twice each day, a priest would enter the holy place, trim the wicks on the lampstand, and burn incense on a small altar in front of a woven veil separating him from the most holy place. It would likely be the one and only time Zacharias would perform this duty, so this was no ordinary day! Obviously, he

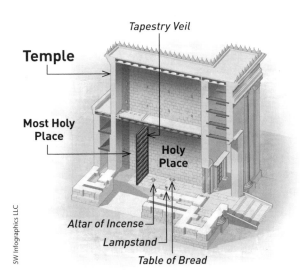

Tapestry Veil

Temple

Most Holy Place

Holy Place

Altar of Incense

Lampstand

Table of Bread

SW Infographics LLC

The diagram shows the interior of the holy place of the temple in Herod's day. Zacharias was the only priest on that day to go into the holy place to trim the wicks on the lampstand and burn incense on the altar before the veil separating that area from the most holy place, where the ark of the covenant was placed.

had no idea how his duties would pale in comparison to what God had in store for him.

Two other priests stirred the coals on the altar of burnt offering in the courtyard and filled Zacharias's censer. He was to enter the holy place, trim the lamps of the menorah, pour the hot coals on the altar of incense, and pour the powdered incense on the coals. He was to *immediately* prostrate himself and then withdraw from the room backwards. Meanwhile, the crowds that gathered in the courtyards for the morning or evening prayers waited for word that the offering had been made.

The Allotment of Priests Serving in the Temple

20,000 PRIESTS:

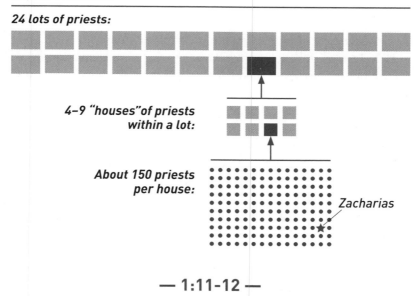

24 lots of priests:

4–9 "houses"of priests within a lot:

About 150 priests per house:

Zacharias

— 1:11-12 —

Perhaps as the initial whoosh of incense smoke cleared, Zacharias saw a heavenly messenger standing to the right of the altar. We don't know what physical form the angel took. The Bible has described the physical appearance of angels in various ways. Sometimes they appear human (e.g., Gen. 18:2, 16; Ezek. 9:2; Dan. 9:21); other times they take bizarrely symbolic forms (e.g., Isa. 6:2; Ezek. 1:6; Rev. 4:7-8). Regardless, his presence shook Zacharias and seized the aging priest with fear.

— 1:13-17 —

The angel calmed Zacharias with wonderful news. Long after his wife's body had passed the age of conception, their lifelong petition for a child would be granted. She would bear a son! The angel instructed Zacharias to give his child the name "John." But the good news didn't stop there. This son would be consecrated as a Nazirite from birth, designating him an uncommon emissary of God—holy and set apart for special use by the Lord.

According to the Law given to Israel through Moses (Num. 6:1-21), a man or woman fulfilling a vow to accomplish something for the Lord would temporarily abstain from anything associated with grapes, including wine and raisins. Someone under the Nazirite vow would refrain from cutting his or her hair until the objective had been completed. The Nazirite would avoid all contact with any dead carcass or corpse. On exceedingly rare occasions, the Lord would designate someone to become a lifelong Nazirite, such as Samson (Judg. 13:5).

The angel also revealed that John would be filled with the Holy Spirit from the moment of his conception, a divine gift more wonderful than the Old Testament believer could have imagined. God sometimes gave the gift of His Spirit to someone for a specific purpose and for a limited time. He also gave His Spirit to the King of Israel as a seal of authenticity. Never before had someone been filled with the Holy Spirit from birth to death.

And if the lifelong designation as a Nazirite and the lifelong gift of the Holy Spirit were not enough blessing, the angel revealed that John would fulfill Malachi's last prophetic promise: "Behold, I am going to send My messenger, and he will clear the way before Me. . . . Behold, I am going to send you Elijah the prophet before the coming of the great and terrible day of the LORD. He will restore the hearts of the fathers to their children and the hearts of the children to their fathers, so that I will not come and smite the land with a curse" (Mal. 3:1; 4:5-6).

Zacharias, as a seasoned priest and an expert in the Hebrew Scriptures, completely understood the implications of the angel's message. John would become the greatest old covenant prophet who had ever lived (Matt. 11:11), a worthy forerunner of the Messiah (Isa. 40:3).

— 1:18-20 —

It is hard to fault Zacharias for his disbelief. The news was almost too much to take in. Not only would his barren, elderly wife conceive a son, but what a son! In typical Old Testament fashion, he asked for a miraculous sign to confirm the authenticity of the messenger and his message (Gen. 15:8; Judg. 6:36-40; 2 Kgs. 20:8; Isa. 7:11). The angel, however, didn't appreciate this seasoned priest's lack of trust. Zacharias, of all people,

No Ordinary Day

LUKE 1:9

In my book, A Bethlehem Christmas, I imagined what Zacharias might have experienced in the temple. He knew it was a special day in the life of a priest, but he had no idea just how special it would be for him!

The Holy Place, with all its gravity and mystery, grabbed Zacharias by the senses and held him captive for what seemed an eternity. He tilted his head back and breathed in the mingled aroma of bread, incense, cedar, and the burnt flesh of sinners' substitutes. Ministering in the Holy Place was a rare opportunity in the life of an ordinary priest, so he consumed every detail with his eyes, fully intending to return there in his mind for years to come.

It was darker than he imagined. Cedar-paneled walls disappeared into the darkness nearly a hundred feet overhead before meeting a ceiling he could barely make out. Finely crafted furniture adorned God's enormous antechamber, and the gold implements appeared to be as holy as their purpose. Seven lights of a large golden lampstand flickered on his left. On the right stood a table with twelve loaves of unleavened bread, neatly arranged in two rows of six. A few steps ahead, the altar of incense. A flat, square surface standing three feet high, and overlaid with pure gold. And within arm's length of the altar, a thick linen veil separated him from the potentially lethal presence of the Almighty.

This was the place where men met God.

His task wasn't complicated. Twice each day, a priest slipped behind the outer veil with a censer of coals from the altar in one hand and a measure of incense in the other. It should take only a few moments, but Zacharias wasn't about to rush anything.

(continued on next page)

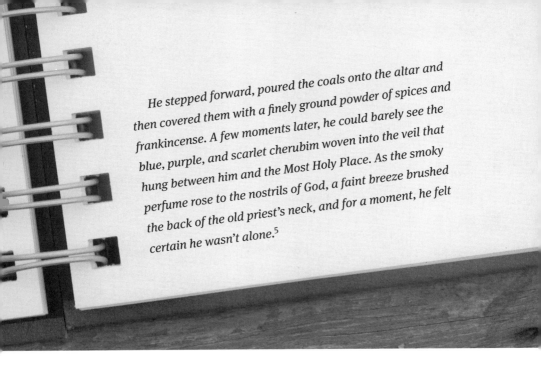

He stepped forward, poured the coals onto the altar and then covered them with a finely ground powder of spices and frankincense. A few moments later, he could barely see the blue, purple, and scarlet cherubim woven into the veil that hung between him and the Most Holy Place. As the smoky perfume rose to the nostrils of God, a faint breeze brushed the back of the old priest's neck, and for a moment, he felt certain he wasn't alone.[5]

should have trusted the word of God, and he should have believed in the power of God to fulfill His promises (Gen. 21:1). His individual reaction to the good news and his personal failure to believe God's word mirrors the failure of Israel to bring the word of God to the nations.

This particular angel—one of only two named in Scripture—identified himself as Gabriel, which means "God's valiant one." We might paraphrase his name "Hero from God." (See also Luke 1:26 and Dan. 9:21.)

Zacharias' doubting objection, "*I* am old!" (Luke 1:18) is mirrored by Gabriel's retort: "*I* am Gabriel!" He said, in effect, "I am all the proof you need. I have seen God face-to-face; I come directly from His throne room with this message. You undoubtedly remember my name from Scripture, so you know I've been doing this work for a long, long time."

The chastisement given to Zacharias is both ironic and symbolic. His disbelief rendered him mute, unable to share the wonderful news he had received from God in His sanctuary. Zacharias—a priest, a divinely ordained intermediary between God and His people—failed to believe God's message, and his lack of trust stole his voice. His nine-month silence reflected the four-hundred-year hush that preceded the fulfillment of God's promises.

— 1:21-23 —

While Zacharias dialogued with God's messenger, receiving wonderful news about the coming of the long-awaited Messiah, the people waited and prayed outside the sanctuary. According to the Mishnah (a second-century AD document recording Jewish traditions), the priests performing the day's duties were to stand on the porch before the people and pronounce a blessing.[6] Unfortunately, Zacharias bore the telltale signs of a man who either had received a divine vision or had profaned the Lord's temple. Clearly he had encountered God, but his inability to speak (or hear [1:62]) could have been interpreted in one of two ways. Both Ezekiel and Daniel temporarily lost the ability to speak after receiving visions from God (Ezek. 3:26; Dan. 10:7-8, 15). Contemporary theology also held, however, that physical ailments were God's punishment for sin. Was Zacharias's condition proof of God's abandonment or evidence of His activity?

The form of the Greek verb *dianeuō* [1269] (the imperfect periphrastic[7]) tells us that, throughout his week of service, Zacharias "kept making signs" (Luke 1:22) as a means of communication, and we also learn that he "was remaining mute" (literal translation). At the end of his appointed time at the temple, the priest returned to his home in the hill country of Judea (1:23, 39-40).

In a small measure, I can identify with Zacharias. The greatest thrill of my life is to proclaim God's message. It is perhaps the greatest joy of my entire existence. To be silenced from that would be the worst of judgments—to be a priest without a message . . . a prophet without a voice.

Imagine the sad frustration Zacharias endured, unable to verbally tell everyone, "My friends, my fellow members of the beloved, patient people of Israel: The words of our prophets are coming to pass. My wife, as barren as Israel these four-hundred years, will conceive and bear the forerunner of the Christ!"

But he could say nothing. He remained powerless to strengthen their faith or to help them endure the dark days of Herod the Great or to herald the day when "the sun of righteousness" would come "with healing in [His] wings" (Mal. 4:2). For no less than nine months and eight days—perhaps longer—he gestured and scribbled notes. His God-imposed silence taught him what years in the priesthood did not: When God speaks, your only responsibility is to trust His word.

— 1:24-25 —

"After these days," Zacharias and Elizabeth conceived. Luke doesn't tell us how long after the priest's return this occurred. Quite likely not long, if Zacharias truly believed what had been told him.

We also don't know for certain why Elizabeth "kept herself in seclusion for five months" after she became pregnant. One clue is that most women begin to show the unmistakable signs of pregnancy around five months. Perhaps Elizabeth wanted to enjoy the first months of her pregnancy away from the killjoy nay-saying of doubters.

Take note of her response (1:25) in contrast to that of her husband. Whereas Zacharias asked, "How shall I know for certain?" Elizabeth responded, in summary, "The Lord has dealt with me in grace" (cf. Gen. 30:23).

APPLICATION: LUKE 1:5-25

Impossible Opportunities

Three lasting lessons emerge from the story of Zacharias and Elizabeth.

First, *our impossibilities set the stage for God to do His best work.*

Do you have a son or daughter who is out of control, too old for you to discipline? Are you in a life-or-death struggle with an incurable disease? Is your marriage spiraling toward divorce? Finances hopelessly upside-down? Stuck in a destructive compulsion or addiction? Whatever your alleged "impossible circumstances," they set the stage for God to show His infinite power and amazing grace, to triumph over evil.

Second, *God's delays are not necessarily His denials.*

Don't misinterpret a "wait" as a "no." Don't think that if something hasn't happened in the time you expect, God has said no. His timing and His method always differ from our own. Rather than letting unmet expectations become a cause for doubt, let them become a means of growth. Use this as a time to pore over the principles you may have taken for granted, and allow the Holy Spirit to apply these truths in ways you never expected. Set aside your impatience and anger with this reassurance:

"The Rock! His work is perfect,
For all His ways are just;
A God of faithfulness and without injustice,
Righteous and upright is He. (Deut. 32:4)

Third, *when God intervenes, His surprises are always for His all-surpassing glory and our ultimate good.*

He created a perfect world, but the sin of humanity turned it into a chaotic mess, for which we are all responsible and to which we are all subject. In other words, we made a mess of God's perfect world, and He has every right to leave us in it. Nevertheless, the Lord didn't abandon us to our sin and destruction. He has promised to intervene.

As the Gospel of Luke will reveal, God intervened by becoming one of us in the person of His Son, Jesus Christ. Through the death, resurrection, and power of Jesus, the Father has promised all who trust Him that He "causes all things to work together for good to those who love God, to those who are called according to His purpose" (Rom. 8:28). "All things" includes unplanned pregnancies, unexpected calamities, unforeseen trials, and even those times when He must say no to a request. Never forget that He will use His "no" to display His glory and to bring about our ultimate good.

The Day Mary Met Gabriel
LUKE 1:26-56

NASB

26 Now in the sixth month the angel Gabriel was sent from God to a city in Galilee called Nazareth, 27 to a virgin ªengaged to a man whose name was Joseph, of the ᵇdescendants of David; and the virgin's name was ᶜMary. 28 And coming in, he said to her, "Greetings, ªfavored one! The Lord ᵇis with you." 29 But she was very perplexed at *this* statement, and kept pondering what kind of salutation this was. 30 The angel said to her, "Do not be afraid, Mary; for you have found favor with God. 31 And behold, you will conceive in your womb and bear a son, and you shall name Him Jesus. 32 He will be great and will be called the Son of the Most High; and the Lord God will give Him the throne of His father David; 33 and He will reign over the house of Jacob forever, and His kingdom will have no end." 34 Mary said to the angel, "How ªcan this be, since I ᵇam a virgin?" 35 The

NLT

26 In the sixth month of Elizabeth's pregnancy, God sent the angel Gabriel to Nazareth, a village in Galilee, 27 to a virgin named Mary. She was engaged to be married to a man named Joseph, a descendant of King David. 28 Gabriel appeared to her and said, "Greetings,* favored woman! The Lord is with you!*"
29 Confused and disturbed, Mary tried to think what the angel could mean. 30 "Don't be afraid, Mary," the angel told her, "for you have found favor with God! 31 You will conceive and give birth to a son, and you will name him Jesus. 32 He will be very great and will be called the Son of the Most High. The Lord God will give him the throne of his ancestor David. 33 And he will reign over Israel* forever; his Kingdom will never end!"
34 Mary asked the angel, "But how can this happen? I am a virgin."
35 The angel replied, "The Holy

NASB

angel answered and said to her, "The Holy Spirit will come upon you, and the power of the Most High will overshadow you; and for that reason the ᵃholy Child shall be called the Son of God. ³⁶And behold, even your relative Elizabeth has also conceived a son in her old age; and ᵃshe who was called barren is now in her sixth month. ³⁷For ᵃnothing will be impossible with God." ³⁸And Mary said, "Behold, the ᵃbondslave of the Lord; may it be done to me according to your word." And the angel departed from her.

³⁹Now ᵃat this time Mary arose and went in a hurry to the hill country, to a city of Judah, ⁴⁰and entered the house of Zacharias and greeted Elizabeth. ⁴¹When Elizabeth heard Mary's greeting, the baby leaped in her womb; and Elizabeth was filled with the Holy Spirit. ⁴²And she cried out with a loud voice and said, "Blessed *are* you among women, and blessed *is* the fruit of your womb! ⁴³And ᵃhow has it *happened* to me, that the mother of my Lord would come to me? ⁴⁴For behold, when the sound of your greeting reached my ears, the baby leaped in my womb for joy. ⁴⁵And blessed *is* she who ᵃbelieved that there would be a fulfillment of what had been spoken to her ᵇby the Lord."

⁴⁶And Mary said:
"My soul ᵃexalts the Lord,
⁴⁷ And my spirit has rejoiced in God
    my Savior.
⁴⁸ "For He has had regard for
        the humble state of His
        ᵃbondslave;
    For behold, from this time on all
        generations will count me
        blessed.
⁴⁹ "For the Mighty One has done
        great things for me;
    And holy is His name.
⁵⁰ "AND HIS MERCY IS ᵃUPON
        GENERATION AFTER
        GENERATION
    TOWARD THOSE WHO FEAR HIM.

NLT

Spirit will come upon you, and the power of the Most High will overshadow you. So the baby to be born will be holy, and he will be called the Son of God. ³⁶What's more, your relative Elizabeth has become pregnant in her old age! People used to say she was barren, but she has conceived a son and is now in her sixth month. ³⁷For the word of God will never fail.*"

³⁸Mary responded, "I am the Lord's servant. May everything you have said about me come true." And then the angel left her.

³⁹A few days later Mary hurried to the hill country of Judea, to the town ⁴⁰where Zechariah lived. She entered the house and greeted Elizabeth. ⁴¹At the sound of Mary's greeting, Elizabeth's child leaped within her, and Elizabeth was filled with the Holy Spirit.

⁴²Elizabeth gave a glad cry and exclaimed to Mary, "God has blessed you above all women, and your child is blessed. ⁴³Why am I so honored, that the mother of my Lord should visit me? ⁴⁴When I heard your greeting, the baby in my womb jumped for joy. ⁴⁵You are blessed because you believed that the Lord would do what he said."

⁴⁶Mary responded,

"Oh, how my soul praises the
        Lord.
⁴⁷   How my spirit rejoices in God
        my Savior!
⁴⁸ For he took notice of his lowly
        servant girl,
    and from now on all
        generations will call me
        blessed.
⁴⁹ For the Mighty One is holy,
    and he has done great things
        for me.
⁵⁰ He shows mercy from generation
        to generation
    to all who fear him.

51 "He has done [a]mighty deeds with His arm;
He has scattered *those who were* proud in the [b]thoughts of their heart.
52 "He has brought down rulers from *their* thrones,
And has exalted those who were humble.
53 "HE HAS FILLED THE HUNGRY WITH GOOD THINGS;
And sent away the rich empty-handed.
54 "He has given help to Israel His servant,
[a]In remembrance of His mercy,
55 As He spoke to our fathers,
To Abraham and his [a]descendants forever."

56 And Mary stayed with her about three months, and *then* returned to her home.

51 His mighty arm has done tremendous things!
He has scattered the proud and haughty ones.
52 He has brought down princes from their thrones
and exalted the humble.
53 He has filled the hungry with good things
and sent the rich away with empty hands.
54 He has helped his servant Israel and remembered to be merciful.
55 For he made this promise to our ancestors,
to Abraham and his children forever."

56 Mary stayed with Elizabeth about three months and then went back to her own home.

1:27 [a]Or *betrothed;* i.e. the first stage of marriage in Jewish culture, usually lasting for a year before the wedding night. More legal than engagement [b]Lit *house* [c]Gr *Mariam;* i.e. Heb Miriam; so throughout Luke 1:28 [a]Or *woman richly blessed* [b]Or *be* 1:34 [a]Lit *will* [b]Lit *know no man* 1:35 [a]Lit *the holy thing begotten* 1:36 [a]I.e. *this is the sixth month to her who* 1:37 [a]Lit *not any word* 1:38 [a]I.e. female slave 1:39 [a]Lit *in these days* 1:43 [a]Lit *from where this to me* 1:45 [a]Or *believed, because there will be* [b]Lit *from* 1:46 [a]Lit *makes great* 1:48 [a]I.e. female slave 1:50 [a]Lit *unto generations and generations* 1:51 [a]Lit *might* [b]Lit *thought, attitude* 1:54 [a]Lit *So as to remember* 1:55 [a]Lit *seed*

1:28a Or *Rejoice.* 1:28b Some manuscripts add *Blessed are you among women.* 1:33 Greek *over the house of Jacob.* 1:37 Some manuscripts read *For nothing is impossible with God.*

Any serious study of Jesus' birth merits an accurate understanding of the one who bore Him. Unfortunately, more confusion surrounds the mother of the Christ child than the baby Himself! Thanks to the artist's brush, the sculptor's chisel and mallet, the author's pen, and the well-meaning imagination of preachers, we know more about the Mary of dogma and legend than the real Mary of Scripture.

The Roman Catholic Church has not helped the situation by adding several unbiblical doctrines to its teaching on Mary. These include:

"Immaculate Conception," the notion that Mary was born without a fallen sin nature, free from original sin.

"Perpetual Virginity," which insists that Mary remained a virgin her entire life.

"Bodily Assumption," the belief that Mary never succumbed to death but was taken directly into heaven in bodily form.

By adding one Mary-exalting dogma to another, the Roman Catholic Church now regards Mary as a co-mediator (or "mediatrix") alongside her Son, Jesus Christ. In the words of Pope John Paul II, "In union with Christ and in submission to him, she collaborated in obtaining the grace of salvation for all humanity."[8]

Protestants during the Reformation and through the first several centuries afterward reacted sharply to Catholic errors, pushing the pendulum too far to the other side. Fearing excessive veneration for Mary, they virtually ignored her, leaving many of us today ignorant about this remarkable woman of God. Fortunately, Luke took great care to preserve her perspective regarding her role in the greatest event in history. We learn all we need to know about Mary by observing her response to a most unusual visit and her subsequent journey to Judea to visit her close relative Elizabeth.

— 1:26-27 —

Luke's account of Gabriel's visit to Mary emphasizes the link between the forerunner and the Christ in three ways. First, this second segment (1:26-56) parallels the structure of the first (1:5-25). Second, Luke established the time of this episode as "in the sixth month," referring to Elizabeth's pregnancy. Elizabeth withdrew from the public for five months; in the sixth month of her pregnancy, her close relative, Mary, experienced something extraordinary. Third, he reveals the name of the angel early in the narrative, emphasizing the fact that the same messenger that came to Zacharias came to Mary as well.

Luke emphasizes Mary's virginity by using the term *parthenos* [3933] twice in the same sentence. Some argue the word indicates merely a young girl eligible for marriage, not necessarily one untouched by a man. But the ancient Greeks prized virginity and used the term quite literally. For instance, Artemis, the goddess of Ephesus, was categorically and zealously virginal. Greeks and Romans looked to Artemis to protect chaste young men and women. Moreover, she symbolized the cultic power of virginity, representing "young and budding life and strict innocence."[9] Consequently, a young, unmarried woman was called a *parthenos*. To be anything other than virgin before her wedding would have been unthinkable, even in pagan society.

At the time of the angel's visit, this virgin was "engaged" to a man named Joseph (1:27). Jewish custom in Israel divided the process of

NAZARETH

LUKE 1:26

The name Nazareth most likely derives from one of two Hebrew terms. *Netser* [H5342] is the Hebrew word for "branch" or "shoot," which forms a wordplay for Isaiah (11:1) and Matthew (2:23). Just as likely is the Hebrew verb *natsar* [H5341], which means "to watch." Nazareth rested in a bowl-shaped depression 1150 feet (350 meters) above sea level. This made it a perfect place to keep watch over the vast Jezreel Valley (also known as the Plain of Esdraelon, the Valley of Megiddo, and Armageddon), roughly 1,000 feet below.

Archeological evidence suggests that, for centuries, no more than two hundred Hebrews farmed land and tended animals in the remote village of Nazareth.

The reputation of the Nazarenes was one of little account. When the disciple Nathanael heard that Jesus grew up in Nazareth, he curled his lip and muttered, "Can any good thing come out of Nazareth?" (John 1:46).

Nazareth Ridge. The village of Nazareth sits atop the mountain range above the Jezreel Valley.

marriage into three stages. First, the choice of a mate. A suitable match would be proposed (typically by parents). The couple and their families would take time to become acquainted and approve the match, after which they entered a formal agreement. This contract often included a dowry. Once the contract had been signed and sealed, usually in a synagogue, the couple entered the second stage: betrothal.

The betrothal period lasted no less than was necessary to make certain the bride was not already pregnant, but could last as long as a year. During this time, the bride and groom were bound to one another as husband and wife, and only a writ of divorce could break the covenant. Furthermore, if the woman was found to be pregnant during the betrothal, she was viewed as an adulteress and might be publicly stoned to punish her sin and to vindicate the groom's honor. The groom had the option to settle the matter privately to avoid a public scandal.

When the waiting period had elapsed and the groom's new living quarters had been prepared to receive the bride, the third stage transpired: A wedding ceremony celebrated the couple's union, and the families hosted a grand feast.

Mary was a betrothed virgin, waiting for the celebration of her vows and the consummation of her union with Joseph.

— 1:28-29 —

The angel's greeting, "Greetings, favored one! The Lord is with you," conveyed the idea of granting grace. Young women occupied a very low status in ancient times, so Mary probably found the angel's greeting to be startlingly gracious.

The Latin Vulgate renders the Greek as *gratiae plena*, or "full of grace." The Roman Catholic Church has taken this to mean that Mary had received an overabundance of grace that she could then bestow upon others. She becomes an intermediate source of grace. The Greek term, however, is best understood as a perfect passive verb, meaning she was the recipient of an action completed by someone else. In short, the greeting is simply emphasizing that Mary was a recipient of God's unmerited favor, a pattern for other believers who would be the recipient of God's free grace. It does not place her in a special position as mediator of overflowing grace.

— 1:30-33 —

The angel explained why Mary could be considered "favored." Heaping grace upon grace, Gabriel revealed five future facts, each more wonderful than the one before.

1. *She will conceive and bear a son (cf. Isa. 7:14).*

Every married Hebrew woman would receive this news with joy. Jews, more than any other ancient culture, cherished their offspring. And the blessing of a son meant the family legacy would continue another generation, and might even become the branch from which the Messiah would spring.

As part of the announcement, Mary was commanded to name the boy Jesus, which is the Greek equivalent of the Hebrew name Yeshua (or Joshua, in English). The name means "YHWH saves" (cf. Matt. 1:21).

2. *He will be great and will be called the Son of the Most High.*

Gabriel's announcement to Mary alludes to his announcement to Zacharias (Luke 1:15) in that the son will be "great." The messenger distinguished Jesus from John, however, by declaring Him to be the "Son of the Most High." We discover later that the title is literal. But the expression was sometimes used in the sense of "special person of God" (6:35; Ps. 82:6; Matt. 5:9). Mary probably heard it this way, only to realize later the full significance.

3. *He will be given the throne of David.*

The expression "son of God" also bore royal significance. The King of Israel was an "anointed one," a "messiah" (little *m*). He was also considered a "son of God" (2 Sam. 7:14; 1 Chr. 22:9-10; Pss. 2:7; 89:27). Gabriel revealed that Mary's son would become the King of Israel, not in the treacherous, illegitimate way Herod (a non-Jew) occupied the throne. Nor would He claim illegitimate kingly authority in the manner of the Hasmonean Dynasty (priests descended from Levi). Jesus would lay legitimate claim to David's throne as a true descendant of David (2 Sam. 7:16) and Judah (Gen. 49:10).

4. *He will be the Hebrew Messiah.*

Gabriel revealed the most amazing news of all. Jesus would not only be a special man of God and a king of Israel; He would be *the* King of Israel. *The* Messiah. The angel's use of these phrases drew upon very familiar Old Testament language associated with the Messiah (2 Sam. 7:13, 16; Ps. 89:36, 37; Isa. 9:6-7; Jer. 23:5-6).

5. *His kingdom will endure forever.*

The kingdom of God is a consistent theme throughout Luke's narrative. The nation of Israel was supposed to become a means or a vehicle of God's ruling the earth, but the people proved unworthy. The Lord chose David to become king, but even this great man failed to serve as God's worthy vice-regent. So, the Lord promised David that his dynasty would endure, eventually under the rule of a worthy king whose kingdom would exist forever (2 Sam. 7:13, 16; see also Dan. 2:44; 7:14, 18, 27). Gabriel promised that Mary's son would be that very king!

Mary knew exactly what Gabriel meant by this. She would become the mother of the Messiah (capital *M*)!

— 1:34-37 —

Mary's question differs dramatically from that of Zacharias. He asked, "How will I know this?" (1:18), and then enumerated the physical difficulties preventing the fulfillment of Gabriel's announcement. His question suggests that a miraculous sign would be enough to win his confidence. Mary's question, on the other hand, reflects genuine confusion. She asked, "How can this be?" She qualified her question by saying, literally, "since I do not know a man."

Her use of the word "know" is a euphemism for sexual relations (Gen. 4:1; 19:8; Judg. 21:12; Matt. 1:25). Her use of the present tense described her status as a virgin. She asked a reasonable, practical question. "How will this happen without a man?" She took the announcement to mean the conception would happen very soon, but her consummation with Joseph was still several months away. Clearly, the Lord didn't expect her to sin!

Gabriel provided a straightforward answer. He declared that this would be a supernatural conception involving no man—it would be the work of the Most High God through the Holy Spirit. God originally created humanity out of nothing, and He would soon create out of nothing what Mary needed to conceive a child.

Within the angel's announcement, we see all three persons of the Trinity referenced. God the Father, by the agency of the Holy Spirit, would bring the Son into the world through Mary. We also see a direct allusion to the beginning of the world. Just as the Spirit of God moved over the surface of the earth's primordial waters and then brought light into the dark, formless void (Gen. 1:2-3), so He would overshadow Mary to bring the Light of the World to humanity.

Gabriel explained how the title "Son of God" was more than an expression. This child—a holy child, free from the contamination of Adam's original sin—was actually the Son of the Most High (cf. Luke 1:32).

While Mary didn't ask for confirmation through a miraculous sign, the angel nonetheless provided something to build her confidence and sustain hope through the difficult days to come. He sealed the announcement with more good news: God had given Zacharias and Elizabeth a miraculous pregnancy as well. And with that, he alluded to the Lord's visit to Abraham and Sarah in their old age, declaring, "Nothing will be impossible with God" (cf. Gen 18:14), perhaps suggesting that even more amazing events would soon take place.

Gabriel's Heavenly Dialogue

LUKE 1:37

The problem of sin and evil creates a unique difficulty. Transgression of God's laws—decrees that reflect His very character—must carry a penalty or the laws are meaningless. Therefore, to simply set aside the penalty of sin would require the Lord to deny His very character. Yet to eradicate sin would destroy the sinner.

Gabriel and the other angels probably struggled to understand the Lord's extraordinary efforts to redeem sinful humanity. And they may have found His plan equally perplexing. If the Lord were to explain why God must become a man in order to redeem humanity, I imagine the conversation might go something like this (from Gabriel's perspective):

Unable to resolve the dilemma, I asked, "How will you destroy sin and preserve the people?"

The Lord glowed with pleasure at the opportunity to reveal the next detail of His plan. "I will provide a substitute—someone to pay the penalty of sin on their behalf."

"But who?" I protested. "How can someone pay for the sins of another if he dies paying for his own?"

"A very astute question," He answered. "The substitute must not have any sin of his own."

I was even more perplexed. "But Lord, the substitute would have to be a human in order to represent humanity, yet all of humanity has been infected with evil. Furthermore, this substitute would have to be superhuman in order to pay the penalty for all people, to die a death that would cover not just one sinner's penalty, but that of the whole multitude! What substitute can possibly suffice?"

After a short silence, God said, "God."

(continued on next page)

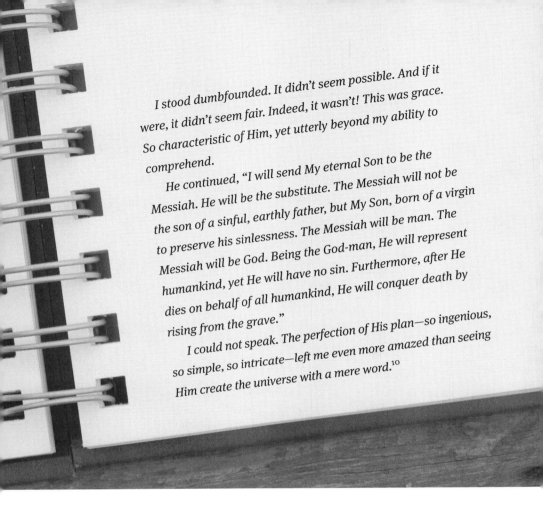

I stood dumbfounded. It didn't seem possible. And if it were, it didn't seem fair. Indeed, it wasn't! This was grace. So characteristic of Him, yet utterly beyond my ability to comprehend.

He continued, "I will send My eternal Son to be the Messiah. He will be the substitute. The Messiah will not be the son of a sinful, earthly father, but My Son, born of a virgin to preserve his sinlessness. The Messiah will be man. The Messiah will be God. Being the God-man, He will represent humankind, yet He will have no sin. Furthermore, after He dies on behalf of all humankind, He will conquer death by rising from the grave."

I could not speak. The perfection of His plan—so ingenious, so simple, so intricate—left me even more amazed than seeing Him create the universe with a mere word.[10]

— 1:38-40 —

Mary responded without hesitation. The Greek word translated "bond-slave" describes a particular kind of servitude common in her day. The term denotes a person who has voluntarily sold himself or herself into slavery, usually to pay a debt or to avoid destitution. She used this word to express her complete submission to the will of her Creator. "Behold, the bondslave of the Lord." In other words, *I willingly commit myself to the unconditional service of the Lord.*

Take note of how the women respond to the miraculous activity of God in the beginning of Luke's account. Mary felt stunned, surprised, humbled, and curious, but never once did she say, "This is impossible! I don't believe what I'm hearing." Nor did she object, "There's no way I'm going to stand before the people of Nazareth and listen to them call my son illegitimate. I refuse to spend the rest of my life defending my honor!"

Quite the opposite! While not understanding all the particulars, she responded with immediate belief, complete submission, and total trust in her Lord. Luke records no hesitation from Elizabeth in believing the Lord could accomplish a miracle. Both women lived in the horizontal dimension, but they never forgot the vertical. They lived in the realities of a broken, sinful world, but they remained open to the intervention of God's grace.

To tie the births of the forerunner and the Christ together, Luke records Mary's visit to the home of Zacharias and Elizabeth (1:39-40). She immediately hastened south from Nazareth to an unnamed city in the hill country of Judea. Luke uses geography strategically, so place names don't appear unless they have theological significance or support his narrative structure. Here, Luke's primary concern is to tell us that Mary went to be with Elizabeth.

— 1:41-45 —

By this time, Elizabeth had begun to feel the kicks of her baby, John. She had emerged from seclusion to allow everyone to see her grandmotherly frame bearing the unmistakable swelling of a baby in her womb, and no doubt she quickly became the talk of Judea. Zacharias had undoubtedly told her, through writing and gestures, the significance of John's birth. So, when Mary entered her home—by now pregnant with the Christ child—and called her name, the forerunner responded in Elizabeth's womb to the presence of the Messiah. The Holy Spirit filled Elizabeth with supernatural knowledge of Mary's condition and gave her words of praise for God.

Luke does not reveal the details of Mary's conversations before departing Galilee, or whether she had revealed anything to her family or even to Joseph. Matthew's account of Joseph's reaction (Matt. 1:18-19) probably describes the response of Mary's family and community as well. Imagine the loneliness she must have felt as she tried to explain the wonderful news of her unique place in history. Imagine the reaction of those who knew her. "Pregnant, yet still a virgin? Just stop and tell us the truth!"

In stark contrast, imagine what Mary must have felt when, without a word from her, Elizabeth knew of her pregnancy and understood its significance. While she gives honor to Mary as the bearer of the Messiah, she focuses on the child. By virtue of Mary's arrival, Elizabeth has received a royal visit from her "Lord" (Luke 1:43).

The title "Lord" in Luke's Gospel is especially meaningful. Of the 202 occurrences of the Greek term kyrios [2962] in the synoptic Gospels

(Matthew, Mark, and Luke), 104 appear in Luke, most frequently in connection with Jesus. While the everyday use of the title could refer to anyone with status or authority (e.g., Luke 13:8; 14:22), Luke's Gospel follows the precedent set by the Septuagint. This Greek translation of the Hebrew Old Testament also uses *kyrios* to refer to humans with status or authority (cf. Gen. 18:12; 23:6; Exod. 21:5-8, 28-29), but in thousands of instances, it uses it to render God's most sacred name, YHWH (Yahweh).

Elizabeth most likely didn't understand the full significance of God's incarnation, just as Mary puzzled over the idea for many years (Luke 2:19). Without a doubt, however, she knew the unborn Messiah had entered her home. She may have referred to the Messiah as "my Lord" (1:43) even if she viewed him as only human. Nevertheless, we cannot overlook the fact that the same word, *kyrios*, in 1:45 can only refer to God. This leaves open the possibility that Elizabeth understood the mystery of the Incarnation before anyone else.

— 1:46-56 —

Mary's response has been given the Latin title *The Magnificat* based on the first Greek word in the response, which means "exalt" or "magnify." Most translations arrange the text in strophes, like poetry, for two reasons. First, the meter and style of the Greek text appears hymnic. Second, much of Mary's song comes directly from Hebrew Scripture, blending quotations and allusions to messianic psalms and Old Testament prophecy.

Lines from *Magnificat*	OT Quotations/Allusions
My soul exalts the Lord	1 Sam. 2:1-2; Ps. 34:2-3
And my spirit has rejoiced in God my Savior.	Pss. 24:5; 25:5; 35:9; Isa. 12:2; Mic. 7:7; Hab. 3:18
For He has had regard for the humble state of His bondslave; For behold, from this time on all generations will count me blessed.	Ps. 138:6
For the Mighty One has done great things for me; And holy is His name.	Ps. 24:8; Zeph. 3:17
AND HIS MERCY IS UPON GENERATION AFTER GENERATION TOWARD THOSE WHO FEAR HIM.	Ps. 103:17
He has done mighty deeds with His arm; He has scattered those who were proud in the thoughts of their heart.	Pss. 98:1; 118:15
He has brought down rulers from their thrones, And has exalted those who were humble.	Job 5:11; Ps. 2

HE HAS FILLED THE HUNGRY WITH GOOD THINGS; And sent away the rich empty-handed.	Ps. 107:9
He has given help to Israel His servant, In remembrance of His mercy,	Isa. 41:8-10
As He spoke to our fathers, To Abraham and his descendants forever."	Gen. 17:19; Ps. 132:11; Isa. 41:8-9

If Mary's hymn of praise tells us anything, it's that she did not consider herself exalted, but rather a woman very much like the rest of humanity: a sinner in need of a Savior. It also reveals a woman very familiar with the Scriptures and desperately longing for the fulfillment of God's covenant promises through the Messiah. Her celebration hymn also shows that while Mary may not have completely understood the significance of the Incarnation, she recognized that the fulfillment of God's promises—all of them from the beginning of time—was growing within her womb. Mary's visit with Elizabeth lasted about three months, but she apparently returned home before John's birth (1:56).

Mary is worthy of our admiration for two very good reasons. First, God chose to honor Mary among all women to bring the Christ child into the world. Though not sinless, though very much a woman in need of a Savior, she was nevertheless chosen as a qualified vessel to bear God's Son.

Second, Mary chose to set aside her own dreams of a normal life to accept the complications of obedience. God's blessings notwithstanding, she accepted an extremely difficult assignment. The rest of Nazareth didn't receive an angelic visit, so Mary would have to endure the sting of false accusations along with the privilege of bringing God's redemptive plan to the world. She would be the bearer of the most wonderful secret in the history of humankind, yet suffer the consequences of being misunderstood.

If we venerate Mary for any reason, let it be for her remarkable example of faith and obedience.

APPLICATION: LUKE 1:26-56

His Will, His Way, His Timing

There is, perhaps, no event or issue more intimately associated with the will of God than the conception of a child. Like most matters, we have some measure of control over the how and when of conception. Medical technology gives us some ability to prevent pregnancy and offers hope to many infertile couples. But neither birth control nor fertility treatments are 100 percent effective. The miracle of new life remains God's special prerogative.

The same can be said about most issues in life. We have varying degrees of influence in matters of wealth, longevity, career, politics, society, and just about any sphere you can name. Yet, we cannot control everything. For all our ingenuity and diligence, we will experience circumstances we did not choose—either because evil occurred or because God intervened. Therefore, we must learn how to adjust to circumstances beyond our control.

In the case of Mary, God intervened to cause the impossible. A virgin conceived a child. Mary's response illustrates two helpful principles.

First, *regardless of the circumstances—whether unpleasant or enjoyable—God is in control.* Mary undoubtedly imagined the challenges she would face when the angel first announced the Lord's plan, but she could not have been prepared for just how difficult it would be. No one would believe the truth no matter how hard she tried to explain the miracle. Whispers and snickering and jokes and scorn would become her closest and most enduring companions. And she had no idea how her betrothed would react to the news. Nevertheless, she submitted to the will of God and trusted that He would see to the details.

Second, *faith is a decision, not a feeling.* Mary responded, "May it be done to me *according to your word*," not "May it be done to me because I 'have a peace about it.'" She made a conscious decision to accept her circumstances because she trusted in the character of God. She didn't wait for her conflicted emotions to settle down. She didn't ask how God would work out all the details before submitting to Him. She didn't ask for time to think it over. She made a decision to trust in the Lord's power and goodness despite the inevitable hardship that lie ahead.

When confronting circumstances beyond our control, a vertical perspective is essential. Submission to the will of God becomes much easier the more we turn our eyes from the horizontal plane to look deeply into His character. Do as the old gospel song invites:

Turn your eyes upon Jesus,
Look full in His wonderful face;
And the things of earth will grow strangely dim
In the light of His glory and grace.[11]

The Prophet of the Most High
LUKE 1:57-80

NASB

57 Now the time ªhad come for Elizabeth to give birth, and she gave birth to a son. 58 Her neighbors and her relatives heard that the Lord had ªdisplayed His great mercy toward her; and they were rejoicing with her.

59 And it happened that on the eighth day they came to circumcise the child, and they were going to call him Zacharias, ªafter his father. 60 But his mother answered and said, "No indeed; but he shall be called John." 61 And they said to her, "There is no one among your relatives who is called by that name." 62 And they made signs to his father, as to what he wanted him called. 63 And he asked for a tablet and wrote as follows, "His name is John." And they were all astonished. 64 And at once his mouth was opened and his tongue *loosed,* and he *began* to speak in praise of God. 65 Fear came on all those living around them; and all these matters were being talked about in all the hill country of Judea. 66 All who heard them kept them in mind, saying, "What then will this child *turn out to* be?" For the hand of the Lord was certainly with him.

67 And his father Zacharias was filled with the Holy Spirit, and prophesied, saying:
68 "Blessed *be* the Lord God of Israel,
For He has visited us and accomplished redemption for His people,
69 And has raised up a horn of salvation for us
In the house of David His servant—
70 As He spoke by the mouth of His holy prophets from of old—

NLT

57 When it was time for Elizabeth's baby to be born, she gave birth to a son. 58 And when her neighbors and relatives heard that the Lord had been very merciful to her, everyone rejoiced with her.

59 When the baby was eight days old, they all came for the circumcision ceremony. They wanted to name him Zechariah, after his father. 60 But Elizabeth said, "No! His name is John!"

61 "What?" they exclaimed. "There is no one in all your family by that name." 62 So they used gestures to ask the baby's father what he wanted to name him. 63 He motioned for a writing tablet, and to everyone's surprise he wrote, "His name is John." 64 Instantly Zechariah could speak again, and he began praising God.

65 Awe fell upon the whole neighborhood, and the news of what had happened spread throughout the Judean hills. 66 Everyone who heard about it reflected on these events and asked, "What will this child turn out to be?" For the hand of the Lord was surely upon him in a special way.

67 Then his father, Zechariah, was filled with the Holy Spirit and gave this prophecy:

68 "Praise the Lord, the God of Israel,
because he has visited and redeemed his people.
69 He has sent us a mighty Savior*
from the royal line of his servant David,
70 just as he promised
through his holy prophets long ago.

71ᵃSalvation FROM OUR ENEMIES,
And FROM THE HAND OF ALL WHO
HATE US;
72 To show mercy toward our
fathers,
And to remember His holy
covenant,
73 The oath which He swore to
Abraham our father,
74 To grant us that we, being
rescued from the hand of our
enemies,
Might serve Him without fear,
75 In holiness and righteousness
before Him all our days.
76 "And you, child, will be called the
prophet of the Most High;
For you will go on BEFORE THE
LORD TO PREPARE HIS WAYS;
77 To give to His people *the*
knowledge of salvation
ᵃBy the forgiveness of their sins,
78 Because of the tender mercy of
our God,
With which the Sunrise from on
high will visit us,
79 TO SHINE UPON THOSE WHO SIT IN
DARKNESS AND THE SHADOW
OF DEATH,
To guide our feet into the way of
peace."
80 And the child continued to grow
and to become strong in spirit, and
he lived in the deserts until the day
of his public appearance to Israel.

1:57 ᵃLit *was fulfilled* 1:58 ᵃLit *magnified*
1:59 ᵃLit *after the name of* 1:71 ᵃOr *Deliverance*
1:77 ᵃOr *Consisting in*

71 Now we will be saved from our
enemies
and from all who hate us.
72 He has been merciful to our
ancestors
by remembering his sacred
covenant—
73 the covenant he swore with an
oath
to our ancestor Abraham.
74 We have been rescued from our
enemies
so we can serve God without
fear,
75 in holiness and righteousness
for as long as we live.
76 "And you, my little son,
will be called the prophet of
the Most High,
because you will prepare the
way for the Lord.
77 You will tell his people how to
find salvation
through forgiveness of their
sins.
78 Because of God's tender mercy,
the morning light from heaven
is about to break upon us,*
79 to give light to those who sit in
darkness and in the shadow
of death,
and to guide us to the path of
peace."
80 John grew up and became strong
in spirit. And he lived in the wilderness until he began his public ministry to Israel.

1:69 Greek *has raised up a horn of salvation for us.*
1:78 Or *the Morning Light from Heaven is about
to visit us.*

You may be waiting patiently for God to work. If the truth were known, perhaps you are waiting *impatiently* for God to work. But you are waiting. Perhaps you are holding onto a promise from God, a message of hope you once found in His Word. And clinging to this promise has kept you from falling into a dark abyss of despair.

Let me encourage you to keep a tight grip on that promise. Hold

The Blessing of Hopelessness

LUKE 1:68-69

In the beginning, God created us to find our greatest contentment in obedience to Him. It is as much a part of us as our DNA. Tragically, however, the fall of Adam in the Garden of Eden changed everything, including human nature. We have inherited Adam's sin-twisted perspective, which doubts the goodness of God and fears that obedience to Him will somehow rob us of happiness. This compulsive drive to serve ourselves prevents us from fulfilling our created purpose. Instead of serving the will of God, we will stop at nothing to nurture our own comfort, and we are powerless to overcome our own selfishness.

To restore us to Himself, God must intervene. He must overpower our love for self and break our habit of looking for contentment in the broken, sinful world around us. Unfortunately, it is a painful, often traumatic process. Only as hope in the world fails do we seek fulfillment in the Lord. We look to Him for provision only when our paychecks stop. We look to Him for healing only when doctors give up. We trust Him for companionship only when betrayal leaves us lonely. Meanwhile, God calmly restates His promises, patiently waiting for hopelessness to complete its work in us.

Then, at just the right time, when we have given up hope in temporal concerns, He offers the gift of Himself. At the end of hope, the Lord issues an invitation to find in Him all that we cannot find in the world.

Thank God for the gift of hopelessness, without which we would forever ignore the hope we have in Him.

onto it, just like the remnant of Israel clung to the closing words of Malachi's oracle through four hundred years of dark silence. Godly men and women waited on the Lord's perfect timing, trusting His Word: "Behold, I am going to send you Elijah the prophet before the coming of the great and terrible day of the LORD" (Mal. 4:5). They waited and watched for the appearing of the forerunner, knowing the dawn of the Sun of Righteousness (Mal. 4:2) would soon dispel the darkness.

It is said that the night is darkest just before the dawn. The "days of Herod, king of Judea" (Luke 1:5) could not have been darker. Then . . . "the time had come for Elizabeth to give birth, and she gave birth to a son" (1:57). What glorious news!

— 1:57-60 —

On the day Elizabeth gave birth, Zacharias could neither speak nor hear (1:62), because he had initially doubted Gabriel's message (1:20). This paralleled the nation of Israel at that time, which had failed to obey and consequently had heard no new message from God and produced not one word from a prophet for four hundred years. With the birth of John, however, the infant cry of a prophet of the Most High pierced the silence. In time, he would bring the word of God to His covenant people and call them to repentance.

God had commanded that a newborn male was to be circumcised on the eighth day of life (Lev. 12:3). In time, this came to be the day on which the baby's name would be announced to the community, as family and friends gathered to rejoice and to witness the new baby's initiation into God's covenant with Abraham (Gen. 17:10-11). The family and friends of Zacharias and Elizabeth fully expected the boy would receive his father's name and carry the family legacy forward (Luke 1:59-61). But Elizabeth had received from Zacharias strict instructions to obey the Lord's command: "You will give him the name John" (1:13).

— 1:61-66 —

The gathered family and friends struggled to understand the happy couple's choice of name for their son. "John" is a perfectly good name, meaning "God is gracious." It was not a rare or unusual name; many men in Judea and Galilee bore the name John. But it was an odd choice because no one in Zacharias's family bore this name—and this was to be their only descendant. Nevertheless, Zacharias confirmed this choice of name in writing (1:63).

The Greek expression translated "all at once" or "immediately" is *parachrēma* [3916], a favorite term for Luke, especially when describing a miracle. Zacharias's discipline didn't last a moment longer than necessary. Just as the angel had foretold, he remained silent until John was born and had been named. His obedience loosened his tongue and opened his ears. And, as often happens when God's children emerge from discipline, Zacharias used his first words to praise God.

For Luke, "fear" with God as the object always refers to awestruck wonder (cf. 5:26; 7:16; Acts 5:11; 9:31; 19:17). In all but one case (Luke 8:37), people struck by this "fear" glorified God and were inspired to worship Him with renewed passion—that's exactly what happened here. The family and friends of the couple undoubtedly heard Zacharias tell the whole story of his experience in the temple sanctuary and the predictions concerning John's role as the forerunner of the Christ. Consequently, the gossip network covering the region of Judea lit up like a Christmas tree!

— 1:67-80 —

Sometime later, Zacharias composed a prophetic psalm, dripping with Old Testament quotations and allusions. Tradition has given this hymn the title "Benedictus," taken from the first word in the Latin translation. Whereas Mary's "Magnificat" is a personal hymn of thanksgiving, Zacharias's "Benedictus" is a hymn of praise on behalf of the nation. Both regard Mary's child as the fulfillment of God's promise concerning the Messiah, but they differ in emphasis. Mary gave thanks for a personal Savior; Zacharias praised God for sending Israel a national Redeemer. Both roles, of course, deserve equal attention. Jesus came to restore God's original created order—to eradicate evil and redeem the world—but this has personal, individual implications for each of us.

To point the people of Israel forward, Zacharias first gained a firm grip on the nation's past. He drew heavily upon Old Testament expressions; rehearsed God's covenant with Abraham, Israel, and David; celebrated God's past victories over Israel's enemies; and alluded to messianic promises (1:68-75). Then, Zacharias considered the future implications of the forerunner's arrival (1:76-79).

Blessed be the Lord God of Israel	1 Kgs. 1:48; Pss. 41:13; 72:18; 106:48
a horn of salvation for us	Pss. 18:2; 132:17
Salvation FROM OUR ENEMIES, And FROM THE HAND OF ALL WHO HATE US	Ps. 18:17 (2 Sam. 22:18); Ps. 106:10

And to remember His holy covenant, The oath which He swore to Abraham our father	Gen. 22:16-18; Pss. 105:8-9, 42; 106:45
you will go on BEFORE THE LORD TO PREPARE HIS WAYS	Isa. 40:3; Mal. 3:1; 4:5
To give to His people the knowledge of salvation By the forgiveness of their sins	Jer. 31:34
the Sunrise from on high will visit us	Mal. 4:2
TO SHINE UPON THOSE WHO SIT IN DARKNESS AND THE SHADOW OF DEATH	Isa. 9:2
To guide our feet into the way of peace	Isa. 59:8

At the heart of his prophetic psalm, Zacharias affirmed the announcement he received from the angel: "You, child, will be called a prophet of the Most High, for you will go before the Lord to prepare His ways." Luke's concluding remarks summarize John's early life to confirm that he did, indeed, become a strong-in-spirit and Spirit-filled (1:15) prophet who later won widespread respect and admiration.

The Lord did not disappoint the faithful remnant of His people living in the dark shadow of Herod's Jerusalem. Though later than His weary people desired, He set events in motion according to His perfect timing. And to keep their hope from fading in the dark hours before the dawning of the Sun of Righteousness, He conspicuously announced the arrival of the forerunner. Astute Jews would not have missed the significance of John's birth. As they watched the remarkable young prophet grow like a wildflower in the wilderness, their hope must have blossomed as well.

APPLICATION: LUKE 1:57-80

The Making of a Servant

The Lord called Israel to be a priestly nation. He set the Hebrews aside from all other peoples, ordaining them to mediate the relationship between heaven and earth, teach the Scriptures, model obedience to the Law, and become an example of living faith in God (see Exod. 19:6). He strategically placed them on a narrow land bridge—through which all the other great civilizations passed when conducting trade or making war—so they could see the *shalom* of Israel and learn of their God. Unfortunately, Israel faltered in their faith and neglected to fulfill their priestly obligations.

Luke's narrative shows Zacharias to have been a type of Israel, in that he, too, answered a priestly call but, due to wavering belief, failed to fulfill his obligations. Consequently, Israel and Zacharias endured similar divine discipline. Both endured an imposed silence.

All servants of God must periodically accept discipline, because service to Him is a high and holy calling. We are, after all, dealing with matters of eternal consequence. Therefore, while the rewards are great, the process of molding can often become intense. If you have answered the Lord's call to serve Him in teaching, preaching, or some other role in spiritual leadership, watch as the following principles become evident in your own experience.

During difficult times of discipline, God's promises keep us hoping (Mal. 3–4).

God had promised Israel a forerunner who would herald the coming of the Messiah. The Jews knew their discipline would eventually yield to celebration. Similarly, Zacharias rested in the knowledge that his imposed silence would end with the birth of his son.

Discipline is not punishment. God doesn't punish His servants—He trains them. The purpose of any divinely ordained difficulty is not retribution, but instruction. Therefore, He offers hope in the midst of a trial, always promising to restore joy when the hardship has accomplished its purpose in us.

When you find yourself under divine discipline—and all servants of God inevitably will—rest assured, your sorrow will turn to dancing in due time. As the psalmist reminds us, "Weeping may last for the night, but a shout of joy comes in the morning" (Ps. 30:5).

When relief comes, God's praise fills our mouths (Luke 1:64, 68-75).

As soon as Zacharias's tongue loosened, praise for the Lord filled his mouth.

God's discipline produces joy and inspires gratitude when the process is complete—always. Never resentment. Never bitterness. In fact, in looking back, I have noticed in myself a serene, wistful acceptance that the Lord's discipline—as difficult as it may have been—was indeed necessary. And I find myself freed from old bondages. When His surgery on my soul is complete, I get back to work with more energy and even greater enthusiasm.

When you emerge from divine discipline, you will praise Him for what He accomplished in you.

When growth occurs, God's lessons become our legacy (1:76-80).

After Zacharias praised God for His faithfulness to Israel, he immediately turned to his son. I don't believe Zacharias merely predicted John's future in ministry; I think he invested himself in preparing the boy for greatness.

When God's discipline accomplishes its transforming purpose, we have a responsibility to pass along the lessons we learn, not only to those we lead, but to any who follow us in ministry. I have found that God's discipline yields the most impactful sermons and most profound contributions to teaching and writing. While the words come from my lips and flow through my pen, I cannot claim credit for the insights. They are the fruit of divine pruning, the lessons I learned through God's discipline.

Nativity Revisited
LUKE 2:1-20

NASB

¹Now in those days a decree went out from Caesar Augustus, that a census be taken of all ᵃthe inhabited earth. ²ᵃThis was the first census taken while ᵇQuirinius was governor of Syria. ³And everyone was on his way to register for the census, each to his own city. ⁴Joseph also went up from Galilee, from the city of Nazareth, to Judea, to the city of David which is called Bethlehem, because he was of the house and family of David, ⁵in order to register along with Mary, who was engaged to him, and was with child. ⁶While they were there, the days were completed for her to give birth. ⁷And she gave birth to her firstborn son; and she wrapped Him in cloths, and laid Him in a ᵃmanger, because there was no room for them in the inn.

⁸In the same region there were *some* shepherds staying out in the fields and keeping watch over their

NLT

¹At that time the Roman emperor, Augustus, decreed that a census should be taken throughout the Roman Empire. ²(This was the first census taken when Quirinius was governor of Syria.) ³All returned to their own ancestral towns to register for this census. ⁴And because Joseph was a descendant of King David, he had to go to Bethlehem in Judea, David's ancient home. He traveled there from the village of Nazareth in Galilee. ⁵He took with him Mary, to whom he was engaged, who was now expecting a child.

⁶And while they were there, the time came for her baby to be born. ⁷She gave birth to her firstborn son. She wrapped him snugly in strips of cloth and laid him in a manger, because there was no lodging available for them.

⁸That night there were shepherds staying in the fields nearby, guarding

flock by night. 9And an angel of the Lord suddenly stood before them, and the glory of the Lord shone around them; and they were terribly frightened. 10But the angel said to them, "Do not be afraid; for behold, I bring you good news of great joy which will be for all the people; 11for today in the city of David there has been born for you a Savior, who is ªChrist the Lord. 12This *will be* a sign for you: you will find a baby wrapped in cloths and lying in a ªmanger." 13And suddenly there appeared with the angel a multitude of the heavenly host praising God and saying,

14 "Glory to God in the highest,
And on earth peace among men
ªwith whom He is pleased."

15When the angels had gone away from them into heaven, the shepherds *began* saying to one another, "Let us go straight to Bethlehem then, and see this thing that has happened which the Lord has made known to us." 16So they came in a hurry and found their way to Mary and Joseph, and the baby as He lay in the ªmanger. 17When they had seen this, they made known the statement which had been told them about this Child. 18And all who heard it wondered at the things which were told them by the shepherds. 19But Mary treasured all these things, pondering them in her heart. 20The shepherds went back, glorifying and praising God for all that they had heard and seen, just as had been told them.

2:1 ªI.e. the Roman empire 2:2 ªOr *This took place as a first census* ªGr *Kyrenios* 2:7 ªOr *feeding trough* 2:11 ªI.e. Messiah 2:12 ªOr *feeding trough* 2:14 ªLit *of good pleasure; or of good will* 2:16 ªOr *feeding trough*

their flocks of sheep. 9Suddenly, an angel of the Lord appeared among them, and the radiance of the Lord's glory surrounded them. They were terrified, 10but the angel reassured them. "Don't be afraid!" he said. "I bring you good news that will bring great joy to all people. 11The Savior— yes, the Messiah, the Lord—has been born today in Bethlehem, the city of David! 12And you will recognize him by this sign: You will find a baby wrapped snugly in strips of cloth, lying in a manger."

13Suddenly, the angel was joined by a vast host of others—the armies of heaven—praising God and saying,

14 "Glory to God in highest heaven,
and peace on earth to those
with whom God is pleased."

15When the angels had returned to heaven, the shepherds said to each other, "Let's go to Bethlehem! Let's see this thing that has happened, which the Lord has told us about." 16They hurried to the village and found Mary and Joseph. And there was the baby, lying in the manger. 17After seeing him, the shepherds told everyone what had happened and what the angel had said to them about this child. 18All who heard the shepherds' story were astonished, 19but Mary kept all these things in her heart and thought about them often. 20The shepherds went back to their flocks, glorifying and praising God for all they had heard and seen. It was just as the angel had told them.

Well-chosen gifts bring great pleasure. Birthday gifts bring joy to children; anniversary gifts say, "I love you." Farewell gifts ease the melancholy of parting, and Christmas gifts bring laughter and fun to the cold, gray-sky season of winter. But there is nothing more delightful than receiving a surprise gift—an unexpected, tangible expression of love on an otherwise ordinary day.

God is the premier gift-giver, and He specializes in surprise gifts. I believe He glows with pleasure when we stumble upon the gifts He leaves in our path. The surprise of an answered prayer. A sudden healing. An unforeseen romance. An unexpected conception (after the shock has worn off, of course!). A financial windfall, like receiving a rebate check or finding a wad of money in an old pair of jeans. As the apostle James wrote, "Every good thing given and every perfect gift is from above, coming down from the Father of lights, with whom there is no variation or shifting shadow" (Jas. 1:17). The Lord showers us with grace at every opportunity, including little surprise gifts, "just because."

No gift, however, can exceed the surprise gift He delivered to the world in a little hamlet outside Jerusalem twenty centuries ago: a tiny, squirming bundle of joy like every other child ever born, yet utterly unique in one remarkable manner. This boy was undiminished deity and true humanity, two natures perfectly united in one extraordinary person. The apostle Paul described God's gift of His Son as an "indescribable gift" (2 Cor. 9:15), a gift too wonderful for words.

Luke, under the prompting and guidance of the Holy Spirit, set out to describe God's indescribable gift in a carefully crafted narrative.

— 2:1-2 —

Luke established the relative time frame, not only for historical purposes, but to establish the social and cultural context of the Messiah's birth. Luke's Gospel habitually connects the events of Jesus' life to the world as a whole. Luke didn't tell the story of a local hero, or even a national figure; he chronicled the life of the King of kings.

On the other side of the Mediterranean Sea, nearly 1,500 miles away, a man calling himself Augustus, "supreme ruler," thought he controlled much of the known world. Luke, however, casts Caesar Gaius Octavian as a pawn of God's providence. His order to count the people of Israel merely served to move Joseph and Mary from Nazareth to Bethlehem in order to fulfill Micah's prophecy:

> But as for you, Bethlehem Ephrathah,
> Too little to be among the clans of Judah,
> From you One will go forth for Me to be ruler in Israel.
> His goings forth are from long ago,
> From the days of eternity. (Mic. 5:2)

THE STAR OF CAESAR AUGUSTUS

LUKE 2:2

On March 15, 44 BC, the same men who had declared Julius Caesar a god conspired against their leader and stabbed him to death. Everything Caesar owned—his property, wealth, and titles—then became the possession of his adopted son and sole heir, Gaius Octavius, a callow nineteen-year-old boy.

Over the next twenty years, Octavius transformed himself into the greatest leader the Roman Empire had ever known. He gradually added

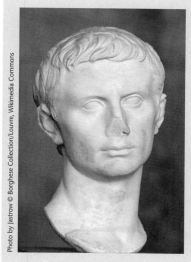
Stone bust of Caesar Augustus

to his titles the designation of *Princeps* ("leading citizen"), *Pontifex Maximus* ("high priest)," and eventually, *Augustus* ("supreme ruler"). While he actively sought these titles and openly placed himself at the center of Rome's global power, he deftly played the part of a humble, reluctant leader.

Then, in the autumn months of 12 BC, as a bright comet painted a blazing stripe across the night sky, Caesar Augustus boldly proclaimed that it was the spirit of Julius entering heaven. The superstitious Romans then affirmed Augustus's claim to deity and supported his suggestion that he, too, should be worshiped. He was, after all, the son of a god.

Some scholars have debated Luke's historical accuracy, arguing that Quirinius did not conduct a census as governor of Syria until AD 6 and that Herod the Great died no later than 4 BC. But historical evidence suggests that Quirinius had been in Syria on a military mission for Augustus from 10–7 BC and that, with Herod's increasing madness, the emperor was poised to bring the region under direct Roman control. Augustus is known to have issued orders for a census in at least three other regions (Syria, Gaul, and Spain), as well as to have maintained the Roman custom of conducting a census every fourteen years. Furthermore, Luke refers to this as the "first" census, most likely indicating it was a separate census conducted prior to the more well-known census of AD 6.

— 2:3-6 —

The census, while Roman in origin, was most likely conducted by conscripted Jews according to Jewish customs, which would have included assembly by tribes and clans.[12] This required the betrothed couple of Nazareth to journey 90 miles south to Bethlehem, the city of David, the pair's ancestral capital. Luke's description "up from Galilee" refers to the rise in elevation, unlike our modern, "north-up" map perspective.

Bethlehem, which likely means "house of bread," sat 2,350 feet (716 meters) above sea level, surrounded by fertile farmland and

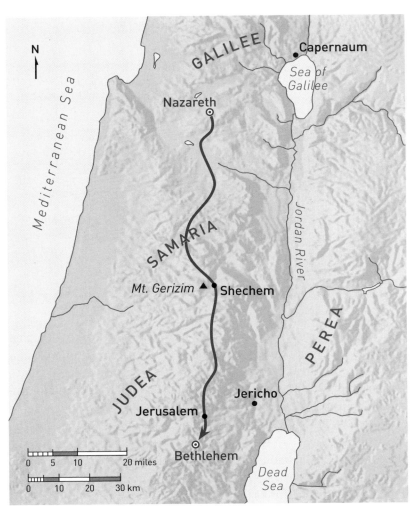

Joseph and Mary lived in Nazareth, but because of a census they traveled to Joseph's ancestral home, Bethlehem (Luke 2:1-4).

grass-covered hillsides. Locals cultivated fig trees, olive groves, and vineyards, while vast flocks of sheep and goats grazed the surrounding valleys. Five to seven miles of rugged terrain separated Bethlehem from Jerusalem, providing the kind of rural isolation typical of farming communities. The census, however, brought throngs of David's descendants from all over Herod's territory.

Luke provides few details about why Mary accompanied Joseph, or why the two would risk being that far from home with Mary so near full term in her pregnancy. Instead, he kept the story simple. Augustus ordered a census, which put the couple in Bethlehem at the time of Jesus' birth, just like the prophecy (Mic. 5:2) had predicted (cf. Luke 2:11).

I speculate that the couple probably intended to stay with family but found their ancestral city overrun with many more distant relatives than they had expected. Furthermore, the registration process probably took much longer than anyone anticipated, so Mary's pregnancy came to term before they could return home to Nazareth.

— 2:7 —

Next Christmas, in churches all across America, children will don bathrobes, sandals, and makeshift headdresses to reenact the Nativity. And much of the plot in these pageants is based on English translations of Luke's almost casual explanation ". . . because there was no room for them in the inn." Consequently, we imagine the hapless couple wandering the streets of Bethlehem, searching in vain for a "vacancy" sign but finding none.

The local inhabitants, following ancient Near Eastern rules of hospitality, would have opened their homes to the visitors, but the poor people of Bethlehem could not have accommodated every traveler. So Mary and Joseph would have sought out an "inn." Thanks to these charming children's pageants, we imagine an "inn" to be an ancient version of a Motel 6. The Greek term *katalyma* [2646], however, derives from a verb that means, literally, "to unyoke" or "to put down." The Septuagint (an ancient Greek translation of the Old Testament) frequently uses the term to mean "resting place." Therefore, *katalyma* generally refers to "lodging," usually rented or borrowed (cf. 9:12; 22:11; Mark 14:14).

It is quite possible that a temporary khan or caravansary was established in Bethlehem to supply lodging for the crowds. These large, walled, open-air courtyards were often seedy establishments run by shady characters, offering slightly better protection from robbery and

Joseph and Mary might have lodged in Bethlehem in a caravansary like this one in Qalaat al-Madiq, Syria.

the elements than sleeping on the street or in the open fields. More truck stop than motel, they were not the kind of place to give birth.

Because none of the expected human lodging was available, Mary laid the child in a *phatnē* [5336] ("feeding trough" or "animal stall"; cf. Luke 13:15), traditionally rendered as "manger," an archaic English term for a feeding trough. Caves often served as such locations, and one tradition suggests that the place of Jesus' birth was a cave, carved out of the limestone by shepherds for use as a stall.[13] Luke stressed this detail to highlight an irony: the King of kings was not born in a palace, like Augustus or Herod, or even in a comfortable home like other Jewish children. He came to earth to save humanity by becoming human, and He brought hope to the lowly by becoming lowly.

After a brief description of the setting and an even briefer sketch of the Lord's birth, Luke turned the lens of his narrative away from geography and politics to focus on a matter of great concern to him: the response to the arrival of the Savior—first by the angels sent to announce His birth (2:8-14), then by the lowly shepherds graced by the good news (2:15-18), and finally by the mother of the Christ child herself (2:19-20).

— 2:8-12 —

As soon as the Savior had entered the world, an angel was dispatched to announce His arrival, though not to kings or dignitaries, as with the birth of an earthly prince. Instead, the angel found shepherds, who customarily camped in the open fields in order to protect their flocks from predators and thieves. According to rabbinic literature from the fifth century AD, shepherds were a despised class, not unlike vagrants and homeless people today. This later tradition stands in stark contrast to the positive image of shepherds in the Old Testament, so it's unclear how Jews in Jesus' day would have regarded them. Given the hypocrisy of the religious authorities described in the Gospels, the ceremonially clean keepers of the temple would not have wanted to rub shoulders with people living among animals in the wilderness.

Whether or not Jewish culture despised shepherds, the point is clear. God sent word of His Son's birth first to people most likely to welcome news of the Messiah, people who wanted a Savior. Augustus held a firm grip on much of the known world, so his immense power blinded him to his own need. Herod the Great strutted around the marble floors of his Roman-style palace, at once complacent in his achievements yet paranoid of potential enemies around him. According to Matthew, Herod considered the Messiah a political rival and tried to have Him assassinated (Matt. 2:13); so, obviously he would not have received the news with joy. The religious authorities who ruled the temple under the puppet master Annas wanted a messiah to affirm their hypocrisy and advance their political agenda; so, they would not have received the news of His humble birth as authentic.

"An angel of the Lord" (not *the* angel of the Lord, as in the Old Testament) appearing to the shepherds may have been Gabriel (Luke 1:19, 26), but it could have been another. Regardless, the angel stood before the humble men of the field, not as a natural human, but as an obviously supernatural vision accompanied by the glory of God's presence. As with Zacharias and Mary, the angel's appearance gripped the shepherds with fear, prompting the reassurance, "Do not fear" (cf. 1:13, 30).

The messenger's announcement begins with a term familiar in the ancient world. The verb *euangelizō* [2097] means "to proclaim news" or "to announce information." This verb described the actions of a messenger bearing official proclamations of the king or announcing news of military victory or the birth of a royal heir. In fact, "the announcement is in rhythmic prose, and finds an interesting parallel in a statement about the birth of Augustus."[14] Strictly speaking, the proclamation could contain bad news, but the term was more often associated with glad tidings. Therefore, the messenger qualified the message with the phrase "great joy." Moreover, this information is "for all the people," implying that the men bore a certain responsibility to do something with the good news they were hearing.

The message contained detailed information about the arrival of the Messiah and specific information leading to His location:

- "today": The waiting is over; the birth has already occurred.
- "in the city of David": Bethlehem was not formally called this. In fact, most people would have considered Jerusalem the city of David. But the shepherds would have recognized the angel's reference in connection with their hometown hero. Furthermore, the announcement deliberately connects the birth of Christ with the bloodline of David in fulfillment of Micah's prophecy (Mic. 5:2) and God's promise (2 Sam. 7:12-13). The Lord's covenant promise to David was immediately fulfilled in the reign of Solomon, but ultimately in the Messiah.
- "born for you": The "you" in Greek is plural because Jesus came to the world to redeem all of humanity. Whereas Matthew presents Jesus as the Jewish Messiah, establishing a worldwide monarchy in which individuals may take refuge, Luke emphasizes His role as the Savior of the world.
- "a Savior, who is Christ the Lord": Luke sandwiched the title "Christ" (*Christos* [5547]) between that of "Savior" and "the Lord." Throughout the Septuagint, the Greek term for "savior" is closely associated with God, who is called both *theos* (God) and *kyrios* (Lord) (cf. Deut. 32:15; Pss. 24:5; 25:5; 62:2, 6-7; 79:9; 95:1). "Christ the Lord" essentially means the same as "Messiah God."[15]
- "wrapped in cloths and lying in a manger": The angelic messenger gave them information that would distinguish the Christ child from other newborn infants they might find. The description highlighted both the ordinary and extraordinary. Like all newborns in that day, Jesus was bundled in strips of cloth. Yet, unlike all other children, this infant lay in a "feeding trough" or "animal stall" (cf. Luke 2:7). If a cave was being used for this purpose, it is possible that it had been in use by these very shepherds.

— 2:13-14 —

"Suddenly" or "unexpectedly" a large group of angels joined the first, which Luke calls a "multitude of the heavenly host"—an image seen in the Old Testament as well (e.g., 1 Kgs. 22:19). The assembled angels represented the awesome power of heaven gathered, on this particular occasion, for peaceful purposes. By leading the celebration of Christ's birth, they showed submission to the infant King of the world and asserted His authority against the powers of darkness. They gave vertical praise to God and affirmed the horizontal effect of His grace.

When the Lord's redemptive plan is complete, He will have restored peace between God and humanity (Rom. 5:1), as well as peace between all individuals. The phrase "with whom He is pleased" comes from a single Greek word, *eudokia* [2107], which is notoriously difficult to translate. It is loosely based on a classical Greek verb meaning "to take pleasure or delight in" but is otherwise not found anywhere outside biblical literature. *Eudokia* appears to have been coined by the translators of the Septuagint to render some instances of the Hebrew term *rātson* [H7522], which often implies divine grace (Pss. 5:12; 51:18; 106:4).

The NASB rendering vaguely suggests that something in humanity pleased God, prompting Him to reward us with His favor. The NIV translation, "on whom his favor rests," captures the expression a little better. Based on no particular merit of our own, God delighted to grace humanity with a Savior.

— 2:15-18 —
Just as suddenly as the angelic host had filled the skies, these celestial celebrants retreated to the invisible realm of heaven, leaving the shepherds in the dark of night—but glowing inwardly. Their harsh, solitary life among the flocks—subject to the elements, overlooked by polite society, on guard against jackals of both the animal and human variety—did not give these men much opportunity to celebrate. But they had just received the greatest news humanity could have heard. They responded immediately to the announcement of a Savior and set off to find their Messiah.

— 2:19-20 —
In the solitude of a 2 a.m. feeding, every new mother ponders the miracle she holds and tries to imagine what kind of person her tiny baby will become. Mary, however, had much more to consider. The shepherds' report of the thunderous praise of countless angels, who had referred to her son as "the Messiah" and who had even affirmed the divine providence involved in the family's pitiful lodging situation, only

further added to the surprising nature of what she had already heard from Gabriel. After the wonderstruck shepherds set off, continuing to spread the wonderful news, she was left in reflection, still staring at her newborn child.

The Greek term translated "treasured" means "to preserve," "to guard," or "to keep watch." The accompanying verb, rendered "pondering," literally means "to bring together," much like someone arranging the pieces of a jigsaw puzzle. For Mary, the last nine months had included an angelic visit, a difficult announcement, the near collapse of her betrothal, and less-than-ideal circumstances for childbirth. She must have recalled Joseph's anguish and his unflinching obedience to the will of God. She probably marveled at the timing of the census, the birth of God's Son in a stable, and the worship of shepherds. Her memories formed a complex and curious puzzle that dared to be solved. For years to come, Mary would arrange and then rearrange everything she had experienced in order to make sense of it all.

Who can blame her? Two thousand years later, we are still coming to terms with the miraculous, inexplicable mystery of a man who is God because God became a man.

Luke's account of the Lord's birth leaves out many details we might like to know. Why did Mary go to Bethlehem so close to the time of delivery? Or did something happen to delay the couple's return to Nazareth? Did she have a midwife, or did Joseph perform an emergency delivery? Did the angels sing in antiphonal voice, or did they shout? I have a dozen more questions, and I suspect you do as well. But the Lord didn't direct Luke's pen to satisfy our curiosity. God prompted Luke to write something simple that would help us recognize His surprise gift. We know from the story that Jesus is a descendant of David and the rightful heir to Israel's throne. We know He was born in Bethlehem in fulfillment of prophecy (Mic. 5:2) yet could also be called a Nazarene as predicted (Matt. 2:23; see also "Nazareth," page 43). We know the angels affirmed His divine nature as Savior-Messiah-Lord. And we know from Mary's response that the unfolding story will reveal much more about this remarkable baby.

God's surprise gift to the world had many more surprises in store.

APPLICATION: LUKE 2:1-20

Your Testimony

I find it interesting that God did not deliver the good news of the Messiah's birth to priests or prophets or kings. Rather than issue an official proclamation from the steps of the temple or the throne of a king, the Lord sent His angels to a group of nameless shepherds. He chose the least influential individuals—humanly speaking—to become the first witnesses to a message "which will be for all the people" (Luke 2:10).

While the shepherds undoubtedly recognized their own lack of status and influence, they nonetheless responded immediately. I find in their example two worthy exhortations for us today.

First, *respond immediately to opportunities*.

As soon as the angels disappeared and the skies closed the men said, "Let us go" (2:15), and they went "in a hurry" to find the Savior (2:16).

Don't wait for special occasions to talk about the Lord. Speak up whenever the opportunity arises. You don't have to be obnoxious by forcing a conversation, but remain continually transparent about your relationship with Christ. Watch for open doors. Don't hesitate; speak freely.

Second, *share your experience*.

God didn't call the shepherds to teach or preach. They had neither the training nor the skills. Instead, the Lord charged them with the responsibility to share what they had seen and heard, to describe their experience. In response, the shepherds "made known the statement which had been told them about this Child" (2:17).

Biblical and theological training is good. I highly recommend it for everyone, regardless of their calling or vocation. But you don't need formal training to tell others about Jesus Christ, any more than you need medical training to tell a friend about a good doctor. If you are a believer, you have a "before-and-after" story of your experience with Jesus Christ. Before you placed your faith in Christ, your life looked one way. After trusting in Him, your life changed. Your "testimony" is simply a description of the before-and-after change you experienced.

If a group of shepherds could do it, so can you. Respond immediately to opportunities and share your experience.

A Sacrifice, a Savior, a Sword
LUKE 2:21-38

NASB

21 And when eight days had passed, [a]before His circumcision, His name was *then* called Jesus, the name given by the angel before He was conceived in the womb.

22 And when the days for their purification according to the law of Moses were completed, they brought Him up to Jerusalem to present Him to the Lord 23 (as it is written in the Law of the Lord, "EVERY *firstborn* MALE THAT OPENS THE WOMB SHALL BE CALLED HOLY TO THE LORD"), 24 and to offer a sacrifice according to what was said in the Law of the Lord, "A PAIR OF TURTLEDOVES OR TWO YOUNG PIGEONS."

25 And there was a man in Jerusalem whose name was Simeon; and this man was righteous and devout, looking for the consolation of Israel; and the Holy Spirit was upon him. 26 And it had been revealed to him by the Holy Spirit that he would not see death before he had seen the Lord's [a]Christ. 27 And he came in the Spirit into the temple; and when the parents brought in the child Jesus, [a]to carry out for Him the custom of the Law, 28 then he took Him into his arms, and blessed God, and said,

29 "Now Lord, You are releasing
　　　Your bond-servant to depart
　　　in peace,
　　According to Your word;
30 For my eyes have seen Your
　　　salvation,
31 Which You have prepared in the
　　　presence of all peoples,
32 A LIGHT [a]OF REVELATION TO THE
　　　GENTILES,
　　And the glory of Your people
　　　Israel."

33 And His father and mother were amazed at the things which

NLT

21 Eight days later, when the baby was circumcised, he was named Jesus, the name given him by the angel even before he was conceived.

22 Then it was time for their purification offering, as required by the law of Moses after the birth of a child; so his parents took him to Jerusalem to present him to the Lord. 23 The law of the Lord says, "If a woman's first child is a boy, he must be dedicated to the LORD."* 24 So they offered the sacrifice required in the law of the Lord—"either a pair of turtledoves or two young pigeons."*

25 At that time there was a man in Jerusalem named Simeon. He was righteous and devout and was eagerly waiting for the Messiah to come and rescue Israel. The Holy Spirit was upon him 26 and had revealed to him that he would not die until he had seen the Lord's Messiah. 27 That day the Spirit led him to the Temple. So when Mary and Joseph came to present the baby Jesus to the Lord as the law required, 28 Simeon was there. He took the child in his arms and praised God, saying,

29 "Sovereign Lord, now let your
　　　servant die in peace,
　　as you have promised.
30 I have seen your salvation,
31 　which you have prepared for
　　　all people.
32 He is a light to reveal God to the
　　　nations,
　　and he is the glory of your
　　　people Israel!"

33 Jesus' parents were amazed at what was being said about him.

were being said about Him. ³⁴ And Simeon blessed them and said to Mary His mother, "Behold, this *Child* is appointed for the fall and ᵃrise of many in Israel, and for a sign to be opposed— ³⁵ and a sword will pierce even your own soul—to the end that thoughts from many hearts may be revealed."

³⁶ And there was a prophetess, ᵃAnna the daughter of Phanuel, of the tribe of Asher. She was advanced in ᵇyears and had lived with *her* husband seven years after her ᶜmarriage, ³⁷ and then as a widow to the age of eighty-four. She never left the temple, serving night and day with fastings and prayers. ³⁸ At that very ᵃmoment she came up and *began* giving thanks to God, and continued to speak of Him to all those who were looking for the redemption of Jerusalem.

2:21 ᵃLit *so as to circumcise Him* 2:26 ᵃI.e. Messiah 2:27 ᵃLit *to do for Him according to* 2:32 ᵃOr *for* 2:34 ᵃOr *resurrection* 2:36 ᵃOr *Hannah* ᵇLit *days* ᶜLit *virginity* 2:38 ᵃLit *hour*

³⁴ Then Simeon blessed them, and he said to Mary, the baby's mother, "This child is destined to cause many in Israel to fall, and many others to rise. He has been sent as a sign from God, but many will oppose him. ³⁵ As a result, the deepest thoughts of many hearts will be revealed. And a sword will pierce your very soul."

³⁶ Anna, a prophet, was also there in the Temple. She was the daughter of Phanuel from the tribe of Asher, and she was very old. Her husband died when they had been married only seven years. ³⁷ Then she lived as a widow to the age of eighty-four.* She never left the Temple but stayed there day and night, worshiping God with fasting and prayer. ³⁸ She came along just as Simeon was talking with Mary and Joseph, and she began praising God. She talked about the child to everyone who had been waiting expectantly for God to rescue Jerusalem.

2:23 Exod 13:2. 2:24 Lev 12:8. 2:37 Or *She had been a widow for eighty-four years.*

I used to skip over certain passages of Scripture when preaching through a book of the Bible. In my younger days, this might have been one of them. At first glance, there isn't much to see—just a lot of mundane details about how Joseph and Mary fulfilled the customary obligations of first-century Judaism. This is the kind of information parents like to tell, but no one wants to hear. Johnny's first haircut. Suzie's first missing tooth. Considering how little detail Luke provided concerning the birth of the Messiah, however, I realized that there might be something worth noticing in these mundane details. After all, Luke included only three stories from the childhood of Jesus, and this is one of them. This seemingly insignificant episode—typically bypassed when telling the story of Jesus—contains some remarkable truths about the Christ child that I summarize in three catchwords: sacrifice (to fulfill the Law; 2:24), Savior (another prophetic declaration about Jesus; 2:30), and sword (the Messiah's destiny; 2:35).

— 2:21-24 —

As we begin to examine this episode in the life of Jesus, take note of Luke's curious repetition:

- "according to the law of Moses" (2:22)
- "as it is written in the Law of the Lord" (2:23)
- "according to what was said in the Law of the Lord" (2:24)
- "the custom of the Law" (2:27)

Luke even transitions from this episode to the next with the summary statement, "When they had performed *everything according to the*

RITUALLY UNCLEAN

LUKE 2:24

According to Jewish Law, a new mother was to remain in seclusion no less than forty days (Lev. 12:2-4) after the birth of a son. During this time, she was considered *ritually* unclean. The adjective "ritually" is vitally important to understand, because it doesn't carry the negative connotations twenty-first-century Westerners imagine.

The Law of Moses declared many routine activities "ritually unclean." Ritual cleansing required copious washing and a waiting period before contact with food or other people. This uncleanness could be related to literal uncleanness, such as when a person touches a carcass or feces (Lev. 5:2). Very often, however, ritual "uncleanness" was symbolic and could include eating certain kinds of food, such as rabbit or shellfish (Lev. 11:6-19). Later, Jesus declared all foods "clean," or ceremonially permissible to eat (Mark 7:14-20). God never had a moral objection to shellfish; rather, He used it and other foods symbolically to teach the Jewish people the concept of consecration.

By declaring women *ritually* unclean during menstruation, the Lord blessed women with time off from the daily routine, providing them with privacy and rest long before feminine hygiene products made normal activities possible. And by declaring new mothers *ritually* unclean for several weeks after childbirth, He protected women and their newborns from potential disease due to contact with the general population.

The God of Israel took good care of His covenant people. They were suffering slaves when He first called them out of Egypt, but within a couple of generations He transformed them into a society charged with showing the world His nature. They observed the rule of law, they enjoyed better health and greater freedom from disease, and they saw lower infant mortality and higher life expectancy than their neighbors. All because God loved them enough to declare some things ceremonially or ritually "unclean" several millennia before modern science taught us how to live longer, healthier lives.

Law of the Lord, they returned to Galilee, to their own city of Nazareth" (2:39, emphasis mine).

Jesus later declared that he did not come "to abolish the Law . . . but to fulfill [it]" (Matt. 5:17), and "It is easier for heaven and earth to pass away than for one stroke of a letter of the Law to fail" (Luke 16:17). From the beginning of His earthly life, even before He could talk or walk or exercise His will as a human, Jesus fulfilled the requirements of God's covenant with the Jews.

On the eighth day of life, a newborn male was to be circumcised (Gen. 17:11-12; Lev. 12:3), at which time parents customarily announced the boy's name. By following this Law of Moses, by bearing the sign of God's covenant with Abraham, Jesus became identified with the nation of Israel. Luke's description parallels his account of John's circumcision (Luke 1:57-66). Upon his circumcision, the couple named him Jesus, as instructed by the angel.

For the next thirty-three days, Joseph and Mary observed Old Testament laws by keeping the new mother and her child away from general contact with people and from daily routines. At the end of this period of ritual uncleanness, the family was to present their firstborn son in the temple and redeem him in recognition of the fact that he belonged to God (Exod. 13:2-15; Num. 3:13; 8:17; 18:15-16). Afterwards, the parents took their child home, but with the reminder that he and they belonged to the Lord. For all children, regardless of birth order, the parents were to bring a sin offering (Lev. 12:6-7). Because Joseph and Mary brought a pair of doves as an offering, we know they were not wealthy (Lev. 12:8).

— 2:25-26 —

Luke abruptly shifts his narrative to tell a remarkable story of a devout Jew anxiously awaiting the arrival of the Messiah. We call the four-hundred-year span between Malachi and the birth of Christ a period of divine silence, meaning that no prophet wrote or spoke to the nation on behalf of God. That's not to say, however, that the Lord had turned His back on His people. He miraculously preserved them through foreign invasion and affirmed their rededication of the temple after it had been desecrated. (Jews today continue to celebrate this event at Hanukkah, or the "Feast of Dedication" [John 10:22; cf. 1 Macc. 4:52-60].) Furthermore, God spoke personally and supernaturally to devout men and women.

While Augustus Caesar strutted the marbled floors of his palace pulling the strings of power to suit his own agenda, while Herod maniacally searched out and destroyed potential rivals to his ill-gotten throne, and while religious leaders skimmed money from the temple treasury and twisted Judaism to suit their perverse lust for power, God's people quietly prayed for the coming of the Messiah. Simeon (Luke 2:25), whose name derives from the Hebrew verb "to hear," lived in daily expectation of "the consolation of Israel," a common messianic reference in Isaiah (Isa. 40:1; 49:13; 51:3; 57:18; 61:2). The Holy Spirit revealed to this member of Israel's believing remnant that he would see the Messiah in his own lifetime.

— 2:27-32 —

In the same way that Simeon knew he would see the Christ before his death, he knew to come to the temple on that particular day, and he knew which couple carried the Christ child. Who knows how long the man had been rehearsing these lines in anticipation of this day? But, when he took the baby in his arms, he offered to the Lord a hymn of praise. The lines of his blessing bear the telltale rhythm and meter of a song, just like the praise songs of Mary (1:46-55) and Zacharias (1:68-79).

His short song can be divided into two sections. The first (2:29-30) celebrates the fulfillment of God's promise to him personally. The second (2:31-32) celebrates the provision of a Savior to the entire world, both Jew and Gentile.

Take note of Simeon's emphasis on eyes, seeing, light, and glory. The archetype of light as a symbol for truth can be traced throughout the Bible. Furthermore, God's "glory" had long been associated with light, with the radiant splendor of His character often being manifested in the light that came to be called the shekinah. Simeon's song draws upon the close association of glory with God's visible presence to declare that this little baby was nothing less than God revealed in physical form.

— 2:33-35 —

Joseph and Mary were "amazed." Luke will use the Greek term *thaumazō* [2296] often as he describes the reaction of witnesses to the miracles of Jesus. It carries the idea of wonder or astonishment.

I am amazed that the couple was amazed. Each had received a personal visit from an angel bearing astounding news. They had experienced a virgin conception and birth. They knew they held the Messiah in their arms and had heard the report of the shepherds, how a host of angels split the heavens and filled the night sky with their praise of "Messiah God." Yet Simeon's song astonished them.

Mary didn't completely comprehend what had happened. In fact, the reality of God becoming a human would take the people who knew Jesus a lifetime to appreciate. We look back at them and wonder how they could be so slow to grasp the truth. But I'm sure if they could see into the future, they would marvel that we are not more amazed!

After blessing the couple, Simeon prophesied the future of the Christ child. He would be both a blessing and a curse to individuals, depending upon how they regarded Him. He would cause some to fall as a stone of stumbling (Isa. 8:14-15), while to others He would be a cornerstone (Isa. 28:16) upon which to build.[16] He would become the means of destruction for those who oppose the redemptive plan of God, but the source of salvation for those who submit to Him.

Simeon predicted the boy's effect on Mary personally and on the nation as a whole. The Messiah's death would be like a soldier's sword to His mother, and it would divide the nation like a broadsword, separating true children of the covenant from unbelievers (cf. Matt. 10:34-39).

— 2:36-38 —

Another fixture of the temple in Jerusalem was a woman named Anna, or, more properly, Hannah, which is Hebrew for "grace" or "mercy." Luke designates her a "prophetess" (cf. Exod. 15:20; Judg. 4:4; 2 Kgs. 22:14; Neh. 6:14; Isa. 8:3), meaning she received revelation from God. She suffered a terrible, yet common, tragedy in that her husband died after only seven years of marriage. Rather than remarry, as women were strongly encouraged to do (1 Tim. 5:14), she devoted the remainder of her very long life to praying, fasting, and worshiping in the temple. Like Simeon, she actively anticipated the coming of the Messiah and the "redemption of Jerusalem" (Luke 2:38)—a figurative way of indicating the nation of Israel as a whole by reference to its capital.

She and Simeon probably knew one another and worshiped with a group of people who eagerly sought the One who would redeem Jerusalem. After Simeon had made his pronouncement, she arrived and gave further prophetic confirmation that the baby was the long-awaited Redeemer, and she excitedly began to announce his arrival to all who had hoped for the Messiah. Luke doesn't reveal how the people responded to her report. We don't know whether they scorned her as a feebleminded, old woman or heeded her words as a prophetess.

Curiously, Luke abruptly ends the episode with a summary of Jesus' first twelve years of life. Perhaps Luke included this brief snippet from Mary's baby book to let us know that the arrival of the Messiah was neither quiet nor unexpected. His birth had been announced to the people most likely to care, and they spread the news like wildfire. Many people anticipated His coming, although none of them occupied positions of power, wealth, or religious influence. So, without much fanfare, the Christ entered the temple to satisfy the requirement of the Law and to take His place alongside His kindred Jews. Only a small remnant understood the importance of what occurred that day.

While the Christ child's visit to His Father's house passed without much notice from the rulers and priests of Israel, we begin to appreciate several truths about Jesus. In the short span of eighteen verses, we discover an important relationship between the Messiah and the Law of God. While the Christ came to usher Israel into a new era of grace, He did not come to invalidate the Law God had given to Israel through Moses. On the contrary, the Messiah came to satisfy the Law on Israel's behalf.

We also see Jesus as a personal and historical linchpin connecting Israel's dismal past with its glorious future. The sin of Israel and its failure to steward the word of God to the nations prevented the nation from receiving all the covenant blessings of the Lord. In the Christ, through His obedience, Israel will finally receive the full measure of peace, prosperity, and power that God had always longed to give His people.

And we learn in the prophetic utterance of a "righteous and devout" (2:25) worshiper that the events of Golgotha trace their beginning to Bethlehem. The Son of God was born to die and destined to rise again.

APPLICATION: LUKE 2:21-38

Clean and Clear

Power has its privileges. Just ask the judge who is stopped for speeding or the magnate who needs a favor from the government. Rules have a way of bending under the feet of powerful people. So, it is especially refreshing when a person of great authority or significance subjects himself or herself to the same rules that govern the rest of us. There is something admirable about a judge paying parking tickets.

Mary and Joseph had just experienced the birth of the Messiah. The

King of all creation lay cooing in their arms, and they had already endured so much. False accusations of impropriety. A long journey to pay an oppressive tax. Less-than-ideal conditions for delivering a child. So, if anyone could or should be excused from purity rituals and temple customs, it certainly would be the mother of God and her husband! Yet, take note of their meticulous obedience to the Law.

- Joseph and Mary circumcised Jesus on the eighth day (2:21; see Gen. 17:12; Lev. 12:3).
- They named Him at the time of his circumcision (Luke 2:21; 1:31).
- Mary observed her forty "days of purification" (2:22; see Lev. 12:6-8).
- Joseph and Mary brought Jesus to the temple to present Him to the Lord (Luke 2:22-23; see Exod. 13:2, 12; Num. 3:13; 8:17).
- Joseph and Mary brought the required sacrifice after childbirth (Luke 2:24; see Lev. 5:7; 12:8).
- The couple "performed everything according to the Law of the Lord" (Luke 2:39).

I once served with an admirable executive pastor who frequently used the expression "clean and clear." It's a good standard. Every decision needs to be clean of any wrongdoing and clear of any future entanglements. It adds a lot of work and sometimes costs extra money, but you can't put a price tag on the peace of mind that comes from knowing everything is done correctly. Joseph and Mary returned to Nazareth "clean and clear," ready to settle down and nurture the Christ child to adulthood.

What about you? Is everything "clean and clear" in your life? Would a tax audit send you into a panic? Would a thorough investigation into your business dealings cause you stress? If you discovered that a private detective had been recording your every move in the last month, would that make you nervous? Would a recording of your computer keystrokes reveal anything shameful? Do you follow company policies? Report your expenses fairly? Behave the same at home as you do at work, at church, and while away on business trips?

Do you apply rules and regulations fairly? In other words, do you subject yourself to the same standards as everyone else, or do you exercise the prerogative of power to overlook some requirements and "conveniently" bend a few rules?

How differently would you live if every decision were "clean and clear"?

The Day the Pupil Stumped the Professors
LUKE 2:39-52

NASB

39 When they had performed everything according to the Law of the Lord, they returned to Galilee, to their own city of Nazareth. 40 The Child continued to grow and become strong, ªincreasing in wisdom; and the grace of God was upon Him.

41 Now His parents went to Jerusalem every year at the Feast of the Passover. 42 And when He became twelve, they went up *there* according to the custom of the Feast; 43 and as they were returning, after spending the full number of days, the boy Jesus stayed behind in Jerusalem. But His parents were unaware of it, 44 but supposed Him to be in the caravan, and went a day's journey; and they *began* looking for Him among their relatives and acquaintances. 45 When they did not find Him, they returned to Jerusalem looking for Him. 46 Then, after three days they found Him in the temple, sitting in the midst of the teachers, both listening to them and asking them questions. 47 And all who heard Him were amazed at His understanding and His answers. 48 When they saw Him, they were astonished; and His mother said to Him, "ªSon, why have You treated us this way? Behold, Your father and I ᵇhave been anxiously looking for You." 49 And He said to them, "Why is it that you were looking for Me? Did you not know that I had to be in My Father's ªhouse?" 50 But they did not understand the statement which He ªhad made to them. 51 And He went down with them and came to Nazareth, and He continued in subjection to them; and His mother treasured all *these* ªthings in her heart.

NLT

39 When Jesus' parents had fulfilled all the requirements of the law of the Lord, they returned home to Nazareth in Galilee. 40 There the child grew up healthy and strong. He was filled with wisdom, and God's favor was on him.

41 Every year Jesus' parents went to Jerusalem for the Passover festival. 42 When Jesus was twelve years old, they attended the festival as usual. 43 After the celebration was over, they started home to Nazareth, but Jesus stayed behind in Jerusalem. His parents didn't miss him at first, 44 because they assumed he was among the other travelers. But when he didn't show up that evening, they started looking for him among their relatives and friends. 45 When they couldn't find him, they went back to Jerusalem to search for him there. 46 Three days later they finally discovered him in the Temple, sitting among the religious teachers, listening to them and asking questions. 47 All who heard him were amazed at his understanding and his answers. 48 His parents didn't know what to think. "Son," his mother said to him, "why have you done this to us? Your father and I have been frantic, searching for you everywhere." 49 "But why did you need to search?" he asked. "Didn't you know that I must be in my Father's house?"* 50 But they didn't understand what he meant. 51 Then he returned to Nazareth with them and was obedient to them. And his mother stored all these things in her heart.

⁵²And Jesus kept increasing in wisdom and ªstature, and in favor with God and men.

2:40 ªLit *becoming full of* 2:48 ªOr *Child* ᵇLit *are looking* 2:49 ªOr *affairs*; lit *in the things of My Father* 2:50 ªLit *had spoken* 2:51 ªLit *words* 2:52 ªOr *age*

⁵²Jesus grew in wisdom and in stature and in favor with God and all the people.

2:49 Or *"Didn't you realize that I should be involved with my Father's affairs?"*

In preparation for writing a book on parenting, I was curious to learn about the childhood of the great biblical figures. I wanted to see how their earliest experiences may have influenced their relationship with the Lord and perhaps guided their adult decisions. So, I began my study in Genesis and searched the pages of the Old and New Testaments looking for helpful information. To my amazement, I didn't find much.

Cain and Abel were born, and the next thing you know, Cain is killing his brother Abel. We first encounter Noah as an adult who "found favor in the eyes of the LORD" (Gen. 6:8). Abraham was old enough to be a grandfather by the time we meet him. Esau and Jacob were born as twins; we are told that Esau loved to hunt while Jacob preferred the comforts of home, but their story begins as young adults. We meet Joseph at seventeen. We are given a few vignettes from the lives of Moses, Samuel, and David. Not much more for Samson, Elijah, Elisha, Ruth, Esther, Solomon, Job, Daniel, Jonah, and all the other prophets.

In the New Testament, we find a single sentence on the entire childhood of John the Baptizer, who apparently spent most of his childhood in the desert. Barnabas: nothing. Silas: nada. We learn that Timothy had a godly mother and grandmother, but nothing about his father or his journey to manhood is shared. Even the early years of Saul of Tarsus remain a mystery. We know zilch about his days in Tarsus as a little Jewish boy or the details of his education under Gamaliel.

I soon realized that much of what I *thought* I knew about these people didn't come from Scripture but from my own imagination.

While the Gospels don't tell us all we would like to know about the childhood of Jesus, we actually have more information about His early years than any other person in the Bible. And what we learn from Him as a child is priceless.

As Luke continues his account of Christ's early years, he speeds past several significant episodes. If Luke knew about the visit of the magi, Herod's desperate attempt to destroy the legitimate King of the Jews, their sojourn in Egypt, and their subsequent return to Nazareth (Matt. 2:1-23), then he deliberately left out these details because they didn't advance his primary purpose in writing. He left these to Matthew, who omitted the birth account in order to focus on Jesus' strained relationship with the national leaders of Israel. (Note Matthew's transition from 1:25 to 2:1.) Luke chose, instead, to focus on the ordinariness of the Lord's childhood, while showing Him to have been an extraordinary child.

— 2:39-40 —

The events of Matthew 2:1-23 fall between Luke 2:38 and 2:39. Joseph, Mary, and Jesus remained in Egypt until the death of Herod the Great in

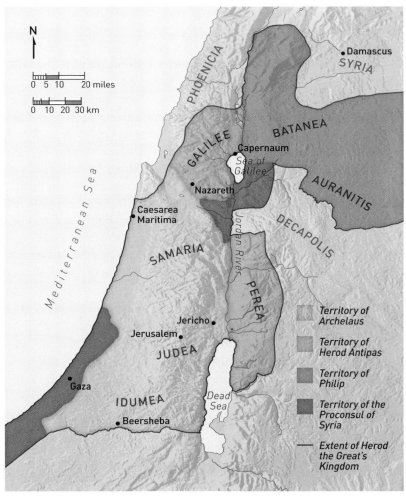

The regions ruled by Herod the Great were divided between his sons when he died in 4 BC.

4 BC and may have planned to then live in Judea permanently. But, upon their return, they discovered that the cruelty of Herod's son Archelaus eclipsed that of his father. According to the Jewish historian Josephus, he "began his reign with the murder of three thousand citizens; as if he had a mind to offer so many bloody sacrifices to God for his government."[17] So, they returned to their original home in Nazareth of Galilee, ruled by the slightly less insane Antipas (Matt. 2:22-23). The town's isolation from mainstream Jewish politics provided the family relatively good protection from the whims of Antipas. (See comments on 1:26-27.)[18]

— 2:41-45 —

According to Jewish law, only men were required to make the journey to Jerusalem for the three great feasts (Deut. 16:16): Passover, Pentecost, and Tabernacles. Nevertheless, particularly devout families made the journey together, and for Joseph, Mary, and Jesus, that would have required a three- or four-day journey from Galilee. Traveling in large caravans protected the pilgrims from robbery during their journey and added to the joy of the celebration.

In this particular year, Jesus was twelve years of age, one birthday shy of manhood according to Jewish custom. At thirteen, young men were considered full-fledged "sons of the covenant," complete with all the rights and responsibilities of adulthood, and were fully responsible to know and follow the Law of Moses.[19] Today, Jews initiate young boys into manhood through the rite of bar mitzvah. The Mishnah is a document compiled between AD 70 and 220 to preserve the oral teaching and practical traditions of the rabbis. It describes a rudimentary form of this rite to be performed on special occasions, such as betrothal and marriage. In such cases, the priests examined a young man or woman's comprehension of the Law before holding them legally accountable for their decisions.[20] This suggests that first-century Jews may have performed some form of this rite as well, but no one can say for certain.

As the week of Passover concluded and the families began their caravan home to Galilee, Jesus asserted His independence. He remained behind in Jerusalem to spend time with the priests in the temple. Meanwhile, Joseph and Mary journeyed north to Galilee along with hundreds of other pilgrims, including dozens of friends and extended relatives, only to discover en route that Jesus had not joined extended family in another part of the caravan. Immediately, Joseph and Mary returned to Jerusalem and after three days of searching, found Jesus in the temple, sitting among the nation's foremost experts in Jewish law.

— 2:46-47 —

Luke describes the religious leaders as "amazed" (*existēmi* [1839]), which literally means "'to remove oneself,' figuratively 'to lose one's wits,' 'go out of one's mind,' 'be terrified out of one's wits.'"[21] We would say, "They were beside themselves." This term is common in the Septuagint when describing a person's response to a manifestation or act of God. Luke uses this term in Luke–Acts almost exclusively for supernatural activity (such as resurrection [8:56; 24:22]; activities of the Holy Spirit [Acts 2:7, 12; 10:45]; and the work of Simon the magician [Acts 8:9, 11, 13]). The NASB translates no fewer than four other Greek terms as "amazed." Luke could have chosen any one of those, but he selected the most theologically loaded term available.

So, "amazed" barely does justice to the utter astonishment and excitement Israel's most gifted teachers experienced upon meeting Jesus. They reacted as we might if we were to hear a five-year-old give a lecture on quantum gravity and string theory and then banter with today's leading minds in particle physics. The priests and leading teachers had encountered a child-savant. The boy theologian was making logical connections to arrive at insights that should have been far beyond any twelve-year-old mind.

— 2:48-50 —

When Joseph and Mary found Jesus in the temple, they understandably spoke to Him like any parent would after searching for three days. Their voices undoubtedly expressed both relief and exasperation. Luke renders Mary's address to Jesus with the Greek word *teknon* [5043] (rendered "Son" in English), which was typically used by a superior to address a subordinate, such as in a teacher-student, master-slave, or parent-child relationship. This form of address was entirely appropriate. Mary forgot whom she was addressing, however, and overstepped herself in two other respects. First, speaking for the couple, she asked a question that mildly suggested insensitivity or even selfishness on the part of Jesus. Second, she referred to Joseph as the father of Jesus.

At first blush, the response given by Jesus might appear disrespectful, but if we could have heard His inflection, undoubtedly we would have heard genuine confusion in His voice. If Joseph and Mary had remembered the message of the angel and the prophecy of Simeon, they should have known exactly where to find the Son of God. Furthermore, His mild rebuke marks a significant turning point in His life by establishing two important facts. He clarified for Mary, Joseph, and the gathered theological experts, first, that His Father was none other than God, and second, that His life was not His own—a divine destiny marked the path before Him and he "had" to follow it obediently (cf. John 4:34; 5:30, 36; 6:38; 17:4; 19:28, 30).

The phrase "in My Father's house" can also be translated "about My Father's business" (NKJV) because the Greek expression does not include the word "house" but rather a pronominal use of the article "the," to be understood in light of the immediate context. "In the [house] of My Father" makes good sense because of where they were standing. "In the [things] of My Father" also makes sense because of what Jesus was doing. In other words, Joseph and Mary should have been able to predict the most likely place to find Jesus if they fully considered His divine identity and divine purpose on earth.

Unfortunately, Joseph and Mary didn't get it: "They did not understand the statement which He had made to them."

— 2:51-52 —

While Joseph and Mary—as firsthand witnesses to angelic announcements, worship by shepherds and magi, and prophetic oracles—did not see Jesus' divine purpose unfolding before them, Jesus did. He, perhaps for the first time, completely understood what He had come to earth to do. Even so, He would have to wait, for He was not yet recognized as a man in Jewish society.[22] Therefore, despite Jesus' realization of His identity, He submitted to the authority of Joseph and Mary without complaint.

The phrase "treasured all these things in her heart" recalls 2:19 and portrays Mary gathering memories into a mental scrapbook. This statement serves to conclude this section of the Lord's biography.

Luke's summary statement in 2:52 describes the years between age twelve and thirty (3:23), the age at which a priest may begin service in the temple (Num. 4:46-47) and the traditional age of full manhood. It also bookends this particular episode with Luke 2:40: "The Child continued to grow and become strong, increasing in wisdom; and the grace of God was upon Him."

These two verses (2:40, 52) both describe Christ's growth using the imperfect tense, which emphasizes ongoing, continual progression. The different verbs in the two verses, however, create for us a "before-and-after" picture, as it were, with a progression implied in 2:41-51. Luke communicates that Jesus came out of this experience very different from how He entered it.

The Greek term rendered "continued to grow" (2:40) emphasizes physical growth. Roughly translated, Luke says He "got bigger." The expressions for "become strong" and "increasing in wisdom" are passive verbs. In other words, Jesus didn't have much to do with getting bigger and becoming strong or wise. Biology was doing the work. In 2:52, however, Luke's choice of verb means "to advance," "to make headway," or "to forge ahead."[23] After this event in Jesus' childhood, Luke portrays Him as actively participating in His own maturation. After His time with the professors in the temple, Jesus emerged fully aware of His identity and purpose.

In between the passive "getting bigger" and the active "forging ahead," Luke's vocabulary reveals a progression in maturity. The word for "child" in 2:40 is *paidion* [3813], which can denote an infant, a toddler, or even a young boy or girl, but not a teenager. Jesus is then referred to as a *pais* [3816], the general term for a youthful person who has not yet reached puberty (2:43). In 2:48, His mother addresses Him as *teknon*, which was used of someone's progeny or of a disciple. It's a term of rank. And then finally, in 2:52, Luke calls Jesus by His proper name, just as he turns the narrative toward the public ministry of the adult Messiah.

I don't think this is a coincidence. As I trace the name Jesus through chapter 2, I find:

- 2:21: The newborn child receives the name Jesus.
- 2:27: "The child (*paidion*) Jesus" is brought to the temple.
- 2:43: "The boy (*pais*) Jesus" remained behind in the temple.
- 2:52: "Jesus" (no qualifier) kept maturing.

When the Son came to earth to become a flesh-and-bone human, He voluntarily laid aside the use of His divine power. He exchanged omnipresence for finitude; He existed fully in one place within a finite human body. He exchanged omnipotence for frailty; He suffered the pain, weakness, hunger, and fatigue that is common to all people. He exchanged omniscience for incomprehension; He "grew in wisdom." (Omniscience cannot grow!)

Like all little boys, He gained weight. He learned manners. He was taught to read. He received instruction in the synagogue and at home. And somewhere in the process of maturity, He became fully aware of His identity as the Son of God and completely conscious of His mission as the Savior of the world.

Luke's description of this event in Jesus' childhood strongly suggests that this may have been the day it all came together.

APPLICATION: LUKE 2:39-52

Practical Thoughts on Growing Up

Although Luke chose to include only three small stories from the childhood of Jesus, we have more than enough to derive some practical principles on parenting and childhood.

For parents: The process of growing up is divinely orchestrated and therefore healthy. Let it happen.

While Jesus' experience in the temple demonstrated uncommon maturity, he came by it quite naturally. As Steven Curtis Chapman sings, "There was the climbin' of trees and the scrapin' of knees, all the fun that a boy's born to have."[24] Meanwhile, Joseph and Mary protected and provided; they "went to Jerusalem every year at the Feast of the Passover" (2:41), suggesting faithful participation in spiritual instruction. Yet, make no mistake, the child's heavenly Father remained in charge of his earthly development.

It is a mistake to think we receive children as lumps of clay to be molded into the image we think best. On the contrary, God has a plan for each child, and He has already begun the molding. Our primary responsibility as parents is to discover how God is molding each child, and then fit our training according to God's working.

That's not to say our role is passive or that we shouldn't actively participate in their development. The Lord has given us a significant stake in their future. Therefore, provide nurturing and nourishment for their bodies, minds, and spirits. Offer reasonable protection from harm. Establish appropriately wide boundaries, and then bring discipline when those limits are crossed. Set a worthy example of godliness, with transparency and authenticity. And then, start releasing children from the first day of life to the day they leave home for good—deliberately, gradually, cooperatively, positively, and consistently. But never forget that God remains in charge of their destiny.

For children: The process of growing up prepares you for independence, but it doesn't nullify your obligation to submit.

If any one person in the world had the maturity and the moral right to rule His home at twelve years of age, it was Jesus. Nevertheless, "He continued in subjection to [Joseph and Mary]" (2:51).

God commands children to defer to parental wisdom and authority. Think about it: Jesus was perfect; His earthly parents were not! Still,

He submitted to their authority until He became fully independent, living on His own.

Submission is easy when we agree with those in authority. It becomes a matter of faith when we don't. We honor Christ when we follow His example.

The Greatest Mortal Who Ever Died
LUKE 3:1-38

NASB

¹ Now in the fifteenth year of the reign of Tiberius Caesar, when Pontius Pilate was governor of Judea, and Herod was tetrarch of Galilee, and his brother Philip was tetrarch of the region of Ituraea and Trachonitis, and Lysanias was tetrarch of Abilene, ² in the high priesthood of Annas and Caiaphas, the word of God came to John, the son of Zacharias, in the wilderness. ³ And he came into all the district around the Jordan, preaching a baptism of repentance for the forgiveness of sins; ⁴ as it is written in the book of the words of Isaiah the prophet,

"THE VOICE OF ONE CRYING IN THE
WILDERNESS,
'MAKE READY THE WAY OF THE
LORD,
MAKE HIS PATHS STRAIGHT.
⁵ 'EVERY RAVINE WILL BE FILLED,
AND EVERY MOUNTAIN AND HILL
WILL BE ᵃBROUGHT LOW;
THE CROOKED WILL BECOME
STRAIGHT,
AND THE ROUGH ROADS SMOOTH;
⁶ AND ALL ᵃFLESH WILL SEE THE
SALVATION OF GOD.'"

⁷ So he *began* saying to the crowds who were going out to be baptized by him, "You brood of vipers, who

NLT

¹ It was now the fifteenth year of the reign of Tiberius, the Roman emperor. Pontius Pilate was governor over Judea; Herod Antipas was ruler* over Galilee; his brother Philip was ruler* over Iturea and Traconitis; Lysanias was ruler over Abilene. ² Annas and Caiaphas were the high priests. At this time a message from God came to John son of Zechariah, who was living in the wilderness. ³ Then John went from place to place on both sides of the Jordan River, preaching that people should be baptized to show that they had repented of their sins and turned to God to be forgiven. ⁴ Isaiah had spoken of John when he said,

"He is a voice shouting in the
wilderness,
'Prepare the way for the LORD's
coming!
Clear the road for him!
⁵ The valleys will be filled,
and the mountains and hills
made level.
The curves will be straightened,
and the rough places made
smooth.
⁶ And then all people will see
the salvation sent from God.'"*

⁷ When the crowds came to John for baptism, he said, "You brood of

warned you to flee from the wrath to come? [8]Therefore bear fruits in keeping with repentance, and do not begin to say [a]to yourselves, 'We have Abraham for our father,' for I say to you that from these stones God is able to raise up children to Abraham. [9]Indeed the axe is already laid at the root of the trees; so every tree that does not bear good fruit is cut down and thrown into the fire."

[10]And the crowds were questioning him, saying, "Then what shall we do?" [11]And he would answer and say to them, "The man who has two tunics is to share with him who has none; and he who has food is to do likewise." [12]And *some* tax collectors also came to be baptized, and they said to him, "Teacher, what shall we do?" [13]And he said to them, "[a]Collect no more than what you have been ordered to." [14]*Some* soldiers were questioning him, saying, "And *what about* us, what shall we do?" And he said to them, "Do not take money from anyone by force, or accuse *anyone* falsely, and be content with your wages."

[15]Now while the people were in a state of expectation and all were [a]wondering in their hearts about John, as to whether he was [b]the Christ, [16]John answered and said to them all, "As for me, I baptize you with water; but One is coming who is mightier than I, and I am not fit to untie the thong of His sandals; He will baptize you [a]with the Holy Spirit and fire. [17]His winnowing fork is in His hand to thoroughly clear His threshing floor, and to gather the wheat into His barn; but He will burn up the chaff with unquenchable fire."

[18]So with many other exhortations he preached the gospel to the

snakes! Who warned you to flee the coming wrath? [8]Prove by the way you live that you have repented of your sins and turned to God. Don't just say to each other, 'We're safe, for we are descendants of Abraham.' That means nothing, for I tell you, God can create children of Abraham from these very stones. [9]Even now the ax of God's judgment is poised, ready to sever the roots of the trees. Yes, every tree that does not produce good fruit will be chopped down and thrown into the fire."

[10]The crowds asked, "What should we do?"

[11]John replied, "If you have two shirts, give one to the poor. If you have food, share it with those who are hungry."

[12]Even corrupt tax collectors came to be baptized and asked, "Teacher, what should we do?"

[13]He replied, "Collect no more taxes than the government requires."

[14]"What should we do?" asked some soldiers.

John replied, "Don't extort money or make false accusations. And be content with your pay."

[15]Everyone was expecting the Messiah to come soon, and they were eager to know whether John might be the Messiah. [16]John answered their questions by saying, "I baptize you with* water; but someone is coming soon who is greater than I am—so much greater that I'm not even worthy to be his slave and untie the straps of his sandals. He will baptize you with the Holy Spirit and with fire.* [17]He is ready to separate the chaff from the wheat with his winnowing fork. Then he will clean up the threshing area, gathering the wheat into his barn but burning the chaff with never-ending fire."

[18]John used many such warnings as he announced the Good News to the people.

people. ¹⁹But when Herod the tetrarch was reprimanded by him because of Herodias, his brother's wife, and because of all the wicked things which Herod had done, ²⁰Herod also added this to them all: he locked John up in prison.

²¹Now when all the people were baptized, Jesus was also baptized, and while He was praying, heaven was opened, ²²and the Holy Spirit descended upon Him in bodily form like a dove, and a voice came out of heaven, "You are My beloved Son, in You I am well-pleased."

²³When He began His ministry, Jesus Himself was about thirty years of age, being, ^aas was supposed, the son of Joseph, ^bthe son of ^cEli, ²⁴the son of Matthat, the son of Levi, the son of Melchi, the son of Jannai, the son of Joseph, ²⁵the son of Mattathias, the son of Amos, the son of Nahum, the son of ^aHesli, the son of Naggai, ²⁶the son of Maath, the son of Mattathias, the son of Semein, the son of Josech, the son of Joda, ²⁷the son of Joanan, the son of Rhesa, the son of Zerubbabel, the son of ^aShealtiel, the son of Neri, ²⁸the son of Melchi, the son of Addi, the son of Cosam, the son of Elmadam, the son of Er, ²⁹the son of ^aJoshua, the son of

¹⁹John also publicly criticized Herod Antipas, the ruler of Galilee,* for marrying Herodias, his brother's wife, and for many other wrongs he had done. ²⁰So Herod put John in prison, adding this sin to his many others.

²¹One day when the crowds were being baptized, Jesus himself was baptized. As he was praying, the heavens opened, ²²and the Holy Spirit, in bodily form, descended on him like a dove. And a voice from heaven said, "You are my dearly loved Son, and you bring me great joy.*"

²³Jesus was about thirty years old when he began his public ministry.

Jesus was known as the son of Joseph.
Joseph was the son of Heli.
²⁴Heli was the son of Matthat.
Matthat was the son of Levi.
Levi was the son of Melki.
Melki was the son of Jannai.
Jannai was the son of Joseph.
²⁵Joseph was the son of Mattathias.
Mattathias was the son of Amos.
Amos was the son of Nahum.
Nahum was the son of Esli.
Esli was the son of Naggai.
²⁶Naggai was the son of Maath.
Maath was the son of Mattathias.
Mattathias was the son of Semein.
Semein was the son of Josech.
Josech was the son of Joda.
²⁷Joda was the son of Joanan.
Joanan was the son of Rhesa.
Rhesa was the son of Zerubbabel.
Zerubbabel was the son of Shealtiel.
Shealtiel was the son of Neri.
²⁸Neri was the son of Melki.
Melki was the son of Addi.
Addi was the son of Cosam.
Cosam was the son of Elmadam.
Elmadam was the son of Er.
²⁹Er was the son of Joshua.

Eliezer, the son of Jorim, the son of Matthat, the son of Levi, ³⁰the son of Simeon, the son of ªJudah, the son of Joseph, the son of Jonam, the son of Eliakim, ³¹the son of Melea, the son of Menna, the son of Mattatha, the son of Nathan, the son of David, ³²the son of Jesse, the son of Obed, the son of Boaz, the son of ªSalmon, the son of ᵇNahshon, ³³the son of Amminadab, the son of Admin, the son of ªRam, the son of Hezron, the son of Perez, the son of Judah, ³⁴the son of Jacob, the son of Isaac, the son of Abraham, the son of Terah, the son of Nahor, ³⁵the son of Serug, the son of ªReu, the son of Peleg, the son of ᵇHeber, the son of Shelah, ³⁶the son of Cainan, the son of Arphaxad, the son of Shem, the son of Noah, the son of Lamech, ³⁷the son of Methuselah, the son of Enoch, the son of Jared, the son of Mahalaleel, the son of Cainan, ³⁸the son of Enosh, the

Joshua was the son of Eliezer.
Eliezer was the son of Jorim.
Jorim was the son of Matthat.
Matthat was the son of Levi.
³⁰ Levi was the son of Simeon.
Simeon was the son of Judah.
Judah was the son of Joseph.
Joseph was the son of Jonam.
Jonam was the son of Eliakim.
³¹ Eliakim was the son of Melea.
Melea was the son of Menna.
Menna was the son of Mattatha.
Mattatha was the son of Nathan.
Nathan was the son of David.
³² David was the son of Jesse.
Jesse was the son of Obed.
Obed was the son of Boaz.
Boaz was the son of Salmon.*
Salmon was the son of Nahshon.
³³ Nahshon was the son of
    Amminadab.
Amminadab was the son of
    Admin.
Admin was the son of Arni.*
Arni was the son of Hezron.
Hezron was the son of Perez.
Perez was the son of Judah.
³⁴ Judah was the son of Jacob.
Jacob was the son of Isaac.
Isaac was the son of Abraham.
Abraham was the son of Terah.
Terah was the son of Nahor.
³⁵ Nahor was the son of Serug.
Serug was the son of Reu.
Reu was the son of Peleg.
Peleg was the son of Eber.
Eber was the son of Shelah.
³⁶ Shelah was the son of Cainan.
Cainan was the son of Arphaxad.
Arphaxad was the son of Shem.
Shem was the son of Noah.
Noah was the son of Lamech.
³⁷ Lamech was the son of
    Methuselah.
Methuselah was the son of
    Enoch.
Enoch was the son of Jared.
Jared was the son of Mahalalel.
Mahalalel was the son of Kenan.
³⁸ Kenan was the son of Enosh.*

NASB

son of Seth, the son of Adam, the son of God.

3:5 ªOr *leveled* **3:6** ªOr *mankind* **3:8** ªOr *in* **3:13** ªOr *Exact* **3:15** ªOr *reasoning* or *debating* ᵇI.e. the Messiah **3:16** ªThe Gr here can be translated *in, with* or *by* **3:23** ªLit *as it was being thought* ᵇLit *of Eli*, and so throughout the genealogy ᶜAlso spelled *Heli* **3:25** ªAlso spelled *Esli* **3:27** ªGr *Salathiel;* names of people in the Old Testament are given in their Old Testament form through v 38 **3:29** ªGr *Jesus* **3:30** ªGr *Judas* **3:32** ªGr *Sala* ᵇGr *Naasson* **3:33** ªGr *Arni* **3:35** ªGr *Ragau* ᵇGr *Eber*

NLT

Enosh was the son of Seth.
Seth was the son of Adam.
Adam was the son of God.

3:1a Greek *Herod was tetrarch.* Herod Antipas was a son of King Herod. **3:1b** Greek *tetrarch;* also in 3:1c. **3:4-6** Isa 40:3-5 (Greek version). **3:16a** Or *in.* **3:16b** Or *in the Holy Spirit and in fire.* **3:19** Greek *Herod the tetrarch.* **3:22** Some manuscripts read *my Son, and today I have become your Father.* **3:32** Greek *Sala,* a variant spelling of Salmon; also in 3:32b. See Ruth 4:20-21. **3:33** Some manuscripts read *Amminadab was the son of Aram. Arni* and *Aram* are alternate spellings of Ram. See 1 Chr 2:9-10. **3:38** Greek *Enos,* a variant spelling of Enosh; also in 3:38b. See Gen 5:6.

The church has hit upon hard times. We live in a day in which success is king. Everything has to work well. We must always have a better year this year than last year. In the parlance of church-talk, our ministries have to be "relevant," which is just another word for "financially and numerically successful." And success on those terms is all about savvy marketing.

Imagine you are the chairperson of a steering committee for a new ministry, and someone from the "Build-n-Grow" ministry marketing firm outlines the following plan of action based on five governing rules:

1. *Don't go to where the people are; make them come to you.*
And should they come, don't provide seating; make them stand. Don't build a building; meet outside.

2. *Dress unattractively.*
Avoid the latest trends. In fact, look weird on purpose.

3. *Speak offensively.*
Insult your listeners and verbally assault your opponents. Use harsh, condemning words. Call your detractors names, like "snakes" and "hypocrites."

4. *Rail against high-ranking officials who don't have integrity.*
Point out their lies and expose their double standards publicly. Don't hedge your words. Expose their sin and call them sinners.

5. *Encourage your followers to follow a worthier leader.*
In fact, admit your utter unworthiness by comparison.

You may not consider this strategy very competent, but the five-point plan comes straight out of John the Baptizer's manual. The advance man for the Messiah prepared the way in just this manner. He broke every ministry-building rule, yet he enjoyed incredible success. The pontiffs and potentates of the day jailed the forerunner and eventually executed him, but Jesus called him the greatest man ever born of a woman (Matt. 11:11).

John took a simple, two-phase approach to his mission:

Phase One: Prepare the way (Luke 3:3-14).
Phase Two: Get out of the way (3:15-20).

— 3:1-2 —

You cannot separate John the Baptizer from his times. And the times were bleak. Like most ancient chronicles, Luke's account establishes the historical context of the narrative, starting with the most important ruler and working his way down the chain of command. These lists of rulers can appear boring because they include unknown names and describe unfamiliar political circumstances. So, we might be tempted to skim over verses like this (3:1-2), but only to our own detriment. Luke included this information because it tells us something about the man John.

John began his ministry during a time of political fracturing in Israel. While priests and procurators vied for power, the people desperately longed for a leader.

When John first appeared, Tiberius Caesar had succeeded Augustus as emperor of the Roman Empire. Also by this time, Herod the Great had died (AD 4), after which Augustus divided the king's territory between three sons: Archelaus (Judea, Samaria, Idumea), Antipas (Galilee and Perea), and Philip (Gaulanitis, Auranitis, Batanea, Trachonitis, Paneas, and Ituraea). (See map, "Israel after Herod the Great," page 82.) Rome absorbed the rest of his territory, placing it under the direct rule of governors.

Just two years later, however, Archelaus was deposed for his cruelty and exiled to Vienna in Gaul. Therefore, his territory came under direct Roman rule through governors as well. (See comments on 2:39-40.) Pontius Pilate became the fifth governor of Judea in AD 26. Meanwhile, Herod Antipas continued to rule Galilee.

Luke names both Annas and Caiaphas when referring to the high priesthood of the temple. Although Caiaphas officially held the office, many recognized his father-in-law, Annas, as the true power behind the office. Annas was originally appointed high priest in AD 6 by Quirinius, but later was deposed by Valerius Gratus in AD 15. Nevertheless, he remained the acknowledged head of a vast empire of organized corruption in Jerusalem. Essentially he was the mafia "Godfather" of the foremost crime family in the capital city. "He and his family were proverbial for their rapacity and greed."[25] After his removal from office, he wielded power through his son Eleazar and then through his son-in-law Caiaphas. In fact, his family held a virtually unbroken line of succession though four more sons after Caiaphas, and then a grandson.

During this bleak time, after four hundred years of divine silence, "the word of God came to John" (3:2). While Jesus matured in Galilee, the Lord prepared John in the rugged wilderness of Judea.

— 3:3-6 —

John fulfilled the prophecy of Isaiah 40:3-5 (quoted here by Luke) by calling on Israelites to repent and to submit to the traditional Jewish rite of baptism. Ordinarily, Gentile converts to Judaism were ceremonially washed by immersion in water as they became, as it were, adopted children of the covenant.[26] John's baptism of repentance required Jews to admit they had forsaken their covenant with God and to approach Him as if for the very first time. By submitting to John's baptism, they were essentially admitting they were no better than Gentiles and needed a fresh start with God.

— 3:7-9 —

John prepared the way for the Messiah by confronting the nation of Israel for their failure to steward God's Word and for despising their covenant with God. According to the Gospel of Mark, John looked, sounded, and acted utterly different from the religious leaders people had grown accustomed to hearing. John didn't dress to impress. Unlike the Sadducees, Pharisees, chief priests, scribes, and Herodians, who draped themselves in the finest linens, he "was clothed with camel's hair and wore a leather belt around his waist, and his diet was locusts and wild honey" (Mark 1:6). While the religious authorities ate the best meat from the sacrifices, John stood gaunt from ascetic living and leathery from the sun.

He asked a penetrating question: "Who warned you to flee from the wrath to come?" (Luke 3:7). The "wrath" is none other than the wrath of God, which Old Testament prophets likened to fire (Isa. 13:9; 26:11; 29:6; 30:27; Jer. 4:4; 5:14; 17:4; Ezek. 21:31; 22:21; Zeph. 2:2; Mal. 3:2; 4:1-5). Some older commentators suggest John drew upon a familiar image from his days of living in the wilderness. He described the people coming to his ministry of baptism as snakes fleeing their holes and rushing to the river before an approaching brush fire. Many had come to believe their Jewish heritage guaranteed them a place in God's kingdom, and that having Abraham as their ancestor made them morally and spiritually acceptable before the Lord. But, as Israel's leaders became more openly corrupt, the people began to fear the worst—and for good reason.

John also compared the people to trees that either bear fruit or do not. The image of a tree without fruit is a picture of uselessness, and fruit growers don't keep worthless trees. The image of fruit also illustrated the concept of "proof." A tree expert can examine the leaves and bark of a tree for the telltale signs of disease. Most can't do that. It doesn't take an expert, however, to see that if a tree doesn't bear fruit, there is something wrong with the tree. If, on the other hand, a tree hangs heavy with good fruit, everyone knows the tree is healthy.

Repentance is the fruit of a heart yielded to God. Not just *regret* because of sin's consequences. Not merely *remorse*, the emotional sorrow of getting caught in sin. Repentance is an ongoing, conscious decision to turn away from sin and to pursue God's plans. Therefore, repentance, like fruit, can be seen. The presence of fruit tells us the tree is alive, healthy, and fulfilling its purpose.

— 3:10-14 —

John's rebuke for those coming for baptism prompted a question. Circumcision symbolized a Jewish man's dedication to God; he bore the physical mark of his consecration. But, according to God, outward circumcision is worthless apart from "circumcision of the heart" (Deut. 10:16; 30:6; Jer. 4:4; Rom. 2:29). Similarly, baptism isn't a magic spell that cleanses evil from the heart, nor does it satisfy God's demand for righteousness. Baptism is merely an outward symbol of what should be true of a person's heart.

John said, in effect, "Don't come to me for baptism thinking that's how you will escape God's wrath; you can find safety only through repentance. Baptism isn't any better than circumcision if your heart remains unchanged." So, naturally, the people wanted to know, "What shall we do?"

John's response depended upon his audience.

To everyone, the fruit of repentance is unselfishness. The human heart is given to selfishness, but a repentant heart will resist the urge to hoard, will share excess with others, and will trust that the Lord will provide for tomorrow.

To tax collectors, the fruit of repentance is honesty. A tax collector paid a large franchise fee to become a *telōnēs* [5057], a universally hated government post (because of its strong association with corruption). He would use Rome's authority to collect as much money as he could without getting himself killed. He turned in the amount actually demanded by Rome and then kept the surplus for himself. Interestingly, John didn't call for tax collectors to surrender their posts; he merely stated that a repentant heart will deal with others honestly and will trust God to provide wealth if He so chooses.

To soldiers, the fruit of repentance is gentleness. There were many inequities among the classes of people in the Roman Empire, and often, powerful people—including soldiers—took what they wanted unless someone more powerful prevented them. Soldiers were paid a salary by the government, but they were encouraged to supplement their income by taking the spoils of battle. This also applied in peacetime. A family could be required to provide room and board for a soldier. If they refused, a soldier could use his power to make their lives miserable.

A repentant heart doesn't use power for the sake of personal gain; repentant hearts use power for good, while depending upon the Lord for provision and protection.

John didn't preach a works-based gospel. He didn't call people to be baptized as a means of salvation. And he didn't call people to behave better as a way to escape God's wrath. John called people to be baptized as a symbol of their believing repentance, while describing the outward evidence of a transformed heart.

— 3:15-18 —

The rank-and-file Jewish citizen desperately wanted godly leadership but could find it neither on the throne nor in the temple. Every visible leader, it seemed, had sold out to Rome. So, when a renowned prophet with John's strong pedigree emerged with God's message on his lips and without a hint of corruption, people naturally began to speculate: *Could this be the Messiah?*

If they had recalled Scripture, they would have known that John did not qualify. The Messiah was to be a descendant of David, not of Levi; John descended from Aaron (Luke 1:5), a descendant of Levi. But since the Hasmonean Dynasty (also of Levi) had ruled Israel for many generations as kings, John's heritage probably didn't matter to them. In their desperate "expectation," they would have made him king anyway.

John quickly set the record straight. He illustrated his worth compared to the Christ by recalling the image of the most menial house slave, whose duty was to remove the dirty sandals of guests when they arrived. Moreover, he compared his ministry to that of the Messiah by recalling the Lord's words, spoken through the pen of Malachi:

> "Behold, I am going to send My messenger, and he will clear the way before Me. And the Lord, whom you seek, will suddenly come to His temple; and the messenger of the covenant, in whom you delight, behold, He is coming," says the LORD of hosts. "But who can endure the day of His coming? And who can stand when He appears? For He is like a refiner's fire and like fullers' soap. He will sit as a smelter and purifier of silver, and He will purify the sons of Levi and refine them like gold and silver, so that they may present to the LORD offerings in righteousness. Then the offering of Judah and Jerusalem will be pleasing to the LORD as in the days of old and as in former years." (Mal. 3:1-4)

John drew again upon the image of fire, highlighting its dual purpose: It destroys what is worthless while refining what is precious. A refining fire purifies precious metals, burning off impurities. On the threshing floor, workers used winnowing forks to toss the grain stalks into the air to separate grain kernels from their husks. The grain was gathered; everything else was burned. John alluded to this dual purpose of fire in order to foretell the Messiah's ministry. The Christ would, with the power of the Holy Spirit, test and divide the nation (cf. Luke 12:49-53). Individuals will either come through the fire purer or be consumed by it.

This was the essence of John's teaching, which he communicated in a number of ways. Luke included these words of John, in part, to foreshadow the baptism of the Holy Spirit, which he records in his second volume (Acts 2:3-4).

— 3:19-20 —

Luke inserts a short summary of John the Baptizer's clash with Herod Antipas before turning his focus to Jesus. Antipas inherited Galilee and Perea after the death of his father, Herod the Great. Originally, he had married the daughter of a Nabatean king to please Augustus, but around the time of John's ministry, he visited his brother Philip on the way to Rome and began an affair with Philip's wife. To complicate matters, she also happened to be his niece. When he returned from Rome, he banished his first wife and married his brother's wife, in clear and shameless violation of Jewish Law (Lev. 18:16; 20:21). When

John publicly condemned Antipas as an adulterer, he was arrested and thrown into prison, where he languished for two years. Were it not for John's immense popularity and Herod's occasionally positive feelings about John's teachings, he would have been executed immediately (Matt. 14:5; Mark 6:20).

John's arrest clearly demonstrates that the Jewish people and their leaders didn't see eye to eye. Whereas the citizens saw a hero of righteousness, the ruling class saw an enemy of the state. The typical solution people would seek in that type of situation would be for someone to heal the breach, to "build consensus," and to unify Israel's fractured populace. But that was not God's plan. John's ministry drove a wedge between those who loved God's Word and their corrupt leaders. And where John widened the gap, Jesus would create a giant chasm.

— 3:21-22 —

Before Antipas arrested John, however, the forerunner fulfilled his ultimate purpose.

Artists typically depict Jesus alone with John in the Jordan River, but Luke's description appears to show Jesus standing at the end of a long line of people. "All the people" doesn't mean "every single person in Israel." For example, the religious authorities refused to submit to a baptism of repentance; they never acknowledged their sin. Rather "all" is likely a hyperbole. John was ministering to a vast number of people at the time that Jesus came to be baptized.

Naturally, we are curious to know why Jesus asked to be baptized. After all, He had no sin for which to repent. Matthew offers a short explanation (Matt. 3:14-15), but it still requires some interpretation on our part, and not everyone agrees on that interpretation. Not to be outdone, I find the following significance in the Lord's baptism, although I cannot say for certain Luke had this in mind: Just prior to entering the most holy place on the Day of Atonement, the high priest was ceremonially purified by the washing of water, consecrating himself for that special service before God (Lev. 16:4). Jesus, our great High Priest (Heb. 2:17; 4:14), may have undergone a similar symbolic washing of baptism to publicly consecrate Himself for His own ministry. This act also made baptism a symbolic doorway to a new kind of life, through which He would be the first to walk. On behalf of the nation, and of all humankind, Jesus received the new covenant (cf. Ezek. 36:25-28. See also Isa. 44:3; 59:21; Jer. 31:31-33; Ezek. 37:14; 39:29; Joel 2:28-29). And by our baptism into Christ, we also demonstrate that we have entered that covenant, consecrating ourselves to His service and partaking of all its blessings.

Returning to Luke's narrative, we note that he places almost no emphasis on the physical aspect of the Lord's baptism. In the Greek, Jesus' baptism is part of a lengthy subordinate clause that provides the setting for the supernatural aspect of the event. In other words, the baptism provides the context for the more important details, which are given preeminence:

1. "Heaven was opened" (Luke 3:21): It is virtually impossible to explain what this means. I cannot begin to imagine what onlookers must have seen that day. Nevertheless, it was an answer to Isaiah's ancient prayer: "Oh, that You would rend the heavens and come down" (Isa. 64:1). The phrase commonly refers to an extraordinarily special moment in time when earth and heaven are not separated (Ezek. 1:1; John 1:51; Acts 7:56; 10:11; Rev. 19:11).

2. "The Holy Spirit descended" (Luke 3:22): The visible manifestation of the Holy Spirit validated the Son's ministry for those who were present. In that moment, we see the Trinity—three distinct persons, each eternally and fully God—interacting with one another. As the Son prayed, and the Holy Spirit descended, the Father affirmed the Christ.

3. "In bodily form like a dove" (3:22): The phrase "bodily form" means that the Holy Spirit took a physical, visible form. Luke's expression does not suggest the Holy Spirit became a dove; Luke merely used a familiar image to describe a unique event in history—something no one had seen before nor will ever see again. Regardless, his choice of analogy is important. Just like today, the dove symbolized peace in the first century.

4. "A voice came out of heaven" (3:22): The voice, of course, belonged to the Father. While the Lord had broken His silence by speaking prophetically through John, onlookers would not have missed the significance of His speaking publicly and audibly to Jesus. Everyone present overheard the Lord's expression of pleasure in Jesus, and they heard for themselves the Father call Jesus "My beloved Son" (cf. John 12:28-30).

5. "My beloved Son, in You I am well-pleased" (Luke 3:22): Most scholars see a direct allusion to Psalm 2:7 and Isaiah 42:1. The Father would again affirm the Son using similar words at the Transfiguration (Luke 9:35).

— 3:23-38 —

With the heavenly pronouncement about Jesus' identity, Luke turns to give a fuller description of the person of Jesus. The Lord had reached the traditional age of maturity (cf. Num. 4), when a man attained "fullness of strength."[27] As Luke is fond of tracing important people and events from their beginning, he includes a genealogy, establishing Jesus' legal right to the throne of Israel through David. He references Joseph as His "supposed" father for legal purposes. Whether Jesus was considered an adopted or a biological child makes no legal difference: Jesus stood to inherit what belonged to Joseph. Unlike Matthew, however, Luke continued his genealogy all the way back to Adam, perhaps to make the point that Jesus, as a descendant of the first man, came to save all of humanity, Jew and Gentile alike.

Luke calls Adam "the son of God" (Luke 3:38), though clearly not in the same way Jesus is the Son of God. Adam had no mother and was not conceived. He was formed from the dust of the ground. By calling Adam "the son of God," Luke reflects the influence of his mentor, Paul, by pointing to Jesus as the second Adam (cf. Rom. 5:14-21; 1 Cor. 15:21-22, 45-49).

Luke's genealogy of Jesus marks His baptism as the beginning of His public ministry and the apex of John's ministry in terms of significance (on John, cf. Luke 5:33; 7:19-29, 33; 9:7-9, 18-19; 16:16; 20:4-7). John, the forerunner, had completed his mission. He didn't set out to win friends or to exert his influence for selfish gain. He set his sights on one objective: to pave the way for the Christ with truth. He fulfilled his calling by confronting Israel's leaders with their sin and by calling the nation to repent. He didn't seek to unify Israel. Instead, with a full and evenhanded application of God's Word, he drove a wedge between the people, who longed for the righteousness of God, and their leaders, who had abandoned it generations beforehand.

Jesus hailed John as a hero (7:19-29, 33), but make no mistake; John didn't rest on his laurels, because he never received them—not in this life anyway. John's reward for faithfulness was arrest by a corrupt king of Galilee, two years of suffering in a dungeon, and finally execution by the manipulative design of Herod's wife during one of Herod's drunken parties (Matt. 14:6-12). No state funeral for John. No national season of mourning. Not even justice for those who had mistreated and murdered the greatest of God's prophets. John's ministry apparently came to nothing as he suffered a cruelly pointless death. At least, that's the view from earth. From heaven's vantage point, however, the forerunner of the Christ was the greatest mortal who had ever died.

APPLICATION: LUKE 3:1-38

Lessons from the Ministry of John

As I review the remarkable ministry of John the Baptizer, three lessons emerge.

First, *those who make an impact must not fear being different.*

John didn't live where other religious teachers lived. He didn't dress like his peers, and he ate a strange diet. Moreover, his method of ministry broke the mold.

If God were happy with the way things were going, He wouldn't send someone to move in a different direction. If you want to make a difference, you will think differently from the crowd. You will have different convictions. You will not agree with the majority. You will stand for things others do not see as important. You will represent a minority voice. You will have another opinion.

Don't fear being different, and don't expect others to understand. Leadership is not for people pleasers; leaders must accept misunderstanding as a normal part of their role.

Second, *agents of change must learn how to be specific.*

John called for repentance. His listeners—including tax collectors and soldiers—wanted to know what repentance looked like. So, John gave them specific examples.

Leaders usually have a fully-formed picture in their minds of what should be, and it's radically different from the status quo. To effect change, leaders must learn how to reproduce their vision in the minds of others, which often requires painstaking explanation of minute details.

Patiently and consistently communicate your vision with as much detail as possible. And don't grow weary of repetition.

Third, *those who risk confronting others dare not forget the consequences.*

People don't like change. Especially those who benefit from the status quo. Consequently, when John challenged those in power, he wound up in jail—and then dead.

Through the centuries, many men and women have suffered the consequences of confronting powerful people. They suffered the loss of freedom. They lost popularity. They often didn't see progress in their lifetimes. And sometimes their leadership took the form of martyrdom.

Therefore, count the cost of leadership. Be sure the change you seek is worth the potential investment. And be certain you are right!

If your convictions demand that you lead others to change, expect hardship. It is inevitable.

The Devil Never Made Him Do It
LUKE 4:1-13

NASB

¹ Jesus, full of the Holy Spirit, returned from the Jordan and was led around ªby the Spirit in the wilderness ² for forty days, being tempted by the devil. And He ate nothing during those days, and when they had ended, He became hungry. ³ And the devil said to Him, "If You are the Son of God, tell this stone to become bread." ⁴ And Jesus answered him, "It is written, 'MAN SHALL NOT LIVE ON BREAD ALONE.'"

⁵ And he led Him up and showed Him all the kingdoms of ªthe world in a moment of time. ⁶ And the devil said to Him, "I will give You all this domain and ªits glory; for it has been handed over to me, and I give it to whomever I wish. ⁷ Therefore if You ªworship before me, it shall all be Yours." ⁸ Jesus answered him, "It is written, 'YOU SHALL WORSHIP THE LORD YOUR GOD AND SERVE HIM ONLY.'"

⁹ And he led Him to Jerusalem and had Him stand on the pinnacle of the temple, and said to Him, "If You are the Son of God, throw Yourself down from here; ¹⁰ for it is written,

'HE WILL COMMAND HIS ANGELS
 CONCERNING YOU TO GUARD
 YOU,'

¹¹ and,
'ON *their* HANDS THEY WILL BEAR
 YOU UP,
SO THAT YOU WILL NOT STRIKE

NLT

¹ Then Jesus, full of the Holy Spirit, returned from the Jordan River. He was led by the Spirit in the wilderness,* ² where he was tempted by the devil for forty days. Jesus ate nothing all that time and became very hungry.

³ Then the devil said to him, "If you are the Son of God, tell this stone to become a loaf of bread."

⁴ But Jesus told him, "No! The Scriptures say, 'People do not live by bread alone.'*"

⁵ Then the devil took him up and revealed to him all the kingdoms of the world in a moment of time. ⁶ "I will give you the glory of these kingdoms and authority over them," the devil said, "because they are mine to give to anyone I please. ⁷ I will give it all to you if you will worship me."

⁸ Jesus replied, "The Scriptures say,

'You must worship the LORD your
  God
 and serve only him.'*"

⁹ Then the devil took him to Jerusalem, to the highest point of the Temple, and said, "If you are the Son of God, jump off! ¹⁰ For the Scriptures say,

'He will order his angels to
  protect and guard you.
¹¹ And they will hold you up with
  their hands

YOUR FOOT AGAINST A STONE.'"

12 And Jesus answered and said to him, "It is said, 'YOU SHALL NOT PUT THE LORD YOUR GOD TO THE TEST.'"

13 When the devil had finished every temptation, he left Him until an opportune time.

4:1 ªOr *under the influence of;* lit *in* 4:5 ªLit *the inhabited earth* 4:6 ªLit *their* (referring to the kingdoms in v 5) 4:7 ªOr *bow down before*

so you won't even hurt your foot on a stone.'*"

12 Jesus responded, "The Scriptures also say, 'You must not test the LORD your God.'*"

13 When the devil had finished tempting Jesus, he left him until the next opportunity came.

4:1 Some manuscripts read *into the wilderness.* 4:4 Deut 8:3. 4:8 Deut 6:13. 4:10-11 Ps 91:11-12. 4:12 Deut 6:16.

Temptation is a universal human affliction. Even as the first man and woman enjoyed the uninhibited goodness of God's creation, evil lurked in the trees of paradise, seeking an opportunity to corrupt His most precious creatures. Before the first sin, there was the first temptation. Just like temptation today, that first temptation involved four distinct phases:

1. The Appeal: Something forbidden promises fulfillment apart from God's provision.
2. The Struggle: Tension builds between the appeal of sin and belief in God's goodness.
3. The Response: A decision is made either to disobey or to wait on God.
4. The Aftermath: The consequences of sin breed despair; the fruit of obedience multiplies blessing.

When seen in this light, it's all so objective isn't it? Having dissected temptation, it's easy to see the utter stupidity of sin and to appreciate the goodness of God—yet how feeble we become when tempted! Dietrich Bonhoeffer made this insightful statement about the sinister appeal of temptation:

In our members there is a slumbering inclination towards desire which is both sudden and fierce. With irresistible power desire seizes mastery over the flesh. All at once a secret, smoldering fire is kindled. The flesh burns and is in flames. It makes no difference whether it is sexual desire, or ambition, or vanity, or desire for revenge, or love of fame and power, or greed for money, or, finally, that strange desire for the beauty of the world, of nature. Joy in God is in course of being extinguished in us and we seek all our joy in the creature. At this moment God is quite unreal to us, he loses all reality, and only desire for the creature is real; the only reality is the devil. Satan does not here fill us with hatred of God, but with forgetfulness of God. And now his falsehood is added to this proof of strength. The lust thus aroused envelops the mind and will of man in deepest darkness. The powers of clear discrimination and of decision are taken from us. . . . It is here that everything within me rises up against the Word of God.[28]

As God incarnate, Jesus was fully human and therefore subject to temptation. He battled sin's appeals daily and emerged victorious, entrusting Himself to God the Father.

— 4:1-2 —

As John the Baptizer fades to the background, the ministry of Jesus comes into focus. At the beginning of His public ministry, the Spirit led Jesus away from public view for forty days.

Jesus was young: only about thirty years old. He was inexperienced: He lived in a tiny, remote town far away from the turmoil of Jerusalem. He was alone: In the wilderness, He didn't have a supporting community to hold Him accountable. He was hungry: His body needed food, which also affected Him mentally, emotionally, and spiritually. Nevertheless, Jesus was "full of the Holy Spirit," meaning He habitually acted in concert with the mind and will of God. While the Spirit did, indeed, dwell within Him, the force of this expression describes one's decision to obey God (cf. Gal. 5:16).

After His baptism, Jesus "was led around by the Spirit in the wilderness." Luke's phrasing recalls the Exodus experience as the Israelites followed the Lord's leading into the wilderness, only to find themselves in desperate need of water (Exod. 17:1-7). The people did not lack water because of disobedience; the Lord led them to a place where there was none. He then miraculously supplied what they needed. It was a lesson God would teach His people time and again throughout their journey from Egypt to the Promised Land (e.g., Exod. 15:22-25; 16:1-4, 8-13). Even so, they did not learn. Their failure to trust the Lord's provision kept them from entering Canaan, and they wandered the wilderness for forty more years (Num. 13:25-33; 14:33). These forty years then became a time of testing for the nation (Deut. 8:2).

Similarly, Jesus followed divine leading into the wilderness, where He suffered physical deprivation. And in this weakened physical state, the devil found an opportunity for temptation.

The term "the devil" (*diabolos* [1228]) is an adjective used as a noun and means "accuser" or "slanderer." When it occurs in the New Testament with the definite article, as it does here, it specifically refers to Satan—evil personified.

The devil attacked Jesus in three ways:

1. A personal temptation (Luke 4:3)
2. A power temptation (Luke 4:5-7)
3. A pride temptation (Luke 4:9-11)

— 4:3 —

A Personal Temptation

The simple suggestion, "If You are the Son of God, tell this stone to become bread," is likely not a direct quote, but rather reflects the gist of Satan's temptation over a period of time, probably couched in attractive terms repeated many times over. The devil tempted Jesus with an activity that could easily be rationalized as victimless. Turning stones to bread wouldn't cause anyone any harm. It merely called upon Jesus to satisfy normal physical needs. What could be wrong with that?

Satan's helpful suggestion is subtly evil in at least three respects. First, the phrase "If you are the Son of God" subtly suggests that Jesus had a right to something the Father had withheld. In the Garden of Eden, humanity began to fall when Adam and Eve first doubted the goodness of God. Second, the temptation suggested that the Son should act independently of the Father, which would violate their unity. Third, the temptation undermined trust in God.

The Spirit of God had led Jesus to forgo food for forty days. God, as the Creator of humanity, certainly knows what humans need to survive. To forsake dependence upon God in this case would have repeated the sin of Eden and the faithlessness of the Israelites in the wilderness.

Jesus, recognizing His position in history, responded to Satan's assault with a quotation from Deuteronomy 8:3, which reads, "He humbled you and let you be hungry, and fed you with manna which you did not know, nor did your fathers know, that He might make you understand that man does not live by bread alone, but man lives by everything that proceeds out of the mouth of the LORD."

— 4:5-8 —

A Power Temptation

The devil took Jesus on a supernatural, whirlwind tour of the world, showing Him all the power He did not—as a human—possess. According to Old Testament prophecy, all power would be given to Him by the Father (Ps. 2:7-9; Dan. 7:13-14; cf. Ps. 72:11; Zech. 9:9-10; Matt. 28:18), so Satan did not offer anything that Jesus was not already going to eventually receive. The temptation was that, in receiving authority from Satan rather than from the Father, He might receive His messianic birthright without the messy details of being the Messiah. The temptation was to receive supreme power over the world without first suffering on behalf of humanity (Luke 24:26).

Satan offered Jesus a shortcut to power. Glory without Gethsemane. The only condition: "Worship before me." He suggested a mere, momentary act, but one with eternal consequences. The simple act of Christ worshiping Satan would separate the Son from the Father and invalidate the Messiah's ability to represent humanity on the cross. Of course, what Satan attempted was impossible. The Trinity cannot be separated, and God cannot sin.

This has caused many to wonder, "If Jesus could not have sinned, what is the purpose of this passage?" Luke didn't relate the story to suggest that the plan of salvation was ever in jeopardy. While the episode creates tension for the reader, the point is *not* that Satan almost foiled God's plan. Luke's point is twofold. First, he wanted to establish, early on, that the Lord came to confront, overcome, and ultimately destroy evil. This opening skirmish sets the tone for the rest of Luke's Gospel, which is essentially an account of the war between the Son of God and Satan. Second, Luke wanted to show that Jesus is one of us. He's human. While He could not have sinned, He nevertheless took the full brunt of Satan's temptation. Consequently, we can be sure "we do not have a high priest who cannot sympathize with our weaknesses, but One who has been tempted in all things *as we are*, yet without sin" (Heb. 4:15, emphasis mine).

Jesus responded to Satan's deception with yet another passage of Scripture, this time from the greatest commandment (Deut. 6:13), derived from the Hebrew statement of faith: "Hear, O Israel! The LORD is our God, the LORD is one!" (Deut. 6:4).

— 4:9-12 —

A Pride Temptation
Satan's third temptation transported Jesus to the "pinnacle" of Herod's temple in Jerusalem. The Greek term translated "pinnacle" denotes the tip or extremity of something. On a building, this could be a ledge. Luke's implication of height suggests a portion of the temple involving a large drop. This could have been a famous overlook from the

southeast corner of the temple complex, described by Josephus as a "vastly high elevation" looking down to the "immense depth" of the Kidron Valley below.[29] But that would not explain why Satan chose the temple and not a more remote precipice.

A clue may lie in the Scripture passage Satan twisted to support his challenge. The extended passage reads,

> For He will give His angels charge concerning you,
> To guard you *in all your ways.*
> They will bear you up in their hands,
> That you do not strike your foot against a stone.
> (Ps. 91:11-12, emphasis mine)

Take note of Satan's omission (in italics). Many have noted this omission, but some have dismissed it, suggesting that Jesus' response ignored Satan's misquote. But the idea of the Messiah's way is important in light of the public and messianic significance of the site of Satan's temptation.

Perhaps Satan chose the temple because of its significance to the Messiah. Again, he introduced the temptation with the conditional clause, "If You are the Son of God," which suggested that, as Messiah, Jesus should naturally accept the challenge. I suggest the "pinnacle" is the top of the Sanctuary, which rose 150 feet (45 meters) above the Court of Priests below. A prophecy in Malachi 3:1 stated that the Messiah would "suddenly come to His temple." Satan's challenge to leap to the busy courtyard below certainly would have created an entrance worthy of the Messiah. The devil's twist on Psalm 91:11-12 cleverly implied that the Jews would immediately recognize the miracle and accept Him as the Messiah. His omission of the key phrase *"in all your ways"* (Ps. 91:11) avoided the issue at hand. This was not the *Messiah's* way. He planned to confront the religious authorities in the temple with truth, not with a show of power. He will come in power sometime later.

Jesus responded, again, with Scripture. He quoted Deuteronomy 6:16, which reads, "You shall not put the LORD your God to the test, as you tested Him at Massah." It's part of Moses' farewell speech to the nation, which continued, "You should diligently keep the commandments of the LORD your God, and His testimonies and His statutes which He has commanded you" (Deut. 6:17).

I cannot help but wonder if Jesus' reply to Satan wasn't also a form of direct address: "Satan, you shall not put [Me], the Lord your God, to the test."

— 4:13 —

The phrase "every temptation" suggests Satan attempted to lure Jesus more than three times. The Greek word translated "finished" means "to complete," "to bring to an end," or "to accomplish." During the Lord's forty days in the wilderness, Satan pressed every temptation to its fullest extent, yet Jesus did not fail. No mere mortal can appreciate the horrors Jesus endured. We break down as the pressure mounts, but Jesus never broke. He suffered the afflictions of temptation like no other human ever has or ever will.

Eventually, the tempter departed and the story continues with an air of optimism, yet tinged with foreboding. An ominous phrase tells us we have not seen the last of the tempter. He will not reappear in person until Luke 22:3. In the meantime, however, the Lord will encounter Satan's minions and confront the palpable presence of evil in humanity as He journeys toward His messianic destiny in Jerusalem.

• • •

As this chapter of Jesus' life closes, Luke opens the next, which follows the Lord's public ministry. Jesus left the wilderness for familiar territory near His boyhood home, and at first, the people of Galilee received Him warmly and responded positively to His teaching in the synagogues. Soon, however, they would discover that Jesus didn't come to establish the kingdom of God on their terms.

Luke's prologue opened with the introduction of the forerunner, whose primary purpose was to prepare Israel for their Messiah and then to move aside. John faithfully accomplished his mission. The next time he surfaces in the narrative, we find him imprisoned in the dungeon of Herod Antipas. Meanwhile, Luke's focus turns away from the forerunner to highlight the public ministry of the Messiah.

APPLICATION: LUKE 4:1-13

Triumphing over the Tempter

I want you to remember something that you would much rather forget. I want you to remember the last time you were tempted and you said yes. The flesh solicited its wicked indulgence and you bought . . . Satan dropped his baited hook and you bit . . . the world waged war against your soul and you surrendered. I know it isn't a pleasant thought. I know you'd rather put it out of your mind. But think about it for a moment.

Now, let's turn to a better thought. Let's consider what you should have done instead of falling to the temptation. In so doing, let's consider a couple of tips for triumphing over the tempter, drawn from the episode of Jesus' temptation in the wilderness. These suggestions are simple, easy to remember, and easy to use—by the power of the indwelling Holy Spirit.

First: *When you are weak, expect a major assault.* Count on it. This means that if you're with people who weaken your resolve, Satan will tempt you. If you're dwelling on thoughts that distract you from mental and emotional vigilance, you'll be attacked. If you're in a place that weakens your discernment, expect an onslaught. The solution is to "be strong in the Lord" (Eph. 6:10). Rest in His strength and expressly wield the Word of God (Eph. 6:17). Get ahold of Scripture. Read it. Memorize it. Christ triumphed over the tempter by the Word of God—the Word that was ready in His mind, in His heart, and on His lips. So be strong. Be prepared.

Second: *When you resist, be ready for a different approach.* Just as we've seen with Christ's temptation, the devil doesn't come once and go away for good. He comes a second time with a different strategy. Then a third. Be on your guard! Satan never runs out of ideas for your destruction. He will try this, then that, to get you to take a second look at that billboard, to linger on the wrong website, or to entertain passing thoughts that should be instantly put out of your mind. So "resist the devil" (Jas. 4:7), and brace yourself for a new form of temptation.

When Satan is resisted, he will "flee from you" (Jas. 4:7), but like a rabid dog kicked away by its prey, he'll always circle back for another bite, or crouch in waiting for "an opportune time" (Luke 4:13). The great reformer Martin Luther put it this way: "The devil takes no holiday; he never rests. If beaten, he rises again. If he cannot enter in front, he steals in at the rear. If he cannot enter in the rear, he breaks through the roof or enters by tunneling under the threshold. He labors until he is in. He uses great cunning and many a plan. When one miscarries, he has another at hand and continues his attempts until he wins."[30]

Temptation is coming. This is a fact. But we need not succumb to it. Though alone we are weak, in Christ we are strong. Though Satan may attack us in various ways, the Holy Spirit is never caught by surprise. And even when the devil pummels us again and again and again, God has promised to never leave us or forsake us (Heb. 13:5).

MINISTERING AND SERVING (LUKE 4:14–9:50)

The stronghearted ministry stalwart Charles Haddon Spurgeon wrote about his early days in ministry in his *Lectures to My Students*: "My success appalled me; and the thought of the career which it seemed to open up, so far from elating me, cast me into the lowest depth, out of which I uttered my *miserere* and found no room for a *gloria in excelsis*. Who was I that I should continue to lead so great a multitude? . . . It was just then that the curtain was rising upon my lifework, and I dreaded what it might reveal."[1] Spurgeon had good reason to dread. Satan doesn't allow ministers much of a "honeymoon" before leveling his attacks. Evil strikes early and hard, at the most inopportune times, and in completely unexpected ways.

Still, nothing can compare to the darkness that surrounded Jesus as He prepared for public ministry. With His hair still wet from baptism, He had retreated to the wilderness for forty days and nights of fasting and communing with the Father, only to be spiritually assaulted by the devil. This was merely the beginning of his confrontation with the kingdom of darkness. No fewer than three times, the tempter had attempted to sink his poisonous fangs into the Savior of the world (4:1-13). Although Jesus withstood each of the devil's vicious assaults, we can hardly call it an escape. If the wilderness was a frying pan, Galilee was the fire. Jesus' ministry in Galilee, which Luke highlights in this portion of his Gospel (4:14–9:50), was marked by challenges and opposition. Here he would begin to proclaim the gospel (4:18; 7:22); he would begin to assert the authority of the kingdom to free humanity from sin.

KEY TERMS IN LUKE 4:14–9:50

mathētēs (μαθητής) [3101] "disciple," "student," "follower"
A *mathētēs* is one who subjects himself or herself to a process of becoming familiarized with something by experiencing, learning, or receiving

direction. This process usually implies the aid of another person, and as the term fully developed, it was inconceivable for one to be a learner without a guide or a master. The term is used to refer to the disciples of rabbis, and those of John the Baptizer, the Pharisees, and Moses (e.g., Mark 2:18; John 9:28). Although we often refer to the twelve apostles as the "twelve disciples," it is important to recognize that this term often refers to all of Jesus' followers (Luke 6:13, 17).

exousia (ἐξουσία) [1849] "authority," "dominion," "jurisdiction," "control"

This term is closely related to *exestin* [1832], which can mean "it is possible" or "it is permitted." One who has *exousia* has unrestricted ability to act upon his or her own discretion. This authority almost always implies power to enforce one's will, either delegated by a higher-ranking authority or possessed in one's own right. In Luke's Gospel, the people marvel at Jesus' authority in word and deed (4:32, 36), and Jesus gives authority to His disciples (9:1).

basileia (βασιλεία) [932] "kingdom," "government," "royal power"

This term denotes the dominion of a lawful king, which the Greeks saw as something derived from Zeus. In the Old Testament, Israel was originally a theocracy, a nation whose king was God. Therefore, Israel was the kingdom of God. Even when a human sat on the throne of Israel, he derived his power from God. The Gospels depict the earth as the dominion of Satan or evil, a usurper to the rightful throne of God. Jesus came to reestablish divine rule (i.e., the kingdom of God).

parabolē (παραβολή) [3850] "parable," "figure," "illustrative comparison"

This word has the basic sense of "set beside" or "stand beside," with the idea that two things should be compared and then understood as similar. In practice, a parable is a narrative or a saying designed to illustrate a truth. Unlike an allegory, in which the figurative people or things have direct, literal counterparts, a parable is intentionally less precise. In parables, the big picture is what is important, not the details.

pistis (πίστις) [4102] "faith," "trust," "confidence," "reliance"

This word denotes confidence in the reliability of a person or thing and can describe one's trust in a person's word, in a compact or treaty, or in a deity (or deities). The term implies both knowledge and action. One may receive knowledge of a certain truth and may even offer verbal agreement, but "trust" or "confidence" is not said to be present until one's behavior reflects that truth. In the Hellenistic period, this word came to connote the conviction that gods do exist and are active. The Greeks worshiped and feared their gods, but they did not have a relationship with them. Luke's readers, however, would also have known the word from the Septuagint (the Greek translation of the Old Testament), where it—and related words, like *pisteuō* [4100], "to believe," "to accept as truth," "to commit one's trust"— is linked to the relationship with Israel's covenant-keeping God. For the Jew, and therefore the Christian, *pistis* became a description of the means by which someone relates to God—so much so that the participial form came to designate members of the church as "believers" (e.g., Acts 2:44; 4:32; 5:14).

akoloutheō (ἀκολουθέω) [190] "to follow," "to go the same way," "to go after"

Literally, this verb means "to go the same way." The metaphorical extension of this idea connotes imitating the thoughts, beliefs, actions, or lifestyle of another. Similarly, we might say of a boy adopting his father's occupation, "He's following in the footsteps of his father." Though the Old Testament makes occasional use of similar imagery (see 1 Kgs. 19:20; for examples of synonyms, see Gen. 5:22; 6:9; Mic. 6:8), the New Testament uses it much more frequently, perhaps because of the accessibility of the human example of Christ and his earthly relationship to his disciples.

Into the Fire
LUKE 4:14-30

NASB

¹⁴And Jesus returned to Galilee in the power of the Spirit, and news about Him spread through all the surrounding district. ¹⁵And He *began* teaching in their synagogues and was praised by all.

¹⁶And He came to Nazareth, where He had been brought up; and as was His custom, He entered the synagogue on the Sabbath, and stood up to read. ¹⁷And the ªbook of the prophet Isaiah was handed to Him. And He opened the ªbook and found the place where it was written,

¹⁸ "THE SPIRIT OF THE LORD IS UPON ME,

BECAUSE HE ANOINTED ME TO PREACH THE GOSPEL TO THE POOR.

HE HAS SENT ME TO PROCLAIM RELEASE TO THE CAPTIVES,

NLT

¹⁴Then Jesus returned to Galilee, filled with the Holy Spirit's power. Reports about him spread quickly through the whole region. ¹⁵He taught regularly in their synagogues and was praised by everyone.

¹⁶When he came to the village of Nazareth, his boyhood home, he went as usual to the synagogue on the Sabbath and stood up to read the Scriptures. ¹⁷The scroll of Isaiah the prophet was handed to him. He unrolled the scroll and found the place where this was written:

¹⁸ "The Spirit of the LORD is upon me,

for he has anointed me to bring Good News to the poor.

He has sent me to proclaim that captives will be released,

AND RECOVERY OF SIGHT TO THE
BLIND,
TO SET FREE THOSE WHO ARE
OPPRESSED,
19 TO PROCLAIM THE FAVORABLE
YEAR OF THE LORD."

20 And He closed the ªbook, gave it back to the attendant and sat down; and the eyes of all in the synagogue were fixed on Him. 21 And He began to say to them, "Today this Scripture has been fulfilled in your ªhearing." 22 And all were ªspeaking well of Him, and wondering at the ᵇgracious words which ᶜwere falling from His lips; and they were saying, "Is this not Joseph's son?" 23 And He said to them, "No doubt you will quote this proverb to Me, 'Physician, heal yourself! Whatever we heard was done at Capernaum, do here in your hometown as well.'" 24 And He said, "Truly I say to you, no prophet is welcome in his hometown. 25 But I say to you in truth, there were many widows in Israel in the days of Elijah, when the sky was shut up for three years and six months, when a great famine came over all the land; 26 and yet Elijah was sent to none of them, but only to ªZarephath, *in the land* of Sidon, to a woman who was a widow. 27 And there were many lepers in Israel in the time of Elisha the prophet; and none of them was cleansed, but only Naaman the Syrian." 28 And all *the people* in the synagogue were filled with rage as they heard these things; 29 and they got up and drove Him out of the city, and led Him to the brow of the hill on which their city had been built, in order to throw Him down the cliff. 30 But passing through their midst, He went His way.

4:17 ªOr *scroll*   4:20 ªOr *scroll*   4:21 ªLit *ears*
4:22 ªOr *testifying* ᵇOr *words of grace* ᶜLit *were proceeding out of His mouth*   4:26 ªGr *Sarepta*

that the blind will see,
that the oppressed will be set
free,
19   and that the time of the LORD's
favor has come.*"

20 He rolled up the scroll, handed it back to the attendant, and sat down. All eyes in the synagogue looked at him intently. 21 Then he began to speak to them. "The Scripture you've just heard has been fulfilled this very day!"

22 Everyone spoke well of him and was amazed by the gracious words that came from his lips. "How can this be?" they asked. "Isn't this Joseph's son?"

23 Then he said, "You will undoubtedly quote me this proverb: 'Physician, heal yourself'—meaning, 'Do miracles here in your hometown like those you did in Capernaum.' 24 But I tell you the truth, no prophet is accepted in his own hometown.

25 "Certainly there were many needy widows in Israel in Elijah's time, when the heavens were closed for three and a half years, and a severe famine devastated the land. 26 Yet Elijah was not sent to any of them. He was sent instead to a foreigner—a widow of Zarephath in the land of Sidon. 27 And many in Israel had leprosy in the time of the prophet Elisha, but the only one healed was Naaman, a Syrian."

28 When they heard this, the people in the synagogue were furious. 29 Jumping up, they mobbed him and forced him to the edge of the hill on which the town was built. They intended to push him over the cliff, 30 but he passed right through the crowd and went on his way.

4:18-19 Or *and to proclaim the acceptable year of the LORD.* Isa 61:1-2 (Greek version); 58:6.

Any minister arriving in a new area to take on new responsibilities must become keenly aware of the expectations of the people there. Quite often, these expectations are unspoken, deeply held demands of which the people themselves are unaware. How well the minister manages these expectations can determine success. One must not necessarily give in to these demands, but one cannot afford to ignore them. A minister cannot allow the hodgepodge of individual expectations to shape the ministry, but they must be taken into account.

When Jesus arrived in Galilee to begin His public ministry in earnest, the religious leaders there were operating in light of centuries of tradition and hundreds of rules that new rabbis were expected to follow. They also had a very clear picture of what the Messiah would look like and what He would do. So, when Jesus stepped onto the public scene and into the pulpit of His home synagogue, He faced His first challenge in ministry.

— 4:14-15 —

Luke introduces the public ministry of Jesus with a summary of His activity in Galilee, where initially He was received with enthusiasm.

The region derives its name from the Hebrew word *galil* [H1550], which means "ring," "cylinder," "circle," or "district." As far back as the time of the Assyrians (Isa. 9:1; cf. Judg. 4:2), this region had been made into a foreign province, and Jewish influence was very weak there. Jews living in this region consequently adopted many non-Jewish ways. Josephus, writing around the time of Jesus, described the Galileans as "ever fond of innovations, and by nature disposed to changes, and delighting in seditions."[2]

Stories of John the Baptizer and his introduction of the Messiah undoubtedly had preceded Jesus. Some eagerly anticipated the Messiah; others simply wanted a leader to overthrow Rome. Regardless, the Galileans welcomed Jesus, probably because they saw His potential to reverse their fortunes (cf. John 6:15, 26).

— 4:16 —

The region of Galilee had no lack of opportunities to teach and to minister. According to Josephus, "The cities lie here very thick, and the very many villages there are here, are everywhere so full of people, by the richness of their soil, that the very least of them contain above fifteen thousand inhabitants."[3] Jesus probably ministered for several weeks, or even months, in Galilee, teaching and healing, before deciding to teach in the synagogue of His hometown, Nazareth.

Luke stresses that Jesus faithfully attended the synagogue on the Sabbath. Furthermore, He participated in the reading of Scripture.

Synagogue worship followed a liturgy, consisting of several parts: benedictions, recitation of the *Shema*, prayers, reading from the Law, and reading from the Prophets, followed by exposition. For each Sabbath, a Jewish lectionary[4] specified which passage to read from the Pentateuch. According to Alfred Edersheim, "Every Sabbath at least seven persons were called up to read, each a portion, which was to consist of not less than three verses. The first reader began, and the last closed, with a benediction. . . . The reading of the law was followed by a lesson from the prophets."[5] While later Jewish lectionaries assigned specific lessons from the Prophets to suit the sections of the Law appointed for the day, first-century synagogues may or may not have done this. It's quite possible the man given the honor of reading from prophecy was allowed to choose which passage to read and then explain.

— 4:17-19 —

The fact that the book of Isaiah was handed to Jesus suggests at least some structure to the readings. Regardless, He located on the scroll the passage we know as Isaiah 61:1-2, although chapter and verse numbers were not in use at the time. As we read the NASB and other translations, the passage in Luke differs somewhat from the Old Testament text.

ISAIAH 61:1-2	LUKE 4:18-19
The Spirit of the Lord GOD is upon me, Because the LORD has anointed me To bring good news to the afflicted; He has sent me *to bind up the brokenhearted,* To proclaim liberty to captives	The Spirit of the Lord is upon Me, Because He anointed Me to preach the gospel to the poor. He has sent Me . . .
And freedom to prisoners; To proclaim the favorable year of the LORD *And the day of vengeance of our God; To comfort all who mourn,*	to proclaim release to the captives, *And recovery of sight to the blind,* To set free those who are oppressed, To proclaim the favorable year of the Lord."

The differences between the Old Testament passage as rendered by the NASB and Luke's reproduction of the reading are quite technical, and are explained very well by my colleague Dr. Darrell L. Bock in his fine commentary on Luke.[6] Luke most likely summarized Jesus' entire reading, which may have included a reading from the closely-related passage, Isaiah 58:6.

Take note of Jesus' decision to end His reading where He did. He stopped short of reading, "And the day of vengeance of our God." He ended His reading on the subject of grace. The purpose of His first coming was to proclaim the good news of salvation by grace through faith in the Messiah. The "day of vengeance" will come soon enough. The day of wrath will occur in the future as predicted by John in Revelation. For now, however, the Lord's anger against sin is held in reserve. Now is the time of grace, during which all who embrace the Messiah as their Savior will find mercy.

— 4:20-22 —

In keeping with good synagogue etiquette, Jesus stood to read Scripture and then sat to teach. After hearing stories of His astounding miracles and authoritative teaching throughout Galilee, the hometown crowd sat with rapt attention. His mother, brothers, sisters, cousins, neighbors, and teachers all wondered what Jesus would say.

His declaration may not have come as a surprise. He unequivocally identified Himself as the object of Isaiah's prediction about the Messiah. But this may have been said often of Him in Nazareth, as Joseph and Mary probably told their story many times. Besides, talk of His ministry had taken all of Galilee by storm. Nevertheless, the crowd marveled at His teaching on grace. God's vengeance they understood well; His grace, on the other hand, may have been difficult to accept, especially with open corruption taking place in the temple.

The people marveled in the same way small-town folk often shake their heads in disbelief when the world considers one of their own a hero. They looked upon Jesus with a mixture of bewildered incredulity and pride.

— 4:23-24 —

A speaker doesn't have to be omniscient to read an audience. When Jesus recognized that the congregation hovered somewhere between bewilderment and anger, He quoted a proverb to characterize their attitude; in today's terms, he was saying, "Practice what you preach! Take some of your own medicine!" Having made the claim to be the Messiah, He sensed that the people wanted Him to prove it. They had heard of His performing miracles elsewhere, but they wanted to see His supernatural power for themselves.

Jesus didn't shy away from performing miracles. He performed miraculous signs throughout Galilee for two reasons. First, compassion.

He healed people to relieve them of their physical, mental, and spiritual burdens, simply because He loved them. Second, authentication. He performed miracles to give the people a tangible reason to believe His words. Each miracle was a "sign," a supernatural validation of His identity. Most importantly, each miracle was an act of His sovereign choice, never in response to coercion or manipulation.

When people came to Jesus wanting to believe, He gave them "signs" to validate their decision. When people came to Jesus looking for a reason to reject Him, He gave them all they hoped to find.

Sometime between Luke 2:51 and 3:1, Jesus had relocated to Capernaum (Matt. 4:13; Mark 2:1). And, because He had performed miracles in Capernaum, the people of Nazareth demanded that He perform signs there as well—not because they wanted to believe His claims, but to overcome their skepticism. Anticipating their unrighteous demand, He turned their objection around. He pointed to Israel's long history of ignoring and even abusing messengers from God.

— 4:25-27 —

To illustrate His point—and to give the skeptics even more justification for their lack of faith—Jesus recalled two particularly dark episodes in Israel's history. He used a phrase ("I say to you in truth") similar to His characteristic phrase, "Truly I say to you," to indicate that His next statement would be authoritative or significant (Luke 4:24; 12:37; 18:17, 29; 21:32; 23:43). And what came next was a scathing indictment of the Nazarenes' character.

He first recalled a time when Ahab and Jezebel ruled the territories later called Galilee and Samaria (1 Kgs. 17:1-24). In addition to their cruelty and corruption, they led the Israelites in the worship of Baal, the storm god. While the ruling classes gave their tacit support, authentic believers in God remained silent. Meanwhile, one man, Elijah, stood alone against Ahab, Jezebel, and the priests of Baal.

To demonstrate the impotence of their storm god, God caused a three-year drought, during which time Elijah depended upon the Lord for provision. God sent the prophet to a Gentile woman living in Sidon, a woman whose supply of food and water had nearly run out. Through Elijah, the Lord promised the woman, "The bowl of flour shall not be exhausted, nor shall the jar of oil be empty, until the day that the LORD sends rain on the face of the earth" (1 Kgs. 17:14). She believed Elijah's words, provided him room and board, and survived the drought.

Jesus also recalled an episode from the life of Elisha in which

Naaman, a Gentile military commander, received cleansing from a skin disease, while Israelites afflicted with the same ailment remained in their condition (Luke 4:27; 2 Kgs. 5).

This cut the Nazarenes to the quick. Jews considered skin diseases to be an outward manifestation of inward corruption. To be cleansed of "leprosy" was to be cleansed of sin. Furthermore, Jesus implied that the Gentile's faith qualified him for divine favor the Jews could not receive. Because first-century Jews believed they were favored by God—and therefore saved—simply because of their ancestry, they rejected Jesus' teaching as heresy. The people of Nazareth were insulted by these two references to Israel's past because Jesus was suggesting that Gentiles, whom the Jews despised, were more worthy of His teaching and healing ministry.

— 4:28-30 —

Not surprisingly, the Nazarenes erupted in a rage and attempted to execute Jesus as a false prophet, lynch mob-style (cf. Num. 15:35; Deut. 13:5). But Jesus "passed through their midst"—a statement that mildly suggests a miraculous escape. Luke doesn't offer any details of His escape; they aren't important. Jesus eluded their grasp because His time to die had not yet come.

Luke used this experience early in Jesus' public career to show the polarizing effect the Lord had on those who encountered Him. While eagerly embraced by the needy, He was flatly rejected by the wealthy, the powerful, the comfortable, and the complacent. His hometown leaders expected preferential treatment. Not only were they Jews, they had known Jesus "back when." But Jesus set the record straight. The Messiah didn't come to rescue only one particular race; He came to save those who wanted a Savior. His domain is the whole world, and His subjects are all those who call Him King.

APPLICATION: LUKE 4:14-30

Swimming against the Tide of Public Opinion

What do you do when the tide of public opinion turns against you? Have you been on one side of people's favor, only to find yourself on the other side because of something you did that—while not wrong— was unpopular? Have friends turned against you? Family members?

Colleagues? Consider these three suggestions for when you find yourself swimming upstream in this type of situation.

First, *don't be surprised.* Some natural responses might be, "I can't believe he said that." "I can't believe they're treating me like this." "I can't believe they thought I was saying such and such." The reasons people turn against you can be bewildering, but take it for what it is: human nature acting selfishly. We are all subject to the whims of human nature to tell us what is important and to resent those who threaten to take it away.

That is no big surprise. In fact, seasoned leaders soon learn to anticipate public backlash and prepare themselves beforehand.

Second, *don't give up.* Luke tells us how Jesus responded to the uprising against Him in the synagogue: "Passing through their midst, He went His way" (4:30). He refused to let one group keep Him from pressing on. He just passed through their ranks with plans to carry His agenda forward. And that's exactly what the balance of this narrative is about.

Don't give up. Listen to opposing opinions and consider them carefully. But, just because "the crowd" is against you, that doesn't mean you're wrong. And if people considered significant don't like you, that doesn't mean you're not pleasing God. If you have determined that the course you have taken is right, stay on it.

Third, *don't get sidetracked.* The story ends, simply, "He went His way" (4:30). He never lost sight of the mission—the cross, redeeming humanity, conquering evil, pleasing the Father.

Fred Seward, the son of Abraham Lincoln's secretary of state, noted that Lincoln took "a genial, philosophical view of human nature, and of national destiny."[7] That attitude placed the judgment of people in the hands of God, allowing the president to rise above petty squabbles and pointless power struggles. Good leaders address dissent when necessary but spend the rest of their time pursuing what they know to be right, taking care to inspire others with their vision.

Ministry at the Grassroots Level
LUKE 4:31-44

NASB
31 And He came down to Capernaum, a city of Galilee, and He was teaching

NLT
31 Then Jesus went to Capernaum, a town in Galilee, and taught there in the synagogue every Sabbath day.

NASB

them on the Sabbath; 32and they were amazed at His teaching, for His ªmessage was with authority. 33In the synagogue there was a man ªpossessed by the spirit of an unclean demon, and he cried out with a loud voice, 34"Let us alone! ªWhat business do we have with each other, Jesus bof Nazareth? Have You come to destroy us? I know who You are—the Holy One of God!" 35But Jesus rebuked him, saying, "Be quiet and come out of him!" And when the demon had thrown him down in the midst *of the people,* he came out of him without doing him any harm. 36And amazement came upon them all, and they *began* talking with one another saying, "What is ªthis message? For with authority and power He commands the unclean spirits and they come out." 37And the report about Him was spreading into every locality in the surrounding district.

38Then He got up and *left* the synagogue, and entered Simon's home. Now Simon's mother-in-law was suffering from a high fever, and they asked Him ªto help her. 39And standing over her, He rebuked the fever, and it left her; and she immediately got up and ªwaited on them.

40While the sun was setting, all those who had any *who were* sick with various diseases brought them to Him; and laying His hands on each one of them, He was healing them. 41Demons also were coming out of many, shouting, "You are the Son of God!" But rebuking them, He would not allow them to speak, because they knew Him to be ªthe Christ.

42When day came, Jesus left and went to a secluded place; and the crowds were searching for Him, and came to Him and tried to keep Him from going away from them. 43But He said to them, "I must preach the

NLT

32There, too, the people were amazed at his teaching, for he spoke with authority.

33 Once when he was in the synagogue, a man possessed by a demon—an evil* spirit—cried out, shouting, 34"Go away! Why are you interfering with us, Jesus of Nazareth? Have you come to destroy us? I know who you are—the Holy One of God!"

35 But Jesus reprimanded him. "Be quiet! Come out of the man," he ordered. At that, the demon threw the man to the floor as the crowd watched; then it came out of him without hurting him further.

36Amazed, the people exclaimed, "What authority and power this man's words possess! Even evil spirits obey him, and they flee at his command!" 37The news about Jesus spread through every village in the entire region.

38After leaving the synagogue that day, Jesus went to Simon's home, where he found Simon's mother-in-law very sick with a high fever. "Please heal her," everyone begged. 39Standing at her bedside, he rebuked the fever, and it left her. And she got up at once and prepared a meal for them.

40As the sun went down that evening, people throughout the village brought sick family members to Jesus. No matter what their diseases were, the touch of his hand healed every one. 41Many were possessed by demons; and the demons came out at his command, shouting, "You are the Son of God!" But because they knew he was the Messiah, he rebuked them and refused to let them speak.

42Early the next morning Jesus went out to an isolated place. The crowds searched everywhere for him, and when they finally found him, they begged him not to leave them. 43But he replied, "I must preach the kingdom of God to the other cities also, for I was sent for this purpose." ⁴⁴So He kept on preaching in the synagogues of ᵃJudea.

4:32 ᵃLit *word*   4:33 ᵃLit *having a spirit*   4:34 ᵃLit *What to us and to you* (a Heb idiom)   ᵇLit *the Nazarene*   4:36 ᵃOr *this word, that with authority... come out?*   4:38 ᵃLit *about her*   4:39 ᵃOr *served*   4:41 ᵃI.e. the Messiah   4:44 ᵃI.e. the country of the Jews (including Galilee)

Good News of the Kingdom of God in other towns, too, because that is why I was sent." ⁴⁴So he continued to travel around, preaching in synagogues throughout Judea.*

4:33 Greek *unclean;* also in 4:36.   4:44 Some manuscripts read *Galilee.*

I don't do my best learning in a classroom. I did well in school. I studied hard, listened well, completed all of my assignments on time and well enough to earn good grades, and I performed admirably on tests. Still, I don't count my hours in the classroom as my best times of instruction. I learn best by observing an expert. I appreciate teachers, but I need a mentor who will take time to show me how it's done. By God's grace, I had the privilege of learning under some of the very best.

This segment of Luke's narrative represents the third of a three-part introduction to the public ministry of Christ. The first (4:14-16) briefly summarizes His activity. The second (4:17-30) clarifies the scope of His mission as the Messiah: to save those who want a Savior. The third (4:31-44) shows specific examples of how Jesus conducted ministry. And what a wonderful model this last segment is for Christians! Jesus demonstrated four activities that, more or less, define Christian ministry. As we examine each activity, watch for the recurring theme of authority.

He taught truth. (4:31-32)
He confronted evil. (4:33-37, 41)
He demonstrated compassion. (4:38-40)
He renewed His strength. (4:42-44)

— 4:31-32 —

After departing His hostile hometown of Nazareth, Jesus resumed His successful ministry in Capernaum. The journey took Him, literally, from high to low, from 1150 feet (350 meters) above sea level to 680 feet (200 meters) below it, by the Sea of Galilee. While He went "down" in elevation, His ministry soared.

The people were amazed by the manner in which Jesus taught, which was unique for its day. Luke writes that He taught with "authority" (*exousia* [1849]), using a Greek word that means "of free choice."

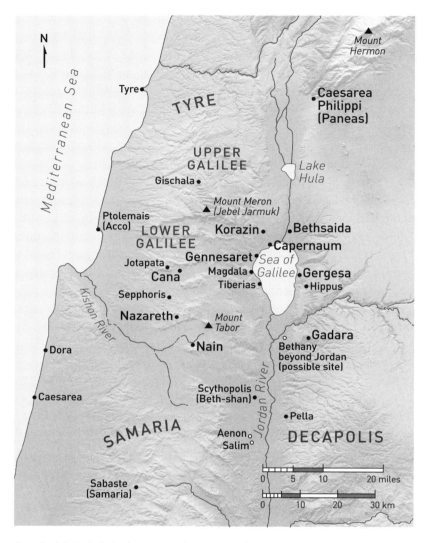

Jesus' ministry in Luke focuses on the region of Galilee. Capernaum functioned as a home base for Jesus and his disciples, but they traveled all over the region teaching and healing.

It is the term used to describe the sovereign, authoritative decision of a king or a judge (cf. Luke 12:5; Acts 1:7; Rom. 9:21; Jude 1:25). Mark's parallel account states, "He was teaching them as one having authority, *and not as the scribes*" (Mark 1:22, emphasis mine). According to Walter Liefeld, "The majority of the rabbis would base their teaching on the chain of tradition, citing the opinions of their predecessors."[8] Sabbath after Sabbath, people heard the scribes drone on: "According to Rabbi

The Jewish synagogue fulfilled many of the same functions in the local community as the modern-day Christian church: worship, instruction, and fellowship. Jesus, as an exceptionally popular rabbi, taught at the synagogue in Capernaum. Today, this white limestone synagogue from the fourth century rests on the foundation of the black basalt synagogue Jesus knew in His day.

so-and-so . . . But Rabbi what's-his-name disagrees, saying . . ." But Jesus didn't appeal to the traditions of men; He taught directly from the Scripture, speaking as the author of the texts in question, without any appeal to human authorities. Luke stresses this with the phrase "His message" (Luke 4:32).

It is true that Jesus enjoyed the unique advantage of being God—no one can exposit a book quite like the author himself. However, I don't think that was Luke's point. What gave Jesus' teaching such authority? He appealed directly to the text, not to particular schools of thought or the opinions of other respected teachers. In our day, we may apply this to Bible helps, such as commentaries, lexicons, and dictionaries. These tools can be very useful, but they were never intended to replace the Bible itself. Furthermore, Jesus not only taught the Scriptures as one who understood their meaning, but He also lived out the timeless principles of the Old Testament. He explained God's Word from His own human experience. In this way, He is our model teacher.

— 4:33-35 —

Luke carries the theme of authority forward in his description of the Lord's encounter with a demon-possessed man. This also happens to be the first of Jesus' miracles recorded in Luke's Gospel.

On this occasion, "a man having a spirit of an unclean demon" (lit.) was in the synagogue at the same time as Jesus. Luke doesn't explain how they happened to meet, but his depiction indicates the demon-possessed man was surprised to see Jesus. The phrase "Let us alone!" in the NASB translates a single Greek interjection, *ea*, the meaning of which is disputed. It could be the imperative form of a verb meaning "to leave" or "to permit" (*eaō* [1439]), or a common emotional interjection—similar to "Ah!"—expressing anger or dismay. Because the latter is common in classical poetry, and Luke appears to have been classically trained, I favor understanding this word as the interjection.

Whereas people struggled to understand or accept Jesus' identity, the demon did not. Note the specific identifiers in his rant: Jesus of Nazareth, the Holy One of God. The title "Holy One of God" is not an official title, but a notable contrast to the demon's own identity. Whereas "holy" things are consecrated—that is, set apart for special use in God's service—the demon was unclean and unacceptable, having dedicated himself to the opposition of God's purposes. Luke's language highlights the meeting of opposites. The literal embodiment of God confronted the literal embodiment of evil. And, ironically, they clashed in the synagogue. The question "What business do we have with each other?" comes from the Greek rendering of a Hebrew idiom, which conveys the idea "What have we in common?" (Josh. 22:24; Judg. 11:12; 2 Sam. 16:10; 19:22; 1 Kgs. 17:18; 2 Kgs. 3:13; cf. Matt. 27:19; Luke 8:28; Mark 5:7; John 2:4). This was the demon's way of telling Jesus to "get lost" or "mind Your own business." Furthermore, the question "Have You come to destroy us?" is rhetorical, expressing both sarcasm and contempt.

For all his blustering, the demon proved impotent before the authority of Christ. The Lord commanded and the demon obeyed.

As with His teaching (Luke 4:32), the people responded with "amazement" at the Lord's "authority" (*exousia*). His message and His power extended beyond mere teaching in the synagogue to overpower the forces of hell. While any mortal man could conceivably teach with authority, this man's authority overcame evil. Other teachers decried the rise of evil; this man put evil in its place.

— 4:38-41 —

Jesus again exercised His authority—this time over the illness of Simon's mother-in-law. Luke's narrative makes it clear that this incident occurred immediately after Jesus had cast out the demon in the

Modern Thinking on the Subject of Satan

LUKE 4:34

What the Bible teaches about demons is neither funny nor phony. It is real. Nevertheless, many Christian theologians and teachers are reluctant to approach the subject, perhaps fearing that it will make them look superstitious or irrational. We live in the age of science because people like Galileo Galilei, Johannes Kepler, and Isaac Newton—all devout believers in the Creator—replaced myth and superstition with rational views of nature. They believed that God created an orderly, mechanical universe in which virtually everything could be described by scientific inquiry. Sometimes they went too far. Since that time, the scientific community has removed God from its equations, and we are currently taught to regard the notion of spiritual darkness—the activity of Satan and his demonic minions—as a shameful relic of our former ignorance.

Today, I am sad to say, intelligent, rational people have very little reason to think seriously about the demonic. Movies and television fictionalize or make jokes about Satan. Countercultural rebels idealize him and then hide behind the indignation it arouses in others. Some tribal cultures still conjure him with ancient ceremonies or try to ward him off with trinkets. And to make matters worse, some well-meaning Christians attach every conceivable evil to his direct, supernatural activity.

Frankly, I think people tend to give Satan too much credit. Environmental disasters are to be expected in a cursed, fallen world. As are diseases, weeds, and—I am convinced—mosquitoes. And when you think of it, the vast majority of human suffering comes at the hands of other humans. No need to blame the devil; as sinful people, we are quite capable of evil without the influence of anyone.

Still, the work of evil powers and principalities in our world is neither phony nor funny. It is real. But we have no reason to fear. Demonic power withers in the presence of God. And Christ is returning soon!

synagogue. Jesus went to Simon's home, and at the request of friends, he proceeded to help the woman's fever. Today, a fever is usually little more than a nuisance, easily treated with over-the-counter medicine. In those days, however, a person suffering a fever could either recover suddenly or die quickly. A fever represented the same kind of uncertainty as a coma might today.

Jesus "rebuked" the fever (same term as 4:35), and just like the demon, the fever departed. Simon's mother-in-law, just like the man in the synagogue, received immediate relief. Luke's parallelism is deliberate. He takes great care to demonstrate that the Lord possesses authority over personified evil (demons) and the problem of evil (human suffering), and that both submit to His word.

Luke reinforces the two events with a summary of Jesus' activity the rest of that Sabbath. The exorcism and the healing were not isolated events. He repeated the miracles many times over for numerous demon-possessed and infirm people. The act of laying on one's hands is an authoritative gesture, most often used to confer blessing or to delegate power (Gen. 48:13-14; Num. 8:10; 27:18; Deut. 34:9; Acts 6:6; 8:17; 1 Tim. 4:14; 2 Tim. 1:6). Moreover, Jesus rebuked the demons, further exercising divine authority.

The phrase "While the sun was setting" clarifies that Jesus healed after the Sabbath had concluded. Jews could neither travel long distances nor carry anything (or anyone) until sunset (cf. Mark 1:32). He waged war on evil throughout the night, receiving all who came for relief, and healing each individual merely for the sake of love.

— 4:42-44 —

In the midst of His ministry of compassion and despite the rapid rise of His popularity, Jesus "left" ministry and "went" toward seclusion. People desperate for relief from the ravages of evil clamored for Jesus' attention, searching for Him and trying to coerce His compassion. Nevertheless, He retreated from public ministry. When God became a man, He voluntarily laid aside the use of His divine attributes, including omnipotence. Human bodies get tired. They wear down, after which they require rest. Jesus recognized His need for physical, mental, emotional, and spiritual renewal. Everyone doing ministry should be wise enough to follow His example!

Jesus, in becoming human, also voluntarily laid aside omnipresence. While the needs in Capernaum could have occupied Him for a decade, other people in other cities needed Him too. Luke concluded this segment with a summary statement of the Lord's ministry in the "synagogues of Judea." While "Judea" is technically the southern province of Israel—distinct from Galilee to the north and Samaria between the two—Luke most likely means the entire nation here. In other words, "Judea" in this case should be understood as "the land of the Jews" (cf. Luke 6:17; 7:17; 23:5), unlike his more specific use in other places (1:39, 65; 2:4; 3:1; 5:17; 21:21). Although Luke structured his narrative geographically rather than chronologically, He does note that Jesus ministered throughout the land of Israel, even in the beginning of His public ministry.

APPLICATION: LUKE 4:31-44

Ministry in the Rough

A great coach knows the value of fundamentals. These are the basics of the game that, when executed well, usually lead to victory. In American football, fundamentals include blocking, tackling, snapping the ball cleanly, and completing a solid handoff or a forward pass. When hitting a baseball, they include keeping your eye on the ball, stepping into the pitch, swinging in a smooth and level manner, and following through. The game of golf is all about the swing; if you know which way to face and can develop a consistent swing, you will do well in the sport.

Jesus boiled Christian ministry down to four fundamentals:

- Teaching truth (4:31-32)
- Confronting evil (4:33-37, 41)
- Demonstrating compassion (4:38-40)
- Renewing one's strength (4:42-44)

Teaching truth (4:31-32). For a minister today, teaching the truth could not be more challenging—or crucial. I have encountered a lot of church-growth manuals, and in my weaker moments, I have even considered a few of the strategies they outline. In principle, I don't have a problem with taking advice from the business world—some churches could use a good lesson in organization—but sheep don't flock to a shepherd because of a great business plan. Sheep follow a shepherd because the shepherd cares for them and leads them to food. In ministry, "food" is none other than truth from God's Word.

All ministers in all forms of ministry have a responsibility to teach the Scriptures, identify timeless principles, and then encourage others to apply what they have learned. This naturally applies to pastors, teachers, missionaries, and evangelists, but not exclusively. The same responsibilities apply to those serving as counselors, worship leaders, writers, chaplains—any role that puts the minister in contact with others.

Confronting evil (4:33-37, 41). Jesus confronted evil in its many forms by releasing others from its grip. He cast out demons, healed broken bodies, denounced false teaching, stood for what is right against those who used evil for selfish gain, and demanded justice for the helpless and mercy for the forgotten. While we do not have His miraculous abilities, we do have His authority to confront evil. With that authority comes responsibility. Ministry requires that we confront evil in all its forms and that we risk our own security to see it defeated.

Dietrich Bonhoeffer took this dimension of Christian ministry very seriously. He had openly opposed Adolf Hitler on several occasions, most notably in a 1933 radio address, just two days after the madman was installed as the Chancellor of Germany. By 1938, the threat to his safety and the prospect of compulsory military service prompted him to accept a teaching post at Union Theological Seminary, safely located across the Atlantic in New York. But his conscience would not be silenced. In July of 1939, He wrote to a friend,

> I have made a mistake in coming to America. I must live through this difficult period of our national history with the Christian people of Germany. I shall have no right to participate in the reconstruction of Christian life in Germany after the war if I do not share the trials of this time with my people. . . . Christians in Germany will face the terrible alternative of either willing the defeat of their nation in order that Christian civilization may survive, or willing the victory of their nation and thereby destroying our civilization. I know which of these alternatives I must choose; but I cannot make that choice in security."[9]

He took the last scheduled steamer back to Germany where he eventually faced the hangman's noose for openly denouncing Adolf Hitler and participating in a plot to rid the world of him.

For most of us, confronting evil will not result in the loss of life;

nevertheless, opposing it is neither safe nor convenient. Not far from where you sit right now, evil has caused suffering, and it continues to spread. More than likely, others in your community have banded together to confront that evil. Perhaps it's time to join them. Or, if you are a ministry leader, gather your resources, call others to join you, and take action.

Demonstrating compassion (4:38-40). You don't have to look far to find someone in need of compassion. And you don't have to go a great distance to find an organization formed to provide tangible relief to the suffering caused by poverty, illness, crime, ignorance, or natural disasters. They would be delighted to hear you say, "I'm here to help. Where can I serve you most effectively?"

If you are a ministry leader and you have too much demanding your attention to begin a new initiative, then establish a relationship with parachurch ministries in your area and encourage others to help. These organizations would welcome the support and cooperation of churches.

Renewing one's strength (4:42-44). Ministry is a tough job! It is a labor of love, and full-time vocational service to the Lord is often invigorating. If, however, you are engaged in too much ministry, you are only so far from burnout. If you have not set aside regular, sustained time for fun, relaxation, rest, and refreshment—including but not limited to vacations, sabbaticals, or furloughs—then you won't be much good for ministry for very long. You will be physically present but increasingly less effective. You must know yourself well enough to say how much is too much, and then—here's the hard part—trust the perspective of someone close to you to help you set limits.

The public will never think what you do is enough, and your critics will begrudge your taking time off. You will be called lazy or uncommitted when you take time for yourself. That's because most people aren't aware of how much you do until their needs go unmet. Consequently, they remain largely ignorant of all that you do around the clock and throughout the week.

Take time. Get away. Schedule downtime like you would an important meeting, and protect it. Eventually, the people you serve will learn to accept that you are unavailable for *anything* during certain times of the day, certain days of the week, and certain times of the year. In fact, they will learn to care for you when they see you taking care of yourself. And they will appreciate the added years of service you render because you didn't quickly burn out.

What It's Like to Fish with Jesus
LUKE 5:1-11

NASB

¹Now it happened that while the crowd was pressing around Him and listening to the word of God, He was standing by the lake of Gennesaret; ²and He saw two boats lying at the edge of the lake; but the fishermen had gotten out of them and were washing their nets. ³And He got into one of the boats, which was Simon's, and asked him to put out a little way from the land. And He sat down and *began* teaching the ªpeople from the boat. ⁴When He had finished speaking, He said to Simon, "Put out into the deep water and let down your nets for a catch." ⁵Simon answered and said, "Master, we worked hard all night and caught nothing, but ªI will do as You say *and* let down the nets." ⁶When they had done this, they enclosed a great quantity of fish, and their nets *began* to break; ⁷so they signaled to their partners in the other boat for them to come and help them. And they came and filled both of the boats, so that they began to sink. ⁸But when Simon Peter saw *that*, he fell down at Jesus' ªfeet, saying, "Go away from me Lord, for I am a sinful man!" ⁹For amazement had seized him and all his companions because of the catch of fish which they had taken; ¹⁰and so also *were* ªJames and John, sons of Zebedee, who were partners with Simon. And Jesus said to Simon, "Do not fear, from now on you will be catching men." ¹¹When they had brought their boats to land, they left everything and followed Him.

5:3 ªLit *crowds* 5:5 ªLit *upon Your word* 5:8 ªLit *knees* 5:10 ªOr *Jacob*

NLT

¹One day as Jesus was preaching on the shore of the Sea of Galilee,* great crowds pressed in on him to listen to the word of God. ²He noticed two empty boats at the water's edge, for the fishermen had left them and were washing their nets. ³Stepping into one of the boats, Jesus asked Simon,* its owner, to push it out into the water. So he sat in the boat and taught the crowds from there.

⁴When he had finished speaking, he said to Simon, "Now go out where it is deeper, and let down your nets to catch some fish."

⁵"Master," Simon replied, "we worked hard all last night and didn't catch a thing. But if you say so, I'll let the nets down again." ⁶And this time their nets were so full of fish they began to tear! ⁷A shout for help brought their partners in the other boat, and soon both boats were filled with fish and on the verge of sinking.

⁸When Simon Peter realized what had happened, he fell to his knees before Jesus and said, "Oh, Lord, please leave me—I'm such a sinful man." ⁹For he was awestruck by the number of fish they had caught, as were the others with him. ¹⁰His partners, James and John, the sons of Zebedee, were also amazed.

Jesus replied to Simon, "Don't be afraid! From now on you'll be fishing for people!" ¹¹And as soon as they landed, they left everything and followed Jesus.

5:1 Greek *Lake Gennesaret,* another name for the Sea of Galilee. 5:3 *Simon* is called "Peter" in 6:14 and thereafter.

At times, the Lord takes special delight in surprising us. When He does, He seems especially pleased to turn impossible situations into times of celebration. Just when we are ready to throw our hands in the air and give up hope; when we have come to the end of our resources, exhausted our energy, run out of ideas, and lost our creativity; when quitting seems like the only remaining option; the Lord pulls off a miracle.

Paul the apostle experienced this so many times that he began to detect a pattern. The best things happen when we run out of options. "I will rather boast about my weaknesses, so that the power of Christ may dwell in me. Therefore I am well content with weaknesses, with insults, with distresses, with persecutions, with difficulties, for Christ's sake; *for when I am weak, then I am strong*" (2 Cor. 12:9-10, emphasis mine).

This would become the first principle of discipleship under Jesus. In most cases, a mentor trains pupils to become autonomous. As the students learn, they become less and less dependent on their master until, finally, they gain enough knowledge to set out on their own. But Jesus had a very different lesson plan for His students. He would teach His followers how to become ever more dependent upon their Master. Their first lesson in dependence began with their calling, when their impossibility gave Him the opportunity to give a surprise gift.

— 5:1-3 —

The phrase "Now it happened" (Luke 5:1) begins a new story. The span of time between the statement of 4:43 and the events of 5:1 could have been hours or months—Luke's summary of Jesus' activity in 4:44 does not imply a long break between the two. I believe 5:1 occurred the morning following the events of 4:42-43. If so, Jesus healed all night (4:40-41), retreated to a secluded place to rest (4:42), was found by the crowds (4:42), and returned to minister near Capernaum (5:1). Unfortunately, the growing multitude began to hinder His effectiveness. So, Jesus used His surroundings to His advantage. He saw a body of water and boats and decided to create an ad hoc amphitheater.

Luke's original audience would have understood the implications of his description of the scene. The men were washing their nets early in the morning because they had been fishing all night, most likely with dragnets, the kind used for deepwater fishing. While they labored through the night with no success (5:5), Jesus had previously (perhaps that very night) labored all night providing relief to countless people. Whereas the fishermen had no success, Jesus could barely keep up with the numbers He had attracted.

Jesus chose to use Simon's boat, probably because it was Simon's house Jesus had used to conduct His healing ministry (4:38). He positioned the boat a short distance from the shore, sat down—the customary posture for teaching—and began to teach. His voice echoed across the still waters of the Sea of Galilee that early morning as hundreds—perhaps thousands—lined the shore to hear Him.

Not far from the Lord, an exhausted, sweat-drenched Simon sat and listened.

— 5:4-7 —

I would love to know what Jesus taught the people from Simon's boat. A lesson on discipleship? Perhaps the joy of fulfilling one's destiny? Or maybe trusting God for provision? Regardless, when He was finished, the Lord instructed Simon to take the boats out to deep water. Jesus asked the men to return to the very place where they had labored in vain.

He further instructed Simon to "let down your (plural) nets for a catch." These deepwater nets required more than one boat to deploy and retrieve, so the Lord's request involved the entire group. We learn from other parts of the New Testament that Simon and his brother, Andrew, ran a fishing enterprise (Matt. 4:18), often partnering with John and his brother, James (Luke 5:10). While other men who served as hired hands probably helped, Luke focused the narrative on Simon, who frequently spoke for the group.

The men undoubtedly found the Lord's command particularly annoying after hauling empty nets all night long. Nevertheless, Simon obeyed, calling Jesus "Master," as the two had been acquainted for some time (John 1:41-42; Luke 4:38). Throughout his narrative, Luke uses the title "Master" in the place of "Rabbi," a title Gentile audiences would not have found significant.

In Simon's mind, this was a fool's errand. Fish retreat to the depths to stay cool during the day. He knew to fish at night when they come to the surface to feed. Not long after deploying the net, however, Simon noticed the top line of the net had become taut to the point of breaking. The sudden transition in the men's demeanor must have been comical as Simon frantically barked orders and the crew scrambled, grunted, and groaned to haul in the net. When the weight of fish nearly pushed the first boat under the waves, the second came to the rescue. Eventually, both crews gingerly rowed toward the shore, their vessels barely visible above the water.

While the story describes actual events, Luke's purpose follows the Lord's. Jesus performed this miracle, not for the sake of the people on the shore, but for Simon and his partners. His object lesson taught the men that good intentions and earnest effort are not enough; only the Lord can make an otherwise futile life productive.

— 5:8 —

The Lord's object lesson brought Simon to his knees as he began to see, perhaps for the first time, that Jesus was not merely a powerful prophet or a supernaturally gifted healer, but superhuman. Simon observed the presence of God. He prostrated himself in worship at Jesus' feet and begged for mercy, much like another man who found himself frozen with fear when confronted by God. Isaiah, the Old Testament prophet, said, "Woe is me, for I am ruined! Because I am a man of unclean lips, and I live among a people of unclean lips; for my eyes have seen the King, the LORD of hosts" (Isa. 6:5). Both men understood the potential consequence of direct contact with God. Sinfulness cannot survive in the presence of divine holiness. Because Simon understood himself to be a man tainted with sin, he feared Jesus.

— 5:9-10 —

Again, Luke describes the response of people in terms of amazement. When God takes control of a situation in our weakness, it amazes everybody—usually because there is no explanation for it, which makes those divine surprises and interventions so magnificent.

As the fishermen trembled before their Messiah, they heard words that would forever change their lives: "Do not fear, from now on you will be catching men" (Luke 5:10). The Greek word rendered "catch" literally means "capture alive." Paul uses the expression in the negative sense of men "held captive" by Satan to do his will (2 Tim. 2:24-26). By contrast, Jesus promised Simon and the others that they would be capturing men to do the will of the Father.

— 5:11 —

The disciples' unprecedented success in business that day didn't prompt them to invite the Lord to become a senior partner in the business. They understood the principle Jesus taught through their massive haul of fish: *With Me, you can do all things; without Me, everything you touch will come to nothing.* When they were ready to accept this truth, they responded to the call of God. The men immediately dropped their nets, left everything behind, and accepted the Lord's invitation to join an inner circle of students.

• • •

It saddens me to know that some reading this will forfeit God's surprises for the illusion of security. Simon and his companions didn't remain in the shallows, content with what they could reasonably expect to receive from their own efforts. Against all reason, they obeyed the Lord's command to do something unusual, something irrational (from a human perspective), something that expert fishermen would otherwise refuse to do. They steered their boats toward deep waters—the wrong part of the lake at the wrong time of the day for catching fish. In response to their faith decision, Jesus pulled off a miracle. Against all odds, the God of lakes, fish, and fishermen exercised His divine authority over creation to give His students a surprise gift.

I wonder how many surprise gifts we forfeit by playing it safe, by depending upon our own expertise, by seeing only impossibilities in the Lord's commands.

Simon, Andrew, James, and John didn't allow the greatest day of their fishing careers to distract them. That day, they determined to follow Jesus anywhere He led and to do anything He commanded. Even if it led them into deeper waters.

APPLICATION: LUKE 5:1-11
Things to Remember When You're in Deep Water

I find in this wonderful section of Scripture no fewer than six observations from the ministry of Christ that help you keep calm when you are in over your head.

1. *Jesus chose not to minister to others all alone.* Jesus had at His disposal the omnipotent power of the Almighty, but He deliberately involved others in His work. He could have pulled up all those fish with one arm with the power of God within Him, but He let Simon and the other fishermen pull up all those fish. He delegated tasks to these disciples in order to show them something about their future in ministry (cf. 5:10). Jesus doesn't need us to do His work. He calls us to work and He uses our efforts

to accomplish His objectives, not because He needs us, but in order to share His victory with us. There is great comfort in that. When you're sharing in His work, He delights to share the fruit of success—if not now, then later.

2. *Jesus uses the familiar to do the incredible.* Jesus met the disciples on their turf; He didn't take them to the edge of heaven. He worked in their familiar scene, the fishing world. He got into their place of work, the boat. He had them use their nets and their skills. He engaged them in their trade. But in using the familiar, He lifted their eyes from the commonplace to glimpse what could be accomplished through His power.

3. *Jesus moves us from the safety of what can be seen, to help us trust Him through the risks of the unseen.* None of the work was done in shallow water. Jesus could have summoned the fish from the deep waters so the men could scoop them up from the shore, but He didn't. He directed the men to row out into the deep before instructing them to lower their nets. Not only is that where the big fish swim, but they had also already fished there and caught nothing. He wanted the men to trust Him, even though they saw no reason to obey.

4. *Jesus sometimes rewards faithfulness by breaking our nets and filling our boats.* None of those veterans of the sea ever dreamed of catching that many fish in one haul. The fruit of their obedience nearly sank their boats. When God's hand is on a ministry, the potential is mind-boggling. We get a glimpse of it every once in a while, and it frightens spiritual leaders to death. "What is God getting us into?" we might ask. "We can't get our arms around it. We can't stop the growth. The revival won't seem to settle down. People's lives are getting changed. There's inner healing going on."

5. *Jesus conceals His surprises until we follow His leading.* Everything was business as usual. Simon sat listening to the Lord's teaching, maybe dozing off a little. Then Jesus nudged him for another casting of the net. Simon didn't see anything supernatural. The water didn't glow. The boat didn't have a little halo over it. Jesus didn't bring nets from heaven that tingle when touched. Simon rowed the same boat he had been in all night, using the same nets that had come up empty. The surprise came when the men put out to the deep and let down their nets *in obedience.* Only then did they see the supernatural working of the Lord.

6. *Jesus reveals His objective to those who are willing to relinquish their security.* After Simon and the other disciples obeyed the Lord's command and experienced His supernatural working, they were permitted to see the greater plan Jesus had for them. Each step of faith revealed more of God's plan. But they had to risk trusting the Lord first.

Great Deeds, Strong Faith, Big God
LUKE 5:12-26

NASB

12 While He was in one of the cities, behold, *there was* a man ᵃcovered with leprosy; and when he saw Jesus, he fell on his face and implored Him, saying, "Lord, if You are willing, You can make me clean." 13 And He stretched out His hand and touched him, saying, "I am willing; be cleansed." And immediately the leprosy left him. 14 And He ordered him to tell no one, "But go and show yourself to the priest and make an offering for your cleansing, just as Moses commanded, as a testimony to them." 15 But the news about Him was spreading even farther, and large crowds were gathering to hear *Him* and to be healed of their sicknesses. 16 But Jesus Himself would *often* slip away ᵃto the ᵇwilderness and pray.

17ᵃOne day He was teaching; and there were *some* Pharisees and teachers of the law sitting *there,* who had come from every village of Galilee and Judea and *from* Jerusalem; and the power of the Lord was *present* for Him to perform healing. 18 And *some* men *were* carrying on a ᵃbed a man who was paralyzed; and they were trying to bring him in and to set him

NLT

12 In one of the villages, Jesus met a man with an advanced case of leprosy. When the man saw Jesus, he bowed with his face to the ground, begging to be healed. "Lord," he said, "if you are willing, you can heal me and make me clean." 13 Jesus reached out and touched him. "I am willing," he said. "Be healed!" And instantly the leprosy disappeared. 14 Then Jesus instructed him not to tell anyone what had happened. He said, "Go to the priest and let him examine you. Take along the offering required in the law of Moses for those who have been healed of leprosy.* This will be a public testimony that you have been cleansed."

15 But despite Jesus' instructions, the report of his power spread even faster, and vast crowds came to hear him preach and to be healed of their diseases. 16 But Jesus often withdrew to the wilderness for prayer.

17 One day while Jesus was teaching, some Pharisees and teachers of religious law were sitting nearby. (It seemed that these men showed up from every village in all Galilee and Judea, as well as from Jerusalem.) And the Lord's healing power was strongly with Jesus.

18 Some men came carrying a paralyzed man on a sleeping mat. They

down in front of Him. ¹⁹But not finding any *way* to bring him in because of the crowd, they went up on the roof and let him down through the tiles with his stretcher, into the middle *of the crowd,* in front of Jesus. ²⁰Seeing their faith, He said, "ᵃFriend, your sins are forgiven you." ²¹The scribes and the Pharisees began to reason, saying, "Who is this *man* who speaks blasphemies? Who can forgive sins, but God alone?" ²²But Jesus, ᵃaware of their reasonings, answered and said to them, "Why are you reasoning in your hearts? ²³Which is easier, to say, 'Your sins have been forgiven you,' or to say, 'Get up and walk'? ²⁴But, so that you may know that the Son of Man has authority on earth to forgive sins,"—He said to the paralytic—"I say to you, get up, and pick up your stretcher and go home." ²⁵Immediately he got up before them, and picked up what he had been lying on, and went home glorifying God. ²⁶ᵃThey were all struck with astonishment and *began* glorifying God; and they were filled with fear, saying, "We have seen remarkable things today."

5:12 ᵃLit *full of*   5:16 ᵃLit *in*   ᵇOr *deserted places*
5:17 ᵃLit *On one of the days*   5:18 ᵃOr *stretcher*
5:20 ᵃLit *Man*   5:22 ᵃOr *perceiving*   5:26 ᵃLit
Astonishment took them all

tried to take him inside to Jesus, ¹⁹but they couldn't reach him because of the crowd. So they went up to the roof and took off some tiles. Then they lowered the sick man on his mat down into the crowd, right in front of Jesus. ²⁰Seeing their faith, Jesus said to the man, "Young man, your sins are forgiven."

²¹But the Pharisees and teachers of religious law said to themselves, "Who does he think he is? That's blasphemy! Only God can forgive sins!"

²²Jesus knew what they were thinking, so he asked them, "Why do you question this in your hearts? ²³Is it easier to say 'Your sins are forgiven,' or 'Stand up and walk'? ²⁴So I will prove to you that the Son of Man* has the authority on earth to forgive sins." Then Jesus turned to the paralyzed man and said, "Stand up, pick up your mat, and go home!"

²⁵And immediately, as everyone watched, the man jumped up, picked up his mat, and went home praising God. ²⁶Everyone was gripped with great wonder and awe, and they praised God, exclaiming, "We have seen amazing things today!"

5:14 See Lev 14:2-32.   5:24 "Son of Man" is a title Jesus used for himself.

"Your God is too small!"

Those five little words graced the plain, blue cover of a book by the late British author J. B. Phillips. They tumbled onto my conscience like a barrel of bricks. I was a seminary student at the time, and after nearly four years of preparing to present the Word of God to others, my world had become much too small—about the size of a syllabus—encompassing no more than a campus and a three-room apartment. I was married, with one child in the crib and another on the way. My solitary purpose in life: to graduate in a couple of weeks.

When your world becomes that small, the God you worship can't be that much bigger. And I didn't realize just how tiny He had become until

Phillips's book enlarged my vision. Little could I have even imagined all that God had planned for the next fifty years!

By the time of Caesar Tiberius, Herod Antipas, Pontius Pilate, Annas, and Caiaphas, Israel's God had been shrunk to the size of a petty, pathetic legalist, scrupulously counting good deeds and deducting points for bad behavior. He seemed to care for neither people nor their suffering, only what they could do to please Him. In many ways, the Almighty Creator had become fashioned like Israel's rulers. To make things even worse, those trained and commissioned to teach the nation about God no longer saw Him as bigger than their problems.

But Jesus came to earth to change all of that. He began with small demonstrations of His power and then gradually revealed the full extent of His authority. On this particular day, God grew bigger for some people. Sadly, however, not for all.

— 5:12-13 —

After recruiting His first disciples, Jesus continued His ministry of teaching and healing. His location is unclear. He could have been far south in Judea or just a few hours' walk from the site of Simon's miraculous catch of fish (5:11). Regardless, something changed. His ministry—at least as presented by Luke—took on a completely new dimension, illustrated first by His encounter with a man "covered with leprosy" (5:12).

The man could have suffered from what we now call Hansen's Disease, or any one of a dozen other skin ailments called leprosy by the Greeks. All the same, we understand skin diseases to be a localized condition. Ancient people, however, considered leprosy a symptom of uncleanness emanating from somewhere within. And for Jews especially, this physical uncleanness merely accompanied the deeper problem of sin. Therefore, a person was not *healed* of leprosy; he was *cleansed*.

The man presented his request to Jesus in the form of a conditional clause, which Greek grammarians describe as a "third class conditional clause." This type of conditional statement indicates that the speaker doesn't presume to know whether the "if" is true or not. The leper didn't doubt Jesus' ability; however, past experience with people—especially religious authorities—caused him to doubt the Lord's willingness to cleanse him. He asked for help with a sense of "I don't blame You, either way." He expected nothing. He didn't bargain with God or try to justify his condition. He merely presented his need to the Lord and remained open to receive whatever Jesus might offer.

Jesus was not only willing; He did the unthinkable. He reached out and literally touched the man society had rejected as untouchable. In other instances, Jesus merely spoke a word and the miracle took effect. In at least one case, He healed from a distance of twenty miles (John 4:46-54). But in this situation, He chose to touch the leper's diseased skin, as if to say, "Your disease doesn't prevent Me from accepting you."

A touch. A miracle. And the man's life changed forever.

— 5:14-16 —

Jesus had to balance His ministry very carefully between miracles and teaching, or He would draw all the wrong people for all the wrong reasons. While Jesus didn't try to maintain total secrecy, He did want the man to maintain his focus on what was important. The Lord's two explanatory phrases reveal His intentions. "Just as Moses commanded" shows that He wanted the former leper to follow the mandate of scriptural Law (Lev. 14:1-32) and then reenter society as a whole man. In the phrase "as a testimony to them," Jesus urged the man to allow his healing and his restored life to do the talking. Furthermore, this would send a message directly to the temple leadership that something special was happening. A tradition among the rabbis held that curing leprosy was as difficult as raising the dead,[10] perhaps because they saw the disease as the physical manifestation of sin's consequences. Therefore, in their minds, to remove the consequences of sin was to absolve the person of sin.

Whether or not the man followed the Lord's instructions—I happen to think he did—the news about Jesus "was spreading" (imperfect tense, Luke 5:15) and great multitudes "were gathering" (imperfect tense, again). Consequently, Jesus found it necessary to retreat from public life to rest, reflect, refresh, and recharge.

— 5:17 —

The message Jesus sent to the temple via the testimony of a healed leper had reached its target. This set the stage for Jesus to add an important dimension to His ministry of teaching and healing. Up to this point, you may have detected a pattern:

Authority in teaching (4:14-32)
Authority to cast out demons (4:33-37, 41)
Authority to heal illnesses (4:38-40)
Authority to command nature (5:1-11)

This particular day was like most others in Jesus' ministry. Multitudes thronged to hear Him teach and to see Him heal the sick. On this day, however, the crowd included teachers and clerics from all parts of Israel. Even the foremost religious authorities of Jerusalem, Israel's political and religious elite, came to see the man who had undeniably cleansed a leper.

— 5:18-19 —

As He taught from the beloved scrolls of the Jewish Scriptures—the Law of Moses, the oracles of the prophets, and the wisdom writings—a small band of men strategized on behalf of their paralyzed friend. They had heard of Jesus' ability to heal the sick but were disappointed to find Him seated near the center of a large house and surrounded by a crowd of Pharisees and religious teachers, none of whom would yield for someone supposedly suffering divine judgment for sin.

The band of men did some creative thinking. They climbed the outside staircase, located the ceiling directly above Jesus' head, and started pulling tiles. Within a few moments, a stretcher slowly descended, bearing a paralyzed man.

— 5:20-21 —

Jesus decided to help the paralytic patient in response to his faith and that of his friends. The men had gone to extraordinary lengths to place their friend before Jesus because they believed He possessed authority over illness. Unlike the scribes and Pharisees, those unnamed friends had a big God for whom no disease or dysfunction was too difficult to cure.

Many had seen Jesus heal before. A brief word, perhaps a touch of the hand, and the sick immediately received perfect health. But on this occasion, Jesus stunned the crowd by saying something different. Surprising words; outrageous words: "Friend, your sins are forgiven you."

The teachers and religious officials immediately understood the immense implications of Jesus' declaration and called it blasphemy—any manner of speech that disregards or disrespects the value of another. This could include curses, slander, or other statements that treat someone with contempt. Jewish leaders reserved the term for those who reviled God. C. S. Lewis explains why the religious leaders had good reason to be upset:

> Now unless the speaker is God, [forgiving sins] is really so preposterous as to be comic. We can all understand how a man forgives offences against himself. You tread on my toe and I forgive you, you steal my money and I forgive you. But what should we make of a man, himself unrobbed and untrodden on, who announced

THE PHARISEES

LUKE 5:17

The most likely meaning of the term "Pharisee" is "separated one."[11] Many trace this sect of Judaism to Daniel and his three friends, who refused to partake of their captors' food (Dan. 1:8-19) or worship the king as a god (Dan. 3:1-30) while exiled in Babylon. Having been taken from the Promised Land and cut off from their temple, they clung to the Law as a means of preserving their identity as distant sons of Abraham. But after more than six hundred years, this admirable loyalty to nationalism and devotion to the Law had taken on a life of its own.

The Pharisees had become a tight-knit brotherhood, a political and religious party that had earned the respect of their fellow Jews. They were meticulous expositors of Scripture and worked tirelessly to apply the general principles of the Law to everyday life. The Law stated, for example, that every Israelite was to set aside the seventh day of the week for resting the body and refreshing the soul (Exod. 20:10-11). So that everyone would know how to apply the Law and to "rest" as they should, the Pharisaic rabbis added a long list of prohibitions. Later, this oral tradition of the Pharisees was preserved in a document called the Mishnah, which contains no fewer than twenty-four chapters *just on how to keep the Sabbath*.

No one rivaled the Pharisees in being religious. No one could!

that he forgave you for treading on another man's toes and stealing other men's money? Asinine fatuity is the kindest description we should give of his conduct. Yet this is what Jesus did. He told people that their sins were forgiven, and never waited to consult all the other people whom their sins had undoubtedly injured. He unhesitatingly behaved as if He was the party chiefly concerned, the person chiefly offended in all offences. This makes sense only if He really was God whose laws are broken and whose love is wounded in every sin. In the mouth of any speaker who is not God, these words would imply what I can only regard as a silliness and conceit unrivalled by any other character in history.[12]

In this way, Jesus added "authority to forgive sins" to His growing list of divine prerogatives. It's worth noting that He waited until he had a houseful of Scripture experts and religious authorities to do it!

— 5:22-23 —

As mentioned before (see commentary on 4:23-24), a seasoned speaker doesn't need supernatural power to read an audience or to anticipate their objections. But Luke's language subtly suggests that Jesus super-naturally perceived the religious leaders' thoughts—the reasoning taking place "in their hearts" (5:22), presumably beyond the awareness of people without supernatural knowledge. Jesus perceived the internal dialogue taking place within these religious experts. Their theological objections would have been compelling if He were not God. So Jesus addressed their concerns directly with an intriguing challenge. His question employs sophisticated logic.

He asked, "Which [statement] is easier to say [if visual validation is not a requirement]?" It's easier for a fraud to say, "Your sins are forgiven," because no one can disprove it or hold the speaker accountable. Who's to say the sins were not indeed forgiven? One can neither prove nor disprove the claim. Therefore, it's more difficult for a fraud to command a paralytic to "get up and walk," since a lack of healing would expose the fraud's powerlessness.

If, on the other hand, someone possessed ultimate authority over all things, He could make either statement with equal ease. Therefore, to offer visual validation for the more difficult statement is to prove both the authority to forgive sin *and* to heal paralysis.

— 5:24-25 —

Before anyone had a chance to answer the question verbally, Jesus brushed aside any theological objections by uttering the apparently more difficult statement. And to be certain no one missed the significance of His action, He said, "So that you (plural—that is, the roomful of theologians) may know that the Son of Man (that is, "the man sitting before you") has authority on earth to forgive sins . . . I say to you (singular—the paralyzed man), get up."

This is the first time in Luke's narrative that Jesus uses the title, "Son of Man." It's a highly significant messianic title in Jewish theology and a particular favorite of Luke. It reminds the listener that Jesus, as a human, identifies with us, but that He came to accomplish great things on our behalf. He is human, yet much more than human. His authority is, in fact, divine in origin.

No sooner did the command leave the Lord's lips than the formerly paralyzed man got up, picked up his stretcher, and left the house—and this is important—"glorifying God." He was brought to Jesus in faith in a great, big God, and he walked away with the concept of an even bigger God.

"SON OF MAN"

LUKE 5:24

Jesus frequently referred to Himself as "Son of Man," a particularly meaningful title with roots deep in the soil of Israel's Scriptures. First, Jesus used it to call attention to His own humanity, which was feeble and fragile (Job 25:6; Pss. 8:4; 144:3; 146:3; Isa. 51:12; Ezek. 2:1; cf. Matt. 26:41 and Mark 14:38). Being human, he suffered the pains of humanity, most especially in the ordeal of the cross.

More significantly, it is the title given by Daniel to the messianic figure in one of his visions. The vision recorded in Daniel 7:1-14 summarizes human history in terms of four great empires, depicted as four fearsome animals. He predicted that God, the "Ancient of Days," would eventually brush these empires aside to establish His own rule on the earth. At that time, a superhuman hero described as "one like a Son of Man" (Dan. 7:13) would receive from the "Ancient of Days" everlasting dominion over all the earth, the authority to rule as its king.

Jews of Jesus' time struggled to understand the dual image of the Messiah presented throughout Old Testament prophecy. Isaiah, for example, described the Messiah as both a conquering king and a sacrificial martyr—a man who would die to save His people, yet reign forever as their king. How could the Messiah be both human and superhuman? How could He die, yet reign eternally? The conundrum seemed so baffling, many theologians have suggested that perhaps the Messiah is really two individuals, one who dies as the "suffering servant" and another who resurrects the first and then reigns as the supreme king.

The Messiah is, in fact, the "Son of God" *and* the "Son of Man"—divine and human—perfectly united in one person without mixture or confusion. He is superhuman because He is God. He is also completely human. While Luke took great pains to establish the divinity of Jesus through the birth narrative, his Gospel emphasizes the Lord's identity with humanity. Therefore, the title "Son of Man" appears twenty-five times in his account (Luke 5:24; 6:5, 22; 7:34; 9:22, 26, 44, 58; 11:30; 12:8, 10, 40; 17:22, 24, 26, 30; 18:8, 31; 19:10; 21:27, 36; 22:22, 48, 69; 24:7), and in each occurrence, draws special attention to His identity as the Messiah or the mission He came to complete.

— 5:26 —

Luke concludes the episode with a summary statement describing the response of the people, including the scribes and Pharisees, who were theological experts and religious authorities. They were all ecstatic and gave glory to God, which matched what Jesus wanted. He came to give glory to the Father through His obedience as the Son. But, in contrast to the account of Simon and his companions in 5:1-11, Luke does not clearly give the specific reason for their awe. Simon fell at Jesus' feet in worship, recognizing His divine identity and responding accordingly (5:8). Rather than respond to Jesus in worship, this audience exclaimed, "We have seen remarkable things today." Well, no kidding! Luke's ending begs the question, "How will the people respond to Jesus in the long run?"

• • •

When God became a man in the person of Jesus Christ, people had the opportunity to see God as He is. As they observed Jesus' character, they saw the heart of God. As they witnessed Jesus' miracles, they saw the power of God. As they listened to Jesus' words, they saw the impact of God on the lives of those who responded in faith. And on this particular day, when the people gathered to see the ministry of Jesus in action, they soon discovered their vision of God was too small, much too limited. The Messiah's miracles of healing represented only one dimension of His ministry. He came not only to heal maladies of the body; He brought cleansing from the deadly spiritual disease of sin.

APPLICATION: LUKE 5:12-26

Two Ways to Maintain a Big-God Mindset

The size of your God will determine the scope of your ministry.

Note that I said "scope" and not "size." Size measures things in terms of head counts, square footage, and digits in a budget. Scope measures the size of a person's vision. If you have a big God, your vision will have no limits. If you have a pipsqueak god in your mind, you will spend your life wringing your hands over trifling matters and never accomplish a thing.

Let me suggest a couple of important perspective-changers to help you expand your notion of God. These might be a little unorthodox, so bear with me.

First, *study astronomy.*

Order a catalog from your local community college and sign up for a class on astronomy. Or find an enthusiast to introduce you to this field of study.

Sometime after childhood, we began to shrink the universe down to the size of our own experience. We draw lines around the scope of our own existence and forget there is a vast universe beyond our perception. Consequently, God becomes a petty ruler of our pathetic, little fiefdom.

The goal in such a course would be to expand our perspective of the universe—if not in astronomy, then in some other field of study of God's immense handiwork. As you consider the size of the cosmos, measured in eons and light-years, you will begin to see God with the proper frame of reference.

Second, *travel farther.*

Get outside your normal sphere of life. Far outside. On-the-other-side-of-the-world outside. Visit people who are very different from your neighbors. Immerse yourself in a culture very different from your own. Experience the needs and suffering of people in distant places. This can be done on vacation, but even better as part of a ministry. There are dozens of organizations that make the logistics simple, even the most difficult part of raising funds. Trust the Lord to make this possible. Make the effort. Take the steps. See what God is doing around the world.

With a bigger view of the universe (with all its immensity and complexity) and a bigger view of the world (with all its suffering and grandeur), I guarantee your view of God will expand. And so will your scope of ministry.

Is It Okay to Party with Sinners?
LUKE 5:27-39

NASB

27 After that He went out and noticed a tax collector named ªLevi sitting in the tax booth, and He said to him, "Follow Me." 28 And he left everything behind, and got up and *began* to follow Him.

29 And Levi gave a big reception for Him in his house; and there was a great crowd of tax collectors and other *people* who were reclining *at the table* with them. 30 The Pharisees and their scribes *began* grumbling at His disciples, saying, "Why do you eat and drink with the tax collectors

NLT

27 Later, as Jesus left the town, he saw a tax collector named Levi sitting at his tax collector's booth. "Follow me and be my disciple," Jesus said to him. 28 So Levi got up, left everything, and followed him.

29 Later, Levi held a banquet in his home with Jesus as the guest of honor. Many of Levi's fellow tax collectors and other guests also ate with them. 30 But the Pharisees and their teachers of religious law complained bitterly to Jesus' disciples, "Why do you eat and drink with such scum?*"

NASB

and ªsinners?" ³¹And Jesus answered and said to them, "*It is* not those who are well who need a physician, but those who are sick. ³²I have not come to call the righteous but sinners to repentance."

³³And they said to Him, "The disciples of John often fast and offer prayers, the *disciples* of the Pharisees also do ªthe same, but Yours eat and drink." ³⁴And Jesus said to them, "You cannot make the ªattendants of the bridegroom fast while the bridegroom is with them, can you? ³⁵But *the* days will come; and when the bridegroom is taken away from them, then they will fast in those days." ³⁶And He was also telling them a parable: "No one tears a piece of cloth from a new garment and puts it on an old garment; otherwise he will both tear the new, and the piece from the new will not match the old. ³⁷And no one puts new wine into old wineskins; otherwise the new wine will burst the skins and it will be spilled out, and the skins will be ruined. ³⁸But new wine must be put into fresh wineskins. ³⁹And no one, after drinking old *wine* wishes for new; for he says, 'The old is good *enough.*'"

5:27 ªAlso called *Matthew* 5:30 ªI.e. irreligious Jews 5:33 ªOr *likewise* 5:34 ªLit *sons of the bridal-chamber*

NLT

³¹Jesus answered them, "Healthy people don't need a doctor—sick people do. ³²I have come to call not those who think they are righteous, but those who know they are sinners and need to repent."

³³One day some people said to Jesus, "John the Baptist's disciples fast and pray regularly, and so do the disciples of the Pharisees. Why are your disciples always eating and drinking?"

³⁴Jesus responded, "Do wedding guests fast while celebrating with the groom? Of course not. ³⁵But someday the groom will be taken away from them, and then they will fast."

³⁶Then Jesus gave them this illustration: "No one tears a piece of cloth from a new garment and uses it to patch an old garment. For then the new garment would be ruined, and the new patch wouldn't even match the old garment.

³⁷"And no one puts new wine into old wineskins. For the new wine would burst the wineskins, spilling the wine and ruining the skins. ³⁸New wine must be stored in new wineskins. ³⁹But no one who drinks the old wine seems to want the new wine. 'The old is just fine,' they say."

5:30 Greek *with tax collectors and sinners?*

Mark Twain is credited with saying, "Having spent considerable time with good people, I can understand why Jesus liked to be with tax collectors and sinners." Sadly, I have to admit that I sometimes find the company of unbelievers more enjoyable than time with "good people." The unbelievers are comfortable with their sin, which makes them less likely to focus on mine. And while I cannot agree with many of their choices, at least they come by their hypocrisy honestly—unlike many believers who live in denial of their own. And let's face it: Non-Christians don't put a guilt-trip on fun. They like to have fun, and they don't feel the need to hide their delight or adorn their fun with something high-minded.

Now, don't get me wrong. I'm not advocating sin. I'm not saying fun is the most important thing in life. And I'm certainly not saying non-believers are morally superior simply because they make no pretense about their sin. I'm simply suggesting that Christians need to loosen up, lighten up, and get out more. (I include myself in this admonishment.)

I've observed a strange phenomenon among many Christians. Before they were born again, they had more frequent contact with non-Christians. They worked and played with nonbelievers, went to the same places, watched movies with them, enjoyed television and sports with them, and perhaps they even went on vacations together. Then, following their conversion, the believer(s) gradually withdrew into church life. Eager to immerse themselves in the things of Christ, these new Christians surrounded themselves almost exclusively with believing friends. By and by, they spend time with friends from church, send their children to Christians schools, read Christian literature, listen to Christian radio, watch Christian television, and conduct business from the Christian yellow pages. Before long, they begin to look down on those rare believers who deliberately engage the nonbelieving world and who go to places Christians typically avoid. In other words, the mentality becomes such that it's okay to go into a bar to hand out Christian literature, but it's not okay to enjoy a soft drink, eat a few peanuts, and hang out with the people there.

Soon after Jesus demonstrated His authority to forgive sins, He found a particularly despised kind of sinner to call as one of His disciples. What He did next shocked the legalistic, rigid religious world.

— 5:27-28 —

According to Matthew and Mark, the healing of the paralyzed man occurred near Capernaum (Matt. 9:1; Mark 2:1), indicating that Levi was a tax collector in, or near, that city. Therefore, Levi had probably heard Jesus teach on more than one occasion.

The Greek term *telōnēs* [5057] refers to a particular kind of tax collector strongly associated with corruption. To become a *telōnēs*, one had to purchase a franchise from a government official. Rome set collection quotas for each month, but a *telōnēs* could use government authority to extort as much as he wanted. The tax money went to Rome; the surplus went into the tax collector's pocket.

To pay for the franchise, a Jew may have sold off land, which seems only reasonable from a Gentile point of view. But Jews drew much of their identity from owning a parcel of the Promised Land. To sell off one's portion of the land given to Abraham was akin to selling one's birthright for a bowl of soup (Gen. 25:29-34). Jews considered this worse than treason. Tax collectors had betrayed their people, rejected their heritage, despised their temple, and renounced their God. Tax collectors had sold themselves to foreigners, which put them on the same level as shameless harlots.

Levi was named after Jacob's third son, who had fathered the Israelite tribe by that name. During the time following the Exodus, the tribe of Levi remained faithful to God while the others bowed before a golden calf (Exod. 32). This prompted God to designate the descendants of Levi as priests. Ironically, Levi the tax collector didn't mediate the relationship between God and Israel; he instead sold his birthright, as it were, to represent the interests of Rome. So it must have come as a shock to everyone when Jesus walked by Levi's booth and called him to become one of His inner-circle students. The tax collector didn't seem surprised, though. His contemporaries must have marveled that he immediately shut down his enterprise, "left everything," and "began to follow" Jesus.

— 5:29 —

Levi wasted no time giving his peers the opportunity to meet their Savior. After responding to Jesus' call, he threw a grand celebration to honor His Master, sending invitations to the only guests who would come: his fellow tax collectors and a broad assortment of sin-stained ragamuffins from around the region.

The text doesn't explicitly say that Jesus had fun that day. Perhaps He conducted a Bible study that may have included an invitation at the end—but that's doubtful. It was Levi's party; he was the host, not Jesus. Luke's report suggests Jesus dined at Levi's table and drank his wine. He probably laughed, told stories, and sang songs with the city's notorious sinners. How great was that? Without stooping to sin, or losing His dignity in raucous, off-color behavior, Jesus nonetheless "lowered Himself" to enjoy the company of sinners and to embrace them as friends. He reclined at their table *in fellowship*.

— 5:30-32 —

Common sense might lead us to believe that the religious leaders in the community would have joined the celebration. After all, a former sinner had seen the light and become a full-time follower of a prominent rabbi! But as the riffraff emerged from the dark corners of Galilee to celebrate their friend's most unusual decision, a group of squint-eyed clerics stood frowning outside the courtyard gates, casting sideways glances toward the house and talking about him in whispers. They hated what they saw!

Eventually, the narrow-minded, legalistic Pharisees could no longer contain their indignation. As the city's moral down-and-outers cele-brated the salvation of Levi, the religious officials grumbled their re-proach. Disgusted and angry, they asked, "Why do you eat and drink with the tax collectors and sinners?"

This question is the first of two similar criticisms that Luke records in this context. The Pharisees had a moral caste system to maintain and political territory to defend. It never occurred to them that God might not be pleased with them.

Jesus' response is sarcastic in that it takes the Pharisees' perspective for granted and then applies the logical consequences accordingly. Of course, the Pharisees were not "well" (Luke 5:31), which was Jesus' point.

Commenting on the Pharisees' skewed perspective, Brennan Man-ning notes, "Paradoxically, what intrudes between God and human be-ings is our fastidious morality and pseudo-piety. It is not the prostitutes and tax collectors who find it most difficult to repent: it is the devout who feel they have no need to repent."[13] Levi and his friends were just the kind of people Jesus came to save: people honest enough to admit they are deathly ill with the disease of sin and want to be healed of it.

— 5:33-35 —

The conversation didn't end. It may have continued there, at Levi's feast, or perhaps in the days that followed. Luke may have compressed a daylong conversation in typical, first-century-narrative fashion. Re-gardless, the Pharisees compared Jesus and His disciples to John the Baptizer and his followers and asked another question. While John's disciples fasted for the sake of prayer, Jesus' attended banquets and thoroughly enjoyed themselves. Why?

The Pharisees prized expressions of piety and self-denial, presum-ing those activities to be more pleasing to God. But their ideas came more from Greek philosophy than Hebrew theology. Virtually all of the religious observances God ordained for the nation of Israel involved feasting and celebrating in community. The Pharisees, however, set aside certain days—Mondays and Thursdays—for fasting. By the time of Jesus, they could no longer distinguish between God's Law and their own oral traditions.

Jesus responded with an analogy set within a question. The Greek construction of the question presupposes a negative response, such as, "You don't want to get sick, do you?" His analogy draws upon the image of a wedding feast and casts himself as the bridegroom. He used this imagery because God had used it often when promising Israel a Redeemer. Their Messiah would be their Bridegroom, despite Israel's unfaithfulness during betrothal (Isa. 54:5-8; 62:4-5; Jer. 2:2; Ezek. 16; Hos. 2:14-23).

The purpose of fasting is to help intensify one's focus on God for a given period of time, usually for the sake of concentrated prayer. Hunger pangs keep the person's mind in a constant state of awareness of the reason for prayer—the specific issue at hand—and help to underscore the person's resolve to set aside, for a season, all temporal concerns. Fasting is important because the tangible world can begin to feel more significant—even more real—than God, who is typically not seen or heard physically. Jesus' point was that the disciples didn't need to fast in order to concentrate on God; they could reach out and touch Him—literally!

The Lord then alluded to His foreordained death for the first time, though Simeon had alluded to it earlier (Luke 2:35).

— 5:36 —

Jesus gave another reason for the differing religious practice of John's disciples and His own. John was technically a prophet of the Old Testament era. His was the last authoritative voice of the old covenant, and he came for the express purpose of introducing the bearer of the new covenant (Jer. 31:31-34). Under the old covenant, a faith response to God took the form of obedience to external laws; one approached God in faith by means of temple rites with the aid of priests as intermediaries. In the new covenant, a faith response to God takes the form of trust in Christ's obedience on our behalf. We approach the Father in faith through the Son, who is our sole intermediary (John 14:6; Acts 4:12; Eph. 2:18; Heb. 2:17; 9:11-15).

He illustrated His reasoning with three word pictures: cloth (Luke 5:36), wineskins (5:37-38), and wine (5:39).

Luke's presentation of the cloth analogy differs slightly from that of Matthew and Mark. The other two Gospels tell the story from the perspective of the old cloth, which suffers greater damage when patched with new cloth. From that perspective, the "old cloth" has suffered enough abuse at the hands of men. Applying new covenant practices to the old covenant would result in more disobedience to the Law, not less. The freedom of the new covenant works because the hearts of new-covenant people are transformed to desire obedience.

Luke's retelling takes the perspective of the new cloth, which not only fits a Gentile viewpoint, it also magnifies the absurdity. Why would someone cut a hole in a new garment and then use that piece of new cloth to repair an old article of clothing? The patch will look ridiculously conspicuous and the new garment will be ruined.

— 5:37-38 —

The Lord's second analogy pictures the process of making wine. Grape juice was poured into a sack created from sheepskin, which is supple and stretchy when first sewn together. As the grape juice ferments, yeast transforms sugar into alcohol and releases carbon dioxide gas. Fortunately, new wineskins stretch to contain the increased volume. Because an old wineskin is brittle instead of elastic, it splits under the pressure. Old wineskins are perfectly suited for old wine in which the fermentation process is complete.

The old covenant simply cannot contain new-covenant practices. Again, both old and new are ruined when mismatched.

— 5:39 —

Jesus' third analogy is pointed at the Pharisees. He turned the old-wine/new-wine image into a challenge—a good-natured taunt—saying in effect, "Complacent people settle for what is merely good enough (old wine), rejecting what is excellent (new wine) simply because it is new."

People fermented wine for practical reasons. Fermentation preserved grape juice for long-term storage in an age without refrigeration, and it was almost always mixed with water. This had the triple advantage of stretching the supply of wine, reducing its potency, and rendering water safer to drink. Therefore, wine was not a delicacy, but a product of necessity. In fact, the art of winemaking originally sought to make the best of an otherwise second-rate situation. Even today, homemade wine is functional in that it's safe to drink, but it rarely tastes good.

In the first century, new wine—that is, fresh grape juice—was a rare treat, enjoyed for just a few days after harvest.

• • •

By the end of this conversation, Jesus had made His point: old covenant, old practices; new covenant, new practices. He, as the Messiah, came to establish a completely new paradigm, a new world order instituted and implemented by the Creator in human form. The religious elite should not have been taken unawares. Prophets had long foretold the coming of a new way that would replace the old (Jer. 31:31-34; Ezek. 11:19-21; 34:23-31; 36:26-27; 37:24-28; Joel 2:12-32), and that this new way would involve God Himself pursuing the unrighteous to bring them to repentance and to restore their broken fellowship with Him (Isa. 61:1; Hos. 2:14-20; Joel 2:18-19; Zech. 8:14-15). Instead of summoning the unrighteous to the temple, He would seek them where they are and save them as they are.

Unfortunately, this new way would not sit well with the old guard. But if they thought Jesus partying with sinners rubbed them the wrong way, they hadn't seen anything yet!

APPLICATION: LUKE 5:27-39

A Challenge to Stretch

After more than fifty years in vocational ministry, some pastors like to say, "I've seen it all." I'm glad to say I haven't! Throughout my career, I have been privileged to serve with forward-thinking men and women who have challenged me to question the way things are and to imagine new ways to advance the kingdom of God. We keep stretching the boundaries of creativity, and I love it! Let me encourage you to do the same with a couple of challenges.

First, *I challenge you to move closer to the unsaved.*

Go to one of your school reunions. Go back through an old yearbook and find a friend that you've dropped. Break the ice with a neighbor. Get to know a co-worker on a personal level. Move closer. Become friends. You may find out that you have some of the most wonderful answers that person is looking for. Chances are good he or she knows you're in the family of God. Move closer. Don't be afraid. They won't bite!

Second, *I challenge you to try new ways of reaching and winning the lost.*

New wine bursts old wineskins. You will quickly discover that you will need to be creative, flexible, open, and willing to adjust if you're serious about reaching lost people. You might want to do something with another Christian friend, and the two of you plan it together. It might be some means of interacting with unbelievers in ways no one has considered. It might take you to places Christians don't normally go. It might require some unorthodox methods that could draw criticism.

I know this can be taken to extremes. But before you criticize a new idea, just do a little analysis of your personal evangelism. If you're in touch with unbelievers and you have ample opportunity to influence the lost, then I commend you. If not, then what's holding you back?

William Barclay writes,

> There is in religious people a kind of passion for the old. Nothing moves more slowly than a church. The trouble with the Pharisees was that the whole religious outlook of Jesus was so startlingly new they simply could not adjust to it.
>
> The mind soon loses the quality of elasticity and will not accept new ideas. "Don't," says Jesus, "let your mind become like an old wineskin." People say of wine, "The old is better." It may be at the moment, but they forget that it is a mistake to despise the new wine, for the day will come when it has matured and it will be the best of all.[14]

Take a look at your interaction with the lost. Now let me ask, "What's new?"

The Defiant Messiah
LUKE 6:1-11

NASB

[1] Now it happened that He was passing through *some* grainfields on a Sabbath; and His disciples were picking the heads of grain, rubbing them in their hands, and eating *the grain.* [2] But some of the Pharisees said, "Why do you do what is not lawful on the Sabbath?" [3] And Jesus answering them said, "Have you not even read what David did when he was hungry, he and those who were with him, [4] how he entered the house of God, and took and ate the [a]consecrated bread which is not lawful for any to eat except the priests alone,

NLT

[1] One Sabbath day as Jesus was walking through some grainfields, his disciples broke off heads of grain, rubbed off the husks in their hands, and ate the grain. [2] But some Pharisees said, "Why are you breaking the law by harvesting grain on the Sabbath?"

[3] Jesus replied, "Haven't you read in the Scriptures what David did when he and his companions were hungry? [4] He went into the house of God and broke the law by eating the sacred loaves of bread that only the priests can eat. He also gave some to

and gave it to his companions?" 5 And He was saying to them, "The Son of Man is Lord of the Sabbath."

6 On another Sabbath He entered the synagogue and was teaching; and there was a man there ªwhose right hand was withered. 7 The scribes and the Pharisees were watching Him closely *to see* if He healed on the Sabbath, so that they might find *reason* to accuse Him. 8 But He knew ªwhat they were thinking, and He said to the man with the withered hand, "Get up and ᵇcome forward!" And he got up and ᶜcame forward. 9 And Jesus said to them, "I ask you, is it lawful to do good or to do harm on the Sabbath, to save a life or to destroy it?" 10 After looking around at them all, He said to him, "Stretch out your hand!" And he did *so;* and his hand was restored. 11 But they themselves were filled with ªrage, and discussed together what they might do to Jesus.

6:4 ªOr *showbread;* lit *loaves of presentation*
6:6 ªLit *and his*   6:8 ªLit *their thoughts*   ᵇLit *stand into the middle*   ᶜLit *stood*   6:11 ªLit *folly*

his companions." 5 And Jesus added, "The Son of Man* is Lord, even over the Sabbath."

6 On another Sabbath day, a man with a deformed right hand was in the synagogue while Jesus was teaching. 7 The teachers of religious law and the Pharisees watched Jesus closely. If he healed the man's hand, they planned to accuse him of working on the Sabbath.

8 But Jesus knew their thoughts. He said to the man with the deformed hand, "Come and stand in front of everyone." So the man came forward. 9 Then Jesus said to his critics, "I have a question for you. Does the law permit good deeds on the Sabbath, or is it a day for doing evil? Is this a day to save life or to destroy it?"

10 He looked around at them one by one and then said to the man, "Hold out your hand." So the man held out his hand, and it was restored! 11 At this, the enemies of Jesus were wild with rage and began to discuss what to do with him.

6:5 "Son of Man" is a title Jesus used for himself.

A wise mentor with many years' experience in the trenches once said to me, "Choose your battles carefully." That would have made perfect sense had it come from one of my commanding officers in the Marine Corps, but I received that counsel under the tutelage of a seasoned mentor in ministry.

Spiritual warfare? Sure, I expected that. But this experienced pastor uttered those words in the context of an upcoming meeting with church elders. He had been through several battles in his years in pastoral ministry and had the scars to show for his wise—and unwise—choices. While he was fortunate to have an excellent group of men leading the church alongside him, he occasionally found himself locked in spiritual combat behind closed doors in the church conference room. Even godly people can be stubbornly wrong in spiritual matters from time to time. Sometimes, a spiritual leader must take a strong stand on principle, even if it means offending powerful people and then suffering the terrible consequences of ungodly wrath. One must take this stand on principle, regardless of whether one can win or whether it involves defying long-standing tradition. Even if it puts one on the losing side of politics. Even if it means having to stand alone. Anyone who doubts this needs only to examine the ministry of Jesus.

The Pharisees never doubted their self-appointed role as God's judge, jury, and executioner in all things related to the Torah. As a result, they expected Jesus to agree with them—perhaps to join their ranks, honor their customs, earn their respect, and lead Israel as the greatest Pharisee of all time. But the relationship between Jesus and the religious authorities in Israel started out strained and only grew worse with time. He never did fit into their ranks. His claiming to be the Messiah rubbed them the wrong way, but they couldn't deny His miracles. He treated them dismissively, brushing aside their teachings and traditions to stand on His own authority when expositing the Scriptures. He healed the kind of people they felt sure God had censured with disease or disfigurement (Exod. 20:5; Luke 13:2; John 9:1-2; Acts 28:4). He exercised authority over demons, diseases, sin, and even nature, in an uncomfortably Godlike way. He forgave sin, which seemed more than a little presumptuous to them, and on top of all that, He *enjoyed* the company of sinners. But, up to this point, He hadn't done anything obviously wrong in their estimation. Questionable, perhaps. Extraordinary, for sure. But nothing overtly out-of-bounds.

Then, one day, He did the unthinkable. He drew a line in the sand the day He defied their authority by challenging their interpretation and application of God's Law. They could accept some things, but the one thing they couldn't accept was a defiant Messiah.

— 6:1-2 —

Jesus and His disciples were not wealthy men. Some of the disciples may have come from upper-middle-class families, and Levi had probably extorted large sums in his career as a tax collector, but the men had left all that behind to follow their Messiah. Fortunately, Jewish Law provided for poor people. Deuteronomy 23:24-25 permitted someone to enter a farmer's field in order to eat one's fill, provided none of the food was taken away. So, in perfect accord with the Law, Jesus and His disciples entered a man's field of wheat or barley to eat lunch. In the minds of the Pharisees, however, the men were laboring on the Sabbath, for "plucking wheat from its stem is reaping, rubbing the wheat heads between one's palms is threshing, and blowing away the chaff is winnowing!"[15] (See also "The Pharisees," page 141.)

The challenge of the Pharisees is revealing. They accused Jesus of doing what was "unlawful"; that is, contrary to God's Law as given through Moses. But there was no scriptural law against what He and His disciples did. The Pharisees could no longer distinguish between their man-made interpretations and traditions and the God-given Law.

Jesus cut down the Pharisees' challenge with a double-edged response: They had misunderstood the intent of God's Law (Luke 6:4-3); and they had wrongfully taken control of the Sabbath, something which was God's (His) to control (6:4).

He then illustrated this twofold declaration by healing a physically deformed man on the Sabbath (6:6-11).

— 6:3-4 —

The construction of Jesus' question implies that they had indeed read the Scripture about David but failed to comprehend the meaning. He then took them back to 1 Samuel 21:1-6, which describes David's actions after his final break from Saul. As he fled into the wilderness with several companions, he approached a priest in Nob, asking for provisions. David told the priest a half-truth to explain why he was traveling with the king's men without Saul, telling him "the king" had sent him on a secret errand. By "the king" David meant himself. Although Saul occupied the throne, he was no longer the legitimate ruler of Israel.

The only food available was bread from the table in the Lord's sanctuary, known as "consecrated bread" (Lev. 24:5-8). Each day, as it was replaced, priests were allowed to consume it as part of their daily sustenance (Exod. 25:30; Lev. 24:9). Therefore, it was a gift normally reserved for them as God's provision for their dedicated service to Him.

While God gave the consecrated bread to the priests exclusively, that did not preclude them from sharing their gift with others, especially those in need. God never intended His exclusive gift to the priests to be so exclusive as to condemn non-priests to death by starvation! Therefore, the priest shared the consecrated bread with David, in deference to kingly authority. Even so, the priest made sure David's men were ritually pure, not having engaged in unrepentant sin for which they had not sacrificed.

Jesus drew upon this Old Testament story to underscore at least two points. First, the Lord established the Sabbath as a gift, not a burden. To let famished people go hungry would have undermined His original purpose for this weekly feast day (Mark 2:27). Second, like David, He was the King of Israel incognito, the legitimate King not yet in possession of the throne.

— 6:5 —

No one dared to challenge the Pharisees' exclusive jurisdiction as police, judge, and jury over all matters related to the Sabbath. That is, until Jesus. His bold claim, "The Son of Man is the Lord of the Sabbath," challenged the authority of the Pharisees, who had stolen the Sabbath from God. He said, in effect, "Because the Law came from God, it can never be greater than God. 'The Lord blessed the sabbath day and made it holy' (Exod. 20:11). [I], the Son of Man, am the Lord of the Sabbath. The Sabbath is not yours to control; it is Mine, because I am God. Therefore, I am taking it back from you."

Luke doesn't tell us how the Pharisees responded, probably because it doesn't matter. Instead, he tells us how Jesus exercised His authority over the Sabbath.

— 6:6-7 —

The scene changes but the story continues. It might have been the next Sabbath, or many Sabbaths later; Luke doesn't say. He merely tells us that the Pharisaical Sabbath rules were in play. In the first scene (Luke 6:1-5), the Pharisees brought the controversy to Jesus. In the second (6:6-7), Jesus deliberately challenged their authority on what they considered their home turf. And His challenge came in the form of kindness.

The Pharisees reluctantly realized that Jesus' authority trumped their own—the power of His miracles could not be denied. It also was becoming painfully evident that His popularity threatened to eclipse their own influence with the people. So, they trailed after Jesus, looking for opportunities to discredit Him or, literally, "speak against" Him. Luke's term translated "watched" carries the connotation of spying or lurking (Ps. 37:12), with the added sense of scrupulously recording observations (Ps. 130:3). They spied on Him to see if He would commit the horrific sin of healing someone *on the Sabbath*. According to the Pharisees' rules, a physician was not allowed to give aid to the sick or practice medicine in any fashion on the Sabbath except in a few extenuating circumstances. If a woman gave birth, a midwife could assist in delivery. And if someone lay at death's door, a physician could administer help. Otherwise, their man-made traditions forbade assistance in non-life-threatening treatments.[16]

As Jesus taught in the synagogue, His eyes fell on a man with a "withered" hand. The Greek term pictures a dried up plant or a leaf in winter (cf. Luke 23:31). The theology of the day interpreted such an ailment as God's irreversible judgment for sin. Moreover, it was his right hand, which was considered the more important hand.

— 6:8-9 —

Just like before (5:22), Jesus "knew their thoughts." This knowledge was not mere intuition; Jesus supernaturally understood their inner reasoning. In spite of that, He called the man with the withered hand forward. He could have dealt with him in private. He could have gestured silently or healed the man with a mere thought. But Jesus deliberately and boldly brought him to the front of the synagogue.

Jesus then challenged the scribes and Pharisees with a question, which the Greek construction presents as two sets of alternatives. The NLT appropriately captures the essence of the Lord's challenge: "Does the law permit good deeds on the Sabbath, or is it a day for doing evil? Is this a day to save life or to destroy it?" It left no room for a middle-ground reply. For Jesus, withholding a cure was just as cruel as deliberately causing harm. It also had the effect of silencing His critics' objections. How were they to reply? "We believe it's best to do evil and to destroy life"?

— 6:10 —

Jesus "looked around" at the men, staring them down, defying their absurd rules, condemning their lack of compassion (Mark 3:5), daring them to interfere. Take note of Jesus' authoritative approach and Luke's emphasis on obedience. Jesus had earlier commanded the man, "Get up and come forward!" The man "got up and came forward" (Luke 6:8). Then Jesus commanded, "Stretch out your hand!" The man "did so" (6:10). And the very act of obedience—extending his twisted, useless hand—demonstrated the Lord's power to heal diseases. Everyone saw the man's hand "restored," yet Jesus had not done work in the manner of a traditional physician. He was clearly responsible for the healing, though He hadn't moved a muscle!

This left His accusers without any condemning testimony. If they took their complaint to the Jewish ruling council to press charges, their description of the events would make them look like fools. What is more, Jesus demonstrated to them beyond any shadow of doubt that He is Lord of the Sabbath.

— **6:11** —

This marked a turning point—or better, the breaking point—in Jesus' relationship with the Pharisees. Whereas they might have hoped to recruit Jesus to join their ranks, He firmly established His authority over everything they held dear. And He disagreed on virtually every point.

Luke describes the strong reaction of Jesus' enemies as their being filled with "rage," which literally means "unreason." It describes a kind of foolishness or folly that bears a moral slant, the kind of anger expressed by a hothead who allows impulsive hostility to overpower logic. In their senseless wrath, the Pharisees were determined to find some expedient way to harm Jesus.

• • •

Jesus didn't look for a fight, but neither did He back down when the Pharisees took the fight to Him. He didn't allow their opposition to deter Him from doing what was right. And when their interests and His met at the moral crossroads of ministry, He demanded they yield the right-of-way to Him, their Prophet (Deut. 18:17-19), their Teacher, their King (2 Sam. 7:12-13), and their God.

APPLICATION: LUKE 6:1-11
Defiance Done Right

If you think that you won't raise the ire of legalists by ignoring their rules, you've never really studied Luke 6:1-11. Don't think you can simply do what you think is right and mind your own business. Legalists won't let that happen. They will ostracize you. They will make life miserable for you. They will single you out, accuse you, mischaracterize you, label you, and try to convince you that you're crazy at best, or sinful at worst. Legalists want everybody to be as miserable as they are.

The fact is, if you don't want your life to be ruled by legalists, you will have to defy their self-appointed authority. Let me suggest some ways to defy legalism constructively.

First, *analyze the issue.*

Is this issue worth fighting for? Most issues of freedom are worth defending, but some are not. Make that determination, recognizing that all freedom comes at the cost of suffering. If you have determined the issue is worth the pain legalists will cause, then bear it with dignity.

Second, *check your motives.*

Sometimes we take a defiant stand because we are stubborn and rebellious, and we prize our autonomy. Other times, restricting our own freedom for the sake of a weaker believer is the right thing to do, but we care more about making ourselves happy. Does love for others guide your actions? This analysis will take honesty and may require the help of a friend to determine the truth.

Third, *pray for wisdom.*

Prayer brings clarity, which is needed when legalists make life difficult. Prayer brings courage, because there is the assurance of God's support. Prayer gives God greater opportunity to align your mind with His. And prayer encourages a submissive, loving spirit, even as you do what causes legalists stress.

"The Twelve" and Their Marching Orders
LUKE 6:12-49

NASB

12 It was ªat this time that He went off to the mountain to pray, and He spent the whole night in prayer to God. 13 And when day came, He called His disciples to Him and chose twelve of them, whom He also named as apostles: 14 Simon, whom He also named Peter, and Andrew his brother; and ªJames and John; and Philip and Bartholomew; 15 and Matthew and Thomas; James *the son* of Alphaeus, and Simon who was called the Zealot; 16 Judas *the son* of James, and Judas Iscariot, who became a traitor.

17 Jesus came down with them and stood on a level place; and *there was* a large crowd of His disciples, and

NLT

12 One day soon afterward Jesus went up on a mountain to pray, and he prayed to God all night. 13 At daybreak he called together all of his disciples and chose twelve of them to be apostles. Here are their names:

14 Simon (whom he named Peter),
Andrew (Peter's brother),
James,
John,
Philip,
Bartholomew,
15 Matthew,
Thomas,
James (son of Alphaeus),
Simon (who was called the zealot),
16 Judas (son of James),
Judas Iscariot (who later betrayed him).

17 When they came down from the mountain, the disciples stood with Jesus on a large, level area, surrounded by many of his followers

a great throng of people from all Judea and Jerusalem and the coastal region of Tyre and Sidon, ¹⁸who had come to hear Him and to be healed of their diseases; and those who were troubled with unclean spirits were being cured. ¹⁹And all the ªpeople were trying to touch Him, for power was coming from Him and healing *them* all.

²⁰And turning His gaze toward His disciples, He *began* to say, "Blessed *are* ªyou *who are* poor, for yours is the kingdom of God. ²¹Blessed *are* ªyou who hunger now, for you shall be satisfied. Blessed *are* you who weep now, for you shall laugh. ²²Blessed are you when men hate you, and ostracize you, and insult you, and scorn your name as evil, for the sake of the Son of Man. ²³Be glad in that day and leap *for joy*, for behold, your reward is great in heaven. For in the same way their fathers used to ªtreat the prophets. ²⁴But woe to you who are rich, for you are receiving your comfort in full. ²⁵Woe to you who ªare well-fed now, for you shall be hungry. Woe *to you* who laugh now, for you shall mourn and weep. ²⁶Woe *to you* when all men speak well of you, for their fathers used to ªtreat the false prophets in the same way.

²⁷"But I say to you who hear, love your enemies, do good to those who hate you, ²⁸bless those who curse you, pray for those who ªmistreat

and by the crowds. There were people from all over Judea and from Jerusalem and from as far north as the seacoasts of Tyre and Sidon. ¹⁸They had come to hear him and to be healed of their diseases; and those troubled by evil* spirits were healed. ¹⁹Everyone tried to touch him, because healing power went out from him, and he healed everyone.

²⁰Then Jesus turned to his disciples and said,

"God blesses you who are poor,
    for the Kingdom of God is yours.
²¹ God blesses you who are hungry now,
    for you will be satisfied.
God blesses you who weep now,
    for in due time you will laugh.

²²What blessings await you when people hate you and exclude you and mock you and curse you as evil because you follow the Son of Man. ²³When that happens, be happy! Yes, leap for joy! For a great reward awaits you in heaven. And remember, their ancestors treated the ancient prophets that same way.

²⁴ "What sorrow awaits you who are rich,
    for you have your only happiness now.
²⁵ What sorrow awaits you who are fat and prosperous now,
    for a time of awful hunger awaits you.
What sorrow awaits you who laugh now,
    for your laughing will turn to mourning and sorrow.
²⁶ What sorrow awaits you who are praised by the crowds,
    for their ancestors also praised false prophets.

²⁷ "But to you who are willing to listen, I say, love your enemies! Do good to those who hate you. ²⁸Bless those who curse you. Pray for those

you. ²⁹ Whoever hits you on the cheek, offer him the other also; and whoever takes away your ^acoat, do not withhold your ^bshirt from him either. ³⁰ Give to everyone who asks of you, and whoever takes away what is yours, do not demand it back. ^{31 a}Treat others the same way you want ^bthem to treat you. ³²If you love those who love you, what credit is *that* to you? For even sinners love those who love them. ³³ If you do good to those who do good to you, what credit is *that* to you? For even sinners do the same. ³⁴If you lend to those from whom you expect to receive, what credit is *that* to you? Even sinners lend to sinners in order to receive back the same *amount.* ³⁵But love your enemies, and do good, and lend, ^aexpecting nothing in return; and your reward will be great, and you will be sons of the Most High; for He Himself is kind to ungrateful and evil *men.* ^{36 a}Be merciful, just as your Father is merciful.

³⁷ "Do not judge, and you will not be judged; and do not condemn, and you will not be condemned; ^apardon, and you will be pardoned. ³⁸ Give, and it will be given to you. They will ^apour into your lap a good measure— pressed down, shaken together, *and* running over. For by your standard of measure it will be measured to you in return."

³⁹ And He also spoke a parable to them: "A blind man cannot guide a blind man, can he? Will they not both fall into a pit? ⁴⁰ A ^apupil is not above his teacher; but everyone, after he has been fully trained, will ^bbe like his teacher. ⁴¹ Why do you look at the speck that is in your brother's eye, but do not notice the log that is in your own eye? ⁴² Or how can you say to your brother, 'Brother, let me take out the speck that is in

who hurt you. ²⁹ If someone slaps you on one cheek, offer the other cheek also. If someone demands your coat, offer your shirt also. ³⁰ Give to anyone who asks; and when things are taken away from you, don't try to get them back. ³¹ Do to others as you would like them to do to you.

³² "If you love only those who love you, why should you get credit for that? Even sinners love those who love them! ³³ And if you do good only to those who do good to you, why should you get credit? Even sinners do that much! ³⁴ And if you lend money only to those who can repay you, why should you get credit? Even sinners will lend to other sinners for a full return.

³⁵ "Love your enemies! Do good to them. Lend to them without expecting to be repaid. Then your reward from heaven will be very great, and you will truly be acting as children of the Most High, for he is kind to those who are unthankful and wicked. ³⁶ You must be compassionate, just as your Father is compassionate.

³⁷ "Do not judge others, and you will not be judged. Do not condemn others, or it will all come back against you. Forgive others, and you will be forgiven. ³⁸ Give, and you will receive. Your gift will return to you in full—pressed down, shaken together to make room for more, running over, and poured into your lap. The amount you give will determine the amount you get back.*"

³⁹ Then Jesus gave the following illustration: "Can one blind person lead another? Won't they both fall into a ditch? ⁴⁰ Students* are not greater than their teacher. But the student who is fully trained will become like the teacher.

⁴¹ "And why worry about a speck in your friend's eye* when you have a log in your own? ⁴² How can you think of saying, 'Friend,* let me help you get rid of that speck in your eye,'

your eye,' when you yourself do not see the log that is in your own eye? You hypocrite, first take the log out of your own eye, and then you will see clearly to take out the speck that is in your brother's eye. [43] For there is no good tree which produces bad fruit, nor, [a] on the other hand, a bad tree which produces good fruit. [44] For each tree is known by its own fruit. For men do not gather figs from thorns, nor do they pick grapes from a briar bush. [45] The good man out of the good [a] treasure of his heart brings forth what is good; and the evil *man* out of the evil *treasure* brings forth what is evil; for his mouth speaks from [b] that which fills his heart.

[46] "Why do you call Me, 'Lord, Lord,' and do not do what I say? [47] Everyone who comes to Me and hears My words and [a] acts on them, I will show you whom he is like: [48] he is like a man building a house, who [a] dug deep and laid a foundation on the rock; and when a flood occurred, the [b] torrent burst against that house and could not shake it, because it had been well built. [49] But the one who has heard and has not acted *accordingly*, is like a man who built a house on the ground without any foundation; and the [a] torrent burst against it and immediately it collapsed, and the ruin of that house was great."

when you can't see past the log in your own eye? Hypocrite! First get rid of the log in your own eye; then you will see well enough to deal with the speck in your friend's eye.

[43] "A good tree can't produce bad fruit, and a bad tree can't produce good fruit. [44] A tree is identified by its fruit. Figs are never gathered from thornbushes, and grapes are not picked from bramble bushes. [45] A good person produces good things from the treasury of a good heart, and an evil person produces evil things from the treasury of an evil heart. What you say flows from what is in your heart.

[46] "So why do you keep calling me 'Lord, Lord!' when you don't do what I say? [47] I will show you what it's like when someone comes to me, listens to my teaching, and then follows it. [48] It is like a person building a house who digs deep and lays the foundation on solid rock. When the floodwaters rise and break against that house, it stands firm because it is well built. [49] But anyone who hears and doesn't obey is like a person who builds a house right on the ground, without a foundation. When the floods sweep down against that house, it will collapse into a heap of ruins."

6:12 [a] Lit *in these days* **6:14** [a] Or *Jacob*, also vv 15 and 16 **6:19** [a] Lit *crowd* **6:20** [a] Lit *the* **6:21** [a] Lit *the* **6:23** [a] Lit *do to* **6:25** [a] Lit *having been filled* **6:26** [a] Lit *do to* **6:28** [a] Or *revile* **6:29** [a] I.e. outer garment [b] Or *tunic*; i.e. garment worn next to body **6:31** [a] Lit *Do to* [b] Lit *people* **6:35** [a] Or *not despairing at all* **6:36** [a] Or *Become* **6:37** [a] Lit *release* **6:38** [a] Lit *give* **6:40** [a] Or *disciple* [b] Or *reach his teacher's level* **6:43** [a] Lit *again* **6:45** [a] Or *treasury, storehouse* [b] Lit *the abundance of* **6:47** [a] Lit *does* **6:48** [a] Lit *dug and went deep* [b] Lit *river* **6:49** [a] Lit *river*

6:18 Greek *unclean*. **6:38** Or *The measure you give will be the measure you get back*. **6:40** Or *Disciples*. **6:41** Greek *your brother's eye*; also in 6:42. **6:42** Greek *Brother*.

"Discipleship" became *the* Christian buzzword of the 1970s. Sermons highlighted the need for Christians to "make disciples." Conferences revolved around the theme of discipleship, and seminars dissected the principles of disciple-making. Countless books, booklets, articles, and pamphlets diagrammed and described innumerable methods to be reproduced in churches. Parachurch organizations launched with the express purpose of equipping spiritual leaders for the long-term commitment of training new believers to become mature Christians.

Many mature Christians today have one or two disciple-making mentors to thank for their spiritual growth. They were discipled by someone who loved them enough to invest time and energy that could have been spent on increasing their own influence or power. For some, that took place in a very structured—perhaps even rigorous—environment. For others, it happened more casually—so informal, in fact, they may not have been aware of the process.

The concept of discipleship may have been de-emphasized or periodically forgotten from time to time in the last two millennia, but it is by no means new. The resurgence of discipleship in the 1970s traced its inspiration to a rediscovery of the Bible's emphasis on personal, up close, relational, spiritual training passed from a seasoned believer to those less experienced. Jesus commanded His followers to "make disciples" (Matt. 28:19), but not before He chose a handful—twelve, to be exact—and then poured His own life into theirs for approximately three years.

— 6:12-13 —

While some found in Jesus all the excuse they needed to reject the Messiah, multitudes saw hope in Him. Having accepted the limitations of human flesh, Jesus could not personally instruct all of His followers. To multiply His ministry, He would need to instruct a select group of men and then charge them with the responsibility to do the same. But before making this crucial selection, Jesus prepared Himself.

Soon after the contentious Sabbath in a Galilean synagogue, Jesus withdrew to a secluded place to pray. The Lord went out, away from public life, to "the mountain," which doesn't likely refer to any specific place, but conveys the idea of silence and solitude. The phrase "spent the whole night" comes from a Greek word used only once in the New Testament (*dianyktereuō* [1273]) to describe spending a whole night engaged in some work. Jesus spent the whole night in prayer before making one of the most important decisions of His entire ministry, although few at the time could have appreciated the gravity of this moment.

By this time, the disciples of Jesus numbered in the thousands, from which He must select a very few to become His closest companions. They would assist in His miracles, share His meals, travel with Him everywhere to witness every moment, hear His sermons repeated a hundred times, learn to replicate His ministry, and ultimately carry on without His physical presence. This up-close-and-personal training would transform a select group of disciples into apostles. Disciples follow and learn. Apostles exercise delegated authority (Luke 9:1-6, 10).

Jesus called His disciples to a meeting and, perhaps after a time of teaching, He named twelve to become apostles.

— 6:14-16 —

Many would have seen Jesus' selection of the Twelve as curious. He didn't search the temple in Jerusalem for the best and brightest scholars. He ignored the schools of meticulous Pharisees who devoted their lives to strict obedience to the Law. Instead, He chose James and John, whom he also referred to as "the sons of thunder" (Mark 3:17) (quite likely because of their bombastic tempers). He chose timid Andrew and his brash, outspoken brother, Simon. He invited the despised tax-collecting sellout, Levi (cf. Luke 5:27 and Matt. 9:9-13; here called Matthew, which means "gift of God"). He picked cynical Bartholomew (also called Nathanael [John 1:45-46]) and Thomas, known to us for his questions and doubts. He hand-selected working-class, uneducated men with obvious flaws. Why would He? How could He? It is important to remember that Jesus saw His men not as what they were, but as what they were to become.

Eleven of the Twelve hailed from Galilee, so far as we know. Luke doesn't make an obvious point of this, although it would fit neatly into his motif of Jesus' journey from Galilee to Jerusalem, which begins at Luke 9:51. Before beginning that journey, Jesus selected His apostles from the simplehearted men of Galilee, more than 70 miles removed from the corruption of the religious authorities.

Ironically, Judas, son of Simon Iscariot (John 6:71), was the only selection that would have made sense to the onlookers of his day—a fine, stronghearted patriot from Kerioth of Judea. How impressive— initially! The name Iscariot most likely derived from the Hebrew *Ish-keriot*, meaning "man of Kerioth"; and the people of Kerioth, a city in southern Judea, probably believed Judas would represent them well in the struggle for independence. He was born and raised in the rugged territory where mighty King David learned to become Israel's greatest shepherd. His name, Judas, bristled with rugged heroism. As one commentator notes, "Judah, or Judas, was the name of one of the twelve sons of Jacob in the Old Testament, and the brilliant uprising for independence in 164 BC was led by a man named Judas. This Judas Maccabaeus was looked upon by all Jews as a sort of George Washington."[17]

The original twelve apostles of Jesus are mentioned in four lists in the New Testament. The lists can be divided into three groupings, with Peter heading the first, Philip leading the second, and James (son of Alphaeus) heading the third. In all the lists, each group names the same persons, although there is some variety after naming the group leader. In all four, Peter leads the list while Judas occupies the bottom slot. As we could expect, the list in Acts omits Judas altogether.

THE TWELVE			
MATTHEW 10:2-4	**MARK 3:16-19**	**LUKE 6:14-16**	**ACTS 1:13**
Simon (Peter)	Simon (Peter)	Simon (Peter)	Peter
Andrew	James (son of	Andrew	John
James (son of	Zebedee)	James (son of	James (son of
Zebedee)	John	Zebedee)	Zebedee)
John	Andrew	John	Andrew
Philip	Philip	Philip	Philip
Bartholomew	Bartholomew	Bartholomew	Thomas
Thomas	Matthew	Matthew	Bartholomew
Matthew	Thomas	Thomas	Matthew
James (son of Alphaeus)	James (son of Alphaeus)	James (son of Alphaeus)	James (son of Alphaeus)
Thaddaeus	Thaddaeus	Simon (the	Simon (the
Simon (the	Simon (the	Zealot)	Zealot)
Zealot)	Zealot)	Judas (son of	Judas (son of
Judas Iscariot	Judas Iscariot	James)	James)
		Judas Iscariot	----

Note that several apostles were called by more than one name. Surnames were uncommon then, so people with similar names were distinguished in other ways. James "the Less" (Mark 15:40) may have been younger or shorter than another James. In other cases, men may have changed their names. Jesus may have given Levi his new name, Matthew; and Judas, the son of James, may have preferred the name Thaddaeus after Judas Iscariot's betrayal.

— 6:17-18 —

Luke states that Jesus came down from the mountain with the apostles, suggesting He had pulled them away from the "large crowd of His disciples" and a "great throng" of other people from all over Israel. His descending the mountain with the disciples to engage the multitudes accomplished two important objectives. First, by virtue of their walking with Jesus, the Twelve were identified publicly as His assistants. Second, the Twelve would see Jesus' ministry in action from a new perspective. Instead of watching the Messiah from the audience, they now stood behind Him, on stage.

As Jesus waded into the sea of people suffering the wounds of evil, the Twelve saw the challenge Jesus had been facing for months. The needs of people were overwhelming, falling into three categories: the need for teaching, the need for healing, and the need for freedom from demons. Immediately, the men saw why Jesus had called them to join His inner circle as "assistant ministers." They were to join Him in combating spiritual ignorance, reversing the effects of evil, and confronting the supernatural minions of darkness.

— 6:19 —

Luke's statement in this verse should be taken hyperbolically, perhaps to describe the motivation for seeking Jesus and to underscore the immensity of the needs in Israel—and the world. As Jesus moved among the people at this stage of His ministry, they jostled and maneuvered to touch Him. Even without His conscious assent, healing power flowed from Him like mist blowing from a huge fountain. This image of Jesus as the source of divine power overcoming sin and evil is an important one in Luke's Gospel, recurring throughout (Luke 5:17; 6:18; 7:7; 8:46-47; 9:11, 42; 14:4; 17:15; 22:51). The image becomes all the more important when Jesus later delegated this power to His followers when commissioning them. "You will receive power when the Holy Spirit has come upon you; and you shall be My witnesses both in Jerusalem, and in all Judea and Samaria, and even to the remotest part of the earth" (Acts 1:8).

— 6:20-22 —

After Jesus and the Twelve came down the mountain and engaged in ministry, Jesus turned toward His broader group of followers—hundreds, if not thousands, of men and women that Luke calls disciples or devoted learners.

Many expositors break the narrative at 6:20, which is unfortunate. Luke probably intended 6:12-49 to be read as a unit, with the calling of the apostles leading into an extended discourse on discipleship (6:20-49), as Jesus explained the implications of following Him. It was as if He said, "If you want to follow Me, this is what you can expect: Take Me or leave Me."

This treatise (6:20-49), which is similar in some ways to the Sermon on the Mount (Matt. 5), represents the essence of Jesus' teaching throughout His ministry. In other words, He taught the principles of God's kingdom repeatedly, at length, using many illustrations and examples. And His teaching very likely followed the style of the day, in which the teacher sat, communicated truth in the form of a quasi-casual lecture, and welcomed dialogue, answering questions and refuting challenges.

This speech as presented by Luke is undoubtedly a condensed version of the Lord's actual teaching that day. Luke didn't insert a transcription of Jesus' lecture and interaction with the audience; instead, he gave us a concentrated sampling of this teaching time. If this were a literal transcription, the Lord's sermon would have lasted less than five minutes!

Jesus opened his discourse with blessings and curses (Luke 6:20-26) that describe the profound difference between His kingdom and the world. In this sense, the sermon is what theologians call "eschatological," having reference to the end times when His kingdom will replace the present world order, which is corrupt and evil. Therefore, His kingdom and the world, as it exists today, are quite opposite. What is good in the world is bad in the kingdom of God. To be blessed by good fortune in one realm is to be cursed in the other.

While the Lord's sermon describes the ultimate fulfillment of end-time promises, He nevertheless invited His disciples to become citizens of his kingdom now. While the consummation of God's kingdom and the fullness of its blessings are yet future, the kingdom of God stood before them in the flesh-and-bone presence of King Jesus. To embrace Jesus as King, however, would necessarily put His disciples at odds with the present world order.

Four blessings and four curses weigh the cost and benefits of discipleship. As one commentary notes, "Originally in Greek usage the word ['blessed'] described the happy estate of the gods above earthly sufferings and labors. Later it came to mean any positive condition a person experienced."[18] It describes transcendent happiness, the kind that neither depends upon earthly fortunes nor falters before temporal hardships. A "blessed" person possesses what we would call "joy."

The blessings of God's kingdom were not held in reserve for poor people only, but for those who are—as expressed by Matthew—"poor in spirit" (Matt. 5:3). Poverty in this sense can be literal; that is, having nothing. Or it can be a figurative description of one's attitude toward temporal wealth. Jesus was poor in spirit when He relinquished the limitless wealth of heaven to become the son of a poor, Galilean teenage girl. Jesus was poor in spirit when He bypassed the opportunity to turn wilderness stones into oven-fresh loaves, by nourishing Himself on God's Word rather than ill-gotten food. Jesus called those "blessed" who emptied their hands of this world's wealth in order to cast themselves headlong upon God's resources.

The second blessing, for those who "hunger," is more complex than it appears. At the superficial level—which is nonetheless true—Jesus promises delayed gratification for those who wait. In the literal sense, those who choose not to nourish themselves on ill-gotten food suffer the pangs of hunger in the short term, but will feast on God's provision in the kingdom to come. It is the promise of an eventual political reversal. The word for "satisfied" means, literally, "fed or filled with enough." But that is the least of the promises. While people seek inward satisfaction through physical, external means, God calls His disciples to seek spiritual satisfaction first (Matt. 6:33). In the figurative sense, those who long for righteousness will be satisfied in time. They will receive righteous standing before God and will witness the Lord flooding the world with His righteousness. Injustice will be washed away in the torrent.

The blessing on those who "weep now," like the second, promises delayed gratification. Presumably, those who weep do so for the same reason the world "groans" (Rom. 8:20-23): because it "was subjected to futility" in judgment for sin, and because it waits eagerly for redemption. In the Old Testament, God honored the tears of those who wept for righteousness. In fact, He saw those tears as seeds that would yield a bumper crop of divine goodness in the future (Ps. 126:5-6). Those who weep over all that is wrong in the world are more likely to commit themselves to making things right.

The fourth blessing, unlike the first three, offers no explicit promise of vindication. From a marketing point of view, it's a disastrous appeal to discipleship, one that highlights the negative with no stated promise for a return on investment! Put bluntly, Jesus promised His followers they would receive hatred, social rejection, verbal reproach, and defamation of character simply by associating with Him. Respectable, leading citizens of this world order will label Jesus' followers enemies of the state and persecute them as outlaws. Surely this raised a few eyebrows among the Twelve.

This "blessing" would resonate especially deep within many Jews, whose worst fear was excommunication from the community. The punishment was financial, social, cultural, and spiritual. To be "cut off from the people" was to live outside a relationship with God (e.g., Gen. 17:14; Exod. 12:15, 19; 31:14; Lev. 7:27). Jesus promised that the opposite was true; excommunication from the world frees a person to enjoy fellowship with God.

— 6:23 —

Jesus concluded His blessings with a dual command: "Be glad" and "spring about" (literally translated). "Be glad" is rendered from the passive form of the Greek term for "rejoice." With tongue-in-cheek hyperbole, He encouraged His followers to leap up and down like they'd won billions in a sweepstakes. Because the world is an upside-down place for disciples of Jesus, a place in which good things are called bad and evil things good, it's a privilege to be reviled by godless men. To receive mistreatment on earth is to wear a badge of honor in God's kingdom. In fact, persecution places believers in the same heroic category as martyred Old Testament prophets (1 Kgs. 19:10; 2 Chr. 24:21; 36:16; Jer. 26:23; Heb. 11:37).

— 6:24-26 —

At the opening of Luke 6:24, Luke marks a sharp change in mood with a particularly strong contrasting conjunction, the Greek word *plēn* [4133]. The interjection "woe" is a mournful moan uttered in response to personal anguish or prompted by pity for the suffering of another. It can also convey a warning, as if to say, "I deeply pity you if this is true."

The strong contrast involves the "rich" as opposed to the "poor" above. Jesus apparently had some wealthy followers who helped keep Him and His men sheltered, fed, and clothed (8:1-3; 23:50-53). As with the "poor," Jesus cares about one's attitude with respect to wealth. To what does one look for sustenance? Does he trust in his paycheck, or does he cling to righteousness, believing God will meet his needs? Will she sacrifice righteousness for a more secure position with the company, or will she do what is right, even if it ruins her career? Penetrating questions, all.

Jesus warned that those who pursue wealth above all else have already received their full "comfort" in this life. Interestingly, the Greek term translated "comfort" is *paraklesis* [3874], a word derived from the same stem as the word used of the Holy Spirit, *parakletos* [3875]. Luke used the most obvious Greek term to translate Jesus' Hebrew or

Aramaic. Still, it is disconcerting because earlier he referred to the Messiah as Israel's "consolation" (2:25)—also *paraklesis*. It's as if Luke took advantage of the word choice to ask the reader, "Which 'comforter' would you prefer in the long run? Money or God?"

The second and third "woes" simply contrast the second and third blessings (6:21). If, unlike Jesus in the wilderness (4:3-4), we feast on ill-gotten food, "hungry" barely describes the anguish waiting for us in eternity.

The fourth "woe" goes to all who seek the acceptance and admiration of godless people or the people of this world order. Again, this is not to suggest we make ourselves offensive and then pat ourselves on the back as good citizens of God's kingdom. Obnoxious Christians rarely, if ever, have a positive impact on nonbelievers. On the contrary, we are to lead quiet, respectable lives and allow our good reputation in the world to become a testimony (Rom. 13; 2 Cor. 8:21; 1 Tim. 3:7).

Jesus warned against people-pleasing. If a disciple's perspective on God, morality, spirituality, and how the world should work doesn't ruffle some non-Christian feathers, there is something terribly wrong. It is quite possible he or she has compromised the message or watered down the gospel for the sake of political or social gain. Woe to that person!

— 6:27-35 —

The blessings and woes embody the stark contrast between the kingdom of God and the present world order. Next Jesus turned to "those who hear" and unpacked the implications of this difference in very practical terms, beginning with relationships. He showed that relationships in the kingdom are altogether different from those in the world at large.

In our dog-eat-dog world, it's common to see business competitors and political combatants fight tooth-and-nail in a no-holds-barred battle to pummel their opposition. While relationships on Main Street may not be as brazenly ruthless as those on Wall Street or Pennsylvania Avenue, the thinking is not much different—just less obvious.

Jesus introduced His teaching with the emphatic phrase "But *I* say to you (plural) who hear . . ." Then He dispensed advice the world calls patently stupid. He urged six specific actions that express unconditional love.

Love your enemies. Do good to those who hate you. The kind of love Jesus called His disciples to express is *agapē* [26], which the New

Testament speaks of often and characterizes as a distinctly Christian kind of love that seeks the greatest good of another. *Agapē* is a word rarely found outside Jewish and Christian writings. The Greek culture celebrated *eros*, which, although used in various contexts, often connoted the intoxicating, impulsive romantic love between men and women. They also honored *philia* [5373], the warm, noble affection of deep friendship. But, for the most part, *agapē* remained an undeveloped term in Greek literature. The human authors of the New Testament needed a Greek word to express God's love—especially the kind of love modeled by Christ and commanded by Him in the upper room. But the most common Greek terms wouldn't suffice. Fortunately, *agapē* was relatively unknown and largely undefined, so it perfectly suited their purposes. Like an empty wineskin, it waited to be filled with distinctly Christian meaning.

Jesus called His disciples to give this selfless kind of love to the most unlovable people of all: their own enemies. These people don't merely seem unfriendly; they act on their bad intentions. Disciples are to respond to hostility with love—practical, Christlike love in action.

Bless those who curse you. The word "bless" literally means "to speak well." It carries the idea of speaking well of someone to others, avoiding the temptation to denigrate or cause others to think ill of a person. In the New Testament the term very frequently has a spiritual connotation. To "bless" someone is to speak well of him or her to God. To "curse," on the other hand, is to call down divine affliction upon someone (cf. Luke 9:54).

Jesus wanted His followers to "speak well" of everyone before God, including those who call down divine calamities and who revile them in public.

Pray for those who mistreat you. The natural response to mistreatment is to seek justice, usually in the form of retribution. Injury for injury and pain for pain. This is especially true in Middle-Eastern cultures, even to this day. In the Old Testament, prophets and poets wisely rested in the promise that God would take just vengeance on their behalf (e.g., Deut. 32:35; Ps. 94:1).

Jesus took this a step further. He not only expected His disciples to leave vengeance in the hands of God, He also called for them to petition the Lord for mercy on the people who cause harm!

Respond to aggression with gentleness. The Greek word rendered "hit" is a general term that can describe any kind of blow ranging from a backhanded slap (Matt. 5:39) to a sharp punch (Acts 23:2). It's very likely Jesus had in mind an insulting slap, not a brutal blow to the face. He wasn't calling His disciples to become the world's punching bag. Moreover, this hit on the cheek might also be figurative, a blow to one's ego. He wanted His disciples to lay aside their pride in deference to non-life-threatening attacks from nonbelievers.

Be generous to those who are selfish. This gentle response to aggression included keeping a loose grip on possessions, which ultimately belong to God anyway. The Lord called for generosity in response to greed. In the kingdom of God, physical possessions are merely a means to an end, and He can easily replace them. The point is to value people far more than things.

Treat others the same way you want them to treat you. Jesus summarized His teaching with what has been called "the Golden Rule." This great standard of kindness toward others, however, is not original to Him. Both Jews and pagans encouraged kindness for the sake of mutual benefit. For example:

> "What you do not want done to yourself, do not do to others." (Confucius)
> "We should behave to our friends as we wish our friends to behave to us." (Aristotle)
> "May I behave to others as they should do to me." (Plato)
> "What you hate, do not do to anyone." (Tobit 4:15)

This give-to-gain mentality is only logical. Loving others in the hope of receiving love in return isn't a sacrifice; it's an investment with a reasonable expectation of reward. Jesus, on the other hand, called for self-giving *without the expectation* of anything in return. His brand of discipleship requires faith, confidence that all good things come from God. The Lord doesn't reward His people for extending grace; that's nothing more than works-based righteousness. Instead, He calls His own to imitate Him, which gives them access to all that is His.

You might call this a grace principle. Those who exist in a grace relationship with God can count on it no less than the law of gravity. Imitate Christ, and we partake in all that is His. As we extend grace, the grace of God comes to us in greater quantities, not only to benefit us, but to shower those around us with the goodness of God.

— 6:36-38 —

Jesus expounded on the grace principle (Luke 6:31) with five specific examples:

1. Be merciful (6:36). The first example reminds us that we have received mercy from the Father, which should, in turn, motivate us to mercy. What we have received freely, we can afford to give away freely. The Greek word carries the sense of strong emotion involving empathy for the difficulties suffered by another. It is not merely the logical decision to avoid retaliation; mercy deliberately withholds punishment out of sympathy.

2. Don't judge (6:37a). This is perhaps one of the least understood—and I might add, the most abused—sayings of Jesus. People under sin's condemnation often deflect responsibility using this statement as their defense. The Greek verb has in mind a person "acting as a judge." Judgment in this sense is the exclusive prerogative of a person who has the qualifications and the power to sit in judgment.

The Lord has reserved judgment over people as His exclusive domain. While we must discern the difference between right and wrong, and never shy away from declaring sinful behavior displeasing to God, we must avoid sitting in judgment over people. We may identify the sin as sin, but God alone is the judge of humanity.

3. Don't condemn (6:37b). If one of Jesus' followers presumes to sit in judgment over those who sin, that person clearly doesn't have an appreciation for the gravity of his or her own sins. A murderer freed from death row who presumes to condemn others to death for their crimes is a hypocrite. A genuine follower of Jesus, on the other hand, understands the great gift he or she has received. Gratitude inspires compassion and renders condemnation unthinkable.

4. Forgive (6:37c). The Greek word translated "pardon" here means, literally, "release" (*apolyō* [630]). This is the essence of forgiveness: release from the consequences of wrongdoing. To forgive a debt is to release the debtor from the obligation to repay. To forgive an offense is to release the offender from any obligation to repair the damage or to suffer similar pain. It also includes releasing the harsh memories of all the offenses.

5. Give in good measure (6:38). In addition to withholding judgment and condemnation, and in addition to releasing people from the demands of justice, Jesus told His followers to take mercy to the next level. Mercy withholds justice after a sin; grace gives sacrificially to the sinner despite his or her wrongdoing. He promised that givers would feel only temporarily the sacrificial sting of giving. Their sacrifice will be restored many times over.

To illustrate the abundance His followers can expect, Jesus pictured a person receiving grain. This scene would have been a familiar sight in His day. Normally, a person expecting to purchase grain would carry a container to the merchant. A person unprepared to receive grain would simply hike up the front of their tunic to form a pouch (a "lap"). So, Jesus' illustration suggests surprise blessing. Furthermore, the expression "pressed down, shaken together, and running over" pictures generosity on the part of the person doling out the grain. They don't merely pour the grain into the lap-pouch; they pack the grain in as densely as possible.

Jesus assured His followers that the grace they give out will come back to them in surprising ways and with overflowing abundance. It is not difficult to see just how radical the teaching of Jesus was.

— 6:39-40 —

The phrase "And He also spoke a parable to them" marks a logical break in Jesus' discourse. The first part of Jesus' discourse (6:20-38) described the difference between the present world order and God's kingdom and explained how citizens of His kingdom should behave. Then, having described discipleship, He turned to the subject of teaching and spiritual leadership. Remember, Jesus had recently come down the mountain with twelve specially designated men in tow. These men, given the title "apostle," were to be trained as their Master's empowered emissaries, charged with the responsibility of building and leading the church. In Jewish terms, these men would begin the work of building the kingdom. Leadership in God's kingdom bears little resemblance to leadership in the world. To describe the difference, Jesus presented three parables:

The blind leading the blind (6:39-42)
The produce of good and bad trees (6:43-45)
The wise builder and the foolish builder (6:46-49)

The first two illustrate the difference between genuine citizens of God's kingdom and those who merely pretend. The third reveals the devastating consequences of disobedience.

Within the first illustration, Luke's narrative contrasts two images that Jesus probably developed at length when teaching. The first paints a comical picture of one blind person presuming to lead another. Normally, a blind individual will take the elbow of a sighted person who leads the sightless person through unfamiliar territory, helping him or her avoid obstacles and pitfalls. But what good is a blind guide?

Matthew's account tells us that Jesus also used this illustration in reference to the Pharisees, who presumed to lead others toward God by presenting themselves as spiritual experts. These self-appointed authorities in all things religious were, in fact, spiritually blind (Matt. 15:14). The truth is, no one becomes the spiritual leader of another by virtue of one's own authority. In God's kingdom, equality replaces hierarchy (Luke 6:40). All disciples stand before Christ equally in need of reformation. Consequently, spiritual leadership takes a completely different form.

While the first image pictures what spiritual leadership *doesn't* look like, the second image (6:40) declares that spiritual leaders lead by example, not by self-appointed and self-proclaimed authority. Jesus is the only authority, our sole Exemplar, our only true Teacher. Leaders in God's kingdom lead others by their own discipleship. Unlike teachers in the world, who stand before their followers, facing them on the basis of their own authority, leaders in Christ's kingdom lead with their backs to their followers in submission to, and in steadfast pursuit of, the Teacher.

— 6:41-42 —

Jesus further highlighted the absurdity of trying to become a spiritual boss on the basis of personal authority by imagining one blind man observing in his peer's eye a "speck" (literally, "a small piece of straw, chaff, or wood")[19] despite the sight-impairing "log" (literally, "a piece of heavy timber such as a beam used in roof construction or to bar a door")[20] in his own eye!

In 6:41, Jesus highlights hypocrisy in leadership, but He didn't leave it there. He pressed the issue further in 6:42, illustrating that all people stand before God with defective eyes; therefore, no one can presume to become a spiritual ophthalmologist to another. The best any of us can do to help another's blindness is escort him or her to the One who can solve the problem.

— 6:43-45 —

Jesus' second illustration establishes a direct correlation between the character and the speech of a spiritual leader. The Greek word rendered "bad" in 6:43 (*sapros* [4550]) means, literally, "rotten" or "decaying." It doesn't take a horticultural expert to know that healthy trees produce healthy fruit, not rotten, decaying fruit. Furthermore, no one expects delicious fruit from a rotten, decaying tree.

The point is clear. What's inside a person determines what is produced on the outside, whether good or bad (Matt. 12:33). Both are the product of one's "heart."

As a general precept, this is obvious. Jesus, however, didn't use this principle in isolation. He used it to connect two other ideas. The first illustration (Luke 6:39-42) highlights the absurdity of criticizing others, using a negative example to say that all disciples—including those in leadership—should be self-critical. This illustration which follows speaks to the issue of obedience (6:46-49). Therefore, we should hear self-criticism from spiritual leaders as they strive for obedience. This is the "good" (*agathos* [18], meaning "useful, beneficial, or pure") from within the good person (6:45).

— 6:46-49 —

The title "Lord" honored someone having both power and authority, such as the patriarch of a family, a court judge, or the ruler of a realm. Doubling the title when calling to someone emphasizes the emotion, strongly implying complete devotion.

Jesus asked, rhetorically, why anyone would express such deeply felt devotion with their lips, yet neglect obedience. While other teachers prized information and judged their students on the basis of their knowledge, Jesus defined learning differently. True disciples heed their Teacher's words and then faithfully apply them. Their examinations come in the form of trials.

Jesus then gave His third illustration, likening a disciple's life to a house. The difference between the wise disciple and a disciple in name only is the presence of a reliable foundation. Those who put the Lord's words into action are building on a solid foundation anchored to an immovable rock. Those who do not, lose everything in the "torrent" (6:49).

Whereas Matthew chose to highlight the end-time consequences of poor building practices with very direct language (Matt. 7:21-23)—declaring insincere, unrighteous disciples to be hell-bound—Luke chose a subtler approach. The image isn't as stark, but the calamity described by Luke is not your everyday thunderstorm. The term for "torrent" literally means "river." People, even stupid people, don't build their houses in rivers. The "torrent" is an unusual, cataclysmic event that pictures end-time devastation.

This is terribly convicting, especially for those of us who have been called to tell people what the Lord said. When these words land in full force, we realize the crux of Christianity is not what occurs in a church sanctuary on a Sunday morning. Real Christ-following occurs during the week, when the church building we attend is miles away and we're in our home or on the road or at the office or in cyberspace. That's where disciples genuinely follow Christ, where citizens willingly obey the King, and where leaders truly lead.

• • •

For Jesus, discipleship involved far more than passing on knowledge from teacher to students or merely training a group of successors to continue what He had started. For Him, disciples are people called out of the present world order to become Christlike citizens of a completely new kingdom. Christian discipleship, therefore, is the process of introducing the citizens of King Jesus to a completely foreign culture in which everything is different—governance, the role of the law, the economy, even the system of jurisprudence. What the world calls foolish is wise in the new kingdom life Jesus offers. Mercy replaces retribution. Grace supplants justice. Sacrificial giving drives the economy—not earning, borrowing, lending, buying, and hoarding (Luke 6:20-38).

As the Messiah, Jesus came not only as a great teacher and *the* Prophet bearing God's Word; He came as the King of Israel whose domain encompasses the whole world. This is not to say, however, that all people will become citizens. Jesus came as the Savior of all people everywhere, but not all people will be saved. Jesus came as the King of all creation, but not all people willingly submit to His sovereign authority. Those who are true disciples—genuine citizens of the new kingdom—demonstrate their allegiance by obeying the King. Therefore, the present world order and God's kingdom are similar in this respect: If you don't obey the king, you are not a citizen of his kingdom; you are an outlaw, and you will be treated like one.

APPLICATION: LUKE 6:12-49

How to Make Disciples

In Matthew 28:19, when He commissions the apostles, Jesus uses the words "make disciples." Jesus made disciples and then commanded them to repeat the process. But what does it mean to "make disciples"? See if you think this makes sense:

Discipleship is a meaningful, hands-on relationship between a person who is qualified and willing to be a mentor and a few who desire to grow stronger in character and deeper in the Christian walk.

To make this clearer, let me offer a few contrasting thoughts to define and describe effective discipleship.

Discipleship is a long-term relationship; it is not a brief set of lessons. Disciples are not made in a week and a half or even six months. Disciples take time to grow, usually over a period of years. Generally speaking, the more frequent the time together, the more rapid the disciple's development. I know some relationships in which gatherings occur just twice a year for a week at a time, but these relationships have lasted more than a decade.

Discipleship is up close and personal; it is not distant. Mentoring takes place in the context of a growing familiarity in which the process of time erodes barriers to honest communication. Disciples need eye-to-eye contact and lots of opportunities for each to see the other at his or her worst. Generally, it's best for men to disciple men and women to disciple women.

Discipleship is relational; it is not formal. It isn't merely memorizing verses of Scripture or completing a prepared curriculum. Mentoring is really teaching by example; so, unstructured time together—accomplishing work, enjoying play, sharing leisure—allows surprising yet important topics of conversation to rise to the surface.

Discipleship is practical; it is not theoretical. Learning begins with theory but quickly transitions to practical application.

Discipleship is coaching; it is not controlling. A mentor who attempts to control disciples creates a cultic environment. Mentors must never forget that their disciples are God's people; mentors are merely one part of the Lord's overall program of transformation. He will shape disciples in the image of Christ, *not the image of the mentor!*

No one ever graduates from a discipleship program. Schools have offered discipleship as part of their curricula, but a syllabus makes true discipleship impossible. Discipleship is less about knowledge and more about seasoning. You will seldom write anything down, you'll never be graded, and the tests are never written. Making disciples is not an academic exercise.

There Is Always Hope
LUKE 7:1-17

NASB

¹When He had completed all His discourse in the hearing of the people, He went to Capernaum.

²And a centurion's slave, ᵃwho was highly regarded by him, was sick and about to die. ³When he heard about Jesus, he sent some ᵃJewish elders asking Him to come and ᵇsave the life of his slave. ⁴When they came to Jesus, they earnestly implored Him, saying, "He is worthy for You to grant this to him; ⁵for he loves our nation and it was he who built us our synagogue." ⁶Now Jesus *started* on His way with them; and when He was not far from the house, the centurion sent friends, saying to Him, "ᵃLord, do not trouble Yourself further, for I am not worthy for You to come under my roof; ⁷for this reason I did not even consider myself worthy to come to You, but *just* ᵃsay the word, and my ᵇservant will be healed. ⁸For I also am a man placed under authority, with soldiers under me; and I say to this one, 'Go!' and he goes, and to another, 'Come!' and he comes, and to my slave, 'Do this!' and he does it." ⁹Now when Jesus heard this, He marveled at him, and turned and said to the crowd that was following Him, "I say to you, not even in Israel have I found such great faith." ¹⁰When those who had been sent returned to the house, they found the slave in good health.

¹¹Soon afterwards He went to a city called Nain; and His disciples were going along with Him, ᵃaccompanied by a large crowd. ¹²Now as He approached the gate of the city, ᵃa dead man was being carried out, the ᵇonly son of his mother, and she was a widow; and a sizeable crowd from the city was with her. ¹³When the Lord saw her, He felt compassion for

NLT

¹When Jesus had finished saying all this to the people, he returned to Capernaum. ²At that time the highly valued slave of a Roman officer* was sick and near death. ³When the officer heard about Jesus, he sent some respected Jewish elders to ask him to come and heal his slave. ⁴So they earnestly begged Jesus to help the man. "If anyone deserves your help, he does," they said, ⁵"for he loves the Jewish people and even built a synagogue for us."

⁶So Jesus went with them. But just before they arrived at the house, the officer sent some friends to say, "Lord, don't trouble yourself by coming to my home, for I am not worthy of such an honor. ⁷I am not even worthy to come and meet you. Just say the word from where you are, and my servant will be healed. ⁸I know this because I am under the authority of my superior officers, and I have authority over my soldiers. I only need to say, 'Go,' and they go, or 'Come,' and they come. And if I say to my slaves, 'Do this,' they do it."

⁹When Jesus heard this, he was amazed. Turning to the crowd that was following him, he said, "I tell you, I haven't seen faith like this in all Israel!" ¹⁰And when the officer's friends returned to his house, they found the slave completely healed.

¹¹Soon afterward Jesus went with his disciples to the village of Nain, and a large crowd followed him. ¹²A funeral procession was coming out as he approached the village gate. The young man who had died was a widow's only son, and a large crowd from the village was with her. ¹³When the Lord saw her, his heart overflowed with compassion. "Don't

her, and said to her, "ᵃDo not weep." ¹⁴And He came up and touched the coffin; and the bearers came to a halt. And He said, "Young man, I say to you, arise!" ¹⁵The ᵃdead man sat up and began to speak. And *Jesus* gave him back to his mother. ¹⁶Fear gripped them all, and they *began* glorifying God, saying, "A great prophet has arisen among us!" and, "God has ᵃvisited His people!" ¹⁷This report concerning Him went out all over Judea and in all the surrounding district.

7:2 ᵃLit *to whom he was honorable*   7:3 ᵃLit *elders of the Jews*   ᵇLit *bring safely through, rescue*   7:6 ᵃOr *Sir*   7:7 ᵃLit *say with a word*   ᵇOr *boy*   7:11 ᵃLit *and*   7:12 ᵃLit *one who had died*   ᵇOr *only begotten*   7:13 ᵃOr *Stop weeping*   7:15 ᵃOr *corpse*   7:16 ᵃOr *cared for*

cry!" he said. ¹⁴Then he walked over to the coffin and touched it, and the bearers stopped. "Young man," he said, "I tell you, get up." ¹⁵Then the dead boy sat up and began to talk! And Jesus gave him back to his mother.

¹⁶Great fear swept the crowd, and they praised God, saying, "A mighty prophet has risen among us," and "God has visited his people today." ¹⁷And the news about Jesus spread throughout Judea and the surrounding countryside.

7:2 Greek *a centurion;* similarly in 7:6.

Survival experts will tell you that someone stranded alone in the wilderness needs at least four things to survive: shelter, water, food, and hope. Stories abound of people who floated helplessly at sea for days without water or lived for weeks in the open without food, yet survived. Hope kept them going until they were rescued. On the other hand, each day in the United States, ninety people lose hope and choose to end their own lives.[21]

This intangible necessity of life called "hope" consists of two elements: a longing for something and the anticipation of fulfillment. Prisoners of war have endured unspeakable suffering and survived because they refused to surrender the expectation of liberation. Childless couples have submitted to bizarre and expensive batteries of procedures, all in the anticipation of conceiving a baby. Students keep their noses to the late-night grindstone, month after month, year after year, striving for the day of graduation. Unemployed workers—some well past middle age—faithfully send out their résumés and consistently follow up on job leads, fully expecting to receive an offer, sooner or later. Hope fuels people's fire.

Despair is the antithesis of hope. As Thornton Wilder wrote, "Hope is a projection of the imagination; so is despair. Despair all too readily embraces the ills it foresees; hope is an energy and arouses the mind to explore every possibility to combat them."[22] Without hope, despair drowns in difficulties, all too often pulling its victim under with it.

After deputizing twelve apostles and instructing His followers on discipleship, Jesus returned to His adopted home of Capernaum. Soon afterward, He began to encounter hopelessness in varying degrees. The stories preserved by Luke illustrate the close connection between hope for the future and confidence in Jesus' power and goodness. The first two stories involve stark contrasts that Luke took particular care to note. Because of this, he placed them side by side in his narrative, even though significant geographic distance separated the two incidents.

7:1-10	7:11-17
Capernaum (Home)	Nain (A day's journey southwest)
Gentile centurion's servant	Jewish widow's only son
Deathly ill	Dead
Jesus responded to a request for help.	Jesus acted on His own compassion.
Jesus never saw the centurion or the servant.	Jesus saw the woman and the casket.
Centurion displayed complete confidence in Jesus' authority	Widow displayed only grief and hopelessness
Jesus healed the servant without a word.	Jesus raised the dead by speaking to the body.

— 7:1-3 —

Sometime after returning to Capernaum, Jesus received word from a messenger of a Roman centurion that the soldier's servant lay deathly ill. A centurion commanded a hundred men in a Roman legion of approximately six thousand soldiers. In terms of modern-day rank, he would be an infantry captain or, perhaps, a major. This medium-rank combat veteran had been stationed somewhere in Galilee, but Luke doesn't say where. It could have been in Capernaum, but not necessarily.

The man who lay dying was the centurion's "slave." The institution of slavery in the Roman Empire, while often brutal, was different from the slavery of seventeenth- and eighteenth-century England and America. In the first century, slaves were bound to a master in one of several ways, only one of which was "man-stealing," the detestable practice more familiar to us today. Some slaves were abandoned children who were adopted and given a home, in which they gladly served. Some sold themselves into servanthood to escape the hardscrabble life of freeborn poverty. And many were born into slavery as the children of slaves. Often Roman masters treated slaves like animals, but some slaves were given respect and opportunities for freedom and social climbing. Most slaves could expect to be freed by the age of thirty—or even sooner—either by purchasing their freedom or as a part of their masters' final testaments.

In this case, the centurion went to extraordinary lengths to save the life of his slave. Because he understood the delicate nature of Jewish-Gentile interaction (due mainly to issues of ritual purity), he asked some Jewish elders—men of influence in the local synagogue—to ask Jesus for help. Luke doesn't tell us why Jesus decided to help the centurion. Similarly, Matthew's account (Matt. 8:5-13) tells us He simply responded, "I will come and heal him" (Matt. 8:7).

— 7:4-5 —

We normally hear the worst about racial interaction, but in this case, the Roman centurion had earned the affection of the Jewish community in his town (wherever that was). The Jewish elders described the centurion as "worthy" of this favor. Luke used the Greek term *axios* [514], which can be rendered "worthy," "fit," or "deserving," based on the idea of a balance scale. They might as well have said, "On the balance scale of good and bad, he tips the scale decidedly toward the good." Because they considered the man morally worthy—on balance—of Jesus' kindness, the men approached the Master, Jew to Jew, citing the man's love of the Jewish people, which he demonstrated by donating enough money to give them a synagogue.

— 7:6-8 —

As Jesus neared the home, the centurion's messengers intercepted Him. The soldier clearly understood that Jews don't normally enter a Gentile's home for fear of ritual contamination. For Jesus to enter might require a time-consuming purification ritual and temporary disqualification from worship in the temple. The centurion hoped to spare Jesus the trouble. Furthermore, he saw himself as unworthy of Jesus' kindness.

Two Greek words describe the centurion's contradiction of the opinion of his Jewish friends in 7:4-5 that he was "worthy." First, the term rendered "worthy" in 7:6 expresses the idea of sufficiency: "I am not sufficient, adequate, or important enough for this honor." He would have said the same if Caesar Tiberius had made the trip. In terms of rank, he did not warrant a visit from someone so much higher on the social scale. Second, a verbal form of *axios* appears in 7:7. The related terms rendered "worthy" in 7:6-7 describe worthiness in a sense that is closer to goodness on the moral balance scale.

He seems not to have intended for Jesus to make the journey at all. As a man of power and influence in the military, he understood the nature of authority. That explains why he demonstrated his complete understanding of Jesus' authority over all things, including whatever causes illness. Compare this to the request of the "royal official" (John 4:46-54) who "implored Him to come down [from Cana to Capernaum] and heal his son."

Although this centurion did not feel worthy of God's kindness, he never doubted the Master's authority to solve his problem. His confidence in Jesus' ability never faltered, yet he refused to presume upon His grace. He hoped the Lord would heal his beloved servant, but he didn't ask with a sense of entitlement. This was quite a man!

— 7:9-10 —

In an interesting twist of terms, Luke then tells us it was Jesus' turn to "marvel." He expressed amazement at the centurion's faith, which He described as the greatest in all of Israel.

While Matthew provides more detail about Jesus' response, Luke chose to keep it simple. The Lord met the man's humility and confidence with a miracle of healing. By the time the centurion's friends returned to the house, the slave had made a full recovery.

— 7:11 —

Luke quickly shifts the setting to the town of Nain, which may be the site of the present-day Arab village of Nein, about 25 miles southwest of Capernaum, just 5 miles from Nazareth. Today, Nein is a tiny village of about two hundred people, and there's no archeological evidence to suggest it was ever much larger. If this is true, Jesus went to a relatively insignificant place in Galilee, perhaps en route to somewhere else. Despite the small size of the town, there were many witnesses; besides the Twelve, a "large crowd" followed Him.

— 7:12 —

Luke mentions that Jesus approached the "gate" of the city, but Nain was a relatively small village and would not have had a large, fortified wall with towers, as did larger cities.[23] Regarding the "gate" of the city, Luke probably used the term in the general sense of "entrance," where local men gathered to do business and where visitors would go first.

A Hymn of Hope

LUKE 7:8

The Bible teaches that hope is tightly bound to confidence in the power and goodness of God. In my experience, they do indeed rise and fall together. I struggle most with despair when I begin to doubt God's ability to solve my problems or when I suspect He doesn't care. More than once, while struggling to overcome a desperate problem, I have thought, Wouldn't it be great if He dropped in for a visit, just to say, "Hi, Chuck. I want to assure you that I'm alive and well, I care about you, and I'm in charge of this." My faith doesn't falter; God keeps that secure. But my confidence could use a boost like that.

While I have yet to open my front door to Jesus' smiling face, and I have yet to hear Him audibly reassure my troubled thoughts, I have heard Him. I honestly believe that one of the reasons God has given us His Word is to keep our hope alive. When my confidence in the Lord ebbs and I need a hope transfusion, I turn to His written Word, and these inspired writings have come to my rescue time after time.

On one particular occasion, I received courage from a pastor who struggled with circumstances more desperate than I can imagine: In the filth of a Roman dungeon, alone and numbering his last days on earth, Paul encouraged his younger associate, Timothy, with a hymn:

> For if we died with Him, we will also live with Him;
> If we endure, we will also reign with Him;
> If we deny Him, He also will deny us;
> If we are faithless, He remains faithful, for He cannot deny Himself.
> (2 Tim. 2:11-13)

My confidence rebounded and hope returned. I remember thinking, Things are tough, Chuck, but not that tough. God has everything under control.

On their way in, Jesus and His followers met a funeral procession that was on its way out of town. The burial custom of the Jews called for the family to wrap the body of the loved one from head to toe in strips of linen soaked in as much as 75 pounds of aromatic spices and resin to counteract the smell of decomposition (see John 19:39, NLT). On the day of burial, friends of the deceased placed the wrapped body on a bier, a lattice frame supported by horizontal poles, which they carried to the family's burial place—possibly a cave hewn from a limestone hill, depending on the wealth of the family.[24] After placing the body on a shelf carved into the wall of the cave, the family would have sealed the entrance of the cave with a large stone. In well-to-do families who had the means to own a burial tomb, sometime later—perhaps upon the death of another family member—the family would gather the deceased person's bones and place them in the family ossuary, or "bone box," along with their forefathers.

Luke includes an important detail that conveys the desperation and hopelessness of the situation: The deceased was the only son of a widow. Unfortunately, for much of history, a woman bereft of the protection and provision of a man could not expect to survive long, as many died from hunger, exposure, or assault. Uncivilized cultures valued people to the extent that they served the community. Women past the age of childbearing couldn't build the population and were too old for labor. Therefore, women feared the prospect of widowhood without children.

Although Jewish culture led the rest of the ancient world in caring for the helpless, such as orphans, widows, and the disabled, they offered just enough help to keep them from utter privation. If the widow of Nain owned land, she didn't have the resources to farm it. And unless the woman had significant money stored away, she faced a dismal future.

Luke describes the funeral crowd as "sizeable," using the same term (*hikanos* [2425]) spoken by the centurion when he declared, "I am not *worthy* for You to come under my roof" (Luke 7:6). Thus Luke's theme of "worthiness" in the centurion's story finds its way into the widow's encounter with Jesus.

— 7:13-15 —

In this case, no one approached Jesus for help. Prompted solely by His own compassion, He halted the funeral procession with an unusual command for a mourner. The Greek command is, literally, "Stop weeping!" He knew she had no reason to grieve or to be hopeless.

He then stepped past the grieving mother to approach the body of the deceased. The English word "coffin" isn't appropriate in this case because Jews didn't place people in boxes for burial in the soil. The correct term is "bier," which is a kind of stretcher or even a simple plank. They placed the wrapped body on a bier in order to carry it to the burial site. Jesus touched the bier to halt the procession and then spoke to the dead man.

Luke described the next event with stark literalism. "The dead man sat up and began to speak" (7:15). The term translated "sat up" was often used in reference to someone formerly incapacitated by illness (cf. Acts 9:40).[25] I remember my parents using the expression similarly. "She's sitting up now" meant "She was very sick and extremely weak, but her strength is returning."

The old expression "Dead men don't talk" obviously didn't apply on this occasion. The man started speaking. What he had to say must have been fascinating! Jesus gave the young man back to his mother, much like Elijah had done after he raised the widow's son in Sidon (cf. 1 Kgs. 17:23; Luke 4:26).

— 7:16-17 —

Just like the audience who witnessed the healing of the paralyzed man (5:26), this crowd was seized by sudden awe—the kind of respectful wonder people experience when encountering God (1:12; 1:65; 5:9). The crowd gave glory to God for what had happened, while recognizing the supernatural presence of Jesus. As yet, however, they did not completely understand who was standing among them. John the Baptizer had given Israel hope, but he languished in Herod's dungeon. Jesus, at the very least, represented a glorious rebirth of hope.

The reaction of the crowd differs dramatically from that of the Pharisees, who plotted His demise after He healed bodies and forgave sins on the Sabbath. The crowd gave praise to God and then dispersed, carrying the news of what they had seen to towns and villages throughout Judea. Luke describes the effect of Jesus' fame on the people of Judea as hopeful, yet we have seen this before (4:14-15).

• • •

Two tragic scenes had siphoned all the hope out of the people who were grieving alongside the afflicted. But when Jesus stepped in, their hope revived. A centurion's sick slave regained complete physical health; and a widow's only son, who had died, returned to life. Small wonder the news of these miracles went out all over Judea and all the surrounding district! We can easily imagine how these two events would become the headline stories on the evening television newscasts across our country today.

APPLICATION: LUKE 7:1-17

Hope . . . Deep Down

Let me pass along a couple of thoughts that stick in my mind after examining these seventeen verses. In doing so, I want to tie in a couple of verses from Romans 8.

> But if we hope for what we do not see, with perseverance we wait eagerly for it. In the same way the Spirit also helps our weakness; for we do not know how to pray as we should, but the Spirit Himself intercedes for us with groanings too deep for words; and He who searches the hearts knows what the mind of the Spirit is, because He intercedes for the saints according to the will of God. (Rom. 8:25-27)

The Holy Spirit not only hears your requests, He intercedes according to God's will. You may present requests and desire certain solutions, many of which are not in your own best interest or do not align with God's will; so, God's own Spirit intercedes for us. He edits the rudimentary words of our prayers, conforming them to the highest good of all, and then sends back to us the right solutions to the problems we face.

Hope is restored when we remember that our Lord is not hindered or limited by the things that make us feel helpless. When we come to a mountain we cannot cross, it's not a hindrance to Him. When we battle a disease for which we cannot find a cure, He doesn't panic. When we are caught in a no-win predicament, He is infinitely resourceful. He specializes in impossible problems.

That is a great source of hope. I know He is greater than the greatest of my problems.

Hope remains when we accept as truth that even though we cannot see God or hear Him or touch Him, He is hard at work on our behalf. This is perhaps the hardest part of faith. Not seeing, not hearing, not having any tangible evidence of God's concern for our problems leaves too much room for the imagination. And, unfortunately, we don't tend

to fill the information void with good thoughts or encouraging anticipation. Satan would have us believe our Creator has abandoned His
creation, leaving us to suffer evil alone and forgotten. When we fall
into the natural pattern of doubt—"God doesn't love me; God doesn't
care"—the circumstances of life will substantiate our worst fears. Consequently, choosing to accept the truth of God's genuine care and active
involvement becomes a discipline. When we choose to trust in His love,
we will see it abound.

In Defense of a Doubter
LUKE 7:18-35

NASB

18 The disciples of John reported to him about all these things. 19 Summoning ªtwo of his disciples, John sent them to the Lord, saying, "Are You the ᵇExpected One, or do we look for someone else?" 20 When the men came to Him, they said, "John the Baptist has sent us to You, to ask, 'Are You the ªExpected One, or do we look for someone else?'" 21 At that ªvery time He cured many *people* of diseases and afflictions and evil spirits; and He gave sight to many *who were* blind. 22 And He answered and said to them, "Go and report to John what you have seen and heard: *the* BLIND RECEIVE SIGHT, *the* lame walk, *the* lepers are cleansed, and *the* deaf hear, *the* dead are raised up, *the* POOR HAVE THE GOSPEL PREACHED TO THEM. 23 Blessed is he ªwho does not take offense at Me."

24 When the messengers of John had left, He began to speak to the crowds about John, "What did you go out into the wilderness to see? A reed shaken by the wind? 25 ªBut what did you go out to see? A man dressed in soft ᵇclothing? Those who

NLT

18 The disciples of John the Baptist told John about everything Jesus was doing. So John called for two of his disciples, 19 and he sent them to the Lord to ask him, "Are you the Messiah we've been expecting,* or should we keep looking for someone else?"

20 John's two disciples found Jesus and said to him, "John the Baptist sent us to ask, 'Are you the Messiah we've been expecting, or should we keep looking for someone else?'"

21 At that very time, Jesus cured many people of their diseases, illnesses, and evil spirits, and he restored sight to many who were blind. 22 Then he told John's disciples, "Go back to John and tell him what you have seen and heard—the blind see, the lame walk, those with leprosy are cured, the deaf hear, the dead are raised to life, and the Good News is being preached to the poor." 23 And he added, "God blesses those who do not fall away because of me.*"

24 After John's disciples left, Jesus began talking about him to the crowds. "What kind of man did you go into the wilderness to see? Was he a weak reed, swayed by every breath of wind? 25 Or were you expecting to see a man dressed in expensive

are splendidly clothed and live in luxury are *found* in royal palaces! 26But what did you go out to see? A prophet? Yes, I say to you, and one who is more than a prophet. 27This is the one about whom it is written,

'BEHOLD, I SEND MY MESSENGER
   aAHEAD OF YOU,
WHO WILL PREPARE YOUR WAY
   BEFORE YOU.'

28I say to you, among those born of women there is no one greater than John; yet he who is aleast in the kingdom of God is greater than he." 29When all the people and the tax collectors heard *this,* they aacknowledged God's justice, having been baptized with the baptism of John. 30But the Pharisees and the alawyers rejected God's purpose for themselves, not having been baptized by bJohn.

31"To what then shall I compare the men of this generation, and what are they like? 32They are like children who sit in the market place and call to one another, and they say, 'We played the flute for you, and you did not dance; we sang a dirge, and you did not weep.' 33For John the Baptist has come eating no bread and drinking no wine, and you say, 'He has a demon!' 34The Son of Man has come eating and drinking, and you say, 'Behold, a gluttonous man and a adrunkard, a friend of tax collectors and bsinners!' 35Yet wisdom is vindicated by all her children."

7:19 aLit *a certain two* bLit *Coming One* 7:20 aLit *Coming One* 7:21 aLit *hour* 7:23 aLit *whoever* 7:25 aOr *Well then, what* bOr *garments* 7:27 aLit *before Your face* 7:28 aOr *less* 7:29 aOr *justified God* 7:30 aI.e. experts in the Mosaic Law bLit *him* 7:34 aOr *wine-drinker* bI.e. irreligious Jews

clothes? No, people who wear beautiful clothes and live in luxury are found in palaces. 26Were you looking for a prophet? Yes, and he is more than a prophet. 27John is the man to whom the Scriptures refer when they say,

'Look, I am sending my
   messenger ahead of you,
and he will prepare your way
   before you.'*

28I tell you, of all who have ever lived, none is greater than John. Yet even the least person in the Kingdom of God is greater than he is!"

29When they heard this, all the people—even the tax collectors—agreed that God's way was right,* for they had been baptized by John. 30But the Pharisees and experts in religious law rejected God's plan for them, for they had refused John's baptism.

31"To what can I compare the people of this generation?" Jesus asked. "How can I describe them? 32They are like children playing a game in the public square. They complain to their friends,

'We played wedding songs,
   and you didn't dance,
so we played funeral songs,
   and you didn't weep.'

33For John the Baptist didn't spend his time eating bread or drinking wine, and you say, 'He's possessed by a demon.' 34The Son of Man,* on the other hand, feasts and drinks, and you say, 'He's a glutton and a drunkard, and a friend of tax collectors and other sinners!' 35But wisdom is shown to be right by the lives of those who follow it.*"

7:19 Greek *Are you the one who is coming?* Also in 7:20. 7:23 Or *who are not offended by me.* 7:27 Mal 3:1. 7:29 Or *praised God for his justice.* 7:34 "Son of Man" is a title Jesus used for himself. 7:35 Or *But wisdom is justified by all her children.*

Contrary to popular opinion, doubting is a normal, healthy, perhaps even necessary experience in spiritual growth. Disciples who never suffer periods of trembling confidence in their God, the Bible, the gospel, or their calling are most likely playing it safe and living in denial. Doubts force us to pursue the truth. Doubts fuel the believer's pursuit of real answers to life's most troubling questions. Doubts make deep divers out of novice swimmers. Doubts cause us to go down into the labyrinthine realm of profound truths to find treasures many people don't even know exist.

Doubters are deep thinkers who need something more than churchy platitudes and folk theology. Doubters crave spiritual truths that *work* rather than clichés that merely decorate their denial. A doubter is no more a heretic than a questioner is a fool. As Pascal wrote, "We must know where to doubt, where to feel certain, where to submit. He who does not do so, understands not the force of reason."[26] Tennyson expressed this poetically:

> There lives more faith in honest doubt,
> Believe me, than in half the creeds.[27]

Many things lead us to honest doubt. Circumstances that appear completely random cause us to question the faithfulness of God. When good people suffer and evil people prosper, we begin to wonder about the fairness of God. The weight of public opinion and the way nonbelievers present scientific evidence can cause us to doubt the existence of God. The shame of our own sinful behavior can lead us to doubt the love of God. And, most perplexing of all, when faithful obedience causes unspeakable suffering, we can begin to doubt everything we once thought true.

While Jesus' ministry in Galilee gathered momentum, drawing disciples by the thousands, John the Baptizer languished in the dungeon of Herod Antipas (Luke 3:20). Not long after John baptized Jesus— perhaps only months later—Antipas captured the forerunner and held him prisoner. Though privately fascinated and amused by his lifestyle and popularity, the despotic ruler of Galilee didn't much care for the prophet's message. John openly declared Antipas's current marriage unlawful because it clearly violated the Law of Moses (Lev. 18:16; 20:21). Antipas had divorced his first wife to marry Herodias, who had been married to his brother Philip. To complicate matters further, Herodias was the niece of both men!

The son of Zacharias and Elizabeth was different from the start. He grew up in the desert, isolated from the easy life, taking his shelter among the caves that once protected David and drawing nourishment solely from the hand of God. He clothed himself in camel's hair, with a leather belt about his waist. He ate locusts and wild honey. And I believe that, while living in the isolation and privation of the wilderness, the eccentric desert preacher heard the voice of God—not mystically, but audibly, in the manner of Old Testament prophets.

The forerunner faithfully proclaimed divine truth and called the weak-willed ruler of Galilee to account. In so doing, he stood in the tradition of the authentic prophets who had gone before him. Samuel stripped disobedient Saul of his dynasty (1 Sam. 13:13-14). Nathan confronted David with his sin (2 Sam. 12:7-12). Elijah spent his career announcing the sins of Ahab and Jezebel (1 Kgs. 18:18-19). Jeremiah called an entire nation to account for their crimes and foretold their doom. Most of these men enjoyed the Lord's protection in response to their faithfulness. John, however, suffered for his uncompromising obedience.

Naturally, John had a few questions for the man he had earlier proclaimed the Messiah.

— 7:18-19 —

John's disciples kept him abreast of "these things"; that is, everything Jesus had been teaching and doing since His baptism.

Like most earnest Jews, John anticipated a new golden age for Israel because the Old Testament prophets had promised nothing less (Isa. 9:1-7; 11; 35; 42:1-9; Jer. 30–31; Dan. 7:14; Zech. 9:9-10). But John, the greatest of the prophets—who once inspired thousands—now languished in prison, forgotten by all. Clearly, truth and power remained bitter enemies in the realm of fallen humanity. The dominion of evil remained evident throughout the world, including in Galilee and amid the religious authorities in Jerusalem. If "the Expected One" had come, nothing appeared to have changed—at least, not as expected. When John didn't see his world changing with the arrival of the Messiah, he began to entertain doubts. As a result, he felt compelled to ask a reasonable question: "Are You the Expected One, or do we look for someone else?"

Luke includes this incident because it is remarkable. This is the same man who had boldly and openly identified Jesus as the Christ. He had known this from the earliest moments of his existence (Luke 1:41). His unique role had been ordained by God: to prepare the way for the Messiah and to identify Jesus as the "Expected One," "the Lamb of God" (John 1:29). The greatest of God's prophets now struggled with doubt!

— 7:20-21 —

When the disciples of John arrived to put the question to Jesus, they found Him in the very act of curing people of their afflictions—a fitting sign of His identity. Luke describes the physical ailments as *nosos* [3554], a general term for maladies that were considered socially devaluing, and *mastix* [3148], which refers to particularly painful conditions. In addition to exercising authority over diseases, Jesus commanded evil spirits to leave their victims.

John's disciples probably bristled at this, if only a little. Who were these people, compared to John? Who of all people in Israel deserved to be relieved of his suffering more than John? Yet Jesus didn't use any of His authority—none of His limitless power—to free John from his dungeon. With a mere word, Jesus could have knocked the doors off of their hinges and crumbled the stone walls of John's prison—but He didn't.

— 7:22-23 —

Jesus reassured John in the spirit of an important Old Testament prophecy. Isaiah reassured his own generation of Israelites, promising them that a future generation of Israelites would encourage one another with the good news of the Messiah.

> Encourage the exhausted, and strengthen the feeble.
> Say to those with anxious heart,
> "Take courage, fear not.
> Behold, your God will come with vengeance;
> The recompense of God will come,
> But He will save you."
> Then the eyes of the blind will be opened
> And the ears of the deaf will be unstopped.
> Then the lame will leap like a deer,
> And the tongue of the mute will shout for joy. (Isa. 35:3-6)

Jesus said, in effect, "Encourage John's 'anxious heart,' *for we are that future generation!* Report to him the fulfillment of Isaiah's messianic promise. Blind eyes see. Deaf ears hear. Mute mouths speak. Lame legs leap. Lepers are cleansed and corpses are revived." (See also Isa. 61:1-2.) He then concluded His exhortation with a benediction: "Blessed (same word as Luke 6:20-22) is he who does not take offense at Me."

The verb translated "take offense" is better rendered with the English expression "come to ruin" or "fall away," as in the NLT. In other words, "Blessed is the person who does not come to ruin because of Me. Blessed are the unoffended when they have to live with earthly iniquities. A special blessing rests upon those who are trapped in a situation they cannot get out of, when it looks as though the world has abandoned them and they are treated unfairly. Blessed are those whose faith is not destroyed under such difficult circumstances."

Jesus pronounced this blessing upon John, but His benediction contains a subtle, implied warning. This will become clearer in 7:29-30. John had not come to his ruin, despite his flagging confidence. His doubt did not diminish his faith, unlike those who gladly saw him imprisoned and hoped to see Jesus join him there.

Jesus was not the kind of messiah the Pharisees wanted. He came to establish a different kind of kingdom, not one founded upon military might or political cunning. He did not come to overthrow Rome, conquer the world, or to establish a Hebrew world empire. At least, not yet. Many early disciples fell away because Jesus refused to be the kind of savior they wanted (John 6:66). They died in their sins, or "came to ruin," by rejecting the Messiah as He had presented Himself.

The true Messiah came to conquer souls first. World conquest, theocratic rule, and the eradication of evil will one day be accomplished— be assured of that. Before all that, however, the Messiah came to transform hearts of stone into hearts of flesh so they would beat in perfect rhythm with the heart of God (Jer. 31:31-33). This would require the conquering King to become a suffering Servant (Isa. 42:1-9; 49:1-13; 50:1-11; 52:13–53:12).

"Tell John," Jesus said, as it were, "these are the works of the Messiah. Judgment will come upon the wicked, and the righteous will be vindicated, but not now. That's later. Tell John I'm right on target."

The Lord's benediction reminded John that to become a citizen of His kingdom is to become like its King.

— 7:24-25 —

After John's disciples carried the Lord's message to his prison cell, Jesus turned to the bystanders to set them straight regarding John's doubt. He chose an intriguing image to describe John. "A reed shaken by the wind" is a double entendre. On one side, the question could be rendered, "What did you go out into the wilderness to see? The foliage?" His rhetorical question leans toward a negative response because the rugged barrenness of the Judean hill country didn't support much beyond the simplest and hardiest plant life. In this way, Jesus reminded the crowd that John was accustomed to hardship, which he chose from his earliest days. Herod's dungeon, as bad as it was, would never break John.

On the other side of the double entendre, the question can be rendered, "What did you go out into the wilderness to see? A common reed trembling and barely able to remain rooted?" Again, no. They tramped into the wilderness to see an unusual sight, a man who stood in contrast to the pampered religious authorities in the temple, and who stood in firm opposition to their puffed-up, pseudo authority. The religious leaders depended upon men for their sustenance and, therefore, nurtured the power of men to maintain their opulent standard of living. John, on the other hand, ate directly from the hand of God and answered to no one but Him. At his lowest moment, John knew which king to seek: King Jesus.

— 7:26-28 —

Jesus repeated His challenge a third time: "But what did you go out to see?" He ridiculed the first two potential answers. This time, He supplied the correct response: "A prophet." Jesus reminded the crowd that John fulfilled Malachi's prediction, the first part of which the Lord quoted (Mal. 3:1).

Despite John's crisis of confidence, Jesus considered him no less than the greatest man who ever lived. Why? Because of his effective preaching? His selfless lifestyle? His courageous, tenacious, voracious love of divine truth? Those certainly made John great, but no. It was because the man remained faithful to his calling and to his God, despite the temptation to quit in the desert and join the creature comforts of the religious elite in Jerusalem. In fact, Jesus was confident John would emerge from this season of doubt as a man of faith.

— 7:29-30 —

Luke inserts a parenthetical note before continuing Jesus' discourse. Luke notes a great divide in the Lord's audience. Many people "heard"; here the verb implies they received Jesus' teaching about John as truth and then responded by believing. The phrase translated "they acknowledged God's justice" is better rendered "they vindicated God." They didn't merely offer verbal affirmation; they vindicated God by their very existence as believers (cf. Luke 7:35).

The other portion of Jesus' audience, the Pharisees and "lawyers" (scribes who were experts in the Law of Moses), "rejected" God's sovereignty over them. The term "rejected" comes from the Greek word meaning "to declare invalid," "to nullify," or "to set aside." Rather than vindicate God by allowing themselves to become examples of His righteousness, they invalidated His "plan" (literal translation) for themselves.

What separated these two groups was their response to John's baptism. Even before the Messiah arrived, each group had made its choice.

— 7:31-32 —

Jesus turned from praising John the Baptizer for his remarkable faith in the face of doubt, to rebuke the Pharisees for their pretend piety. He directed His criticism to "this generation," meaning the general population of Jews in Israel, who venerated the Pharisees and blindly followed their lead. He likened the religious authorities in Israel to a collection of children playing in the marketplace—certainly a familiar scene across the nation and down through the ages. Children like to play pretend games.

When I was a child, the girls wanted to play "house." My friends and I preferred "war." If a girl was especially pretty, we might be persuaded to drop our wooden weapons to be the husband in her game. Otherwise, we hid behind bushes and planned sorties to ambush the enemy. "Bang! Bang! I got you!" one would yell. "No, you didn't! You missed!" another shouted in protest. And so the pretend war ended and the real conflict ensued. Eventually, the older kids won the argument, not because they were right, but because they barely tolerated the younger, and the younger wanted to keep playing.

Jesus likened the Pharisees to squabbling children who complain that everyone doesn't play their phony games. The older kids played the flute for a mock celebration, but some refused to dance. Then, the older kids wanted to play funeral, but some declined to mourn. Like petulant brats, the Pharisees derived fun from making others play by their rules rather than from the joy of play itself. They remind me of the guy in our neighborhood who made the rest of us play his special brand of baseball because he owned the bat!

— 7:33-35 —

Jesus applied His analogy to the Pharisees, quoting their conflicting complaints. They criticized John because he preferred the wilderness to the temple, calling sinners to receive a convert's baptism. He ate locusts and wild honey provided by God rather than rely upon the corrupt economy

Never Satisfied

LUKE 7:35

As I read "The Parable of the Brats" (7:31-35), I am reminded of some unbelievers I have encountered over the years. No matter what is said, they find fault. "Oh, if you knew the guy I worked with who goes to church, you wouldn't come on so strong about this Jesus stuff. I mean, this guy is really a hypocrite." And if that didn't work, they'd say, "Oh, well, listen. I had a friend in my fraternity. You should have known this guy. I mean, he'd quote verses all the time, but in the final analysis he wasn't really what he claimed to be."

Some people will contort their own minds to find fault with everything associated with Christ, and they're always picking at something here or there to excuse their unwillingness to believe. "John? Too extreme. Jesus? Too sociable."

What will they say at death? What will be their plea upon entering the chasm of time called eternity? Jesus said, "Wisdom is vindicated by all her children." Wisdom's children are those who wisely accept the message of John and Jesus. In the end, the truth vindicates itself, either to the everlasting joy of the wise or to the eternal sorrow of the foolish.

I admit, you will not find a perfect person among the ranks of God's children, but you will find change among all of us. If, in fact, you do not see a gradual change for the better in a person, I suggest you're not looking at a genuine son or daughter of God. God reforms those He saves. Perfection awaits us in eternity, but until then, we must rest our case with Him.

of Jerusalem. He lived beyond the reach of their control, so when his influence outstripped their own, they had no recourse but to denounce him as an emissary of Satan. When Jesus, on the other hand, took His ministry to the people, enjoying banquets and partying with sinners—the opposite of John's approach, yet not in line with the Pharisees'—these same condemning clerics called Him a drunkard and a glutton.

His point was simple. The Pharisees merely pretended to care about God's rules. In truth, they cared only about their own. The only kind of obedience the religious experts in Israel wanted was obedience to *their* authority. If you refused to submit, they took their bat and went home—or worse.

Jesus closed His discourse with an axiom: "Wisdom is vindicated by all her children." We have a perspective today the Pharisees did not. From our vantage point centuries in their future, we see the results of their choices. We know what will happen less than three years after the Pharisees denounce John as a demonized heretic and dismiss Jesus as a drunkard and a glutton. Jesus will rise from the dead to vindicate His innocent death on behalf of all humanity, He will prove His identity as God in human flesh, and He will ascend to heaven to take His rightful place in power. Less than forty years after that event, while Emperor Titus's soldiers dismantled the Jewish temple, block by block, the Messiah's church would continue to spread in every major city in the realm. And today, thousands of years later, most everyone in the world knows the name Jesus Christ—but very few can recall the name of a single first-century Pharisee.

People with power often *think* they have truth, so they feel justified quashing anyone who dares to disagree. But wisdom is vindicated by all her children. Time will reveal who has believed correctly, as opposed to those who have rejected God's purpose for themselves.

• • •

Luke doesn't reveal John's reaction to Jesus' reassurance. We know only that he remained in prison until beheaded by Herod Antipas, the ruler of Galilee (9:9; Matt. 14:1-12). From an earthly point of view, John's ministry came to nothing as he suffered a cruelly pointless death. From heaven's vantage point, the Baptizer remained the greatest mortal who ever died. Regardless, it was John's trust in Christ that gave him unshakable confidence during his lonely last days. He drew his nourishment directly from the Lord Himself and found Him sufficient. Though shaken by doubt, he never blew away.

APPLICATION: LUKE 7:18-35

Lessons in Doubt

Some doubting is healthy. Doubt can force us to pursue the truth rather than just being gullible and believing whatever we are told. Doubts occasionally fuel our curiosity and drive us deeper into the mysteries of divine truth.

I take three lessons from John's struggle with confidence.

First, *doubting may temporarily disturb but it does not permanently destroy a relationship with Christ.*

John the Baptizer's lapse in confidence didn't invalidate his faith. Remember Blaise Pascal's observation? "We must know where to doubt, where to feel certain, where to submit."[28] I'm sure when the Baptizer's disciples returned with the Lord's message, he submitted. We would expect nothing less from this great prophet, so Luke regarded it as a point that went without saying. The opposite reaction would have merited comment from Luke.

You may be in a period of doubt. It may be the most difficult, melancholy period of your life. If so, may the grace and mercy of God sustain you. As friends walk away shaking their heads, and as other people talk about you (or preach to you), may the Lord sustain you through this period of doubt. Your doubts notwithstanding, this is part of your growth. Trust that the Lord will hold you close. Seek the truth, no matter what. I can say with confidence that, if you follow truth, it will lead you to God.

Second, *special blessings rest upon those who can live with earthly inequities, knowing there are heavenly purposes.*

I will admit that tragedies reported in the news can affect me deeply. I occasionally ask the Lord, "Where are You?" When someone in our congregation loses a child or succumbs to cancer or experiences the heartbreak of infidelity or must declare bankruptcy, the anguish I feel can be overwhelming. And in those times, I have to recognize that I cannot see what God sees. My perspective on life is like looking through a straw. Not allowing the world's innumerable inequities to undermine your trust in God's sovereignty and goodness will prepare you for surprising, special blessings.

Third, *being childlike is commendable; being childish is unacceptable.*

Our Lord tells us to be like little children in our guileless trust of Him. When frightened, children run to their parents for safety. They don't analyze dangers, rationalize them away, or talk themselves out of fear—not until after they climb into Mom's or Dad's arms!

When John the Baptizer struggled with doubts, he sent his disciples to Jesus with his questions. He didn't take them to rival teachers, false religions, pagan philosophers, or other doubters; nor did he keep them to himself. He ran to the arms of God, as it were, like a good child should.

The Love and Grace of Jesus
LUKE 7:36-50

NASB

36 Now one of the Pharisees was requesting Him to ªdine with him, and He entered the Pharisee's house and reclined *at the table.* 37 And there was a woman in the city who was a ªsinner; and when she learned that He was reclining *at the table* in the Pharisee's house, she brought an alabaster vial of perfume, 38 and standing behind *Him* at His feet, weeping, she began to wet His feet with her tears, and kept wiping them with the hair of her head, and kissing His feet and anointing them with the perfume. 39 Now when the Pharisee who had invited Him saw this, he said to himself, "If this man were a prophet He would know who and what sort of person this woman is who is touching Him, that she is a ªsinner."

40 And Jesus answered him, "Simon, I have something to say to you." And he ªreplied, "Say it, Teacher." 41 "A moneylender had two debtors: one owed five hundred ªdenarii, and the other fifty. 42 When they were unable to repay, he graciously forgave them both. So which of them will love him more?" 43 Simon answered and said, "I suppose the one whom he forgave more." And He said to him, "You

NLT

36 One of the Pharisees asked Jesus to have dinner with him, so Jesus went to his home and sat down to eat.* 37 When a certain immoral woman from that city heard he was eating there, she brought a beautiful alabaster jar filled with expensive perfume. 38 Then she knelt behind him at his feet, weeping. Her tears fell on his feet, and she wiped them off with her hair. Then she kept kissing his feet and putting perfume on them. 39 When the Pharisee who had invited him saw this, he said to himself, "If this man were a prophet, he would know what kind of woman is touching him. She's a sinner!"

40 Then Jesus answered his thoughts. "Simon," he said to the Pharisee, "I have something to say to you."

"Go ahead, Teacher," Simon replied.

41 Then Jesus told him this story: "A man loaned money to two people—500 pieces of silver* to one and 50 pieces to the other. 42 But neither of them could repay him, so he kindly forgave them both, canceling their debts. Who do you suppose loved him more after that?"

43 Simon answered, "I suppose the one for whom he canceled the larger debt."

have judged correctly." 44Turning toward the woman, He said to Simon, "Do you see this woman? I entered your house; you gave Me no water for My feet, but she has wet My feet with her tears and wiped them with her hair. 45You gave Me no kiss; but she, since the time I came in, has not ceased to kiss My feet. 46You did not anoint My head with oil, but she anointed My feet with perfume. 47For this reason I say to you, her sins, which are many, have been forgiven, for she loved much; but he who is forgiven little, loves little." 48Then He said to her, "Your sins have been forgiven." 49Those who were reclining *at the table* with Him began to say ato themselves, "Who is this *man* who even forgives sins?" 50And He said to the woman, "Your faith has saved you; go in peace."

7:36 aLit *eat* 7:37 aI.e. an immoral woman
7:39 aI.e. an immoral woman 7:40 aLit *says*
7:41 aThe denarius was equivalent to a day's
wages 7:49 aOr *among*

"That's right," Jesus said. 44Then he turned to the woman and said to Simon, "Look at this woman kneeling here. When I entered your home, you didn't offer me water to wash the dust from my feet, but she has washed them with her tears and wiped them with her hair. 45You didn't greet me with a kiss, but from the time I first came in, she has not stopped kissing my feet. 46You neglected the courtesy of olive oil to anoint my head, but she has anointed my feet with rare perfume.

47"I tell you, her sins—and they are many—have been forgiven, so she has shown me much love. But a person who is forgiven little shows only little love." 48Then Jesus said to the woman, "Your sins are forgiven."

49The men at the table said among themselves, "Who is this man, that he goes around forgiving sins?"

50And Jesus said to the woman, "Your faith has saved you; go in peace."

7:36 Or *and reclined.* 7:41 Greek *500 denarii.*
A denarius was equivalent to a laborer's full
day's wage.

Love and grace have a lot of qualities in common. For me, one quality towers above the rest as the most crucial in a genuinely fulfilling relationship: acceptance. Grace allows others to be who they are. Love—deeply fulfilling, ultimately satisfying love—accepts others without conditions or stipulations. True love doesn't try to mold others in the image of one's self, doesn't nitpick another's flaws, and doesn't give or withhold presence based on merit. Acceptance means being free of prejudice, remaining open to the potential good in others despite the appearance of defects. Acceptance is the grace to let others *be*—"warts and all."

Many years ago, I read a wonderful description of acceptance that resonated so deeply, I kept it near my desk until the print became too faded to read. I've shared it many times from the pulpit, and it still fills me with contentment to read it.

Acceptance. It means you are valuable just as you are. It allows you to be the *real* you. You aren't forced into someone else's idea of who you really are. It means your ideas are taken seriously since they reflect you. You can talk about how you feel inside and why you feel that way—and someone really cares.

Acceptance means you can try out your ideas without being shot down. You can even express heretical thoughts and discuss them with intelligent questioning. You feel safe. No one will pronounce judgment on you, even though they don't agree with you. It doesn't mean you will never be corrected or shown to be wrong; it simply means it's safe to be *you* and no one will destroy *you* out of prejudice.[29]

Acceptance is a rare quality to find, even in the home and at church, where we should find acceptance in abundance. Instead, we seem to find greater freedom to be ourselves among strangers. Perhaps we—and we're *all* guilty of this—fail to give others unqualified acceptance because we're afraid they'll take advantage of the situation and behave in sinful or destructive ways. We live under the reasonable, albeit mistaken, notion that by keeping a close watch on one another's sin and by holding one another strictly accountable for errant behavior, we can inspire those we love to be better people. But acceptance is not permissiveness. Jesus proved that. In fact, His acceptance of sinners gave them greater freedom to acknowledge their own wrongdoing and to seek from Him a remedy for their sinfulness. His acceptance opened the door to repentance.

Throughout His earthly ministry, Jesus never compromised the righteousness of God, yet He remained utterly accepting of deeply flawed people. No incident illustrates this better than the day a prostitute crashed the Pharisees' party.

— 7:36 —

While Jesus' ministry of teaching and healing continued to ignite Galilee, drawing multitudes of followers, the Pharisees felt increasingly marginalized. Every time Jesus exercised His divine authority, their credibility waned. Each time Jesus forgave a sinner, the religious leaders lost their power to condemn. He contradicted their teaching, exposed their pride and hypocrisy, rejected their interpretation of Scripture, exposed the errors in their traditions, and even ridiculed them as petulant little brats. Nevertheless, a Pharisee invited Jesus to a banquet.

He could have been an admirer, but it's doubtful, especially as the story unfolds. He might have planned to trap Jesus and hand Him over to His enemies, but that's equally doubtful. A banquet would have attracted too much attention for the arrest of an immensely popular rabbi. More likely, the Pharisee was simply curious or perhaps trying to appear magnanimous by hosting a political or religious rival. Regardless, Jesus graciously accepted the man by accepting his invitation to dinner. After all, He had enjoyed the company of other sinners!

The phrase "reclined at the table" describes the traditional posture for eating in the ancient Near East. They didn't sit in chairs at a high table; they lay down around a low table, propped on the left elbow with a cushion for support and with their feet angled away from the food. They ate with their hands, not a fork and knife.

— 7:37-38 —

Having set the scene, Luke introduces the surprise element, especially for a room full of Pharisees. As Jesus ate, a "sinful woman" crept toward the table, fell at His feet, and drenched Him with her tears. Then, in an extravagant gesture of worship, she anointed His feet with expensive perfume, pouring out the entire container. Try to imagine the scene.

Luke doesn't reveal what justified calling the woman sinful. Tradition has suggested she was a former prostitute by incorrectly identifying her with Mary Magdalene,[30] whose identity as a prostitute is itself absent in Scripture. Whatever her sin, she was not welcome in the presence of Pharisees, so it's safe to assume she had not been invited. Based on Jesus' response later in the story, she was most likely redeemed from her life of sin and forgiven.

Martin Luther called the woman's tears "heart water."[31] Tears of gratitude soaked the Lord's feet as she sobbed uncontrollably, lost in wonder, love, and praise. Luke used the imperfect tense to describe her continual weeping, wiping, kissing, and anointing, suggesting that she carried on for an uncomfortably long time. Moreover, her actions depict worship so profuse and so unrestrained as to border on self-humiliation. In the ancient Near East, only the lowest slaves touched the feet of another, and almost always for washing. A woman's hair represented her dignity (1 Cor. 11:6, 15) and, if married, she never took it down in public. So, the woman's hair touching Jesus' feet represented the most extreme act of humility possible.

While tears, hair, and kisses showered the Lord's feet, the woman added "perfume." The Gospels of Mark and John add that the perfume was pure nard, a highly prized extract from the spikenard plant, native to India and imported at great expense. Normally, the perfume was intended for anointing one's head, which was most likely the woman's intent until her overwhelming emotions took over. Hers was spontaneous worship—unguarded, surprising, intimate.

— 7:39 —

While the narrative doesn't say this outright, it strongly implies that Jesus allowed the woman to worship Him, perhaps for some time. While the woman worshiped, the Pharisee condemned. His thought consists of what grammarians call a "second class conditional clause," which is an "if . . . then" statement that presumes a negative condition. When used like this, the speaker intends to disprove the positive. For example, in the statement "If Mr. Jones were rich, he wouldn't be driving a cheap car," the implication is that Mr. Jones is not rich because he *does* drive a cheap car.

In this case, the Pharisee decided that Jesus could not be a genuine emissary of God because He not only tolerated the presence of a sinner, He welcomed her devotion.

— 7:40-43 —

"Jesus answered." Note that the Pharisee had not spoken out loud. No doubt, the man maintained a composed, dignified façade despite his inward disgust. (Pharisees—even those today—hone this skill with daily practice.)

As before (Luke 5:21-23), Jesus knew this man's heart and addressed his objections, referring to the host by name. Simon was a very common name, which the Pharisee shared in common with the Lord's disciple Simon Peter.

Ever the Teacher, Jesus confronted the man with a parable of two indebted men, one who owed the equivalent of five hundred days' wages. The other owed fifty days' wages. (A common laborer earned one denarius for each full day of work.) Both represented large sums of money, but the difference was dramatic: the money a man could earn in one and a half months versus one and a half years.

In Jesus' parable, *both* men were unable to pay and *both* received grace in the form of forgiveness. Their responses to their gracious lender, however, differed by the amount of debt they had. In truth, the lender could have tossed *both* men into debtor's prison. In those days, a person who failed to repay a loan was kept in prison until his family came up with the money. So, theoretically, both debts could have received the same punishment. Yet, because one had less money to pay back, he didn't feel as grateful.

The application of Jesus' parable is straightforward. The debt is sin and the debtors are sinners. God is the gracious moneylender who released the men from their obligation to repay what they could not, in fact, afford.

Jesus' parable invites listeners to identify themselves in the metaphor. If the listeners identified with the man in deeper debt, they would view the woman with compassion. If the listeners identified with the man with smaller debt, they should at least feel rebuked.

— 7:44-47 —

Upon His arrival at Simon's house, Jesus should have received the customary welcome of a guest, beginning with a basin of water in which to rinse road dust from His feet. This was not required, but a gracious host with good manners would have provided this for each arrival. An especially honored guest typically received the assistance of a servant or someone in the household, who removed his sandals, washed his feet, dried them with a towel, and then applied a small amount of perfume. This was not expected, but upper-class hosts typically displayed this kind of refinement.

A typical Middle Eastern greeting—even today—involves a kiss on both cheeks, the Western equivalent of a handshake or a casual embrace among friends. Furthermore, a special courtesy included anointing the head with a small amount of inexpensive olive oil.

Jesus turned to the woman while directing His comments to Simon. His body language punctuated the irony of what He would say next. He simultaneously rebuked the Pharisee's low-class hosting and approved the despised woman's high-class treatment. On a superficial level, Jesus evened the social playing field, showing the socially unwelcome woman to be more socially acceptable than the socially privileged Simon. On a deeper level, Jesus demonstrated the woman's superior spiritual awareness. Where Simon saw a false prophet, the woman recognized God in human flesh.

While talking to Simon, the Lord looked at the woman. It was a look of affirmation. It was a look of acceptance. It was a look of appreciation. He then compared her actions to Simon's inaction. As Luke translates the Lord's Hebrew or Aramaic into Greek, he places grammatical emphasis on "no water," "no kiss," and "no oil."

Simon did not offer the basic courtesy of a water basin for Jesus' feet, but the woman washed them with her humility. Simon did not greet Jesus with even the perfunctory kiss of a causal acquaintance, but the woman showered His feet with kisses. Simon offered neither perfume for Jesus' feet nor the mild honor of an olive oil anointing, but the woman emptied her entire treasure of expensive ointment on Jesus' feet.

Whereas the other Gospel narratives emphasize the extreme value of the woman's gift—nearly a year's wages for a middle-class laborer (Mark 14:5; John 12:5)—Luke focused on her humility. She had anointed Jesus' head as well (cf. Matt. 26:7; Mark 14:3), but by highlighting the Lord's feet, Luke emphasized the contrasting value of the woman's most prized offerings (her hair, her kisses, and her extraordinarily expensive perfume) and the Lord's lowest extremities. In other words, she offered her best to the Lord's least.

Still speaking to Simon ("I say to you"), Jesus declared the woman's sins forgiven ("her sins, which are many"). Jesus didn't excuse the woman's sins, and He didn't minimize the truth. He never denied her wrongdoing or that her sins offended God and required forgiveness. He nevertheless accepted the woman, not in spite of her sins, but with them.

Jesus then connected His parable with the present situation—again without revealing the man's inner thoughts, although most could have guessed the Lord's meaning. By calling the woman one who "loved much," Jesus identified her as the greater debtor in the parable. But He left the "he who is forgiven little" ambiguous.

Ironically, the one "who is forgiven little" remains the perspective of the proud. Only people lacking humility would see themselves owing a small debt to God. Little need for forgiveness (in the mind of the proud) yields little love for God. Therefore, following this logic, those who pride themselves as God's favorites have the least devotion for Him.

Jesus subtly turned the Pharisee's claim to superiority upside down. These self-appointed religious experts prided themselves as favored by God because of their excessive devotion. Their devotion led them to believe they were religiously superior to everyone else, who had shown an obvious lack of devotion through sin. But Simon's own statement proved that the woman's devotion to God far exceeded his!

— 7:48-50 —

The Lord's discourse with Simon and the woman's roomful of detractors ended. The Lord pushed the world aside for a private moment between a sinner and her God. While the religious world rejected the "sinful woman," Jesus accepted her. While the religiously pure had nothing to offer her but frowning condemnation, Jesus' unqualified acceptance not only prompted her repentance, but it also provided what she needed most: divine pardon for her hopeless debt of sin. Grace superabounds!

Luke highlights yet another contrast. While the woman wept with abandon out of gratitude for her God's forgiveness, the other guests asked, in effect, "Who does this guy think he is, presuming to forgive sins as if he were God?" Luke's description doesn't reveal whether each man asked this silently or murmured this to one another. The similarity to the incident in Luke 5:21 suggests they murmured aloud. While the men indignantly questioned Jesus' authority to pardon sin, Jesus declared unambiguously, "Your faith has saved you." In the context of sin and forgiveness, this refers to salvation from damnation. In this case, the woman faced no particular danger in the temporal sense, only in the eternal, cosmic sense.

Jesus' final benediction, "Go in peace," most likely used the profoundly important Hebrew term *shalom* [H7965].

• • •

Ironically, the woman didn't find pardon among those whose official task was to proclaim God's Word, the scribes and Pharisees. The Lord had established the temple as a means of restoring lost sinners to Himself, but she didn't go near there. She would not have found welcome among the priests. The burdens and restrictions of religion kept the "sinful woman" on the fringes of Jewish life until the Messiah, her Savior, accepted her as is. While the Lord restored the wayward woman, many of Israel's most devout men began to distance themselves from the Son of God.

APPLICATION: LUKE 7:36-50

What Kind of Life?

With whom do you identify most in this story? Your answer may not be the one you tell your friends or admit openly in a Bible study group. But, in the quiet of this moment, as you read these pages by yourself, give that question some thought. The answer holds the key to your future happiness, the health of your relationships, and—most important of all—your eternal destiny.

As I compare and contrast the Pharisee and the sinful woman, two principles emerge that may explain why you identify with one more than the other.

First, *pride holds us hostage to sin.* Pride is, in part, a futile attempt to ignore our own sins by concentrating on the sins of another. Therefore, pride blinds the eyes of the soul so that we cannot see the gift of grace the Lord longs to give us. What we refuse to see, we refuse to accept. And by refusing to acknowledge our need for freedom, we remain bound by sin. In addition to the eternal ramifications of pride, we bring upon ourselves unnecessary strife. Refusing to acknowledge sinful behavior keeps us perpetually on the run from truth, constantly at odds with those who should be closest to us, and always justifying ourselves in the court of public opinion. What an unhappy way to live!

Second, on the other hand, *humility sets us free.* Humility accepts the truth of what we are. And that acceptance creates the opportunity to receive what we need: We receive God's grace, which has an eternal impact; and here on earth, we receive the forgiveness of family, friends, co-workers, even complete strangers.

One of the marvelous things about working with terribly sinful yet utterly humble people is the joy of witnessing their responses when they realize they're forgiven. Jesus said to the woman, "Your faith has saved you; *shalom* (go in peace)." She left in peace, most likely as the happiest woman in the city. Forgiven, freed from sin, free to live without shame.

Now, *that's* the life for me!

Where Are You in This Picture?
LUKE 8:1-21

NASB

¹Soon afterwards, He *began* going around from one city and village to another, proclaiming and preaching the kingdom of God. The twelve were with Him, ²and *also* some women who had been healed of evil spirits and sicknesses: Mary who was called Magdalene, from whom seven demons had gone out, ³and Joanna the wife of Chuza, Herod's steward,

NLT

¹Soon afterward Jesus began a tour of the nearby towns and villages, preaching and announcing the Good News about the Kingdom of God. He took his twelve disciples with him, ²along with some women who had been cured of evil spirits and diseases. Among them were Mary Magdalene, from whom he had cast out seven demons; ³Joanna, the wife of Chuza, Herod's business manager;

and Susanna, and many others who were contributing to their support out of their private means.

4 When a large crowd was coming together, and those from the various cities were journeying to Him, He spoke by way of a parable: 5 "The sower went out to sow his seed; and as he sowed, some fell beside the road, and it was trampled under foot and the birds of the ªair ate it up. 6 Other *seed* fell on rocky *soil,* and as soon as it grew up, it withered away, because it had no moisture. 7 Other *seed* fell among the thorns; and the thorns grew up with it and choked it out. 8 Other *seed* fell into the good soil, and grew up, and produced a crop a hundred times as great." As He said these things, He would call out, "He who has ears to hear, ªlet him hear."

9 His disciples *began* questioning Him as to what this parable meant. 10 And He said, "To you it has been granted to know the mysteries of the kingdom of God, but to the rest *it is* in parables, so that SEEING THEY MAY NOT SEE, AND HEARING THEY MAY NOT UNDERSTAND.

11 "Now the parable is this: the seed is the word of God. 12 Those beside the road are those who have heard; then the devil comes and takes away the word from their heart, so that they will not believe and be saved. 13 Those on the rocky *soil are* those who, when they hear, receive the word with joy; and these have no *firm* root; ªthey believe for a while, and in time of temptation fall away. 14 The *seed* which fell among the thorns, these are the ones who

Susanna; and many others who were contributing from their own resources to support Jesus and his disciples.

4 One day Jesus told a story in the form of a parable to a large crowd that had gathered from many towns to hear him: 5 "A farmer went out to plant his seed. As he scattered it across his field, some seed fell on a footpath, where it was stepped on, and the birds ate it. 6 Other seed fell among rocks. It began to grow, but the plant soon wilted and died for lack of moisture. 7 Other seed fell among thorns that grew up with it and choked out the tender plants. 8 Still other seed fell on fertile soil. This seed grew and produced a crop that was a hundred times as much as had been planted!" When he had said this, he called out, "Anyone with ears to hear should listen and understand."

9 His disciples asked him what this parable meant. 10 He replied, "You are permitted to understand the secrets* of the Kingdom of God. But I use parables to teach the others so that the Scriptures might be fulfilled:

'When they look, they won't
  really see.
When they hear, they won't
  understand.'*

11 "This is the meaning of the parable: The seed is God's word. 12 The seeds that fell on the footpath represent those who hear the message, only to have the devil come and take it away from their hearts and prevent them from believing and being saved. 13 The seeds on the rocky soil represent those who hear the message and receive it with joy. But since they don't have deep roots, they believe for a while, then they fall away when they face temptation. 14 The seeds that fell among the thorns represent those who hear the

NASB

have heard, and as they go on their way they are choked with worries and riches and pleasures of *this* life, and bring no fruit to maturity. ¹⁵But the *seed* in the good soil, these are the ones who have heard the word in an honest and good heart, and hold it fast, and bear fruit with ᵃperseverance.

¹⁶"Now no one after lighting a lamp covers it over with a container, or puts it under a bed; but he puts it on a lampstand, so that those who come in may see the light. ¹⁷For nothing is hidden that will not become evident, nor *anything* secret that will not be known and come to light. ¹⁸So take care how you listen; for whoever has, to him *more* shall be given; and whoever does not have, even what he ᵃthinks he has shall be taken away from him."

¹⁹And His mother and brothers came to Him, and they were unable to get to Him because of the crowd. ²⁰And it was reported to Him, "Your mother and Your brothers are standing outside, wishing to see You." ²¹But He answered and said to them, "My mother and My brothers are these who hear the word of God and do it."

8:5 ᵃLit *heaven* 8:8 ᵃOr *hear!* Or *listen!* 8:13 ᵃLit *who believe* 8:15 ᵃOr *steadfastness* 8:18 ᵃOr *seems to have*

NLT

message, but all too quickly the message is crowded out by the cares and riches and pleasures of this life. And so they never grow into maturity. ¹⁵And the seeds that fell on the good soil represent honest, good-hearted people who hear God's word, cling to it, and patiently produce a huge harvest.

¹⁶"No one lights a lamp and then covers it with a bowl or hides it under a bed. A lamp is placed on a stand, where its light can be seen by all who enter the house. ¹⁷For all that is secret will eventually be brought into the open, and everything that is concealed will be brought to light and made known to all.

¹⁸"So pay attention to how you hear. To those who listen to my teaching, more understanding will be given. But for those who are not listening, even what they think they understand will be taken away from them."

¹⁹Then Jesus' mother and brothers came to see him, but they couldn't get to him because of the crowd. ²⁰Someone told Jesus, "Your mother and your brothers are standing outside, and they want to see you."

²¹Jesus replied, "My mother and my brothers are all those who hear God's word and obey it."

8:10a Greek *mysteries*. 8:10b Isa 6:9 (Greek version).

In our day, size and success are synonyms. That's certainly true in the business world. If you rise through the ranks of a large, profitable corporation, your competitors will envy and admire you. If you turn a huge profit, magazines will post your mug on their front covers and hail you as an economic messiah. Size means success. In the professional world, if you build a large practice with clients begging for your expertise, you're a success. The size of your practice makes it so.

The formula is simple: Size = Success = Income.

Sadly, the same mentality has attached itself to the world of Christian ministry. Pastors of small churches often envy pastors of large churches. Leaders of small parachurch ministries feel outclassed by ministries that run on eight-figure budgets. People in ministry often *try* to keep their priorities straight and might work hard to push pride and shame out of the picture. They very much want to define success in terms of maturity—but the world's paradigm is hard to shake.

As Jesus continued His ministry, traveling from town to town, up and down the narrow strip of land called Israel, the multitudes of followers increased geometrically. But Jesus never considered this a sign of success. Quite the opposite, He became more concerned that the size of His following would allow superficial faith and unholy motives to fester undetected. Some people followed Him to get their stomachs filled. Others followed Him to watch Him do wonderful works. Many attached themselves to Him to be part of a crowd that was following a famous personality. And, while ministers today would be flattered and would be quick to join the church-growth conference circuit, Jesus began to see the size of His ministry as a *threat* to success, not a validation of achievement. Consequently, He decided the time had come to thin the ranks. He changed His style of teaching from straightforward lecture and dialogue to speaking in parables.

Matthew reports that when Jesus was asked why He switched to speaking to the crowds only in parables, He said, "To you it has been granted to know the mysteries of the kingdom of heaven, but to them it has not been granted. For whoever has, to him more shall be given, and he will have an abundance; but whoever does not have, even what he has shall be taken away from him. Therefore I speak to them in parables; because while seeing they do not see, and while hearing they do not hear, nor do they understand" (Matt. 13:11-13).

— 8:1-3 —

At this point in the story, Luke inserts an editorial note about the practical expression of faith on the part of genuine disciples. With His ministry on the move, the Twelve ministered alongside Jesus, while a band of women also followed—women whom Jesus had healed, released from demonic possession, or redeemed from sin and shame. The men had left their livelihoods to devote themselves to exclusive training as apostles. The women gave out of their own financial means to support the practical needs of Jesus and the Twelve. Like the "sinful woman" in the previous segment, these people gave tangible expression to their faith in the Messiah.

While many are not named, Luke called attention to three particular women, perhaps to establish the identity of two of the women for later, when they will witness the Lord's resurrection (Luke 23:49, 55-56; 24:5, 10; Acts 1:14), or perhaps because they were people of special interest in the early church.

Mary Magdalene had been freed from demon possession. The name Magdalene may be a reference to her home in the region of Magdala on the western shore of the Sea of Galilee, roughly 3 miles north of Tiberius. Church tradition often has labeled her a former prostitute, and unreliable exegetes frequently have confused her with the Mary who washed Jesus' feet (John 12:3). But nothing in Scripture suggests she was any different from the many people Jesus had cleansed of demons. The Gospels indicate that she followed Jesus by faith, not for selfish reasons.

Joanna was the wife of a highly placed official in the court of Herod Antipas, perhaps the chief administrator of his estate. Susanna remains a mystery to this day. While the early church may have known her well, we know nothing more than that she followed Jesus, provided tangible support for His ministry out of her own financial resources, and may have been among the women who prepared the body of Jesus for burial.

— 8:4-8 —

The short segment praising these genuine believers in Jesus concludes Luke's emphasis on faith in action. What follows is a parable of Jesus, told to describe the different kinds of people who followed Him and what would become of them. While Jesus had used metaphors and illustrations, this is the first true parable in Luke's narrative.

At this point in the narrative, Jesus' ministry is on the move more than ever before. He had been based primarily in Capernaum, but now He traveled from town to town almost nonstop. When people in a given region discovered where Jesus was, they converged on His location to see His miracles and hear His teaching. But, instead of receiving a straightforward lesson, they listened to a story.

The Lord described a familiar scene in Galilee: a farmer scattering grain seeds across a field prepared for planting. In the ancient Near East, farmers prepared a field by plowing just before the rainy season—not to create rows of deep furrows like we would see today, but to loosen the soil and break up clods. Wooden plows dug shallow furrows, merely scratching the surface. After this, clumps could be broken up and the surface leveled with a hoe or, if it was a large field, by dragging a comblike harrow over the surface. Sowing grain consisted of walking

PARABLES

LUKE 8:4

Of all the teaching tools available to a teacher, none has greater power to convey deep spiritual truths than the parable. And none has greater ability to confuse. That's why Jesus preferred the art of storytelling when teaching a mixed audience of disciples and detractors. He loved stories!

The term "parable" is a transliteration of the Greek word *parabolē* [3850b], which means "to throw alongside," and it's always used for the purpose of comparison. Telling a parable is simply the art of teaching through narrative, such that the familiar is thrown alongside the unfamiliar in order to shed light on something. The speaker uses common, everyday circumstances to communicate unfamiliar things, even supernatural things. The images appear simple and obvious, but the truths they convey are neither. Two factors make interpretation possible for the hearer.

First, a willingness to understand. An unteachable spirit will find it easy to twist a parable into nonsense and then use it to prove the teacher a fool. As a result, those who wanted to reject Jesus found more than enough justification in His parables.

Second, spiritual discernment. The parables of Jesus reveal truths that exist beyond the natural realm. His lessons cannot be accessed through scientific research. They must be revealed by someone able to transcend the natural world to comprehend the supernatural. Therefore, the listener must have the aid of the Holy Spirit to understand the parables of Jesus. Fortunately, the Lord has promised to teach anyone willing to learn.

Jesus used parables in mixed audiences because this unique form of story accomplished two important objectives: Parables repelled hostile skeptics and equipped serious disciples.

"He who has ears to hear, let him hear" (Luke 8:8; 14:35).

through the field, scooping a handful of seed from a sack hanging over the shoulder, and then broadcasting the seed in wide arcs. Afterward, the seed would be covered by smoothing the soil, either by hand or by another implement.[32]

In the story, as the sower threw his seed, some dropped onto the footpath running through the farmland. Seed that survived the trampling of passersby became a treat for birds. From the start, it never showed promise.

Other seed fell on shallow patches of soil covering a large slab of limestone just beneath the surface. Early growth on this thin shelf of dirt soon withered because the roots couldn't push down into the soil, draw nourishment, and anchor the plant. Initial promise gave way to early disappointment.

Other seed fell outside the planned planting area among the natural ground cover, which may have included brambles, which could grow as high as six feet, and native grasses, which grew densely at ground level. The grain stalks couldn't compete with these briars and weeds, causing them to wither and die before producing fruit.

But some seed fell on good soil, which gave the grain stalks ample opportunity to grow. Despite the farmer's many losses, this seed made his effort worthwhile, returning a harvest many times greater than his initial investment.

As Jesus taught in parables, He often chose not to explain the parable immediately to the broader audience. He merely punctuated this story with the exhortation, "He who has ears to hear, let him hear." In other words, "If you get the point, apply it!"

The fact is, many didn't get the point. And this, of course, was the point. The words of the parable were like seeds broadcast over the crowd and landing on all kinds of soil. The harvest would, in time, reveal which kind of soil the seed found in each person. Would their hearts look to the Lord for more, or turn away?

— 8:9 —

The disciples who heard this parable did not immediately understand it, so Jesus interpreted the meaning for them. This is important: Jesus didn't speak in parables to be deliberately obscure. He didn't set out to frustrate ears eager to hear. He used parables to make His teaching less interesting to those not genuinely interested. Curiosity-seekers found little to entertain them. In fact, Jesus will answer the critic who suggests He reserved His teaching for favored people (8:16-18) and Luke will prove it (8:19-21).

— 8:10 —

The disciples didn't understand the parable, but they accepted Jesus at face value—a critical factor that set them apart from the Lord's critics. Because of their earnest desire to comprehend the word picture, Jesus interpreted the images. Luke includes the Lord's explanation for the sake of the reader. The Lord's explanation establishes a pattern by which to discern the meaning of later parables.

If the Word of God is a sword, then the parables of Jesus are its razor-sharp edge. Jesus confirmed to His disciples that parables would separate genuine disciples from curiosity-seekers, pretenders, bandwagon jumpers, and hypocrites. He also affirmed that they had been granted the gift of divine understanding—the "ears to hear"—the ability to understand revealed truth. The parables would confound those who did not want to receive and obey God's Word. Yet these same stories would instruct those who had chosen to place their trust in the Son of God.

The idiom "seeing they may not see, and hearing they may not understand" is an allusion to Isaiah 6:9, which records the first words of God to the recently commissioned prophet. He challenged Isaiah to rebuke the leaders of Israel with sarcastic reverse psychology.

> [The Lord] said, "Go, and tell this people:
> 'Keep on listening, but do not perceive;
> Keep on looking, but do not understand.'
> "Render the hearts of this people insensitive,
> Their ears dull,
> And their eyes dim,
> Otherwise they might see with their eyes,
> Hear with their ears,
> Understand with their hearts,
> And return and be healed."
> (Isa. 6:9-10)

The Lord's allusion to this frustrating time in Israel's history confirms that everyone in Jesus' audience had the *ability* to understand, but not the *desire*. It was a problem of the heart, not the head. The parables were relatively easy for willing hearts to comprehend, but impossible for the rebellious. Still, the average natural mind cannot grasp all the things that God has for the people of God. He has prepared His people—those whom He draws to Himself (John 6:44, 65; 12:32)—with the apparatus to comprehend those things the natural mind cannot grasp.

— 8:11-12 —

Jesus explained the meaning of the parable in simple terms. The seed represents God's message. The sower is the same throughout. The seed is the same throughout. Only the soil changes, which affects everything. Interestingly, Jesus didn't identify the sower, probably because it's not important to the meaning of the parable. The farmer could be anyone: a pastor, an evangelist, a writer, a Christian in the workplace, a teacher—anyone communicating God's truths. Success depends upon the soil, not the sower.

The asphalt-hard soil on the footpath represents those who never let the seed penetrate the surface. The Word of God is never given a chance to sprout and put down roots because the person remains impervious, allowing the devil to pluck it from the surface. Consequently, these "beside-the-road-soil" people *will not* believe and, therefore, cannot be saved.

— 8:13 —

The second kind of soil, a thin layer of dirt over a slab of limestone, represents those who receive God's message and show early signs of genuine discipleship, but succumb to temptation, fail to mature, and never bear fruit. Superficial enthusiasm evaporates at the first sign of difficulty. The literal meaning of the Greek term for "fall away" is "not stand." It's variously used to describe desertion, withdrawal, departure, and related ideas. Luke uses the middle voice, which indicates that the subject of the verb acts upon itself to complete the action.[33] It could be translated "and in time of temptation withdrew themselves."

— 8:14 —

The third kind of soil, the "choked-with-thorns soil," illustrates people whose lives are filled with competing concerns in the temporal realm, such as anxieties (presumably over the potential loss of something), wealth (or, more precisely, the relentless pursuit of it), and fleshly delights (of the short-term variety). These concerns can preoccupy our minds, drain us of energy, and poison our joy. Current concerns, well-intentioned though they may be, have a way of siphoning our interest in God's Word, and other priorities outgrow our desire for spiritual things. Politics, crime statistics, school debates, civic battles that never seem to end, squabbling neighborhood associations, compulsions, habits, and activities—on and on it goes, until before you know it, the "worries of the world" cover and choke our spiritual lives like Deep South kudzu.

The process is gradual and steady. Just as weeds grow slowly, just as thorns slowly entangle themselves around other plants, so these thorns slowly engulf a life. These weeds and briars keep the Word from growing normally and producing fruit.

— 8:15 —

The good soil describes those who have heard with honest, open, and willing hearts, ready to receive God's Word and then put it into action.

Neither defensive nor resistant, these "good-soil" people eagerly seek truth and welcome reproof, even when it's painful. They "hold it firmly" and produce fruit with fortitude, patience, endurance, and steadfastness.

Clearly, this last example represents genuine disciples who are saved from their sin through their faith. And, just as clearly, the first example—the "beside-the-road soil"—depicts people who are not saved due to their rebellious resistance to the Word of God. The middle two examples, however, defy a simple explanation. Good theologians have debated the eternal fate of "rocky-soil" people and "choked-with-thorns" people for generations, yet without a satisfactory answer.

The issue isn't clear because Jesus didn't make it clear. And if He didn't make it clear, it's probably not important. The point of the parable was not to unravel the mysteries of eternal salvation or to settle, once and for all, the predestination versus free will debate. Jesus commended only the last kind of soil, while rebuking the first three. Fallen, selfish humanity wants to know the minimum standard to get into heaven. How much is enough? But the primary thrust of Jesus' parable is maturity and the production of fruit. Clearly His major concerns are the obstacles to the Word's full potential.

— 8:16-18 —

After hearing the parable of the soil, the seed, and the sower, one might begin to wonder if Jesus deliberately restricted His teaching to people already "in the know." He did, after all, suggest that the disciples were given a privileged glimpse into divine mysteries (Luke 8:10), implying a kind of favoritism. After explaining the meaning of the parable, however, Jesus immediately dispelled any notion that the gospel is for only a privileged few by the illustration of a lamp and its purpose.

Sermons and Bible lessons on the topic often conclude with the interpretation of the parable of the soils, but the Lord continued, declaring His intention for all people to understand the parable and become good soil for the gospel. The image of lighting a lamp and then blocking its light is absurd. The very purpose of light is to dispel darkness while making all things visible; covering a lamp defeats its purpose.

While Matthew emphasized the practical application of the image— "Let your light shine before men in such a way that they may see your good works, and glorify your Father who is in heaven" (Matt. 5:16)—Luke emphasized the effect of Jesus' teaching of truth. Throughout the Bible, the image of light represents truth. While Jesus taught in parables to confound the rebellious, He nevertheless broadcast the truth of the gospel like a sower scatters seed. He is a lamp; His purpose is to shine light. And light exposes all things formerly hidden in darkness.

The phrase "So take care how you listen" (Luke 8:18) is literally, "Therefore, *see* how you *hear*." This cleverly links the "hearing" of the gospel so prominent in 8:4-15 with the act of "seeing" the truth in 8:16-18. Taking both images together—the parable of the soils and the illustration of lighting a lamp—we discover that how one receives God's message and then responds to the truth reveals one's chosen disposition toward God. The gospel is not given to the chosen few alone; it is given to all. The "good-soil" few are revealed by their response to the gospel.

While the truth of the gospel will be vindicated in the end, the primary point is the accountability placed upon the hearer to respond correctly. Jesus concluded His teaching with another somber warning to emphasize the grave responsibility of choice. Those who respond to the light they have been given will receive more light. Those who reject the light they have been given, choosing darkness instead, will lose what they *think* they have.

The specific qualification "what he thinks he has" refers to the spiritual insight foolish people—those who reject God's Word—think they possess. Imagine a man sitting in a dark room, proudly clutching what he believes to be a massive stack of bills which he estimates to be worth at least ten thousand dollars. Then imagine someone turning on the overhead light to reveal that nothing is printed on the paper. The fool suddenly lost his illusion of wealth. The light of truth took from him what he thought he had.

— 8:19-21 —

Because Luke didn't shift the setting of these verses to a different time or place, we should see the arrival of Jesus' blood relatives as a continuation of the same episode. On the heels of Jesus' illustration of light and hearing—receiving God's Word and heeding it—the Lord's family enters the narrative.

Neither Luke nor the other Gospel writers comment on the spiritual condition of Jesus' mother and brothers in this context (cf. Matt. 12:46-50; Mark 3:31-35). We know from other contexts that His half brothers (fathered by Joseph and born of Mary) didn't believe in Him (John 7:5) until after His resurrection (Acts 1:14; 1 Cor. 9:5; Gal. 1:19).

Mark reported that "His own people" tried to take Jesus into custody on the grounds He had "lost His senses" (Mark 3:21). Presumably, "His own people" refers to His blood relatives, which may have included Mary. Joseph had apparently died before the start of Jesus' public ministry.

Regardless, Luke, Matthew, and Mark simply use this circumstance to set the stage for Jesus' comment. The throng of people surrounding Jesus prevented His blood relatives from getting close to Him. This illustrates the immensity of His popularity at this point in His ministry. In the same way that it would be difficult to see a celebrity at a public event today, the Lord's family was physically separated from Him by the mass of people. When word reached Jesus that His mother and brothers wanted to see Him, He took the opportunity to clarify the objective of His ministry. Without dishonoring His human family, Jesus elevated the status of those who receive the gospel and then put it into action, those "who hear the word of God and do it." He didn't rebuff His mother and brothers; He merely used the occasion to announce how *anyone* can gain access to Him.

Luke 8:21 marks the end of a single episode before a change of setting. The entire segment opens with a seemingly disjointed reference to the devotion of disciples and the tangible support of dedicated women (Luke 8:1-3). Jesus then taught that receptive hearts bear the fruit of the gospel while others fail to yield anything (8:4-15). He taught that the gospel is for everyone and that everyone is responsible for their response to the light they receive because, one day, they will be held accountable (8:16-18). Jesus concluded His discourse by emphasizing obedience, which is the fruit of God's Word.

Jesus defined success in ministry by a very different standard from that of today's size-obsessed church culture. He broadcast the good news, knowing that many hearts—perhaps even the majority—would not receive the Word, grow to maturity, and bear fruit. Yet, like the farmer, He sowed seed for the sake of finding good ground. And the yield from "good-soil" hearts made His mission worth the investment. For Jesus, success meant having a relatively few "good-soil" people producing fruit.

Jesus is our model for ministry. He labored for the sake of maturity, not multitudes.

APPLICATION: LUKE 8:1-21
Ministry Success Starts with You

God has painted a word picture that includes every one of us. Where are you in the parable?

Do you see yourself as a productive, persevering Christian? Don't be needlessly modest in your answer. You may be. That doesn't mean you're perfect; it means you cling to the truth and seek to apply it consistently. You're open and honest, responsive to the prompting of Scripture, grateful for grace, and hungry for righteousness. You are growing toward maturity, and that's a good thing.

Do you see yourself as a busy, preoccupied believer? That's a very convicting question. When you look at the priorities of your life, do you see thorns that have choked out the good Word and kept it from being the best, the top priority? Are you so involved in the pursuit of temporal happiness that anxiety drains your energy? Do you have the "gift of worry"? Does your lack of contentment hinder you from experiencing peace within?

God is ready to hear your prayer. He's ready to help you clear away the thorns and thistles of temporal cares.

Do you see yourself in the shallow soil of a superficial seeker? If so, you're rootless and unstable. You responded to an emotional appeal or followed a crowd or did something to please a friend, or you like the company you now keep; but it wouldn't take much to change your mind. You're a hearer, but not a doer. You're not really a believer.

Are you the hard-hearted, stubborn soul who has no interest in spiritual things? If that's you, a day will come when you'll regret your proud, self-willed attitude. Tragically, it'll be too late.

Your response to divine truth depends on the condition of your heart.

Freedom from Bondage
LUKE 8:22-39

NASB
22 Now on one of *those* days Jesus and His disciples got into a boat, and He said to them, "Let us go over to

NLT
22 One day Jesus said to his disciples, "Let's cross to the other side of the lake." So they got into a boat and

220

the other side of the lake." So they launched out. ²³But as they were sailing along He fell asleep; and a fierce gale of wind descended on the lake, and they *began* to be swamped and to be in danger. ²⁴They came to Jesus and woke Him up, saying, "Master, Master, we are perishing!" And He got up and rebuked the wind and the surging waves, and they stopped, and ᵃit became calm. ²⁵And He said to them, "Where is your faith?" They were fearful and amazed, saying to one another, "Who then is this, that He commands even the winds and the water, and they obey Him?"

²⁶Then they sailed to the country of the Gerasenes, which is opposite Galilee. ²⁷And when He came out onto the land, He was met by a man from the city who was possessed with demons; and who had not put on any clothing for a long time, and was not living in a house, but in the tombs. ²⁸Seeing Jesus, he cried out and fell before Him, and said in a loud voice, "ᵃWhat business do we have with each other, Jesus, Son of the Most High God? I beg You, do not torment me." ²⁹For He had commanded the unclean spirit to come out of the man. For it had seized him many times; and he was bound with chains and shackles and kept under guard, and *yet* he would break his bonds and be driven by the demon into the desert. ³⁰And Jesus asked him, "What is your name?" And he said, "Legion"; for many demons had entered him. ³¹They were imploring Him not to command them to go away into the abyss.

³²Now there was a herd of many swine feeding there on the mountain; and *the demons* implored Him to permit them to enter ᵃthe swine.

started out. ²³As they sailed across, Jesus settled down for a nap. But soon a fierce storm came down on the lake. The boat was filling with water, and they were in real danger.

²⁴The disciples went and woke him up, shouting, "Master, Master, we're going to drown!"

When Jesus woke up, he rebuked the wind and the raging waves. Suddenly the storm stopped and all was calm. ²⁵Then he asked them, "Where is your faith?"

The disciples were terrified and amazed. "Who is this man?" they asked each other. "When he gives a command, even the wind and waves obey him!"

²⁶So they arrived in the region of the Gerasenes,* across the lake from Galilee. ²⁷As Jesus was climbing out of the boat, a man who was possessed by demons came out to meet him. For a long time he had been homeless and naked, living in the tombs outside the town.

²⁸As soon as he saw Jesus, he shrieked and fell down in front of him. Then he screamed, "Why are you interfering with me, Jesus, Son of the Most High God? Please, I beg you, don't torture me!" ²⁹For Jesus had already commanded the evil* spirit to come out of him. This spirit had often taken control of the man. Even when he was placed under guard and put in chains and shackles, he simply broke them and rushed out into the wilderness, completely under the demon's power.

³⁰Jesus demanded, "What is your name?"

"Legion," he replied, for he was filled with many demons. ³¹The demons kept begging Jesus not to send them into the bottomless pit.*

³²There happened to be a large herd of pigs feeding on the hillside nearby, and the demons begged him to let them enter into the pigs.

NASB

And He gave them permission. ³³ And the demons came out of the man and entered the swine; and the herd rushed down the steep bank into the lake and was drowned.

³⁴ When the herdsmen saw what had happened, they ran away and reported it in the city and *out* in the country. ³⁵ *The people* went out to see what had happened; and they came to Jesus, and found the man from whom the demons had gone out, sitting down at the feet of Jesus, clothed and in his right mind; and they became frightened. ³⁶ Those who had seen it reported to them how the man who was demon-possessed had been ªmade well. ³⁷ And all the people of the country of the Gerasenes and the surrounding district asked Him to leave them, for they were gripped with great fear; and He got into a boat and returned. ³⁸ But the man from whom the demons had gone out was begging Him that he might ªaccompany Him; but He sent him away, saying, ³⁹ "Return to your house and describe what great things God has done for you." So he went away, proclaiming throughout the whole city what great things Jesus had done for him.

8:24 ªLit *a calm occurred* 8:28 ªLit *What to me and to you* (a Heb idiom) 8:32 ªLit *them* 8:36 ªOr *saved* 8:38 ªLit *be with*

NLT

So Jesus gave them permission. ³³ Then the demons came out of the man and entered the pigs, and the entire herd plunged down the steep hillside into the lake and drowned.

³⁴ When the herdsmen saw it, they fled to the nearby town and the surrounding countryside, spreading the news as they ran. ³⁵ People rushed out to see what had happened. A crowd soon gathered around Jesus, and they saw the man who had been freed from the demons. He was sitting at Jesus' feet, fully clothed and perfectly sane, and they were all afraid. ³⁶ Then those who had seen what happened told the others how the demon-possessed man had been healed. ³⁷ And all the people in the region of the Gerasenes begged Jesus to go away and leave them alone, for a great wave of fear swept over them.

So Jesus returned to the boat and left, crossing back to the other side of the lake. ³⁸ The man who had been freed from the demons begged to go with him. But Jesus sent him home, saying, ³⁹ "No, go back to your family, and tell them everything God has done for you." So he went all through the town proclaiming the great things Jesus had done for him.

8:26 Other manuscripts read *Gadarenes;* still others read *Gergesenes;* also in 8:37. See Matt 8:28; Mark 5:1. 8:29 Greek *unclean.* 8:31 Or *the abyss,* or *the underworld.*

Our world is a violent, chaotic, unpredictable, dangerous place to live. It wasn't always this way. God created the world to be a hospitable place for people to thrive. Under His original world order, physical needs found abundant supply, freeing humanity to love one another and to enjoy their Creator. Then, humanity twisted His original, created order into something grotesque. In addition to the direct consequences of our individual acts of disobedience, we collectively suffer the cosmic fallout of Adam's sin (Gen. 3). Because of the Fall, we live under the dominion of evil, which subjects humanity to diseases, disasters, discord, death, and decay—evil caused by no one in particular and shared by everyone in common.

God could have left us in the mess we made. He could have turned away or, worse, tossed the whole lot of us into eternal damnation to suffer the just penalty of our rebellion. But He didn't. He made "the problem of evil" His own by becoming one of us in the person of His Son, Jesus Christ. The Son of God came to suffer the world's evil alongside us and to reestablish His dominion.

The first phase of Jesus' campaign to retake the world began with His public announcement in Nazareth, in which He proclaimed that the era of the Messiah had begun (Luke 4:14-30). As the Messiah, He asserted His authority over the synagogue (4:14-37), over demons (4:31-37), over nature (5:1-11), over sin (5:17-26; 7:36-50), over the Sabbath (6:1-11), over disease (4:38-41; 5:12-26; 7:1-10), and over death (7:11-17). And up to this point in the narrative, Luke has emphasized the effect of Jesus' ministry on an individual scale. He provided relief from suffering to thousands of people, but the greater problem of evil remained. While many would have been happy for things to continue as they were, coming to Jesus whenever they needed relief from this affliction or that, Jesus had a greater plan in mind. Healing a few thousand people was only the beginning. He had come to overthrow evil's dominion, to eradicate evil altogether, not merely undo its damage one person and one problem at a time.

Luke 8:22 marks a subtle shift in the public ministry of Jesus. His miracles had been mere skirmishes in His war on evil. Soon, He would take His fight to the source (9:51). In the meantime, His miracles took on a heightened meaning. Instead of merely freeing individuals from the temporal effects of evil, Jesus offered eternal refuge under His dominion, through which His followers could ultimately prevail with Him.

— 8:22 —

At some point, Jesus determined to travel from His present location (not specified by Luke) to "the other side of the lake." The lake was none other than the Sea of Galilee, and His destination, a region lying southeast of the sea. He most likely started out from the harbor in His adopted hometown of Capernaum, but not necessarily. His itinerant ministry could have placed Him anywhere in Upper Galilee. Regardless, it called for a boat ride across a notoriously unpredictable body of water.

Today we view the ocean and other large bodies of water as a necessary part of the planet's health. But to many ancient peoples, the sea was a mysterious, dangerous place, characterized by chaos and possessing the power to kill without warning. And no fate could have been worse than to be swallowed by the sea and have one's remains eaten by fish. To some biblical writers, the sea acted as a symbol, "a principle of disorder, violence, or unrest that marks the old creation" (cf. Ps. 107:23-27; Isa. 57:20; Ezek. 28:8).[34] Even for experienced fishermen, launching out into the middle of the Sea of Galilee was to propel oneself into the unknown.

— 8:23 —

The Sea of Galilee is situated 686 feet (209 meters) below sea level in a deep rift between the Arabian Desert and the Mediterranean Sea. Winds unexpectedly whip through the gorge and churn the sea into a choppy nightmare, especially for the crude sailing craft of the first century. Even today, captains of powered vessels keep a close check on weather reports.

The vessel taken by Jesus and His disciples, which likely included more than just the Twelve, must have been substantial for the time, perhaps even a Roman trade ship. Luke reports that Jesus slept, oblivious to the fierce wind and choppy sea, suggesting He had gone below deck in the hold of the ship. Mark adds the detail that He was *in* the stern, *on* a cushion (Mark 4:38). During their voyage, the boat began to take on water.

Imagine the experience. The vessel was already riding low in the water, loaded with people. The wind caused the boat to list heavily to one side while waves lapped over the hull. All hands on deck frantically bailed water, but more sea poured in than they could remove. Is there any more helpless image than a sinking ship? The disciples became overwhelmed with panic.

— 8:24 —

The double use of the title "Master" heightens the sense of urgency, as does Luke's choice of Greek vocabulary—the term translated "perish" is an extreme word, more dismal and terrifying than "die." The term appears several times in Luke's narrative in reference to damnation (e.g., Luke 4:34; 9:25; 13:3, 5; 15:24, 32; 17:33; 19:10).

Jesus stood up, perhaps came onto the deck (if He indeed was below), and "rebuked" the storm. The Greek term refers to calling attention to wrongdoing and assigning responsibility. It's a close cousin to "reprove" (e.g., 2 Tim. 4:2), except that the desired response is humility instead of conviction. Rebuking also implies the possibility of a consequence, making it the ideal word to describe an authority figure bringing a subordinate back into line. In essence, Jesus woke from His sleep and spoke strong words to the whipping wind and crashing waves: "Oh, shut up!"

Immediately, the wind and waves stopped and "a calm came to be" (literally rendered). The silence must have been deafening. No howling wind. No treacherous waves. Only an eerie stillness of the water as the boat slowly stopped rocking.

— 8:25 —

The Master looked into the faces of His disciples and gently rebuked them with the rhetorical question, "Where is your faith?" The obvious implication was that His followers had no reason to fear the tempest because, with Jesus' presence, they were no longer subject to its destructive power. They were under the dominion of a new King more powerful than the sea.

The men (and perhaps women) stood in "fear" (cf. Luke 5:8-10, 26; 7:16) and "wonder" (*thaumazō* [2296]; see Key Terms on page 25). Their question to one another indicates they didn't fully comprehend Jesus' identity. They had come to accept Him as a prophet—perhaps *the* Prophet (Deut. 18:15-19)—exercising divine authority, but they didn't yet see the full extent of the Lord's mission. As we might say, they failed to connect the dots.

— 8:26-27 —

The "country of the Gerasenes" refers to a region also known as the Decapolis (cf. Mark 5:20), so named for ten Greek city-states settled originally after the conquest of Alexander the Great. The historian Pliny, writing in the first century, listed these cities as Canatha, Damascus, Dion, Gadara, Gerasa, Hippos, Pella, Philadelphia, Rephana, and Scythopolis.[35] Jesus probably landed near the beautiful harbor town known today as Ein Gev. The town of Hippos lay just 2 miles (3.2 kilometers) away on a plateau 1720 feet (525 meters) above the shore.

Soon after arriving, Jesus encountered a man "having demons" (literally translated). It appears that the demons compelled the man to do very unnatural things, things that damage the body and oppose every standard of civilized behavior. He didn't wear clothing. He lived where corpses lie rather than in houses among the living. Matthew adds that he and another like him were violent (Matt. 8:28). Mark's account shares Luke's comment that the attempts to chain him had failed (Luke 8:29), and Mark also states that the townspeople could hear his tormented shrieking day and night as he cut his own flesh with stones (Mark 5:3-5). Furthermore, the demons spoke through the man—using the man's vocal chords—interacting with Jesus as though using the man like a puppet.

— 8:28-29 —

Ironically, the Lord's disciples had asked in fear and astonishment, "Who is this man?" (Luke 8:25, NLT), while the demons had no difficultly recognizing in Jesus the supremacy of God (8:28). The demons' fear, however, was not worshipful awe of the Almighty, but a selfish dread of destruction. Just like before, in Capernaum, the demons tried to intimidate Jesus and then flatter Him (cf. 4:34, 41). These demons tried to suggest He had neither the authority to cast them out nor a vested interest in their activity, but they quickly switched tactics, bowing before Him in feigned worship. Unlike the previous demons mentioned in Luke, these begged for mercy, asking not to be "tormented," a punishment referred to in Revelation 20:10: "And the devil who deceived them was thrown into the lake of fire and brimstone, where the beast and the false prophet are also; and they will be tormented day and night forever and ever."

— 8:30-31 —

When asked their name, the demons answered, "Legion." At the time of Caesar Augustus, a Roman "legion" numbered in the thousands, perhaps in the neighborhood of 6,800![36] Luke doesn't tell us how many demons the man had within him, but suffice it to say, there were many. The man was completely given over to the forces of darkness and helpless to resist their control. When Jesus arrived, however, everything changed. Whereas the demons had brought fear to the man and the people of the region, now the arrival of Jesus caused the demons to tremble. They begged Jesus not to send them to the "abyss."

The word "abyss" comes from the Greek word *abyssos* [12], which literally means "bottomless." Old Testament Jews used this term to refer to the place of the dead, not knowing exactly where it was or what it was like. In the New Testament, the term appears only twice outside of the book of Revelation (here and in Rom. 10:7). Revelation describes "the abyss" as the place from which evil forces come to wage war (Rev. 9:1-2, 11; 11:7; 17:8). The activity of Satan and his demons will crescendo during the Great Tribulation, after which they will be thrown into the *abyssos* for a thousand years (Rev. 20:1-3). During that time, Christ will reign on the earth as its rightful King. After this millennial reign, Satan and his fallen angels will be released for a brief time before meeting their final end: eternal suffering in "the lake of fire"—a place originally prepared for them (Rev. 20:10).

— 8:32-33 —

We can only guess why Jesus allowed the demons to enter the herd of swine (two thousand pigs, according to Mark 5:13) instead of sending them to the abyss. Perhaps He took advantage of their compromise to illustrate the reality of what opposed Him and His followers. Behind the evils of disease, disasters, discord, death, and decay lie the forces of darkness. Evil has a personality—its name is Satan (Luke 4:1-13). He has followers no less dedicated to the destruction of God than their leader is.

When the multitude of demons left the one man and entered the massive heard of swine, the destructive power became too much for the animals to bear. The carnage must have been gruesome to see as a couple thousand (cf. Mark 5:13) screaming, terrorized pigs violently ran (the same word used in Acts 7:57 and 19:29 to describe rioting mobs) down an embankment and plunged into the depths. The sound must have disturbed onlookers as the animals' collective squealing gradually diminished as each disappeared beneath the sea. The symbolism of the spectacle undoubtedly resonated with every disciple watching. Unclean spirits entered unclean animals and then plunged involuntarily into the abyss of the sea. Jesus had condemned evil to drown in its own chaos.

— 8:34-36 —

The herdsmen saw the destruction of their livestock and ran off to report the loss—presumably to the owners of the animals and local officials ("in the city")—as well as spread the gossip throughout the countryside. Their story must have sounded insane, so the herd owners, the town officials, and other people who heard the tale came to see for themselves. While Jesus had condemned the demons to a bottomless, chaotic torment, the man they once tormented finally found freedom from bondage. No longer naked, but clothed. No longer uncontrollable, but seated. No longer living among the tombs, but in his right mind. Moreover, the image of his sitting at the feet of Jesus pictures discipleship. He had become an instant follower.

— 8:37-39 —

The man was unquestionably freed of the demons; no observer could deny it. Yet the townspeople reacted to Jesus' display of divine power with fear (cf. Luke 5:8-10, 26; 7:16; 8:25), though not of the worshipful variety. Luke offers no explanation for the people's fear; he simply describes their request. Moreover, it was not merely the herd owners who sought to prevent further loss of property; "all the people" of the neighboring city and the surrounding territory asked the Lord to depart.

Jesus didn't try to convince them otherwise; He simply left.

The man, contrary to his countrymen, begged Jesus to allow him to join His followers. The imperfect tense suggests the man repeatedly and continually pleaded. Jesus didn't reject the man; He simply had other plans for him. Furthermore, the man was likely a Gentile, which would have unnecessarily complicated the Lord's mission at this stage.

In accordance with the Lord's emphasis on faith yielding obedience, the man did exactly as he was instructed. Jesus said, "Return to your house" and the man "went away." Jesus also said, "Describe what great things God has done for you" and the man "proclaimed" (that is, "preached") to everyone what Jesus had done for him.

• • •

Two miracles down; four to go. The six miracles of Luke 8 and 9 demonstrate that the old world order—the fallen world of disease, disasters, discord, death, and decay—falls impotent before the unlimited power of God, which, of course, Jesus possesses in full. He commands the elements of nature and He wields ultimate authority over the forces of evil. Luke next demonstrates the Lord's power over disease and death.

APPLICATION: LUKE 8:22-39

Arming Yourself for Spiritual Warfare

Spiritual warfare is a serious matter, and I would never want to be guilty of minimizing the threat or underestimating the enemy. On the other hand, a constant focus on spiritual warfare can become a distraction. Some well-meaning theologians, pastors, and teachers have built entire ministries around combating the forces of darkness. Some of the teaching is quite good, and I have gleaned valuable methods from it that I use in my own life and ministry. Unfortunately, the majority of teaching on demonic activity and spiritual warfare is flawed in two respects.

First, *it makes too much of sparse scriptural evidence.* The Bible doesn't give us much information about Satan and demons. Nevertheless, what we have is sufficient. Scripture tells us they are real, they are evil, they traffic in fear and deception, and they are relentlessly opposed to everything God desires. We have no reason to fear, so we can overcome them with confidence in God's power and with truth.

Second, *much of the teaching on spiritual warfare pays too much attention to the wrong spiritual power.* Jesus never went looking for demonic activity, yet He dealt with it immediately and directly when it came looking for Him. We would do well to follow His example. We shouldn't look for demonic activity going on around us. We don't need to wonder if the invisible presence of demons is behind any particular problem. Rather than obsessing over the problem of evil, we are encouraged to fix our gaze on the unequaled power of Jesus Christ (Heb. 12:1-2).

So, how do we respond to the threat of personified evil? I have four observations to summarize and apply.

First, *expect struggles with the forces of darkness.* This world does not operate according to God's rules; it is infected with the presence of evil. Satan and his angels will not relent from their destructive schemes until Christ returns and banishes them to the abyss. Until then, Christian, we are at war and fighting behind enemy lines.

Second, *stand firm by actively living out your faith.* You have nothing to fear. Satan and his minions tremble before the awesome power of God. If you are a believer in Jesus Christ, you have that power living within you in the person of the Holy Spirit. Pursue truth, do what is right, take courage in your salvation, trust in the inevitable victory that God will win over evil, and study His Word so that you can skillfully divide truth from fiction.

Third, *resist the forces of darkness.* If you have dabbled in the occult or sought power from Satan, I must warn you. You have trifled with forces that are far beyond our mental grasp. The occult is not something you can study and harness like electrical energy. Satan is not an inanimate phenomenon of nature. He has a mind, he has been in the business of destroying lives for many thousands of years, and he will not be outwitted by the likes of us. However, he is neither omnipotent nor omnipresent. Our only recourse is to claim God's promise: "Resist the devil and he will flee from you" (Jas. 4:7). We do that by going to the Lord in prayer for everything, resisting the forces of darkness by the power of the Holy Spirit.

If you have experimented with the occult, if you have consciously welcomed the involvement of Satan in your life, I recommend you take a firm stand right now. Here is a prayer that will help orient you in the right direction. It is a prayer, not an incantation or a magic formula. The words have no power in themselves. A prayer is communication with God, and in this case, you are asking for His help.

Find a quiet place where you can spend a few moments in prayer.

My Heavenly Father,

I do here and now renounce any and all allegiance I have ever given to Satan and his demons. And I refuse to accept anything from them, to be influenced by them, or to be used by them in any way whatsoever. I reject all their attacks upon my mind and my body.

I place myself under Your power, and I stand on the truth that the sacrifice Christ made on the cross has paid the penalty of my sins. I understand that, because of the death and resurrection of Jesus, Satan and his angels are defeated foes. I understand that, because I am Yours, Satan and his angels cannot defeat me.

In the name of Jesus Christ, I ask that You protect me from the forces of darkness, that You overcome their power by Yours, and that You remove any influence they would have upon me. I stand upon the promises in Your Word. And in humble faith, I ask that You give me a strong spirit and a wise mind to resist the devil.

I pray this in the name of Jesus Christ. Amen.

When you feel oppressed or fearful, recall the time and place you first prayed this prayer. You don't need to repeatedly ask God for salvation from your sins, but you can regularly ask for His protection and renew your commitment to stand against evil.

Finally, *never forget that believers in Jesus Christ fight on the winning side in the war between good and evil.* We will be injured on occasion, and we will suffer setbacks, but we will certainly have freedom from spiritual bondage. And because we know the outcome, we have every reason to live with confidence.

Never Too Little, Never Too Lost
LUKE 8:40-56

NASB

[40] And as Jesus returned, the [a]people welcomed Him, for they had all been waiting for Him. [41] And there came a man named Jairus, and he was an [a]official of the synagogue; and he fell at Jesus' feet, and *began* to implore Him to come to his house; [42] for he had an [a]only daughter, about twelve years old, and she was dying. But as He went, the crowds were pressing against Him.

[43] And a woman who had a hemorrhage for twelve years, and could not be healed by anyone, [44] came up behind Him and touched the fringe of His [a]cloak, and immediately her hemorrhage stopped. [45] And Jesus said, "Who is the one who touched Me?" And while they were all denying it, Peter said, "Master, the [a]people are crowding and pressing in on You." [46] But Jesus said, "Someone did touch Me, for I was aware that power had gone out of Me." [47] When the woman saw that she had not escaped notice, she came trembling and fell down before Him, and declared in the presence of all the people the reason why she had touched Him, and how she had been immediately healed. [48] And He said to her, "Daughter, your faith has [a]made you well; go in peace."

[49] While He was still speaking, someone came from *the house of* the synagogue official, saying, "Your daughter has died; do not trouble the Teacher anymore." [50] But when Jesus heard *this,* He answered him, "Do not be afraid *any longer;* only believe, and she will be [a]made well." [51] When He came to the house, He did not allow anyone to enter with Him,

NLT

[40] On the other side of the lake the crowds welcomed Jesus, because they had been waiting for him. [41] Then a man named Jairus, a leader of the local synagogue, came and fell at Jesus' feet, pleading with him to come home with him. [42] His only daughter,* who was about twelve years old, was dying.

As Jesus went with him, he was surrounded by the crowds. [43] A woman in the crowd had suffered for twelve years with constant bleeding,* and she could find no cure. [44] Coming up behind Jesus, she touched the fringe of his robe. Immediately, the bleeding stopped.

[45] "Who touched me?" Jesus asked.

Everyone denied it, and Peter said, "Master, this whole crowd is pressing up against you."

[46] But Jesus said, "Someone deliberately touched me, for I felt healing power go out from me." [47] When the woman realized that she could not stay hidden, she began to tremble and fell to her knees in front of him. The whole crowd heard her explain why she had touched him and that she had been immediately healed. [48] "Daughter," he said to her, "your faith has made you well. Go in peace."

[49] While he was still speaking to her, a messenger arrived from the home of Jairus, the leader of the synagogue. He told him, "Your daughter is dead. There's no use troubling the Teacher now."

[50] But when Jesus heard what had happened, he said to Jairus, "Don't be afraid. Just have faith, and she will be healed."

[51] When they arrived at the house, Jesus wouldn't let anyone go in with

NASB

except Peter and John and James, and the girl's father and mother. [52]Now they were all weeping and lamenting for her; but He said, "Stop weeping, for she has not died, but is asleep." [53]And they *began* laughing at Him, knowing that she had died. [54]He, however, took her by the hand and called, saying, "Child, arise!" [55]And her spirit returned, and she got up immediately; and He gave orders for *something* to be given her to eat. [56]Her parents were amazed; but He instructed them to tell no one what had happened.

8:40 ªLit *crowd*   8:41 ªLit *ruler*   8:42 ªOr *only begotten*   8:44 ªOr *outer garment*   8:45 ªLit *crowds*   8:48 ªOr *saved you*   8:50 ªOr *saved*

NLT

him except Peter, John, James, and the little girl's father and mother. [52]The house was filled with people weeping and wailing, but he said, "Stop the weeping! She isn't dead; she's only asleep."

[53]But the crowd laughed at him because they all knew she had died. [54]Then Jesus took her by the hand and said in a loud voice, "My child, get up!" [55]And at that moment her life* returned, and she immediately stood up! Then Jesus told them to give her something to eat. [56]Her parents were overwhelmed, but Jesus insisted that they not tell anyone what had happened.

8:42 Or *His only child, a daughter.*   8:43 Some manuscripts add *having spent everything she had on doctors.*   8:55 Or *her spirit.*

My friend and the former president of Taylor University, Jay Kesler, once boasted with a wink, "I have an office full of pictures in which I'm shaking hands with great dignitaries, all of whom are looking at someone else." Truly great leaders take time to focus on individuals despite the constant pressure to please the masses. If Jesus were to shake your hand, He would look directly through your eyes into your soul because to Him, you matter. In our Lord's eyes, no one is ever too little; no one is ever too lost.

As Jesus came ashore from a trip to the region of the Decapolis, the needs of two very different women demanded His attention. One was the daughter of a prominent leader in the Jewish community; the other an anonymous social outcast. How He would address their competing needs would define His ministry in many ways. Would He favor the one promising greater political advantage? Would He help the helpless at the risk of alienating powerful friends? Or would class distinctions carry any weight at all with Jesus? Would He address the most pressing need and leave the less urgent for later? Or would He recognize that each individual sees his or her need as vital?

All great leaders face this dilemma at some point in their rise to power. They gain momentum by focusing on individuals, but at some point along the way, a choice has to be made. Will they begin to treat their followers as parts of a collective, or will they see people as individuals, each with unique, deeply felt needs?

As Jesus came ashore after a disappointing rejection and a difficult voyage, a dilemma awaited Him.

— 8:40-42 —

Jesus had been asked to leave the Gentile region of the Decapolis, but He returned to an enthusiastic welcome from a multitude keeping watch on the harbor, eagerly anticipating His return. Luke doesn't specify where Jesus landed, but it was most likely Capernaum, His base of operations in Galilee.

By this time in Jesus' ministry, everyone knew that one touch could change everything. Hundreds, perhaps thousands, had experienced a surge of divine power coursing through their bodies, causing maladies of every conceivable kind to vanish. Among the crowd stood an "official of the synagogue." Most likely he was not a rabbi but an elder, a layman responsible for the administration of the synagogue, which included the arrangement of worship services, the selection of teachers, building maintenance, and community affairs. Jewish culture revolved around the leadership of local elders.

The man, Jairus, was undoubtedly well known in the community. While probably wealthy, there's no reason to assume he wasn't devout. The anxious father came to Jesus with a problem no mere human could solve, one that every parent fears. His "one and only" or "only begotten" daughter lay dying in his home. Luke highlights the fact that the girl was twelve years old, the traditional age of consent, the very beginning of adulthood.[37] Unfortunately, the most learned physicians could not help her, so he hoped his influence would convince the renowned healer of Galilee to grant him a favor—one famous man to another. The community leader groveled at Jesus' feet, begging Him to make the journey, which may have been a day's walk or more.

Immediately, Jesus started out, pressing against the crush of bodies surrounding Him.

— 8:43-44 —

As Jesus made His way to the official's house, a woman on the fringes of the crowd took a very different approach from that of Jairus. She didn't ask Jesus for healing; instead, she hoped to siphon some of His power secretly. A continual flow of blood from her womb rendered her perpetually unclean (Lev. 15:25-30). This miserable malady not only kept her from participating in Jewish religious life, but it also prevented her from joining normal social activity. Everyone refused to touch her to avoid becoming ritually unclean themselves. Living the past twelve years on the periphery of society, shunned by all—perhaps her husband as well—had most likely left her doubtful of receiving the Lord's kindness. So, her faith, intermingled with superstition, prompted her to slip between the crush of bodies to steal a touch.

Interestingly, she had been struggling with this illness for as long as the elder's daughter had been alive. During the same twelve years that this little girl had been the sunshine of Jairus's home, a hopelessly ill woman suffered in humiliation and discouragement. The official's only daughter—and perhaps only child—enjoyed privileged status in Jewish society; her father's wealth made her the potential prize of every suitor in Galilee. The unnamed woman, on the other hand, existed on the periphery of the community and was not permitted to be intimate with any man (Lev. 15:24).

A desperate lunge allowed her fingers to touch the "fringe" of Jesus' robe, which most likely refers to a tassel. In those days, devout Jews wore an outer tunic that had four tassels hanging from the hem. Traditionally, the tassels represented the Lord's commands (Num. 15:37-40; Deut. 22:12).[38] The woman probably touched the tassel hanging over Jesus' shoulder.

The word for "touch" (*haptō* [681]) is the same term used for the Lord's healing touch throughout Luke's narrative. As the desperate woman's fingers contacted the tassel of Jesus' tunic, she immediately felt a sudden rush of tingling vitality flow through her limbs, warm the center of her body, and stop the seeping of blood from her body. Imagine! In that moment of time, a dozen years of chronic bleeding, baffled doctors, and shunning neighbors suddenly ended.

— 8:45-48 —

Jesus felt the surge of healing power too. He stopped immediately to ask, "Who is the one who touched Me?" At first, His question may have sounded accusatory. Everyone denied it, despite the fact that a crowd of people had been pressing Him from all sides, which Peter pointed out. Peter said, in effect, "With all of these people pushing and grabbing, who *hasn't* touched You?" But Jesus had sensed the flow of divine power leaving His body, so He continued to search the crowd.

The woman remained silent until she realized her touch hadn't been overlooked in the commotion of bumping and jostling. Then, with her face to the ground, trembling with fear, she explained everything: How she had suffered for so long, how she had tried in vain to reach Him through the crowd, how she knew beyond any fear that one touch from Him would make her whole. She may have expected a rebuke to rain down from Jesus and His followers, but she heard, instead, words of kindness flowing from a heart of compassion.

Jesus called the woman "daughter," not the more formal "woman" as was the custom. He called her by a term of familial endearment, despite the fact He may have been younger than she. He declared that her faith had made the difference. This did not take anything away from divine ability; Jesus merely commended her faith as the component most often missing when people came to Him.

The term translated "made well" is *sōzō* [4982], which literally means "to save," but has a broad range of uses in addition to spiritual salvation. Perhaps, in this case, it is a double entendre. The woman had been saved from her physical condition and, at the same epochal moment, saved from sin. At any rate, the Lord sent her off with a final blessing, "Go in peace," probably using the Hebrew term *shalom* (cf. Luke 7:50).

— 8:49 —

Soon after the word "daughter" fell from Jesus' lips, someone from the synagogue official's house arrived with sad news. The messenger could have been a family member or, more likely, a servant. He bore the news every parent dreads. Jairus's daughter had died. Since the girl was already dead, the messenger saw no reason for the Lord to trouble Himself with a wasted trip.

At this point, it would seem that Jesus had wasted time on an unknown nobody while allowing an important elder's daughter to die. He appeared to have delayed rushing to the emergency situation in order to deal with a less serious problem that had lasted for a dozen years. Dealing with her could have waited. Besides, He didn't have to stop to address the woman. He could have let her have her healing without breaking stride, continued quickly toward Jairus's house, and put forth more effort to arrive before she died.

Take note of the messenger's lack of faith. Luke doesn't comment on the father's thoughts, but the messenger probably said what everyone was thinking: It's too late for the girl; sickness is one thing, death is another. The woman, on the other hand, never doubted the Lord's ability to heal her condition. Earlier, a centurion didn't trouble Jesus with continuing the journey to his home, because he trusted in the limitless power of the Lord to heal, regardless of severity, distance, or any other complication (7:6-9).

— 8:50-51 —

Jesus answered "him" (8:50). The referent is unclear. "Him" could be the messenger or Jairus. It really doesn't matter. The Lord's reassurance was intended for all. Luke's translation of Jesus' reply is short and to the point, consisting of six Greek words.

Mē phobou, monon pisteuson, kai sōthēsetai.
Don't fear, only believe, and she will be saved (my translation).

The term rendered "made well" in the NASB is the same word as in 8:48. In other words, the same faith that saved the woman will save the girl. Sickness or death, it doesn't matter; the result is the same.

When Jesus arrived at the synagogue official's home, He left the crowd behind. In fact, He left the majority of the disciples outside, allowing only Peter, John, and James to enter with Him. This is the first time Jesus gave these three exclusive access to a special event in His ministry, but it would not be the last (9:28; Matt. 17:1; 26:37; Mark 9:2; 14:33). Neither Luke nor the other Gospel accounts reveal the reason for this exclusion, or why these three men in particular; but it seems clear the Lord did this here out of respect for the family. He saw no reason to overburden the house with the jostling mob that had accompanied Him.

— 8:52-53 —

While the multitude remained outside, the house was nevertheless filled with mourners who were present to grieve the girl's death. In keeping with ancient Near Eastern custom, the mourners were "weeping" and "lamenting." The Greek term for "weep" here is different from the term used by John's Gospel to describe that "Jesus wept" (John 11:35). The latter term emphasizes the shedding of tears. The term used here by Luke refers to audible wailing. The term for "lamenting" means "to beat," as in beating the chest as an overt expression of sorrow.

Jesus hushed the cacophony of mourning with the surprising announcement, "She has not died, but is asleep."

Some scholars see this as an example of the Lord's omniscience, announcing the girl was only in a coma. Luke's description of her revival contradicts this, however. "Her spirit returned" to her body (Luke 8:55), indicating that, in death, her spirit had departed. In truth, Luke made clever use of a common euphemism for death (cf. John 11:11-13) to foreshadow the experience of all who place their faith in Christ (1 Cor. 15:20; 1 Thes. 4:13-14). People who die "in Christ" will awaken to new life.

In a moment, the mourners began laughing; not from joy, but in sarcastic, cynical derision. They knew a dead body when they saw one. They were convinced the girl had died and, like every other corpse, would stay dead.

— 8:54-55 —

Ignoring all of that, Jesus took the girl's lifeless hand, which would have rendered Him ritually unclean under normal circumstances. But, as with the unclean touch of the sick woman, divine power trumps tradition every time! He commanded her, "Child, arise!"

Luke again uses the term "immediately" in response to the action of Jesus (Luke 4:39; 5:25; 8:44, 47). Her spirit returned as if summoned, her eyes fluttered open, and without hesitation, she stood up. To help the girl and everyone associated with her to return to normal, Jesus ordered her a meal. As a physician, Luke understood that a restored appetite signaled a return to health.

— 8:56 —

Luke uses the rarer Greek term for "amazed" (*existēmi* [1839]) to describe the reaction of the girl's parents (cf. 2:47; 24:22). It literally means "to remove oneself." Figuratively it means "to lose one's wits" or "go out of one's mind"[39] We would say, "They were blown away." In response, Jesus counseled the couple to tell no one.

Luke doesn't reveal the reason Jesus wanted the couple to remain silent about what had happened. The story lends a few clues, but no one can say conclusively. His counsel stands in sharp contrast to the cleansing of the demoniac in the Decapolis. In that case, the Gentiles feared Jesus' divine power and sent Him away. In Galilee, however, the Lord's popularity made it difficult for Him to move about freely (despite His thinning the ranks by speaking in parables). Telling everyone about the resuscitation of the girl would not have advanced His mission.

Another strong motive lay in the fact that many followed Jesus for selfish motives or were swept up in the excitement His miracles inspired. He had already explained that discipleship is costly; citizenship in the kingdom of God calls for radically countercultural thinking and behavior (6:20-49). In fact, He would soon shift the emphasis of His message. In response to excitement over the benefits of following the Messiah, He would begin to highlight the responsibilities and difficulties (9:22-27, 57-62; 12:11-12; 14:27). It's very possible Jesus wanted to deemphasize the sensational in order to highlight the more sobering aspects of following Him.

• • •

Our King has unlimited power, which gives Him the superhuman ability to address the needs of each person individually, without sacrificing His mission. The Savior came to earth to reclaim His creation from the clutches of evil, yet He never forgot the needs of individuals. The scope of His mission is cosmic, yet in His kingdom, there are no insignificant people.

APPLICATION: LUKE 8:40-56

Not Just Living, but *Really* Living

We are very busy people. We move at a pace that's too fast, say yes too often, engage in too many activities, and commit to too many obligations. We have forgotten how to say no, or we're afraid it's rude to set appropriate limits on our time. As a result, the "to-do" list never gets any shorter, and what's really important rarely makes it to the top. Do you question that? Take a look at *your* to-do list.

Obviously, we have a lot to learn from the One who managed His life well rather than allowing demands to manhandle Him. (We never read that Jesus "hurried" anywhere.) The next time you're "too busy," I have a couple of challenges for you.

First, *realize that all your life is directed by the Lord, not just the things you have planned.*

A couple expects one baby; they get two. A man expected one set of duties in his job; he got another. A woman anticipated living in one place; she had to move—three times! A vacation turns into car repairs. A nest egg becomes a safety net. An MRI report reveals a tumor. A career becomes a new start. All of life—including the unplanned, unexpected, even unwanted circumstances—is directed by God, not just the parts you want. Embrace *every* experience as part of His plan for your life.

Second, *refuse to discount unexpected interruptions.*

How easy it is to view interruptions as distractions from real life when we are in a hurry! If you are living such an efficient life that you have no time for interruptions, then you are missing some of God's best opportunities. Since interruptions are unavoidable—as much as we hate to admit it—maybe it would be wise to build into our schedules some extra room for interruptions. Remember, God's mission cannot ultimately be defeated; the twists and turns in your path are very often your opportunities to show the personal care for individuals that bears witness to God's care for each of us.

Welcome to the War
LUKE 9:1-11

NASB

[1] And He called the twelve together, and gave them power and authority over all the demons and to heal diseases. [2] And He sent them out to proclaim the kingdom of God and to perform healing. [3] And He said to them, "Take nothing for *your* journey, neither a staff, nor a [a]bag, nor bread, nor money; and do not *even* have [b]two tunics apiece. [4] Whatever house you enter, stay there [a]until you leave that city. [5] And as for those who do not receive you, as you go out from that city, shake the dust off your feet as a testimony against them." [6] Departing, they *began* going [a]throughout the villages, preaching the gospel and healing everywhere.

[7] Now Herod the tetrarch heard of all that was happening; and he was greatly perplexed, because it was said by some that John had risen from the dead, [8] and by some that Elijah had appeared, and by others that one of the prophets of old had risen again. [9] Herod said, "I myself had John beheaded; but who is this man about whom I hear such things?" And he kept trying to see Him.

[10] When the apostles returned, they gave an account to Him of all that they had done. Taking them with Him, He withdrew by Himself to a city called Bethsaida. [11] But the crowds were aware of this and followed Him; and welcoming them,

NLT

[1] One day Jesus called together his twelve disciples* and gave them power and authority to cast out all demons and to heal all diseases. [2] Then he sent them out to tell everyone about the Kingdom of God and to heal the sick. [3] "Take nothing for your journey," he instructed them. "Don't take a walking stick, a traveler's bag, food, money,* or even a change of clothes. [4] Wherever you go, stay in the same house until you leave town. [5] And if a town refuses to welcome you, shake its dust from your feet as you leave to show that you have abandoned those people to their fate."

[6] So they began their circuit of the villages, preaching the Good News and healing the sick.

[7] When Herod Antipas, the ruler of Galilee,* heard about everything Jesus was doing, he was puzzled. Some were saying that John the Baptist had been raised from the dead. [8] Others thought Jesus was Elijah or one of the other prophets risen from the dead.

[9] "I beheaded John," Herod said, "so who is this man about whom I hear such stories?" And he kept trying to see him.

[10] When the apostles returned, they told Jesus everything they had done. Then he slipped quietly away with them toward the town of Bethsaida. [11] But the crowds found out where he

NASB

He *began* speaking to them about the kingdom of God and curing those who had need of healing.

9:3 ªOr *knapsack* or *beggar's bag* ᵇOr *inner garments* 9:4 ªLit *and leave from there* 9:6 ªOr *from village to village*

NLT

was going, and they followed him. He welcomed them and taught them about the Kingdom of God, and he healed those who were sick.

9:1 Greek *the Twelve;* other manuscripts read *the twelve apostles.* 9:3 Or *silver coins.* 9:7 Greek *Herod the tetrarch.* Herod Antipas was a son of King Herod and was ruler over Galilee.

Jesus came to earth to overthrow the dominion of evil and to reestablish the kingdom of God. Throughout His ministry, He exercised His authority to that end, but He always intended to replicate His ministry. He called twelve men to become His apprentice soldiers in the war on evil and gave them ample opportunity to watch and learn. The apostles-in-training assisted, but up until now, the Lord had done all the ministering. The Twelve brought people to be healed, and Jesus touched their diseased or distorted bodies. The Twelve probably took care of Jesus' physical needs and arranged the details of His travel so He could concentrate on teaching. The Twelve observed, listened, questioned, and learned, but Jesus instructed. It was Jesus who cast out the evil spirits. All that would now change. The time had come for His trainees to put their learning into practice. It was time for the Twelve to enter the battle, firsthand.

— 9:1-2 —

Jesus called the Twelve together and charged them with a mission. They were to replicate His ministry of proclaiming the kingdom of God. Furthermore, they were to illustrate the reality of God's kingdom on earth by casting out demons and healing diseases—just like Jesus had done.

To prepare them for ministry, Jesus delegated to the Twelve His divine power and His divine authority. These two things may sound the same, but they are quite different. The first is *dynamis* [1411] ("power"), the divine ability to accomplish the impossible. He infused them with capabilities they did not have on their own (cf. 4:14, 36; 5:17; 6:19; 8:46). The second is *exousia* [1849] ("authority"), the right to carry out the Lord's mission.

A good way to illustrate the difference is to imagine a police officer directing traffic. He wears a gun, which gives him the power or the ability to physically subdue a criminal. Without the power of his weapon, he would have a more difficult time overpowering a violent thug. But he also wields authority delegated to him by the city. He lacks the power to stop a car physically—2,000 pounds of metal going 45 miles per hour would kill him instantly—but by merely holding out his hand, he stops cars by *command.* Drivers must obey his authoritative commands or suffer the consequences brought down by the government that authorized him.

Jesus granted the Twelve the power to accomplish humanly impossible feats, and He delegated His divine authority so they could command diseases and demons to depart. He equipped them to accomplish a specific task: to proclaim the kingdom of God and to back up their preaching with miraculous, divine kindness. They were to proclaim the word and perform good works—two essential duties of discipleship in general, and vocational ministry in particular.

The Greek word for "proclaim" is *kēryssō* [2784], an activity that was accomplished by a *kēryx* [2783], a herald. Today we have public media. To hear from the president, prime minister, or monarch, we turn to the television, the radio, or the Internet. In ancient days, the herald appeared in the city square or public kiosk to speak on behalf of the government. Based on his delegated authority, the words of the herald carried the full weight of the law.

Jesus proclaimed the kingdom of God, but He did so on His own authority as its King. Now He sent the Twelve with His authority to proclaim and His power to back up their proclamation.

— 9:3-4 —

After defining their mission and equipping the Twelve, Jesus gave them specific advice. First, travel light. He counseled against the normal preparation for travel, which included at least five items forbidden by Jesus: a staff, a knapsack, food, money, and a change of clothes. Each item represents a different need that He wanted the men to trust God to provide.

A staff made walking easier, but it was used as a weapon of defense as well. Travelers faced the very real danger of robbery, especially in remote areas. To keep themselves safe, people banded together, hoping their large numbers would discourage outlaws. They carried a long pole to fight off attacks, when necessary.

The Greek word translated "bag" is *pēra* [4082], which one lexicon defines as "the open sack carried on the left hip by a strap over the right shoulder and used by peasants, shepherds, beggars, and wandering philosophers."[40] Jesus not only wanted them to avoid any symbolic association with beggars and wandering philosophers, He wanted the Twelve to travel without provisions. Today, He would say, "Don't pack even so much as a carry-on bag."

Ancient speakers and writers often used the word "bread" to mean food in general. And "money" is self-explanatory. He told the men to go out with no means of providing their own next meal.

A "tunic" was an inner garment worn next to the skin under an outer garment. By telling the men not to take an extra tunic, He said, essentially, "Don't even pack a change of underwear."

When you put it all together, it becomes reasonably clear that Jesus intended this as hyperbole, exaggeration for the sake of effect. Today, He might say, "Get going right away. Don't worry about safety, don't pack an overnight bag, don't bother with food or money, don't even take a change of underwear. Just go." His point was twofold. First, the mission can't wait; people need to hear the proclamation of the gospel *now*. Second, God will provide for the people in His service; trust Him.

While the men were not to depend upon their own resources, Jesus did expect them to make full use of ancient Near Eastern hospitality, which every household offered as a sacred duty. Moreover, the men were to avoid moving around unnecessarily. Once they arrived in a city, they were to focus on the mission, not accommodations. Additionally, He wanted them to avoid the appearance of sponging off the local residents or seeking better hosts.

In short, He counseled the men to *travel light and trust God.*

— 9:5 —

He also prepared His men for the inevitable. They had seen the poor reception Jesus received in the country of the Gerasenes (8:37). If people rejected the Son of God, certainly they would reject His emissaries. If they proclaimed the gospel in the synagogue of a city and the leaders rejected their message or asked them to leave, the Twelve were to leave.

The act of shaking off the dust of a place symbolized a complete break in association. Jews leaving Gentile soil often shook the dust from their feet as a token of rejecting Gentile uncleanness.[41] Jesus used the image to encourage the Twelve to put rejection behind them and to pursue their cause wherever opportunities arose.

He counseled the Twelve to *toughen up and stay focused.* Frankly, that's excellent advice to all who minister today. I've said for years that the best combination is a tender heart and a tough hide.

— 9:6-9 —

The Twelve did exactly as they were told. According to Mark's Gospel, the men worked in pairs (Mark 6:7). Six teams of two traveled all over Galilee. They may have gone into Judea, but all three synoptic Gospels focus on Galilee at this stage in Jesus' ministry. Luke's presentation implies an extended time of travel, requiring several weeks or perhaps even months.

Word of the Lord's ministry conducted by the Lord and His disciples eventually traveled to the palace of the Galilean ruler. "Herod the tetrarch" is Herod Antipas. The title "tetrarch" refers to the divided rule of Herod the Great after his death, whereby each of three sons received a territory of his own. (See map, "Israel after Herod the Great," page 82.) Instead of a "monarchy" (rule by one), Israel became a "tetrarchy" (rule by four). The fourth ruler was Rome, which retained direct control over lands not given to a son of Herod the Great.

Herod Antipas grew nervous when he heard these reports, worrying that his old nemesis John the Baptizer had risen from the dead. John's public scorn for Antipas's unlawful affair with and marriage to his brother's wife resulted in Antipas's throwing John in prison for two years (see Luke 3:19-20 and comments there). Antipas's impulsive execution of John, which Luke does not record (cf. Matt. 14:6-11; Mark 6:17-28) but is aware of, is implied in the present passage. Suddenly, it seemed Herod's problems had come back to haunt him, literally.

Other reports suggested Elijah had reappeared. Elijah had been the nemesis of Ahab, an idolatrous, debauched king of Israel, who just happened to rule over the same territory given to Antipas. Whether Herod believed the reports or not, he had to take public opinion seriously. Therefore, the tetrarch was "seeking to see Him" (literally rendered), meaning he made repeated attempts to see Jesus in person. Most likely, this means he sent several messages to Jesus requesting a visit or perhaps proposing a meeting. Apparently, Jesus ignored all of the ruler's requests.

— 9:10-11 —

Several weeks or even months later, the Twelve returned to Capernaum. To escape the crowds and to debrief His trainees in private, Jesus took them about 4 miles (6.4 kilometers) northeast to Bethsaida, the hometown of Andrew, Peter, and Philip (John 1:44; 12:21). Its name means "place of hunting," and it was a small village until Philip the tetrarch, the brother of Antipas, enlarged it to support a private residence.

According to Josephus, the tetrarch was buried there in AD 34 and the town was later renamed Bethsaida Julias in honor of Augustus's daughter.[42] The town lay near the bank of the Jordan River and offered a quiet retreat from the bustle of Capernaum.

Jesus gave the men a chance to unwind and "give an account" of their experience. He undoubtedly evaluated their work, gave constructive criticism, affirmed their many successes, answered their questions, explained the broader context of their work, and calmly prepared them for the future. Then they left to retreat in Bethsaida.

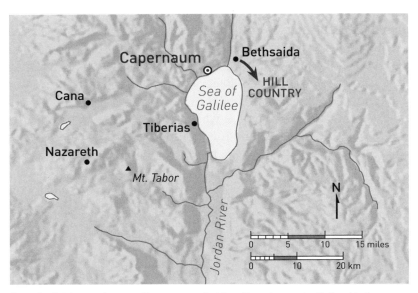

Jesus' ministry center was Capernaum, but he slipped away to Bethsaida for some quiet time with his disciples. In the countryside, He taught the crowds that followed him, but as evening approached, the disciples wanted to send them back to Bethsaida and other nearby villages for food.

During the debriefing process, Jesus and the Twelve apparently started out in Bethsaida and then retreated farther into the hill country (cf. Luke 9:12). Meanwhile, the multitudes found out where Jesus had gone and followed Him. By the time the crowds caught up with Jesus and the apostles, they were in the remote hill country on the eastern side of the Sea of Galilee.

Jesus didn't rebuke the crowd or say, "Why don't you leave us alone? Give us a break—we're trying to get just a little time to ourselves!" Ever the accessible and patient Savior, He welcomed them and continued His ministry of proclaiming the kingdom of God and reversing the effects of evil.

APPLICATION: LUKE 9:1-11

Secrets of a Lasting Ministry

The instructions Jesus gave His disciples before sending them out were specific to them—their time, their mission, their circumstances, their particular needs in the training process. Still, I find in the Lord's words some helpful guidelines for ministry today—or for any vocation, for that matter.

First, *prepare well, but travel light*. That's a difficult balance to maintain. We tend to think of good preparation as packing more stuff for the journey, but Jesus sent the disciples out with nearly nothing. I don't think He did this to teach them a new model of ministry: "Don't plan; just go; wing it." In fact, later, when announcing His departure from the earth, He gave them different instructions (22:35-36). Instead, He used this exercise to help them achieve some balance. He sent them out with no provisions, telling them to travel light and stay focused on the mission.

If we're not careful, we'll get so caught up in planning for every contingency that we'll forget about the mission itself. By traveling light, as it were, we spend less time thinking about *how* we meet the objectives and focus more on actually getting them accomplished.

Second, *lighten up and get tough*. Jesus knew before the disciples departed that rejection would be waiting for them in a number of towns. He encouraged them to spend little time trying to overcome objections and more time finding receptive hearts.

Not everyone *wants* the truth. Not everyone will like what you have to say or how you get something done. Listen to objections and take in constructive criticism, but don't fear what people think or say in response. If you do, you'll spend more time thinking about what critics think than what Christ thinks. Ask God for thicker skin and learn to laugh at yourself. It will help.

Third, *invite the evaluation of people you trust and respect*. When the disciples returned, they debriefed the mission with Jesus. In fact, He took them on a disciples' retreat in order to rest and reflect. Getting the people you trust and respect to offer helpful critique and constructive praise will help you plan better and worry less. In addition, the carping criticism of others will carry less weight.

A Shocking Agenda
LUKE 9:12-27

NASB

¹²Now the day ªwas ending, and the twelve came and said to Him, "Send the crowd away, that they may go into the surrounding villages and countryside and find lodging and get ᵇsomething to eat; for here we are in a desolate place." ¹³But He said to them, "You give them *something* to eat!" And they said, "We have no more than five loaves and two fish, unless perhaps we go and buy food for all these people." ¹⁴(For there were about five thousand men.) And He said to His disciples, "Have them ªsit down *to eat* in groups of about fifty each." ¹⁵They did so, and had them all ªsit down. ¹⁶Then He took the five loaves and the two fish, and looking up to heaven, He blessed them, and broke *them,* and kept giving *them* to the disciples to set before the ªpeople. ¹⁷And they all ate and were satisfied; and ªthe broken pieces which they had left over were picked up, twelve baskets *full.*

¹⁸And it happened that while He was praying alone, the disciples were with Him, and He questioned them, saying, "Who do the ªpeople say that I am?" ¹⁹They answered and said, "John the Baptist, and others *say* Elijah; but others, that one of the prophets of old has risen again." ²⁰And He said to them, "But who do you say that I am?" And Peter answered and said, "The ªChrist of God." ²¹But He ªwarned them and instructed *them* not to tell this to anyone, ²²saying, "The Son of Man must suffer many things and be rejected by the elders and chief priests and scribes, and be killed and be raised up on the third day."

NLT

¹²Late in the afternoon the twelve disciples came to him and said, "Send the crowds away to the nearby villages and farms, so they can find food and lodging for the night. There is nothing to eat here in this remote place."

¹³But Jesus said, "You feed them."

"But we have only five loaves of bread and two fish," they answered. "Or are you expecting us to go and buy enough food for this whole crowd?" ¹⁴For there were about 5,000 men there.

Jesus replied, "Tell them to sit down in groups of about fifty each." ¹⁵So the people all sat down. ¹⁶Jesus took the five loaves and two fish, looked up toward heaven, and blessed them. Then, breaking the loaves into pieces, he kept giving the bread and fish to the disciples so they could distribute it to the people. ¹⁷They all ate as much as they wanted, and afterward, the disciples picked up twelve baskets of leftovers!

¹⁸One day Jesus left the crowds to pray alone. Only his disciples were with him, and he asked them, "Who do people say I am?"

¹⁹"Well," they replied, "some say John the Baptist, some say Elijah, and others say you are one of the other ancient prophets risen from the dead."

²⁰Then he asked them, "But who do you say I am?"

Peter replied, "You are the Messiah* sent from God!"

²¹Jesus warned his disciples not to tell anyone who he was. ²²"The Son of Man* must suffer many terrible things," he said. "He will be rejected by the elders, the leading priests, and the teachers of religious law. He will be killed, but on the third day he will be raised from the dead."

23 And He was saying to *them* all, "If anyone wishes to come after Me, he must deny himself, and take up his cross daily and follow Me. 24 For whoever wishes to save his ªlife will lose it, but whoever loses his ªlife for My sake, he is the one who will save it. 25 For what is a man profited if he gains the whole world, and loses or forfeits himself? 26 For whoever is ashamed of Me and My words, the Son of Man will be ashamed of him when He comes in His glory, and *the glory* of the Father and of the holy angels. 27 But I say to you truthfully, there are some of those standing here who will not taste death until they see the kingdom of God."

9:12 ªLit *began to decline* ᵇLit *provisions* 9:14 ªLit *recline* 9:15 ªLit *recline* 9:16 ªLit *crowd* 9:17 ªLit *that which was left over to them of the broken pieces was* 9:18 ªLit *crowds* 9:20 ªI.e. Messiah 9:21 ªOr *strictly admonished* 9:24 ªOr *soul*

23 Then he said to the crowd, "If any of you wants to be my follower, you must give up your own way, take up your cross daily, and follow me. 24 If you try to hang on to your life, you will lose it. But if you give up your life for my sake, you will save it. 25 And what do you benefit if you gain the whole world but are yourself lost or destroyed? 26 If anyone is ashamed of me and my message, the Son of Man will be ashamed of that person when he returns in his glory and in the glory of the Father and the holy angels. 27 I tell you the truth, some standing here right now will not die before they see the Kingdom of God."

9:20 Or *the Christ. Messiah* (a Hebrew term) and *Christ* (a Greek term) both mean "anointed one." 9:22 "Son of Man" is a title Jesus used for himself.

The Twelve followed their Master to Bethsaida and then beyond, into the hill country, eager to report their experiences and—best of all—to enjoy a period of much-needed rest. They had returned with mixed emotions: exhausted after long days of ministry but energized by their experiences. After watching Jesus exercise divine authority over the dominion of evil, healing the sick and commanding demons to release their victims, they never dreamed of having that kind of power themselves. They had contented themselves with the privilege of assisting the Messiah, perhaps one day ruling under His administration. But then they received power and authority from Jesus. For several weeks, the Twelve fanned out across Galilee, proclaiming the arrival of God's kingdom and validating their message with Messiah-like miracles. While physically demanding, those weeks on the road must have felt absolutely intoxicating!

But before they could process all that had happened, and before they had a chance to regain their strength, a sea of people washed up to their hips, bringing with them waves of human need. Suddenly, in spite of their recent infusion of divine power, the Twelve found themselves powerless to meet the most basic human need of all: the need to eat.

— 9:12 —

When the Twelve had returned from their travels, the Lord invited them to join Him on a retreat to Bethsaida, a small village 4 miles northeast of Capernaum (9:10). From there, the men withdrew into the hill country along the northeast shore of the Sea of Galilee (9:12). In the remote yet relatively fertile wilderness, Jesus and His men would camp under the stars and be able to spend the time in reflection and easy conversation. But word spread of their whereabouts, drawing thousands of followers into the wilderness after them (9:11).

Jesus graciously received the crowd of disciples. After all, ministry is rarely convenient. And after a long day of teaching and healing, the crowd needed provisions. This was a teachable moment that Jesus was not about to waste.

As the sun began to set, the Twelve urged Jesus to send the crowd away. It is possible that they had reached their physical and emotional limits and were thinking only about their own needs rather than the needs of the people. Of course, all people have their limits, including apostles—and preachers, evangelists, music pastors, children's leaders, and certainly counselors. Let's face it: Even the Son of God had physical limits during His earthly ministry. Jesus didn't use this teachable moment to turn the Twelve into holy workaholics. He understood the need for ministers to retreat from ministry. He regularly pulled away from the crowds to pray, and He savored Sabbath rest each week as God had intended. Nevertheless, the burden of ministry never sleeps. So, what's a minister to do? There isn't a Christian worker reading these words who hasn't asked that very question again and again and again!

— 9:13-14 —

The disciples had been proclaiming, healing, and casting out demons for weeks, but they knew their limitations. Jesus surprised them with a challenge, knowing the task exceeded their ability. According to the Gospel of John, "This He was saying to test him [Philip], for He Himself knew what He was intending to do" (John 6:6).

The Twelve searched for what they could find and found nothing but a mere five loaves of bread and two small fish. John's narrative tells us the food had been brought by a young boy, and he would not likely carry a large amount, so neither the loaves nor the fish could have been very large. The apostles also considered purchasing food, but the size of the multitude made this impractical. Luke adds the parenthetical note that there were five thousand men, which didn't include women and children (Matt. 14:21). The crowd could have been as many as twelve to fifteen thousand people. Unfortunately, not one of the disciples thought to ask Jesus for provision.

He instructed them to organize the multitude for food distribution.

— 9:15-16 —

The disciples divided the multitude into groups and arranged an efficient distribution plan. Jesus gave thanks for God's provision and began breaking the bread and pulling off pieces of fish . . . again and again and yet again. For hours, He multiplied the little boy's supply (John 6:9) and passed the abundance to His team of disciples, who "gave them something to eat!" (see Luke 9:13).

As the men made dozens of trips, carrying baskets of food from Jesus to the multitude, their paradigm of ministry undoubtedly changed. They had indeed received power and authority from the Messiah to carry out His ministry, but only as they continually came to Him for provision. Their power to proclaim, to heal, and to cast out demons could never be separated from ongoing dependence upon their Master. The formula remains sound to this day: He is the supply; His disciples are the conduit.

— 9:17 —

As the requests for food dwindled to nothing, Jesus completed the ministry lesson with a final task. The Twelve gathered the leftover pieces of bread and fish the Lord had broken, presumably those that remained after all the people were full. Each of the disciples gathered enough to fill a *kophinos* [2894], a wicker basket used by travelers to carry enough provision for a journey of two or three days (Judg. 6:19; Ps. 81:6).

Do the math. Twelve men. Twelve baskets of provisions for a journey. Far more than each had with him when Jesus first sent them off to minister in pairs (Luke 9:3).

Jesus taught the men to embrace their inadequacies as an opportunity to let the power of God flow through them and accomplish the impossible. He taught His apprentice ministers, the future leaders of God's kingdom, to lead with empty, upturned hands. He taught the apostles to face with complete abandon the impossible tasks they would soon encounter, admitting their own inadequacies in order to receive the Lord's overabundant supply.

All four Gospels report the miracle of Jesus feeding the multitude in the wilderness. Four men share four perspectives to make four different points. All of them true, of course, but different in their emphases and choice of details. Compared to the others, Luke's narrative is very brief, comprising only six verses to John's fourteen. Rather than focus on the event itself, he used the incident as a bridge between the disciples' victory over evil and the Lord's revelation of His true agenda.

- The disciples minister in power throughout Galilee. (9:5-11)
- Jesus feeds the multitude through the disciples. (9:12-17)
- Jesus explains the need for the Messiah to suffer, die, and rise again. (9:18-22)
- Jesus defines discipleship as joining the Messiah in His suffering. (9:23-27)

— 9:18 —

Luke's characteristic phrase "And it happened" is his way of changing the setting and scenery while continuing the story. In other words, the story spans a break in the action, which may have been days or even weeks in duration. We know from the other Gospel accounts that other events took place immediately after Jesus fed the multitude.

Jesus habitually pulled away from ministry among the multitudes for solitary prayer (5:16; 6:12; 9:28), although the Twelve were never far away. In the quiet of their retreat, He asked a loaded question, "Who do the people say that I am?" The term for "people" here is literally "crowds." Jesus asked about the consensus of the rumor mill.

— 9:19-20 —

Luke's placing this question in such close proximity to the feeding of the crowd is crucial to understanding the issue at hand. The Gospel of John reports that the multitude present for the feeding miracle called Him "the Prophet" (Deut. 18:15-18) and "were intending to come and take Him by force to make Him king" (John 6:14-15). The broader populace, including those who did not follow Jesus closely, agreed that Jesus was someone special, but each had his or her own theory as to how or why. John the Baptizer back from the dead (Luke 9:7)? An ancient prophet returning to announce the revival of Israel (Mal. 4:5-6)? As theories abounded, only a very few thought of Jesus as the Messiah. Answers from the rumor mill reflected the sad truth. Even after weeks of ministry in their midst, ignorance and superstition dominated the collective mind of Galilee. The apostles probably shook their heads and remarked, "We still have a lot of work to do." But Jesus cared more about what His own students thought. He turned the question to them. "Who do you [plural] say that I am?"

Peter gave the right answer—the perfect answer, in fact—"the Christ of God." But time would prove that the brash disciple understood his confession like I understand $E=mc^2$. I can quote it. I know it is Einstein's mass-energy equation. I know it is the basis of atomic power, and that it has changed our thinking forever. But please don't ask me to explain it!

The word "Christ" comes from the Greek term *Christos* [5547], the Greek translation of the Hebrew word *mashiach* [H4899], which we transliterate as "Messiah." Both words mean "anointed one." In many ancient Near Eastern cultures, a person receiving special recognition would participate in a ceremony in which a small amount of olive oil was poured over the head. The honor came as a reward for valor on the battlefield or victory over a national enemy. The Hebrews eventually reserved it for commissioning their national leader. In Israel, "the Lord's anointed" (e.g., 1 Sam. 2:10) was none other than the reigning king.

For centuries, hopeful Jews looked for a very special king—an ultimate Messiah, promised by prophets of old, who would supersede all of Israel's past "anointed ones." This person would not be merely *a* christ, but *the* Christ. Isaiah and other prophets predicted that this ultimate king of Israel would lead God's people to a glorious future. His reign would launch an unprecedented period of agricultural and economic superabundance. He would free the nation from foreign tyranny, and he would expand his dominion to bring the entire world under his sovereign rule. Consequently, people looking for the Messiah, the Christ, expected a political figure who would raise an army, recapture the glory days of David and Solomon, subdue the Romans, and establish a worldwide Jewish empire.

— 9:21-22 —

Sharing such Messianic claims would not have served Jesus' agenda very well. The Jewish people were already chafing under Roman domination. Many zealots were itching for revolt. On more than one occasion a man had called himself the messiah and then led his hapless insurrectionists to a pathetic death. Jesus didn't want to incite the multitudes. Besides, He had a radically different plan, a shocking agenda that didn't propel Him to the top of Jewish politics. On the contrary, He planned to be crushed beneath Jerusalem's body politic. His path led to the cross.

Jesus told the men to keep His identity as the Messiah quiet until they understood everything as they should. Until then, their proclamation of the Messiah would have been neither accurate (in terms of what it meant) nor productive. He then gave His closest followers difficult news, critical information He had withheld until now. This message is a fourfold one.

The compound sentence of Luke 9:22 is structured with four infinitive verbs that tell what must happen. "It is necessary," the Lord said, "that the Son of Man should":

- "Suffer"—Not only does this predict His immediate future, the image also alludes to Isaiah's "suffering servant" song (Isa. 52:13–53:12).
- "Be rejected"—This idea harkens back to the many Old Testament predictions that the Jewish rulers will reject the Messiah. The stone rejected by Israel's builders will become the chief stone (Ps. 118:22; Luke 20:17). The "elders and chief priests and scribes" are those men who comprised the Sanhedrin, Israel's ruling council.
- "Be killed"—In light of their misplaced messianic expectations, the disciples would have found this most confusing of all. How can a dead man vanquish Israel's foes and rule the world?
- "Be raised"—Astute expositors call this kind of passive verb a "divine passive." Both the lack of a specific object and the context imply that God will complete the action of the verb. God will do the raising.

This was not the agenda the apostles had in mind for Jesus. In their experience, the future looked bright. Jesus had been winning victories at every turn. He silenced His critics with flawless logic. He healed thousands. He put demons to flight everywhere He went. He taught spellbinding lessons. As a result, He attracted more followers with each passing day. Besides all that, the disciples were just beginning to imitate their Master.

Just when things started looking hopeful, Jesus announced that He—their one and only leader—would soon die!

— 9:23 —

Let's face it: Almost anyone would be willing to sacrifice his or her old life for the chance to rule with the Messiah in His worldwide, Jewish empire. That's a risk well worth taking. Who wouldn't trade a mundane, middle-class, workaday existence for ultimate power, immense popularity, and fabulous wealth in the king's administration? Were the disciples in for a surprise!

Jesus clarified what becoming a part of His kingdom entailed. He was brief and to the point. His triumphant march into the capital city would not end in victory, at least not in the short term. Not in *this* life. To join the Lord's conquering force was to follow Him into suffering. This required obedience to three explicit commands.

First, a disciple must deny himself or herself. Denial doesn't necessarily mean depriving oneself of earthly pleasures. Following Christ may or may not require that. The emphasis on "denying oneself" is submission to His agenda, saying no to what we want and saying yes to what He wants. Christianity is not obedience to a set of rules or the adoption of a certain philosophy; Christianity is absolute obedience to the person of Jesus Christ.

Second, a disciple must take up his or her cross. Executioners forced a condemned person to carry the implement of death to the place of execution. Therefore, to take up one's cross was to die to one's own agenda. Furthermore, the disciple had to do this daily.

Third, a disciple must follow Christ. The Greek term means, literally, "to move behind someone in the same direction, come after."[43] The main idea is to do as He did, to follow in His footsteps. He gave all for the sake of the kingdom of God, holding loosely all earthly things. For Him, the path led to death. The path of His disciples may or may not lead there, but true disciples must be willing to walk behind their Master regardless.

— 9:24 —

Jesus offered three logical reasons to accept His threefold challenge. Luke begins each with the Greek explanatory particle *gar* [1063], which expresses cause. It is often translated "for" or "because."

The first reason involves a paradox about the concept of life. For Jesus, physical life subject to the dominion of evil is no life at all. It only makes sense to spend one's physical life in such a way as to guarantee eternal, spiritual life in the kingdom of God. The Greek word translated "life" in 9:24 is *psychē* [5590], which can mean either "life" or "soul." Therefore, we can paraphrase the paradox two ways, both of which are correct.

> Whoever wishes to save his physical life will lose his spiritual life, but whoever turns over his physical life for My agenda, he is the one who will get to keep his spiritual life.

And/or

> Whoever wishes to save his soul will lose his soul, but whoever turns over his soul for My agenda, he is the one who will get to keep his soul.

The first rejects selfishness. The second rejects self-righteousness.

— 9:25 —

The second logical reason Jesus gives compounds the first by comparing the worth of one's eternal life to all the wealth in the world. ("The whole world" is a metonym[44] for vast wealth. "Himself" is a metonym for the soul.) The rhetorical question asks if someone makes a wise investment by forfeiting himself—his or her existence—for vast riches. It's an absurd question because someone who does not exist cannot enjoy riches or anything else! In today's terms, "How stupid is *that*?"

— 9:26 —

The third reason involves a sober warning. The idea of shame here points back to 9:23, which pictures crucifixion, the most shameful death imaginable in the first century. The Romans developed this manner of execution into a gruesome art form. They designed the whole process (from beginning to end) to heighten pain and to maximize shame. Victims were cruelly ridiculed during scourging, stripped naked, made to carry their own cross, suspended high enough for passersby to see, hung beneath a sign declaring their crimes, taunted on the cross, and then left to rot after death.

To refuse to partake in Christ's suffering and selflessness is to reject Him as Master. When the Lord returns in power, vindicated in the end, He will reject those who have rejected Him.

— 9:27 —

Jesus concluded His discourse with a bold reassurance. Some of the Twelve—but not all!—would see the kingdom of God inaugurated in their lifetimes. Inaugurated, though not consummated. There's a big difference.

Some fine expositors suggest that the Lord's promise refers to His transfiguration eight days later, that His bodily transformation and His meeting with Moses and Elijah was a temporary manifestation of God's kingdom on earth. As such, three of the disciples did, indeed, "see" the coming kingdom of God. They received a foretaste of the kingdom before tasting death. But I don't find this suggestion satisfying for a couple of reasons.

First, this seems like a stingy fulfillment of a big promise, not unlike promising a child he will get to "see" Disney World soon, only to give him a video documentary of the park for his birthday. Luke's account highlights the anticipation of every godly Jew for the coming of God's kingdom, the righteous rule of the Messiah (1:68; 2:25, 38; 23:51). It was a matter of singular importance to genuine believers. The Transfiguration, as glorious as it was, would not have met the expectations Jesus created in the minds of His disciples.

Second, the Lord's choice of words suggests He had a later event in mind. He qualified "some" with two phrases: "standing here" and "will not taste death." If He had intended the Transfiguration just eight days later, the phrase "will not taste death" seems odd. If, however, he intended to exclude Judas, who died before the Lord's resurrection, His ascension, and the coming of the Holy Spirit (Acts 1:6-8), the double qualification makes better sense.

Luke's understanding of the kingdom of God tends to favor the coming of the Holy Spirit as the appearance of the kingdom, the church age as the period of spiritual growth of the kingdom (cf. Luke 13:18-21), and the end-time events as the consummation of the physical kingdom. Just before Jesus ascended to heaven, His followers asked, "Is it at this time You are restoring the kingdom to Israel?" (Acts 1:6). The Lord's answer makes it clear that the kingdom of God has come to earth, but it has not yet come in its complete form (Acts 1:7-8). The King has been crowned, but He has not yet taken His place on His earthly throne. A usurper continues to reign on earth as though he were our legitimate ruler. Jesus does not yet rule over Israel; the descendants of Abraham, Isaac, and Jacob have yet to possess all of the land promised to them; and the dominion of evil continues to dominate the world. Many of the prophecies concerning the Messiah's triumphant reign have not yet been fulfilled. Nevertheless, there is a sense in which some of the disciples "saw" the kingdom of God in their generation just as we "see" the kingdom today.

While the full, literal fulfillment of the kingdom promises will occur when Christ returns "in His glory, and the glory of the Father and of the holy angels," His followers can become citizens of His kingdom now. In the weeks and months to come, as Jesus began His journey toward Jerusalem (Luke 9:51–19:27), He would explain how.

APPLICATION: LUKE 9:12-27

Critical Issues of Discipleship

Not all who attend church and call themselves Christians are disciples. They should be. We have been called, instructed, encouraged, and equipped, yet many choose to sit on their haunches and wait for the kingdom to come. While salvation is by grace alone, through faith alone, in Christ alone, the requirements of discipleship described by Jesus should serve as a warning.

> "If anyone wishes to come after Me, he must deny himself, and take up his cross daily and follow Me." (9:23)

> "Whoever loses his life for My sake, he is the one who will save it." (9:24)

> "Whoever is ashamed of Me and My words, the Son of Man will be ashamed of him when He comes in His glory." (9:26)

I take from these statements that discipleship is not a *requirement* of salvation as much as it is *proof* of salvation. Therefore, I offer two principles to consider as you think about your relationship with Christ.

First, *following Christ means more than believing Him; it includes obeying Him.*

One becomes a convert by trusting in Him, but that's just the beginning. Birth necessarily leads to living! Believing leads to learning; learning leads to transforming; transforming leads to obeying. This is the progression of a Christian, without which, one is not likely a genuine believer.

Second, *living obediently means more than accepting truth; it includes commitment.*

People live according to the truths they genuinely believe. If one genuinely believes what Jesus has taught, one's life will show evidence through daily behavior. That's not to say disciples obey perfectly. It's simply to affirm the need for commitment to learning and applying God's Word.

As believers, we cannot achieve perfect obedience or total commitment, and the Lord has not required this of us; but we should see progress. If not, perhaps we need to revisit our decision to trust in Christ.

The Ultimate Close Encounter
LUKE 9:28-36

NASB

28 Some eight days after these sayings, He took along Peter and John and James, and went up on the mountain to pray. 29 And while He was praying, the appearance of His face became different, and His clothing *became* white *and* ᵃgleaming. 30 And behold, two men were talking with Him; and they were Moses and Elijah, 31 who, appearing in ᵃglory, were speaking of His departure which He was about to accomplish at Jerusalem. 32 Now Peter and his companions had been overcome with sleep; but when they were fully awake, they saw His glory and the two men standing with Him. 33 And as ᵃthese were leaving Him, Peter said to Jesus, "Master, it is good for us to be here; let us make three ᵇtabernacles: one for You, and one for Moses, and one for Elijah"—not realizing what he was saying. 34 While he was saying this, a cloud ᵃformed and *began* to overshadow them; and they were afraid as they entered the cloud. 35 Then a voice came out of the cloud, saying, "This is My Son, *My* Chosen One; listen to Him!" 36 And when the voice ᵃhad spoken, Jesus was found alone. And they kept silent, and reported to no one in those days any of the things which they had seen.

9:29 ᵃLit *flashing like lightning* 9:31 ᵃOr *splendor*
9:33 ᵃLit *they* ᵇOr *sacred tents* 9:34 ᵃLit *occurred*
9:36 ᵃLit *occurred*

NLT

28 About eight days later Jesus took Peter, John, and James up on a mountain to pray. 29 And as he was praying, the appearance of his face was transformed, and his clothes became dazzling white. 30 Suddenly, two men, Moses and Elijah, appeared and began talking with Jesus. 31 They were glorious to see. And they were speaking about his exodus from this world, which was about to be fulfilled in Jerusalem.

32 Peter and the others had fallen asleep. When they woke up, they saw Jesus' glory and the two men standing with him. 33 As Moses and Elijah were starting to leave, Peter, not even knowing what he was saying, blurted out, "Master, it's wonderful for us to be here! Let's make three shelters as memorials*—one for you, one for Moses, and one for Elijah." 34 But even as he was saying this, a cloud overshadowed them, and terror gripped them as the cloud covered them.

35 Then a voice from the cloud said, "This is my Son, my Chosen One.* Listen to him." 36 When the voice finished, Jesus was there alone. They didn't tell anyone at that time what they had seen.

9:33 Greek *three tabernacles.* 9:35 Some manuscripts read *This is my dearly loved Son.*

As skepticism spreads and radical atheism grows more outrageously vocal, interest in the supernatural continues to deepen. While some people steadfastly claim nothing exists beyond the realm of the material universe, others desperately search for meaning, hoping that something—*anything*—transcends our otherwise pointless existence. More television shows than ever explore the mysteries of UFO sightings and search for tangible proof of spirits walking among us. Books and movies tease our imaginations with the possibility of experiencing the supernatural realm. It's big business because it touches some of our deepest needs: the need to know we are not alone, that our existence has a purpose, that we matter to someone greater than ourselves.

Our desire to touch the supernatural realm goes as far back as time itself. Throughout recorded history, as the evidence shows, people of every age and in every culture search the heavens for something or someone greater than the problems of humanity. This universal human instinct compels us to explore the supernatural because we know there has to be more than what we see in the material world. It is human nature to look to the supernatural when we need hope.

After hearing the difficult news of Jesus' shocking agenda, the disciples began to wonder what the future held. They expected the Messiah to gather a great following, overtake corrupt Jerusalem, overthrow cruel Rome, and return Israel to its glory days. But Jesus predicted a completely different path to glory. The path He followed led downward, through suffering and into death. To encourage the Twelve, Jesus promised that most of them would "see the kingdom of God" before dying. He then decided to give three of His students a foretaste of the kingdom, a close encounter with the supernatural, a behind-the-scenes glimpse of the heavenly agenda they had joined. They understood they had become an important part of something great, but they had no concept of its magnitude.

— 9:28-29 —

Roughly a week after the disciples learned their Messiah would suffer and die, Jesus retreated up a mountain to pray, taking along His three most trusted apostles, Peter, John, and John's brother, James. Apparently, Jesus spent quite a bit of time in prayer, because the three apostles were "overcome with sleep" (9:32). After they woke, something very strange occurred. Both Mark and Matthew used the word *metamorphoō* [3339] to describe a change in Jesus' physical state (Matt. 17:2; Mark 9:2). The English word "metamorphosis" is a transliteration of this Greek word. Many translations render this verb as "transfigure." Jesus' body transformed in some way while retaining its basic appearance.

Luke describes what the disciples saw. Jesus' face "became different." Although Luke doesn't say specifically how, Matthew records that "His face shone like the sun" (Matt. 17:2). Moreover, His clothing turned white and literally "flashed like lightning" (*exastraptō* [1823]).

How to Prove the Existence of God

LUKE 9:28-36

I remember when the Russian cosmonaut Yuri Gagarin climbed into a rocket and left the earth's atmosphere to become the first man in space. He was later quoted as saying, "I looked and looked but I didn't see God."[45]

Many struggle to accept the existence of God because they deny the existence of the supernatural realm—that is, the existence of things beyond time, space, and the five senses. They believe only in the material realm for three basic reasons.

First, the supernatural realm defies empirical testing. By definition, anything "supernatural" is above and beyond the natural forces of nature. It cannot be measured or weighed, recorded or analyzed, captured or manipulated. When the supernatural realm briefly and rarely does touch the natural, those who experience it report bizarre phenomena. Consequently, their reports are hard to believe.

Second, the supernatural realm is as different from ours as life inside the womb is from life in the world. Existence beyond the space-time constraints of our universe would boggle the mind; we cannot possibly hope to comprehend it in our limited state. Attempts to discuss existence outside our limited universe defy description. How can we have a vocabulary for what we have not experienced and cannot understand?

Third, the supernatural realm has only one kind of evidence in its favor: the experience of relatively few witnesses. Unfortunately, witnesses have proven to be the least reliable form of evidence, generally speaking. In addition to the biblical accounts of God's activity in the sensory realm, many people have reported out-of-body experiences, such as contact with the dead, trips to heaven and back, and encounters with ghosts, monsters, and aliens. The credibility of a witness's testimony rests completely on his or her trustworthiness as a person, and some people are not entirely sane. This doesn't help otherwise open-minded people accept the possibility of the supernatural.

I can sympathize with skeptics. Still, the existence of the supernatural doesn't depend upon our believing or not believing it is there. Many things are hard to believe; nevertheless, reality will hold us accountable for our beliefs. One Sunday following Yuri Gagarin's voyage into the heavens and his supposed quip about not seeing God, W. A. Criswell,

(continued on next page)

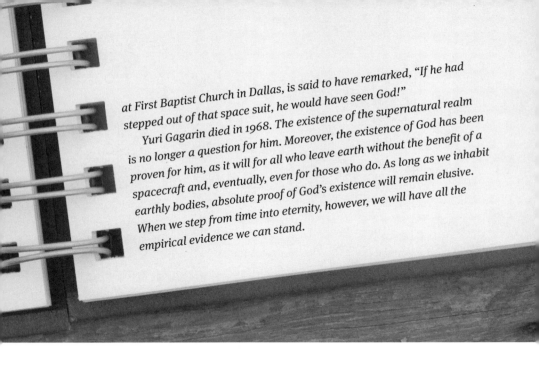

at First Baptist Church in Dallas, is said to have remarked, "If he had stepped out of that space suit, he would have seen God!"

Yuri Gagarin died in 1968. The existence of the supernatural realm is no longer a question for him. Moreover, the existence of God has been proven for him, as it will for all who leave earth without the benefit of a spacecraft and, eventually, even for those who do. As long as we inhabit earthly bodies, absolute proof of God's existence will remain elusive. When we step from time into eternity, however, we will have all the empirical evidence we can stand.

Garments in those days could easily get dirty. Streets weren't paved, so very quickly the hems became filthy. People lay on their sides to eat meals and typically sat on the ground when not indoors. When they slept under the stars, the outer garment often served as a pillow. But, in a moment, His garments "became radiant and exceedingly white, as no launderer on earth can whiten them" (Mark 9:3).

Clearly, this was not a normal, earthly experience. People don't suddenly change in appearance during prayer. Garments don't whiten themselves or flash like lightning. No natural explanation suffices. The three men were not merely superstitious, mistaking a natural event for something mysterious. They truly did witness a supernatural event.

— 9:30-31 —

If that weren't eerie enough, Luke records the appearance of two other figures, Moses and Elijah, who joined Jesus in a conversation. He describes the men as "appearing in glory," which in this context is a visible expression of God's presence. That the men's appearance looked similar to that of Jesus doesn't give them equal status with God, but it does imply they are more like Him now than when they walked the earth.

Why Moses and Elijah? Why not Abraham and Isaiah? Why not Jeremiah and Daniel? Jacob, Joseph, David, or one of the patriarchs along with another prophet? Why not John the Baptizer? Why these two men in particular? Potential explanations will require conjecture because we are not given the answer in Scripture. I observe that Moses was considered the father of the Law, while Elijah was the archetypical prophet. Together, the two men embodied the spirit of "the Law and the Prophets" in Old Testament Scripture. Moses represented the beginning of Israel as a nation, leading them out of Egypt and to the Promised Land, while Elijah represented their consummation by returning before "the great and terrible day of the Lord" (Mal. 4:5-6). The two men also departed the earth in unusual ways. God buried the body of Moses in a secret location (Deut. 34:5-6), and Elijah was taken directly into heaven, presumably without experiencing death (2 Kgs. 2:11-12, 15-18). We know the answer to the question is not important because God never included it in Scripture. What's important is that two departed Old Testament believers stood with Jesus, alive and well, in bodies that were recognizable yet otherworldly in nature. Moses had died more than fourteen hundred years earlier. Elijah departed around nine hundred years prior to this event. Both now stood on earth in visible form, but without the normal earthly restrictions.

Luke reveals that Moses and Elijah conversed with Jesus about His impending "departure," which (interestingly enough) is the Greek word *exodos* [1841]. Jesus would "accomplish" this departure in Jerusalem. The choice of wording characterizes the Lord's future action as the fulfillment of a plan or the completion of a task. His destiny lay in Jerusalem, where He would depart the earth.

I like to imagine that these stalwart heroes of Old Testament faithfulness came to encourage Jesus, to affirm His agenda. After this conversation, Jesus made Jerusalem His focus, which Luke notes several times from this point on (Luke 9:51, 53; 13:33; 17:11; 18:31). But, in truth, we don't know the specifics of their conversation. If it were important, the Lord would have revealed it to Luke or to the other human authors. The more important detail was that Jesus, while still alive, glowed with the same glory and manifested the same otherworldly characteristics as Moses and Elijah. He stood on earth with a foot in each realm, as it were. For a relatively brief time, the kingdom in its glorious fullness existed on that mountain, shared by those three men.

— 9:32-33 —

Peter, John, and James had been sleeping (or had been extremely drowsy) during part of the supernatural encounter, but woke soon enough to witness it. When Peter saw Moses and Elijah beginning to depart, he blurted out an offer to build a "tabernacle" for each of them.

A "tabernacle" was a small, temporary lodging or a hut, similar to those the Jews erected each year in Jerusalem during the Feast of Tabernacles. This festival commemorates the wilderness wanderings and anticipates the messianic kingdom (Lev. 23:42-43; Neh. 8:14-17; Zech. 14:16-21).

Peter instinctively reacted to their leaving with an offer of hospitality, much like a host might say to visitors looking at their watches, "Don't rush off! Stay for supper. We have plenty." Luke adds the explanation "not realizing what he was saying" because as endearing and thoughtful as Peter's suggestion had been, it was absurd. Moses and Elijah were supernatural beings, having bodies that do not need shelters, even if they did want to stay on earth a little longer. Peter's outburst contributes a couple of interesting thoughts.

First, classical Greek writers used the image of a tent as a metaphor for the body, which we inhabit temporarily during our sojourn on earth. Paul drew upon this image as well (2 Cor. 5:1-4). Moses and Elijah didn't need huts any more than they needed flesh-and-bone bodies. They had kingdom-style bodies (1 Cor. 15:50-54; Phil. 3:21; 1 Jn. 3:2). Why go back to the old model when you have the new and much improved version?

Second, Peter's offer to have Moses and Elijah stay longer expresses an honest desire we all share. We want the kingdom in its fullness to come now and to remain forever (Rev. 22:20). The kingdom will indeed come and remain, but only at the cost of great suffering and only when the time is right. Jesus would have to journey to Jerusalem and suffer for the sake of His kingdom (Isa. 52:13–53:12).

— 9:34-35 —

As Peter's voice trailed off, a cloud descended and enveloped the scene. This cloud is reminiscent of several Old Testament scenes, especially those connected with the exodus of Israel from Egypt (Exod. 13:21-22; 16:10; 19:16; 24:15-18; 40:34-38; Isa. 4:5; Dan. 7:13). Naturally, this provoked the men to fear, a common reaction when people encounter a manifestation of God (Isa. 6:5; Dan. 8:17; 10:7-10; Luke 1:12; 5:8; Rev. 1:17).

When the cloud had descended, the voice of the Father spoke audibly for a second time in the Gospel (cf. Luke 3:22), saying, "This is My Son, My Chosen One; listen to Him!" Luke uses a grammatical construction called the "restrictive attributive," which places extra emphasis on the adjective "Chosen." It's as if God had said, "Make no mistake, My Son is My Chosen One!" The Father's endorsement recalls the promise of a Prophet, to whom the people were duty bound to listen (Deut. 18:15).

After hearing about the Lord's plan to enter Jerusalem and then suffer on behalf of His people instead of conquering the city, the disciples probably started getting cold feet. They needed the reassurance that could only come from the voice of God. Note that the Father didn't speak to Jesus; He addressed the disciples. God staged the event for a purpose. This close encounter with the supernatural provided the men all the reassurance they lacked before. Thanks to the Father's endorsement, any doubts they might have harbored dissipated like a morning fog.

— 9:36 —

As the echoes of God's voice dissolved and the cloud vanished, no trace of the supernatural remained.

Note that the men didn't rush down the mountain to tell the other disciples what they had witnessed. According to Mark and Matthew, the Lord asked them to keep it to themselves until after His resurrection (Matt. 17:8-9; Mark 9:8-10); nonetheless, the men didn't appear eager to share their experience. Today, people who claim to encounter the supernatural rush to the nearest media outlets, or hire a publicist, or contact an agent. They're all over the morning news programs, selling their stories to anyone willing to pay. But Peter, John, and James—like other people in the Scriptures—kept the vision to themselves for their own edification, their own instruction. Later, when the time was right, they described their close encounter with the kingdom of God so others—including you and me—might receive the benefit of their experience.

• • •

What was the purpose of the Transfiguration? I think the Father had two objectives in mind—one for Christ and another for the disciples. First, the Father brought reassurance to the Son that the way of suffering was the best and only plan of salvation. In the weakness of His humanity, Jesus depended upon His Father for support and encouragement (cf. Luke 22:43).

I think the Father also wanted to remind the disciples that Jesus was indeed the Christ, His "Chosen One." The disillusionment they had suffered almost certainly undermined their belief. God gave the leading apostles a close encounter with the future kingdom of God to shore up their confidence, to put steel in their spines for the difficult days ahead. He knew they would need it.

APPLICATION: LUKE 9:28-36

His Will, His Way, All the Way

The message the Lord gave the three disciples is a message for us today. I see no fewer than three implications of the Transfiguration that every follower of Christ should hold closely.

First, *in the kingdom of God, death has no power*. For a few brief moments, the kingdom of God appeared on earth in all its glory. This glimpse of the kingdom revealed the living and the dead sharing a special kind of existence, communing with ease, no longer separated by the veil separating the earthly and spiritual realms. While many—if not most—Jews in the first century believed in resurrection and anticipated life after death, their doctrines hung on very thin wires. These three disciples received firsthand experiential proof of the afterlife.

Second, *in the kingdom of God, our bodies will not experience the effects of evil*. The living body of Jesus and the bodies of two long-departed believers took on the same supernatural attributes. This glimpse of the future kingdom of God assures us that we will have bodies, but they will be impervious to pain, suffering, hunger, thirst, privation, injury, disease, and death. We will have no need of shelter, food, or medicine.

Third, *victory is assured despite the path of suffering before us*. We can have confidence—despite the many challenges to our faith—that pursuing God's plan is always best, even if it leads through suffering, pain, and perhaps even death. While we endure the dominion of evil now, a glorious future awaits the faithful. Some pay a huge price for their decision to follow Christ. Some lose contact with their families, some endure social and cultural rejection, some even risk losing their lives for the sake of trusting in Christ. Others may not face such extreme difficulties, but the decision to become a follower of Jesus Christ opens the believer to spiritual attacks. Apart from those difficulties, life can be just plain hard. In fact, sometimes the decision to forsake Christ can appear easier. The Transfiguration is our reminder today: Stay with God's plan! There is none better. Even if it means suffering and pain, even to death. Stay the course. The glory of God awaits you at the end of your journey.

Snapshots from an Amazing Album
LUKE 9:37-50

NASB

37 On the next day, when they came down from the mountain, a large crowd met Him. 38 And a man from the crowd shouted, saying, "Teacher, I beg You to look at my son, for he is my ªonly *boy,* 39 and a spirit seizes him, and he suddenly screams, and it throws him into a convulsion with foaming *at the mouth;* and only with difficulty does it leave him, mauling him *as it leaves.* 40 I begged Your disciples to cast it out, and they could not." 41 And Jesus answered and said, "You unbelieving and perverted generation, how long shall I be with you and put up with you? Bring your son here." 42 While he was still approaching, the demon ªslammed him *to the ground* and threw him into a convulsion. But Jesus rebuked the unclean spirit, and healed the boy and gave him back to his father. 43 And they were all amazed at the ªgreatness of God.

But while everyone was marveling at all that He was doing, He said to His disciples, 44 "Let these words sink into your ears; for the Son of Man is going to be ªdelivered into the hands of men." 45 But they ªdid not understand this statement, and it was concealed from them so that they would not perceive it; and they were afraid to ask Him about this statement.

46 An argument ªstarted among them as to which of them might be the greatest. 47 But Jesus, knowing ªwhat they were thinking in their heart, took a child and stood him by His side, 48 and said to them, "Whoever receives this child in My name receives Me, and whoever receives Me receives Him who sent Me; for the one who is least among all of you, this is the one who is great."

NLT

37 The next day, after they had come down the mountain, a large crowd met Jesus. 38 A man in the crowd called out to him, "Teacher, I beg you to look at my son, my only child. 39 An evil spirit keeps seizing him, making him scream. It throws him into convulsions so that he foams at the mouth. It batters him and hardly ever leaves him alone. 40 I begged your disciples to cast out the spirit, but they couldn't do it."

41 Jesus said, "You faithless and corrupt people! How long must I be with you and put up with you?" Then he said to the man, "Bring your son here."

42 As the boy came forward, the demon knocked him to the ground and threw him into a violent convulsion. But Jesus rebuked the evil★ spirit and healed the boy. Then he gave him back to his father. 43 Awe gripped the people as they saw this majestic display of God's power.

While everyone was marveling at everything he was doing, Jesus said to his disciples, 44 "Listen to me and remember what I say. The Son of Man is going to be betrayed into the hands of his enemies." 45 But they didn't know what he meant. Its significance was hidden from them, so they couldn't understand it, and they were afraid to ask him about it.

46 Then his disciples began arguing about which of them was the greatest. 47 But Jesus knew their thoughts, so he brought a little child to his side. 48 Then he said to them, "Anyone who welcomes a little child like this on my behalf★ welcomes me, and anyone who welcomes me also welcomes my Father who sent me. Whoever is the least among you is the greatest."

NASB

49John answered and said, "Master, we saw someone casting out demons in Your name; and we tried to prevent him because he does not follow along with us." 50But Jesus said to him, "Do not hinder *him;* for he who is not against you is ªfor you."

9:38 ªOr *only begotten*   **9:42** ªOr *tore him*   **9:43** ªOr *majesty*   **9:44** ªOr *betrayed*   **9:45** ªLit *were not knowing*   **9:46** ªLit *entered in*   **9:47** ªLit *the reasoning;* or *argument*   **9:50** ªOr *on your side*

49John said to Jesus, "Master, we saw someone using your name to cast out demons, but we told him to stop because he isn't in our group."
50But Jesus said, "Don't stop him! Anyone who is not against you is for you."

9:42 Greek *unclean.*   **9:48** Greek *in my name.*

NLT

The greatest story ever told is about the greatest person who ever lived. Yet we do not possess an exhaustive account of Jesus' life. As John indicates (John 20:30), he and the other Gospel writers had to select which information to convey out of a vast pool of material. So, instead of a written transcript of the Lord's earthly ministry or uninterrupted hours of film footage, the information about His life comes to us in small, select segments, like snapshots in a photo album. Matthew, Mark, Luke, and John have assembled four distinct photo essays, as it were, sometimes selecting the same scenes, other times different scenes. Each has cropped and centered the photographs to highlight certain details while omitting others, all to convey a particular perspective. Each Gospel presents the truth without error, yet no single writer records the whole story.

Immediately after describing the close encounter that Peter, John, and James experienced with the kingdom of God, Luke selects four snapshots, as it were, from the ministry of Christ to prepare the reader for His journey to Jerusalem.

Jesus frees a demonized boy after the disciples fail to do so. (Luke 9:37-43a)
Jesus announces His betrayal and suffering. (9:43b-45)
Jesus corrects the disciples' definition of greatness. (9:46-48)
Jesus corrects the disciples' understanding of leadership. (9:49-50)

These scenes serve to clarify the role of the Twelve in the kingdom of God, as well as explain the nature of godly leadership.

— 9:37-40 —

The first snapshot captures a tragic scene, filled with the pathos of a father desperate to free his only child from the grip of evil. This occurred the day after Peter, John, and James witnessed the Lord's

Transfiguration and heard the voice of God affirm Jesus as the Messiah. With their confidence restored, they felt ready to reengage in ministry, to follow Jesus without question, and to submit to His agenda.

Reminiscent of the day Jesus came down the mountain with the newly appointed Twelve following close behind (6:12-19), the Lord and His top three returned to find a large crowd waiting for Him. One man among the crowd begged for Jesus' personal attention to his only son, who was tormented by a demon.

Modern science would analyze his symptoms and conclude that he suffers from severe grand mal seizures, now called tonic-clonic seizures, the kind most often associated with epilepsy. In fact, some modern-day expositors have accused the first-century witnesses, including Luke and Jesus, of superstition. But they base their conclusions on the general assumption that ancient people always filled the gaps in their knowledge by attributing maladies to evil spirits.

Luke was a physician. While medical science had a long, long way to go, Dr. Luke was not necessarily given to superstition. Furthermore, epilepsy was a known condition that, although poorly understood, was seen as distinct from demon possession (Matt. 4:24). Ancient people were more likely to see epilepsy as a symptom of insanity than to suspect evil spirits.

In this case, the boy's fits appeared epileptic but were in fact the manifestation of a demon. In Matthew's account (Matt. 17:14-21), the father apparently misdiagnosed the boy as an epileptic and had come to the disciples for a cure. The disciples correctly identified the true source of the child's suffering but could not exorcize the demon.

At this point in Luke's narrative, we see a dramatic contrast between the power of Jesus revealed on the mountaintop and the impotence of His disciples at the bottom.

— 9:41-43a —

Jesus bristled at the disciples' inability to exercise the power He had delegated to them, calling them an "unbelieving and perverted" people. Both terms describe the effects of the fall of Adam, the curse of sin. I can't help but see a subtle allusion to the Lord's exasperation with the people of Israel during their time in the wilderness following the exodus from Egypt (Exod. 32:7-10; Num. 14:27; Deut. 32:5). Yet, despite Jesus' disappointment and frustration, He compassionately invited the man to bring his afflicted son to Him.

Luke describes the boy's fit as the rebellion of the demon within him, which Jesus rebuked (cf. Luke 4:35, 39, 41; 8:24). With apparent ease, the Lord cured the boy of all physical injuries caused by the demon and returned him to his father. Who knows how long the disciples took turns trying to free the boy from the demon? When the crowd saw the Lord's effortless command over evil, they were "amazed" (cf. 2:48; 4:32) at the "greatness of God."

The Greek word for "greatness" literally means "full of splendor, magnificence." The Son derives His power from the Father, and He continually gives glory to the Father. This, apparently, was the disciples' mistake. They tried to exercise the power of God independently, as if it were theirs to command (Mark 9:28-29). The crowd witnessed the difference.

— 9:43b-45 —

Luke takes the opportunity to draw a crucial contrast between Jesus' perspective and that of "everyone"—that is, His disciples and the general population observing His ministry. Luke's use of the imperfect tense "was marveling" refers to an ongoing response as Jesus continued to assert His authority over evil. While the general population continued to marvel, Jesus prepared His disciples—which may have included the Twelve and the broader group of devoted followers—for His journey to Jerusalem (Luke 9:30-31). So far, every confrontation with evil had resulted in an easy victory for Jesus; soon, He would begin a journey to confront evil in a fight to the death—His own death.

Jesus called Himself "the Son of Man," a favorite title for the Messiah that emphasizes His identity with humanity. He revealed that He would be "delivered" into the hands of men. This verb means, literally, "handed over" and has two predominant uses. The first is "to transfer responsibility" (1:2; 10:22; 12:58; 23:25). The second is "to betray" (21:16; 22:4, 6, 21-22, 48). Jesus will be handed over in both senses of the word. God will hand Him over to men, who will not receive Him as their king but unjustly condemn Him to death. In the process, He will be betrayed by Judas and delivered to the Sanhedrin, who will hand Him over to the Romans, who will then try to give responsibility to another (Herod) but will eventually hand Him over to the executioners. These future events would disillusion those expecting Jesus to accomplish in Jerusalem what He had been doing in Galilee.

His followers understood neither the meaning nor the purpose of His warnings. Luke explains that the statement, specifically the meaning and purpose, "was concealed from them so that they would not perceive it" (9:45). The passive "was concealed" might simply describe the disciples' inability to fully understand, but I favor the alternative, which is that it is a "divine passive," which implies the action is completed by God.

In other words, the meaning of the Lord's statement was divinely concealed from the disciples so that they would not comprehend all its implications. Luke also implies that they were aware they didn't understand fully but were afraid to ask further. But why did the Lord say anything at all if they were not to understand fully?

Two reasons. First, He wanted to prepare them for a future that would not play out like they expected or hoped. He didn't paint a rosy picture of their expedition to Jerusalem. His confrontations with evil in Galilee, reversing the physical effects of sin and casting out demons, were mere skirmishes compared to the darkness He would encounter in Judea.

Second, He wanted to plant an important seed in their memories. When the corrupt courts of the religious leaders condemn Jesus, when the morally bankrupt civil leaders turn a blind eye to justice, when He is condemned to suffer the shameful death of the lowest criminal, when He lies cold in a tomb, the Savior wants His followers to know that none of it had been a mistake. He didn't miscalculate and then improvise a victory. When He rose from the dead, He wanted His people to remember what He had said. Everything had gone exactly according to plan.

The Lord's followers were prevented, most likely by God, from comprehending His statement. But let's be realistic; they didn't want to think about the implications. They feared to ask Jesus to explain, not because they feared His angry response, but because they didn't want to know the answer to the question "What do you mean by that, Jesus?" As we would say today, it would result in TMI (too much information).

— 9:46 —

Luke seamlessly weaves this scene in with the previous one, but we know from Matthew that some time had passed (Matt. 17:22–18:1). Luke has linked the interpretation of these two teachings: Jesus had explained that it was necessary for the Messiah to suffer and die; now He would redefine the meaning of "greatness."

The disciples—most likely referring to the Twelve—were discussing the pecking order of the new kingdom. They dialogued and debated the merits of each man in order to determine who should hold which office when Jesus establishes the new kingdom. Who would be the prime minister? Who would assume the duties of the secretary of the interior, or the ministry of war, or the secretary of state? While pride and conceit undoubtedly fueled the conversation, the discussion revolved around rank, privilege, and responsibility in the new government.

— 9:47-48 —

The response by Jesus is priceless. Sometimes he sharply admonished them for petty conversations like this. Other times He may have let their foolishness pass without comment. In this case, He rebuked them by embracing a child, someone too small, too weak, too helpless to be great. With the little boy standing with Him, Jesus rearranged the worldly pecking order. He upset the normal conventions of hierarchy in leadership. His speech was simple, consisting of three statements (Luke 9:48):

"Whoever receives this child in My name receives Me."

The act of "receiving" someone must be understood in the context of ancient Near Eastern hospitality. It means to welcome as family and to care for one's needs. That's delightful to do for an important dignitary or a celebrity. Imagine a knock at your door. The person pleads to come in because he has been robbed at gunpoint, has no money, and has no means of getting help on his own. Be honest with yourself as you answer this question: How would you respond if you recognized the man as the world's wealthiest business mogul? By contrast, how would you respond if he were a mentally disabled vagrant?

Let's face it: We are eager to help the powerful, yet reluctant to help the helpless. Doing favors for powerful people might reap a handsome reward or advance our personal agendas. But helping someone with no resources?

The phrase "in My name" links our motivation to His. To do something in someone's name was to act on his or her behalf. The act of receiving the helpless is our duty as members of the new government. We do this because our leader commands it. Furthermore, in the kingdom of God, you don't rise to power by helping the powerful. You serve the weakest, least deserving people, with no expectation of reward.

"Whoever receives Me [by receiving the least powerful] receives Him who sent Me."

God sent Jesus to be the ultimate example of someone helping the helpless. Jesus receives humanity, welcoming sinners despite their sin and meeting the deepest needs of the least deserving. This practice essentially removes worthiness as a criterion for anything in the new government. People are to be welcomed and served because of their relationship to the King, not because of their rank, power, or ability to benefit those who treat them nicely.

"For the one who is least among all of you, this is the one who is great."

The "least" can be identified in two ways. First, the least powerful receive the greatest honor and privilege in the kingdom because the hierarchy has been turned upside down. In the present world order, everyone serves the monarch, who receives the best of everything. In the kingdom of God, the least powerful receive the kindness of the most powerful. In this way, the least is greatest.

The second interpretation, however, is the most important. Because the hierarchy has been inverted in the new kingdom, the true leaders act like servants. In fact, the King, the greatest of all leaders in the kingdom of God, is the One who made Himself the servant of all humanity, suffering our penalty for sin, receiving all who trust in Him, and giving us eternal life. Those who imitate the King share a measure of His kingly status. The way up in the kingdom of God is to serve others as though they were kings.

— 9:49-50 —

John responded with what appears to be an obtuse statement. He reported that the disciples had seen someone confronting evil, apparently with some success. He didn't say the man was *trying* to cast out demons. The disciples attempted to stop him because he was not part of their group. John essentially asked, "What about those who aren't in our organization? Where do they fit in terms of governmental structure?"

Jesus used this opportunity to reorganize the disciples' organizational chart. Citizens don't become part of the kingdom by passing a test or receiving a membership card or reporting to another citizen or accepting an appointment to office. People become citizens by acknowledging the King's authority and receiving His kindness. They identify themselves as citizens by carrying out the King's agenda. Furthermore, they answer directly to the King, not to the next stratum in the organizational hierarchy. The unknown exorcist not only accomplished the Master's work, he did it in the Master's name and with the Master's power, even though he didn't happen to be among the Twelve.

APPLICATION: LUKE 9:37-50

Kingdom Leadership

The snapshots in this passage change the normal concept of delegated authority. Let's contrast the world's concept of leadership with that of Christ's kingdom. The differences are stark and in many ways convicting. Certainly, as we reflect on them, we're implicitly called to make a decision between the ways of this world and the ways of Christ.

First, the present world order prefers hierarchy, with the best and the brightest (or at least the strongest and most ruthless) dictating from the top. But the kingdom of God calls the humblest and most dependent to serve others from the bottom. Presently, governments, businesses, and, yes, even churches and ministries, embrace a rigid top-down structure in order to enforce their demands. But Peter, who learned his leadership style from the Lord himself, urges future church leaders to avoid "lording it over" those among whom they are called to serve as shepherds (1 Pet. 5:3).

Second, in the present world order, leaders delegate authority to subordinates and give them directives, expecting them to operate independently while holding them accountable for their actions. Excessive dependence upon the leader is considered a weakness. In the kingdom of God, however, authority is delegated for the purpose of service, and authority and dependence upon the Leader are inseparable. We are to go to Him, constantly seeking His will through His Word, expressing our needs through prayer, and relying on His strength by the Holy Spirit.

Third, in the present world order, the lowly underling in an organization may never meet the man or woman at the top. A chain of command separates him or her from the highest rungs of the organization. Sometimes the lowest members of a sprawling corporation may not even know the names of their highest executives, much less recognize them if they showed up on the jobsite. Not so with the kingdom of God! Each member of the body is directly related to the Head—and each one has a relationship with and is accountable to the King. While all members of the body of Christ are accountable to one another (Eph. 5:21; 1 Pet. 5:5), ultimately each citizen of God's kingdom answers directly to the Christ (2 Cor. 5:10).

In our lives and ministry, do we view our actions in terms of service to Christ's kingdom? Do we train leaders to trust God like children, to accept seeming failure, and to look for God at work in the ministry of others we are not connected with? Or do we reflect the values and methods of the kingdom of this world?

INSTRUCTING
AND SUBMITTING
(LUKE 9:51–19:27)

An imaginary line runs from Seward Peninsula in Alaska, along the Rocky Mountains of Canada and the United States, through the deserts of the American Southwest and the Mexican Sierra Madre Occidental, along the ridge of the Andes in South America, finally dropping into the Atlantic Ocean at Cape Horn—the Great Continental Divide. Although imaginary, this line serves a practical purpose: It indicates which ocean the rainwater will seek and which direction rivers will tend to drain, whether westward toward the Pacific or eastward toward the Atlantic. Most people have neither the desire nor the need to know about the Great Divide. In fact, if signs didn't mark the boundary, few would notice anything significant. Nevertheless, this watershed line is profoundly important to geologists.

In my Bible, a line separates Luke 9:50 from 9:51, with a little red cross drawn in the margin. We might call it "The Gospel of Luke Great Divide." Many readers don't see the line because most English versions seamlessly transition from Jesus' statement, "Do not hinder [the one who casts out demons but does not follow along with us]; for he who is not against you is for you" (9:50), to Luke's statement about Jesus' determination to journey to Jerusalem. While the line is barely perceptible, it is profoundly important to the story.

In Luke's narrative, this statement marks the beginning of the Christ's march to the Jewish capital. You won't, however, read the story of a frenzied, angry gathering of violent revolutionaries riding a groundswell of resentment. Jesus didn't lead that kind of insurrection. He didn't intend to fight earthly fire with earthly fire, evil with evil. His revolution looked like none other, a form of insurrection as different as the kingdom of God is from the dominion of evil. And the enemy didn't know what to do with Him.

Jesus had already been to Jerusalem many times, both to attend the feasts mandated by the Law and as a part of His itinerant ministry. But this trip was different. This expedition to Jerusalem was the next phase in His campaign to reclaim the world from the dominion of evil; to expose and condemn the usurping tyrant Satan; and to reestablish the kingdom of God on earth. He would undertake this journey, not as a rank-and-file Jew, but as the leader of a holy, spiritual invasion force. When He arrived, He would, in effect, press Jerusalem and its inhabitants to accept or reject the kingdom He had been proclaiming. During this journey, His disciples would come to grips both with the grim reality of this conflict against evil and with God's dynamic power to overcome it.

KEY TERMS IN LUKE 9:51–19:27

***apostolos* (ἀπόστολος)** [652] "apostle," "sent one," "official envoy," "commissioner"

This noun, related to the verb *apostellō* (ἀποστέλλω [649], meaning "to send" or "to send with a commission/with authority"), described an official government envoy, who might carry official news or read proclamations to the general public across the empire. Greek religion and philosophy later used the term for divinely sent teachers. In Christianity, it came to describe both the function and the official capacity of certain men; to be called an "apostle," one must have personally encountered Jesus Christ after His resurrection and received His commission to bear the good news to others.

***metanoeō* (μετανοέω)** [3340] "to change one's mind," "to regret," "to repent," "to be converted"

Words with well-known general meanings can take on very specific, technical meanings within a particular community. In secular Greek, this verb means "to change one's thinking," "to regret," or "to have remorse." Within the Gospels, however, it almost exclusively carries the idea of being reconciled to God after turning away from sin.[1] Therefore, in Luke and Acts, when one repents, one is saved, converted, and added to the ranks of genuine believers. In Luke, the related noun form *metanoia* [3341] usually describes an ongoing state of mind and depicts someone in right relationship with God.

***ochlos* (ὄχλος)** [3793] "crowd," "multitude," "throng"

This term is used exclusively in the Gospels and Acts, except for four instances in Revelation. It means, simply, "crowd," referring to a relatively large number of people gathered in one place. Secular Greek writers sometimes use the term to mean "commoners" or "rabble," which may have influenced the Gospels. In the synoptic Gospels, a "crowd" contains a mixture of dedicated followers, curiosity-seekers, potential believers, critics, and outright enemies. Luke typically distinguishes the "crowd," which contains various followers, from "disciples," the large number of dedicated followers.

***sōzō* (σώζω)** [4982] "to save," "to rescue," "to preserve a person's well-being"

To "save" someone in the general sense of the word is to act on behalf of that person's well-being, which can include physical healing. The notion "to save from eternal condemnation" is a technical meaning. The Gospels very often use the term as a kind of double entendre (though not always), such that a person receives healing as an outward sign of spiritual deliverance from sin and hell.

A Face Like Flint
LUKE 9:51-62

NASB

51 When the days were approaching for His [a]ascension, He [b]was determined to go to Jerusalem; 52 and He sent messengers on ahead of Him, and they went and entered a village of the Samaritans to [a]make arrangements for Him. 53 But they did not receive Him, because [a]He was traveling toward Jerusalem. 54 When His disciples James and John saw *this,* they said, "Lord, do You want us to command fire to come down from heaven and consume them?" 55 But He turned and rebuked them, [[a]and said, "You do not know what kind of spirit you are of; 56 for the Son of Man did not come to destroy men's lives, but to save them."] And they went on to another village.

57 As they were going along the road, someone said to Him, "I will follow You wherever You go." 58 And Jesus said to him, "The foxes have holes and the birds of the [a]air *have* [b]nests, but the Son of Man has nowhere to lay His head." 59 And He said to another, "Follow Me." But he said, "Lord, permit me first to go and bury my father." 60 But He said

NLT

51 As the time drew near for him to ascend to heaven, Jesus resolutely set out for Jerusalem. 52 He sent messengers ahead to a Samaritan village to prepare for his arrival. 53 But the people of the village did not welcome Jesus because he was on his way to Jerusalem. 54 When James and John saw this, they said to Jesus, "Lord, should we call down fire from heaven to burn them up*?" 55 But Jesus turned and rebuked them.* 56 So they went on to another village.

57 As they were walking along, someone said to Jesus, "I will follow you wherever you go."

58 But Jesus replied, "Foxes have dens to live in, and birds have nests, but the Son of Man has no place even to lay his head."

59 He said to another person, "Come, follow me."

The man agreed, but he said, "Lord, first let me return home and bury my father."

60 But Jesus told him, "Let the spiritually dead bury their own dead!*

NASB

to him, "Allow the dead to bury their own dead; but as for you, go and proclaim everywhere the kingdom of God." 61 Another also said, "I will follow You, Lord; but first permit me to say good-bye to those at home." 62 But Jesus said to him, "No one, after putting his hand to the plow and looking back, is fit for the kingdom of God."

9:51 ªLit *taking up* ᵇLit *set His face* 9:52 ªOr *prepare* 9:53 ªLit *His face was proceeding toward* 9:55 ªEarly mss do not contain bracketed portion 9:58 ªOr *sky* ᵇOr *roosting-places*

NLT

Your duty is to go and preach about the Kingdom of God."

61 Another said, "Yes, Lord, I will follow you, but first let me say good-bye to my family."

62 But Jesus told him, "Anyone who puts a hand to the plow and then looks back is not fit for the Kingdom of God."

9:54 Some manuscripts add *as Elijah did.* 9:55 Some manuscripts add an expanded conclusion to verse 55 and an additional sentence in verse 56: *And he said, "You don't realize what your hearts are like. ⁵⁶For the Son of Man has not come to destroy people's lives, but to save them."* 9:60 Greek *Let the dead bury their own dead.*

The 1984 Summer Olympics in Los Angeles will forever live in my memory, mostly because of a single marathon runner by the name of Gabriela Andersen-Schiess. The race is grueling enough without complications, but when she entered the stadium to complete the final 400 meters, heat exhaustion and dehydration had reduced her body to rubber. For nearly six minutes, she willed herself forward, step-by-agonizing-step, determined to finish what she had started. Doctors attempted to help her, but she waved them off; she had come too far to accept disqualification now. Twenty-six miles behind her, just a few hundred meters to go.

Eventually, she staggered across the finish line and collapsed into the arms of physicians. While her body failed, determination kept her going. Until she had completed the course, the finish line became her sole objective, and nothing would deter her or distract her from reaching it.

As Luke's narrative crests the "Great Divide," he pauses for a moment to set the theme for the Lord's journey. The entire "travel section" of Luke's Gospel (9:51–19:27) must be understood in light of this statement: "It came about in the approaching fulfillment of the days of His ascension that Jesus set His face to travel to Jerusalem" (9:51, my literal translation). His destiny waited for Him in the capital city, where spiritual corruption reigned supreme, and nothing could keep the Son of Man from fulfilling His purpose.

— 9:51 —

Luke marks the beginning of this new section with his characteristic use of the term *egeneto* (from *ginomai* [1096]), meaning "It came about" or "It happened." What "came about" was the approaching fulfillment of Jesus' destiny. "Fulfillment" reflects Luke's use of the verb *sympléroö* [4845], typically used in a literal sense to describe a ship that is either swamped with water or, more positively, fully provisioned with cargo and crew. Luke likened the Lord's destiny to a ship being made ready for a voyage, and he characterized Jesus as a man beginning a long journey to the wharf to meet it. In other words, Jesus moved toward Jerusalem like a man determined not to miss the date of his sailing.

The phrase "He was determined" reflects a colloquialism drawn from the Old Testament: "I have set my face." In Isaiah's "servant song," in which the Lord's Servant bears unspeakable abuse in His quest to redeem the people of Israel, He says to His abusers,

> The Lord GOD has opened My ear;
> And I was not disobedient
> Nor did I turn back.
> I gave My back to those who strike Me,
> And My cheeks to those who pluck out the beard;
> I did not cover My face from humiliation and spitting.
> For the Lord GOD helps Me,
> Therefore, I am not disgraced;
> Therefore, I have set My face like flint,
> And I know that I will not be ashamed.
> He who vindicates Me is near;
> Who will contend with Me? (Isa. 50:5-8)

Jesus "set His face" to go to Jerusalem. He not only determined to make the journey; He resolutely tightened His lips, set His jaw, and fixed His eyes on the cross and His resurrection. Every story He told, every miracle He performed, and every conversation in which He engaged, from this point on, had the cross pulsating in the back of His mind.

— 9:52-53 —

En route to Jerusalem, Jesus would pass through Samaria. To Pharisees and most other Jews, Samaritans were idolatrous half-breeds—ethnically polluted, religiously confused, and morally debased. During a particularly dark period in Israel's history, the Hebrew inhabitants of this region intermarried with Gentiles and established their own temple to rival the one in Jerusalem. Consequently, most Jews—particularly Pharisees—would not set foot on Samaritan soil. To avoid ritual contamination, most Jews traveling between Galilee and Judea chose to cross the Jordan River and pass by to the east of Samaria rather than

The Samaritans believed that Mount Gerizim was the location that God had chosen for his temple, instead of Jerusalem, so they worshiped God there. Pictured here are Samaritan ruins from the Hellenistic period and ruins of a Byzantine church that was built over the older ruins.

journey through it, straight to Jerusalem. Unlike His pharisaical counterparts, however, Jesus embraced the Samaritans as people in need of saving, not unlike their Jewish cousins.

Unfortunately, there was no love lost on the part of the Samaritan people. They despised Jews as religious snobs and took issue with their building a temple in Jerusalem since God had been worshiped on Mount Gerizim for centuries. Therefore, when the inhabitants of one Samaritan town heard that Jesus was headed for Jerusalem instead of Gerizim, they did the unthinkable: They refused hospitality—a sacred duty that only the basest, most despicable people neglected (Deut. 23:3-4; Judg. 8:5-17; 1 Sam. 25:2-38).

— 9:54-56 —

We find in the reaction of John and James the reason for their nickname "the sons of thunder" (Mark 3:17). Their suggested remedy of calling down fire from heaven is an allusion to 2 Kings. 1:9-14, in which King Ahaziah sent men to arrest the prophet Elijah. When they arrived, the prophet called down fire from heaven, which consumed two separate groups of fifty men and their captains. King Ahaziah, of course, was the king of Samaria.

John and James probably thought the Lord would be pleased by their zeal, but instead He rebuked them. The verb "to turn" (*strephō*

Barry Beitzel

A BRIEF HISTORY OF SAMARIA

LUKE 9:52

Originally, the Hebrew nation settled the Promised Land and thrived for several centuries as twelve tribes united by worship at one tabernacle, located in Shiloh, about 10 miles from Mount Gerizim. Eventually, Solomon, Israel's third king, constructed a permanent temple in Jerusalem.

Shortly after Solomon's death, the northern ten tribes rejected the legitimate successor to the throne, chose an idolatrous, rebellious general to lead them, formed a separate nation, and claimed the name Israel for themselves. The southern tribes of Benjamin and Judah remained loyal to Solomon's son and became known as Judah. The northern kingdom and the southern kingdom fought intermittently for the next two hundred years, until Israel was distracted by repeated assaults from the Assyrian king Tiglath-pileser (also known as Pul) (2 Kgs. 15:19-20, 29; 1 Chr. 5:26). Finally, Shalmaneser (2 Kgs. 17:3-6) and his successor, Sargon, finished off Israel by deporting the northern tribes and causing them to intermarry with other conquered nations, virtually breeding them out of existence. After 721 BC, only a small remnant of the Israelite tribes remained in the northern territory, and most of them had begun to intermarry with Gentiles.

After the people of Judah were exiled to Babylon (606–587 BC) and later returned under the leadership of Ezra and Nehemiah, they found the northern region inhabited by Samaritans, people of mixed Hebrew and Gentile heritage. By then, the returning people of Judah had become known as Jews. Tensions mounted when the Samaritans opposed the rebuilding of Jerusalem and the temple; and the final breach occurred when the Samaritans built their own temple on Mount Gerizim, claiming it, not Jerusalem, to be the authentic place of worship. This temple was destroyed by the Jewish high priest John Hyrcanus in 128 BC,[2] and its location was, like that of the Jerusalem temple, further desecrated by Emperor Hadrian's erection of pagan shrines in the second century AD.

[4762]) usually accompanies a statement of correction (Luke 7:9, 44; 14:25-26; 22:61; 23:28). The "kind of spirit" they had adopted stood in sharp contrast with that of the Son of Man, whose conquest would not follow the pattern of marauding generals. He said, in effect, "Don't get sidetracked by others' responses. Press on."

The men probably remembered His earlier instructions concerning their ministry in Galilee (9:5). The act of shaking dust from one's feet not only expressed contempt, it also warned of future judgment. While Jesus did come to save and "not to destroy men's lives," judgment will be a part of His plan after His return at the end of days (10:13-16; 17:20-36).

— 9:57-58 —

Luke reveals the Lord's mind on the topic of discipleship with three short vignettes, each playing heavily on literary irony. The reader knows the end of the story. We know where the Lord's journey will take Him—the depths of suffering He will endure and the glorious triumph He will achieve—and that knowledge colors how we understand these sayings. Jesus was probably less enigmatic in His actual responses to the people. Luke, however, condenses Jesus' sayings to make a point.

The Messiah's disciples and would-be disciples came to Him with certain expectations that differed markedly from His. They expected a Messiah to reestablish the kingdom of God, to free them from foreign tyranny, to restore God's Law and uphold godly justice, and to usher in another economic boom—*all for their sakes*. In other words, they were willing to follow Jesus into battle, expecting a return on their investment. But, unlike the kings and conquerors of the world's kind, Jesus didn't offer perks in exchange for allegiance. He didn't come as a manorial lord seeking serfs. This Messiah called for three qualities in His disciples with *no* promise of earthly benefits. Jesus called for unreserved sacrifice (9:57-58), undivided devotion (9:59-60), and unwavering commitment (9:61-62).

The first vignette involves an offer to follow Jesus anywhere, with the implication that the prospect of danger didn't diminish the man's loyalty. Jesus depicted His experience as less enviable than that of animals. In His day, generals lived quite well during their military campaigns, and their troops usually grew wealthy as they collected the spoils of war. Even a nonviolent, political campaign to claim the throne would have resulted in a trickle-down effect of wealth and power.

Jesus called for unreserved sacrifice in the pursuit of His cause, with no promise of anything beneficial, at least in the worldly sense. He had no temporal wealth or power to promise since He, Himself, lived in poverty.

— 9:59-60 —

In another vignette, Jesus invited a man to follow Him, to join His band of disciples in their quest to confront evil in Jerusalem, and to become a citizen of God's kingdom. The man asked for permission to bury his father first. The phrase "bury my father" can be taken in one of two ways. First, the father has recently died, and the son must prepare the body and then remain ritually unclean for seven days before rejoining normal society (Num. 19:11). Because Jews had a limited time to prepare a body and then get it into a tomb, it is unlikely the encounter with Jesus took place between the father's death and his burial.

Second, and more probable, the father was nearing death, either due to advanced age or a terminal illness. The phrase "bury my father" was a colloquialism meaning "take care of my father until his death, see that he is buried with dignity, and dispose of his estate according to his wishes" (Gen. 49:29). In this case, the would-be disciple asked for an indefinite delay, unlike Levi, Peter, Andrew, James, and John, who immediately left behind their temporal duties.

Jesus' response appears callous. He replied to the man's request with a double entendre in which the "dead" plays off the man's specific request, but He extends the term to describe those who are not disciples. Per this saying, those who do not follow and who place temporal concerns over the demands of the kingdom of God are nothing more than walking dead people. Jesus placed two duties side by side and called the man to choose: Join the dead in their pursuit of vain temporal concerns, or proclaim the kingdom of God as a fully alive citizen. The choice was between mundane futility and everlasting life.

Jesus called for undivided devotion to Him. Of course, because Jesus is inherently good, His followers can follow Him with complete confidence and devotion, knowing that He will always have them do what is right. If the man had expressed complete devotion, Jesus may have compelled him to stay behind, take care of his temporal duties, and bear witness to his community (cf. Luke 8:38-39).

— 9:61-62 —

A third vignette has a would-be disciple committing to follow Jesus, but only after bidding his hometown family and friends good-bye. Again, this appears to be a reasonable concession. Presumably, this encounter took place some distance from the man's home, and he wanted to bid them farewell instead of simply disappearing with Jesus. And, again, the Lord's response appears unnecessarily harsh. But, as usual, there's more going on than we see at first glance.

The Lord's response alludes to a well-known episode in the life of Elijah, a recurring figure in Luke's narrative (1:17; 4:25-26; 9:8, 19, 30-36). In 1 Kings 19:19-21, the prophet found Elisha, the man destined to be his successor, supervising a huge farming enterprise—twelve plow teams, each consisting of two oxen, a plow, and a plowman. Elijah threw his cloak—a symbol of his prophetic office—over the shoulders of Elisha. In response to this unspoken commissioning as Elijah's disciple, Elisha requested—perhaps with his hand still on the plow— "Please let me kiss my father and my mother, then I will follow you" (1 Kgs. 19:20).

Here's what Elisha meant: He sacrificed his pair of oxen over a fire kindled by the wood of his plows, threw a grand celebration for his community, and then "followed Elijah and ministered to him" (1 Kgs. 19:21). He said good-bye to his community while looking forward, not with a wistful glance backward at everything he was leaving. Jesus said, in effect, "I wish you had the heart of Elisha in asking to say good-bye to your people at home." He wanted from His disciples unwavering commitment, declaring that anything less would make for a bad "fit." Anyone not completely committed to the cause of the kingdom would never find a home it in. In fact, the demands of citizenship will chafe uncommitted shoulders like an ill-fitting yoke.

• • •

As the Messiah braced Himself for His fateful conflict with spiritual darkness, the time had come to separate true disciples from casual followers, the determined from the doubtful. Kingdom-building is tough business, calling its citizens to live in foreign territory, according to different—often opposing—standards, among hostile enemies bent on violence, in the expectation of future vindication. In the meantime, the followers of the King must become like Him, determined to confront evil and ready to suffer its backlash, to harden their faces against the fury of hell as they commit themselves to the establishment of God's kingdom on earth.

APPLICATION: LUKE 9:51-62

Press On!

At one point in the Lord's ministry, He knew the time had come to make His way to Jerusalem. He had been there countless times before, but this was different. This time, He would enter the city as its King, not merely a faithful worshiper. Luke drew upon the imagery of Isaiah 50:7, writing, "He set His face toward Jerusalem."

He resolutely tightened His lips, set His jaw, and fixed His eyes upon His destiny. Every student of the Gospel of Luke will tell you this is a hinge in Luke's account. From this point to the end, Jesus has the cross on His heart. Every story He told, every miracle He performed, every conversation He engaged in, every decision He made, took Him ever closer to His goal.

When a Samaritan town refused hospitality, the disciples wanted to bring down retribution upon them. But Jesus refocused them on the mission at hand, encouraging them to ignore others' responses and to press on.

That's good advice for anyone resolved to accomplish something great. Don't get sidetracked because other people won't take you in. Press on! Don't become distracted when others don't support you. Press on! Don't allow detractors and old enemies to make life miserable for you. Press on!

A little later, a new disciple joined the ranks of the faithful, saying, "I will follow You wherever You go" (Luke 9:57). This man, who has such strong confidence in his expression, appears to have a highly charged, fervent devotion. Jesus responded with a realistic assessment of the hardships involved. We have no idea whether the person joined the ranks. In the end, it doesn't matter. Jesus pressed on.

Don't be intimidated by others' zeal. Press on! If other people seem more devoted than you, don't compare. Press on! If others seem to seek attention, you aren't responsible for their sincerity. You have your own attitude to manage. Press on!

Jesus said to another, "Follow Me." The man responded with what would seem to be a legitimate excuse: "Permit me first to go and bury my father." This was likely an idiom meaning "Let me care for my father until he dies." The Lord responded with a call to set and maintain proper priorities. And then He pressed on.

Don't get distracted by a lesser loyalty. You will be surrounded by people who appear to have the same priority as you and say they work for the same goal, but their choices reveal otherwise. And this creates tension. Regardless, don't let the fuzzy, conflicted, wishy-washy priorities of others distract you from your own. Press on!

Twenty centuries have passed and the greatest story ever told continues to be told. That's because Jesus taught His disciples well. Of the Twelve, all but Judas pressed on after His death, burial, resurrection, and ascension. Each dedicated himself to the mission of the kingdom, even to the point of martyrdom.

Today, we have the same mandate as the first-century followers of Christ. So press on!

Practical Talk to Those in Ministry
LUKE 10:1-16

¹Now after this the Lord appointed ᵃseventy others, and sent them in pairs ahead of Him to every city and place where He Himself was going to come. ²And He was saying to them, "The harvest is plentiful, but the laborers are few; therefore beseech the Lord of the harvest to send out laborers into His harvest. ³Go; behold, I send you out as lambs in the midst of wolves. ⁴Carry no money belt, no ᵃbag, no shoes; and greet no one on the way. ⁵Whatever house you enter, first say, 'Peace *be* to this house.' ⁶If a ᵃman of peace is there, your peace will rest on him; but if not, it will return to you. ⁷Stay in ᵃthat house, eating and drinking ᵇwhat they give you; for the laborer is worthy of his wages. Do not keep moving from house to house. ⁸Whatever city you enter and they receive you, eat what is set before you; ⁹and heal those in it who are sick, and say to them, 'The kingdom of God has come near to you.' ¹⁰But whatever city you enter and they do not receive you, go out into its streets and say, ¹¹'Even the dust of your city which clings to our feet we wipe off *in protest* against you; yet ᵃbe sure of this, that the kingdom of God has come near.' ¹²I say to you, it will be more tolerable in that day for Sodom than for that city.

¹³"Woe to you, Chorazin! Woe to you, Bethsaida! For if the ᵃmiracles had been performed in Tyre and Sidon which occurred in you, they would have repented long ago, sitting in ᵇsackcloth and ashes. ¹⁴But it

¹The Lord now chose seventy-two* other disciples and sent them ahead in pairs to all the towns and places he planned to visit. ²These were his instructions to them: "The harvest is great, but the workers are few. So pray to the Lord who is in charge of the harvest; ask him to send more workers into his fields. ³Now go, and remember that I am sending you out as lambs among wolves. ⁴Don't take any money with you, nor a traveler's bag, nor an extra pair of sandals. And don't stop to greet anyone on the road.

⁵"Whenever you enter someone's home, first say, 'May God's peace be on this house.' ⁶If those who live there are peaceful, the blessing will stand; if they are not, the blessing will return to you. ⁷Don't move around from home to home. Stay in one place, eating and drinking what they provide. Don't hesitate to accept hospitality, because those who work deserve their pay.

⁸"If you enter a town and it welcomes you, eat whatever is set before you. ⁹Heal the sick, and tell them, 'The Kingdom of God is near you now.' ¹⁰But if a town refuses to welcome you, go out into its streets and say, ¹¹'We wipe even the dust of your town from our feet to show that we have abandoned you to your fate. And know this—the Kingdom of God is near!' ¹²I assure you, even wicked Sodom will be better off than such a town on judgment day.

¹³"What sorrow awaits you, Korazin and Bethsaida! For if the miracles I did in you had been done in wicked Tyre and Sidon, their people would have repented of their sins long ago, clothing themselves in burlap and throwing ashes on their heads to show their remorse. ¹⁴Yes, Tyre and

will be more tolerable for Tyre and Sidon in the judgment than for you. ¹⁵ And you, Capernaum, will not be exalted to heaven, will you? You will be brought down to Hades!

¹⁶ "The one who listens to you listens to Me, and the one who rejects you rejects Me; and he who rejects Me rejects the One who sent Me."

10:1 ᵃSome mss read *seventy-two* 10:4 ᵃOr *knapsack* or *beggar's bag* 10:6 ᵃLit *son of peace*; i.e. a person inclined toward peace 10:7 ᵃLit *the house itself* ᵇLit *the things from them* 10:11 ᵃLit *know* 10:13 ᵃOr *works of power* ᵇI.e. symbols of mourning

Sidon will be better off on judgment day than you. ¹⁵ And you people of Capernaum, will you be honored in heaven? No, you will go down to the place of the dead.*"

¹⁶ Then he said to the disciples, "Anyone who accepts your message is also accepting me. And anyone who rejects you is rejecting me. And anyone who rejects me is rejecting God, who sent me."

10:1 Some manuscripts read *seventy*; also in 10:17. 10:15 Greek *to Hades*.

Often I have wondered why God involves people in His work when He can do everything Himself. Furthermore, He can do the job better, accomplishing any task completely and perfectly. When I want a job done right, I look for the best and the brightest; I don't give critical and complicated tasks to people sure to let me down. So, why does the Lord entrust fallible, fickle, faith-challenged people with something as important as building His kingdom?

That question will probably remain unanswered until we see Jesus face-to-face. His rationale remains a mystery, yet His method cannot be denied. From the very beginning of His ministry on earth, Jesus established a pattern that would become the *modus operandi* of the kingdom. Beginning in Galilee, He won the hearts of a small army of disciples and then commissioned twelve of them to receive on-the-job training in how to minister just like Him (9:1-6, 10).

Despite the relative success of that decision, Jesus never intended to conquer the world with just twelve followers. Soon after "setting His face to go to Jerusalem," Jesus decided to multiply His kingdom agenda by commissioning an additional seventy followers, challenging them to join His world-redeeming enterprise.

— 10:1-2 —

Jesus formed thirty-five teams of disciples—in addition to the Twelve—and sent them ahead of Him to prepare the cities for His visit. Notably, He sent these disciples out in pairs. We were taught in the Marines that when you dig a foxhole before a battle, always dig it big enough for two men. Two men fighting in the trenches strengthen and encourage each other. They maintain level heads. They are more effective in fighting and have a much better chance for survival. On the other hand, one warrior in combat can easily become discouraged and retreat from the fight. In pairs, soldiers enjoy the benefits of companionship, protection, affirmation, and encouragement.

Ministry isn't easy work. When Jesus outlined the mission for the seventy, He made this clear. The labor force is small (10:2). The competition is fierce as wolves (10:3). The travel amenities are not ideal (10:4a). The time is limited (10:4b). The pay depends upon others (10:7). The message can be rejected (10:10). And obedience can be alienating (10:11). He wasn't recruiting workers for a Fortune 500 corporation! Nevertheless, Jesus encouraged these seventy disciples by giving them a realistic evaluation of the mission, twice calling them "laborers."

Jesus was extremely frank at the end of Luke 9, and He was no less frank here. Doing the work of the kingdom of God is labor. Even so, He freed these laborers from the burden of success. By calling Himself the "Lord of the harvest," He reminded the laborers that the harvest—or lack thereof—belongs to Him, not to the laborer. That helps the workers maintain a healthy perspective. The seventy didn't need to stay awake at night worrying over whether their efforts would succeed. God is responsible for the harvest; His laborers are responsible to labor faithfully.

Because the work to be done is so overwhelming compared to the number of workers, He charged them with the responsibility to pray. They were to ask the Lord of the harvest to call and appoint more laborers.

— 10:3-4 —

Jesus then specified how he wanted these seventy followers to behave while engaging in ministry. It is virtually the same methodology He gave to the Twelve apostles (9:1-10). His official appointment, "Behold, I send you . . . ," uses the Greek verb *apostellō* [649], which is related to the noun "apostle" (*apostolos* [652]). An "apostle" was someone commissioned and sent forth to accomplish a task on behalf of another. For example, a king might send an envoy to carry out his wishes in a certain area. The official envoy's authority was to be obeyed like that of the sender. Consequently, people were expected to treat the envoy as though he were the king or, otherwise, suffer the king's wrath.

Despite their delegated power, these envoys were like harmless lambs among bloodthirsty wolves. Just as the Samaritan village rejected the King (9:51-56), so others would certainly reject His envoys.

Therefore, though doing the same with the Twelve (9:3), it would seem odd that He would send them out with little or no provisions instead of loading them down with plenty of money and food to help them survive if no one offers hospitality. While the seventy went out as lambs among wolves, carrying no provisions, they were neither helpless nor poor. Jesus challenged them to live as He did, dependent upon God for safety and sustenance. He wanted them to be rich and secure because of their connection with God, just like Him.

He also impressed upon the seventy a sense of urgency. The ancient Near Eastern custom of greeting involved the giving and receiving of hospitality and could last for hours or even days (Judg. 19:4-9; cf. 2 Kgs. 4:29). Jesus told the seventy not to get caught up in long, extended greetings. Be polite, but pursue the task with urgency.

— 10:5-6 —

Just as the seventy were to depend upon God for their provision and protection, so they were to rely upon God to send them to the right audience. Jesus subtly reminded His appointees that they must not be choosy about where they go or to whom they speak. They were to be on mission at "Whatever house" they entered. Regardless of the location, the size of the house, or the culture of the town, they were to bid them peace and proclaim the kingdom message. The seventy didn't know what houses they would enter, and Jesus didn't want them to care. It didn't matter. The kingdom of God isn't for one select and special audience. The invitation is open to all people.

The blessing "Peace be to this house" is culturally rooted in the Hebrew word *shalom* [H7965]. The meaning goes deeper than just the absence of war, battles, or arguments. It carries the idea of wholeness and prosperity in every aspect of life. For the Jew, the term *shalom* described the quality of life promised in the kingdom of God.

The apostles' blessing also served another purpose. How the message was received revealed the hearts of the listeners. The phrase "man of peace" is literally "son of peace" in the original language. The idea of sonship carries the implication of likeness or similarity. In the same way a son bears his father's features, so a son of peace will bear the likeness of peace. Moreover, the message of kingdom *shalom* should find a place to rest within the heart of a person seeking the kingdom.

Jesus said, in effect, "Cast the message of kingdom peace toward the people; it will bounce off of those who have no interest in the kingdom. Then you know to whom you are speaking."

— 10:7-9 —

Jesus repeated the advice He gave to the Twelve (Luke 9:4), except with greater detail and further explanation. He wanted them to stay in the first household that welcomed them and to gratefully receive whatever hospitality they were offered. This was to avoid any accusation that the apostles were out for personal gain and to distinguish themselves from itinerant philosophers.

While Jesus didn't want the seventy to focus on what they could get rather than what they had to give, He did expect their physical needs to be met: "The laborer is worthy of his wages." He expected them to receive enough compensation for their work to provide what they genuinely needed. The advice "Eat what is set before you" encourages contentment. He wanted them to keep their focus on the mission of proclaiming the kingdom of God and to become models of contentment rather than examples of greed or restlessness. In terms of ministry, contentment gains the respect of those who hear the message.

In each city they entered, the envoys were to use their delegated power to reverse the physical effects of evil. And when performing a healing miracle, they were to announce that the miracle was just a foretaste of the Messiah's reign. The phrase "the kingdom of God has come near to you" uses the perfect tense, indicating a lasting effect. The divine rule of the Messiah has commenced, but the fullness of the kingdom is still in the future. His reign will be consummated when He returns in power.

— 10:10-12 —

An unfortunate reality of life in a fallen world is that God's message of *shalom* will sometimes be rejected. Jesus therefore did not hesitate to prepare the seventy for inevitable resistance. In the face of rejection, the seventy were to stand fast in the truth with confidence. Moreover, they were to pronounce judgment against the city by shaking its dust from their shoes and declaring the nearness of the kingdom of God. Jews shook dust from their feet when leaving Gentile territory to symbolize their rejection of Gentile customs.

To reject an envoy of the king is to reject the king, and to reject a king is to invite his wrath. Jesus announced the consequences of rejecting Him as King and despising His kingdom. That city would suffer judgment more severe than the fire that consumed Sodom (Gen. 19:24-25) because it had received a more complete revelation of divine truth than the Old Testament city. Strong words indeed!

— 10:13-15 —

The idea of rejection prompted Jesus to pronounce a series of "woes" on cities that poorly received His representatives. "Woe" (cf. "What sorrow awaits," NLT) is an interjection of mournful pain and inexpressible sadness, commonly uttered at funerals. It also served as a warning, as if to say, "Your present course will lead to your demise, so I will mourn your destruction now."

All of the cities Jesus mourned lay near Capernaum, although the precise location of Chorazin has been lost to history. He compared their stubborn rejection to the cities of Tyre and Sidon, which notoriously rejected God and received the condemnation of Israel's most revered prophets (Isa. 23:1-18; Jer. 25:15-17, 22; 47:4; Ezek. 26:1–28:23; Joel 3:4-8; Amos 1:9-10). He further stated that if Tyre and Sidon had received the same revelation that was given the cities near Capernaum, the inhabitants would have repented, even going so far as to debase themselves with the familiar symbol of mourning and penitence: "sackcloth and ashes" (Josh. 7:6; 1 Kgs. 20:31-32; Esth. 4:2-3; Job 2:8; 42:6; Isa. 58:5; Jon. 3:6-8).

The expression of "woe" conveys warning, but not wrathful condemnation. In fact, if we had heard the inflection of the Lord's voice, we would have heard sorrow. The cities that rejected the kingdom message had doomed themselves to inevitable, unavoidable damnation. He didn't pronounce this woe oracle to convince the rebellious cities; Jesus mourned their loss to bolster the courage of the seventy. Those who reject the apostles' message would bring condemnation down on themselves; therefore, the apostles should not take the rejection personally.

— 10:16 —

Jesus concluded His commissioning speech by underscoring their divine appointment. As envoys of the king, they were due the same respect owed to Jesus. But, more importantly, the seventy could take neither the credit nor the blame for the people's response to their message. People worship God and receive His Word because they love Him, not because the messenger is particularly tactful or lovable. Many people reject the Lord despite His utter goodness, not because the messenger failed in some way. If the messenger has faithfully delivered the message, nothing more could have been done.

• • •

Jesus' interactions with the citizens of Israel didn't fit the mold of a politician. He didn't set out to win friends and influence people; instead, He determined to free souls from bondage and then empower them to influence others. He didn't plan to conquer the world by laying siege to cities; He elected to capture the hearts of people. Jesus, however, never intended to do all of the work Himself. We learn from His example that the work of ministry in the kingdom of God is not the responsibility of a select few. He didn't set aside a group of clergy to do all the work of evangelism, care, teaching, and the myriad of other tasks in ministry. While He does call some to devote their vocational lives to leading others in this way, the Messiah expects *all* citizens of His kingdom to shoulder the burden of displacing the dominion of evil and restoring God's original order on earth. While the Lord can complete the task without our help, He nonetheless has given *all* of His people a genuine stake in His agenda.

APPLICATION: LUKE 10:1-16
Faithful and Accountable

Earlier, Jesus sent out the Twelve to replicate His ministry of proclaiming the kingdom, healing diseases, and casting out demons (9:1-6). Then He sent out several dozen more to do the same. As we reflect on their work, let me offer two thoughts.

First, to all who minister to others: *Be faithful to Him who called you.*

That borders on cliché, I realize, but we need this simple reminder. God has called us. And those He has called, He has equipped. He didn't call us to fail; He didn't even call us to "succeed" (whatever *that* means). He called us to be faithful to Him. Don't give in. Don't give up. Don't burn out. Don't quit. Stay at it.

Second, to you who are ministered to: *Be accountable to those who serve you.*

When one of their flock has gone far astray and is in danger of becoming a reproach to Christ or a danger to others, a shepherd is right to take the initiative in holding that person accountable. In that case, a worthy servant of Christ will lovingly and humbly confront the one who has strayed (Gal. 6:1-2). We who are under their care and protection should be willing to submit.

Over four hundred years ago, the reformer Martin Luther provided a reflection on ministry. Much has changed, yet culturally, ministry remains very much the same. Luther wrote,

It is a wearisome office for anyone to have general oversight as to how the sheep live, so as to direct and help them. There must be oversight and watchfulness night and day, so the wolves do not break in; so that body and life must also be devoted to it. Therefore [Peter] says, "you are not to do it of constraint." True it is that no one should force himself uncalled into the ministry; but if he is called and required for it, he should enter it willingly, and discharge the duties his office demands. For they who do it of constraint, and who have no appetite and love for it, will not properly discharge the duties of the ministry.³

Thank you, Lord, for Martin Luther.

Joyful Return, Insightful Response
LUKE 10:17-24

NASB

¹⁷The ᵃseventy returned with joy, saying, "Lord, even the demons are subject to us in Your name." ¹⁸And He said to them, "I was watching Satan fall from heaven like lightning. ¹⁹Behold, I have given you authority to tread on serpents and scorpions, and over all the power of the enemy, and nothing will injure you. ²⁰Nevertheless do not rejoice in this, that the spirits are subject to you, but rejoice that your names are recorded in heaven."

²¹At that very ᵃtime He rejoiced greatly in the Holy Spirit, and said, "I ᵇpraise You, O Father, Lord of heaven and earth, that You have hidden these things from *the* wise and intelligent and have revealed them to infants. Yes, Father, for this way was well-pleasing in Your sight. ²²All things have been handed over to Me by My Father, and no one knows who the Son is except the Father, and who the Father is except the Son, and

NLT

¹⁷When the seventy-two disciples returned, they joyfully reported to him, "Lord, even the demons obey us when we use your name!"

¹⁸"Yes," he told them, "I saw Satan fall from heaven like lightning! ¹⁹Look, I have given you authority over all the power of the enemy, and you can walk among snakes and scorpions and crush them. Nothing will injure you. ²⁰But don't rejoice because evil spirits obey you; rejoice because your names are registered in heaven."

²¹At that same time Jesus was filled with the joy of the Holy Spirit, and he said, "O Father, Lord of heaven and earth, thank you for hiding these things from those who think themselves wise and clever, and for revealing them to the childlike. Yes, Father, it pleased you to do it this way.

²²"My Father has entrusted everything to me. No one truly knows the Son except the Father, and no one truly knows the Father except

anyone to whom the Son wills to reveal *Him*."

²³ Turning to the disciples, He said privately, "Blessed *are* the eyes which see the things you see, ²⁴for I say to you, that many prophets and kings wished to see the things which you see, and did not see *them*, and to hear the things which you hear, and did not hear *them*."

10:17 ªSome mss read *seventy-two* 10:21 ªLit *hour* ᵇOr *acknowledge to You*

the Son and those to whom the Son chooses to reveal him."

²³ Then when they were alone, he turned to the disciples and said, "Blessed are the eyes that see what you have seen. ²⁴I tell you, many prophets and kings longed to see what you see, but they didn't see it. And they longed to hear what you hear, but they didn't hear it."

In the early nineties, a few years after Desert Storm, General Norman Schwarzkopf wrote an autobiography titled *It Doesn't Take a Hero*. The book is a fascinating read for anyone who has spent any time in the military. Near the middle of the book he recounts his thoughts as he headed for his first combat command position in Vietnam. Schwarzkopf, a West Point graduate, headed to Vietnam with high hopes, stars in his eyes, full of zeal and energy. He had gone to Vietnam, in his own words, "for God, country, and Mom's apple pie."

But later in the book he paints a different picture. After a second tour of duty, he left the battle-scarred landscape of Southeast Asia—where many young men under his command had either died or lost parts of their bodies to landmines—only to return to a divided United States. He wrote with realism, "I realized then I was really tired of being a commander . . . I thought, *Thank God it's over*. I'd saved as many lives as I could . . . I wanted to get home to my family."[4]

Same geography, same circumstance; but what a difference in the man himself, between first going to war and returning home!

After their time of ministry, the seventy "sent ones" whom Jesus had commissioned returned with their own "war stories" to tell. He had charged these special envoys of the Messiah with the task of proclaiming the *shalom* of God's kingdom and healing the sick, both physically and spiritually. He empowered them and authorized them to minister on His behalf in preparation for His personal visit on the way to Jerusalem. Furthermore, He reminded them of several truths: The message is God's. The harvest is God's. Their protection and provision are God's responsibility.

When they completed their task, these battle-tested ministers of the kingdom returned different from when they left. But, unlike Stormin' Norman Schwarzkopf, they had joyful stories to tell.

EXCURSUS: THE LEGEND OF LUCIFER

LUKE 10:18-20

Satan. The devil. Lucifer. Belial. Beelzebul. The Father of Lies. The Accuser. The Prince of the Power of the Air.

In the Old Testament, he's a shadowy figure at best. Including the introduction of the deceiving serpent in Genesis, only four clear references give us a glimpse of this personification of evil.

The serpent in Genesis 3 is generally regarded to be Satan taking the form of a creature or inhabiting an otherwise benign animal in the Garden of Eden. Interestingly, the text doesn't specifically identify the serpent, but John later alludes to the Garden serpent in Revelation, calling Satan "the dragon, the serpent of old" (Rev. 12:9, 15; 20:2).

In Job, a personage known as Satan presented himself before God alongside the "sons of God," which are presumably angels. God's treatment of Satan suggests he is an angelic being, but out of place among the others (Job 1:6-12). In response to God's affirmation of Job as "a blameless and upright man, fearing God and turning away from evil," Satan lived up to his name, which means "accuser" or "adversary." Satan then afflicted Job in order to prompt him to sin.

The prophet Zechariah described Satan as an angelic figure standing before the "angel of the LORD," accusing the high priest of being unfit to serve because of past sins (Zech. 3:1-7).

And finally, Satan moved David to sin by taking a census to assess his military strength rather than trust the Lord's protection (1 Chr. 21:1-2).

These are the only Old Testament mentions of an evil personage appearing in any context other than two debatable allusions in the oracles of Isaiah and Ezekiel. In Isaiah's poem, the Lord reassured Israel that the nation would rise again after its destruction by Babylon. To help the people prepare for that great day of celebration, in which the king of Babylon would suffer punishment for the evil he committed, God wrote His people a taunt song. The poem describes the king's terrible experience in a place of torment beyond the grave, and then sings,

> "How you have fallen from heaven,
> O star of the morning, son of the dawn!
> You have been cut down to the earth,
> You who have weakened the nations!
> "But you said in your heart,
> 'I will ascend to heaven;
> I will raise my throne above the stars of God,
> And I will sit on the mount of assembly
> In the recesses of the north.
> 'I will ascend above the heights of the clouds;
> I will make myself like the Most High.'
> "Nevertheless you will be thrust down to Sheol,
> To the recesses of the pit. (Isa. 14:12-15)

While the song clearly refers to a human king, not Satan, later Jewish literature regards this as allusion to the origins of Satan before Genesis 1:1. The same can be said of Ezekiel's condemnation of the King of Tyre (Ezek. 28:11-19), which draws upon the image of the deceiving serpent in the Garden of Eden, essentially calling the human king the embodiment of evil.

(continued on next page)

While Ezekiel's words applied directly to the mortal ruler of Tyre, most theologians (past and present) see previously undisclosed truths about Satan in the prophet's imagery.

Between the Old and New Testaments, Jewish writers turned Satan into a fairy-tale monster not unlike a vampire or the bogeyman, using a disturbing blend of scriptural clues and Jewish mythology. For example, a passage from the pseudepigraphical book of 2 Enoch reads,

> And one from out . . . the order of angels, having turned away with the order that was under him, conceived an impossible thought, to place his throne higher than the clouds above the earth, that he might become equal in rank to my power. And I threw him out from the height with his angels, and he was flying in the air continuously above the bottomless . . .[5]

Another fanciful book purporting to be the writing of Solomon describes Satan and demons in detail, complete with interviews. Take note of the imagery:

> I questioned the demon, saying: "Tell me how you can ascend into heaven, being demons, and amidst the stars and holy angels intermingle." And he answered: "Just as things are fulfilled in heaven, so also on Earth (are fulfilled) the types of all of them. For there are principalities, authorities, world-rulers, and we demons fly about in the air; and we hear the voices of the heavenly beings, and survey all the powers. And as having no ground (basis) on which to alight and rest, we lose strength and fall off like leaves from trees. And men seeing us imagine that the stars are falling from heaven. But it is not really so, O king; but we fall because of our weakness, and because we have nowhere anything to lay hold of; and so we fall down like lightnings in the depth of night and suddenly. And we set cities in flames and fire the fields. For the stars have firm foundations in the heaven, like the sun and the moon."[6]

Mainstream rabbis dismissed these writings as folklore; however, they did regard the king of Babylon in Isaiah 14 as an illustration of Satan's future condemnation—and correctly so. While Jesus didn't affirm or support the fairy-tale depiction of Satan, He did draw upon a rich tapestry of literary imagery to describe the devil's demise.

— 10:17 —

Luke doesn't reveal how long these seventy followers were gone, where they went, to whom they ministered, how often they had to kick dust from their sandals, or how many received their message of *shalom* (see comments on Luke 10:5-6). We learn only that they returned with joy, not unlike children desperate to tell their parents about some new wonder they have discovered. Luke preserves their sense of excitement, summarizing their report, "Lord, even the demons are subject to us in Your name."

When Jesus sent out the Twelve, He gave them "power and authority over all the demons and to heal diseases" (9:1). As core members of the Lord's leadership team, this made perfect sense. It was a surprising yet reasonable move. When Jesus sent out the seventy, however, He made no reference to wielding power over demons. They were told to heal the sick and to declare that the kingdom of God had come near (10:9). When they returned, bursting with excitement, we discover they were able to command demons to bow before the name of Christ. Their authority paralleled that of their Master (4:41) and His core leadership (9:6).

— 10:18-20 —

The Lord's vivid depiction of Satan falling from his place of power is, without question, symbolic of the effect Jesus and His disciples were having on the world. His imagery alludes to Isaiah 14:12, which many interpret as a reference to Satan's fall from the heavenly realm in punishment for his rebellion, an event that occurred before Genesis 1:1. At the end of days, Satan will fall from his place of dominion over the world and suffer eternal torment (Rev. 20:10), a consequence of his final defeat. Jesus saw the ministry of the seventy as part of that final fall.

Jesus used the imagery of Isaiah 14 to affirm the disciples' exuberance and to clarify the scope of His mission. He came not merely to become the Messiah of the Jews, or even Ruler of the world, but to transform all of creation on a cosmic scale. He came to conquer the dominion of evil.

Jesus continued His affirmation of their past ministry in order to encourage boldness in the future. The perfect tense of the phrase "I have given you" indicates a past action with continuing effect. He had already given them authority over evil, the evidence of which they had already seen, and this authority remained with them for future ministry. The image of treading on serpents and scorpions recalls a common Old Testament colloquialism for divine protection in which people are seen trampling dangerous animals under foot (Ps. 91:13; see also Isa. 11:8). The specific reference to serpents and scorpions also points to God's protection of Israel in the wilderness after the Exodus (Deut. 8:15).

His imagery also recalls the curse placed upon Satan in the Garden of Eden:

> And I will put enmity
> Between you and the woman,
> And between your seed and her seed;

He shall bruise you on the head,
And you shall bruise him on the heel. (Gen. 3:15)

While Jesus is undoubtedly the woman's "seed," the consummate victor over Satan, He nevertheless calls His disciples to join Him in the trampling of evil (Rom. 16:20).

Even as Jesus rejoiced with the disciples, celebrating their victory over evil, He lifted their eyes from the immediate to view everything with an eternal perspective. Their ability to command demons to depart is but a temporal triumph. The victory of eternal consequence is their eternal life in the kingdom of God. Moreover, their significance in the kingdom doesn't come from their accomplishments in ministry, but that God has claimed them as His people.

— 10:21 —

Having praised His followers for their success in ministry, Jesus responded to the prompting of the Holy Spirit and broke out in spontaneous praise to His Father. Luke describes all three persons of the Trinity in close interaction, celebrating the triumph of the Father's paradoxical plan. The Lord didn't reserve His truth for the minds of the intellectually gifted or the culturally wise. He didn't favor those who are wealthy, sophisticated, noble, or privileged. While humanity seeks wisdom from centers of higher learning to give us answers and lead the way, and while earthly leaders recruit only the brightest and the best, Jesus chooses the least qualified, unworthy individuals to achieve supernatural victory.

This is not to suggest that God looks down on education or that there's something wrong with learning more and more. Accomplishing great deeds through people of average intelligence or minimal education doesn't disparage the contributions of geniuses or diminish the benefits of knowledge. The Father's choice of ordinary people simply magnifies His power over evil. Furthermore, the Lord honors those who remain like babes with open hearts and teachable minds, regardless of their I.Q.

On the other hand, those who are impressed by their own superior intellect, who no longer have any place in their heart for God, and who reject faith as an affront to wisdom have no place in the kingdom of God. That's because worldly wisdom cannot make sense of the Cross (1 Cor. 1:18-23). Therefore, in calling His disciples "infants," Jesus extended the greatest compliment possible in the kingdom of God. In His economy, the least are the greatest.

— 10:22 —

If anyone doubted Jesus' identity before, He left little room for mis-understanding with His boldest claim to deity thus far. The phrase "all things," when used without specific reference to a particular realm (such as "all things *in the sea*" or "all things *which are written*"), almost always means "everything in the universe" (John 1:3; Acts 17:24; Eph. 3:9; Col. 1:16). Jesus affirms to the Father in the hearing of the disciples that all things—authority over the entire universe—have been handed to Him, in fulfillment of Daniel 7:13-14. The ultimate consummation of Christ's dominion will take place at the end of days (Rev. 19:11-21); in the meantime, a tension exists between the Messiah's ownership of the world and His actual possession of it. At the time of Jesus' prayer—as is true today—Satan sits on the throne of the world as a usurper of power, an illegitimate ruler (John 12:31; Eph. 2:2; 6:12).

Because Jesus is the true King of all creation and the sole person with pure knowledge of the Father, He is the only means by which humanity can know God. Luke's choice of phrasing emphasizes Jesus' sovereignty as the sole mediator between God and man. We do not have control over revelation. We see the Father only as the Son reveals Him, and the Son is under no moral obligation to reveal anything. By the Son's sovereign choice, people receive the knowledge of God through Him.

— 10:23-24 —

The context of a private statement indicates that "disciples" here is a small group, most likely the Twelve. Thus, Jesus finished addressing the seventy and then turned to say something privately to the Twelve. They had certainly heard what Jesus said to the seventy and, while it applied to them as well, He gave something special to His inner circle of future earthly leaders. I call this the "beatitude of privilege."

In the Old Testament, after the monarchy was established, no one was more important than the king. Kings were entitled to all honor and received the best of everything. Their authority could not be questioned or challenged, and they counted everything in the realm as their personal property. Yet none of their wealth and privilege could compare to the benefit of experiencing the presence of God's Son in the flesh and seeing the reestablishment of His kingdom on earth.

In Old Testament lore, no figure loomed larger than the prophet, whose supernatural knowledge made him frightfully powerful among men. Prophets spoke with God in person and through dreams or visions.

Prophets possessed secrets of future events and wielded miraculous power. Yet their knowledge paled in comparison to what the Twelve had seen and heard in person. They saw the miracles Jesus performed. They heard divine mysteries revealed. The Twelve saw the Father-Son relationship of Jesus like no others had. Besides this, they witnessed firsthand the testimony of the "seventy" whom the Lord had sent out in the power of the Holy Spirit (Luke 10:1-24).

APPLICATION: LUKE 10:17-24

What Disciples Do

The seventy disciples returned with stories to tell of lessons learned on the road. If we were sitting around the campfire as Jesus debriefed their experiences, what might we have learned from them?

Walt Kelly used to draw a syndicated cartoon strip called "Pogo." In one strip, Pogo sits beside the swamp fishing. Before long, a little duck swims to the shore, waddles up, and sits down beside him.

"Has you see'd my cousin?" asks the duck.

"Your cousin?"

"Yep. He's migrating north by kiddy car," says the duck.

"By kiddy car?" Pogo asks. "Why don't he fly?"

"Oh, he's afraid of flying. He's afraid he's gonna fall off."

Pogo looks at the duck. "Then why don't he swim?"

"Oh, he never swims. When he swims he gets seasick."

Incredulously, Pogo looks at the duck and makes the great statement, "When your cousin decided to be a duck, he entered the wrong business."

Sometime ago my friend Haddon Robinson provided a beatitude for that little cartoon. "Blessed is the duck who, when he decides to be a duck, does what ducks are supposed to do!" And if I may borrow from my friend's line, "Blessed is the disciple who, when he or she decides to be a disciple, does what a disciple is supposed to do—to hear, to see, and to believe."

Perhaps you began this journey with Jesus Christ well. Maybe you felt a rush of excitement and a release of emotional burdens when you came to the cross of Calvary and felt the weight of sin lifted from your shoulders; you saw your guilt washed away by the crimson blood of

Christ, never to be held against you again. Through His resurrection you have been given power to live on a level you never dreamed possible. And you hit the ground running, doing what disciples are supposed to do, telling people about the Savior. You were excited about the new life that had been given, thrilled over sins forgiven, and rejuvenated to serve Him and to represent Him.

Today, you return from a portion of your journey to do some evaluation. Have you gotten sidetracked? Have you discovered that you have begun to place your emphasis on nonessentials rather than on the essentials? When you decided to be a disciple, you didn't enter the wrong business, did you? No, you didn't. You made the right choice. But it's time to decide to do what a disciple's supposed to do: Obey the Master and follow the Leader. That's what a disciple's supposed to do.

What About My Neighbor's Neighbor?
LUKE 10:25-37

NASB

25 And a ªlawyer stood up and put Him to the test, saying, "Teacher, what shall I do to inherit eternal life?" 26 And He said to him, "What is written in the Law? ªHow does it read to you?" 27 And he answered, "YOU SHALL LOVE THE LORD YOUR GOD WITH ALL YOUR HEART, AND WITH ALL YOUR SOUL, AND WITH ALL YOUR STRENGTH, AND WITH ALL YOUR MIND; AND YOUR NEIGHBOR AS YOURSELF." 28 And He said to him, "You have answered correctly; DO THIS AND YOU WILL LIVE." 29 But wishing to justify himself, he said to Jesus, "And who is my neighbor?"

30 Jesus replied and said, "A man was going down from Jerusalem to Jericho, and fell among robbers, and they stripped him and ªbeat him, and went away leaving him half dead. 31 And by chance a priest was going

NLT

25 One day an expert in religious law stood up to test Jesus by asking him this question: "Teacher, what should I do to inherit eternal life?"

26 Jesus replied, "What does the law of Moses say? How do you read it?"

27 The man answered, "'You must love the LORD your God with all your heart, all your soul, all your strength, and all your mind.' And, 'Love your neighbor as yourself.'"*

28 "Right!" Jesus told him. "Do this and you will live!"

29 The man wanted to justify his actions, so he asked Jesus, "And who is my neighbor?"

30 Jesus replied with a story: "A Jewish man was traveling from Jerusalem down to Jericho, and he was attacked by bandits. They stripped him of his clothes, beat him up, and left him half dead beside the road.

31 "By chance a priest came along.

NASB

down on that road, and when he saw him, he passed by on the other side. 32 Likewise a Levite also, when he came to the place and saw him, passed by on the other side. 33 But a Samaritan, who was on a journey, came upon him; and when he saw him, he felt compassion, 34 and came to him and bandaged up his wounds, pouring oil and wine on *them;* and he put him on his own beast, and brought him to an inn and took care of him. 35 On the next day he took out two ªdenarii and gave them to the innkeeper and said, 'Take care of him; and whatever more you spend, when I return I will repay you.' 36 Which of these three do you think proved to be a neighbor to the man who fell into the robbers' *hands?*" 37 And he said, "The one who showed mercy toward him." Then Jesus said to him, "Go and do ªthe same."

10:25 ªI.e. an expert in the Mosaic Law
10:26 ªLit *How do you read?* 10:30 ªLit *laid blows upon* 10:35 ªThe denarius was equivalent to a day's wages 10:37 ªOr *likewise*

NLT

But when he saw the man lying there, he crossed to the other side of the road and passed him by. 32 A Temple assistant* walked over and looked at him lying there, but he also passed by on the other side.

33 "Then a despised Samaritan came along, and when he saw the man, he felt compassion for him. 34 Going over to him, the Samaritan soothed his wounds with olive oil and wine and bandaged them. Then he put the man on his own donkey and took him to an inn, where he took care of him. 35 The next day he handed the innkeeper two silver coins,* telling him, 'Take care of this man. If his bill runs higher than this, I'll pay you the next time I'm here.'

36 "Now which of these three would you say was a neighbor to the man who was attacked by bandits?" Jesus asked.

37 The man replied, "The one who showed him mercy."

Then Jesus said, "Yes, now go and do the same."

10:27 Deut 6:5; Lev 19:18. 10:32 Greek *A Levite.* 10:35 Greek *two denarii.* A denarius was equivalent to a laborer's full day's wage.

In 1959, Vince Lombardi inherited the Green Bay Packers at the lowest point of their history as a professional football team. After losing ten of their twelve games the previous season, it seemed they had nowhere to go but up. But, after losing five straight games, Lombardi began to wonder. He gathered the team and announced his intention to get back to basics. He then picked up a ball and said, "Gentlemen, *this* is a football!"

Max McGee, a notorious cutup, replied from the back of the squad, "Uh, Coach, could you slow down a little. You're going too fast for us."[7]

Lombardi laughed, but quickly refocused the team. Though surrounded by tons of football experience, the time had come to wipe the slate clean and start from scratch. The most ingenious playbook in the league won't help a team win if the players have forgotten how to block, tackle, pass, catch, and run.

By the time Jesus stepped onto the religious scene in Israel, the most visible examples of Judaism had reduced godliness to a list of rules and rituals so complicated that no one could maintain it. Even worse, the rules and rituals caused these religious experts to forget the basics, including the most fundamental principles of God's Law. As Jesus praised His disciples for a job well done and declared the kingdom of God officially begun, one of these experts wanted to know what was required of him to join. The question gave Jesus a teaching opportunity He couldn't ignore.

— 10:25-26 —

Luke's narrative has quickly shifted from a private conversation with the Twelve to a public setting. Luke chose to place this story shortly after the report of the seventy to make an important connection. Or, perhaps it might be better to call it a *dis*connection. For the past several weeks or months, the disciples had been proclaiming the arrival of God's kingdom on earth. This prompted a "lawyer," an expert in Jewish laws and traditions, to ask a loaded question.

It's loaded for two reasons. First, it inappropriately combines the idea of "doing"—that is, working to gain a benefit—and the idea of "inheriting." He asked what one must *do* to *inherit* eternal life, which Jews correctly understood as living in God's kingdom. One does not work to gain an inheritance; an estate already belongs to the inheritor and is guaranteed to become his or her property in due time. First-century Jews believed they automatically inherited eternal life as children of Abraham, who had received the unconditional covenant of God.

Second, the question challenged the central message given by Jesus throughout His ministry. On several occasions, He had forgiven sins, cast out demons, and rescued people from the physical effects of evil, declaring that their faith had saved them (5:20; 7:9, 50; 8:48)—that is, given them relief from the temporal consequences of evil *and* the eternal punishment for sin. In other words, they inherited eternal life because of their faith, despite their lives of sin.

The lawyer didn't ask the question as a person seeking a genuine answer. He threw the question down like a gauntlet, challenging Jesus to a theological duel, as it were. That's because the official representatives of Judaism had long ago disconnected from the fundamental truths of God's kingdom. Luke described lawyers, along with Pharisees, as men who had "rejected God's purpose for themselves, not having been baptized by John" (7:30).

Jesus did what an insightful teacher always does; He turned the question back toward the lawyer. Instead of disputing the lawyer's faulty assertions, He probed the lawyer's understanding of the Law and its role in the life of a genuine citizen of the kingdom. One does indeed inherit eternal life by grace through faith, but that does not invalidate the Law or render it useless.

— 10:27-29 —

Particularly pious Jews wore on their wrist or head a small leather pouch or box—known as a phylactery—containing selected texts from the Torah. They did this in literal obedience to God's command, "You shall bind [My words] as a sign on your hand and they shall be as frontals on your forehead" (Deut. 6:8), and as a practical means of keeping the Law foremost in their minds. By Jesus' time, however, this practice had become a conspicuous sign of spirituality. Therefore, it's quite possible the lawyer was wearing a phylactery when challenging Jesus.

Jesus asked the man what role he thought the Law played in the kingdom of God. In response to Jesus' question, the lawyer quoted two Old Testament texts that may have been bound to his head or wrist: "You shall love the LORD your God with all your heart, and with all your soul, and with all your strength, and with all your mind" (Deut. 6:5),

GPO Photo by Mark Neyman/Wikimedia Commons

This man is wearing one of the *tefillin*, also known as a phylactery, a small box that holds a portion of the Torah and is worn by Jewish men on their foreheads or hands, attached with small leather straps. The origins of wearing phylacteries are found in Exodus 13:16 and Deuteronomy 6:8; 11:18.

and "[you shall love] your neighbor as yourself" (Lev. 19:18). In other words, the lawyer correctly understood the heart of the Law.

Jesus responded, in effect, "You have your answer. Now, get after it!"

It is possible to deserve eternal life by obedience to the Law of God—in theory. In other words, anyone who is morally perfect does indeed deserve eternal life in the kingdom of God. Morally perfect people don't need grace. In alluding to Old Testament precedents (Lev. 18:5; Ezek. 20:11), Jesus invited the man to practice what he preached and to bank on his good works being enough to earn eternal life in the kingdom.

At this point, the attorney—like all good practitioners of the law—started looking for loopholes. He knew he had not kept the Law perfectly, nor could he. He knew he had long ago lost the moral perfection battle. So, he attempted to do what all Pharisees did. Recognizing that the moral standard of heaven is too high, he looked for a way to lower the bar. "Wishing to justify himself," he sought to define the term "neighbor" in the most convenient way possible.

In the Old Testament, before the Exile and whenever Israel was not sharing the Promised Land with invaders, a Jew's neighbor was almost certainly another Jew. The man probably thought, *If the definition of "neighbor" includes those people I like and with whom I am most comfortable, then I'm doing just fine!* But Jesus didn't come to lower the bar; He came to raise the standard of righteousness (Matt. 5:17-48).

To answer the lawyer's question, Jesus told a story.

— 10:30 —

Jesus gave the story a setting His audience would immediately recognize. When Jews traveled from Judea in the south to Galilee in the north, they typically traveled east, down the mountains toward the Jordan River basin in order to go around Samaria, which lay between Judea and Galilee. Such was their loathing of the Samaritans that they preferred this longer, more treacherous route. Jerusalem sits nearly 2,100 feet (630 meters) above sea level; Jericho in the Jordan River valley is 850 feet (260 meters) below sea level. The 2,950-foot (900-meter) drop in less than 20 miles (32 kilometers) made for a bad road. The path wound its way through terrain perfect for bandits to ambush unwary travelers. For centuries, people called it "the bloody way."

Jesus described a man who was beaten senseless, naked, broke, and left for dead by robbers—completely helpless. Notably, the man is left anonymous. He could have been anyone. The lawyer, like all his high-minded religious friends, had taken the road to Jericho many times, though never alone. Everyone feared suffering this man's fate. Jesus heightened the pathos of the story so the lawyer would see himself lying there in the wilderness.

— 10:31-32 —

"By chance," hope came in the person of a priest, a man called by God to mediate the relationship between Himself and humanity, who was also an expert in the Law. Certainly, he had memorized Leviticus 19:18, "[You shall love] your neighbor as yourself." Alas, the dying man's hope passed *on the other side* of the road, perhaps to obey Leviticus 21:1-3:

> Then the LORD said to Moses, "Speak to the priests, the sons of Aaron, and say to them: 'No one shall defile himself for a dead person among his people, except for his relatives who are nearest to him, his mother and his father and his son and his daughter and his brother, also for his virgin sister, who is near to him because she has had no husband; for her he may defile himself.'"

If so, the priest chose to ignore the "greater commandment" and to soothe his conscience with the knowledge he had obeyed the lesser.

"Likewise" (that is, "by chance"), hope came again in the person of a Levite. Levites could be considered "assistant priests," attending to the less critical duties in the temple. They therefore had less reason to worry about ritual purity. But he, too, passed by *on the other side* of the road.

— 10:33-35 —

The hero of the story comes as a surprise. Luke's choice of word order places emphasis on the word "Samaritan." A hated Samaritan—of all people!—"saw" exactly what the priest and the Levite had seen, but he responded with compassion. Whereas the other two travelers passed by on the other side of the road, the Samaritan "came to him." Moreover, the Lord describes the Samaritan's care as tender, conscientious, thorough, and sacrificial. He gave the best care of the day, washing the wounds in wine to ward off infection, bathing the raw flesh in soothing olive oil, and bandaging the injuries to protect them. He took the bruised man to safety and cared for him until morning. He even left the innkeeper two days' wages, charging him to care for the injured man, promising to return and cover any additional expenses. His grace toward the unknown victim was extraordinary!

— 10:36-37 —

For a third time, Jesus turned the debate toward the lawyer, placing him in the role of decision maker. Jesus' question reveals a greater concern for the lawyer's application of the Law than his ability to distill it to something pithy and easy to manage. Jesus' question also made it difficult for the man to lower the standard of righteousness to something convenient and self-justifying.

Jesus notably asked who "proved to be a neighbor to the man" as a clever means of recalling the Golden Rule: "Treat others the same way you want them to treat you" (Luke 6:31). The lawyer knew how he would want to be treated if he were the helpless man in the story. Consequently, he was cornered. He had no choice but to offer the obviously correct answer. He might not have considered the hated half-breed his neighbor, but the morally superior Samaritan would have treated him with compassion.

Jesus ended the encounter with the challenge, "Go and do the same," knowing the man could not consistently apply such an impossibly high standard of goodness—at least not day after day and person by person. Jesus' challenge put all hope of salvation by works completely out of reach.

In the end, Jesus took the expert in the Law of God back to the basics. He demonstrated beyond any doubt and above any objection that the man had failed morally. For all his knowledge and despite his meticulous attention to legal minutiae, he was less righteous than a hated Samaritan. Jesus proved that, while earning one's way into the kingdom of God is a theoretical possibility, it is a practical impossibility. All have fallen short of the standard. All have failed to obey the most basic principles of the Law. Therefore, all need grace. Only those who trust in the unmerited favor of God's Son can become citizens of God's kingdom.

APPLICATION: LUKE 10:25-37

A Crucial Principle for Ministry

A lingering idea from this passage leads to a crucial principle for ministry.

The lingering idea we dare not miss: What you are determines what you see, and what you see determines what you do.

All three passersby saw the man, but only one was compassionate. On the basis of something deep within him, prompted by his empathy, he saw human need, and whether the one in need was Samaritan or not was immaterial. As a result, he did something different from the others. What you are determines what you see, and what you see determines what you do.

This leads to a crucial principle for all Christians, but especially those in ministry. Nothing is more basic to Christianity than this, and all of us would do well to remember it when planning to reach another with the gospel: *People will not care how much we know until they know how much we care.*

Let me explain by way of a personal illustration.

Toward the end of my seminary education—four years of intense study at Dallas Theological Seminary—Cynthia and I were almost certain our unborn child would not see life outside the womb. The financial and personal strains of those years were difficult enough without the anguish of potentially losing a child.

I needed a friend, someone to care. So, late one evening, after studying in the library until closing, I thought I would find a professor who would put his arms around me—any of the men I had been studying under and following for nearly four years. I remember knocking on a door and no one answered. I walked a little farther and knocked, but no one answered. I saw a light shining underneath another door, so I knocked on that door.

After a moment, a professor I had known during those years opened his door a crack. "Yes?" he stared at me. Had I known it was him, I don't believe I would have disturbed him. I learned long ago that he didn't have the capacity to understand. He had a brilliant mind, a magnificent capacity to teach the Greek language. I had taken several courses from him, and we knew each other well from the classroom.

"Yes, Chuck. What do you want?"

I stood there, and tears just ran from my eyes. But I could hear in his voice he didn't want to talk to me. I said, "Am I disturbing you?"

"Yes, you're disturbing me. What do you want?"

I said, "Nothing. I don't want anything."

"Fine," he said, and closed the door.

I needed somebody. I wanted somebody who would simply listen to what I was going through. I've wondered since then if anyone will receive a reward for how much Greek they know.

The next morning, while I was still trying to find my way through the labyrinth of my feelings and get up on my own feet from the depression and fear of losing our baby and maybe even losing my wife, Dr. Howie Hendricks walked up to me and put his arms around me and won my heart. He has held onto it to this day. He listened, he empathized, and he told me of the miscarriage he and his wife experienced and how they recovered from that tragedy. And from that day forward, I wanted to know what he knew, because I knew how much he cared.

Exchanging What's Good for What's Best
LUKE 10:38-42

NASB

38 Now as they were traveling along, He entered a village; and a woman named Martha welcomed Him into her home. 39 She had a sister called Mary, who was seated at the Lord's feet, listening to His word. 40 But Martha was distracted with ªall her preparations; and she came up *to Him* and said, "Lord, do You not care that my sister has left me to do all the serving alone? Then tell her to help me." 41 But the Lord answered and said to her, "Martha, Martha, you are worried and bothered about so many things; 42 but *only* one thing is necessary, for Mary has chosen the good part, which shall not be taken away from her."

10:40 ªLit *much service*

NLT

38 As Jesus and the disciples continued on their way to Jerusalem, they came to a certain village where a woman named Martha welcomed him into her home. 39 Her sister, Mary, sat at the Lord's feet, listening to what he taught. 40 But Martha was distracted by the big dinner she was preparing. She came to Jesus and said, "Lord, doesn't it seem unfair to you that my sister just sits here while I do all the work? Tell her to come and help me."

41 But the Lord said to her, "My dear Martha, you are worried and upset over all these details! 42 There is only one thing worth being concerned about. Mary has discovered it, and it will not be taken away from her."

One of the endearing qualities of the Bible is its down-to-earth approach to life. The characters of the Bible are not portrayed as plaster saints or untouchable members of a royal family; instead, they are real-life people with whom anyone can identify. I often wonder if these biblical characters knew that their family lives would be preserved for everyone to see. I'm sure they would have perspired thinking about centuries of readers around the world analyzing their most intimate family moments.

Luke gives us a peek inside the home of two sisters engaged in a brief family squabble, not to embarrass them, but to illustrate a point. In fact, I have little doubt Luke heard this story straight from the lips of an elderly Martha and Mary, years after the Lord's departure, and gained their permission to use it. It perfectly balances a dominant theme in the disciples' training, in which Jesus called His followers to engage in good deeds. The Lord had been clear that citizenship in the kingdom is received by grace through faith in the Messiah. Still, there was room for confusion. After all, the final challenge Jesus laid before the lawyer suggested he work overtime if he expected to do enough to earn eternal life (10:36-37). So, just in case the reader missed the Lord's mild sarcasm, Luke allowed a minor tiff between sisters to become a teachable moment for all of Christendom.

— 10:38-39 —

Luke doesn't tell us where Martha and Mary lived because it isn't important to the story. Nevertheless, we know from John's Gospel that the sisters lived either with, or near, their brother Lazarus, in a village called Bethany about 2 miles northwest of Jerusalem. Situated on the eastern slope of the Mount of Olives, it was a perfect place for Jesus to retreat from the crush of Jerusalem, yet stay close enough to teach in the temple every day. On this occasion, the Lord elected to stay in the home of these three siblings, as He often did, apparently, and it's clear He considered them family. This little house in Bethany was as close to a home as He could get.

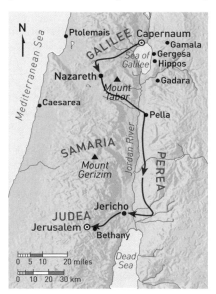

Jesus was on his way to Jerusalem, but along the way from his ministry base in Galilee, he stopped by Mount Tabor (the traditional location for the Transfiguration). Later, He sent out seventy of his disciples to minister in the cities he would visit. Then He stopped in Bethany to see his friends Lazarus, Martha, and Mary before heading to Jerusalem.

Luke's phrasing, "Now as they were traveling along," suggests Jesus and His disciples made an unannounced visit. He doesn't tell us if Jesus came alone or with several followers

Hurry-Up Listening

LUKE 10:39

I had been intense through the evening meal. In fact, I had been intense since arriving home. My packed-out schedule had me on rocket-powered roller skates all day long, and my momentum kept me in hurry-up mode well into the evening. So, I was talking fast, I was spitting out one-word answers, I was barking commands, and I was doing this and doing that. In the midst of my harried exchanges with Cynthia, our daughter Colleen caught up with me, wanting to tell me something about her day. Picking up on my urgency, she said, "Daddy, I want to tell you something about school, and I'll talk real fast. I'll tell you real quick. I won't take much time. I promise I'll talk real, real fast."

I took a deep breath and said, "Now wait a minute. Hold on. Talk slowly." She looked at me with her little girl intensity and said, "Well, Daddy, then listen slowly."

in tow, but the ensuing scene would make better sense if Martha panicked over the number of guests. Regardless, "Martha welcomed Him into her home," a decision characteristic of ancient Near Eastern hospitality. Her name derives from an Aramaic word meaning "lady" or "mistress," as in the "lady of the house." Her name fits her personality: responsible, serious, and perhaps a little intense.

Mary, her sister, appears to be her opposite. When Jesus arrived, Mary sat at Jesus' feet to listen to His teaching, a position normally reserved for official disciples of a teacher and never for a woman.

Note their difference: Martha, the energetic, responsible hostess versus Mary, the attentive, conscientious listener. With these two divergent personalities in the center of a bustling social situation with tasks to be done, the scene was set for conflict.

— 10:40 —

While Mary contentedly soaked in the Lord's teaching, Martha frenetically hustled to meet the needs of her guests, "distracted with all her preparations." The key word "distracted" comes from the Greek term *perispaō* [4049], which also can mean "dragged away."[8] Luke used the word in a more figurative sense to show that Martha was pulled away from Jesus' teaching because she was overburdened with busyness.

Some people naturally focus on tasks when relating to others. Eager to serve, they exercise almost superhuman ability to spot needs without asking and supply what's lacking without the slightest thought of self. There's nothing wrong with task-oriented temperaments. Without them, the world would grind to a halt. Martha's problem was that she was paying so much attention to the preparations for her guests that she stopped paying attention to the Guest.

Martha, feeling overwhelmed by the burden of hosting—perhaps with a streak of perfectionism fueling her frustration—and feeling abandoned by her sister, lashed out at the two people least deserving it. She accused both Mary and the Lord of callously disregarding her at a time when Mary should have pitched in to help. Martha expected the Lord to rebuke Mary for her laziness or selfishness, but instead she received a surprising response.

— 10:41-42 —

Martha's attempt to pull Jesus to her side of the dispute backfired. Rather than hear Jesus affirm to everyone in the house her sacrificial service, she heard a mild rebuke, beginning with "Martha, Martha."

The doubling of her name at the beginning of an address expresses deep emotion—not disappointment, not condescension, not even disapproval, but rather compassion. He understood the circumstances and the effect they had on her personally. He also appreciated her sincere desire to serve everyone. He even acknowledged her efforts, noting only that she was "worried," which resulted in her feeling upset. He said, in effect, "I can see that you care Martha, but you care too much!"

Rather than lecture Martha on the foolishness of worry or scold her for lashing out, He reduced her burden. Martha was fretting over many matters, yet neglecting the only important matter: listening to Jesus. Martha was scurrying to prepare a large meal when something simple would have sufficed, allowing her to enjoy spending time with Jesus. Everyone was in the room with Jesus, except one: Martha.

Rather than rebuke Mary, Jesus chose to praise her example. She had chosen the good part of his unexpected visit, the part that cannot be taken away. She set aside temporal concerns to focus on the eternal. She ignored trivial matters to immerse herself in the teaching of Christ on the kingdom of God.

When this familiar story is connected with the Lord's interaction with the lawyer in the previous episode, an important insight emerges. Throughout His ministry, Jesus urged His disciples to engage in kingdom work, to be responsible citizens by joining His world-redeeming enterprise. He also encouraged obedience to the Law—not to justify oneself or to earn eternal life, but because that's what good citizens do: They obey their king. Even so, He never intended for good deeds and obedience to replace "the good part": a personal relationship with the King. We don't obey the Law to become His citizens; we obey the King because we are His citizens.

APPLICATION: LUKE 10:38-42

Principles for Priorities

As we turn our attention from the ancient home of Martha and Mary to our homes today, it appears little has changed! The same time pressures exist. The same tension between tasks and relationships distracts us. The same personality conflicts come between us. The same clashes among family members over priorities still occur. The Holy Spirit has preserved this vignette for approximately twenty centuries because it still shows us what our priorities should be. Here are two observations worth noting.

First, *when facing a test, it's easy to let our temperament dictate the agenda*. I am, by nature, a task-oriented kind of man. For me, a deadline is a deadline, punctuality is a virtue, and rules are for following; and I cannot rest when tasks remain undone. That's my temperament. It is a valuable part of my constitution that has helped me succeed where others have failed. But that strength can also become my undoing.

Your temperament may be different. You may be more naturally relational when the pressures of life bear down. You may become contemplative or serene in the face of life's demands. But, just like me, you may find your temperament a liability at times.

When tested by circumstances, our default mode may not be the best response. To keep your natural strengths from becoming a liability, become an impartial observer of your own temperament—perhaps enlisting the help of trusted friends—and evaluate when your natural inclinations are helpful and when they cause problems. The people closest to you have probably tried to say something important that you need to hear, but you've shut them out because your way of doing things has always worked before and you're not open to suggestions. Perhaps it's time to hear what they have to say.

Second, *when life gets complicated, it's helpful to remember that simplicity is the best policy*. Even as a pastor, setting aside time to be alone and silent with God can be one of the most difficult choices I must make. Spiritual leadership doesn't make this choice any easier; believe me, the pressure to keep busy is as powerful in ministry as it is anywhere. There are a million and one reasons to leave the Master's feet in the name of doing His work. At least that's the story we tell ourselves. To simplify, I have made one amazingly powerful word a regular part of my vocabulary. The word is *no*.

Believe it or not, a kind, polite, respectful no can be your key to unlocking the power of the spiritual disciplines. Perhaps it's time to back out of a few commitments. Let your no to others free you to say yes to God.

Lord, Teach Us to Pray
LUKE 11:1-13

NASB

1 It happened that while ᵃJesus was praying in a certain place, after He had finished, one of His disciples said to Him, "Lord, teach us to pray just as John also taught his disciples." 2 And He said to them, "When you pray, say:

'ᵃFather, hallowed be Your name.
Your kingdom come.
3 'Give us each day our ᵃdaily
bread.
4 'And forgive us our sins,
For we ourselves also forgive
everyone who is indebted
to us.
And lead us not into
temptation.'"

5 Then He said to them, "ᵃSuppose one of you has a friend, and goes to him at midnight and says to him, 'Friend, lend me three loaves; 6 for a friend of mine has come to me from a journey, and I have nothing to set before him'; 7 and from inside he answers and says, 'Do not bother me; the door has already been shut and my children ᵃand I are in bed; I cannot get up and give you *anything.*' 8 I tell you, even though he will not get up and give him *anything* because he is his friend, yet because of his ᵃpersistence he will get up and give him as much as he needs.

9 "So I say to you, ᵃask, and it will be given to you; ᵇseek, and you will find; ᶜknock, and it will be opened to you. 10 For everyone who asks, receives; and he who seeks, finds; and to him who knocks, it will be opened. 11 Now ᵃsuppose one of you fathers is asked by his son for a ᵇfish; he will not give him a snake instead of a fish, will he? 12 Or *if* he is asked for

NLT

1 Once Jesus was in a certain place praying. As he finished, one of his disciples came to him and said, "Lord, teach us to pray, just as John taught his disciples."

2 Jesus said, "This is how you should pray:*

"Father, may your name be kept
holy.
May your Kingdom come soon.
3 Give us each day the food we
need,*
4 and forgive us our sins,
as we forgive those who sin
against us.
And don't let us yield to
temptation.*"

5 Then, teaching them more about prayer, he used this story: "Suppose you went to a friend's house at midnight, wanting to borrow three loaves of bread. You say to him, 6 'A friend of mine has just arrived for a visit, and I have nothing for him to eat.' 7 And suppose he calls out from his bedroom, 'Don't bother me. The door is locked for the night, and my family and I are all in bed. I can't help you.' 8 But I tell you this—though he won't do it for friendship's sake, if you keep knocking long enough, he will get up and give you whatever you need because of your shameless persistence.*

9 "And so I tell you, keep on asking, and you will receive what you ask for. Keep on seeking, and you will find. Keep on knocking, and the door will be opened to you. 10 For everyone who asks, receives. Everyone who seeks, finds. And to everyone who knocks, the door will be opened.

11 "You fathers—if your children ask* for a fish, do you give them a snake instead? 12 Or if they ask for an

NASB

an egg, he will not give him a scorpion, will he? ¹³If you then, being evil, know how to give good gifts to your children, how much more will *your* ªheavenly Father give the Holy Spirit to those who ask Him?"

11:1 ªLit *He* 11:2 ªLater mss add phrases from Matt 6:9-13 to make the two passages closely similar 11:3 ªOr *bread for the coming day* or *needful bread* 11:5 ªLit *Which one of you will have* 11:7 ªLit *with me* 11:8 ªLit *shamelessness* 11:9 ªOr *keep asking* ᵇOr *keep seeking* ᶜOr *keep knocking* 11:11 ªLit *which of you, a son, will ask the father* ᵇTwo early mss insert *loaf, he will not give him a stone, will he, or for a* 11:13 ªLit *Father from heaven*

NLT

egg, do you give them a scorpion? Of course not! ¹³So if you sinful people know how to give good gifts to your children, how much more will your heavenly Father give the Holy Spirit to those who ask him."

11:2 Some manuscripts add additional phrases from the Lord's Prayer as it reads in Matt 6:9-13. 11:3 Or *Give us each day our food for the day;* or *Give us each day our food for tomorrow.* 11:4 Or *And keep us from being tested.* 11:8 Or *in order to avoid shame,* or *so his reputation won't be damaged.* 11:11 Some manuscripts add *for bread, do you give them a stone? Or [if they ask].*

When all else fails, read the instructions.

I have lived the better part of my life by that little axiom and, to be perfectly honest, it usually works for me. Boxes labeled "Some Assembly Required" don't intimidate me; I rarely have any trouble figuring things out for myself. Occasionally, however, I get in over my head and need help.

One Christmas Eve, after the kids were tucked away, I dragged a box from its hiding place, unpacked and arranged all the parts, and began assembling a kit with the cool efficiency of a surgeon. The pieces came together with ease as the finished product started to take shape—at least as I had it in my mind's eye. In time, however, it became obvious that the work of my hands didn't look like the product on the box. With dawn approaching, I admitted my failure and then searched for the instructions in the trash. Humbled and teachable, I started reading from the top of the page where, to my dismay, a sarcastic sage had written in very small, inoffensive type, "Now that you have made a mess of things, please start over and follow these instructions."

After over fifty years in pastoral ministry, I can say with confidence that most people approach life the same way: "When all else fails, pray." It is part of our fallen, selfish, proud disposition to do things *our* way, and only when the consequences of failure overwhelm us do we seek help.

The disciples noticed that Jesus followed a completely different pattern of prayer. He prayed for different reasons, at different times, with different language, and with a different attitude. After hearing the Lord pray on one occasion, one of His followers asked to learn how to pray like the Son of God.

— 11:1 —

Luke again transitions to a new setting with the word *egeneto* (from *ginomai* [1096]), meaning "It came about" or "It happened." We have no way of knowing for certain where this event took place. For prayer, Jesus appears to have favored a few locations near Galilee (5:16; 6:12; 9:28), and we know He frequently retreated to a garden on the western slope of the Mount of Olives with a good view of Jerusalem (21:37; 22:39). It's quite possible Jesus had been praying in the garden of Gethsemane.

The disciples kindly waited for Jesus to finish, then one approached Him with this revealing request: "Lord, teach us to pray just as John also taught his disciples." It was not uncommon in first-century Israel for religious groups to adopt and memorize a liturgical prayer to express their identity and encourage unity. John the Baptizer may have composed such a prayer, and this may have prompted the disciples to ask for their own. The imperative "teach us," however, may imply a sense of urgency, as in "teach us *now*," suggesting that perhaps something else prompted their request.

No doubt, they noticed His prayers differed greatly from their own. Something about His words, His motivation, His attitude, or His expectations provoked the disciples to become dissatisfied with their own manner of prayer and to seek a different way of communicating with God.

— 11:2-4 —

Jesus didn't hesitate to meet the disciple's request. The prayer as given here is shorter than the version in the Gospel of Matthew, probably because Jesus answered the question more than once, and He never intended it to be offered verbatim. This is a model prayer, given as a general example of how we should approach God. Despite its shorter length, Luke's rendering includes the same irreducible essentials of a complete prayer as in Matthew's narrative. This is the basic outline:

1. Give reverence to God the Father.
2. Submit to God's agenda for the world.
3. Do not hesitate to ask for your needs to be met.

First, *give reverence to God the Father.* The model prayer doesn't begin by calling God "Friend," as though we are His equals. It doesn't call God "Master," as though we are His slaves. Jesus didn't call Him "King," as though we are merely His subjects. The model prayer doesn't open with "Teacher," as though we simply come to Him for knowledge. Although God is indeed Friend, Master, King, and Teacher, Jesus instructed us to address God as He does: *pater* in Greek, *abba* in Aramaic (Mark 14:36; Rom. 8:15; Gal. 4:6), "Father" in English. The title is intimate, familial, and honorific. It recognizes authority, but in the context of a trusting relationship of life-giving love. It welcomes God's offer of provision, protection, guidance, and affirmation.

While the title "Father" is familiar, Jesus expressed reverence. The archaic phrase "be hallowed" derives from the Greek verb *hagiazō* [37], which means "sanctify, make holy, consecrate." It appears here as a passive, and may in fact be a "divine passive," which implies God will carry out the action of the verb. Moreover, the verb is imperative, calling upon God to make His own name holy. We might paraphrase the line as "Father, consecrate your name; make it holy, a sanctified name in my life and in the world." While it's a command (imperative), the line is nonetheless submissive, calling upon God to do what He has declared He will do. In the same spirit, we might "command" God, "Make me Your servant!"

Second, *submit to God's agenda for the world.* Jesus concluded the opening address of this prayer with the phrase "Your kingdom come," which expresses two basic thoughts. The first is an affirmation of the Lord's redemption and reformation of the world under His authority. It's an exclamation of respect and support, not unlike "Long live the king!" Second, it serves to place the prayer in the proper attitude. Again, one's mental-emotional posture is bowed in submission, accepting God's plan and purposes, reminding the one who prays of a program greater than any human agenda. While the Lord cares about our concerns, we will find greater comfort and fulfillment by adopting His.

Third, *do not hesitate to ask for your needs to be met.* The model prayer quickly turns from the high and mighty to the practical and personal. Some well-intentioned, yet misguided, theologians suggest there's no place for personal concerns or physical needs in prayer— that all communication with God should be limited to praise, confession, and adoration. Nothing more. No supplication. But the Lord's example specifically includes a request for the Lord to meet our daily need for food.

One might argue, Why ask God for what He's already promised to provide? In response, I ask, Do you really think the purpose of prayer is to convince God to do something He wouldn't otherwise do? We don't pray to bend God's will to ours. We pray to make His will alive in us and to conform to His agenda. Prayer is a meeting of the minds in which we adopt His way of thinking in practical terms. In this spirit, Jesus said, in effect, "Don't hesitate to ask for your needs." These include:

A. *Basic physical needs.* "Daily bread" alludes to God's provision of manna in the wilderness, between the Exodus and the establishment of Israel in the Promised Land (Exod. 16:1-7). As such, it symbolizes everything needed to survive—clothing, water, shelter, all the essentials of physical life. Note that, like the manna, this provision is daily and continual—abundant to satisfy completely and promised each day in turn (see Prov. 30:7-9).

B. *Daily spiritual renewal.* Just as our bodies need food to survive, so our souls need nurturing—daily cleansing and feeding. This includes—but is not limited to—receiving forgiveness and forgiving others. Without the daily maintenance of forgiveness, we inevitably become bitter, vengeful, burdened, self-loathing souls, destructive to others and poisonous to ourselves. Note that Jesus joined the request for God's forgiveness to our extending forgiveness to others. That's because they are intimately connected.

The Lord makes our forgiveness conditioned upon our willingness to forgive others (Matt 6:14; 18:35; Mark 11:25-26). The one whose pride and selfishness prevents him or her from extending forgiveness to others cannot possibly understand the meaning of grace. And how can one receive what one cannot comprehend? In truth, we all have this in common: We all have someone we can blame for something, and we all deserve blame for harming and/or hurting someone else. And, in the same way that someone is indebted to us for wrongdoing, we are indebted to God all the more!

He also commands forgiveness because it is basic to maintaining the soul. Enemies and their evil deeds can become the focus of life unless we voluntarily remove them through forgiveness.

C. *Protection from temptation.* The request "lead us not into temptation" bothers some people because it seems to imply that God might lead people into compromising situations. But Greek grammar experts identify the phrase "lead us not" as a permissive imperative: "Do not permit us to be led into temptation." Furthermore, a study of extrabiblical religious literature reveals that to "enter temptation" means to succumb to temptation—the idea being that one enters and even embraces temptation. Therefore, the final request of the prayer can be paraphrased, "Cause us not to give in to temptation."[9]

The Greek word for "temptation" (*peirasmos* [3986]) originally referred to a kind of test that proves the character of something, not unlike weighing a gold coin to be certain it isn't fraudulent. Later, pagan writers used the term to describe the ordeals humans endured at the hands of capricious gods. In time, it came to mean "to attempt to make one do something wrong." Of course, the one true God always leads away from temptation, and frequently against our will. This request affirms the Lord's desire and unites our will with His.

To complete His lesson on prayer, Jesus told two parables—the first to encourage persistence in prayer (Luke 11:5-10) and the second to defend the goodness of God (11:11-13).

— 11:5-8 —

Jesus frequently used examples of poor human behavior to illustrate the Lord's supreme goodness and unreserved love, usually following this pattern: "Even humans will behave righteously in this circumstance; therefore, you can trust that God, who is righteous, will behave even more righteously."

The first parable places the disciples in the role of a petitioner, banging on his neighbor's door in the middle of the night. The reason—unexpected guests and the unforeseen need for food—is not important to the story other than to convey the idea of need and urgency. Jesus inserted several details to draw the listener into the story; these details have no deep symbolic meaning. The host in need of bread obviously represents the disciple seeking something from God; the reluctant neighbor is a caricature of God as we often imagine Him: stingy, cantankerous, distracted by His own desires, and reluctant to release blessings He can obviously afford.

Notably, the surprised host doesn't ask for anything for himself in the parable; he merely asks his neighbor to help him honor the ancient Near Eastern duty of hospitality: feeding and sheltering a tired, hungry traveler. In fact, the reluctant neighbor would have been duty-bound to open the door for the traveler; so his unwillingness to let his neighbor in—a man he knows and presumably likes—is incomprehensible. Jesus' parable cleverly heightens the contrast between the honorable host and his disgraceful neighbor.

The Lord's explanation fills in the rest of the details. The neighbor said, "I cannot"; Jesus clarified that he *would* not, dismissing the man's objection as an excuse. And while the selfish neighbor would not do what is right for his relationship with the host, he finally obliged in order to end the midnight banging on his door. Where honor failed, persistence overcame.

The Greek word for "persistence" (*anaideia* [335]) is used in the New Testament only this once; in other contexts it generally means "shamelessness," "impudence," "impertinence," or "ignoring of conventional etiquette." The host didn't care that his neighbor had chosen to behave poorly, and he disregarded the man's opinion of him. His obedience to his duty outweighed the neighbor's selfish desire for sleep. And it finally persuaded him to do what is right.

The Lord's point is twofold. First, when we are doing what God considers good, we can boldly come to Him for provision, even if it feels like impudence (Eph. 3:12; Heb. 10:19; 1 Jn. 3:21-22). Second, if boldness moved an unrighteous man to do what is right, how much more can we rely upon God—who is uncompromisingly good—to support our efforts?

This final point prompted Jesus to tell a second parable.

— 11:9-10 —

Just in case the disciples missed the point, Jesus reinforced it, as expressed through the linking of three imperative verbs to three corresponding indicative verbs[10] with the conjunction "and." This construction indicates that the results are conditioned upon the command and are guaranteed to work. In other words, we could paraphrase the three commands this way:

If only you will ask the Father, *then* your request will be given to you.
If only you will seek[11] the Father's will, *then* you will find it.
If only you will knock, *then* the Father will open the door to your request.

— 11:11-13 —

After comparing God the Father to a negative human example, Jesus used the image of a caring earthly father to illustrate the goodness of God. In fact, He made the connection even more poignant by having His listeners imagine their own children coming to them with a request for a basic necessity. The fish, snake, egg, and scorpion have no deep symbolic meaning. They merely give the story enough everyday realism to help the men connect.

In each case, the child's reasonable request for something to eat is met with the opposite of care. The father who gives his children snakes and scorpions is sadistically cruel, which is barely conceivable in a human father, much less a righteous, loving, heavenly Father. On the contrary, God delights to give the gift of Himself. He promised as much in the announcement of the new covenant (Jer. 31:31-34). God will *always* behave righteously. In fact, He wants nothing more than for us to do what is right, and He will not withhold anything to help us behave righteously. And where we fail, He has promised to succeed through His Holy Spirit.

• • •

Centuries of tradition have taught us to call the prayer of Luke 11:2-4 "The Lord's Prayer," but that's a misnomer. If anything, we should call it "The Disciples' Prayer," or better, "The Model Prayer." Jesus gave it and the two parables that follow as an example of how we should approach God. Not as beggars, but as sons and daughters. Not as owners of a magic genie, but as worshipers of the sovereign, almighty Creator. Not as people seeking to bend the will of God to suit our purposes, but as citizens eager to see the King's agenda become the law of the land.

I think if we came to our heavenly Father as Jesus taught, we would never again complain that God doesn't hear our prayers.

APPLICATION: LUKE 11:1-13

Trust God and Ask Boldly

When I studied this passage, I felt rebuked. I wish I could serve as a good model in this area, but this is an area of continual growth for me—as it is for many, I believe. Nevertheless, let me offer these two thoughts. They have helped me a great deal.

First, *always count on God to answer clearly*.

Now, I did not say quickly. For some reason, I'm one of those people who seldom gets a quick answer. Some people do. They might ask at breakfast, "Lord, please provide the rent money," and they go to the mailbox that afternoon to find it waiting. I rarely have that happen. I make a request and then there's a fairly long period of waiting. And in the waiting period, I grow. My trust in God expands. I become increasingly more persistent—and admittedly more impatient. But I have learned through the years to count on God to answer clearly . . . always.

Second, *never hesitate to be bold, even though the odds are stacked against you*.

You are talking to a Father who has never met His match. Never hesitate to be bold in His presence! Now, I don't mean impudent. I'm not suggesting that we stick our hands on our hips and strut ourselves in front of heaven as though God is supposed to do as we demand. I refer, instead, to a gentle boldness, a confident boldness that comes from assurance in the goodness of God. His answer may be no, but He will nonetheless honor your confidence in His ability.

The Kingdom of Light and the Kingdom of Darkness
LUKE 11:14-28

NASB

¹⁴And He was casting out a demon, and it was mute; when the demon had gone out, the mute man spoke; and the crowds were amazed. ¹⁵But some of them said, "He casts out demons by Beelzebul, the ruler of the demons." ¹⁶Others, ᵃto test *Him,* were demanding of Him a ᵇsign from heaven. ¹⁷But He knew their thoughts and said to them, "ᵃAny kingdom divided against itself is laid waste; and a house *divided* against ᵇitself falls. ¹⁸If Satan also is divided against himself, how will his kingdom stand? For you say that I cast out demons by Beelzebul. ¹⁹And if I by Beelzebul cast out demons, by whom do your sons cast them out? So they will be your judges. ²⁰But if I cast out demons by the finger of God, then the kingdom of God has come upon you. ²¹When ᵃa strong *man,* fully armed, guards his own house, his possessions are ᵇundisturbed. ²²But when someone stronger than he attacks him and overpowers him, he takes away from him all his armor on which he had relied and

NLT

¹⁴One day Jesus cast out a demon from a man who couldn't speak, and when the demon was gone, the man began to speak. The crowds were amazed, ¹⁵but some of them said, "No wonder he can cast out demons. He gets his power from Satan,* the prince of demons." ¹⁶Others, trying to test Jesus, demanded that he show them a miraculous sign from heaven to prove his authority.

¹⁷He knew their thoughts, so he said, "Any kingdom divided by civil war is doomed. A family splintered by feuding will fall apart. ¹⁸You say I am empowered by Satan. But if Satan is divided and fighting against himself, how can his kingdom survive? ¹⁹And if I am empowered by Satan, what about your own exorcists? They cast out demons, too, so they will condemn you for what you have said. ²⁰But if I am casting out demons by the power of God,* then the Kingdom of God has arrived among you. ²¹For when a strong man is fully armed and guards his palace, his possessions are safe—²²until someone even stronger attacks and overpowers him, strips him of his weapons, and carries off his belongings.

NASB

distributes his plunder. ²³ He who is not with Me is against Me; and he who does not gather with Me, scatters.

²⁴ "When the unclean spirit goes out of ᵃa man, it passes through waterless places seeking rest, and not finding any, it says, 'I will return to my house from which I came.' ²⁵ And when it comes, it finds it swept and put in order. ²⁶ Then it goes and takes *along* seven other spirits more evil than itself, and they go in and live there; and the last state of that man becomes worse than the first."

²⁷ While ᵃJesus was saying these things, one of the women in the crowd raised her voice and said to Him, "Blessed is the womb that bore You and the breasts at which You nursed." ²⁸ But He said, "On the contrary, blessed are those who hear the word of God and observe it."

11:16 ᵃLit *testing* ᵇOr *attesting miracle*
11:17 ᵃLit *every* ᵇLit *a house* 11:21 ᵃLit *the* ᵇLit *in peace* 11:24 ᵃLit *the* 11:27 ᵃLit *He*

NLT

²³ "Anyone who isn't with me opposes me, and anyone who isn't working with me is actually working against me.

²⁴ "When an evil* spirit leaves a person, it goes into the desert, searching for rest. But when it finds none, it says, 'I will return to the person I came from.' ²⁵ So it returns and finds that its former home is all swept and in order. ²⁶ Then the spirit finds seven other spirits more evil than itself, and they all enter the person and live there. And so that person is worse off than before."

²⁷ As he was speaking, a woman in the crowd called out, "God bless your mother—the womb from which you came, and the breasts that nursed you!"

²⁸ Jesus replied, "But even more blessed are all who hear the word of God and put it into practice."

11:15 Greek *Beelzeboul;* also in 11:18, 19. Other manuscripts read *Beezeboul;* Latin version reads *Beelzebub.* 11:20 Greek *by the finger of God.* 11:24 Greek *unclean.*

What most people living in our culture know about Satan and demons comes from movies, literature, and video games. The same could be said of angels. That's because our twenty-first-century dedication to science and technology has dismissed these invisible creatures as figments of fantasy, mirages of myth. But according to the Bible, these creatures are very real and should not be taken lightly. They are, in fact, powerful combatants in what Donald Grey Barnhouse called "The Invisible War."

Soon after God created the world in perfect splendor, Satan usurped the throne of creation when he enticed Adam and Eve to believe him instead of God (Gen. 3:1-6). On that day, all of creation fell under Satan's dominion (John 12:31; Eph. 2:2; 6:12). Now we are subject to the physical effects of sin in this life (Rom. 8:19-22) and to eternal punishment for rebellion in the life to come (Rev. 20:11-15; 21:8). Now we suffer disasters, diseases, death, and decay. Now we live in a world order characterized by chaos, selfishness, violence, and fear. Jesus came to change all of that, but Satan will not give up without a fight to the bitter end. Consequently, we live in a combat zone.

The Bible presents this cosmic war like this:

THE KINGDOM OF LIGHT	THE KINGDOM OF DARKNESS
Ruler: Living Triune God	Ruler: Satan, the Devil
Destination: New Heaven, New Earth, Eternal Joy	Destination: Hell, Lake of Fire, Eternal Torment
Strategy: Redemption of Sinners by Grace and the Creation of a New Heaven and New Earth	Strategy: Deception, False Hope, Death without Faith
Ultimate End: Success	Ultimate End: Failure

Throughout His ministry, Jesus exercised His divine authority over the dominion of evil, what we might also call the kingdom of darkness. He reversed the physical effects of sin, resuscitated victims of death, and cast demons into the abyss; but, up to this point in the narrative, Luke has not called attention to the big picture. Now, for the first time, Luke connects the Lord's healing ministry to the broader context of this great struggle between the kingdom of light and the kingdom of darkness.

— 11:14-16 —

The episode begins with Jesus casting out a demon, which by now has become almost routine for the reader. Luke even describes the miracle with a slight air of humdrum. We know from other recorded encounters with demons that they manifest themselves in a variety of ways, including otherwise normal physical ailments. In this case, the demon controlled the man's vocal cords, preventing him from speaking. However, this agent of evil was no match for the power and authority of Jesus, and immediately, the man began to speak.

Unfortunately, this encounter with one kind of evil put Jesus on a collision course with another kind. Whereas the seventy "sent ones" believed in Jesus' divine authority, and therefore received it as a gift from Him, a very different set of men attributed the Lord's power to the kingdom of darkness.

The name "Beelzebul" derives from 2 Kings 1, where the name of a foreign god is "Baal-zebub." "Baal" in Hebrew means "ruler," "lord," or "god." "Zebub" means "flies." Put together, the terms form the derisive name "Lord of the Flies," commonly identified as none other than Satan. In other words, Jesus' critics accused Him of acting with the power of Satan rather than the power of God (cf. Luke 7:33).

Another group—perhaps some of them were connected with the first group—demanded of Jesus to prove that His power came from heaven instead of hell. To prove that His power was divine, they asked for a "sign," a corroborating miracle—an absurd request. He had already performed a miracle, but they suspected it was of evil origins. How would another miracle help?

— 11:17-18 —

Jesus answered both the accusation and the challenge with logic:

A. Satan desires to control people, as evidenced by demonic possession.
B. The mute man has been relieved from possession.
C. The power to remove demonic possession must be against Satan's desires.
D. If this act was Satan's idea, then his entire plan will fail.

If any organization hopes to remain intact and achieve its goals, everyone involved must rally together in unity. If, on the other hand, some work for the objectives while others work against them, failure is inevitable. Satan is evil. And Satan is foolish for thinking he can defeat almighty God. But he isn't stupid. He wouldn't send an agent to destroy his own troops if he really expects to win the invisible war.

— 11:19-20 —

Jesus pressed the argument even further. He pointed out that if He cast out demons by the power of Satan, then the work of other exorcists comes under similar suspicion. By the same token, if Jesus cast out demons by divine power, then so do the other exorcists, whether approved by the temple authorities or authorized by Jesus. He also noted that the flawed logic of His challengers might backfire, not only angering their own political and religious allies, but also placing them under the condemnation of God. If indeed His power comes from God, then His authority over demons proves that He is the Messiah and that He has brought the kingdom of God to earth; so rather than doubting Him, the critics should receive Him as their King.

— 11:21-23 —

Jesus illustrated His warning with a description of siege warfare, which aptly describes His mission on earth: first to declare liberation and rally His citizens, and then to return with crushing, overwhelming power to decimate the kingdom of darkness. He painted a before-and-after picture showing the aftermath of His invasion and subtly warned His critics to be certain they fight for the winning side.

His illustration depicts Satan as a feudal lord who has fortified his home. Luke uses the Greek word *aulē* [833], which generally refers to an enclosed open space—such as a courtyard—and often refers to a palace (cf. NLT), which fits the context here. This "strong man" may feel confident that his realm and possessions are impervious to invasion behind his fortifications and troops. The phrase translated "undisturbed" in the NASB is literally "in peace." In this way, Jesus subtly suggested that His audience stands within the walls of this evil strong man's castle, feeling confident with him that all is well simply because they enjoy peace.

After the palace has been conquered, the very things that once gave the "strong man" and his army a sense of security become the spoils of war for the invader. The implication is this: Peace can suddenly come to an end, so don't become overly confident that you are fighting for the right side just because things are going well.

It was not uncommon for a commander about to lay siege to a fortress to shout a word of both warning and promise to the inhabitants: "When I breech the walls, those who lay down their swords will be spared, but those who fight will be tortured mercilessly." Jesus clarified His position in this invisible, cosmic war with the dominion of evil. There is no middle ground (see also 9:50). Everyone must choose a side: either the kingdom of God led by Christ, or the kingdom of darkness led by Satan. Furthermore, each person must decide well, for the consequences of that choice are eternal.

The ease with which Jesus disposed of the demon should have served notice to all witnesses that the "strong man's" days of peace were about to end.

— 11:24-26 —

Jesus returned to the topic of demon possession with a parable illustrating the futility of trying to remain neutral in the invisible war. In this case, a person becomes a dwelling which cannot remain empty for long. The Lord used Jewish folklore to depict an exorcised demon wandering through "waterless places" to find another person to inhabit. According to extra-biblical literature and superstition, evil spirits lurked in barren wilderness areas like robbers, waiting for unwary victims to possess.

Unable to find another host, the demon returns to his original home to find the person doing quite well. In fact, his living situation has improved. The place is renovated and empty! To be certain he doesn't suffer eviction again, he brings companions, making life for the poor victim worse than before. If, on the other hand, the demon had returned to find God living there, the host would continue to enjoy freedom.

In practical terms, no one can remain neutral in the war between light and darkness. Everyone must be inhabited by someone, either God's Spirit or the spirits of Satan.

— 11:27-28 —

While Jesus addressed this mixed audience of critics and supporters, men and women, a woman shouted a word of affirmation to Jesus. Her blessing on His mother was considered an especially high compliment in an age characterized by honoring parents. Her beatitude said, in effect, "Your mother is a blessed woman for having such a wonderful son; she must have done something right!"

In response to the woman's blessing, Jesus offered a counter blessing, expressing His desire for responsiveness to God's word. Those who hear God's message and then heed it are the ones most deserving of honor.

• • •

This portion of Luke's narrative draws an indelible line through the universe, dividing the kingdom of God from the dominion of evil—God's side of the conflict from Satan's. Having done so, Luke invites the reader to engage with each character in the narrative and then determine which side of the line to choose. With this cosmology firmly established, Luke now turns to the conflict with the Pharisees.

Early in the narrative, the Pharisees and other religious authorities presented mild opposition to Jesus, yet these challenges forebode of greater conflict. For several chapters, they have receded to the background of the story—there has been no mention of the Pharisees since the end of chapter 7. Nevertheless, the Lord's ministry put Him on a collision course with the religious authorities in Jerusalem. Consequently, the remaining narrative will prominently feature His conflict with the Pharisees, begging the question of those involved (and of us), "Which side of this conflict have you chosen for yourself?"

APPLICATION: LUKE 11:14-28
Preparation for Battle

We do not fight an enemy we can see, and that fact will play games with our minds if we allow it to. Fortunately, we have the power of Christ on our side, which guarantees victory. Still, to withstand the attacks of the adversary, keep these three thoughts at the forefront of your mind.

First, *if we wish to understand Satan's strategy, we need information.*

The information you can count on is the Word of God. Open a concordance, find the words "devil," "Satan," "demons," and related terms, and then conduct your own search-and-discover study. See what the Scriptures teach about the enemy. You will be amazed, not only at what is revealed, but by how much of your knowledge *doesn't* come from Scripture. If we wish to do battle, and if we wish to understand the enemy's strategy, we need reliable information. And that's found in the Word of God.

Second, *if we plan to withstand enemy attacks, we need protection.*

We need more than information; we need divine protection. God has listed our primary implements of war in Ephesians 6:11-18. It's all spelled out for you. Learn about the "armor of God," and learn to use it.

Third, *if we hope to be protected from demonic invasion, we need salvation.*

Placing one's faith and trust in Christ for salvation and eternal life is step one. Nothing else matters if you don't belong to Him. In fact, the battle doesn't even begin for you until you have sided against Satan by giving your life to the Lord.

Grave Warnings for the "In" Crowd
LUKE 11:29-36

NASB

29 As the crowds were increasing, He began to say, "This generation is a wicked generation; it seeks for a ªsign, and *yet* no ªsign will be given to it but the ªsign of Jonah. 30 For just as Jonah became a ªsign to the Ninevites, so will the Son of Man be

NLT

29 As the crowd pressed in on Jesus, he said, "This evil generation keeps asking me to show them a miraculous sign. But the only sign I will give them is the sign of Jonah. 30 What happened to him was a sign to the people of Nineveh that God had sent

NASB

to this generation. ³¹ The Queen of the South will rise up with the men of this generation at the judgment and condemn them, because she came from the ends of the earth to hear the wisdom of Solomon; and behold, something greater than Solomon is here. ³² The men of Nineveh will stand up with this generation at the judgment and condemn it, because they repented at the preaching of Jonah; and behold, something greater than Jonah is here.

³³ "No one, after lighting a lamp, puts it away in a cellar nor under a basket, but on the lampstand, so that those who enter may see the light. ³⁴ The eye is the lamp of your body; when your eye is ᵃclear, your whole body also is full of light; but when it is ᵇbad, your body also is full of darkness. ³⁵ Then watch out that the light in you is not darkness. ³⁶ If therefore your whole body is full of light, with no dark part in it, it will be wholly illumined, as when the lamp illumines you with its rays."

11:29 ᵃOr *attesting miracle* 11:30 ᵃOr *attesting miracle* 11:34 ᵃOr *healthy* ᵇOr *evil*

NLT

him. What happens to the Son of Man* will be a sign to these people that he was sent by God.

³¹ "The queen of Sheba* will stand up against this generation on judgment day and condemn it, for she came from a distant land to hear the wisdom of Solomon. Now someone greater than Solomon is here—but you refuse to listen. ³² The people of Nineveh will also stand up against this generation on judgment day and condemn it, for they repented of their sins at the preaching of Jonah. Now someone greater than Jonah is here—but you refuse to repent.

³³ "No one lights a lamp and then hides it or puts it under a basket.* Instead, a lamp is placed on a stand, where its light can be seen by all who enter the house.

³⁴ "Your eye is like a lamp that provides light for your body. When your eye is healthy, your whole body is filled with light. But when it is unhealthy, your body is filled with darkness. ³⁵ Make sure that the light you think you have is not actually darkness. ³⁶ If you are filled with light, with no dark corners, then your whole life will be radiant, as though a floodlight were filling you with light."

11:30 "Son of Man" is a title Jesus used for himself. 11:31 Greek *The queen of the south.* 11:33 Some manuscripts do not include *or puts it under a basket.*

By this point in Luke's story, Jesus' name had become a household word in Israel. First, John the Baptizer drew large crowds and then pointed them toward the Christ. Jesus then shined brighter than any prophet. He fed multitudes with abundance taken from virtually nothing. He worked hundreds, perhaps thousands, of miracles. He cleansed lepers. He raised the dead. He cast out demons. He commanded nature. And He also spoke out against the hypocrisy and legalism of the religious authorities, especially the Pharisees. He humbled the self-righteous and denounced their evil. He also empowered and commissioned numerous followers to minister just as He had, a move that threatened to upset the delicate balance of power in Israel. His grassroots movement became a force to be feared in Jerusalem.

While many took no time in rejecting the Messiah, many others hesitated, perhaps wondering which way the political winds would blow. Most people choosing sides in a revolution don't make their decisions based on principle, but by aligning themselves with the one most likely to win. There can be severe consequences to being on the losing side of a revolution, whether in politics, a boardroom, a church, a school, or a residential association. Consequently, the people Jesus encountered wanted a sign, a token of heavenly assurance that He would indeed win. That way, they could enjoy all the benefits of the kingdom without having to risk life, limb, or even their own comfort.

As the crowds grew, Jesus felt it was time to give them another reality check, starting with a look inside.

— 11:29-30 —

Successful leaders—spiritual or otherwise—run a great risk of corruption whenever throngs of people sing their praises. Even when leaders keep their emotions in check and steer clear of vanity, the pursuit of success can become an obsession. Charles Haddon Spurgeon writes, "Success exposes a man to the pressure of people and thus tempts him to hold on to his gains by means of 'fleshly' methods and practices, and to let himself be ruled wholly by the dictatorial demands of incessant expansion."[12] But as Jesus' popularity grew exponentially, He recognized that many were following not because of devotion to Him, but for what they might gain. He also accepted that many who did not follow remained uncommitted because they wanted assurances. They had their own ideas about what the kingdom should be and how the King should rule it, and they wanted to be certain of their future before switching sides.

Jesus therefore confronted His followers, calling "this generation" (*genea* [1074])—an indirect reference to His audience—"wicked." The Greek word translated "wicked" generally means "bad," "harmful," "unserviceable," or "useless" in the practical sense, and in the moral sense, it connotes the opposite of God. Ironically, He used two examples from their history in which Gentile people of questionable character responded correctly to the word of God without any visible assurances.

The "sign of Jonah" has a dual meaning, one of which remains hidden at this point in the narrative. Jonah was buried, as it were, in the belly of a giant fish before emerging on the third day to proclaim the word of God to Nineveh. Jesus would be swallowed by the earth for three days and emerge victorious over death (Matt. 12:40). The second meaning points to Jonah's warning, which Jesus called a "sign," or a truth-affirming miracle.

God had sent the prophet Jonah to the astoundingly cruel, shockingly bloodthirsty people of Nineveh to convey a warning: "Yet forty days and Nineveh will be overthrown" (Jon. 3:4). And surprisingly, the Ninevites repented.

> Then the people of Nineveh believed in God; and they called a fast and put on sackcloth from the greatest to the least of them. When the word reached the king of Nineveh, he arose from his throne, laid aside his robe from him, covered himself with sackcloth and sat on the ashes. (Jon. 3:5-6)

The people of Nineveh, despite their Gentile blood, their idolatry, and their vicious treatment of enemies, proved to be morally superior to "this generation" of Abraham's sons.

— 11:31-32 —

Jesus pulled a second illustration from Israel's history. The "Queen of the South" is the queen of the Arabian kingdom of Sheba (a.k.a. *Saba'*). During the reign of Solomon, she traveled to Jerusalem to verify stories of his immense wealth and to test his wisdom with riddles. When Solomon exceeded her expectations, she exclaimed, "How blessed are your men, how blessed are these your servants who stand before you continually and hear your wisdom. Blessed be the LORD your God who delighted in you to set you on the throne of Israel; because the LORD loved Israel forever, therefore He made you king, to do justice and righteousness" (1 Kgs. 10:8-9).

Jesus affirmed her moral superiority over "this generation" because she traveled far to see Solomon and returned home believing. He imagined her standing at the final judgment to bear witness to their stubborn refusal to believe what was plainly evident and to add her voice to the chorus of condemnation against them.

He then added the people of Nineveh to the chorus of condemnation. They responded to the word of God with humble repentance instead of a demand for proof that Jonah's words were true. One greater than Solomon and more trustworthy than Jonah stood in their midst, yet "this generation" wanted more signs, more proof, more assurances.

Ministry Is No Joke

LUKE 11:29

I like to laugh, even in the pulpit, which brought no shortage of criticism in the beginning of my ministry. But when something's funny, I laugh. I determined early on that I would never preach with a stained-glass, sonorous voice and then talk like the real Chuck everywhere else; and if something struck me as funny, I would laugh. But I never wanted humor to distract from the message.

When I served as the senior pastor of a church in Southern California, I joined our ministry team on an annual tour of other ministries up and down the coast. Each year we gained valuable insight into our ministry by observing the ministry of others. We discovered what to do differently or better, and—just as important—we learned what not to do.

At one church, the pastor shared some of his secrets to success in ministry. He said, "Always keep 'em laughing. One of the most intense things I do all week is find that final joke to tell 'em so they leave laughing. People come back when you entertain 'em."

Hogwash! Ministry can be fun and some sermons are funny. But proclaiming the Word of God is no joke.

I have nothing against funny stories, and sometimes the congregation needs a good belly laugh. Some preachers are genuinely funny and bring an infectious sense of humor to the pulpit. And that's exactly what they should do: present themselves authentically before the congregation as they preach the Word without compromise. But as soon as entertainment becomes the "most intense" part of sermon preparation, it's time to find another vocation.

These two painful examples of righteousness on the part of Gentile pagans must have sent the Pharisees into a rage.

— 11:33-34 —

To sum up His discourse, Jesus recalled His earlier use of light as a metaphor for divine truth, the revelation of God (Luke 8:16). As before, He pointed out that one does not light a lamp to conceal it. Lamps shed light on the whole room so that everyone can see everything clearly. The Father sent the Son into the world to be light; therefore, no one can claim to be left in the dark.

In the former example (8:16-18), the light revealed what each person had, whether valuable or useless. In this case, Jesus compared people to houses and their eyes to windows. Some windows are "clear." The Greek word for "clear" (*haplous* [573]) means "simple," "sincere," "straightforward," "without an agenda." Some translations use the word "healthy," but this misses the aspect or intention of Luke's chosen term. Clear windows to a person's inner self are intentionally clear, not accidentally or haphazardly so.

The word for "bad" is the same as "wicked" used in 11:29. Because the word for "clear" expresses intentionality and is parallel in the word picture to the word for "bad," the implication is that bad windows block the light because someone decided to draw the shades.

— 11:35-36 —

Jesus then applied the illustration with a command. The imperative carries an implied warning, much like the suggestion "Don't play with fire" implies "or you'll get burned." The implied consequences include condemnation at the final judgment (11:31-32). "Watch out" emphasizes the idea of being attentive—while the windows either block light or let it in, it is the person who is responsible to decide whether to block out the light.

If, on the other hand, a person decides to keep his or her windows clear, the light of God's Word will flood the soul and nothing—no intentions, desires, values, or agendas—will remain hidden.

Jesus could have looked into the soul of each person present and openly revealed everything. He could have pointed to each person within His field of vision and said, in succession:

> "You want to look good in front of your peers."
> "You're a genuine seeker of truth."
> "You're afraid that following Me will cost you power."

"You're a traitor."

"You will sacrifice anything to follow Me."

"You're desperate for forgiveness, and you hope I will not reject you."

He could have probed and exposed each heart, but He didn't. Instead, He challenged His listeners to let the light of God's revelation flood their souls to reveal everything. He gave them the opportunity to be their own judges.

APPLICATION: LUKE 11:29-36
The Perils of Success

Jesus never shied away from delivering a straightforward message to His growing and emotionally charged crowd of followers. Not a word of flattery, not a hint of compromise, and no patronizing. Just plain, understandable talk without regard for the negative consequences it was sure to bring. He refused to play the role others expected. He told the truth—always. He provided substance rather than entertainment; He placed the responsibility for obedience before people; and He warned against self-enlightenment.

As I reflect on the Lord's rise to popularity and the notion of "success" as the world defines it, let me name a few perils that come with success and some counteracting principles.

The first peril is personal: It's what I call *the peril of image-making.* As growth occurs, it is easy for ministry leaders to get their images wrapped up in what's happening and to forget who's really in charge of this spiritual work. But if God isn't in it, you and I should want out of it. And if Christ isn't the star—if Christ isn't Lord—it won't last, and it won't result in good things. Dripping from this peril is pride, pride, pride. The emphasis is on doing, not being. It's obsessed with programs, rather than lives or meeting needs. The focus becomes impressing people with adequacy rather than freely confessing one's own inadequacy.

The counteractive principle is accountability. Someone in a position of equal or greater power must have the freedom to keep that leader's focus on reality. Who is this about? What is important? What isn't? Am I getting in the way of what God wants to do? Am I emphasizing numbers more than I should? Am I seeking the attention?

Back in 1988, *Christianity Today* did an interview with Richard Dortch, who had been a member on staff at the Christian television network PTL when it was growing in popularity. In the article "I Made Mistakes," Dortch says, "We were so caught up in God's work that we forgot about God."[13]

A second peril is what I would call organizational: *the peril of turning ministry into a business*. The business world has some valuable insights, but ministry is not a business. Beware the steady encroachment of business terms and a marketing mentality. Beware the temptation to use the world's methods to attain spiritual objectives. Guard against corporate terminology and titles. It's a dead end. Before long, a steady beat will drum the words into your head: "competition, comparison, competition, comparison, competition, comparison." John Piper is correct: "Brothers, we are not professionals."[14]

To counteract this peril, keep studying Christ. Keep going back to what Christ did, to what Christ said. Observe how He did what He did. Watch how He handled things. Look at how He treated people. Imitate Him. Be a shepherd, not a CEO.

Third, I point to *the peril of tradition*. Tradition is good. It keeps us from chasing the wind. But tradition can cause us to ignore the true condition of the heart. Life becomes business as usual as we go through the religious motions. We conduct the meetings. We keep the show going. And the inevitable result is apathy. The congregation grows in numbers, feeling good about itself, yet the people's hearts wither away.

Sometimes, we need to break with tradition if for no other reason than to wake up the congregation. The remedy for the peril of tradition is creativity—scary in many circles, but very much needed in most.

Clean from the Inside Out
LUKE 11:37-54

NASB

37 Now when He had spoken, a Pharisee asked Him to have lunch with him; and He went in, and reclined *at the table.* 38 When the Pharisee saw it, he was surprised that He had not first ^aceremonially washed before the ^bmeal. 39 But the Lord said to

NLT

37 As Jesus was speaking, one of the Pharisees invited him home for a meal. So he went in and took his place at the table.* 38 His host was amazed to see that he sat down to eat without first performing the handwashing ceremony required by Jewish custom. 39 Then the Lord said to

him, "Now you Pharisees clean the outside of the cup and of the platter; but ªinside of you, you are full of robbery and wickedness. ⁴⁰You foolish ones, did not He who made the outside make the inside also? ⁴¹But give that which is within as charity, and ªthen all things are clean for you.

⁴²"But woe to you Pharisees! For you pay tithe of mint and rue and every *kind of* garden herb, and *yet* disregard justice and the love of God; but these are the things you should have done without neglecting the others. ⁴³Woe to you Pharisees! For you love the chief seats in the synagogues and the respectful greetings in the market places. ⁴⁴Woe to you! For you are like ªconcealed tombs, and the people who walk over *them* are unaware *of it*."

⁴⁵One of the ªlawyers said to Him in reply, "Teacher, when You say this, You insult us too." ⁴⁶But He said, "Woe to you lawyers as well! For you weigh men down with burdens hard to bear, ªwhile you yourselves will not even touch the burdens with one of your fingers. ⁴⁷Woe to you! For you build the ªtombs of the prophets, and *it was* your fathers *who* killed them. ⁴⁸So you are witnesses and approve the deeds of your fathers; because it was they who killed them, and you build *their tombs*. ⁴⁹For this reason also the wisdom of God said, 'I will send to them prophets and apostles, and *some* of them they will kill and *some* they will ªpersecute, ⁵⁰so that the blood of all the prophets, shed since the foundation of the world, may be ªcharged against this generation, ⁵¹from the blood of Abel to the blood of Zechariah, who was killed between the altar and the

him, "You Pharisees are so careful to clean the outside of the cup and the dish, but inside you are filthy—full of greed and wickedness! ⁴⁰Fools! Didn't God make the inside as well as the outside? ⁴¹So clean the inside by giving gifts to the poor, and you will be clean all over.

⁴²"What sorrow awaits you Pharisees! For you are careful to tithe even the tiniest income from your herb gardens,* but you ignore justice and the love of God. You should tithe, yes, but do not neglect the more important things.

⁴³"What sorrow awaits you Pharisees! For you love to sit in the seats of honor in the synagogues and receive respectful greetings as you walk in the marketplaces. ⁴⁴Yes, what sorrow awaits you! For you are like hidden graves in a field. People walk over them without knowing the corruption they are stepping on."

⁴⁵"Teacher," said an expert in religious law, "you have insulted us, too, in what you just said."

⁴⁶"Yes," said Jesus, "what sorrow also awaits you experts in religious law! For you crush people with unbearable religious demands, and you never lift a finger to ease the burden. ⁴⁷What sorrow awaits you! For you build monuments for the prophets your own ancestors killed long ago. ⁴⁸But in fact, you stand as witnesses who agree with what your ancestors did. They killed the prophets, and you join in their crime by building the monuments! ⁴⁹This is what God in his wisdom said about you:* 'I will send prophets and apostles to them, but they will kill some and persecute the others.'

⁵⁰"As a result, this generation will be held responsible for the murder of all God's prophets from the creation of the world—⁵¹from the murder of Abel to the murder of Zechariah, who was killed between the altar and the

NASB

house *of God;* yes, I tell you, it shall be ªcharged against this generation.'

⁵² Woe to you ªlawyers! For you have taken away the key of knowledge; you yourselves did not enter, and you hindered those who were entering."

⁵³ When He left there, the scribes and the Pharisees began to be very hostile and to question Him closely on many subjects, ⁵⁴ plotting against Him to catch ªHim in something He might say.

11:38 ªLit *baptized* ᵇOr *lunch* 11:39 ªLit *your inside is full* 11:41 ªLit *behold* 11:44 ªOr *indistinct, unseen* 11:45 ªI.e. experts in the Mosaic Law 11:46 ªLit *and* 11:47 ªOr *monuments to* 11:49 ªOr *drive out* 11:50 ªOr *required of* 11:51 ªOr *required of* 11:52 ªI.e. experts in the Mosaic Law 11:54 ªLit *something out of His mouth*

NLT

sanctuary. Yes, it will certainly be charged against this generation.

⁵² "What sorrow awaits you experts in religious law! For you remove the key to knowledge from the people. You don't enter the Kingdom yourselves, and you prevent others from entering."

⁵³ As Jesus was leaving, the teachers of religious law and the Pharisees became hostile and tried to provoke him with many questions. ⁵⁴ They wanted to trap him into saying something they could use against him.

11:37 Or *and reclined.* 11:42 Greek *tithe the mint, the rue, and every herb.* 11:49 Greek *Therefore, the wisdom of God said.*

Max Lucado wisely wrote, "Legalism is the search for innocence—not forgiveness. It's a systematic process of defending self, explaining self, exalting self, and justifying self. The obsession with legalism? Self. Not God. Legalism has no pity on people. Legalism makes my opinion your burden, makes my opinion your boundary, and makes my opinion your obligation."[15] If he had lived during Jesus' day, he could have replaced the word "legalism" with "pharisaism." Pharisees had raised legalism to a form of art—an exclusive art form, of course.

Their polished exterior, impressive theological knowledge, daunting ability to debate, and rigorous adherence to Jewish traditions gave these consummate examples of "piety" immense authority among working-class Jews. Furthermore, they stood on centuries of accumulated conventions that had set like concrete. To be sure, changing the status quo was a God-sized task. No one dared challenge the Pharisees for fear of excommunication, a social death sentence for a Jew that allegedly carried eternal consequences as well. No one dared to question their traditions; after all, experts in the Scriptures claimed they fell from God's lips. And who has the right to doubt the wishes of God?

As Jesus continued His assault on the dominion of evil, He squared off against Satan's first line of defense: religion.

— 11:37-38 —

Luke provides less background information on the Pharisees and their customs than Matthew and Mark do, and we learn nothing about this particular Pharisee who had invited Jesus to his home for lunch. I like to think the man felt some level of conviction through the Lord's teaching and began to wonder if his theology had been wrong all these years. But it's just as likely he hoped to challenge Jesus in a more controlled setting.

Jesus accepted the invitation as another opportunity to teach. He entered the home and took His place at the table, lying down, propped on His left elbow, in keeping with ancient Near Eastern custom. But He bypassed the station set up by the Pharisee for ritual handwashing, a complicated invention of devout Jews, the details of which had accumulated over five centuries.

In 586 BC, the Babylonian Empire had sacked the city of Jerusalem and carried many Jews into exile in Babylon. While there, devout Jews wanted to know how to apply the Law of Moses in their new, strange surroundings. Separated from their land, cut off from their temple, and desperate to retain their Jewish identity, they turned to the men whose job it had been to copy and preserve God's written Word. These "scribes" were asked to teach the Law and apply its principles in practical, definable terms.

Over time, however, this initial desire to honor God's Law took on a life of its own. Practical guidelines became tradition, and tradition took on the character of law. A few centuries later, few distinguished between "the traditions of the elders" (Mark 7:1-4) and the Law of God. Literally hundreds of rules, regulations, standards, and guidelines governed Jewish life, such that the idea of having a personal relationship with God became unthinkable: *God is to be obeyed, not enjoyed.*

After the temple in Jerusalem was destroyed in AD 70 and the Jews dispersed after AD 135, a number of rabbis preserved an extensive body of their oral tradition in a document called *The Mishnah.* We learn from this document that pious Jews washed their hands, not for hygiene, but for ceremonial or ritual purity. Before each meal and even between courses, the men returned to special jars consecrated for ritual washing. Alfred Edersheim summarized the tradition this way:

> As the purifications were so frequent, and care had to be taken that the water had not been used for other purposes, or something fallen into it that might discolour or defile it, large vessels or jars were generally kept for the purpose. These might be of any material, although stone is specially mentioned. It was the practice to draw water out of these with what was called a *natla, antila,* or *antelaya,* very often of glass, which must hold (at least)

a quarter of a log—a measure equal to one and a half "egg-shells." For, no less quantity than this might be used for affusion. The water was poured on both hands, which must be free of anything covering them, such as gravel, mortar, &c. The hands were lifted up, so as to make the water run to the wrist, in order to ensure that the whole hand was washed, and that the water polluted by the hand did not again run down the fingers. Similarly, each hand was rubbed with the other (the fist), provided the hand that rubbed had been affused; otherwise, the rubbing might be done against the head, or even against a wall. But there was one point on which special stress was laid. In the 'first affusion,' which was all that originally was required when the hands were not Levitically 'defiled,' the water had to run down to the wrist. If the water remained short of the wrist, the hands were not clean. Accordingly, the words of St. Mark can only mean that the Pharisees eat not "except they wash their hands to the wrist."[16]

What appears excessively detailed to us—even bordering on obsessive-compulsive—was for the Pharisee an expression of love for God's Law. A Pharisee endured this kind of tedium in every sphere of life, six days a week and even more so on the Sabbath, all for the sake of pleasing God. So, when Jesus reclined at table for the meal, He stunned His host. Luke doesn't tell us what the Pharisee said, if anything. Regardless, Jesus responded to the man's objection.

— 11:39-41 —

Jesus used another tradition of the Pharisees involving the ritual cleansing of utensils. They meticulously guarded the inside of containers against ceremonial contamination by the outside. Therefore, Jesus' statement would have been untrue if taken literally. He clearly intended the "cup" and the "platter" to be symbols of the Pharisees themselves. They meticulously observed their man-made, outward symbols of piety while ignoring their internal corruption; they bandaged the symptoms of disease while ignoring the infection. They observed the rules and regulations of ceremonial cleanliness with polluted hearts, a practice that God has always found repulsive (Isa. 1:10-17; 58:4-8; Amos 5:21-24; Mic. 6:6-8). Furthermore, they mistakenly believed their outward deeds could cleanse their inner corruption.

The exact meaning of the Greek phrase rendered "give that which is within" is unclear today, whereas Luke's audience probably understood the colloquialism perfectly. Jesus had criticized the Pharisees for devoting so much attention to good behavior while ignoring their internal sinfulness. Ironically, these men protected the insides of ceremonial vessels from contamination from the vessels' exterior surfaces. They knew it was impossible to cleanse the inside of a cup with anything that had contacted the outside. It appears from *The Mishnah* that a vessel must be immersed in ceremonially clean water to be considered clean. Therefore, Jesus probably meant "give charity (or alms) from the inside" or "give from the heart."

First-century Jewish society considered no deed more merciful and Godlike than giving alms to the poor. Therefore, the Pharisees made a great show of giving money to the temple or directly to the needy. Jesus clarified the role of good deeds in the lives of God's people. If one gives with pure motives, one doesn't have to obsess over what is clean and what is not. If, on the other hand, a person tries to cleanse his or her inner self by doing good things, then the inside remains corrupted or "unclean."

— 11:42-44 —

Two other times before this, Luke records warnings from Jesus in the form of "woes" (Luke 6:24-26; 10:13-15; cf. comments there). "Woe" is a deep moan uttered in response to personal anguish or prompted by pity for the suffering of another. It can also convey a warning, as if to say, "I deeply pity you if this is true." Jesus had warned those who value earthly riches over kingdom wealth (6:24-26), and He had mourned the cities surrounding Capernaum for their lack of response to the Messiah (10:13-16). Now, Jesus warned the Pharisees openly, not only to expose their sin, but also to prompt some to repent.

He pronounced three "woes" over the Pharisees:

First, they emphasized minor issues while ignoring what God desires most (11:42).

To illustrate the Pharisees' meticulous adherence to the letter of the Law, Jesus used hyperbole, exaggeration for the sake of effect— although, His specific example may not have been much of an overstatement! They observed the Jewish law of tithing, by which a farmer was expected to give the first tenth of a crop to the temple, acknowledging that all sustenance comes from the Lord (Lev. 27:30). According to Jesus, the Pharisees counted the sprinkles of herbs from their garden and faithfully offered it to the temple. Meanwhile, they overlooked matters of justice, allowing their neighbors to suffer without an advocate, and they failed to love God as He wants to be loved.

Obeying rules should be the result of loving God, not a replacement for a relationship with Him. As a father, I wanted my children to honor my wishes out of love for me, as a natural part of a close relationship. I would have been heartbroken if any of them had said, "Here, Dad. Write down what you expect of me so that I won't risk losing my inheritance." That's not a relationship! A genuine relationship can't be reduced to a list of rules.

The Pharisees merely pretended to serve God, patting themselves on the back for their meticulous rule-keeping. But they neither knew God's heart nor cared to submit their desires to His will.

Second, they used their leadership for personal gain rather than service to God's people (Luke 11:43).

The "chief seats" in the synagogue were those closest to the front and occupied by the most respected members of the community. Moreover, these "chief seats" faced the congregation, giving the elders a sense of authority over the congregation and putting them in the religious limelight.

Extrabiblical Jewish literature, such as the Talmud, prescribed profuse greetings for teachers of the Law. For the Pharisees, who generally came from working-class families, Pharisaism became their best chance of receiving the kind of respect reserved for the wealthiest nobles in Israel. Their vocation also became their means of living well, often through donations. Achieving religious status also gratified their need for the applause of people. They didn't devote themselves to religious life to serve others; they expected everyone to serve them.

Third, they became agents of defilement rather than mediators of redemption (11:44).

Jesus gave the Pharisees' obsession with ritual cleanliness an ironic twist, one that cut to the core of their values and identity. He called them hidden tombs or, literally, "memorials." The Pharisees considered nothing more potentially defiling than a corpse, which they avoided at all cost. They believed that one became defiled even when one's shadow crossed a dead body or a grave. Consequently, each spring, tombs were coated with a limestone-and-water mixture to make them highly visible to passersby.[17]

This is not a depiction of destruction. He didn't suggest people would fall into the graves and die. While spiritual leaders do have a great impact on others and will be held accountable for their teaching, each person is responsible for his or her own response to God. By calling them "concealed tombs," Jesus accused the Pharisees of leading God's

Reverend Doctor Jerk

LUKE 11:45

I was doing a favor for a friend. He had asked me to participate in a little television panel discussion. My friend, who was producing the show, said, "Would you meet so-and-so at the plane this afternoon? We have too many guys to meet and bring to the studio, and not enough time. Maybe you and your buddy could meet one of the panelists. He's the president of a little Bible school."

My buddy and I were in blue jeans, T-shirts, and jackets. The two of us stood at the gate (pre-9/11) waiting for the plane to unload, and unfortunately, we failed to notice the man we were waiting for. So I said to my buddy, "Well, we'd better go down to baggage claim and meet him there." On the way down we saw a guy with his hat pulled down tight, his tie cinched up tight, and his shirt starched stiff as a board, all decked out in a three-piece suit. I nudged my friend and said, "That's gotta be him."

So I walked up, and I called him by his first name. "Are you so-and-so?"

He replied, "DOCTOR so-and-so, if you don't mind." And he put his bags down for us to carry.

My buddy and I picked up his bags, and I said, "We thought you looked like the man we were looking for."

He said, "Oh, really? Tell me . . . what does a president look like?" I wanted to say, "A JERK—a first-class JERK!" But I exercised some restraint.

If you find yourself craving the limelight and listening for public applause, do us all a big favor: Don't do it in the name of religion. Find another vocation. You'll hurt the cause.

people to become unclean in His eyes. In other words, the Pharisees were unclean and spreading their uncleanness throughout the ranks of God's covenant people.

— 11:45-46 —

One of the Pharisee's other lunch guests objected to the Lord's condemnation of Pharisaism, reminding Him that these men merely carried out what the "lawyers" had determined was genuine piety. "Lawyers" were usually scribes, men who dedicated their lives to meticulously copying the Hebrew Scriptures to preserve them from decay or corruption. Consequently, their constant contact with God's Word made them extremely knowledgeable men, called upon to explain and apply the Law.

The scribe didn't voice his objection to express sorrow or hurt. He meant this as a warning, saying, as it were, "You attack one of us, You attack all of us. If You crush this stone, the entire temple is likely to come down on You!" Note the lawyer addressed Jesus as "Teacher" before threatening His career.

The scribe—probably well established in the religious hierarchy—thought it would be a good idea to bring Jesus back into line with correction. But Jesus didn't flinch. Instead, He pronounced three more "woes" even more severe than the first three. Whereas the Pharisees led the people, which heightened their accountability before God, the lawyers led the Pharisees, teaching them everything they knew. Therefore, the scribes could be called "super-Pharisees."

Jesus accused them of "weighing men down with burdens hard to bear." Luke's translation of the Lord's indictment uses words from the same root three times, all related to the verb *phortizō* [5412], a term often used in shipping, with the meaning "to load." It pictures a ship or an animal heavily burdened by a great weight. A frugal merchant could maximize profit by using a limited number of pack animals so that each was laden with as much cargo as it could bear. The word translated "burdens" is the noun form of this verb. He intensified this idea of burden with an adjective—used only once in the New Testament—meaning "cumbersome," "intolerable," or "hard to bear."

Jesus used this image to characterize the lawyers as sadistic hypocrites, men loading down others while bearing no burdens themselves. The implication is that they purposely made the laws difficult to follow in order to bring about moral failure in others. The Jews of first-century Israel labored under a man-made burden of religiosity, an endless list of rules that governed virtually every aspect of life—all of them based on laws handed down by God, but twisted and inflated to serve the desire of one group of people to dominate another. Earnest Jews were spiritually demoralized and incapable of meeting further demands. In the end, the scribes remained kings of the moral hill by pushing down earnest Jews.

The first "woe" was enough to finish Jesus' career as a teacher, if such a career had been His motivation. He declared the scribes' very existence a fraud of the highest order. Undaunted, He continued with indictments even more severe.

— 11:47-51 —

Jesus accused the scribes—those who taught Jewish tradition beyond (or in place of) the authentic teaching of God's Law—of contributing to murder. Their intellectual fathers killed God's emissaries of divine truth, and the scribes affirmed the murders by burying the victims. Jesus meant this figuratively of course. The scribes had not killed anyone or buried anyone in reality. They did, however, possess the same murderous spirit, such that, according to Jesus, they would have joined their predecessors in murder and, given the chance, will do so in the future.

The images of father and son express both likeness and inheritance. Sons look like their fathers, and sons receive the benefit of their fathers' decisions.

"The wisdom of God" is not an actual entity, but the personification of God's sovereign decision to do one thing or another (Prov. 1:20-33; 8:1-36). This was Jesus' way of saying that God, in His wisdom, trumped the so-called wisdom of the scribes by sending emissaries bearing His authentic teaching. He sent these divine messengers, knowing they would be persecuted and killed, as a means of revealing the true nature of His enemies. He put His word in human flesh, as it were, to give rebellious hearts something tangible to kill, thus revealing what had been hidden. The potential of their sin became actualized when these leaders of Israel destroyed God's messengers.

Jesus accused the scribes of being the embodiment of a spirit of murder that had been on earth from the first generation after Creation. Abel was the first murder victim, slain by his own brother, who seethed with envy because "the LORD had regard for Abel and for his offering; but for Cain and for his offering He had no regard" (Gen. 4:4-5). Abel was not a prophet in the specific sense of carrying God's message to others; his life, however, indicted Cain for rebellion and became the catalyst for Cain's murderous spirit.

Zechariah was the last martyred prophet recorded in the Old Testament (2 Chr. 24:20-21). Undoubtedly, others followed him, but Jesus restricted His examples to those in the Jewish Scriptures.

Jesus declared that "this generation"—that is, the Hebrew men and women during Jesus' lifetime, represented by the religious leaders—would answer for the murderous spirit that had reigned since Cain's murder of Abel. That hardly seems fair, but it turned out to be both prophetic and promising.

It was prophetic in that Jesus is the consummate example of God's Word in human flesh. Whereas the prophets and apostles merely carried divine truth, Jesus *is* divine truth. His presence on earth was the ultimate fulfillment of everything that had once been potential; and by killing Him, "this generation" would bring upon itself the weight of all the world's sin combined. All are guilty; none are innocent. Beating within the chest of everyone—from the greatest to the least—is a murderous heart.

The condemnation by Jesus was also promising because the result of the actions alluded to by the indictment is the offer of forgiveness. His own murder would become the means of redemption for all of humanity. While "this generation" in first-century Israel condemned the Savior to die, every individual contributed to His murder. And by His voluntary sacrifice at the hands of humanity, all of humanity may find salvation.

— 11:52 —

The Lord sealed His earthly fate—in full knowledge of the outcome, mind you—by pronouncing a final woe against the scribes. He named the lawyers as ones holding "the key of knowledge" and, in this sense, they represent Israel as a whole. God called the descendants of Jacob to steward His Law, to become a priestly nation (Exod. 19:6), to mediate the relationship between Himself and the nations (Gen. 12:1-3; 22:18; 26:4; 28:14; Acts 3:25; Gal. 3:8), to shine the light of truth. But Israel squandered its birthright.

Similarly, the scribes had unlimited access to the Word of God, but they read into the text what they wanted to see and thereby kept others from seeing the truth. They ignored the God of grace they found on those pages, and they reduced Him to a petty, vindictive, cosmic accountant keeping a tally of righteous and evil deeds. They should have recognized the Messiah on sight, as did Simeon and Anna (Luke 2:25-32, 36-38); but Jesus didn't fit their self-serving expectations.

If knowledge is a door, then the scribes locked it tight, hid the key, and remained outside with all those who trusted them for entrance.

— 11:53-54 —

In general, it can be said that people react one of two ways to conviction. Caught in their guilt, they either weep in broken, sorrowful repentance, or they lash out at the ones who uncovered their sin. In this case, the scribes and Pharisees became "very hostile." Furthermore, Luke declares that this was just the start of their hatred for Jesus.

From this point on, they would "question Him closely." Luke uses the rare verb *apostomatizō* [653], meaning "to interrogate" or "to question someone with hostile intent." They would "plot against Him" (*enedreuō* [1748]), which is the same term used in Acts 23:21 to describe a plot in which forty men lay in wait, ready to ambush Paul. Here the Pharisees were waiting to "catch" something directly from Jesus' mouth that they could use against Him.

• • •

And so the battle for Jerusalem began. Jesus encountered Satan's perimeter defense network, a dug-in battalion of religious experts, fortified by centuries of religious tradition and armed to the teeth with righteous-sounding rules and customs. Luke concludes this segment with a summary that bristles with murderous intent, although it is primarily political at this point. The religious authorities may have thought they could simply discredit the rabbi from Nazareth, after which they were sure the people would ignore Him. Regardless, they decided they would have to eliminate Jesus as a threat—if not politically, then in some other way.

APPLICATION: LUKE 11:37-54

Never and Always

How can we avoid the mistakes of the Pharisees? I seldom use the words "never" and "always," but I think it's safe to use them in these two suggestions.

First, *never try to cover wrong within by cleaning up the externals of your life*. Never!

Diseases aren't removed with cotton swabs and Band-Aids. And criticizing the physician who shows you a fateful X-ray image won't cure your condition. I realize how absurdly obvious this advice might sound, but for millennia, religious people have been trying to cover sin by looking good externally.

Second, *always pay more attention to the inside of your life*. Always! Externals can help discern what's going on inside, but get to the heart. Our cosmetic-focused culture offers all kinds of things to decorate our surface, but let's pay attention to the core. Let's ask some hard questions: Why do we do what we do? Why do we not tell the truth? Why is that person's opinion of me so powerful? Why is our family so unhappy and dysfunctional, while everybody in the church thinks we're fine? How long can we continue the pretense?

Before we cluck our tongues and wag our fingers at the Pharisees of old, remember that Pharisees live on today—and closer to home than we think!

Marching Orders for True Disciples
LUKE 12:1-12

NASB

¹ Under these circumstances, after ªso many thousands of ᵇpeople had gathered together that they were stepping on one another, He began saying to His disciples first *of all,* "Beware of the leaven of the Pharisees, which is hypocrisy. ² But there is nothing covered up that will not be revealed, and hidden that will not be known. ³ Accordingly, whatever you have said in the dark will be heard in the light, and what you have ªwhispered in the inner rooms will be proclaimed upon the housetops.

⁴ "I say to you, My friends, do not be afraid of those who kill the body and after that have no more that they can do. ⁵ But I will ªwarn you whom to fear: fear the One who, after He has killed, has authority to cast into ᵇhell; yes, I tell you, fear Him! ⁶ Are not five sparrows sold for two ªcents?

NLT

¹ Meanwhile, the crowds grew until thousands were milling about and stepping on each other. Jesus turned first to his disciples and warned them, "Beware of the yeast of the Pharisees—their hypocrisy. ² The time is coming when everything that is covered up will be revealed, and all that is secret will be made known to all. ³ Whatever you have said in the dark will be heard in the light, and what you have whispered behind closed doors will be shouted from the housetops for all to hear!

⁴ "Dear friends, don't be afraid of those who want to kill your body; they cannot do any more to you after that. ⁵ But I'll tell you whom to fear. Fear God, who has the power to kill you and then throw you into hell.* Yes, he's the one to fear.

⁶ "What is the price of five sparrows—two copper coins*? Yet God

Yet not one of them is forgotten before God. [7] Indeed, the very hairs of your head are all numbered. Do not fear; you are more valuable than many sparrows.

[8] "And I say to you, everyone who confesses Me before men, the Son of Man will confess him also before the angels of God; [9] but he who denies Me before men will be denied before the angels of God. [10] And everyone who [a] speaks a word against the Son of Man, it will be forgiven him; but he who blasphemes against the Holy Spirit, it will not be forgiven him. [11] When they bring you before the synagogues and the rulers and the authorities, do not worry about how or what you are to speak in your defense, or what you are to say; [12] for the Holy Spirit will teach you in that very hour what you ought to say."

12:1 [a] Lit *myriads* [b] Lit *the crowd* 12:3 [a] Lit *spoken in the ear* 12:5 [a] Or *show* [b] Gr *Gehenna* 12:6 [a] Gr *assaria*, the smallest of copper coins 12:10 [a] Lit *will speak*

does not forget a single one of them. [7] And the very hairs on your head are all numbered. So don't be afraid; you are more valuable to God than a whole flock of sparrows.

[8] "I tell you the truth, everyone who acknowledges me publicly here on earth, the Son of Man* will also acknowledge in the presence of God's angels. [9] But anyone who denies me here on earth will be denied before God's angels. [10] Anyone who speaks against the Son of Man can be forgiven, but anyone who blasphemes the Holy Spirit will not be forgiven.

[11] "And when you are brought to trial in the synagogues and before rulers and authorities, don't worry about how to defend yourself or what to say, [12] for the Holy Spirit will teach you at that time what needs to be said."

12:5 Greek *Gehenna.* 12:6 Greek *two assaria* [Roman coins equal to ⅟₁₆ of a denarius]. 12:8 "Son of Man" is a title Jesus used for himself.

As Jesus looked toward His future, He saw the cross looming ever larger on the horizon. And with a glance over His shoulder, He saw a massive collection of followers without a clue as to where He was going. What could He tell them? They had seen Him heal diseases, renew broken bodies, cast out demons, feed multitudes, and even bend nature to His will. The multitudes following their Messiah into Jerusalem must have felt invincible. How could the temple leaders deny His divine authority? How could the ruling class do anything but bend the knee to the long-awaited Christ? What chance did the armies of Rome stand against a man who could silence storms? The future of Israel had never looked brighter.

But Jesus knew His destiny. Glory lay on the other side of suffering. God the Father had chosen to reclaim His Creation by giving His Son over to death. Soon, the multitudes following Jesus would witness divine truth fall before human power. They would watch the most powerful man on earth become subjected to the injustice of corrupt religious leaders. They would see their Messiah shamefully betrayed, illegally tried, brutally tortured, and cruelly killed.

What could Jesus tell His true disciples, scattered among the multitudes of fair-weather followers? They needed direction from their leader, marching orders that would carry them through the difficult journey to the cross and then beyond.

— 12:1-2 —

The phrase "under these circumstances"—Luke's transition from a particular episode to a broader perspective of Jesus' ministry—gives us a good chance to summarize His circumstances. We can set the context with four statements.

First, the setting was hostile.

The final statement of the previous segment bristles with hostility on the part of the scribes and Pharisees, who together formed the backbone of Jewish culture and religion. These men would position themselves wherever Jesus went, waiting for a mental lapse or a slip of the tongue, something they could use to discredit and then marginalize their enemy.

A member of the president's cabinet once said to me, "How would you like to step out of your office to find thirty-eight microphones capturing your every word for the purpose of holding something against you? That's how my workday starts." But his workday, as stressful as it was, couldn't compare to the Lord's.

Second, the time was short.

In this "journey section" (Luke 9:51–19:27) of Luke's Gospel, Jesus' ministry approaches Jerusalem like a roller coaster climbing the first hill. His ascent to Israel's capital was gradual and steady, but less than seven days after entering the city in triumph, He would hang lifeless on a Roman cross. He had so much to teach His followers, but he had just a few more weeks—maybe less—for ministry in the flesh.

Third, the crowd was large.

Luke alludes to a steadily growing multitude following Jesus along the way. Luke uses the Greek word *ochlos* [3793], typically translated "crowd." At this stage, he adds the qualifier *myrias* [3461], from which we derive the English word "myriad." It literally means "ten thousands."

While the number of followers was impressive, Luke describes them negatively, portraying them as heedlessly trampling one another (12:1). The same Greek term appears in Matthew 5:13 and 7:6 and Hebrews 10:29 to convey the idea of mob-mentality chaos. A purely human perspective would see Jesus at the head of a great populist movement, destined to topple the existing government. But the Lord knew better.

He knew His destiny, and He understood the fickleness of mobs who don't get their way.

Fourth, His instruction was vital.

The instruction Jesus gave could be compared to the final instructions of a commander before storming a beach or dropping behind enemy lines. Jesus would have to address the crowds while targeting true disciples. The phrase "He began saying" shows this teaching as a process. In other words, Jesus didn't give just one speech; He taught His closest disciples first and then began inserting this new instruction into His lectures as He taught crowds of different sizes in various locations. His instructions took the form of four commands:

Beware of living as a hypocrite. (Luke 12:1-3)
Don't fear physical pain; fear God. (12:4-7)
Confess the Son of Man openly, boldly, and freely. (12:8-10)
Don't become distracted about defending yourself; God will stand in your defense. (12:11-12)

His first point: Be on guard against the pervasive, gradual, imperceptible spread of hypocrisy, which had corrupted the Pharisees.

Jesus didn't view the Pharisees as the great enemy of true discipleship; he detested the hypocrisy that had led them so far astray. The word used illustrates the profound difference between the world system and God's order. "Hypocrisy" (*hypokrisis* [5272]) referred to a person's words, posture, and gestures taken together, as in public debate or theatrical acting. Secular Greek writers could use the term positively or negatively, depending upon the situation. In a positive sense, one may dutifully portray a character on the stage, wearing a public mask over one's true face. When used negatively, one might say "the stage is a sham world and actors are deceivers."[18] Greeks and Romans deeply despised deception.

Jewish writers almost always used the term negatively, describing hypocrites as people who had fallen away from God's revealed truth yet pretended otherwise. Therefore, to be a hypocrite was to lie through behavior instead of speech.

Leaven is yeast. As a literary image, leaven usually represents something unwanted, but not always. Virtually everyone in ancient times knew how to bake bread. A baker who wants his loaf to be light and airy will insert a lump of leavened dough from a previous batch into the fresh dough he's preparing. Before baking, the baker will set the leavened dough aside in a dark, cool place, where the yeast microorganisms will multiply and spread, permeating the whole batch.

Jews were encouraged to make and enjoy leavened bread through-out the year. Each spring, however, in preparation for Passover, Jewish families meticulously swept their houses clean of all dust to be certain that no speck of yeast remained. Just a small amount could find its way into a batch of ceremonial "unleavened bread" and ruin the holiday.

The idea of "leaven" is not to imply something good or bad; rather, it represents something that is gradual and unstoppable once introduced.

— 12:2-3 —

Jesus explained the danger of hypocrisy and the futility of hiding the truth. In the present world order, secrets and dark corners conceal sin and give cover to evil intentions. When the kingdom of God comes, however, everything will be exposed to the light of divine truth. All secrets will be revealed, every heart exposed to open examination, all intentions presented for public scrutiny. If one lives the life of a phony, it will become known.

I am convinced that God would rather face a blunt, honest sinner than deal with an insincere Christian who looks good but in reality loves his or her sin. In the end, when the Messiah returns in power to eradicate evil, hypocrisy will have proved futile. Truth will eventually expose sin, so why not simply be transparent now?

— 12:4-5 —

His second command: Don't be afraid of people; their ability to cause harm is temporal. Instead, fear God, who can hold people accountable for their sins for eternity.

Jesus addressed his disciples as "My friends," which doesn't exclude the wider group of followers but suggests He intended this command specifically for His disciples. He gives a negative command paired with a positive one. First, don't be afraid of people and the harm they can do; even if they torture and kill the body, their ability to cause suffering is limited. That's not particularly comforting until we consider the second imperative.

The NASB rendering, "But I will warn you whom to fear," unduly casts the second command in a negative light. A literal rendering of the Greek phrase would be "But I will *show* you whom to fear." The verb for "show" (*hypodeiknymi* [5263]) means simply "to indicate," "to point out," or "to give instruction." The reason for this fear is God's ability to kill and then cause suffering for eternity.

The second imperative statement can be taken to imply two differ-ent things:

1. "Don't fear people; fear God because He can hurt you worse than people."
2. "Don't fear people; fear God because He will hold all people accountable for the evil they do."

The first suggests we should fear God because He is crueler than people, and we should serve our own interests by pleasing the more powerful person. The second is more likely because it better fits Jesus' apparent desire to reassure His people despite the coming hardship. Furthermore, the second option reassures God's people—many of whom will die a martyr's death in the years to come—that their tormenters will be held accountable for their evil deeds. All people should fear God because "all have sinned and fall short of the glory of God" (Rom. 3:23).

God, as the only perfectly righteous being in the universe, has the sole authority to judge sin and then condemn the sinner. The religious leaders in Jerusalem had claimed that right and exercised it liberally to maintain their hold on power, but they had no moral authority. Because Jesus shares real authority with the Father, He could speak against their hypocrisy with confidence.

— 12:6-7 —

Perhaps to be certain His disciples didn't misunderstand His reference to hell and then wonder if God is cruel, Jesus defended the character of His Father. Moreover, He wanted to reassure those who remained faithful that when they suffer, they do not suffer alone. God is neither absent nor distracted. He cares deeply for His own.

He first compared people to sparrows—the boniest, cheapest food sold in the markets. Five scrawny birds could be purchased for two *assaria* [787], copper coins worth one-sixteenth of an unskilled laborer's daily wage.[19] The Creator cares for each of these nearly worthless birds; not one "is forgotten." In the simplest sense, the verb rendered "forgotten" means "to not recall something." In this context, however, it carries the added implication of acting upon the recollection. While death is a part of life in this fallen creation, even the plight of sparrows doesn't escape the compassionate care of their Creator. Consequently, His disciples, whom He values far more than birds, can rest assured He will take note of their suffering. Nothing escapes His omniscient attention, not even details about ourselves that we take no time to notice.

— 12:8-10 —

The third command: Openly affirm Christ and claim His teaching as your rule of life.

The Greek word translated "confess" is *homologeō* [3670], which means, literally, "to say the same." It indicates consent with what was said before. In legal circles, this verbal affirmation operated much like a pledge of allegiance or an oath of loyalty to the king. In religious contexts, this "confession" identified one with the tenets and values of a sect or its leader.

The act of confessing Christ before men bears the implications of risk and negative consequences. At the same time, the Lord's confession in heaven of true disciples suggests great reward. Obedience to this command, however, is not a *means* of salvation; it is an *indication* of salvation. One is saved by grace alone, through faith alone, in Christ alone. One cannot earn entrance to heaven by volunteering for martyrdom or by shouting the name of Christ in open court.

True disciples prove their mettle when they boldly proclaim Jesus as their Messiah, Savior, King, and God.

While denial or failure to confess Jesus before others will be answered in kind in heaven, Jesus added a grave warning for blasphemy against the Holy Spirit. The Greek word is *blasphēmeō* [987], meaning to "curse," "slander," or "treat someone with contempt." Blasphemy is any manner of speech that disregards or disrespects the value of another. When applied to God, it takes on frightening consequences. A single act of blasphemy, however, doesn't doom someone to hell. If that were true, then Paul had no hope of heaven (1 Tim. 1:13).

William Hendriksen does a splendid job of explaining this "unpardonable sin." He writes:

> Their sin is unpardonable because they are unwilling to tread the path that leads to pardon. For a thief, an adulterer, and a murderer there is hope. The message of the gospel may cause him to cry out, "O God be merciful to me, the sinner." But when a man has become hardened, so that he has made up his mind not to pay any attention to the promptings of the Spirit, not even to listen to his pleading and warning voice, he has placed himself on the road that leads to perdition. He has sinned the sin "unto death" (1 Jn. 5:16; see also Heb. 6:4-8). . . .
>
> The blasphemy against the Spirit is the result of gradual progress in sin. Grieving the Spirit (Eph. 4:30), if unrepented of, leads

to resisting the Spirit (Acts 7:51), which, if persisted in, develops into quenching the Spirit (1 Thes. 5:19).[20]

Obviously, this cannot happen to a believer. A believer is "in Christ." Once a believer has given his or her heart to the Lord Jesus, that relationship is secure throughout eternity. But a person who chooses to reject Christ, who stays with that rejection, and who continues on in hardness and callousness, becomes like Pharaoh, who subjected himself to wrath before God.

I've had people ask, "Could I have possibly committed the unpardonable sin?" My response: "Not so long as you're concerned about it."

— 12:11-12 —

Jesus' fourth command in this section: Do not worry about how to confess Christ before others; the Holy Spirit will be your guide.

Jesus didn't introduce this command with "if," but "when." The terms "synagogues," "rulers," and "authorities" refer to tribunals that can have a huge impact on the futures of true disciples. Synagogues were the ecclesiastical courts of their day, ruling on matters both religious and civil. Excommunication didn't merely bar a Jew from coming to the synagogue; it expelled them from all social and commercial contact as well. A person "cut off" from the people could not buy food or supplies, earn a wage, receive medical attention, or even sell property.

"Rulers" and "authorities" included civil government officials, like Herod Antipas, Pontius Pilate, and Tiberius. Obviously, these men and their deputies could send people to their deaths—or could institute flogging, imprisonment, banishment, or debilitating fines—with the wave of a hand. "When" true disciples face these potentially life-changing encounters, Jesus' divine promise could serve as reassurance. He said, in effect, "When you are brought before the tribunals and you are expected to give an answer for your faith, don't think you have to prepare an eloquent speech; simply speak from the heart. Because the Holy Spirit lives in you, you will say what needs to be said."

• • •

While Jesus was a flesh-and-bone human just like us, He could not have been more different. He is perfect while we are imperfect; He remained true to His mission while we flip-flop and falter; He enjoyed uninhibited communion with the Father while we doubt God's goodness and question His sovereignty; He came for the express purpose of dying, while we doggedly defend our right to be comfortable. How could any of the thousands who followed Jesus hope to be like Him?

APPLICATION: LUKE 12:1-12

How to Live Like a True Disciple

We can lift four clear commands from these verses:

Beware of living as a hypocrite.
Don't fear physical pain; fear God.
Confess the Son of Man openly, boldly, and freely.
Don't become distracted about defending yourself; God will stand in your defense.

Now, how do they apply? Three thoughts come to mind.

First, *if you're a phony, admit it.*

You know whether or not you're a phony; start by admitting it to yourself. Look in the mirror as soon as possible and say—out loud—"(Your Name), you are a phony." And once you get the courage to say it to yourself, say it to someone you know well—who already knows this, by the way. Come into the light and admit what you are. You'll quickly find you're in good company, and change will come more easily.

Second, *if you're fearful, redirect it.*

Turn your fear from the horizontal plane to the vertical. Start fearing the living God and stop fearing others. I've learned that fear steals my courage and makes me timid. If hypocrisy makes me trite, fear makes me timid. Believe me, the enemy isn't timid. Shameless things occur regularly and are becoming more prevalent—whether on screen, in the media, on handheld devices, or even in one's own school or neighborhood. Timidity is not the response we need. If you're fearful of other people, choose instead to fear God.

Third, *if you're worried, pray about it.*

The Lord gave us a marvelous antidote to worry: prayer. I have found that my best response to every worried thought is to turn it into a prayer. "Worry about nothing; pray about everything" (see Phil. 4:6). Rather than let it churn in my stomach, I turn it over to the One who can actually do something about it. It's a difficult habit to form—turning worry into prayer—but in time, I realized that I gained energy as I reduced stress through prayer.

The Testimony of a Fool
LUKE 12:13-34

NASB

13 Someone ªin the crowd said to Him, "Teacher, tell my brother to divide the *family* inheritance with me." 14 But He said to him, "Man, who appointed Me a judge or arbitrator over you?" 15 Then He said to them, "Beware, and be on your guard against every form of greed; for not *even* when one has an abundance does his life consist of his possessions." 16 And He told them a parable, saying, "The land of a rich man was very productive. 17 And he began reasoning to himself, saying, 'What shall I do, since I have no place to store my crops?' 18 Then he said, 'This is what I will do: I will tear down my barns and build larger ones, and there I will store all my grain and my goods. 19 And I will say to my soul, "Soul, you have many goods laid up for many years *to come;* take your ease, eat, drink *and* be merry."' 20 But God said to him, 'You fool! This *very* night ªyour soul is required of you; and *now* who will own what you have prepared?' 21 So is the man who stores up treasure for himself, and is not rich toward God."

22 And He said to His disciples, "For this reason I say to you, ªdo not worry about *your* ᵇlife, *as to* what you will eat; nor for your body, *as to* what you will put on. 23 For life is more than food, and the body more than clothing. 24 Consider the ravens, for they neither sow nor reap; they have no storeroom nor barn, and *yet* God feeds them; how much more valuable you are than the birds! 25 And which of you by worrying can add a *single* ªhour to his ᵇlife's span? 26 If then you cannot do even a very little thing, why do you worry about other matters? 27 Consider the lilies, how they grow: they neither toil nor spin;

NLT

13 Then someone called from the crowd, "Teacher, please tell my brother to divide our father's estate with me."

14 Jesus replied, "Friend, who made me a judge over you to decide such things as that?" 15 Then he said, "Beware! Guard against every kind of greed. Life is not measured by how much you own."

16 Then he told them a story: "A rich man had a fertile farm that produced fine crops. 17 He said to himself, 'What should I do? I don't have room for all my crops.' 18 Then he said, 'I know! I'll tear down my barns and build bigger ones. Then I'll have room enough to store all my wheat and other goods. 19 And I'll sit back and say to myself, "My friend, you have enough stored away for years to come. Now take it easy! Eat, drink, and be merry!"'

20 "But God said to him, 'You fool! You will die this very night. Then who will get everything you worked for?'

21 "Yes, a person is a fool to store up earthly wealth but not have a rich relationship with God."

22 Then, turning to his disciples, Jesus said, "That is why I tell you not to worry about everyday life—whether you have enough food to eat or enough clothes to wear. 23 For life is more than food, and your body more than clothing. 24 Look at the ravens. They don't plant or harvest or store food in barns, for God feeds them. And you are far more valuable to him than any birds! 25 Can all your worries add a single moment to your life? 26 And if worry can't accomplish a little thing like that, what's the use of worrying over bigger things?

27 "Look at the lilies and how they grow. They don't work or make

NASB

but I tell you, not even Solomon in all his glory clothed himself like one of these. 28 But if God so clothes the grass in the field, which is *alive* today and tomorrow is thrown into the furnace, how much more *will He clothe* you? You men of little faith! 29 And do not seek what you will eat and what you will drink, and do not keep worrying. 30 For ªall these things the nations of the world eagerly seek; but your Father knows that you need these things. 31 But seek His kingdom, and these things will be added to you. 32 Do not be afraid, little flock, for your Father has chosen gladly to give you the kingdom.

33 "Sell your possessions and give to charity; make yourselves money belts which do not wear out, an unfailing treasure in heaven, where no thief comes near nor moth destroys. 34 For where your treasure is, there your heart will be also.

12:13 ªLit *out of*   12:20 ªLit *they are demanding your soul from you*   12:22 ªOr *stop being worried* ᵇLit *soul*   12:25 ªLit *cubit* (approx 18 in.) ᵇOr *height*   12:30 ªOr *these things all the nations of the world*

NLT

their clothing, yet Solomon in all his glory was not dressed as beautifully as they are. 28 And if God cares so wonderfully for flowers that are here today and thrown into the fire tomorrow, he will certainly care for you. Why do you have so little faith?

29 "And don't be concerned about what to eat and what to drink. Don't worry about such things. 30 These things dominate the thoughts of unbelievers all over the world, but your Father already knows your needs. 31 Seek the Kingdom of God above all else, and he will give you everything you need.

32 "So don't be afraid, little flock. For it gives your Father great happiness to give you the Kingdom.

33 "Sell your possessions and give to those in need. This will store up treasure for you in heaven! And the purses of heaven never get old or develop holes. Your treasure will be safe; no thief can steal it and no moth can destroy it. 34 Wherever your treasure is, there the desires of your heart will also be.

Senator Paul Tsongas considered himself a "pro-business liberal." He said in an interview, "On traditional Democratic issues, human rights, civil rights, women's rights, the environment, I am a liberal, and I make no apology for that."[21] And for ten years, he served in both houses of Congress, fighting hard for what he believed to be right. Then, tragically, in 1984 he announced an early retirement from politics so he could battle cancer. A friend affirmed the senator's decision in a letter, adding, "No man ever said on his deathbed, 'I wish I had spent more time at the office.'"[22]

Sometimes it takes a brush with death to clarify what's important and what merely appears to be crucial. Jesus wanted His disciples to live *each day* with the perspective of a man brushed by death. That's because people with a keen awareness of their mortality live by different priorities. They cherish people more and possessions less. They embrace relationships and savor time with those they love, and they use work, possessions, and wealth as a means to that end. People close to death cling to life and live it fully, but remain ever aware of the life to come.

Jesus wanted this for His disciples, not only because He was their Messiah, but also because death loomed nearer for Him than any realized.

— 12:13 —

Luke sometimes inserts a grammatical clue to indicate a change of setting; very often he doesn't. Sometimes the context makes it clear that Jesus had moved to a different time or place; frequently we must speculate, as in this case. Jesus had concluded a somber discourse on the inevitable persecution His followers would face, most likely at the hands of religious and civil authorities, especially the Pharisees. The abrupt change in subject at Luke 12:13 strongly suggests the scene has shifted. If the scene had not changed, the man's request for Jesus to arbitrate a matter of probate would have been terribly tactless.

On the other hand, this may have been Luke's point. By stitching these two stories together so seamlessly, he shows the incredible contrast between the Lord's eternal perspective and the petty, temporal concerns of His followers. From the crowd, a man appealed to Jesus, asking Him to use His authority to compel the man's brother to divide their father's estate. First-century Jews would never think to settle their disputes in a civil court presided over by a Gentile. Nor would they ask someone unfamiliar with God's Law or Jewish traditions to arbitrate a case. Instead, they sought out an expert, a "teacher" of the Law, a rabbi. The unknown man regarded Jesus as a suitable judge and, in calling Him "Teacher," he officially presented his complaint for adjudication.

Jewish tradition made the distribution of a man's estate a fairly routine matter. The dead man's holdings were to be equally divided among his living sons, with the eldest son receiving a double portion (Deut. 21:17; Mishnah *Bekhorot* 8.9[23]) along with the right to take his father's place as the patriarch. Usually, complicated matters were to be settled within thirty days. So, on the surface, at least, the man's request appears solid.

The Lord's response could be taken as a discourse against greed and covetousness, suggesting the man sought more than His fair share or wanted it immediately. As someone once said, "Where there is an inheritance, people become wolves." That's a reasonable and common interpretation, one I have preached myself. After all, Jesus opened His discourse with the warning, "Beware, and be on your guard against every form of greed." A deeper look, however, leads me to believe Jesus had a subtler point to make.

We tend to think of greed as *excessive* desire for wealth and material possessions, which we measure on a sliding scale—and a completely subjective scale, at that! Each of us measures greed differently and, coincidentally, we never find ourselves guilty of covetousness. Jesus, on the other hand, didn't define greed as excess desire for wealth; He saw greed as a matter of priorities. *Any* desire for wealth that lacks the kingdom of God as its motivation is greed. To seek money and possessions as a means of satisfying self is covetousness.

Jesus told a parable of an ordinary man (Luke 12:16-21) and taught about utter dependence upon God (12:22-34) in order to suggest a radical new way of running the household finances: *Pour your funds into the kingdom of God and trust Him to satisfy your material needs.* This eternal, kingdom-oriented perspective then becomes the grid through which we interpret the entire passage (12:13-34).

— 12:14 —

Jesus used the man's question to address all of His listeners. He directed His opening question to "him" (singular) but asked, "Who appointed Me a judge or arbitrator over you (plural)?" It was a double-edged rhetorical question. In the temporal sense, Jesus rejected the role of arbiter over earthly matters; He did not come to earth to become a run-of-the-mill rabbi settling petty material disputes. He came to be the judge of every man and woman in matters of eternal significance. In the spiritual sense, the Lord's rhetorical question challenged the man to consider the eternal implications of appealing to the Messiah. He asked, in effect, "If you choose Me as your judge and arbitrator over material matters, are you aware of what you're asking?"

If Jesus did arbitrate the matter, he would have likely focused on something other than possessions. In what follows, He emphasizes the importance of preparing for God's kingdom rather than seeking to obtain the temporal rights under the laws of men.

— 12:15 —

Jesus then shifted His gaze away from the individual to scan the crowd. The Greek verbs are plural, showing that He addressed all who were listening. The term "Beware" (*horaō* [3708]) means to "be perceptive" or "use your powers of observation." He redoubled this charge, saying, "Be on your (plural) guard against every form of greed"—implying "no matter how small or insignificant it seems." The Greek term translated

Dying to Be Rich

LUKE 12:15

From times when men were iron and ships were wood comes an old story about a group of men on a boat who made their way to an island supposedly full of gold. They divided into two groups, those who would dig for gold and those who would plant seeds, cook, and make arrangements for the sustenance of life on the island. But as they began to find the gold, they got more of the men who were involved in planting seeds to start digging for gold. As time progressed, there were fewer cooks and planters, and more men hauling gold.

Eventually, they began to use parts of the ship to reinforce the shaft so they could dig deeper and find more gold. And, as the story concludes, others arrived on the island years later only to find a group of skeletons draped over great treasures of gold.

There's nothing wrong with having. There's nothing wrong with having much. Jesus never attacked wealth; He always addressed motives.

"greed" is *pleonexia* [4124], a word used in classical literature to denote avarice or an insatiable desire for more. Jesus added the qualification "every form," which removes the idea of degrees and forbids the "desire for more" in every sphere of life, not just wealth.

The Lord forbids the "desire for more," but more than what? Jesus said, in so many words, "Even if one were to gain possession of every molecule of riches in the universe, one's life consists of something different." That is to say, a person's life does not consist of "something plus possessions," but of something completely distinct from material wealth. As Walter Liefeld writes, "Greed seeks possessions, which are not to be equated with true 'living.' In fact, they become a substitute for the proper object of man's search and worship—God."[24]

— 12:16-21 —

To illustrate His harsh denunciation of greed and to better explain His unique definition of the term, Jesus told a parable. He never lingered too long in the realm of the theoretical. When He gave people a principle, He usually followed with a story anyone could understand. And in this case, He told the story of a man everyone would envy. In fact, the description of the land as "very productive" indicated the Lord's blessing according to first-century Jewish theology, and it implied that the man somehow deserved to be divinely favored.

The man pondered a problem: too much grain in storage and not enough space to hold it all. In the ancient world, grain in the silo was as good as money in the bank. I would paraphrase the story in today's terms like this:

> The business of a wealthy entrepreneur was off the chart. Every idea worked. Every decision succeeded. He added new accounts each month, and the money rolled in. He began thinking, *This is a gold mine. My major problem is out-of-control growth. I'm running out of space. There seems to be no end in sight. This is my plan: I'll enlarge headquarters and multiply my staff. I will add a warehouse nearby and open several branches each year for the next ten years, exactly as my consultant has suggested. As the business continues to grow, I will slip further and further out of the picture and leave the work in the hands of my efficient executive staff, and I will just take the profits and enjoy them. I might even retire early!*

Take note that our Lord does not—here or elsewhere—criticize an individual for succeeding in hard work, certainly not if it is earned fairly and legally and for the right motive. The problem was not his success. The Lord didn't condemn the man's decision to plan ahead, either. God encourages good planning and wise stewardship. He did, however, frown upon two mistakes.

First, the man didn't understand himself or his own needs. The phrase "Eat, drink, and be merry" not only reflects hedonism, it recalls the self-indulgent Jews in Isaiah 22:12-14 (see also Isa. 56:12) who partied when they should have been repenting. No amount of bodily pleasure would bring peace to his soul or reconcile him to his Maker. He thought only in terms of the tangible, the immediate, that which he could grasp, consume, or store.

Second, he didn't care about others. He hoarded. He built bigger barns rather than distribute his surplus to those with none. He set his sights on retiring early instead of helping a struggling neighbor. He thought only of himself. In fact, his soliloquy contains no fewer than fourteen references to himself ("I," "me," "my," "soul," "you," "your"). Furthermore, he never prayed for divine guidance nor expressed gratitude for the sun, rain, fertility of the soil, or the protection of his farm.

In the midst of the man's reveling in self-indulgent plans, the words "But God" come like a freight train. The word translated "fool" literally means "mindless." It describes someone who refuses to use his or her brain in practical matters. For all his planning, the man failed to plan for the one, universal, 100-percent-certain event each person must face: death. The Lord didn't require grain or money or possessions; He required the man's soul. And, ironically, others would enjoy the financial bounty of his planned retirement.

Jesus summed up the parable with a heavenly definition of greed. The man had stored up treasure for himself, which robbed him of a rich relationship with God. Clearly, there is a conflict between self-interest and dependence on God. If one looks to earthly treasure for security, sustenance, or significance, one will not seek satisfaction from God. And, according to this parable, it's dangerous to seek security in anything but the Lord. Consequently, it can be said that a person is not ready to live until they're ready to die.

— 12:22-26 —

The Greek word translated "and" is *de* [1161], and here it indicates a change in audience. In Luke 12:14, Jesus addressed the man who wanted him to arbitrate. In 12:15, He taught the crowd. In 12:22, He turns to His dedicated followers. Jesus anticipated His disciples' objection,

"If I don't look after my needs, then who will?" While the principles outlined here might apply to all people everywhere, they are a solemn promise to those who serve the King and advance His kingdom. Furthermore, it is doubtful anyone but a true disciple has the capability to follow this advice. The ability to live the kingdom life is theoretically possible for a nonbeliever, but a practical impossibility. Vertical living in a horizontal world requires the supernatural enabling of the Holy Spirit, whom the nonbeliever has rejected.

The Lord gave His disciples instructions to help them overcome three specific enemies: worry (12:22-31), fear (12:32), and selfishness (12:33-34).

Jesus gave two commands in this section on worry—one at the beginning and one near the end—both offering virtually the same advice: "Do not worry" (12:22) and "Do not keep worrying" (12:29). The Greek words for "worry" are slightly different, however. The first word is *merimnaō* [3309], a common word for the mind being distracted, and one that appears often in the New Testament. Jesus, according to Luke 10:41, said to Martha, "You are worrying yourself to the point of distraction about many things" (my translation). When we worry, our minds become a jumble of facts, details, "what-if" scenarios, and possible solutions.

The second word translated "worry" is used only one time in the New Testament; it is the verb *meteōrizomai* [3349], which is related to the adjective that gave us the English word "meteor." The verb means, literally, "to be up in the air" or "to be suspended in space." We might say that someone who is so preoccupied with worry has "spaced out."

Jesus pointed to two issues that keep us worried. First, we fret over matters that are not our responsibility (12:23-24). Stop and think of the hours you spend focusing on food and clothing, the most basic bodily needs. Jesus didn't say not to pay any attention at all to these things; we are commanded to work in order to eat (2 Thes. 3:10-12). There's nothing wrong with dressing attractively. It's not more spiritual to walk around looking like an unmade bed. But the answer is not to focus too much on where the next meal is coming from or on keeping current with the style of the minute.

God takes care of birds; He'll take even better care of people who rely upon Him.

Second, we fuss over what we cannot change (Luke 12:25-26). The meaning of the phrase "add a single hour to his life's span" is disputed. The word rendered "hour" can measure either time or length.

It's frequently used of a cubit, a measurement of roughly 18 inches. The word translated "life span" can mean either "stature" or "maturity." Therefore, "add a single hour to his life's span" is just as likely to be "add a single cubit to his stature." Most translations choose the former because adding 18 inches to one's height doesn't seem like something most people would want.

While taking reasonable care of our bodies may help to extend physical life, worry can only shorten physical life. God, in His sovereignty, has marked the date of our death, and we'll live not a day shorter if we trust in Him.

— 12:27-31 —

Flowers don't have brains, yet they survive. Rooted in soil nourished by God, watered by rains sent by God, blooming in sunshine new every morning, the most tender of plants flourish in the season ordained for them. Jesus compared these short-lived examples of beauty and contentment to the astounding wealth and privilege of Solomon (1 Kgs. 10:4-7; 2 Chr. 9:3-6), who struggled with the apparent futility of life (Eccl. 1:1-11).

The Lord challenged His fledgling disciples to mature in their faith. He called them to stake their lives on their belief in God's sovereignty. Worrying about the future to the point of distraction expresses doubt in the Lord's ability to take care of those who rely upon Him.

At the end of his earthly pursuits—despite the astounding wealth he had accumulated—Solomon arrived at this simple statement of faith: "The conclusion, when all has been heard, is: fear God and keep His commandments, because this applies to every person. For God will bring every act to judgment, everything which is hidden, whether it is good or evil" (Eccl. 12:13-14). This advice is essentially the same as that expressed here by the Lord. Pour your energy, your time, your money, your every earthly resource into God's great kingdom enterprise; and He will adorn you, feed you, console you, and eventually give you unfettered access to all that is His. That is the fundamental meaning of "seek His kingdom."

— 12:32 —

Arthur Somers Roche stated, "Anxiety is a thin stream of fear trickling through the mind. If encouraged, it cuts a channel into which all other thoughts are drained."[25] Jesus addressed the second enemy of true discipleship: fear. Ironically, to reassure them, He didn't call them lions or giants or warriors. On the contrary, by referring to them as a "flock," He associated His disciples with sheep or goats, the most helpless animals in the ancient Near East. Herd animals need close supervision, protection, and constant care. Moreover, the disciples were a "little" flock. Individually, they were defenseless, and their numbers did nothing to help.

The disciples had nothing to fear because their Shepherd never fails to protect and He's always faithful to provide. The kingdom belongs to true disciples, if only they will remain under the watchful care of God.

— 12:33-34 —

The third and final enemy Jesus addressed in His discourse was selfishness. Wealth in the kingdom of God is not measured by what you own or how much you take in, but by how much you give. Jesus commanded His disciples to sell what they had and give the proceeds to "charity."

The Lord doesn't expect His disciples to sell everything, give it all away, and then leave themselves destitute. He still expects parents to provide for their families through honest work. He didn't counsel ridiculous extremes in anything, except perhaps radical faith. Rather, he called His followers to shift the balance of their perspectives to see giving as the measure of wealth and to accumulate possessions on an as-needed basis.

The Lord described the benefits in ironic terms. Earlier, He sent His disciples to minister without a "money belt" (Luke 10:4). In this setting, He counseled them to make heavenly money belts, as it were. Giving away money and possessions on earth creates deposits in heaven, where nothing decays or dwindles, where nothing can be robbed or destroyed.

He then concluded His teaching with a universal principle: You keep your heart where you keep your treasure. The word translated "treasure" actually refers to a treasure house, the place where valuables are kept. Therefore, it's not a matter of *whether* you keep something in your storehouse, but *what* you keep in there! For Jesus, the only treasure that matters is allegiance to the King and devotion to His cause (the kingdom). And with that, He brought the discussion full circle, back to the issue of values.

Charles Spurgeon paraphrased the Lord's teaching this way: "Seek with your whole soul, first and foremost, 'the kingdom of God,' as the place of your citizenship, 'and His righteousness' as the character of your life. As for the rest, it will come from the Lord Himself without your being anxious concerning it."[26]

• • •

I opened this segment with Senator Paul Tsongas's life-changing decision. There's more to the story. After retiring from public life to battle cancer, he made a full recovery. Then, in 1992, he followed his passion back into politics, even seeking his party's nomination for the office of president. But five years later, his cancer returned, and on a cold winter's day in 1997, he died. Politics no longer divided him from his fellow man. Political friends and adversaries alike gathered for a final good-bye, united by sorrow for his family, bonded by a shared realization that all differences evaporate at the graveside. Issues ceased to be important. Temporal causes mattered no more. Career, money, power, possessions, hobbies, habits, and ambitions—all irrelevant. He is where we all shall go: eternity.

Fortunately, before he left this life for the next, Paul Tsongas heeded some very good advice from a friend. He set aside what was important for what was *more* important. And I doubt he lay on his deathbed regretting time away from the office.

APPLICATION: LUKE 12:13-34
How to Live with the Curse of Material Blessing

It is probably safe to say that none of us is any richer than we can stand to be. The Lord doesn't have anything against wealth *per se*, but if we are following Him, He will never allow us to have more than we can handle without it stunting our growth or undermining our obedience. Some Christians are fortunate enough to be very wealthy yet don't seem to struggle with the inherent dangers of material abundance.

After studying Scripture and observing some of my wealthy Christian friends, I have a few suggestions.

First, *when you are blessed with much, give generously.*

Our Lord does not reserve His strongest words for people blessed with wealth. He reserves His strongest words for those who are innately selfish and who hoard rather than give. And if you get more, give more. That doesn't mean you have to give it all away. You can enjoy your money and share it.

As I was preparing these thoughts, a man and his wife were blessed with an unexpected windfall, and they immediately wrestled with the issue of whether to upgrade their furniture or buy some for a missionary friend. I asked, "What did you do?"

"As a matter of fact," he said, "we did both."

They bought new furniture that was less expensive and bought some for the missionary as well. I thought, "Wise decision."

Second, *when you plan for the future, think terminally.*

George Bernard Shaw said, "The statistics on death are quite impressive. One out of one die." Plan with your own end in mind. You will realize that your mass of fortune—little or great—will simply become the property of those who did not work for it and who will not appreciate it nearly as much as you. Enjoy your possessions, but keep them in perspective. What will become of your things when you are gone?

Third, *whether you have much or little, hold it loosely.*

Everything you have belongs to God. He owns it all. If you maintain that perspective, then your grip on things automatically loosens. And you begin to discover that God doesn't care how much you have, whether a little or a lot; He simply wants your unquestioned devotion to Him above all, and for you to use that which He has given you for His kingdom.

People, Get Ready
LUKE 12:35-48

NASB

35 "aBe dressed in readiness, and *keep* your lamps lit. 36Be like men who are waiting for their master when he returns from the wedding feast, so that they may immediately open *the door* to him when he comes and knocks. 37Blessed are those slaves whom the master will find on the alert when he comes; truly I say to you, that he will gird himself *to serve,* and have them recline *at the table,* and will come up and wait on them. 38Whether he comes in the asecond watch, or even in the bthird, and finds *them* so, blessed are those *slaves.*

39 "But abe sure of this, that if the head of the house had known at what hour the thief was coming, he

NLT

35 "Be dressed for service and keep your lamps burning, 36 as though you were waiting for your master to return from the wedding feast. Then you will be ready to open the door and let him in the moment he arrives and knocks. 37The servants who are ready and waiting for his return will be rewarded. I tell you the truth, he himself will seat them, put on an apron, and serve them as they sit and eat! 38He may come in the middle of the night or just before dawn.* But whenever he comes, he will reward the servants who are ready.

39 "Understand this: If a homeowner knew exactly when a burglar was coming, he would not permit

would not have allowed his house to be [b]broken into. [40]You too, be ready; for the Son of Man is coming at an hour that you do not [a]expect."

[41]Peter said, "Lord, are You addressing this parable to us, or to everyone *else* as well?" [42]And the Lord said, "Who then is the faithful and sensible steward, whom his master will put in charge of his [a]servants, to give them their rations at the proper time? [43]Blessed is that slave whom his [a]master finds so doing when he comes. [44]Truly I say to you that he will put him in charge of all his possessions. [45]But if that slave says in his heart, 'My master [a]will be a long time in coming,' and begins to beat the slaves, *both* men and women, and to eat and drink and get drunk; [46]the master of that slave will come on a day when he does not expect *him* and at an hour he does not know, and will cut him in pieces, and assign him a place with the unbelievers. [47]And that slave who knew his master's will and did not get ready or act in accord with his will, will receive many lashes, [48]but the one who did not know *it,* and committed deeds worthy of [a]a flogging, will receive but few. From everyone who has been given much, much will be required; and to whom they entrusted much, of him they will ask all the more.

12:35 [a]Lit *Let your loins be girded* 12:38 [a]I.e. 9 p.m. to midnight [b]I.e. midnight to 3 a.m.
12:39 [a]Lit *know* [b]Lit *dug through* 12:40 [a]Lit *think, suppose* 12:42 [a]Lit *service* 12:43 [a]Or *lord*
12:45 [a]Lit *is delaying to come* 12:48 [a]Lit *blows*

his house to be broken into. [40]You also must be ready all the time, for the Son of Man will come when least expected."

[41]Peter asked, "Lord, is that illustration just for us or for everyone?"

[42]And the Lord replied, "A faithful, sensible servant is one to whom the master can give the responsibility of managing his other household servants and feeding them. [43]If the master returns and finds that the servant has done a good job, there will be a reward. [44]I tell you the truth, the master will put that servant in charge of all he owns. [45]But what if the servant thinks, 'My master won't be back for a while,' and he begins beating the other servants, partying, and getting drunk? [46]The master will return unannounced and unexpected, and he will cut the servant in pieces and banish him with the unfaithful.

[47]"And a servant who knows what the master wants, but isn't prepared and doesn't carry out those instructions, will be severely punished. [48]But someone who does not know, and then does something wrong, will be punished only lightly. When someone has been given much, much will be required in return; and when someone has been entrusted with much, even more will be required.

12:38 Greek *in the second or third watch.*

Sometimes the future brings fun surprises—like when the man who had no idea he would win the lottery bought a ticket and stuck it in his pocket with a fatalistic shrug. He had forgotten all about his impulsive decision to buy a ticket with his other purchases at the convenience store, only to discover a few days later that he would never have to work for a paycheck again.

Other bolts from the blue aren't so happy. For example, on March

18, 1979, Stephanie May received a visit from her pastor, bearing tragic news. A twin-engine airplane crashed just after takeoff near Aspen, Colorado, and in a twinkling, she lost her husband, John Edward, age 51, CEO and chairman of the board of May Petroleum. Stephanie also lost her son, Davin Edward, age 22, a senior at the University of Texas; her daughter Karla Emily, age 18, a senior at Highland Park High School in Dallas; and her son-in-law, Richard Owen Snyder, age 27. Suddenly, Stephanie's circle of significant loved ones shrank by four. What crushing news!

How do you prepare for such a moment?

For the next two months, Stephanie kept a journal, into which she poured her grief and sorted her thoughts. Near the end, she wrote,

> My burden is heavy, but I don't walk alone. My pain is unrelenting, but I thank God for every moment that He blessed me with. I pray that my life will be used for His glory, that I might carry my burden with Christian dignity, and that out of my devastation may His kingdom become apparent to someone lost and in pain. I close this diary, and with it goes all my known ability and capacity for love. I cannot replace or compare my loss. It is my loss. I am not strong. I am not brave.
>
> I am a Christian with a burden to carry and a message to share. I have been severely tested, but my faith has survived, and I have been strengthened in my love and devotion to the Lord. O God, my life is Yours—comfort me in Your arms and direct my life. I have walked in hell, but now I walk with God in peace. John Edward, Davin, Karla, and Richard are in God's hands. I am in God's arms. His love surrounds me. This rose will bloom again.[27]

Stephanie May didn't prepare for March 18, 1979, on March 17. Her preparation for this devastating moment began long beforehand, and her spiritual grounding sustained her through the worst.

Jesus spent much of His ministry teaching His disciples about their ultimate future—the kingdom to come and their eternal citizenship in it. On this day, however, He showed His followers that this hope in the hereafter has practical application in the here and now. After commanding them not to worry, not to be anxious, not to seek what the world seeks, not to be concerned with the things that you can buy or touch or feel, He exhorted His followers, "Be dressed in readiness." But what does that mean? And how can that help us today, in an earthly realm dominated by evil?

— 12:35 —

The command "Be dressed in readiness" literally refers to keeping one's loins continually girded. No one wore pants in the first century; both men and women wore tunics, outer garments that extended well below the knees. When a man needed to run, climb, work, fight—any activity that required nimble movement—he gathered the material in the back of his tunic, pulled it forward between his legs, and tucked it into his belt. Consequently, it became an image of readiness for action.

Similarly, the command "keep your lamps lit" urges the disciples to keep themselves in a perpetual state of awareness. People who have experience in camping understand the importance of light. They douse the lantern only when they're certain it's safe. If campers suspect something might wander into their area during the night, they keep the pilot flame burning and sometimes take turns keeping watch.

After two picturesque commands, Jesus illustrated "readiness" with two metaphors taken from everyday life. The first scenario involves the arrival of someone expected (12:36-38); the second, someone unexpected (12:39-40).

— 12:36-38 —

It's difficult to see in the English of 12:36, but the Greek grammar places great emphasis on the pronoun "you." I would paraphrase the command like this: "You there! Yes, you! Be like men who are waiting for their master." The emphasis grabs one by the shoulders and shakes the reader with each syllable. "This is for *you*. Wake up. Be ready."

The first illustration imagines a well-to-do man attending a wedding feast, which can last up to a week, although guests may elect to leave early. Upon his return, he should not have to bang on his own outer gates like a beggar. The head steward should post a lookout who will warn the rest of the household when the master appears on the horizon. One servant should open the gate upon his arrival, while another helps him into the house. The house should have been kept clean and orderly, and the routine chores completed with due diligence. As a crew unloads his belongings, the table should be set with the appropriate meal of the hour.

Jesus promised faithful followers who live in eager anticipation of His return that He would turn around the tables of service. While the household servants in the illustration are prepared to serve their master, the Messiah will "gird Himself" for service. In the modern vernacular, He will roll up His sleeves to become a waiter. In the Lord's image, the servants recline at the table to eat while the wealthy homeowner pampers them!

He then pronounced a blessing on those servants who diligently keep themselves ready for His return to earth.

— 12:39 —

The Lord's second illustration is not the joyful return of an expected master, but the surprise break-in of an unexpected intruder. Burglars don't send postcards announcing the time and place of their next target, so the homeowner must remain alert at all times. Moreover, first-century thieves usually gained entrance by digging a hole in an exterior wall, which was usually constructed from mud. Consequently, the head of a household had to keep watch over every inch of the home, not just the doors and windows.

We need not read too deeply into the meaning of the illustration. Jesus neither equated himself to a thief nor characterized His return as malicious. He merely alluded to a common idiom for something "unexpected" (cf. 1 Thes. 5:2; 2 Pet. 3:10; Rev. 3:3; 16:15).

— 12:40 —

Jesus applied the metaphors to His own return, using His characteristic self-designation "Son of Man" (Luke 5:24; 6:5, 22; 7:34; 9:22, 26, 44). He had already told His disciples that His mission would take an unexpected path (9:22). In fact, the divine conquest would be no less counterintuitive from an earthly perspective than living as a citizen of God's kingdom—expressed, for example, in 6:27-29: "Love your enemies, do good to those who hate you, bless those who curse you, pray for those who mistreat you."

Jesus had revealed that He must "be killed and be raised up on the third day" (9:22; see also 9:44), although this declaration of His divine mission apparently fell on deaf ears. The full meaning of His going away and then returning would not sink in until much later, after many of His predictions were fulfilled (9:45). Nevertheless, throughout His earthly ministry, Jesus placed some intellectual time bombs in the consciousness of His followers. In due time—at the right time—these memories would explode in the minds of the kingdom's future leaders, giving them a complete understanding of what had happened and a supernatural confidence to take up their Master's cross and to follow His downward path to glory.

Stay Ready!

LUKE 12:38

Before enlisting in the United States Marine Corps, I worked as an apprentice in a machine shop, working for more than four years as a machinist. I worked directly behind a man on a row of turret lathes. I'll never forget Tex and the pouch of chewing tobacco he kept in his back pocket. He used to leave the pouch open to make it easier to pinch a wad of that brown leaf and tuck it into his cheek.

While we were working second shift one night, a little cricket hopped across the floor in front of me, and I thought, *That cricket is the same color as Tex's tobacco.*

I grabbed the cricket, pulled off its head, dropped it in the top of his tobacco pouch, and waited. Not long after that, Tex shoved a couple of callused fingers into the pouch and jammed a big chaw of tobacco into his mouth. He either didn't know or didn't care about the cricket. I never asked and he never said.

Anyway, Tex always washed up just before the final whistle. He was every employer's nightmare, ready to leave before time was up. I asked him, "Tex, how do you do it?" And he said, "Let me tell you something, Sonny. I just stay ready to keep from gettin' ready."

Bad work ethic. Good theology.

— 12:41 —

Peter, as usual, said out loud what others only dared to think. And in so many words, he asked the question on every student's mind: "Is this going to be on the test?" In other words, "Who are the servants in Your metaphor? Us Twelve? Kingdom leaders? All of Your followers? Everyone in the world? Who is responsible for the never-ending task of maintaining constant readiness for the Master's return?"

— 12:42-44 —

In keeping with the teaching style of the day, Jesus responded to Peter's question with another question. Of course, His question was rhetorical. It contained the answer Peter needed to hear: The "faithful and sensible steward" can be anyone who chooses to fulfill the role, and one's qualifications can be seen by one's actions. Those in the Lord's hearing had a duty to ask themselves, "Am I a faithful and sensible steward?"

In the ancient Near East, the steward of the household (*oikonomos* [3623]) wielded almost unlimited power within his master's sphere of influence. He managed the day-to-day affairs of the estate, represented

SLAVERY IN THE FIRST CENTURY

LUKE 12:43

Slavery had been around a long time by the time of Jesus, dating back as far as humans have kept records. Civilizations have been carrying prisoners of war off to slavery for millennia. The Athenians and Romans, however, transformed the practice into a state-sponsored institution, complete with detailed legal codes, sophisticated economic procedures, and complex social customs. The institution of slavery in the Roman Empire, while often brutal, was different from the slavery of seventeenth- and eighteenth-century England and America because it was not based on race.

Slaves came under bondage in one of four primary ways:

1. Prior to the death of Augustus and the end of Rome's foreign expansion, slaves were either captured in war or kidnapped by pirates and then sold at auction. Paul listed engagement in this kind of slavery among other detestable practices, such as sexual immorality, homosexuality, and perjury (1 Tim. 1:10; see also Exod. 21:16).
2. After the death of Augustus, bearing children became the primary source of slavery. According to Roman law, children of enslaved women were bound to their masters as well.

3. An extremely common means of escaping the hardscrabble life of freeborn poverty was to sell oneself into slavery. Many non-Romans chose slavery as a way to gain work skills, climb socially, earn citizenship after manumission—a reasonable expectation, according to Roman law—and even serve in public office. Many believe this had been the path chosen by Erastus (Rom. 16:23), the city manager of Corinth.

4. A common method of dealing with an unwanted pregnancy was to give birth and then abandon the infant to the elements, a practice called "exposure." Infants, primarily baby girls, found alive were often taken to be raised as slaves. Extremely poor parents might elect to sell their child into slavery instead; not necessarily for the money, but as a crude form of adoption.

Roman law considered slaves to be property. A slave could be owned, traded, or sold, like an animal. A slave could not legally marry, bring a suit against someone in court, inherit property or money, or essentially do anything without the master's consent. While slaves received more severe punishment for crimes than their free counterparts, they technically had some legal protection from excessive abuse, not unlike our laws against animal cruelty. Enforcement, however, was inconsistent.

Some slaves could own property, which they legally controlled without interference from their masters. Some acquired their own slaves, whom they sold for a profit. Slaves could also accumulate wealth and then use it to purchase their own freedom, a common method of wiping out debt and reentering life with advanced social status.

Legally, slaves occupied a decidedly subordinate status in Roman society, but sometimes they rose to relatively high ranks. In fact, few could distinguish slaves from freeborn workers-for-hire who carried out the same kinds of duties.

In Greco-Roman households slaves served not only as cooks, cleaners, and personal attendants, but also as tutors of persons of all ages, physicians, nurses, close companions, and managers of the household. In the business world, slaves were not only janitors and delivery boys; they were managers of estates, shops, and ships, as well as salesmen and contracting agents. In the civil service slaves were not only used in street-paving and sewer-cleaning gangs, but also as administrators of funds and personnel and as executives with decision-making powers. . . . As such, in stark contrast to New World slavery in the 17th–19th centuries, Greco-Roman slavery functioned as a process rather than a permanent condition, as a temporary phase of life by means of which an outsider obtained a place within a society.[28]

Most slaves could expect to be freed by the age of thirty, or even sooner, as many owners set all their slaves free as a part of their final testaments.

his master in business dealings, supervised the staff, and even exercised some authority over the owner's wife and children, insofar as he carried out the patriarch's desires and upheld his values. A "sensible" (*phronimos* [5429]) steward used his head to understand his master's will. Jesus pronounced a blessing upon the steward who carries out His wishes with faithful sensibility.

— 12:45-46 —

The unwise steward commits two errors. First, he says to himself, "I will do as I please while my master is away"; and second, he says, "I have plenty of time to put things right before my master returns." Notably, Jesus adjusted His terminology when comparing the unwise steward to his faithful counterpart. Both men serve their master's interests, and both hold the rank of "slave" or "bond-servant." In the first example, Jesus referred to the slave as a "steward"; in the second, however, the slave is never more than a slave despite the power delegated to him. The Master may return at any moment, proving the unwise steward's assumptions to be fatally flawed. He may not do as he pleases, he has less time than he imagines, and the reckoning for his presumption is both swift and severe.

— 12:47-48 —

Jesus summarized the parable and then applied a double-edged, universal principle to give Peter's initial question a direct answer:

> Edge 1: Those who behave badly in ignorance will receive less punishment than those who knew God's expectations and then flouted them.

> Edge 2: Those who receive a greater portion of divine revelation bear a proportionally greater weight of responsibility.

We are responsible for the truth that comes to us. For example, as soon as I know the bridge is down, I am responsible to stop and to stop every car behind me. That's responsible living in light of the warning. Jesus' followers understand that Christ is real, the Bible is true, hell is a factual place, and eternity is long; therefore, we are held responsible to do something with this information.

• • •

We isolated this discourse in order to analyze it, but Luke never intended it to be read out of context. It belongs to a longer discussion on the importance of kingdom living in the present world. Let's summarize what Jesus taught in this section.

It only seems as though evil rules the world with impunity; God sees all and He will reward those who openly declare allegiance to His coming kingdom (Luke 12:1-12). Do not live in the present dominion of evil as though it will remain forever; give your earthly wealth and possessions to the kingdom of God, and you will enjoy a millionfold return on your investment when the Messiah topples the kingdom of Satan (12:13-21). Don't worry that you won't have enough to eat or wear or that you will be homeless; God values you, and He will faithfully provide for all who depend upon Him (12:22-34). Live each day in this dominion of evil as though it were your last; live each day like the kingdom of God is here already. For all you know the King will arrive within the next five minutes (12:35-40). What's that, Peter? To whom does this apply? All who have heard this teaching are responsible to live by it. If that's you, take heed (12:41-48)!

The followers of the King must begin living in the current dominion of evil as though the kingdom of God were present now in its fullness. Satan continues to rule the earth, but another King will arrive "on a day when we do not expect him and at an hour we do not know" (12:46). And we will be held accountable for how we have chosen to live. Did we live according to the paradigm of the present world of sin, or did we adjust our behavior to fulfill the expectations of our returning Master?

This choice not only affects how the Master will receive us when He returns, but it also impacts how we navigate the ebb and flow of life in this era—here and now in the world ruled by Satan—where tomorrow may bring great fortune or unspeakable tragedy. That's why Stephanie May's words mean so much to so many. When the tragedy struck, she didn't lose her bearings. Her kingdom perspective gave her the hope and strength she needed to survive March 18, 1979, and March 19, and March 20. In fact, she has seen her rose bloom and wither many times since that terrible day. Nevertheless, she remains faithful and sensible. And one day, perhaps in the not too distant future, she will hear her Master say, "Sit down to dinner, My loyal and loving daughter, and let Me serve you."

APPLICATION: LUKE 12:35-48

Vertical Living in a Horizontal World

The philosopher Søren Kierkegaard urged that life can only be understood backwards, but it must be lived forwards.[29] That is, for the most part, true—at least from a two-dimensional perspective. People who observe the precepts of God are given an understanding about life that comes from above. While we live on the horizontal plane, moving in linear fashion from the past into the future, God brings vertical wisdom, insight, and perception, which we would not otherwise have. And His is an upward call. So, our goal is to live vertically in a horizontal world.

If we are to do this, what has to change? Let me suggest two things that speak directly to me.

First of all, *we have to change how we think before things happen.* We have to program ourselves to be ready for whatever happens by choosing our perspective ahead of time—vertical, eternal, theological. Think first of the kingdom when you wake up in the morning. Think first of God as you drive to work. Think first of His will and His plan when you encounter whatever you do on your job or in your school. First: His kingdom, His righteousness. Think first of what He would have you do in a situation that's threatening and difficult and, frankly, worrisome. We must change how we think before something happens.

Second, *we must change how we react when things do happen.* People in law enforcement learn how to keep from panicking when they hear screams, alarms, or gunfire. They immediately go into action. Similarly, astronauts are trained to handle the liftoff just as comfortably as they handle the orbiting. They're trained to react in a calm and deliberate manner. They're trained not to panic.

For the believer, this vertical perspective doesn't come overnight. It comes through experience—failure, evaluation, adjustments, improvement—so that over time, one learns how to see things from God's perspective: vertically, top down. Eventually, if you are a disciple of Christ learning to see all circumstances as God sees them, you won't have to understand life backwards; you can understand it (to some degree, anyway) here and now.

It's Time to Get Real
LUKE 12:49-59

NASB

49 "I ᵃhave come to cast fire upon the earth; and ᵇhow I wish it were already kindled! 50But I have a baptism to ᵃundergo, and how distressed I am until it is accomplished! 51Do you suppose that I came to grant peace on earth? I tell you, no, but rather division; 52for from now on five *members* in one household will be divided, three against two and two against three. 53They will be divided, father against son and son against father, mother against daughter and daughter against mother, mother-in-law against daughter-in-law and daughter-in-law against mother-in-law."

54And He was also saying to the crowds, "When you see a cloud rising in the west, immediately you say, 'A shower is coming,' and so it turns out. 55And when *you see* a south wind blowing, you say, 'It will be a hot day,' and it turns out *that way*. 56You hypocrites! You know how to analyze the appearance of the earth and the sky, but ᵃwhy do you not analyze this present time?

57"And why do you not even on your own initiative judge what is right? 58For while you are going with your opponent to appear before the magistrate, on *your* way *there* make an effort to ᵃsettle with him, so that he may not drag you before the judge, and the judge turn you over to the officer, and the officer throw you into prison. 59I say to you, you will not get out of there until you have paid the very last ᵃcent."

12:49 ᵃOr *came* ᵇLit *what do I wish if...?*
12:50 ᵃLit *be baptized with* 12:56 ᵃLit *how*
12:58 ᵃLit *be released from him* 12:59 ᵃGr *lepton;* i.e. 1/128 of a denarius

NLT

49 "I have come to set the world on fire, and I wish it were already burning! 50I have a terrible baptism of suffering ahead of me, and I am under a heavy burden until it is accomplished. 51Do you think I have come to bring peace to the earth? No, I have come to divide people against each other! 52From now on families will be split apart, three in favor of me, and two against—or two in favor and three against.

53 'Father will be divided against son
and son against father;
mother against daughter
and daughter against mother;
and mother-in-law against daughter-in-law
and daughter-in-law against mother-in-law.'*"

54Then Jesus turned to the crowd and said, "When you see clouds beginning to form in the west, you say, 'Here comes a shower.' And you are right. 55When the south wind blows, you say, 'Today will be a scorcher.' And it is. 56You fools! You know how to interpret the weather signs of the earth and sky, but you don't know how to interpret the present times.

57"Why can't you decide for yourselves what is right? 58When you are on the way to court with your accuser, try to settle the matter before you get there. Otherwise, your accuser may drag you before the judge, who will hand you over to an officer, who will throw you into prison. 59And if that happens, you won't be free again until you have paid the very last penny.*"

12:53 Mic 7:6. 12:59 Greek *last lepton* [the smallest Jewish coin].

Peter traveled with the Lord and listened to His teaching, but he didn't understand the full significance of the movement he had joined. Like many others, Peter thought Jesus would enter Jerusalem to claim David's throne by politics, by intrigue, or by force, backed by a steadily growing horde of followers. In truth, the scope of Jesus' mission had been much greater. He didn't come to administer the daily activities of a city or restore a country to its former greatness or even rule the world as a Caesar; His kingdom agenda was—and still is—cosmic in scale.

Throughout His ministry, Jesus gradually revealed the full magnitude of His mission, and this extended discourse on kingdom living was no exception. It began with a warning that all that is hidden now will be revealed one day (12:1-12). Then, the misplaced priorities of a man seeking justice (12:13-15) launched a series of lessons featuring a "then vs. now" theme, all pointing to the arrival of a very different era. Jesus signaled the conclusion of this extended discourse with a shocking statement that merely hinted at the magnitude of His plan.

— 12:49-50 —

Jesus frequently spoke prophetically; that is, He uttered big-picture statements about the future while stressing the importance of godly conduct in the present. Sometimes His emotions prompted Him to express His hatred for sin and what it had done to His creation. As He pondered the coming of His kingdom and surveyed the perversion of evil, He longed for everything to be put right immediately.

Peter heard his Master's statement, "I have come to cast a fire upon the earth," but at the time he could not have known what it meant. Later, he did. After all the events of Jesus' earthly ministry—including His crucifixion, burial, resurrection, commission, and ascension—the apostle realized that the Son of God had arrived in the flesh, in part, to announce the end of the world as we know it. All of human history is moving toward an unimaginably cataclysmic, transformational event that will reorder the universe—everything from atoms to galaxies. Years later, Peter warned,

> Know this first of all, that in the last days mockers will come with their mocking, following after their own lusts, and saying, "Where is the promise of His coming? For ever since the fathers fell asleep, all continues just as it was from the beginning of creation." For when they maintain this, it escapes their notice that by the word of God the heavens existed long ago and the earth was formed out of water and by water, through which the world

at that time was destroyed, being flooded with water. But by His word the present heavens and earth are being reserved for fire, kept for the day of judgment and destruction of ungodly men.

But do not let this one fact escape your notice, beloved, that with the Lord one day is like a thousand years, and a thousand years like one day. The Lord is not slow about His promise, as some count slowness, but is patient toward you, not wishing for any to perish but for all to come to repentance. But the day of the Lord will come like a thief, in which the heavens will pass away with a roar and the elements will be destroyed with intense heat, and the earth and its works will be burned up. (2 Pet. 3:3-10)

Fire will consume the universe as we know it, so that this old earth and the old heavens will cease to exist. In their place a new earth and a new heaven will emerge (Rev. 21:1), and all of it will be freed from the disease of sin and the dominion of evil. But as Jesus stood somewhere between Galilee and Jerusalem, lamenting the suffering that grips the world both then and now, He expressed impatience with the unfolding of His own plan: "And how I wish [the end-time fire] were already kindled!"

I find great comfort in knowing that the Lord laments each second that evil continues to exist. He could, at any moment, eliminate all pain, suffering, disasters, disease, death, sorrow, mourning, and decay. But that would also mean the end of us! His plan of redemption must tolerate the continued existence of evil for a time—just enough time to make a way for salvation and to collect all those who will choose to trust in Christ.

Jesus hated evil, but His love for humanity won the day. His future "baptism" refers to an immersion into suffering—the ordeal of Gethsemane, the cross, and the sepulcher—before His triumphant rise. He described His state of mind as "distressed" (synechō [4912]) until the plan was accomplished. The apostle Paul used this same Greek verb to describe being "hard-pressed" (or torn) by two alternative desires (Phil. 1:23). Both Jesus and Paul held themselves together while enduring great affliction.

We can only imagine the Lord's inner conflict. On a personal level, He left the pristine holiness of a perfect heaven to live in the cesspool of creation. While we hate evil because of the harm it causes us, God hates evil because it violates His very nature and corrupts everything—everyone—He loves. On another level, the Lord found

Himself conflicted by His abhorrence for the continued existence of sin and His compassion for people. He "held Himself together" despite being torn between righteousness and patience.

— 12:51-53 —

When the angels announced the arrival of the Messiah, they praised God, saying, "Glory to God in the highest, and on earth peace among men with whom He is pleased" (2:14). So, the Lord's sobering clarification of His mission could appear to conflict with His birth announcement. Which is true? Did He come to bring peace or division?

The answer depends upon your perspective. From the divine point of view, Jesus came to redeem humanity from the clutches of sin and to restore all people to a right relationship with God. He has opened the offer of salvation to all people everywhere. Unfortunately, some do not want reconciliation with God. Some people like things the way they are. Many reject God as King, fearing the loss of wealth or power or significance or pleasure or autonomy. While the intent of heaven is unity, earthly realities routinely transform the message of peace into a declaration of war.

The fact is, truth does not unite people; it divides people. Truth unites people who desire truth, but it stirs violence in the hearts of those who don't. And no earthly relationship, regardless of how close, can survive the crisis of truth.

Peace comes to the hearts of men and women whose hearts are right with God. That's where peace happens. Pursue peace on earth, but don't be surprised when it's short-lived. Don't be discouraged because peace on earth remains elusive; pursue peace regardless. After all, if you are a true disciple of Jesus Christ, you are a child of peace. It is in your new nature to desire harmony with others.

The division of which Jesus spoke has both an immediate and ultimate fulfillment. In the immediate, the truth of Christ will divide people for the reasons stated above. Ultimately, believers will be removed from this earth (1 Thes. 4:13-18; 2 Thes. 2:1-4), leaving unbelievers to endure a horrible time of tribulation, a time of unprecedented lawlessness the likes of which this world has never known (Dan 12:1; Matt 24:21; Mark 13:19; Rev. 13:5-18). Families will again be divided.

Because divine truth divides people, we should be very careful not to say to the individuals we lead to Christ, "Come to the Lord and all of your problems will be solved, all of your difficulties will be removed, all pain will soon be erased." While the healing power of God's forgiveness is immense, and the transforming power of the Holy Spirit makes all things new, we still live in a dark, sin-twisted world. Therefore, I warn new believers, "You need to understand: you will be misunderstood. Not everyone is ready, as you have been, to give their hearts to Christ. You need to know this could bring a division between you and those with whom you once enjoyed peace and harmony."

— 12:54-56 —

While we must accept that truth divides, Jesus nevertheless urged His followers to pursue peace. He began with an illustration of urgency and awareness (Luke 12:54-56), and then, in light of the approaching end, commanded us to accept whatever peace we can negotiate (12:57-59).

The phrase "He was saying" uses the imperfect tense, which may indicate an ongoing or repetitive action. In other words, while He taught His followers to expect strife on account of their faith in Jesus as the Messiah, He continued to challenge the mixed crowds listening to His teaching. He chastised their unwillingness to acknowledge the unfolding of events that fulfill the predictions of the Old Testament.

Jesus equated observing His ministry to noting daily weather patterns. Both offer unmistakable signs of what is to come. In the past, a cloud forming over the Mediterranean has always brought rain. A south wind has always brought heat. Past experience with certain signs should help an attentive person predict the immediate future. In similar fashion, the Lord's audience had exposure to the Hebrew Scriptures, including prophecies concerning the Messiah, His mission, His death, His triumph, and many references to His kingdom. He chastised their failure to analyze and interpret the signs of their times.

Ample indications about the future lay within their grasp, yet they failed to take hold of the truth. The kingdom of God is coming, at which time the Ultimate Judge will resolve all disputes. Individuals will not seek justice from one another but will stand as individuals before God to receive justice, not only for what they are due from others, but for what they owe.

— 12:57-59 —

Jesus appealed to the crowds to settle their disputes, particularly where they were in the wrong. To illustrate the wisdom of making peace, He used the analogy of two people resolved to settle a debt in court. Prior to appearing before the judge, the debtor should either appeal to the lender's mercy to be freed from the debt or try to reach a settlement.

There's no guarantee the debtor will be released from the balance that cannot be repaid, but it is better than facing certain condemnation from the judge.

APPLICATION: LUKE 12:49-59

Getting Real in the Here and Now

People tend to respond in one of three ways to a study of end-time events. Two are extreme; one strikes the right balance.

One extreme response is to live completely and totally for the future. Some individuals carry the mandate to "be alert" to such extremes that they live as though the earth is finished now. Not surprisingly, they often struggle with deep emotional and mental troubles. And unfortunately, they tend to gather around themselves a group of fearful minions.

The second extreme completely ignores end-time prophecy as either total nonsense or complete allegory. Apathy becomes the state of mind. Jesus said these people are like those who perished in the ancient flood: "They were eating, they were drinking, they were marrying, they were being given in marriage, until the day that Noah entered the ark, and the flood came and destroyed them all" (17:27).

Rather than fall into one of those two extremes, let's live wisely and joyously in the present, never forgetting that He's coming back. How can we do that? Let me give you a couple of very practical ideas.

First, the next time you see the word "peace," whether it's written on a stamp or whether it's part of a slogan someone's passing around, remember that the only place there can be lasting peace is in the human heart, through faith in Christ. Each time you see the word "peace," let it remind you that, because of Christ, peace can exist in the heart. When the heart is changed, life can change.

Second, each time you watch the weather report, remember that Christ's return could occur that day. When the weather patterns unfold as the forecast had warned, remember that the return of Christ will fulfill the promises of Scripture. "The trumpet will sound, and the dead will be raised imperishable, and we will be changed" (1 Cor. 15:52). "We who are alive and remain will be caught up together with them in the clouds to meet the Lord in the air, and so we shall always be with the Lord (1 Thes. 4:17).

What a Difference Jesus Makes!
LUKE 13:1-17

NASB

¹Now on the same occasion there were some present who reported to Him about the Galileans whose blood Pilate had ªmixed with their sacrifices. ²And Jesus said to them, "Do you suppose that these Galileans were *greater* sinners than all *other* Galileans because they suffered this *fate?* ³I tell you, no, but unless you ªrepent, you will all likewise perish. ⁴Or do you suppose that those eighteen on whom the tower in Siloam fell and killed them were *worse* ªculprits than all the men who live in Jerusalem? ⁵I tell you, no, but unless you repent, you will all likewise perish."

⁶And He *began* telling this parable: "A man had a fig tree which had been planted in his vineyard; and he came looking for fruit on it and did not find any. ⁷And he said to the vineyard-keeper, 'Behold, for three years I have come looking for fruit on this fig tree ªwithout finding any. Cut it down! Why does it even use up the ground?' ⁸And he answered and said to him, 'Let it alone, sir, for this year too, until I dig around it and put in fertilizer; ⁹and if it bears fruit next year, *fine;* but if not, cut it down.'"

¹⁰And He was teaching in one of the synagogues on the Sabbath. ¹¹And there was a woman who for eighteen years had had a sickness caused by a spirit; and she was bent double, and could not straighten up at all. ¹²When Jesus saw her, He called her over and said to her, "Woman, you are freed from your sickness." ¹³And He laid His hands on her; and immediately she was made erect again and *began* glorifying God. ¹⁴But the synagogue official, indignant because Jesus had healed on the Sabbath, *began* saying

NLT

¹About this time Jesus was informed that Pilate had murdered some people from Galilee as they were offering sacrifices at the Temple. ²"Do you think those Galileans were worse sinners than all the other people from Galilee?" Jesus asked. "Is that why they suffered? ³Not at all! And you will perish, too, unless you repent of your sins and turn to God. ⁴And what about the eighteen people who died when the tower in Siloam fell on them? Were they the worst sinners in Jerusalem? ⁵No, and I tell you again that unless you repent, you will perish, too."

⁶Then Jesus told this story: "A man planted a fig tree in his garden and came again and again to see if there was any fruit on it, but he was always disappointed. ⁷Finally, he said to his gardener, 'I've waited three years, and there hasn't been a single fig! Cut it down. It's just taking up space in the garden.'

⁸"The gardener answered, 'Sir, give it one more chance. Leave it another year, and I'll give it special attention and plenty of fertilizer. ⁹If we get figs next year, fine. If not, then you can cut it down.'"

¹⁰One Sabbath day as Jesus was teaching in a synagogue, ¹¹he saw a woman who had been crippled by an evil spirit. She had been bent double for eighteen years and was unable to stand up straight. ¹²When Jesus saw her, he called her over and said, "Dear woman, you are healed of your sickness!" ¹³Then he touched her, and instantly she could stand straight. How she praised God!

¹⁴But the leader in charge of the synagogue was indignant that Jesus had healed her on the Sabbath day.

NASB

to the crowd in response, "There are six days in which work should be done; so come during them and get healed, and not on the Sabbath day." [15] But the Lord answered him and said, "You hypocrites, does not each of you on the Sabbath untie his ox or his donkey from the stall and lead him away to water *him?* [16] And this woman, a daughter of Abraham as she is, whom Satan has bound for eighteen long years, should she not have been released from this bond on the Sabbath day?" [17] As He said this, all His opponents were being humiliated; and the entire crowd was rejoicing over all the glorious things being done by Him.

13:1 ªI.e. shed along with 13:3 ªOr *are repentant*
13:4 ªLit *debtors* 13:7 ªLit *and I do not find*

NLT

"There are six days of the week for working," he said to the crowd. "Come on those days to be healed, not on the Sabbath."

[15] But the Lord replied, "You hypocrites! Each of you works on the Sabbath day! Don't you untie your ox or your donkey from its stall on the Sabbath and lead it out for water? [16] This dear woman, a daughter of Abraham, has been held in bondage by Satan for eighteen years. Isn't it right that she be released, even on the Sabbath?"

[17] This shamed his enemies, but all the people rejoiced at the wonderful things he did.

Many skeptics and atheists point to what philosophers have termed "the problem of evil" as justification for their rejection of God. "Why would a good, all-powerful God allow evil to continue?" they ask. "Either He is not really good or He is not very powerful; otherwise, He would have eliminated suffering long ago." And to be perfectly honest, their argument finds a ready "Amen!" when bad things happen to good people—especially when those good people happen to be the ones we love. Furthermore, when we watch the wicked continue to prosper, it makes obedience to the kingdom of God a monumental exercise of faith.

As Jesus journeys to Jerusalem, the problem of evil becomes ever more evident in Luke's narrative. In fact, Luke 13 marks yet another subtle transition in the story. From this point on, the physician presents Jesus more as a storyteller than a miracle-worker. Miracles decrease while parables increase. Divine power still flows through the Lord's hands, but the frequency of overt miracles appears to taper off as the narrative takes Jesus ever closer to Jerusalem. This suggests that the darkness surrounding the so-called "holy city" and the absence of the people's faith resulted in a decrease in Jesus' willingness to perform signs and wonders in Jerusalem and the surrounding area (cf. 5:20; 7:9; 7:50; 8:48; 17:19; 18:42).

From a human perspective, it would seem that God had forsaken

Jerusalem, leaving the "holy city" in the unclean hands of unholy priests. Evil ruled from the temple with impunity, which caused some to wonder about the goodness or sovereignty of God. On one occasion, when a group of listeners lamented the murder of righteous men by their wicked Roman occupiers, Jesus took the opportunity to set the record straight. We have within our grasp the ultimate solution to the "problem of evil," and it begins with a change in perspective.

— 13:1 —

Luke indicates this discussion took place "on the same occasion" as the discourse of 12:54-59, in which Jesus warned the crowds about the coming final judgment. Using the image of a debtor walking to court with his lender, Jesus urged everyone to seek mercy. He said, in effect, "All of you are indebted to Me because of your sin; admit your inability to pay and ask Me for forgiveness. Seek mercy now because justice is coming soon!"

The promise of coming judgment often brings out the Pharisee in us. We immediately think of all those who have harmed us and feel comforted by the thought of their being called to account by God's withering rebuke. We rarely see ourselves in the role of abuser, defrauder, adulterer, slanderer, or liar. Along those lines, someone in the crowd—speaking for many others, no doubt—pointed to the atrocity of Pontius Pilate, who had murdered a group of righteous Galileans as they tried to sacrifice.

The phrase "whose blood Pilate had mixed with their sacrifices" refers to an incident that we have no historical record of; nevertheless, it is in keeping with the procurator's sadistic brutality. He had, on more than one occasion, slaughtered defenseless Jews who dared to protest his policies (see Josephus, *Wars of the Jews* 2.9.2-4 [169–177]; *Antiquities* 18.3.1-2 [55–62]; 18.4.1 [85–87]). Whether Galileans were literally slaughtered while sacrificing or killed for some reason in connection with the sacrifice doesn't much matter. The phrase highlights the irony of people being murdered while behaving righteously. The report of Pilate's atrocity paints the Galileans as innocent victims deserving justification and the Romans as the prospering wicked who deserve condemnation.

Again, the Jews expected a political, military Messiah who would establish a Jewish world empire and then hold Rome accountable for its sins. In reporting Pilate's evil deed, the people wanted to know how Jesus would handle this foreign-policy crisis.

— 13:2-3 —

At the root of the people's expectations lay a theological presupposition. First-century Jews—like most everyone living in the twenty-first century—believed that good things happen to good people and bad things happen as a result of sin. So, when bad things happened to good people, it left them confused. Had God fallen asleep at the helm? Or were the ostensibly "good people" actually bad?

As usual, Jesus brushed aside the foreign-policy question to address the deeper spiritual issue. He began by probing their perspective, asking, "Were those who suffered and died worse sinners than their neighbors who didn't die?" (my paraphrase). His answer not only presumed the impeccable character of God, but it went straight to the heart of the issue: self-righteousness. He said, in effect, "The Galilean victims were not worse sinners than you; it's better to say that you are just as bad as them, and you will suffer the same fate if you don't make things right with God."

— 13:4-5 —

Jesus raised another difficult issue involving the deaths of eighteen people in a tragic accident. "Siloam" probably refers to the reservoir situated beyond the southeast corner of Jerusalem, and the accident may have involved the collapse of a tower supporting an aqueduct that fed the city. Again, the specific incident became well known in Israel but has been lost to history. Regardless, everyone can appreciate the theological problems of such an incident.

In the first example, people died for doing something righteous while their murderer, Pilate, continued to prosper. In the second example, moral certainty becomes more confused. Jesus chose an event that occurred in Jerusalem to neutralize any regional prejudices. His question delineated the theological difficulty raised by the seemingly random tragedy. If God is utterly good and completely sovereign over all events in life, then the eighteen who perished must have been "culprits" who deserved their tragic, "accidental" deaths. The Greek word translated "culprits" is literally "debtors" (see the related word in 7:41; 11:4), a common figurative expression for "sinners."

Some may have accepted this theological reasoning, while perhaps others didn't. Jesus insisted that our reasoning must remain consistent. We can't say in one instance, "Those depraved sinners had it coming!" then, in another, ask, "Why do the good suffer while the wicked prosper?" Either God is sovereign over all, or He is not. Either God is just, or He is not. However we choose to explain the continuing presence of evil and suffering in the world, we must apply it consistently. Jesus' response to both hypothetical answers is identical: "I tell you, no, but unless you repent, you will all likewise perish."

If people's sin puts them in danger of misfortune or calamity, then we should not be amazed that a few people die as a result; rather, we should be surprised that the majority of humanity continues to live! If sin reaps adversity, then no one should prosper. If sin is the basis of calamity, then everyone deserves a gruesome end. Consequently, Jesus issued a warning with a double meaning:

> First: If you believe that sin is the basis of all calamities, then you should repent right away; your calamity might be next!

> Second: Sin does indeed lead to calamity—at the final judgment. Repent!

Jesus also might have intended a third meaning. The collective sin of Israel put the people in danger of national calamity. He saw the inevitable future that was coming if the religious and national leaders continued their folly of the past several decades. Jerusalem sat on a seething cauldron of intrigue, seditions, internal rivalries, external alliances, and a growing tension between the ruling and working classes. Compromising politicians and bloodthirsty zealots left Israel ripe for a false messiah to lead them to their deaths. In AD 70, the first Jewish-Roman War ended with the destruction of the temple; by AD 135, two more defeats left the Jewish nation without a home.

— 13:6-9 —

Jesus corrected the faulty theology of His listeners by telling a parable. This simple story explains why a good, all-powerful God allows evil to remain, for now.

Let's call the vineyard owner "Justice." In order to enjoy figs, Justice reserved space for a fig tree, setting aside valuable real estate that could have been used to grow more grapes. A fig tree, unlike most fruit trees, frequently bears fruit in its first season, with full production expected by the third year of cultivation. So it's understandable that Justice would consider cutting down the plant after three years of nonproduction. It was the logical thing to do.

Justice said to Mercy, the vineyard keeper, "Cut down the tree" (see 3:9). Mercy replied to Justice, "Let me give it a little extra nurturing this year; if it doesn't respond, then cut it down."

Jesus wanted His listeners to accept three changes in perspective. First, the world is full of suffering, not because God created (i.e., planted) it that way, but because humanity corrupted the world with sin (Gen. 3:1-19; Rom. 5:12; 1 Cor. 15:21). We should stop blaming God as though He is responsible for the problem of evil. Second, we perpetuate the problem of evil through continual sin. The vast majority of the world's suffering—disasters and diseases notwithstanding—could be reduced to virtually nothing if all people everywhere stopped sinning and followed the Lord's kingdom guidelines (e.g., Luke 6:27-38). Third, evil is not "out there"; it lives in the heart of every person. If God were to eradicate all evil, all of us would disappear from the face of the earth to face the just penalty of our sin.

Mercy has delayed justice to give all people an opportunity to repent. But, as they say in the world of commerce, it's "free for a limited time."

By God's grace, evil people (i.e., you and I) remain alive. By God's grace, we have the mental capacity to come to terms with what we're hearing. By God's grace, we can turn from sin and turn toward Christ. By God's grace, we are given time for the fruit of repentance to emerge. But there will come a day when He will say, "Cut it down," and time will be no more. Eternity will dawn, and the unrepentant soul must stand without Christ before God to give an answer for sin.

— 13:10-13 —

Luke quickly shifts the setting to another time and location, but he maintains a close connection between the Lord's parable and His next encounter with suffering. While teaching in one of the synagogues on the Sabbath—for the final time in Luke's narrative—Jesus saw a woman suffering the physical effects of evil. An evil spirit caused a physical condition that compromised her dignity as a human and, in some ways, symbolized the spiritual condition of Israel. She was bent double as though straining to carry the burden of sin. Luke emphasizes the pathos of her condition by telling us she had suffered this affliction for eighteen years.

Unlike many of His other recorded miracles, Jesus initiated the encounter. As presented by Luke, the sight of her pathetic condition may have interrupted His lesson: "He was teaching. . . . And there was a woman. . . ." He noticed her, called her over, and performed a physical and spiritual miracle, freeing her from both the demon and the physical consequences of its presence.

His liberating declaration is significant. It's expressed in the perfect passive form of *apolyō* [630], which can be understood to mean "You have been loosed." She was not simply set on a path to eventual freedom, given the means for self-liberation, or merely called free. At the utterance of His voice, the Lord loosed her. Period. She immediately stood up straight and gave glory to God. The visual lesson began with a person who had been reduced to an animal-like posture by an evil spirit and ended with her restoration to former dignity as an upright bearer of God's image.

— 13:14 —

The protest by the head of the synagogue is surprising on a human level, yet we have come to expect it in Luke's narrative (see 6:6-11). Why wouldn't somebody in ministry rejoice to see a minion of evil defeated and a member of the community be released from a long-term physical burden? Why would this man not greatly rejoice to see God glorified in his synagogue? Instead, his "indignant" response reflects anger at a perceived wrong (cf. Matt. 20:24; 26:8; Mark 10:14).

The contrast between the woman's response and that of her spiritual leader could not have been more dramatic. She danced for joy; he vainly tried to recapture his audience, which had understandably been swept up in the woman's euphoria. (Note that he addressed *the audience* in response to what had occurred.) He reached into the desiccated crypt of his memory, found the appropriate proof text, and gave it a convenient twist, saying in effect, "Six days you shall labor and do all your work (Exod. 20:9; 34:21; 35:2-3; Lev. 23:3; Deut. 5:13); it is most important that we keep the Law!"

The leader called Jesus' deed of kindness "work," overlooking the fact that Jesus merely spoke and the woman's healing came from God. If the One who was the Lord of the Sabbath had disapproved of such "work," He would not have healed her.

— 13:15-16 —

While the leader of the synagogue railed against the crowd for allowing a situation of healing to arise, Jesus leveled His response against the leader and his cronies, calling all of them hypocrites (the "you" is plural). He noted that the traditions of the Pharisees permitted them to lead their livestock to a water source on the Sabbath (see Mishnah, *Shabbat* 5)—extending the most basic kindness even to animals—yet prevented them from the kind of work that would bring relief to a woman afflicted by a demon. To drive the point deeper, Jesus referred to her as "a daughter of Abraham," elevating her status in the eyes of her kindred Jews.

— 13:17 —

Luke's summary of the episode sets the stage for the rest of the narrative. Jesus' opponents—referring to the religious leaders—"were being humiliated" while their congregation "was rejoicing." Jesus had exposed their love for rules and their contempt for suffering people. Throughout the rest of the narrative, those who opposed Jesus would continue to experience humiliation and contempt while those who were drawn to Jesus would continue to experience joy.

• • •

What a difference Jesus makes! He is the solution to "the problem of evil." While God could have solved the sin problem by cutting down the fig tree, as it were, He grants us mercy by delaying judgment. Moreover, God made "the problem of evil" His own personal problem by sending His Son to suffer as we suffer, to die the death we deserve, and to conquer what had defeated us: sin and death.

How great is our God! He is all-powerful, and He will eradicate evil in due time. Until then, we must endure with patience and join the Lord in His plea, "Unless you repent, you will all likewise perish" (Luke 13:3, 5).

APPLICATION: LUKE 13:1-17

What's the Difference?

Jesus, in His teachings, corrects and broadens our perspective. Jesus, in His timing, waits patiently in grace for us to amount to something. Jesus, with His touch, frees us from that which held us in its clutches for so many years.

I have three questions for you to consider.

First: *What teaching has broadened and corrected your perspective?* The sovereignty of God? Oh, I hope that's one! The faithfulness and forgiveness of God? I hope that's another one. The grace and mercy of God? How about the holiness of God? Has the teaching corrected your perspective so you can see that surprising, unexpected events may, in fact, be the plan of God?

Second: *What timing has played a major part in your growth?* God has patiently and graciously preserved you with life during times of rebellion and resistance, times of impatience and harshness. Where has the timing played a major part in your growth? And how gracious of Him to give you, even this very moment, an opportunity to believe.

Third: *What touch from His hand has set you free?* In what way has He touched you and made you whole? This is all part of your testimony to the difference Jesus can make.

Maybe it's time to write your answers down for the benefit of another. Maybe it's time to share the story of your lostness and God's faithfulness in a setting where others can benefit from your experience. Ask the Lord for an opportunity like that and begin preparing now.

Straight Talk for Saints and Sinners
LUKE 13:18-35

NASB

18 So He was saying, "What is the kingdom of God like, and to what shall I compare it? 19 It is like a mustard seed, which a man took and threw into his own garden; and it grew and became a tree, and THE BIRDS OF THE ᵃAIR NESTED IN ITS BRANCHES."

20 And again He said, "To what shall I compare the kingdom of God? 21 It is like leaven, which a woman took and hid in three ᵃpecks of flour until it was all leavened."

22 And He was passing through from one city and village to another, teaching, and proceeding on His way to Jerusalem. 23 And someone said to Him, "Lord, are there *just* a few who are being saved?" And He said to them, 24 "Strive to enter through the narrow door; for many, I tell you, will seek to enter and will not be able. 25 Once the head of the house gets up and shuts the door, and you begin

NLT

18 Then Jesus said, "What is the Kingdom of God like? How can I illustrate it? 19 It is like a tiny mustard seed that a man planted in a garden; it grows and becomes a tree, and the birds make nests in its branches."

20 He also asked, "What else is the Kingdom of God like? 21 It is like the yeast a woman used in making bread. Even though she put only a little yeast in three measures of flour, it permeated every part of the dough."

22 Jesus went through the towns and villages, teaching as he went, always pressing on toward Jerusalem. 23 Someone asked him, "Lord, will only a few be saved?"

He replied, 24 "Work hard to enter the narrow door to God's Kingdom, for many will try to enter but will fail. 25 When the master of the house has locked the door, it will be too late. You will stand outside knocking

NASB

to stand outside and knock on the door, saying, 'Lord, open up to us!' then He will answer and say to you, 'I do not know where you are from.' 26 Then you will begin to say, 'We ate and drank in Your presence, and You taught in our streets'; 27 and He will say, 'I tell you, I do not know where you are from; DEPART FROM ME, ALL YOU EVILDOERS.' 28 In that place there will be weeping and gnashing of teeth when you see Abraham and Isaac and Jacob and all the prophets in the kingdom of God, but yourselves being thrown out. 29 And they will come from east and west and from north and south, and will recline *at the table* in the kingdom of God. 30 And behold, *some* are last who will be first and *some* are first who will be last."

31 Just at that time some Pharisees approached, saying to Him, "Go away, leave here, for Herod wants to kill You." 32 And He said to them, "Go and tell that fox, 'Behold, I cast out demons and perform cures today and tomorrow, and the third *day* I ªreach My goal.' 33 Nevertheless I must journey on today and tomorrow and the next *day;* for it cannot be that a prophet would perish outside of Jerusalem. 34 O Jerusalem, Jerusalem, *the city* that kills the prophets and stones those sent to her! How often I wanted to gather your children together, just as a hen *gathers* her brood under her wings, and you would not *have it!* 35 Behold, your house is left to you *desolate;* and I say to you, you will not see Me until *the time* comes when you say, 'BLESSED IS HE WHO COMES IN THE NAME OF THE LORD!'"

13:19 ªOr *sky*   13:21 ªGr *sata*   13:32 ªOr *am perfected*

NLT

and pleading, 'Lord, open the door for us!' But he will reply, 'I don't know you or where you come from.' 26 Then you will say, 'But we ate and drank with you, and you taught in our streets.' 27 And he will reply, 'I tell you, I don't know you or where you come from. Get away from me, all you who do evil.'

28 "There will be weeping and gnashing of teeth, for you will see Abraham, Isaac, Jacob, and all the prophets in the Kingdom of God, but you will be thrown out. 29 And people will come from all over the world—from east and west, north and south—to take their places in the Kingdom of God. 30 And note this: Some who seem least important now will be the greatest then, and some who are the greatest now will be least important then.*"

31 At that time some Pharisees said to him, "Get away from here if you want to live! Herod Antipas wants to kill you!"

32 Jesus replied, "Go tell that fox that I will keep on casting out demons and healing people today and tomorrow; and the third day I will accomplish my purpose. 33 Yes, today, tomorrow, and the next day I must proceed on my way. For it wouldn't do for a prophet of God to be killed except in Jerusalem!

34 "O Jerusalem, Jerusalem, the city that kills the prophets and stones God's messengers! How often I have wanted to gather your children together as a hen protects her chicks beneath her wings, but you wouldn't let me. 35 And now, look, your house is abandoned. And you will never see me again until you say, 'Blessings on the one who comes in the name of the LORD!'*"

13:30 Greek *Some are last who will be first, and some are first who will be last.*   13:35 Ps 118:26.

The religious environment in Israel was not openly pugnacious. On the contrary, the Sadducees, Pharisees, scribes, and priests projected a respectable and pious demeanor. These smooth-talking religious experts not only waxed eloquent on "the Law, the Prophets, and the Writings," but they also cleverly wrapped their individual, self-serving agendas in Bible passages and theological reasoning. And because they wielded the considerable power of excommunication, no one dared step into their intellectual arena to challenge their hypocrisy.

Then Jesus arrived.

The true Messiah didn't fit the mold cast by the religious elite in first-century Israel. Jesus accepted people as they were, and He addressed their real needs. He dined with the lowly, sought after the outcast, embraced religious untouchables, and stood with Israel's commoners against their mannerly taskmasters. He also gave His followers the dignity of plain talk. He drew thousands of followers with straightforward answers to their honest questions about life and death, the kingdom of God and the dominion of evil, heaven and, yes, even hell. In addition to all that, He remained unimpressed with the religious leaders and unintimidated by their power.

Even as the Lord's "opponents were being humiliated" (13:17) by His public victories, Jesus kept a level head concerning His mission. While His supporters felt affirmed and empowered for the first time in their lives, their Master knew the difficulties that awaited them. He had already thinned the ranks when his emphasis shifted from performing signs and wonders to speaking in parables. Plain talk about the kingdom (13:18-21), salvation (13:22-30), and the difficulties of His mission (13:31-35) would reduce their numbers even more. Even so, they deserved nothing less than the truth—plain and simple.

— 13:18-19 —

In his account of Jesus' continued march toward Jerusalem, Luke emphasizes Jesus' teaching on the kingdom of God, beginning with two analogies drawn from everyday life in Israel. The first illustrates the humble beginnings of something great (13:18-19); the second, its inevitable transformation of the world (13:20-21).

In the first analogy, Jesus conjures the image of a seed, perhaps the most fitting symbol of potential.

The kingdom of God is both spiritual and earthly—spiritual in that people may become citizens by trusting in Jesus as their Messiah, and earthly in that Jesus will one day sit upon a literal throne and establish a literal administration over the world (Ps. 2; Isa. 2; 9:6-7; 11:1-5; Jer. 33:14-26; Dan. 7; Mic. 5:2-15). At that time, the kingdom of God will have fully come indeed. Evil will have been vanquished; the earth will enjoy peace, justice, tranquility, and fulfillment. With the removal of the curse, there will be complete communion between creation and Creator (Rev. 19:11–20:6).

Not unlike a seed falling to the ground, the literal kingdom of God came to earth in the person of its King, Jesus Christ. Like a seed, however, there is a delay between its planting and its fulfillment. A seed goes into the ground, and from the perspective above the soil, nothing happens. Eventually, however, something insignificant in size becomes something magnificent. In secret, potential yields to actuality.

The ultimate fulfillment of the earthly, literal reign of King Jesus was *initiated* by His first advent—what some theologians have termed "the Christ Event." They use this term to designate the totality of His earthly ministry: His birth, life, teaching, death, resurrection, commissioning of the disciples, and sending of the Holy Spirit. The spiritual aspect of His kingdom on earth began at that time, opening the way for people to become citizens now. Still, the physical kingdom is yet to be fulfilled and consummated.

The Lord used the illustration of a mustard seed because first-century teachers and writers commonly used it to emphasize the smallness of something. The black mustard seed is so small, one can easily mistake it for a speck of dirt. Nevertheless, it produces a plant that can grow as tall as 15 feet (4.6 meters) under ideal conditions. To highlight the contrast from small beginnings to grand fulfillment, Jesus used an illustration of kingdom greatness found in Old Testament passages in which a tree gives refuge to birds (Judg. 9:15; Ps. 104:12-13; Ezek. 17:22-24; 31:3-14).

Within forty years of Jesus' resurrection—a single lifetime—the gospel had reached all of the great metropolitan centers of the Roman empire and had even reached innumerable villages and hamlets along the trade routes between these large cities. And it can be argued that, by the end of the second century, the entire known world had been exposed to the gospel.

— 13:20-21 —

Jesus also compared the kingdom to a portion of leaven—more commonly known as yeast—which a baker kneads into a batch of dough. "Three pecks [*saton* (4568), 13:21] of flour" is roughly 10.3 gallons (39 liters) of dry flour, which would weigh about 45 pounds (20.6 kilograms). That's a significant baking operation!

The Lord's emphasis is not the *gradual* conversion of the dough but its *inevitable* transformation. The kingdom changes believers from the inside out with the promise of inevitable and complete transformation. Likewise, the world will be fundamentally changed. It is only a matter of time.

Jesus introduced both of these images to answer a critical question and to prepare true disciples for the future. The critical question "Why does God allow evil to continue?" was answered earlier with the parable of the fruitless tress. He has delayed final judgment to allow everyone an opportunity to repent and to receive forgiveness. To prepare His followers for the difficult, even disillusioning, events to come, Jesus warned that the kingdom is like a seed, which appears dormant for a time; and it's like leaven, which works imperceptibly. Yet both inevitably prevail.

Luke uses these two images to introduce two incidents, each foreshadowing future difficulties.

— 13:22-24 —

The first potential difficulty comes in the form of an honest question.

Luke shifts the setting to observe Jesus and His followers in the course of ministry (as well as on the way to Jerusalem). One person noted that many heard the gospel, yet relatively few responded. This prompted a reasonable question: "Just how successful is this kingdom enterprise that we have committed to advance?"

The Lord's reply reframed the issue. In response to the question "What about *them*?" Jesus said, "*You* strive to enter the narrow door." "Strive" is a plural verb in this instance, so He addressed this to all of His followers. And it's an imperative, expressing a command. The term rendered "strive" is *agōnizomai* [75], which Greek writers frequently used to describe the efforts of an athlete in competition, straining for the goal, or of a warrior compelling every cell of his body to obtain the victory. Such discipline and effort is "agonizing."

The image of the narrow door most likely refers to a small entryway set within the larger door of a house. We shouldn't place too much emphasis on the narrowness of the door. It simply refers to the approved entrance to the home. To protect the property from intruders, a reasonably well-off family home featured a walled courtyard with a large, solid door, which was opened only to allow animals or carts to enter and leave. Family members and guests routinely entered and exited through the smaller, inset door.

Jesus never offered people the message, "Look, just be sincere. Simply adhere to the religion of your choice and think positively about God. Look deep within yourself to find the good and accentuate the positive; that's good enough for God, and He'll let you into heaven when you die." On the contrary, to enter heaven, one must approach the approved entrance, which usually remained open during daylight hours and was closed at night.

— 13:25-27 —

Jesus continued His analogy and emphasized the limited time in which people may enter the household door. Like the city gates, when the door closed for the night, it remained closed until daylight. People returning to the city after dark had to find lodging outside the city walls, regardless of their identity or social status. And the same was true of a household. To open the door at night placed the entire household at risk for invasion by robbers; therefore, once the door was closed, it remained closed. The homeowner's reply, "Depart from Me, all you evildoers," alludes to Psalm 6:8-10, in which David finds both safety from his enemies and vindication for their abuse.

The Lord applied the illustration to those who want to enter the kingdom. The door remains open, but God will slam it shut one day, after which no one may enter. An individual's death closes the door; for that person, the opportunity to enter has passed. On a cosmic scale, God will close the door on salvation at the end of days. The new creation (Rev. 21–22) will be the eternal home of those who entered before it became too late.

— 13:28-30 —

When describing God, people generally err on the side of either mercy or justice. They either emphasize God's loving-kindness to the exclusion of His anger toward sin, or they depict Him as only vengeful to the exclusion of mercy. In truth, His anger is filled with grace, and His mercy has limits. He has provided a means of salvation that is open to all and completely free, yet the consequences of sin remain a real danger to those who do not receive His gift.

"That place" is nothing less than eternal torment in a place separated from God's mercy. The "kingdom of God," on the other hand, is a place of eternal feasting with a vast array of people of every race from all parts of the globe, from all walks of life, and from every era of history since the beginning of time.

— 13:31-33 —

The transitional phrase "Just at that time" closely connects the theological significance of these two events. While Luke reported the events as they occurred—that is, in close chronological sequence—he also wanted to stress their logical connection.

While many Pharisees opposed Jesus and hoped to see Him discredited or even killed, some followed Him in secret (Luke 23:50-51; John 19:38-39). The men who came to warn Jesus could have been either secret followers or enemies hoping to frighten Jesus away. The latter is more probable as Jesus gave the men a message to carry back to the king of Galilee. Regardless, the Pharisees brought accurate information: Herod Antipas wanted Jesus dead.

From a political and military point of view, this was disheartening news, dispelling any hope of cooperation with anyone among the Jewish ruling class. For Jesus to become king of Israel, He would have to depend upon the support of the commoners, which He had in great numbers . . . for now. But Jesus didn't plan to leverage His assets in a bid for the throne of David. Instead, He predicted spiritual victory through political failure. His path to the throne lay through the valley of death. Therefore, Herod's threat merely confirmed the Lord's ultimate victory.

Jesus sent a message back to Herod, calling him "that fox," the precise meaning of which is uncertain. Foxes then, like now, were small, predatory animals that used stealth to subdue their prey. In rural America, they sneak into barns and chicken coops at night to pilfer the small farm animals. Consequently, they're seen as cowardly pests that prey upon the defenseless.

Jesus sent a message that put all evil forces on notice. He said, in effect, "You cannot stop, alter, interrupt, or ignore the objective God has sent Me to achieve. I will continue to battle evil during the time I have left, and I will keep My appointment with the cross in Jerusalem." And in so doing, He intended to culminate Jerusalem's lengthy history of killing God's messengers. At the end of a long line of martyred prophets stood the invincible Word of God incarnate.

— 13:34-35 —

If the walls of Jerusalem could speak, they could repeat countless sermons from one godly prophet after another whose blood had been spilled for the sake of God's word. And each unjust death brought further condemnation against the city. Consequently, Jesus lamented the squandered opportunities afforded the city. Throughout history, its kings rebuffed the Lord's promise of provision and protection. Its priests exchanged hope for the true Messiah with a line of illegitimate rulers, and they set aside God's grace for a list of man-made traditions. Moreover, the city—particularly its political and religious leaders—was in need of changing its ways; otherwise, it faced future desolation.

Jesus punctuated His lament with a quotation from Psalm 118, part of which reads:

> The stone which the builders rejected
> Has become the chief corner stone.
> This is the LORD's doing;
> It is marvelous in our eyes.
> This is the day which the LORD has made;
> Let us rejoice and be glad in it.
> O LORD, do save, we beseech You;
> O LORD, we beseech You, do send prosperity!
> Blessed is the one who comes in the name of the LORD;
> We have blessed you from the house of the LORD.
>   (Ps. 118:22-26)

Because Jesus used illustrations foreign to our modern, Western, twenty-first-century experiences, we may not find His "plain talk" as plain as we would like. But His listeners clearly understood His teaching. He didn't paint a rose-colored picture of the future. The path to the kingdom would traverse dark valleys and take dangerous turns. Victory would not come instantaneously or easily but through an arduous process requiring diligence and patience (Luke 13:18-21). The kingdom will be populated with a remnant of refugees from the dominion of evil, never a majority (13:22-30). And the Messiah's personal journey to kingdom glory would require His death (13:31-33), a God-ordained martyrdom to bring a final, fatal indictment against the powers of darkness ruling the world and pervading God's own temple (13:34-35).

Plain talk. Straight talk. Tough talk. But the words of life always are.

APPLICATION: LUKE 13:18-35

Straight Talk for Tough Times

I don't speak Christianese. I do have the ability to understand the special languages of denominational meetings, pastors' conferences, and Christian tradeshows; and I am familiar with several dialects. I simply choose not to speak Christianese. I much prefer plain talk. And it seems Jesus did too. He engaged in at least three conversations in this passage, and I discern at least three principles at work in His communication, which I'll express as suggestions.

First, *speak plainly* (13:18-21). Jesus loved the sophisticated art of the parable for its unique ability to explain heavenly mysteries in down-to-earth terms. He chose images from everyday life, experiences every one of His listeners could recall seeing or doing recently. He revealed divine truth in such plain, ordinary terms that it sounded like common sense.

When communicating the truths of Scripture, speak the language of your audience. I don't mean Spanish, French, Russian, or Texan; that much is obvious. I mean the language they use at home and work. Engineers and dentists don't use the same terms. One is not smarter than the other; they simply communicate differently. Know the vocabulary and speaking style of your audience and then adapt. And be careful with Greek and Hebrew terms. If they help make the point, use them; but don't show off.

Second, *speak candidly* (13:22-30). When someone asked Jesus a frank question, He gave a candid answer. The questioner essentially asked, "If you have such a great thing going, then why don't you have more customers?" This was a very forthright question that acknowledged the obvious: The percentage of converts was low. Jesus responded plainly with some harsh realities: The truth is not popular (13:24), the offer expires (13:25-27), and while the consequences of rejection are terrifying (13:28), the rewards are eternal (13:29).

When skeptics challenge or seekers probe, resist the urge to make Christian theology pretty. Yes, there is a hell; and yes, God will send you there if you don't repent. God is love, but His wrath is fearsome; don't cross Him. God is patient and merciful, but both qualities have limits. These are truths many don't like to hear, but they are true nonetheless.

Third, *speak boldly* (13:31-35). When the Pharisees arrived with news that Antipas wanted Him dead, Jesus recognized it as a threat and answered it without flinching. He laid out His plan for the next several days and beyond, saying, in effect, "I will be doing what I have been doing; I will go to Jerusalem as planned and complete My mission; and I don't care what you think about it."

Critics and enemies will try to intimidate. They may, in fact, have the power to harm you. If your plan is biblically sound, supported by the wisdom of trusted advisors, honors God, and advances His agenda, threats cannot dissuade you. Even upon pain of death, you have no choice but to pursue the path before you, and you should say so.

Spiritual Table Manners
LUKE 14:1-24

NASB

¹ It happened that when He went into the house of one of the ᵃleaders of the Pharisees on *the* Sabbath to eat bread, they were watching Him closely. ² And ᵃthere in front of Him was a man suffering from dropsy. ³ And Jesus answered and spoke to the ᵃlawyers and Pharisees, saying, "Is it lawful to heal on the Sabbath, or not?" ⁴ But they kept silent. And He took hold of him and healed him, and sent him away. ⁵ And He said to them, "ᵃWhich one of you will have a son or an ox fall into a well, and will not immediately pull him out on a Sabbath day?" ⁶ And they could make no reply to this.

⁷ And He *began* speaking a parable to the invited guests when He noticed how they had been picking out the places of honor *at the table*, saying to them, ⁸ "When you are invited by someone to a wedding feast, do not ᵃtake the place of honor, for someone more distinguished than you may have been invited by him, ⁹ and he who invited you both will come and say to you, 'Give *your* place to this man,' and then in disgrace you ᵃproceed to occupy the last

NLT

¹ One Sabbath day Jesus went to eat dinner in the home of a leader of the Pharisees, and the people were watching him closely. ² There was a man there whose arms and legs were swollen.* ³ Jesus asked the Pharisees and experts in religious law, "Is it permitted in the law to heal people on the Sabbath day, or not?" ⁴ When they refused to answer, Jesus touched the sick man and healed him and sent him away. ⁵ Then he turned to them and said, "Which of you doesn't work on the Sabbath? If your son* or your cow falls into a pit, don't you rush to get him out?" ⁶ Again they could not answer.

⁷ When Jesus noticed that all who had come to the dinner were trying to sit in the seats of honor near the head of the table, he gave them this advice: ⁸ "When you are invited to a wedding feast, don't sit in the seat of honor. What if someone who is more distinguished than you has also been invited? ⁹ The host will come and say, 'Give this person your seat.' Then you will be embarrassed, and you will have to take whatever seat is left at the foot of the table!

place. ¹⁰But when you are invited, go and recline at the last place, so that when the one who has invited you comes, he may say to you, 'Friend, move up higher'; then you will have honor in the sight of all who ᵃare at the table with you. ¹¹For everyone who exalts himself will be humbled, and he who humbles himself will be exalted."

¹²And He also went on to say to the one who had invited Him, "When you give a luncheon or a dinner, do not invite your friends or your brothers or your relatives or rich neighbors, otherwise they may also invite you in return and *that* will be your repayment. ¹³But when you give a ᵃreception, invite *the* poor, *the* crippled, *the* lame, *the* blind, ¹⁴and you will be blessed, since they ᵃdo not have *the means* to repay you; for you will be repaid at the resurrection of the righteous."

¹⁵When one of those who were reclining *at the table* with Him heard this, he said to Him, "Blessed is everyone who will eat bread in the kingdom of God!"

¹⁶But He said to him, "A man was giving a big dinner, and he invited many; ¹⁷and at the dinner hour he sent his slave to say to those who had been invited, 'Come; for everything is ready now.' ¹⁸But they all alike began to make excuses. The first one said to him, 'I have bought a ᵃpiece of land and I need to go out and look at it; ᵇplease consider me excused.' ¹⁹Another one said, 'I have bought five yoke of oxen, and I am going to try them out; ᵃplease consider me excused.' ²⁰Another one said, 'I have married a wife, and for that reason I cannot come.' ²¹And the slave came *back* and reported this to his master. Then the head of the household became angry and said to his slave, 'Go out at once into the streets and lanes of the city and bring in here the poor

¹⁰"Instead, take the lowest place at the foot of the table. Then when your host sees you, he will come and say, 'Friend, we have a better place for you!' Then you will be honored in front of all the other guests. ¹¹For those who exalt themselves will be humbled, and those who humble themselves will be exalted."

¹²Then he turned to his host. "When you put on a luncheon or a banquet," he said, "don't invite your friends, brothers, relatives, and rich neighbors. For they will invite you back, and that will be your only reward. ¹³Instead, invite the poor, the crippled, the lame, and the blind. ¹⁴Then at the resurrection of the righteous, God will reward you for inviting those who could not repay you."

¹⁵Hearing this, a man sitting at the table with Jesus exclaimed, "What a blessing it will be to attend a banquet* in the Kingdom of God!"

¹⁶Jesus replied with this story: "A man prepared a great feast and sent out many invitations. ¹⁷When the banquet was ready, he sent his servant to tell the guests, 'Come, the banquet is ready.' ¹⁸But they all began making excuses. One said, 'I have just bought a field and must inspect it. Please excuse me.' ¹⁹Another said, 'I have just bought five pairs of oxen, and I want to try them out. Please excuse me.' ²⁰Another said, 'I just got married, so I can't come.'

²¹"The servant returned and told his master what they had said. His master was furious and said, 'Go quickly into the streets and alleys of the town and invite the poor, the

NASB

and crippled and blind and lame.' ²²And the slave said, 'Master, what you commanded has been done, and still there is room.' ²³And the master said to the slave, 'Go out into the highways and along the hedges, and compel *them* to come in, so that my house may be filled. ²⁴For I tell you, none of those men who were invited shall taste of my dinner.'"

14:1 ªI.e. members of the Sanhedrin   14:2 ªLit *behold*   14:3 ªI.e. experts in Mosaic Law   14:5 ªLit *Whose son of you...will fall*   14:8 ªLit *recline at*   14:9 ªLit *begin*   14:10 ªLit *recline* at the table   14:13 ªOr *banquet*   14:14 ªOr *are unable to*   14:18 ªOr *field* ᵇLit *I request you*   14:19 ªLit *I request you*

NLT

crippled, the blind, and the lame.' ²²After the servant had done this, he reported, 'There is still room for more.' ²³So his master said, 'Go out into the country lanes and behind the hedges and urge anyone you find to come, so that the house will be full. ²⁴For none of those I first invited will get even the smallest taste of my banquet.'"

14:2 Or *who had dropsy.*   14:5 Some manuscripts read *donkey.*   14:15 Greek *to eat bread.*

Certain settings lend themselves to breaking down interpersonal barriers and creating opportunities to teach—and none serves better than the dinner table. Something about sharing a meal allows people to lower their defenses, perhaps because it reminds us that, despite our social or economic differences, we all share the same biological needs and suffer the same weaknesses. We also use mealtimes to push aside the cares of the world to nurture our bodies, and when people share this personal experience, the result can only be a more intimate closeness.

Throughout His ministry, Jesus clashed with the religious authorities in both Galilee and Judea, and eventually, the clerics' animosity became a barrier to constructive change. At the end of the day, Jesus didn't come to earth to win arguments; He came to redeem people from their sin. And that included the Pharisees, whose tenacious hold on legal tradition kept them from grasping the spirit of God's Law, which is grace. When you brush aside the jots and tittles of man-made traditions, cut through the fleshy sinews of rules and regulations, and penetrate the center of Old Testament Law, you find the heart of God—and you discover it beats for people.

The Pharisees had forgotten this and had wandered far afield of God's original purpose in giving the Law. Jesus broke bread with these wayward legalists to bring them home again. But in that casual setting, would they heed the Lord's call?

— 14:1-2 —

Luke sets the scene as innocent enough. Jesus had accepted the invitation of a leading Pharisee after Sabbath services in the local synagogue.

In what town, we do not know, but the incident could have played out in a number of places in Israel. It should have been a pleasant afternoon of dining, fellowship, and relaxation in God's gift of the Sabbath if not for a sinister undercurrent created by the religious leaders. Luke adds, "They were watching Him closely."

The Greek word for "watching closely" is *paratēreō* [3906]. It sometimes means "to observe," as in the observation of a holiday or the rules of etiquette, or "to be on the lookout," as with a guard in a watchtower. But often it carries the idea of malicious intent, as in "to lie in wait" or "to watch insidiously." The circumstances don't favor any particular interpretation of this term until Luke calls attention to the presence of one individual: "a man suffering from dropsy."

Today we call the condition "edema," an abnormal accumulation of fluid that causes swelling in tissues, joints, and body cavities. The condition frequently causes the feet, ankles, and legs to appear puffy and larger than normal, which can seriously affect major organs. It's a painful and potentially deadly disease. The Pharisees would have responded very negatively to the physical deformity caused by the malady and probably would have objected to the man's presence in the temple.

The scribes and Pharisees knew where Jesus stood on the issue of healing on the Sabbath. Not long before this, He had healed a suffering woman, and when a minor religious official chastised Him, Jesus rebuked the man for his misplaced priorities (13:12-16). This prompted the people to rejoice while their leaders were humiliated (13:17). Now, to raise the stakes, the "leaders of the Pharisees" orchestrated another opportunity for Jesus to violate their rules. These "leaders" were none other than members of the Sanhedrin, the Jewish high council—the functional equivalent of a supreme court and parliament combined.

While the invitation to dine appeared pleasant, the religious authorities used it as an opportunity to say, in effect, "Okay, big shot, *now* let's see how boldly You trample our traditions!"

— 14:3-4 —

Jesus answered the unspoken challenge of the Sanhedrin. But before taking action, Jesus asked the assembled experts in the Law of God to weigh in: "Is it lawful to heal on the Sabbath, or not?"

It was a loaded question, similar to the one posed in 6:9. It was a brilliant move. They had tried to put Jesus in a public no-win scenario, but He turned the tables. He publicly asked them to choose between their traditions and common kindness. (I call it "common kindness" because even pagan Gentile idolaters would have chosen to relieve the man's suffering if they had the power.) If they said, "No, it is not permitted to show compassion on the Sabbath," they would have to admit that their traditions were more precious than people. If they said, "Yes, it is permitted," then they would have authorized Jesus to violate their rules! Caught in Jesus' ethical checkmate, the religious leaders remained silent.

Jesus "took hold of him." We might picture Jesus pulling the man to Himself with both arms in a compassionate embrace. After healing him, Jesus released the man. The term translated "sent him away" is the antonym of "took hold of him," and it means, literally, "released." It has a wide range of meaning, including "send away" (8:38), "pardon" (6:37), and even "divorce" (16:18), but it can hardly be coincidence that Luke used the same term as in 13:12: "Woman, you are *freed* from your sickness." The physician linguistically linked the two healings to make a point: Jesus didn't shy away from healing on the Sabbath just because the nation's most powerful men happened to be watching.

— 14:5-6 —

Jesus not only healed on the Sabbath, just as He did before (13:10-17), but He also repeated the lesson for the religious experts. Earlier, He pointed out that since the Pharisees' customs allowed them to water their livestock on the Sabbath (13:15), releasing "a daughter of Abraham" from a demon should be even more permissible. After freeing the man from his edema, Jesus appealed to the same logic. The grammatical form of the question anticipates a positive answer: "Yes, of course we would save a son or an ox on a Sabbath."

The Lord's rhetorical question not only exposed the men's inconsistent application of the Law; it showed their reasoning to be self-serving. The man with edema was *somebody's* son who needed saving on a Sabbath day. But because he wasn't the son of a leader, the rule didn't apply. To the callous rulers of petty legalism, the man became nothing more than a pawn in their pathetic scheme to trap a political adversary.

— 14:7 —

After healing the man, and perhaps after the tension of the moment dissipated, Jesus turned the tables again. Whereas the Pharisees had been watching Jesus, Jesus began watching the Pharisees. He observed their "picking out the places of honor." Almost every culture has a seating etiquette, and Jewish society was no exception. Generally speaking, the most honored guest reclined to the left of the host while the next honored guest reclined on his right. Beyond that, it's not clear how Jewish custom viewed the other seats.

Given the rigid rule-keeping of the Pharisees, we can assume they sat according to rank. If so, Jesus observed the men sizing up their peers to determine instinctively who ranked where in the religious pecking order. The jostling pride that filled the room must have been almost comical.

When the room had settled—some guests preening over their coveted spots and others nursing their wounded pride—Jesus used the opportunity to teach them.

— 14:8-11 —

Luke calls this discourse of Jesus a parable, although it doesn't take the form of a story like many others. Instead, Jesus exposited a Hebrew proverb:

> Do not claim honor in the presence of the king,
> And do not stand in the place of great men;
> For it is better that it be said to you, "Come up here,"
> Than for you to be placed lower in the presence of the prince,
> Whom your eyes have seen. (Prov. 25:6-7)

While this bit of practical wisdom from Solomon has useful, earthly relevance, Jesus used the proverb and its application to warn about the eternal consequences of pride. The Pharisees compared their own relative worth to that of their peers, not only to determine seating arrangements at a banquet, but also to judge worthiness in God's eyes. God, however, doesn't judge worth based on deeds, and He doesn't assign rank according to the same standards by which we judge greatness. In heaven, humility receives praise; sacrifice receives glory; motive trumps action. Pride, on the other hand, results in public disgrace.

The Lord's summary statement highlights the stark contrast between the kingdom of God and the dominion of evil. In the kingdom of God, bowing low puts the humble on the fast track to the top. And Jesus Himself would become the consummate model of humility, subjecting Himself to the humiliation of the cross for the sake of humanity. He is our King because He lowered himself to become our Servant (Phil. 2:5-11).

— 14:12-14 —

Jesus redirected His discourse to focus on the host. Speaking minister to minister, Jesus challenged the man to use his official station and its attendant privileges for something other than political gain. Just like today, first-century politicians and socialites sought to elevate their standing in the community by hosting social events, strategically inviting the "right people" while snubbing the "wrong people" with equal discretion. By hosting parties and reciprocating invitations, a man could build social alliances and advance his standing.

Minister to minister, the Lord suggested the member of the Sanhedrin take a different approach to ministry. Rather than use his assets to further his career, he should use them to benefit those who cannot help themselves. Of course, this was tantamount to committing social suicide for the sake of kingdom reward. Pharisees affirmed the doctrine of resurrection, however, and believed God reserved eternal reward for those who obeyed the Law and did good deeds. Jesus' request merely called upon the man to live consistently with his beliefs.

With the ball squarely in the host's court, an uncomfortable, awkward silence undoubtedly lingered in the air.

— 14:15-20 —

Someone at the table tried to relieve the tension with what he thought was a slogan everyone could affirm. Indeed, his theology was spot-on, but the timing left a little to be desired. I would paraphrase his comment: "Hey, how about that kingdom? Won't that be great?"

Jesus responded with a parable in which a man hosted a meal, not unlike the one everyone was enjoying. To elevate his status, the man had invited all the right guests; unfortunately, all of them begged off, one by one. Each had a perfectly legitimate excuse for not attending. A big real estate transaction requires close attention. "Five yoke of oxen" was a sizeable investment for a large farming operation; the owner wanted to take them on a test run. And who can blame a newlywed for wanting to stay at home?

While each turned down the invitation to dine because of pressing issues, they committed a serious breach of etiquette. Because they had committed to the initial invitation, the host made preparations based on their RSVP. While each excuse cited pressing circumstances, none could be considered unavoidable and to renege at the last minute left the host with wasted food. In the end, each guest made a priority judgment that left the host in a difficult position.

— 14:21-24 —

The jilted host had every right to feel indignant, and no one in the room could fault the man for rescinding his invitation. With food cooked and going to waste, his next decision seems only reasonable. He opened his home to the least desirable and least deserving people in the community, the very same categories of people Jesus suggested His pharisaic host invite: the poor, the crippled, the lame, and the blind (Luke 14:13). Furthermore, when the fictional host noticed he had provisions for more guests, he expanded the search to include outlying, remote areas.

Jesus cleverly crafted His parable to allow His host and the gathered religious leaders to feel empathy for the fictional host. The man in the Lord's parable behaved righteously and reasonably, just as every man in the room undoubtedly would have. When his intended guests reneged, he used the food to benefit the indigent and helpless.

The Lord told this parable to place the religious leaders of Israel on notice. They rested in a calm assurance that their heritage—their Hebrew DNA—would grant them automatic citizenship in the coming kingdom of God. They also believed that the pursuit of their own moral agendas would grant them seats of honor at His banquet table. How wrong they were! The host in Jesus' parable is God. He has indeed prepared the kingdom for His covenant people—the descendants of Abraham, Isaac, and Jacob (see 13:28)—and the inhabitants of that coming kingdom will indeed recline at the table of a great feast (13:29). But one gains entrance to the banquet only by responding to the Lord's invitation. While the banquet was prepared for God's originally invited guests, they are not entitled to the meal; it is a gift. If, by pursuing their own agendas, they do not respond to the final gracious call to eat, then their places at the table will be given to others—the least desirable guests in human terms: "the poor, the crippled, the lame, and the blind" (14:13). "And they will come from east and west and from north and south, and will recline at the table in the kingdom of God. And behold, some are last who will be first and some are first who will be last" (13:29-30).

The Lord concluded His parable with a chilling warning—perhaps with a glance to the man who blurted out, "Blessed is everyone who will eat bread in the kingdom of God!" (14:15). None who feel entitled to citizenship in the kingdom shall eat a morsel, but only those who respond to the Lord's gracious invitation. Only they will find a place at His table, and they are *all* places of honor!

• • •

The Jewish leader's Sabbath banquet didn't turn out quite as he had expected. It began with a failed attempt to intimidate Jesus into compromising His earlier stand. Jesus turned the tables to rebuke the misplaced priorities of legalism. God made laws because He loves people. When man-made rules cause suffering, they no longer reflect the heart of God; therefore, we should reexamine them (14:1-6).

When the other dinner guests began lining up by rank, Jesus rebuked their pride (14:7-11). The kingdom of God assigns rank by humility, and genuine humility doesn't think about self at all. Genuine humility concerns itself with the welfare of others. This rebuke then led to an exhortation to use earthly privilege for the benefit of the needy (14:12-14), suggesting the seating chart in the kingdom will reflect our estimation of human worth today.

Jesus' final parable left everyone at the banquet with a personal, private question: *What is the nature of my commitment to the kingdom of God?* As His journey toward the cross continued, true disciples would sense increasing tension between comfort in this world and joy in the next. Most of the men at the banquet table had already made their decision: comfort *now*. What would the Messiah's disciples choose?

APPLICATION: LUKE 14:1-24
Lessons à la Carte

I think these four scenes yield four lessons.

The first lesson (scene one: 14:1-6): *Legalism blinds and makes us shortsighted*. We give ourselves a list; we then require it of other people. When they don't live up to it, we criticize. That's legalism, and it blinds us so that we become a circle of "us four and no more." It makes us shortsighted. I've never seen a legalist with a real vision for the whole world. Legalists tend to live in the tight radius of their own rules and regulations.

I'll spend the rest of my life in ministry standing against legalism. I don't know of anything that ruins a church fellowship quicker and more severely than legalism.

The second lesson (scene two: 14:7-11): *Pride backfires and makes us selfish*. Invariably your pride will backfire and, one of these days, someone will call your bluff and you'll be embarrassed. One of these days someone will realize you're really applauding yourself, that your statements are really self-serving, that you really did clamor for that front spot, or that you really were offended because someone didn't know your name.

The third lesson (scene three: 14:12-15): *Compassion blesses and makes us sensitive.* The longer I live and the more I study the life of this magnificent God-man, the more I'm impressed with one thing: His compassion. He never let an external distraction keep Him from his internally driven work. God help us to be more like that! He never checked the color of skin and then responded. He never checked to see if a person was in good health or had a fat wallet or ran with the big group. Jesus was compassionate and lived His life sensitive to the needs of people.

The fourth lesson (scene four: 14:16-24): *Salvation beckons and forces us to select.* You have to choose between your busy world and eternal life. You have to choose between the demands and needs of family and the offer of salvation. You have to choose between your yoke of oxen (whatever that may be) and Jesus' promise of eternal life. And this may be your last day to choose, because there is not only a heaven, and there is not only a hell; there is a hurry.

Exacting Expectations
LUKE 14:25-35

NASB

25 Now ᵃlarge crowds were going along with Him; and He turned and said to them, 26 "If anyone comes to Me, and does not ᵃhate his own father and mother and wife and children and brothers and sisters, yes, and even his own life, he cannot be My disciple. 27 Whoever does not carry his own cross and come after Me cannot be My disciple. 28 For which one of you, when he wants to build a tower, does not first sit down and calculate the cost to see if he has

NLT

25 A large crowd was following Jesus. He turned around and said to them, 26 "If you want to be my disciple, you must, by comparison, hate everyone else—your father and mother, wife and children, brothers and sisters—yes, even your own life. Otherwise, you cannot be my disciple. 27 And if you do not carry your own cross and follow me, you cannot be my disciple.

28 "But don't begin until you count the cost. For who would begin construction of a building without first calculating the cost to see if there is

NASB

enough to complete it? ²⁹Otherwise, when he has laid a foundation and is not able to finish, all who observe it begin to ridicule him, ³⁰saying, 'This man began to build and was not able to finish.' ³¹Or what king, when he sets out to meet another king in battle, will not first sit down and consider whether he is strong enough with ten thousand *men* to encounter the one coming against him with twenty thousand? ³²Or else, while the other is still far away, he sends ᵃa delegation and asks for terms of peace. ³³So then, none of you can be My disciple who does not give up all his own possessions.

³⁴"Therefore, salt is good; but if even salt has become tasteless, with what will it be seasoned? ³⁵It is useless either for the soil or for the manure pile; it is thrown out. He who has ears to hear, ᵃlet him hear."

14:25 ᵃLit *many* **14:26** ᵃI.e. by comparison of his love for Me **14:32** ᵃOr *an embassy* **14:35** ᵃOr *hear!* Or *listen!*

NLT

enough money to finish it? ²⁹Otherwise, you might complete only the foundation before running out of money, and then everyone would laugh at you. ³⁰They would say, 'There's the person who started that building and couldn't afford to finish it!'

³¹"Or what king would go to war against another king without first sitting down with his counselors to discuss whether his army of 10,000 could defeat the 20,000 soldiers marching against him? ³²And if he can't, he will send a delegation to discuss terms of peace while the enemy is still far away. ³³So you cannot become my disciple without giving up everything you own.

³⁴"Salt is good for seasoning. But if it loses its flavor, how do you make it salty again? ³⁵Flavorless salt is good neither for the soil nor for the manure pile. It is thrown away. Anyone with ears to hear should listen and understand!"

Most people are capable of handling far greater challenges than we ever place before them. Great leaders understand that people need the inspiration of high expectations. Expect nothing of people and that is exactly what they will produce.

If most of us are honest, we will admit that the times we accomplished the greatest good were those times when an influential person or a distressing circumstance challenged us to do something great. We long to hear the voice of God—but we must be careful what we ask for. When He speaks, the challenge to one's faith can become a life-defining crisis, but it always leads to greatness.

He challenged Noah to defy the people of his generation by building a massive ship on dry land (Gen. 6:5-22). He challenged an aging patriarch to sacrifice his only son on an altar (Gen. 22:1-19), presumably ending any hope of fulfilling God's covenant (Gen. 12:1-3). He challenged a speech-impaired fugitive to become Israel's spokesman in Egypt (Exod. 3:10). He challenged a callow, young shepherd boy—widely considered the runt of the litter—to stand on the field of battle against a man literally twice his height (1 Sam. 17:36). He challenged the hyper-zealous Pharisee, Saul of Tarsus, to renounce his impressive moral résumé to become "Paul, the small" in the cause of the kingdom (Acts 9:15-16).

Each of these God-ordained crises pushed the individual to the brink, forcing them to choose between fear and faith, comfort and commitment. Noah's faith preserved humanity from utter destruction. Abraham's faith made him the spiritual father of all those who believe in God. Moses' faith helped establish the nation of Israel. David's faith put Israel on the map . . . literally. "Paul, the small" became arguably the greatest apostle the church has ever known.

People do great things when pushed beyond their human limits to become conduits of God's power. At some point along their journey, however, they must count the cost of discipleship and commit themselves to the call of God to trust in Him—not in part, but in totality.

As Jesus journeyed closer to Jerusalem, spiritual darkness would grow, and the multitudes that followed Him would be put to the test. Difficult choices would winnow the crowds, sifting the chaff from the precious kernels of true disciples. To prepare them, Jesus clarified the three exacting expectations of God's kingdom, without which one is not able to "be His disciple" (note the phrase repeated in Luke 14:26-27, 33). The Lord introduced each qualification with a negative condition:

"If anyone . . . does not" (14:26)

"Whoever does not" (14:27)

"None . . . who does not" (14:33)

The conditions should not be understood as works necessary for salvation but as evidence of commitment following conversion. In other words, Jesus listed these conditions as a kind of litmus test of genuine discipleship, issuing them for two purposes. First, He challenged each individual to put their own attitude to the test. Second, He warned all who would consider following that discipleship is costly. All three conditions call for the true disciple to give Christ priority over all other things—including relationships (14:26) and plans (14:27-32)—which necessarily leads to the sacrifice of possessions (14:33).

— 14:25 —

As usual, Luke establishes the context before describing the Lord's actions or teaching. He typically defines the circumstances, the audience, and the place (though not always in terms of exact locale). In this case, Jesus was in motion, presumably toward Jerusalem, and the crowds were "going along" with Him. Luke undoubtedly writes this in the literal sense of "traveling with." The phrase "He turned and said" usually introduces a rebuke, a correction, or a clarification (7:9, 44; 9:55; 10:23). Jesus would not have discouraged the act of following; He did, however, challenge the motivation.

— 14:26 —

Priority in Relationships

In order to interpret the Lord's words correctly, one must be familiar with the ancient Near Eastern concept of "hate," which is very different from our modern, Western use of the term. In twenty-first-century America, hate is "intense hostility and aversion usually deriving from fear, anger, or sense of injury; extreme dislike or antipathy."[30] In the ancient literature of Near Eastern cultures, hate is a matter of priorities. For example, Esau "despised" his birthright when he chose a bowl of soup over his covenant blessing (Gen. 25:29-34). Esau didn't have intense negative emotions about his birthright—he certainly didn't "hate" it as we would use the term—in fact, he fought hard to regain what he had lost and was inconsolable when he failed.

In another example, Genesis 29 tells the story of Jacob's two wives and how he "loved" Rachel and "hated" her sister, Leah. Again, the term indicates Jacob's choice to favor one over the other. He couldn't have been too repulsed by Leah. He did, after all, conceive seven children with her! The issue is choice or priority, irrespective of one's feelings. You could say that hatred is as hatred *does*.

Jesus didn't want His disciples to cultivate a deep loathing for people or to treat others cruelly. He called for them to a make a clear, definable, decisive choice to make Him their number one priority over all other relationships, including love for self.

— 14:27-32 —

Priority in Plans

When the Romans executed a prisoner by crucifixion, they made the entire process as humiliating as it was excruciating. After stripping the victim naked for flogging, they hung a sign around their neck listing their crimes. The victim was then forced to carry the implement of their own death through the city streets to the place of execution. Therefore, to "carry one's own cross" is to bear the public scorn of discipleship and to accept the inevitable suffering it brings.

Note the phrase "and come after Me." It expresses the idea of getting in line behind someone. In the same manner the masses followed Jesus on His way to Jerusalem, true disciples place their feet in His footsteps—all the way up to Golgotha, the place of crucifixion. The Lord's call includes a commitment to the kingdom cause that's as selfless and complete as His own. In a practical sense, discipleship requires placing all other goals, objectives, plans, and personal desires under those of the Father. The truly committed follower releases their own will while embracing the Father's will. Later, in the garden of Gethsemane, Jesus would prostrate Himself before His Father and pray, "Father, if You are willing, remove this cup from Me; yet not My will, but Yours be done" (22:42).

Jesus offered two analogies to illustrate conscious, eyes-wide-open commitment. Both depict people making all-or-nothing decisions before proceeding. Jesus didn't want foolhardy promises; fickle disciples do more harm than good to the cause. No, He wants only those who take on the hardships with a reasonable understanding of the cost.

— 14:33 —

Priority in Possessions

"Health and wealth," "word of faith" hucksters love to camp out on this verse. Of course, they mean to have everyone sell their possessions for cash and send it in to them! But that's not what Jesus had in mind. We have to interpret this teaching in conjunction with other passages, such as "If anyone does not provide for his own, and especially for those of his household, he has denied the faith and is worse than an unbeliever" (1 Tim. 5:8).

The point here is to avoid an emotional attachment to money or possessions. Again, it's a matter of priorities. In the realm of relationships, Christ comes first. When planning your life, subject all of your plans to the will of your King (Jas. 4:13-15). And in terms of your possessions, commit them to God's service, whether they remain in your possession or not. Disciples must let no *thing* possess them. Hold everything loosely.

While I don't believe Jesus called all followers to live a spartan, bare-bones lifestyle, nearly all of us in developed countries possess far more than we need.

— 14:34-35 —

The Lord concluded His discourse on the cost of discipleship with a vivid illustration of uselessness. What good is salt that has lost its essential, defining quality of saltiness? Jesus recalled three specific uses for salt in His era, two of which are not well understood today. People continue to use salt for seasoning and preservation, but what about its use in fertilizer and with manure?

Israeli salt, which was refined for various uses, most likely came from the Dead Sea. Processed one way, it yields sodium salt for seasoning. Processed another way, it is inedible but retains high concentrations of minerals beneficial to plants. Additionally, "Farmers added salt to animal dung to slow down the fermentation process so they could preserve it as fertilizer until they needed to use it."[31] Archeologists and historians have discovered dozens of other uses for salt in first-century Israel.

The idea that salt could lose its saltiness is absurd. Salt cannot change its defining quality without changing its molecules to become something else. Jesus used this illustration of impossibility to make two points. First, the kingdom doesn't need useless disciples any more than a household needs to stockpile a useless substance. Second, disciples who do not possess the essential qualities Jesus just described are, by definition, not disciples. They are something else. Therefore, people who do not possess these qualities should seriously question their status as disciples; or, if they have committed themselves to true discipleship, then they should rise to the occasion.

APPLICATION: LUKE 14:25-35

Great Expectations

We should aim high. Our problem is not that we are over-challenged; it's that we're under-challenged. If you will permit me, I need to be forthright with a couple of statements. They don't apply to everyone at all times, so I'll leave it to you to decide whether they apply to you.

First, *stop indulging your laziness.*

Start getting involved with children or teenagers or the aged. Volunteer for services at the church that you attend. If your church doesn't have something for you to do (which I highly doubt), then your community needs you. God didn't call you into His family to serve your-self or to sit on the sidelines. Dust off your rear end and get going!

Second, *start demonstrating your devotion.*

Don't write about it. Don't sing about it. Don't read about how to do it. Do it! Give generously to ministries or causes you respect. Give until it hurts, and then give until it starts feeling good again—and it will. Devote your time and energy to helping someone in need.

You are either a loyal disciple of Christ or you are a lost sinner. You are one or the other—there's no middle category. So, if you're not a lost sinner, then it's time to aim high and become what you are.

How to Make the Angels Laugh
LUKE 15:1-10

NASB

¹Now all the tax collectors and the ᵃsinners were coming near Him to listen to Him. ²Both the Pharisees and the scribes *began* to grumble, saying, "This man receives sinners and eats with them."

³So He told them this parable, saying, ⁴"What man among you, if he has a hundred sheep and has lost one of them, does not leave the ninety-nine in the ᵃopen pasture and go after the one which is lost until he finds it? ⁵When he has found it, he lays it on his shoulders, rejoicing. ⁶And when he comes home, he calls together his friends and his neigh-bors, saying to them, 'Rejoice with me, for I have found my sheep which was lost!' ⁷I tell you that in the same way, there will be *more* joy in heaven over one sinner who repents than over ninety-nine righteous persons who need no repentance.

⁸"Or what woman, if she has ten ᵃsilver coins and loses one coin, does not light a lamp and sweep the house and search carefully until she finds it? ⁹When she has found it, she calls

NLT

¹Tax collectors and other notorious sinners often came to listen to Jesus teach. ²This made the Pharisees and teachers of religious law complain that he was associating with such sinful people—even eating with them!

³So Jesus told them this story: ⁴"If a man has a hundred sheep and one of them gets lost, what will he do? Won't he leave the ninety-nine others in the wilderness and go to search for the one that is lost until he finds it? ⁵And when he has found it, he will joyfully carry it home on his shoulders. ⁶When he arrives, he will call together his friends and neighbors, saying, 'Rejoice with me because I have found my lost sheep.' ⁷In the same way, there is more joy in heaven over one lost sinner who repents and returns to God than over ninety-nine others who are righteous and haven't strayed away!

⁸"Or suppose a woman has ten sil-ver coins* and loses one. Won't she light a lamp and sweep the entire house and search carefully until she finds it? ⁹And when she finds it, she

NASB

together her friends and neighbors, saying, 'Rejoice with me, for I have found the coin which I had lost!' [10]In the same way, I tell you, there is joy in the presence of the angels of God over one sinner who repents."

15:1 ªI.e. irreligious Jews   15:4 ªLit *wilderness*
15:8 ªGr *drachmas*, one drachma was a day's wages

NLT

will call in her friends and neighbors and say, 'Rejoice with me because I have found my lost coin.' [10]In the same way, there is joy in the presence of God's angels when even one sinner repents."

15:8 Greek *ten drachmas*. A drachma was the equivalent of a full day's wage.

In a challenging book on wholehearted devotion to discipleship, Keith Miller and Bruce Larson write,

> The neighborhood bar is possibly the best counterfeit there is to the fellowship Christ wants to give His church. It is an imitation, dispensing liquor instead of grace, escape rather than reality, but it is a permissive, accepting, and inclusive fellowship. It is unshockable. It is democratic. You can tell people secrets and they usually don't tell others or even want to. The bar flourishes not because most people are alcoholics, but because God has put into the human heart the desire to know and be known, to love and be loved, and so many seek a counterfeit at the price of a few beers.
>
> With all my heart I believe Christ wants His church to be a fellowship where people can come in and say, "I'm sunk!" "I'm beat!" "I've had it!"[32]

That may explain why another friend in the ministry tells me he feels much more comfortable in a bar than he does in a church. He's no cynic, however. He is, in fact, a graduate of Dallas Theological Seminary and is very much involved in ministry. Just the same, he admits he finds his bar friends truthful in most respects, transparent about their flaws, generally accepting of others, confidential, generous, affable, and a lot of fun to be around. They also tend to be vulnerable, even forthright, about their troubles, which many try to wash away with alcohol; and most have difficulty with long-term relationships. Consequently, my friend has found in his neighborhood watering hole a mission field ripe for the harvest. And I, for one, am glad he's there cultivating relationships, building trust, and presenting Christ as their best and only hope.

His method and place of ministry make some Christians uncomfortable. They would feel more assured if my friend simply passed out tracts and browbeat some of the patrons into heaven—gingerly, of course—rather than actually sit on a stool or play darts or cheer on the local sports team. Unfortunately, these believers would find themselves in good company among Jesus' critics, the scribes and Pharisees. They didn't care for His method or choice of friends or place of ministry either.

The religiously proper folk called Jesus a glutton and a drunk because He socialized with tax collectors and other people who openly rejected the Law of Moses (Luke 7:34). He was an irreverent revolutionary because He didn't fall in line with their uptight, legalistic system. He experienced greater joy in the company of those who were shamelessly lost than with the self-appointed guardians of religious decorum. He didn't merely conduct holy sorties into the society of these "sinners"; He lingered just to enjoy their company. And He welcomed them into His. So is it any surprise that sinners liked to be around Jesus?

When challenged by His peers in the religious community, Jesus found another opportunity to teach them as well as His disciples about the true nature of ministry and God's vision for the kingdom. With two short analogies, He revealed the heart of heaven, subtly inviting His legalistic friends to loosen up, to love the unlovely, to learn to redeem sinners rather than condemn them, and to dance with the angels.

— 15:1 —

Luke's opening sentence doesn't offer a specific. It's a summary statement describing a growing trust for Jesus among Israel's social outcasts. Gaining their trust was no easy feat. The temple had forsaken these men and women, so they had naturally returned the favor. By the time Jesus arrived, a great divide separated the equally sinful, stubbornly entrenched, and mutually hostile groups. Religious leaders stood on one side bellowing, "Unworthy!" while tax collectors and sinners shouted in return, "Hypocrites!" Some things never change.

In the first two of three stories, Jesus appealed to the needs of blatant sinners, recognizing that almost nothing can penetrate the leathery, emotional hide of those who have been beaten down by the morality of the self-righteous. *Almost* nothing. Jesus, the only thoroughly righteous man, knew the secret. He knew the only way to win their trust was to distinguish Himself from the temple leaders while maintaining a high standard of righteousness. For months, Jesus had been building a track record of gentle approachability. Without compromising morality or obedience to the Law, Jesus systematically challenged the hypocrisy of the religious leaders; and he socialized with irreligious Jews, accepted them as they were, ministered to their needs, and even stood with them against hypocritical condemnation. His consistency paid off. They "were coming near to listen to Him."

— 15:2 —

On the other side of the great divide stood the scribes and Pharisees, men who referred to sinners as "people of the land." This term became especially derisive during the time of Ezra and Nehemiah, who led the Jews back to Israel after seventy years of exile in Babylon. When this godly remnant tried to rebuild the temple and fortify the city of Jerusalem, they found resistance among the mixed-race inhabitants in the surrounding regions (Ezra 4:4; 10:2, 11; Neh. 10:28-31). As the nation of pure-blooded Jews reestablished its dominance, the social and religious elite used the term "people of the land" to refer to all other Jews. By the time of Jesus, the scribes and Pharisees rejected any Jew who didn't observe their traditions, treating them as disdainfully as they treated Samaritans and Gentiles.

Ironically, the Lord had concluded with the invitation "He who has ears to hear, let him hear" (Luke 14:35), and now it was the outcasts who "were coming near Him to listen to Him" ("listen" is the same Greek verb as "to hear"). The scribes and Pharisees began to grumble (cf. 5:30). The term translated "grumble" (*diagongyzō* [1234]) is an emphatic form of the verb *gongyzō* [1111], which sounds like the grumbling that it describes. (Repeat the word "*gon-GOO-zoe*" aloud several times in a low, quiet tone.)

The scribes and Pharisees criticized Jesus for "receiving" (*prosdechomai* [4327]) these undesirables. The Greek term most often has one of two meanings: first, "to welcome favorably" and, second, "to look forward to" or "to wait for." Jesus longed for the company of sinners, waited for them to overcome their suspicions, and then embraced them eagerly. He even socialized with them!

— 15:3 —

Jesus stood in the great divide, hearing as it were the laughter of a party on one side and the muttering consternation of the religious authorities on the other. This prompted three parables about loss and redemption, separation and reconciliation. The first tells the story of a shepherd and a lost sheep (15:4-7), the second, a woman searching for a lost coin (15:8-10), and the third, a deeply moving tale of a father and two rebellious sons (15:11-32). Each story attempts to give the religious experts a glimpse into the heart of God. Take note of the audience: "Them" refers to the grumbling "Pharisees and the scribes."

— 15:4-7 —

As He often did, Jesus described the good behavior of flawed humanity to illustrate the superior goodness of God. His rhetorical question highlights the expected compassion of a shepherd searching for a single lost sheep. In the same way that a man doesn't regard one missing sheep out of a hundred an acceptable loss, the Lord isn't willing to accept the loss of one human soul. Moreover, the story conveys the supreme value God places on each individual. No one is disposable, not even the foolish who wander from the fold.

Jesus applied the illustration by revealing the heart of heaven. God and His angels rejoice over the restoration of one lost soul because they value each individual. And He compared this elation to the joy felt for "righteous persons who need no repentance." In truth, there are no such persons, but the Pharisees counted themselves among the ninety-nine "faithful" sheep who didn't wander off. Jesus obliged their flawed, self-righteous perspective—for now. He didn't want to distract from the main point: God values the very sinners that Israel's religious authorities despised.

— 15:8-10 —

Jesus continued with a second story, perhaps because the Pharisees and scribes remained unmoved. Again, Jesus appealed to the men's sense of common decency with a rhetorical question regarding the response of a woman who had lost a coin. The coin was a *drachma*, a Greek silver coin worth about a day's wages or the cost of one sheep, depending upon the economy. It was a modest amount of money, yet the woman set aside all other activity and diligently searched the house until she found it.

Both stories use similar vocabulary, both involve a search, and both conclude with a celebration; the two stories contain only a slight difference in emphasis. Jesus told these parables to convey the idea of value. God treasures the repentance of lost sinners because He loves people—all of them, individually and specifically.

• • •

Stop and think of the impact of news like this on the person who feels forsaken by God. The desperately down-and-out need no reminder that good people consider them undesirable. Consequently, they hide their shame behind a steely, hollow gaze and dare the world to judge their only trustworthy companion: sin. They would seek help among the righteous, but nicely dressed church people can appear sanctimoniously superior and often profess a religion that merely promises to exchange one burden for another. So, it should surprise no one that they keep their distance from anything remotely religious.

In the lines of two short stories, Jesus reassured hardened sinners—people who, in today's terms, were searching for hope at the bottom of cocktail glasses and seeking comfort in one-night stands—that God has not forsaken them. He is, in fact, searching for them because He treasures them as much as, if not more than, He does those who have not gone astray.[33] Jesus also demonstrated to the religiously upright that it's okay—in fact, more than okay—to seek the lost; the Father rejoices when just one lost person is found!

APPLICATION: LUKE 15:1-10

Compassion First, Then Evangelism

If you really want to engage in evangelism, I have a few suggestions.

The first suggestion for all of us who are children of God by His grace is to *stay in touch with the world of the lost*. This not only keeps us relevant; we need their presence for other reasons. Nonbelievers keep us honest. They spot our phoniness. They are not impressed with our Christian vocabulary. In fact, if you stay too long in the exclusive world of Christians, you'll grow numb to the need for Christ in the world, and you'll stop thinking creatively.

Second, *treat non-Christians well*. If you owe them money, pay your bills. If you hear hate from them, remember that we're to forgive the sinner, not strike back. If they represent a lifestyle that turns you off, understand that's the only thing they know. Stop judging, start loving, and treat them well.

Third, *be very patient*. Remember that God is at work. He'll take account of their actions and their decisions, either by forgiving them in grace or by judging their sin at the end of time. Either way, they are His responsibility, not yours. Don't push. Be available. And keep your patience.

It has been my experience that, in the end, people respond to compassion. And when they see how much you care, your evangelistic words will find a ready home in their hearts.

Two Rebels under One Roof
LUKE 15:11-32

NASB

11 And He said, "A man had two sons. 12 The younger of them said to his father, 'Father, give me the share of the estate that falls to me.' So he divided his ªwealth between them. 13 And not many days later, the younger son gathered everything together and went on a journey into a distant country, and there he squandered his estate with loose living. 14 Now when he had spent everything, a severe famine occurred in that country, and he began to be impoverished. 15 So he went and ªhired himself out to one of the citizens of that country, and he sent him into his fields to feed swine. 16 And he would have gladly filled his stomach with the ªpods that the swine were eating, and no one was giving *anything* to him. 17 But when he came to ªhis senses, he said, 'How many of my father's hired men have more than enough bread, but I am dying here with hunger! 18 I will get up and go to my father, and will say to him, "Father, I have sinned against heaven, and ªin your sight; 19 I am no longer worthy to be called your son; make me as one of your hired men."' 20 So he got up and came to ªhis father. But while he was still a long way off, his father saw him and felt compassion *for him,* and ran and ᵇembraced him and kissed him. 21 And the son said to him, 'Father, I have sinned against heaven and in your sight; I am no longer worthy to be called your son.'

NLT

11 To illustrate the point further, Jesus told them this story: "A man had two sons. 12 The younger son told his father, 'I want my share of your estate now before you die.' So his father agreed to divide his wealth between his sons.

13 "A few days later this younger son packed all his belongings and moved to a distant land, and there he wasted all his money in wild living. 14 About the time his money ran out, a great famine swept over the land, and he began to starve. 15 He persuaded a local farmer to hire him, and the man sent him into his fields to feed the pigs. 16 The young man became so hungry that even the pods he was feeding the pigs looked good to him. But no one gave him anything.

17 "When he finally came to his senses, he said to himself, 'At home even the hired servants have food enough to spare, and here I am dying of hunger! 18 I will go home to my father and say, "Father, I have sinned against both heaven and you, 19 and I am no longer worthy of being called your son. Please take me on as a hired servant."'

20 "So he returned home to his father. And while he was still a long way off, his father saw him coming. Filled with love and compassion, he ran to his son, embraced him, and kissed him. 21 His son said to him, 'Father, I have sinned against both heaven and you, and I am no longer worthy of being called your son.*'

NASB

22 But the father said to his slaves, 'Quickly bring out the best robe and put it on him, and put a ring on his hand and sandals on his feet; 23 and bring the fattened calf, kill it, and let us eat and celebrate; 24 for this son of mine was dead and has come to life again; he was lost and has been found.' And they began to celebrate.

25 "Now his older son was in the field, and when he came and approached the house, he heard music and dancing. 26 And he summoned one of the servants and *began* inquiring what these things could be. 27 And he said to him, 'Your brother has come, and your father has killed the fattened calf because he has received him back safe and sound.' 28 But he became angry and was not willing to go in; and his father came out and *began* pleading with him. 29 But he answered and said to his father, 'Look! For so many years I have been serving you and I have never ªneglected a command of yours; and *yet* you have never given me a young goat, so that I might celebrate with my friends; 30 but when this son of yours came, who has devoured your ªwealth with prostitutes, you killed the fattened calf for him.' 31 And he said to him, 'Son, you ªhave always been with me, and all that is mine is yours. 32 But we had to celebrate and rejoice, for this brother of yours was dead and *has begun* to live, and *was* lost and has been found.'"

15:12 ªLit *living*   15:15 ªLit *was joined to*   15:16 ªI.e. of the carob tree   15:17 ªLit *himself*   15:18 ªLit *before you*   15:20 ªLit *his own* ᵇLit *fell on his neck*   15:29 ªOr *disobeyed*   15:30 ªLit *living*   15:31 ªLit *are always with me*

NLT

22 "But his father said to the servants, 'Quick! Bring the finest robe in the house and put it on him. Get a ring for his finger and sandals for his feet. 23 And kill the calf we have been fattening. We must celebrate with a feast, 24 for this son of mine was dead and has now returned to life. He was lost, but now he is found.' So the party began.

25 "Meanwhile, the older son was in the fields working. When he returned home, he heard music and dancing in the house, 26 and he asked one of the servants what was going on. 27 'Your brother is back,' he was told, 'and your father has killed the fattened calf. We are celebrating because of his safe return.'

28 "The older brother was angry and wouldn't go in. His father came out and begged him, 29 but he replied, 'All these years I've slaved for you and never once refused to do a single thing you told me to. And in all that time you never gave me even one young goat for a feast with my friends. 30 Yet when this son of yours comes back after squandering your money on prostitutes, you celebrate by killing the fattened calf!'

31 "His father said to him, 'Look, dear son, you have always stayed by me, and everything I have is yours. 32 We had to celebrate this happy day. For your brother was dead and has come back to life! He was lost, but now he is found!'"

15:21 Some manuscripts add *Please take me on as a hired servant.*

The parable of the Prodigal Son is perhaps the best-known, yet least-understood, story Jesus ever told. It resonates deeply with readers because they so readily see their own experiences reflected in the wayward son's choices, and they long for the kind of grace shown to him by his father. Furthermore, we all know wayward people who have caused intense heartache; so, this powerful story of forgiveness challenges us to imitate the gentle, merciful father, who is truly the hero of the story. Yet lurking in the shadows is a figure we all know: a frowning, finger-wagging, petulant enemy of grace who never fails to spoil a good story of reconciliation. Who does this older brother represent? The answer is both obvious and surprising.

The story unfolds in three acts:

Act 1: Wayward Lad and Waiting Dad (15:12-16)
Act 2: Repentant and Restored (15:17-24)
Act 3: Resentful Brother and Insightful Father (15:25-32)

— 15:11 —

The parable of the Prodigal Son is the third in a series of three stories featuring the recovery of something valuable. In the first two, a foolish sheep wanders from the fold and a coin rolls into the shadows of a woman's home. A diligent search restores what had been lost to the owner, who then invites family and friends to rejoice. This third tale, while involving similar elements, differs dramatically from the first two.

In the first two parables, Jesus opened with a rhetorical question, inviting His listeners to identify with God, who searches for lost sinners. He broke the pattern in this third parable, opening instead with a simple, sobering statement: "A man had two sons." Now the stakes have been raised. Lost sheep can be written off and lost coins replaced, but not sons. Furthermore, the moral component intensifies. Sheep wander off and coins roll away; they simply behave according to their natures. But sons are responsible for their choices. How does God deal with lost people?

— 15:12-13 —

Hebrew estate planning was not a complicated procedure. The patriarch simply divided his estate among his living sons, with the eldest receiving a double portion and the right to succeed him as the family leader. While neither the Law of Moses nor Jewish customs permitted a man to break with tradition on the basis of favoritism (Deut. 21:15-17), it did allow certain flexibility in other respects (Num. 27:8-11). Later tradition expanded this flexibility, permitting him to distribute his estate before death as a kind of early inheritance. The father may elect to do this of his own free will, but for a child to demand his inheritance was an outrageous and presumptuous act of rebellion. By demanding his inheritance early, the younger son essentially divorced his father. Henceforth, there would be no relationship, no submitting to his authority, no responsibility to carry on the family legacy, and no communication. Put bluntly, he treated the father as though he were already dead.

The father in the story proved merciful from the beginning. According to Old Testament Law, the son proved himself "stubborn and rebellious" and deserved public condemnation by his hometown elders (Deut. 21:18-21). Instead, the father willingly transferred two-thirds of the estate to the older son, liquidated the remainder, and gave it to the younger son in the form of cash. The boy loaded up a cart with all his belongings and the lump of cash and put a long distance between himself and home, perhaps burning bridges all along the way.

The callow youth had a pocket full of money and a head full of dreams, although neither amounted to much. His dreams of dissipation came true, which quickly consumed his bankroll. The adjective "loose" translates the Greek term *asōtōs* [811], which in this context means "wasteful"; it also has a strong connotation of immorality. In other words, the boy didn't merely live off the money until it was gone or commit to unwise investments; he used it to fuel his rebellion.

— 15:14-16 —

About the time his money ran out, a severe famine prevented him from earning more. This was no mere economic downturn or even a depression. The word *famine* struck fear in the hearts of all ancient people. Historians record the bizarre depths to which starving people sink in order to survive, including their willingness to eat grass, shoe leather, garbage, and even the flesh of recently deceased neighbors. Scribes and Pharisees would have interpreted this famine as divine retribution for sin.

Driven to survive by any means possible, the boy hired himself out and took a job feeding swine—a role most Gentiles would not have wanted, to say nothing of a Hebrew. While Jesus' audience cringed at the thought of his ritual defilement, the rebellious youth probably didn't care; after all, he had rejected his former way of life in favor of sinful living in a Gentile country. Eventually, however, the pressing need to eat brought him to his senses. Swineherding paid next to nothing, and he found himself envying the pigs' diet of carob pods. These were hard, bean-like seeds encased in leathery pods, barely edible for humans and not even the first choice for livestock.

— 15:17-19 —

Remorse for his rebellion didn't move the boy. Regret for his dissipation didn't rattle his conscience. The humiliation of tending swine didn't trigger his Jewish scruples. But the realization that pigs enjoyed a superior lifestyle to his own sparked a moment of clarity. The opening of Luke 15:17 reads, literally, "He came to himself," which is to say that his reason returned. As C. S. Lewis wrote, "[Pain] plants the flag of truth within the fortress of a rebel soul."[34] The boy looked at the pigs and then recalled the status of his father's household servants. The vivid comparison suggested a reasonable solution.

Take note of the humility in his rehearsed speech. He acknowledged his affront without minimizing or justifying or shifting blame. He didn't say, "I made a mistake." He took responsibility for making a wrong moral decision, one that estranged him from his father and his God. He also acknowledged the consequences of his decision. His admission, "I am no longer worthy to be called your son," wasn't a platitude; it was a fact. He had legally forfeited his status as the man's son. Later Jewish tradition permitted parents in similar circumstances to hold a funeral service for their children. Moreover, the son's request for mercy was equitable for the father. He left his lofty expectations in the pigsty with his sin. Instead of asking to be restored as a son, he offered to become a hired hand.

The boy's speech demonstrated maturity, responsibility, humility, and compassion for those he harmed. He truly "returned to his senses."

— 15:20-24 —

During the boy's absence, his father continued with life but kept an eye on the horizon. This story of our Father God doesn't depict Him with arms folded and brow furrowed in disapproval. One day the father caught sight of his son on the distant horizon. Rather than wait for the foolish boy to come crawling, this father threw aside his own dignity and ran to meet his returning son, something *no* Near Eastern father would have done.

As if hiking up his robes and running to meet the unworthy son didn't already obliterate the man's dignity, he "fell on his neck" (15:20, literally rendered) and kissed him.

While people set up lengthy and strict systems of probation, God receives the sinner instantly. The son barely started his speech before his father began restoring him. His son appearing on the horizon was repentance enough. The greathearted father immediately gave his son three symbols of restored status as a son: a robe, a ring, and sandals. And everyone in the Lord's audience understood their significance.

The robe given to the son was a long, flowing garment typically associated with wealth. The ring bore the family's signet and was not merely a token of authority; the signet gave the son literal authorization to conduct business on behalf of the family.[35] The sandals were the finishing touch. No deep significance here. Poor people didn't have shoes and the man's son was no longer poor.

The father punctuated his act of restoration with words similar to those used in 15:6 and 15:9. What had been lost is now found. This alone called for a celebration. Ancient households typically selected an animal from the herd to fatten up in anticipation of a special occasion. They kept it in a special pen and fed it wheat grain for a month or longer. A well-fed calf would have provided for dozens of people, so the father envisioned a huge celebration.

This should have been the end of the story. In the first parable, the shepherd found his lost sheep and everyone celebrated. In the second story, the woman found her missing coin and everyone celebrated. When the prodigal son returned home, everyone celebrated—except for one person.

Act 3 begins.

— 15:25-27 —

While the prodigal had lived in a foreign land, squandering his portion of the family fortune, the older son had been at home tending the family enterprise. "In the field" speaks of labor and responsibility. The description also suggests the elder son habitually went to the field and had returned home according to his custom. The verb translated "inquiring" means "to acquire information by questioning," and the imperfect tense indicates action in process. So, a good paraphrase would be:

> While the household celebrated the return of the "worthless son," the responsible son came home from his daily work on behalf of the family enterprise. When he heard the noise of celebration, he cornered a servant and began grilling him for information (my paraphrase).

In response, the servant simply outlined the facts as if explaining something that should be obvious.

— 15:28-30 —

Upon hearing the reason for the music and dancing, he became visibly enraged. The mental picture is not unlike a pot of boiling water, which becomes more and more volatile and then suddenly overflows.

Ironically, when the prodigal brother was "out," the older brother felt "in." With the prodigal celebrating within, however, the older brother refused to go in. And again, the father took the initiative to pursue the "out" brother. He began "pleading" with him (15:28), imploring him to come in. In response, the older brother recounted his years of faithful service and his consistent obedience to his father's commands. To underscore that fact, he used the term *douleuō* [1398] ("to serve as a slave"); he essentially said, "For years, I have been slaving for you." And to emphasize his moral superiority, he compared his worthiness to the prodigal's unworthiness. Note his manner of referring to the younger son: "this son of yours," not "my brother." And don't miss the older brother's embellishment: "devoured your wealth with prostitutes." The Lord's story mentioned nothing about harlots, so the older brother could only have *presumed* that particular detail. The proud often have a dirty imagination.

His resentment over the party had less to do with his brother than the deeper issue of justice. The prodigal son didn't deserve a "welcome home" celebration; he deserved to be tried, convicted, and excommunicated, at least. The Law called for stoning (Deut. 21:18-21)! If anyone deserved a reward, it was the faithful brother.

Let's just admit that something in the older brother's argument strikes a reasonable chord. He had indeed remained by his father's side, diligently serving the needs of the household, living obediently as a good son should. He undoubtedly won the approval of his peers and the entire town. In fact, compared to his wasteful brother, he looked like a saint. And why shouldn't he be celebrated? It would seem the younger son had been rewarded for his sin. It wasn't fair.

The older son's apparent concern for justice sheds light on an even deeper issue: his own estrangement from His father. His brash speech reveals a profound sense of entitlement. He didn't serve and obey his father out of love, but for what he stood to gain. He obviously kept meticulous records. He tried to reduce the father-son relationship to a system of rewards in exchange for services rendered. Furthermore, he didn't respect his father's values, or he would have adopted them himself. Consequently, his attitude put him on the level of an employee rather than a son.

Clearly, the older son bears many of the same qualities as the Pharisees in their relationship with God. It was their grumbling that prompted the series of parables in the first place (Luke 15:2). And, like the older brother, they objected to the Lord receiving tax collectors and sinners rather than rejoicing with Him over their repentance. And they undoubtedly felt the sting of the Lord's rebuke.

— 15:31-32 —

The father's response drips with pathos, expressing both sadness and disappointment. He first addressed the fairness issue by clarifying the nature of their relationship. Employees depend upon fairness, receiving just compensation for deeds rendered. Sons live in grace, enjoying full access to everything their fathers own. The older son could have slaughtered a calf and celebrated with his friends anytime he wanted. As a son, he owns the whole herd!

The father then addressed the issue of values. Whereas he valued the son's life more than possessions, barely giving any thought to the fortune squandered, the older son couldn't see past the fairness issue long enough to celebrate his brother's return. This fact proved beyond any shadow of doubt that the older brother was no less a wayward sinner than the prodigal who actually left the country.

Sadly, there were two rebels living under one roof. They just carried out their rebellion in different ways. In the end, however, the father gained a genuine son for the first time. Repentance and forgiveness gave birth to an authentic father-son relationship based on grace. The future of the other son, however, remains in doubt by the end of Jesus' story. The Lord left the ending unresolved, most likely to prompt a response from the Pharisees. In the first parable, the shepherd "called together his friends and neighbors" to rejoice with him. In the second, the woman "called together her friends and neighbors" to rejoice with her. Both stories use almost identical language, suggesting everyone responded. After all, why would they not?

The father's explanation that he "had to celebrate" left the son with a decision: either continue in his own brand of rebellion or repent and join the celebration.

• • •

Interestingly, I rarely encounter people who see themselves reflected in the older son. Almost everyone identifies with the prodigal's need for grace, and they long for the father's response to their sinful, selfish wanderings. As Christians mature, they often identify with the father as they must learn to forgive deep hurts caused by estranged loved ones. But only a rare few recognize that they, too, share the older son's arrogant sense of entitlement.

In truth, we play all three parts. We are foolish sinners in need of God's forgiveness, and we owe many apologies to the people we have harmed and hurt. We also know many people who need our forgiveness. The father's example calls us to extend grace to others with eagerness and to restore them as quickly as wisdom allows. But let's not overlook the ugly reality that lurking in the shadows of every heart is the sulking older brother who feels entitled to just rewards for good deeds. We resent trials when we feel like we have been so faithful. We consider grace an entitlement, and we dispense justice like it's our right. How seldom do we rejoice when others rejoice! How suspicious we can be of another's repentance!

Beware the pointing finger of the older brother. The finger is yours, and it invariably points to everything resembling yourself.

APPLICATION: LUKE 15:11-32
Two Rebels, One Repentance

The parable of the Prodigal Son tells the story of *two* rebellious sons, not just one. Whereas one sinned openly, the other maintained a respectable façade to conceal his prideful, selfish, condemning nature. Both needed to seek the forgiveness of the father, albeit from different sides. Therefore, I find two principles at work to help guide the actions of those who love wayward sinners.

First, *detestable rebels must face the painful reality of their insanity before they will repent*. For those of us who love a detestable rebel, patience is key. We can nag, pressure, cajole, beg, or bribe, but that simply distracts them from the truth they need to face. Instead, without adding to their burden, we must allow the consequences of their sin to crush their foolishness. And then, when the detestable rebel is ready, we must receive them in grace.

Second, *respectable rebels must face the awful ugliness of their pride before they can repent*. For those of us who love a respectable rebel, courage is key. We must be willing to say what needs to be said, regardless of the backlash or the manipulation or the browbeating. And while they don't appear to hear the painful truth of their pride, our words—wrapped in love—can become tools in the hands of the Holy Spirit to crack the defensive barrier they have erected around their sin. And when respectable rebels are ready to repent, we must show them tenderness.

What's at the Core of Life?
LUKE 16:1-18

NASB

[1] Now He was also saying to the disciples, "There was a rich man who had a manager, and this *manager* was [a]reported to him as squandering his possessions. [2] And he called him and said to him, 'What is this I hear about you? Give an accounting of your management, for you can no longer be manager.' [3] The manager said to himself, 'What shall I do, since my [a]master is taking the management away from me? I am not strong enough to dig; I am ashamed to beg. [4] I know what I shall do, so that when I am removed from the management people will welcome me into their homes.' [5] And he summoned each one of his [a]master's debtors, and he *began* saying to the first, 'How much do you owe my master?' [6] And he said, 'A hundred [a]measures of oil.' And he said to him, 'Take your bill, and sit down quickly and write fifty.' [7] Then he said to another, 'And how much do you owe?' And he said, 'A hundred [a]measures of wheat.' He said to him, 'Take your bill, and write eighty.' [8] And his [a]master praised the unrighteous manager because he had acted shrewdly; for the sons of this age are more shrewd in relation to their own [b]kind than the sons of light. [9] And I say to you, make friends for yourselves by means of the [a]wealth of unrighteousness, so that when it fails,

NLT

[1] Jesus told this story to his disciples: "There was a certain rich man who had a manager handling his affairs. One day a report came that the manager was wasting his employer's money. [2] So the employer called him in and said, 'What's this I hear about you? Get your report in order, because you are going to be fired.'

[3] "The manager thought to himself, 'Now what? My boss has fired me. I don't have the strength to dig ditches, and I'm too proud to beg. [4] Ah, I know how to ensure that I'll have plenty of friends who will give me a home when I am fired.'

[5] "So he invited each person who owed money to his employer to come and discuss the situation. He asked the first one, 'How much do you owe him?' [6] The man replied, 'I owe him 800 gallons of olive oil.' So the manager told him, 'Take the bill and quickly change it to 400 gallons.*'

[7] "'And how much do you owe my employer?' he asked the next man. 'I owe him 1,000 bushels of wheat,' was the reply. 'Here,' the manager said, 'take the bill and change it to 800 bushels.*'

[8] "The rich man had to admire the dishonest rascal for being so shrewd. And it is true that the children of this world are more shrewd in dealing with the world around them than are the children of the light. [9] Here's the lesson: Use your worldly resources

they will receive you into the eternal dwellings.

¹⁰ "He who is faithful in a very little thing is faithful also in much; and he who is unrighteous in a very little thing is unrighteous also in much. ¹¹ Therefore if you have not been faithful in the *use of* unrighteous ªwealth, who will entrust the true *riches* to you? ¹² And if you have not been faithful in *the use of* that which is another's, who will give you that which is your own? ¹³ No ªservant can serve two masters; for either he will hate the one and love the other, or else he will be devoted to one and despise the other. You cannot serve God and ᵇwealth."

¹⁴ Now the Pharisees, who were lovers of money, were listening to all these things and were scoffing at Him. ¹⁵ And He said to them, "You are those who justify yourselves ªin the sight of men, but God knows your hearts; for that which is highly esteemed among men is detestable ªin the sight of God.

¹⁶ "The Law and the Prophets *were proclaimed* until John; since that time the gospel of the kingdom of God ªhas been preached, and everyone is forcing his way into it. ¹⁷ But it is easier for heaven and earth to pass away than for one ªstroke of a letter of the Law to fail.

¹⁸ "Everyone who ªdivorces his wife and marries another commits adultery, and he who marries one who is ᵇdivorced from a husband commits adultery.

16:1 ªOr *accused* 16:3 ªOr *lord* 16:5 ªOr *lord's* 16:6 ªGr *baths*, a Heb unit of measure equaling about 7 1/2 gal. 16:7 ªGr *kors*, one kor equals between 10 and 12 bu 16:8 ªOr *lord* ᵇLit *generation* 16:9 ªGr *mamonas*, for Aram *mamon* (mammon); i.e. wealth, etc., personified as an object of worship 16:11 ªGr *mamonas*, for Aram *mamon* (mammon); i.e. wealth, etc., personified as an object of worship 16:13 ªOr *house-servant* ᵇGr *mamonas*, for Aram *mamon* (mammon); i.e. wealth, etc., personified as an object of worship 16:15 ªLit *before* 16:16 ªLit *is preached* 16:17 ªI.e. projection of a letter (serif) 16:18 ªOr *sends away* ᵇOr *sent away*

to benefit others and make friends. Then, when your possessions are gone, they will welcome you to an eternal home.*

¹⁰ "If you are faithful in little things, you will be faithful in large ones. But if you are dishonest in little things, you won't be honest with greater responsibilities. ¹¹ And if you are untrustworthy about worldly wealth, who will trust you with the true riches of heaven? ¹² And if you are not faithful with other people's things, why should you be trusted with things of your own?

¹³ "No one can serve two masters. For you will hate one and love the other; you will be devoted to one and despise the other. You cannot serve God and be enslaved to money."

¹⁴ The Pharisees, who dearly loved their money, heard all this and scoffed at him. ¹⁵ Then he said to them, "You like to appear righteous in public, but God knows your hearts. What this world honors is detestable in the sight of God.

¹⁶ "Until John the Baptist, the law of Moses and the messages of the prophets were your guides. But now the Good News of the Kingdom of God is preached, and everyone is eager to get in.* ¹⁷ But that doesn't mean that the law has lost its force. It is easier for heaven and earth to disappear than for the smallest point of God's law to be overturned.

¹⁸ "For example, a man who divorces his wife and marries someone else commits adultery. And anyone who marries a woman divorced from her husband commits adultery."

16:6 Greek *100 baths . . . 50 [baths]*. 16:7 Greek *100 korous . . . 80 [korous]*. 16:9 Or *you will be welcomed into eternal homes*. 16:16 Or *everyone is urged to enter in*.

I find it difficult—almost impossible—to enjoy gangster movies. Even a masterpiece of storytelling like *The Godfather* gives me trouble because I find myself empathizing with the protagonists, who are always the worst kinds of criminal. They scheme, they torture, they murder, they escape justice, they thrive—it just doesn't seem right to cheer them on. My strong sense of right and wrong keeps me from enjoying the plot.

The Lord's parable of the unrighteous steward reads like a gangster story. It features dishonest people behaving in questionable ways, and that makes this parable of Jesus one of the most difficult to interpret. It seems incomprehensible that a righteous teacher would use unrighteous characters to illustrate godly behavior. Yet, He sometimes did (see 11:5-8, 11-13; 18:1-5). In this case, Jesus told a comical story of two scoundrels leveraging the rules of the fallen, sinful world to get the best of one another. As such it is a splendid piece of satire and a classic example of teaching by negative example. He might have titled it "How to Get Ahead in the Dominion of Evil."

Interpreting this parable will be easier if we keep a few things in mind. First, throughout His ministry, Jesus had been explaining the profound differences between the dominion of evil (our present world system) and the kingdom of God. They operate according to completely different sets of rules.

Second, Luke places this parable directly after a powerful story of forgiveness and grace. Therefore, Jesus had relationships in mind when telling this parable—relationships between God and man, and between individual people.

Third, Jesus told the parable of the Prodigal Son primarily for the benefit of His enemies, the scribes and Pharisees. He directed this lesson, however, toward His followers, although His enemies listened nearby.

— 16:1-2 —

The story involves a wealthy man who hired a professional we would call a "money manager" today. He retained this man's services to direct his business affairs, which often included writing personal loans in exchange for interest or for a financial stake in someone's enterprise. But instead of investing the money wisely, the manager "squandered" (same verb as 15:13) his employer's money. When the wealthy man heard rumors of the fraud, he announced his intention to fire the manager and demanded a full accounting of the losses, implying he would seek restitution either in court or through more direct means.

Take note of what prompted the wealthy man's action: The manager was "reported"—literally "accused" (the verb is *diaballō* [1225])—by unnamed sources. The manager apparently did not enjoy a good reputation in the community.

— 16:3-7 —

The manager quickly assessed his options. He knew an audit would reveal his poor management, but the employer didn't yet know just how bad the damage was. He stood no chance of charming the employer out of firing him and then hauling him to court; so, with nothing to lose, he devised a plan that would minimize the damage to the employer's account, leaving him a smaller restitution to pay. It also had the great advantage of reforming his dismal reputation by currying favor with several people in the community.

He summoned the first client to settle his account for 50 percent of the total amount owed, most likely a figure based on the man's ability to pay right away. He then summoned the second client and settled the bill for 80 percent. The manner of storytelling suggests he did this with each client, settling their accounts with a generous discount, while simultaneously minimizing the amount he would owe his boss.

The unscrupulous manager applied the first rule of politics: *Always be generous with other people's money.* He left his former position to find help among people who would be grateful to him! What is more, he had each client write the adjusted amount in their own handwriting, making them complicit in the scheme.

— 16:8-9 —

From a worldly point of view, it was a brilliant plan. Even the employer had to admit the manager had acted shrewdly. Note, however, that Jesus didn't praise the manager; in fact, He called him "unrighteous." By placing praise for the manager on the employer's lips, Jesus established two facts about the story. First, the employer and his manager were the same kind of man: unscrupulous in their dealings. Second, the manager's actions were praiseworthy according to the rules of the present world system.

Jesus drew three lessons from the story (16:8, 10, 13). The first begins with the statement "The sons of this age are more shrewd in relation to their own kind than the sons of light." The parable isn't really a story about business principles; it's a story about what's at the core of a person's life and about deciding which set of rules to play by. According to Jesus, we have two choices: the dominion of evil (inhabited by "the sons of this age") and the kingdom of God (populated by "the sons of light"). Unfortunately, "the sons of this age" consistently live what they believe, while "the sons of light" are often wishy-washy about their beliefs. The "sons of this age" play by the rules of the present world order with ruthless abandon, while the "sons of light" switch back and forth.

Lesson number one: If we were as eager and ingenious to attain wisdom and goodness as the unsaved are to attain money and comfort, our lives would show dramatic change. If we were as relentless in our pursuit of forgiveness and grace as the unsaved are in their pursuit of winning, our relationships would also show dramatic change.

— 16:10-12 —

Jesus established another principle not found in the details of the story but derived from its application. He drew a parallel between "little" and "much," between "unrighteous wealth" and "true riches." The categories correspond to the two realms: this age and the coming kingdom of God.

DOMINION OF EVIL	KINGDOM OF GOD
"Little"	"Much"
"Unrighteous wealth"	"True riches"
"That which is another's"	"That which is your own"

Lesson number two: How we handle the "little" we have at our disposal in this world determines how, or whether, we will handle "much" in this realm and in the age to come.

— 16:13 —

Jesus concluded the discourse with lesson number three: You cannot serve both God and money. Jesus used the terms "wealth" and "money" as a figure of speech known as metonymy, in which a concept is not called by its proper name but by something closely associated with it. For example, when a reporter writes, "The White House expressed concern for the economy today," they mean the president or someone in their administration. In this case, "money" stands for the methods and values associated with the present age. Money itself can neither dominate someone nor do anything evil; "wealth" in this case refers to one's devotion to material gain as a means of serving self.

The story teaches that in the dominion of evil, all is fair in relationships, war, politics, business, religion, board games, and any other realm in which there are winners and losers. Therefore, if you want to get ahead in the present world order—if obtaining money and success is your number one goal in life—you have to play by the world's rules, and you'll have to play ruthlessly. Make no mistake: This is the world we inhabit and there is no middle way. As a result, each individual must choose which he or she will serve: "money" or the kingdom.

— 16:14-15 —

Luke inserts a parenthetical note to indicate a shift in audience. Jesus concluded His lesson for genuine followers and then turned to address the Pharisees, who were "lovers of money." Naturally, Luke meant this in the manner Jesus had just described. The religious leaders played by the rules of the present age; they were thoroughly entrenched in the dominion of evil.

In response to His teaching, the religious leaders "scoffed." This Greek verb (*ekmyktērizō* [1592]) means, literally, "to turn up one's nose." Most likely, the Pharisees used a combination of body language, derisive laughter, and taunts—not only to discredit Jesus but also to intimidate His audience with their official repudiation. But Jesus didn't shrink from their challenge. His first statement, "You are those who justify yourselves in the sight of men," identified them as principal players in the parable He had just told. They were the scoundrels Jesus had in mind, men who shrewdly and ruthlessly play by the world's rules to gain money and power. And while the Pharisees tried to cover their greed with false piety, they could not fool God.

Jesus then reiterated the sharp division between the dominion of evil and the kingdom of God. What is considered "good" on earth is "detestable" in heaven. In this way, He called the Pharisees detestable in the sight of God.

— 16:16-17 —

The Pharisees made a good show of their obedience, but in truth, they didn't take God seriously. Jesus proved His point by citing the failure of the Pharisees to honor the Law of God. Throughout His ministry, they had accused the Lord of violating the Sabbath and flouting the Law of Moses; now, He turned the accusation around to claim that the religious leaders had discounted two eras of divine revelation. First, while "The Law and the Prophets" were proclaimed until the ministry of John the Baptizer, the Pharisees tried to dilute the Word of God with a deluge of man-made rules and contrived traditions. Second, the kingdom of

God had been preached by its King in their presence, and throughout His ministry the Pharisees continually discouraged those who would hear Jesus and heed His call.

Despite their efforts to dilute "the Law and the Prophets," and regardless of their campaign to deny entrance to would-be citizens of God's kingdom, Jesus promised they would fail. While the Pharisees claimed to uphold the Law and accused Jesus of violating it (because He rejected their rules and traditions), Jesus set the record straight. The universe will dissolve before the Law of God passes away. He had come to fulfill the Law, not to destroy it (Matt. 5:17-18).

— 16:18 —

Jesus closed His case against the Pharisees by citing God's ordination of marriage as a lifelong bond between a man and woman (see Gen. 2:24), an institution they had virtually erased from the Old Testament with their self-serving rules. The *Mishnah* preserves the oral tradition of the rabbis, two of whom, Shammai and Hillel, lived shortly before the time of Jesus. Here is a short example of their deliberations on this topic:

> The House of Shammai say, "A man should divorce his wife only because he has found grounds for it in unchastity, since it is said, *Because he has found in her indecency in anything* (Deut. 24:1)." And the House of Hillel say, "Even if she spoiled his dish, since it is said, *Because he has found in her indecency in anything*. R. Aqiba says, "Even if he found someone else prettier than she, since it is said, *And it shall be if she find no favor in his eyes* (Deut. 24:1)."[36]

According to the Pharisees, who favored the teaching of Hillel (naturally!), marriage could be created on a whim and dissolved just as flippantly. Make no mistake: They knew full well what they were doing. Jesus didn't need a long, drawn-out discourse to prove His point. When He merely alluded to the marriage–divorce issue and their absurd dismantling of God's design, the Pharisees wisely shut their mouths—at least for the time being. He had just proved beyond any reasonable doubt that the Pharisees subordinated the Word of God to serve their own desires.

• • •

The Lord's parable of the scoundrels might lead to the conclusion that one can succeed in this world only through a ruthless disregard for morality, but that was not His point. Lots of successful nonbelievers find success while maintaining an admirable sense of fair play. Many, if not most, are genuinely nice people. In fact, businesses grow and businesspeople generally succeed through honest hard work and aboveboard dealings—most of the time. Jesus told the story to prompt His audience to ask themselves a crucial, life-defining question: "What is my primary goal in life, and how will I achieve it?"

If "money" is your primary goal, then the kingdom of God is not. And your choices will reflect your priorities. Fortunately, most decision-making opportunities do not force us to choose between "money" and the kingdom of God. Generally speaking, moral choices are the best way to make money and please God. Obedience to the law and honest dealings are not only right, but they also pay good dividends—usually. Sometimes, however, the choice is not so simple. Sometimes doing what is right leads to suffering or requires us to sacrifice worldly success. And *that's* when we come face-to-face with an ugly truth: We typically make decisions that serve the interests of "money" and then feel relieved when our choices also happen to be morally right.

The Lord's parable asks the rhetorical question, "What choice will you make when the interests of 'money' and the kingdom of God conflict? Which master will you serve when kingdom living doesn't get you ahead in the world?"

Citizens of God's kingdom side with integrity, even when it hurts.

APPLICATION: LUKE 16:1-18

Core Issues

As Jesus continued His march toward the cross, He impressed upon His disciples the need to maintain a sharp focus on the kingdom of God. This would not be easy; they faced no fewer than three specific challenges that continue among His followers to this day. Fortunately, each challenge has a solution.

First, *competing voices of authority call us to turn this way or that, each claiming divine endorsement.*

Jesus warned that men and women will emerge in the last days claiming to speak on behalf of God. Thankfully, we have all the revelation we need until we see Jesus face-to-face. We have the sixty-six books of the Bible, God's only inspired, infallible, inerrant Word. Some will attempt to downgrade it or marginalize it or discredit it, but don't believe them. A book containing a mixture of divine truth with a few errors is a book you can't trust. If you have a book you can't trust, *you* have to discern which parts convey truth and which parts lead to error, and that requires *you* to become the authority!

Because God has spoken clearly and without error, we can depend upon His Word to hold accountable anyone claiming to speak for God.

Second, *our sinful nature invariably tries to emphasize external matters rather than deal with internal realities.*

God has promised salvation to all who receive His grace through faith in His Son, but as long as we live on planet Earth, we still struggle with sin. It's easier to focus on external matters, such as image, appearance, popularity, rules, or respectability. If we devote enough time and energy to religious practice, we can eventually convince ourselves we no longer need a savior. We might even begin to fool our peers!

Before leaving His disciples, Jesus promised we would not be left alone. He sent the Holy Spirit to take up residence in the hearts of believers to teach us, convict us of sin, apply Scripture, transform us, and provide encouragement. He has been sent to help us focus on internal matters, such as character, integrity, genuine love for God, and humility. If we ask for His supernatural inward focus, we will receive it.

Third, *Satan is a tenacious former master; he continually tries to reassert his authority.*

He won't show up in a red suit with horns and a pitchfork. He keeps himself well hidden behind good intentions and clever rationalizations. He dangles old desires in front of us, triggers old habits, and plays upon deep-seated fears. He may not suggest you deny Christ; he may simply and subtly suggest you can serve two masters.

We have God's Word and we have His Holy Spirit. As we depend upon both, the solution to this challenge is discipline: our daily decision to lay aside everything, take up our own cross, and follow Him. When my own thinking becomes cloudy and my eyes begin to lose focus on the kingdom of God, and when I need a reminder of who I am and whom I serve, I read Philippians 3:10-11, preferably from the Amplified Bible:

> [For my determined purpose is] that I may know Him [that I may progressively become more deeply and intimately acquainted with Him, perceiving and recognizing and understanding the wonders of His Person more strongly and more clearly], and that I may in that same way come to know the power outflowing from

His resurrection [which it exerts over believers], and that I may so share His sufferings as to be continually transformed [in spirit into His likeness even] to His death, [in the hope] that if possible I may attain to the [spiritual and moral] resurrection [that lifts me] out from among the dead [even while in the body].

The Subject Everybody Ignores
LUKE 16:19-31

NASB

19 "Now there was a rich man, and he habitually dressed in purple and fine linen, joyously living in splendor every day. 20 And a poor man named Lazarus was laid at his gate, covered with sores, 21 and longing to be fed with the *crumbs* which were falling from the rich man's table; besides, even the dogs were coming and licking his sores. 22 Now the poor man died and was carried away by the angels to Abraham's bosom; and the rich man also died and was buried. 23 In Hades he lifted up his eyes, being in torment, and saw Abraham far away and Lazarus in his bosom. 24 And he cried out and said, 'Father Abraham, have mercy on me, and send Lazarus so that he may dip the tip of his finger in water and cool off my tongue, for I am in agony in this flame.' 25 But Abraham said, 'Child, remember that during your life you received your good things, and likewise Lazarus bad things; but now he is being comforted here, and you are in agony. 26 And ªbesides all this, between us and you there is a great chasm fixed, so that those who wish to come over from here to you will not be able, and *that* none may cross over from there to us.' 27 And he said, 'Then I beg you, father, that you send him to my father's house— 28 for I have five brothers—in order that he may warn them, so that they

NLT

19 Jesus said, "There was a certain rich man who was splendidly clothed in purple and fine linen and who lived each day in luxury. 20 At his gate lay a poor man named Lazarus who was covered with sores. 21 As Lazarus lay there longing for scraps from the rich man's table, the dogs would come and lick his open sores. 22 "Finally, the poor man died and was carried by the angels to sit beside Abraham at the heavenly banquet.* The rich man also died and was buried, 23 and he went to the place of the dead.* There, in torment, he saw Abraham in the far distance with Lazarus at his side. 24 "The rich man shouted, 'Father Abraham, have some pity! Send Lazarus over here to dip the tip of his finger in water and cool my tongue. I am in anguish in these flames.' 25 "But Abraham said to him, 'Son, remember that during your lifetime you had everything you wanted, and Lazarus had nothing. So now he is here being comforted, and you are in anguish. 26 And besides, there is a great chasm separating us. No one can cross over to you from here, and no one can cross over to us from there.' 27 "Then the rich man said, 'Please, Father Abraham, at least send him to my father's home. 28 For I have five brothers, and I want him to warn

NASB

will not also come to this place of torment.' 29 But Abraham said, 'They have Moses and the Prophets; let them hear them.' 30 But he said, 'No, father Abraham, but if someone goes to them from the dead, they will repent!' 31 But he said to him, 'If they do not listen to Moses and the Prophets, they will not be persuaded even if someone rises from the dead.'"

16:26 ªLit *in all these things*

NLT

them so they don't end up in this place of torment.'

29 "But Abraham said, 'Moses and the prophets have warned them. Your brothers can read what they wrote.'

30 "The rich man replied, 'No, Father Abraham! But if someone is sent to them from the dead, then they will repent of their sins and turn to God.'

31 "But Abraham said, 'If they won't listen to Moses and the prophets, they won't be persuaded even if someone rises from the dead.'"

16:22 Greek *to Abraham's bosom.* 16:23 Greek *to Hades.*

"Death is a part of life," the old saying goes. That's true now, but it wasn't always that way. When God created the world and pronounced it "very good" (Gen. 1:31), there was no place for death. He didn't create human bodies to wear down or catch diseases or suffer accidents. And He certainly didn't fashion people in His image for them to die and then decay. No, sin caused death. The Creator warned His first creatures that if they disobeyed His one and only prohibition, they would "surely die" (Gen. 2:16-17). They rebelled, and the death that they and all their descendants inherited is worse than they could have imagined.

In the beginning, the world was God's kingdom, and it operated according to His ways. After Adam and Eve sinned, however, everything changed. Their disobedience subjected the world to the dominion of evil, which subjects us to diseases, disasters, death, and decay. But the effects of sin didn't stop with physical death; sin also brought spiritual death, from which the only escape is salvation by grace through faith.

Old Testament writers understood all of this, but not much more. Their knowledge extended to the grave and not much further. They had vague notions of an afterlife (Ps. 17:15; Job 14:14) and even a resurrection (Job 19:26); but for the most part, they referred to all experiences beyond death as *sheol* [H7585], a mysterious netherworld as foreboding as the watery depths of the ocean. The Pharisees had developed a rich doctrine of rewards and punishments pertaining to the hereafter, but like a lot of their teaching, it was puffy with speculative hot air and was almost entirely self-serving. Their political rivals, the Sadducees, believed the soul perished with the body and that the concept of resurrection was a Gentile myth. So the people largely remained in the dark concerning the afterlife.

When Jesus spoke of the kingdom of God, His audiences naturally thought of a physical kingdom on earth, similar to the Roman Empire but ruled by Jewish Law. Indeed, it will be established on earth but only after this world as we know it comes to an end, and it will be unlike any form of government ever conceived. Having explained the profound differences between the present age and the kingdom to come, Jesus needed to fill in a significant gap: What happens between now and the end-time establishment of God's kingdom on earth? If the kingdom will not come until then, why live according to the rules of grace now? If we must live in the dominion of evil until then, why should we not accept its rules and use them to our advantage?

Jesus answered these questions with new revelation; for the first time, people on this side of the grave would know the details of what happens after death and how their behavior in this world affects their experience on the other side.

— 16:19 —

In the previous segment, Jesus warned His followers that one must play by the rules of either this age or the age to come (Luke 16:1-12). Playing by the rules of the present world order requires a ruthless devotion to self and, therefore, the only rule is to win. The rule of the kingdom is grace: humility regarding self, compassion for others, using wealth to advance the status of the poor, using power to uphold truth, and accepting God's free gift of eternal life in exchange for nothing but belief in Him. Furthermore, one *must* choose which kingdom to serve (16:13). He then rebuked the scoffing Pharisees for choosing to serve the dominion of evil while pretending to advance the kingdom of God (16:14-18). With His enemies dizzied by this rebuke, Jesus began a story that would set the record straight in another respect. Because they undermined God on earth (16:16), they would experience His wrath after death.

The story begins as a study in contrast between the two main characters: a man who enjoys great material wealth and a man who has nothing—a billionaire and a beggar. According to the Pharisees, the billionaire's wealth is proof positive of God's favor, which he evidently earned at some point. *Because God is just,* they reasoned, *He does not reward sinfulness; so if a man has great earthly blessing, then God must be very pleased with him.* They also believed, conversely, that poverty or disease indicated God's displeasure. After all, a just God would not allow a just person to suffer unjustly, would He?

Jesus vividly described the billionaire's delight in life. Fine linen lay against his skin while the finest, most expensive material adorned his outer garments. Of all the colors, none were as expensive and scarce as purple. The Greek term translated "splendor" (*lamprōs* [2988]) describes ostentatious luxury, the kind of audacious spending most people can scarcely imagine.

— 16:20-21 —

While the rich man remains anonymous, Jesus named the beggar Lazarus, which raises a question as to whether this is a parable or an actual, metaphysical event about which Jesus had knowledge. The very common name Lazarus derives from the Hebrew name *lazar*, which is a truncated form of Eleazar, meaning "God helps." Because the name has ironic significance in the story, it's likely a parable.

The name is ironic because it appears to run contrary to conventional thinking. A man named "God helps" lies helpless at the gate of the billionaire's home. The expression translated "was laid at his gate" uses the pluperfect, passive form of the verb *ballō* [906] and strongly suggests he was abandoned there. We would say, "He had been dumped at [the rich man's] gate." In ancient cultures—as well as many Eastern societies today—disabled people were taken by family or friends to beg at the entrance of public venues, especially places of worship. At night, they were returned home. In this case, however, Lazarus was not left in a high-traffic, public location but was dumped on the doorstep of a billionaire, not unlike when a baby is left on the doorstep of a hospital. The way Jesus framed the story strongly suggests that Lazarus had become the rich man's responsibility.

Jesus emphasized the contrast between the two men with His description of Lazarus's condition. While the rich man's body was dressed in the finest apparel, the poor man's body was covered in painful abscesses. While the rich man indulged his every appetite, the food which fell from his table would have cured Lazarus's malnourishment. The image of Lazarus longing in vain for food will resurface later. The further detail of dogs licking his wounds makes the image even more pathetic. Jewish society thought of dogs the same way modern city dwellers regard rats: wild, unclean, detestable, worthless creatures.

— 16:22 —

Eventually, both men succumbed to the universal curse of physical death. Note the emphasis given to what happens to the poor man after death. Jesus' audience knew that Lazarus's earthly body would have been carried away to Gehenna (or "the Valley of Hinnom") and burned with the rest of the city's refuse. But whereas the rich man is described as simply being buried, Lazarus was carried by angels to "Abraham's bosom."

The exact meaning of "Abraham's bosom" is disputed, giving rise to a number of elaborate explanations, some more credible than others. In the Old Testament, one was said to be "gathered to his fathers." This notion portrayed the ancient Near Eastern burial custom in which a person was laid to rest on a shelf in the family tomb. Much later, after complete decomposition, the bones of the deceased were gathered up and placed in an ossuary (bone box) along with the bones of their ancestors. So, the literal process of one's bones being gathered to those of one's ancestors became a euphemism for death as well as a poetic image of one's soul being reunited with departed loved ones.

The Lord's expression is sweet. It pictures rest. It suggests vindication in that Lazarus went where Abraham, the Hebrew father of faith, now lives. It says Lazarus is surrounded by the community of God's faithful, whereas he had died alone.

By contrast, the rich man "was buried." The difference in their funerals would have been dramatic. Lazarus would have been unceremoniously hauled to the city dump while the rich man received an elaborate send-off. Five brothers dressed in mourning. Family, friends, associates, city officials, and professional mourners all gathered to weep. Linen burial clothes and a hundred pounds of aromatic spices wrapped the body, which was carefully placed in the burial cave. All this was unspoken by the Lord but undoubtedly vivid in the minds of His audience.

— 16:23-26 —

The contrast on earth is frighteningly reversed after death. While Lazarus rests in the company of God's faithful, the rich man suffers in "torment" or in torture (*basanos* [931]) in "Hades." The Greek term "Hades" (*hadēs* [86]) designated the mythological god of the underworld and was also a generic term roughly equal to *sheol* [H7585], indicating the shadowy netherworld of the dead. In the Gospels of Matthew and Luke, "Hades" is the opposite of "heaven" (Matt. 11:23; 16:18; Luke 10:15).

Hades is a place associated with Satan but not ruled by Him. Eventually, the devil and his demons will be tormented there as well. We might picture Hades as a metaphysical Gehenna ("Valley of Hinnom"), the place where the spiritually dead are burned with other cosmic refuse.

The Lord's imagined dialogue takes place between the rich man and Abraham, not Lazarus or even God. Jesus probably chose Abraham as a means of heaping rebuke on the Pharisees, who believed their pure-blooded, Hebrew pedigree guaranteed their acceptance in God's kingdom. He also wanted to dramatize the separation of faithful and unfaithful Jews. The "great chasm fixed" (16:26) between them not only heightens the sense of distance; it is something no human can span or eliminate, suggesting that God put it there.

Now the roles are reversed. While Lazarus longed for crumbs from the rich man's table, the billionaire begs for a drop of water. Their suffering cannot compare, however; while Lazarus's agony ended, the rich man's will endure for all eternity. And the rich man's suffering is intensified by his overwhelming regret. Jesus placed on the lips of Abraham a rebuke for the billionaire's apathy during life. He could have eased Lazarus's pain, but Abraham is powerless to help him. The time for compassion is before death, never after.

— 16:27-31 —

When convinced of his eternal, perpetual doom, the rich man became greatly concerned for his brothers, who apparently were like him and therefore headed for the same dismal fate. Throughout his life, he had cared only for himself. With money enough to burn, he denied any help to the man dying on his doorstep. With the flames of consequence tormenting his soul, he finally understood in death the truths he had chosen to ignore in life, and he desperately wanted others to make a different choice.

The mention of five brothers introduces a desperately needed element of hope in the story. Perhaps they can be spared this eternal torment, if only a message could be carried to them from the spirit realm. Abraham reminds the rich man that the Lord already sent messages into the physical realm in the form of Scripture—"Moses and the Prophets." In reply, the billionaire suggests that someone returning from the dead will carry irrefutable testimony that no one can ignore. Of course, this foreshadows the Lord's own resurrection. But, Abraham objects, those who don't listen to the Law and the Prophets will be no more likely to change as a result of seeing such a supernatural phenomenon.

• • •

The men and women present that day must have felt dazed by the sudden, completely unexpected glimpse behind the veil separating life from the afterlife. But Jesus didn't give this new revelation simply to satisfy their curiosity. He had no fewer than three specific aims.

First, Jesus wanted to reconnect two ideas the Pharisees had separated: obedience to God and compassion for people. The Pharisees' explanation of evil in the world didn't square with God's. They didn't mind throwing a few crumbs to needy people to make themselves look good or feel good, but some taught that compassion for the needy might interfere with God's retribution for their supposed sin. Jesus called this *hogwash*. The rich man suffered in Hades because He didn't have a relationship with God. His lack of compassion proved it.

Second, Jesus used the negative example of the rich man to warn the Pharisees. They were represented by the five brothers the tormented billionaire wanted to warn. Of all the characters in the story, only the rich man used the word "repent." His anguished cry from beyond the grave became the Lord's appeal to the religious leaders. He said, in effect, "Don't interpret your life of abundance and success to mean that God is pleased with you."

Third, Jesus reaffirmed the superiority of Scripture to all other supposed authorities. Rules and regulations can be helpful. Rituals can help us concentrate on what is meaningful. Traditions can help keep chaos from taking over. But nothing must contradict or supplant God's Word. It is more convincing than the testimony would be of one who comes back from beyond.

APPLICATION: LUKE 16:19-31
Our First Responsibility

The two men in the Lord's parable approached life very differently. We know very little about how Lazarus lived; we know only the tragic way in which he died. The rich man, however, gave himself to two priorities to the exclusion of everything else. He lived to acquire more wealth and then to enjoy it fully. There's nothing wrong with wealth and enjoying it. The problem was his priorities. While he lived sumptuously, a man lay helpless and dying at his gate.

In life, the rich man overlooked his first responsibility: the destiny of his soul. In that regard, I have three statements I trust you will accept as true, if you haven't already.

First, *God's written Word is the most important evidence a person can examine.*

For anyone who would say, "I don't believe all this stuff about Christ, heaven, and hell," I would simply issue a challenge. Don't delve into a lot of religions. Don't start asking for miracles. Don't expect supernatural phenomena to take place. Don't start waiting for visions and dreams. Study the Word of God. Begin reading about what you propose to reject. Examine the evidence and let it say what it says, and then we'll talk about your eternal soul. We'll see what God does in your heart as a result of the study of the Scriptures.

Second, *God's written Word contains the most compelling information to prepare us for death.*

Consider what Scripture says about death. If you are a believer, you will find your fears calmed. Assurance replaces panic. You will see confusion lifted. You will discover there is literally an eternal dwelling place for those who know the Lord Jesus Christ, and God's arms are open.

Third, *the person who ignores the Word of God in life will not be ignored by the God of the Word in eternity.*

Just as there is a heaven to gain, there is a hell to shun. You may not believe it today. Someday you will—I hope, before it's too late.

How Not to Be a Stumbling Block
LUKE 17:1-19

NASB

[1] He said to His disciples, "It is inevitable that ᵃstumbling blocks come, but woe to him through whom they come! [2] It ᵃwould be better for him if a millstone were hung around his neck and he were thrown into the sea, than that he would cause one of these little ones to stumble. [3] ᵃBe on your guard! If your brother sins, rebuke him; and if he repents, forgive him. [4] And if he sins against you seven times a day, and returns to you seven times, saying, 'I repent,' ᵃforgive him."

NLT

[1] One day Jesus said to his disciples, "There will always be temptations to sin, but what sorrow awaits the person who does the tempting! [2] It would be better to be thrown into the sea with a millstone hung around your neck than to cause one of these little ones to fall into sin. [3] So watch yourselves!

"If another believer* sins, rebuke that person; then if there is repentance, forgive. [4] Even if that person wrongs you seven times a day and

⁵The apostles said to the Lord, "In-crease our faith!" ⁶And the Lord said, "If you ªhad faith like a mustard seed, you would say to this mulberry tree, 'Be uprooted and be planted in the sea'; and it would ᵇobey you.

⁷"Which of you, having a slave plowing or tending sheep, will say to him when he has come in from the field, 'Come immediately and ªsit down to eat'? ⁸But will he not say to him, 'Prepare something for me to eat, and *properly* ªclothe yourself and serve me while I eat and drink; and ᵇafterward you ᶜmay eat and drink'? ⁹He does not thank the slave because he did the things which were com-manded, does he? ¹⁰So you too, when you do all the things which are com-manded you, say, 'We are unworthy slaves; we have done *only* that which we ought to have done.'"

¹¹While He was on the way to Jeru-salem, He was passing ªbetween Sa-maria and Galilee. ¹²As He entered a village, ten leprous men who stood at a distance met Him; ¹³and they raised their voices, saying, "Jesus, Master, have mercy on us!" ¹⁴When He saw them, He said to them, "Go and show yourselves to the priests." And as they were going, they were cleansed. ¹⁵Now one of them, when he saw that he had been healed, turned back, glorifying God with a loud voice, ¹⁶and he fell on his face at His feet, giving thanks to Him. And he was a Samaritan. ¹⁷Then Jesus answered and said, "Were there not ten cleansed? But the nine—where are they? ¹⁸ªWas no one found who returned to give glory to God, ex-cept this foreigner?" ¹⁹And He said to him, "Stand up and go; your faith ªhas made you well."

each time turns again and asks for-giveness, you must forgive."

⁵The apostles said to the Lord, "Show us how to increase our faith."

⁶The Lord answered, "If you had faith even as small as a mustard seed, you could say to this mulberry tree, 'May you be uprooted and be planted in the sea,' and it would obey you!

⁷"When a servant comes in from plowing or taking care of sheep, does his master say, 'Come in and eat with me'? ⁸No, he says, 'Prepare my meal, put on your apron, and serve me while I eat. Then you can eat later.' ⁹And does the master thank the ser-vant for doing what he was told to do? Of course not. ¹⁰In the same way, when you obey me you should say, 'We are unworthy servants who have simply done our duty.'"

¹¹As Jesus continued on toward Jerusalem, he reached the border between Galilee and Samaria. ¹²As he entered a village there, ten men with leprosy stood at a distance, ¹³crying out, "Jesus, Master, have mercy on us!"

¹⁴He looked at them and said, "Go show yourselves to the priests."* And as they went, they were cleansed of their leprosy.

¹⁵One of them, when he saw that he was healed, came back to Jesus, shouting, "Praise God!" ¹⁶He fell to the ground at Jesus' feet, thanking him for what he had done. This man was a Samaritan.

¹⁷Jesus asked, "Didn't I heal ten men? Where are the other nine? ¹⁸Has no one returned to give glory to God except this foreigner?" ¹⁹And Jesus said to the man, "Stand up and go. Your faith has healed you.*"

17:1 ªOr *temptations to sin* 17:2 ªLit *is* 17:3 ªLit *Take heed to yourselves* 17:4 ªLit *you shall forgive* 17:6 ªLit *have* ᵇLit *have obeyed* 17:7 ªLit *recline* 17:8 ªLit *gird* ᵇLit *after these things* ᶜLit *will* 17:11 ªLit *through the middle of; or along the borders of* 17:18 ªLit *Were there not found those who* 17:19 ªLit *has saved you*

17:3 Greek *If your brother.* 17:14 See Lev 14:2-32. 17:19 Or *Your faith has saved you.*

The Lord's running discourse cycled back and forth between His followers and His enemies, between people who earnestly followed Him and those seeking opportunities to destroy Him. Each group heard the discourses directed toward the other, so Jesus made the most of each occasion to teach. When instructing the faithful, He warned His adversaries. And when rebuking the unfaithful, He taught His followers by negative example.

In the previous discourse, Jesus encouraged His followers to pursue the kingdom of God with uncompromising loyalty and devotion (16:1-13) and rebuked the scribes and Pharisees for their devotion to the dominion of evil (16:14-31). He even accused the religious authorities of blocking others' access to the kingdom of God with their man-made rules, rituals, and traditions (11:52; 16:16).

After His sobering appeal for the religious leaders to repent (16:19-31), Jesus turned again to His followers. With the negative example of the scribes and Pharisees still fresh on their minds, Jesus warned these potential leaders—those who might lead His budding kingdom on earth—to avoid becoming like His enemies. To help them steer a straight course and become positive examples for others to follow, He suggested four specific actions or attitudes to adopt:

Protect your relationships against lingering resentments. (17:3-4)
Grow toward maturity in faith. (17:5-6)
Serve the kingdom without expectations. (17:7-10)
Cultivate a grateful attitude. (17:11-19)

— 17:1-2 —

Jesus acknowledged the presence of "stumbling blocks" along the path to the kingdom. The Greek term is *skandalon* [4625], which has the literal sense of a stick holding open a baited trap, like a trip wire. Biblical writers, drawing from the Greek translation of the Old Testament, used the term figuratively to describe any means by which a person is brought to their end. In this context, Jesus depicts potential believers walking along a path toward the kingdom's entrance and succumbing to various traps and pitfalls.

Some traps occur naturally. Greed, pride, fear, addictions, compulsions, temptations, distractions—the dangers are legion. Just the same, Jesus warned, "Don't allow yourself to become a danger to others." And He uttered His characteristic, mournful "woe" (6:24-26; 10:13; 11:39-47, 52) upon those who lay traps. He then intensified the seriousness of the sin by calling potential believers needing instruction "little ones," a

Wrong-Way Chuck

LUKE 17:1

I remember when I was a boy of about nine or ten, I ran around with a couple of other fellows, Eugene and Freddy. My mother used to say, "Charles, every time you get with Eugene and Freddy, you get into trouble." I have a feeling that Eugene's mother said, "Eugene, every time you run around with Freddy and Charles, you get into trouble." When we were together, we didn't just get into trouble; we were the trouble.

I remember on one occasion we found a signpost on a street corner that you could turn, and it was a very busy fork in the road. A simple turn of the sign and we could send all kinds of people in the wrong direction. Having been lost in unfamiliar territory many times since then, I regret the frustration we undoubtedly caused. Now that I'm an adult, a man called by God to point the way to the truth, I'm careful to keep all signs pointed in the right direction.

common expression for helpless, innocent children. The image refers to those with the greatest need for instruction or compassion: those who are needy or emotionally wounded or downtrodden by life or ignorant of spiritual matters.

The punishment for contributing to the eternal downfall of another is nothing less than spiritual destruction. Jesus graphically illustrated this punishment with a horrific death. A millstone was a large, exceedingly heavy stone used to grind grain into flour. Jesus combined this with a terrifying archetypal image of chaos and evil in ancient literature: the sea. Moreover, folklore suggested that a body lost to the sea could not be resurrected in the last day, so the thought of sinking to the sea bottom with no hope of surfacing illustrated hopeless, eternal doom.

Barry Beitzel

Ancient millstones were used for grinding grain or pressing olives to produce olive oil.

— 17:3-4 —

Protect your relationships against lingering resentments. Jesus transitioned from the theoretical to the practical with the command "Be on your guard!" The verb (*prosechō* [4337]) means "to be in a state of alert, be concerned about, care for, take care."[37] The present imperative tense calls for an ongoing alertness. To keep from falling into the same destructive patterns as the Pharisees, believers must remain continually vigilant; we do, after all, have the same sinful nature and struggle with the same temptations.

His first area of concern: relationships. Jesus specifically targeted relationships between "brothers"—that is, fellow believers—but not exclusively. His principles have a broad application. Relationships require constant maintenance; otherwise, petty resentments can fester into full-blown feuds, and serious offenses can lead to our downfall. He counseled believers to keep short accounts with others: "If your brother sins, rebuke him."

Presumably, the "sin" is an offense against the person doing the rebuking, not necessarily sin in general. Otherwise, the corresponding command, "Forgive him," would not be appropriate. We do not forgive sins committed against other people or against God. Therefore, Jesus wasn't calling for mutual accountability in general—at least not here.

"Rebuke" expresses the idea of calling attention to wrongdoing and assigning responsibility. The term is a close cousin to "reprove," except the desired response is humility instead of conviction. It carries a strong connotation of warning, implying the possibility of a consequence; therefore, the person confronting a fellow believer must state the sin and define its consequences if the rebuke is ignored.

The Greek verb is an aorist imperative, calling for instantaneous action or action to begin at once. An offense that lingers without redress is like an open wound; even a tiny cut can become infected, jeopardizing the entire body.

Additionally, if the person repents, Jesus called for believers to "forgive him," or literally, "release him." In other words, "Unbind him from his obligation to repay the debt, make up the loss, or suffer retribution." To "release" someone is to set them free from justice. As before, this command occurs as an aorist imperative, pointing to an immediate, instantaneous action. We are to confront immediately and then forgive just as quickly.

His next statement seems to counsel foolishness. Realistically, someone repenting and apologizing nearly fifty times each week would begin to suggest a lack of sincerity; and, in a practical sense, we might want to limit our exposure to continual offenses. Fortunately, He didn't mean that we should continually volunteer for repeated hurt; He used hyperbole—exaggeration for the sake of effect—to emphasize our willingness to forgive.

— 17:5-6 —

Grow toward maturity in faith. The twelve apostles asked for increased faith. They apparently thought of faith as a kind of fuel to accomplish supernatural or superhuman feats, a common misunderstanding today—the idea being "More faith equals greater ability." In His reply, Jesus modified their request to "having faith." To illustrate the unimportance of quantity, He recalled the mustard seed, a common image of insignificance in Jewish teaching and literature. (See comments on 13:19.) To illustrate the power of faith, He pointed to a nearby mulberry tree (related to the sycamore tree of 19:4), known for its resilient, tenacious hold on the soil. Mulberry trees were known for their incredible longevity. The combined illustration portrays the barest traces of faith accomplishing the near-impossible.

Because the twelve apostles (eleven of them, at least) had demonstrated faith by believing in the Messiah and following Him, they already had the faith they needed. It was a matter of exercising their faith. Jesus encouraged them to use the faith they already possessed and to cultivate that skill as they grew toward maturity.

— 17:7-10 —

Serve the kingdom without expectations. Any illustration involving slavery poses a problem for expositors today because of that dark era in American and British history in which people were ripped from their homelands, forced into labor, and treated like chattel. The Greek word *andrapodistēs* [405], or "man-stealing," describes this kind of slavery, which both the Old and New Testaments condemned (Exod. 21:16; 1 Tim. 1:10). While this kind of slavery comprised a sizable population of slaves during Jesus' time, there were at least two other kinds of "slavery" common to ancient economic systems that were practiced in Israel. Slavery could denote "voluntary indenture," and sometimes slavery resulted in adoption. In both cases, a person voluntarily attached themselves to a family, vowing to serve them in exchange for room, board, protection, and community. (See "Slavery in the First Century," page 372.)

The Lord asked a rhetorical question of his disciples that anticipated a no. In the first-century world, slaves were bound to their masters; it was their duty to serve them with wholehearted devotion. I would paraphrase His question this way: "Which of you—if you had a slave—would feel obligated to reward the slave for doing his duties?" The obvious answer is "none." The master-slave relationship maintained certain rules of conduct. If the slave did what was required of him, then the master did not have to reward him with any special privileges or gifts.

Jesus' point is simple. This should be the kind of wholehearted devotion—the kind that does not expect extra reward—that we give to the Lord. God is our superior; we are not His master. We serve Him, not the other way around. He already has brought us into His household as a gift of grace; service is our duty, our responsibility, our privilege. Service to Him is its own reward. He may—and undoubtedly will—reward us with *far* more than any master ever gave a slave, but we have no right to expect anything from our Superior.

The Pharisees, on the other hand, taught an elaborate system of rewards and punishments in their relationship with God. In their self-serving concept of divine justice, God rewarded good behavior with material blessing and punished sin with poverty, disease, disfigurement, and calamities. Therefore, by their reckoning, good deeds put God in the position of debtor!

— 17:11-19 —

Cultivate a grateful attitude. The Greek term translated "leprosy" in the New Testament refers to a wide range of skin diseases, not just what we know today as Hansen's Disease. The evidence for these ten men having this terrifying form of "leprosy," however, is strong. Apparently they had banded together for the sake of mutual care and support, which was necessary in extreme cases; and nine of the ten men were Jews living in Samaria, suggesting their disease made them objects of scorn. Regardless, the label "leper" was a social death sentence. Shame left them few options for survival.

Upon hearing their cry for mercy—from a distance—Jesus commanded them to present themselves to their local priests in obedience to Leviticus 14:1-32. The narrative suggests He did this without even calling the men over. They immediately understood the significance of His order and started out for the nearest synagogue. Luke's grammar suggests the cleansing didn't take place until the men responded to the Lord's command. Literally rendered, the phrase is "In their departing, they were cleansed."

All ten obeyed the Lord's command, expressing belief before seeing the first sign of cleansing. This was good. One returned to express gratitude. This was better. He glorified God, worshiped at Jesus' feet, and expressed gratitude for His gift—an expected response considering the suffering he had escaped as a result of the Lord's compassion. His gratitude is not surprising. The real surprise is that the other nine *didn't* return!

Luke adds the short clarification "He was a Samaritan," which would have caused the Lord's Jewish disciples to wince. The person least likely to behave in a godly way outshined his Jewish counterparts. In this story, Luke offered a gentle, yet poignant, rebuke to his Christian readers. Once again, the person forgiven the most expressed the greatest love and the most gratitude (7:40-47). What could be a greater "stumbling block" to nonbelievers than a Christian with a spirit of entitlement? How much more attractive is a grateful child of God!

• • •

When reading about the Pharisees in the Gospels, it's easy to vilify these leaders of the Jewish community. Two thousand years removed, the modern imagination has them skulking about in black capes, stealing candy from little children. But to people living in first-century Israel, no figures better portrayed godly devotion than these refined, polished, genteel, earnest-looking, vocational ministers of Holy Scripture. The scribes spent hours each day meticulously copying the Scriptures, carefully preserving each jot and stroke in one scroll after another with painstaking accuracy. Because of their dedication, we have trustworthy copies of "the Law, the Prophets, and the Writings." And the Pharisees, for all their pedantic rule-keeping and traditions, did in fact help preserve the nation's Jewishness from evaporating into the ether of Gentile paganism. The scribes and Pharisees were all "good men" as most would judge goodness today.

When we read about the religious leaders in the Gospel accounts, and we hear the Lord's rebukes of them resounding down through the ages, we must not forget their apparent goodness. If we can maintain this balance—as the first-century Jews undoubtedly did—then the Lord's lessons have greater impact. He didn't rebuke obvious villains; He called to account men who thought themselves good.

Jesus said to the men and women who followed Him—all of whom thought themselves good because they followed the Messiah—"Woe to him [or her] through whom [stumbling blocks] come!" (17:1), and "Be [continually] on your guard!" (17:3). He warned all of His followers, for within each of them—and within each of us—there lurks a Pharisee who thinks himself good and must be rebuked daily. And He gave His followers no fewer than four specific ways to keep the Pharisee within in check. If we fail at these, we run a grave risk of becoming the very villains who stood condemned before Christ. (God forbid!)

My Time in the Leper Colony

LUKE 17:12

When I served on the island of Okinawa, I was a member of the Third Division Marine Corps Band. On one occasion, we were invited to a leprosarium on the north end of Okinawa to play a concert, and the memory of those men and women will never leave me.

There we sat in precise rows, decked out in our dress blues, our instruments polished and gleaming. And there they sat, slumped under the weight of pain and fatigue. Mangled bodies bearing the remnants of human faces. Their limbs wrapped in strips of cloth, some of them oozing blood. Many of them tried to cover their deformed faces with their stumps in a pathetic attempt to cover shame and unworthiness. It broke my heart to see them feeling so unworthy because of a condition they neither caused nor deserved.

While we played, the desperately ill men and women listened in rapt attention. I could barely play my instrument through the sadness weighing upon my heart, seeing bodies horrifically distorted by the disease we now call Hansen's. I'll never forget the sound of their applause, which they offered by banging stumps of limbs together or tapping their crutches on the floor or against their chairs.

I would have given almost anything to have the power of healing that day. What a joy it must have been for Jesus to reach down into the sea of human depravity and snatch a soul from the clutches of disease! One day soon, Jesus will empty the hospitals, the leper colonies, and even the graveyards of the world. Then we will live in a world without darkness, sin, suffering, disease, and death. We have His promise on that. And I, for one, can't wait for Him to return!

APPLICATION: LUKE 17:1-19

Clearing the Way

Evangelism is the Lord's job. He will be faithful to bring all who are His into the kingdom (John 6:37, 39). He has called us to join Him in this great, kingdom-building enterprise and has given us a genuine stake in its success. But, ultimately, He is responsible for saving people, regardless of what we do. In other words, if God wants to save someone, they will be saved, often in spite of our failures.

Even so, He will hold us accountable for the influence we have on others and their decision to either accept His gift of grace or reject Christ. The Lord's grave warning against becoming a hindrance should prompt us to examine the influence we have on others. We have two broad areas to consider.

First, *small matters*. Of course, egregious sins like murder, adultery, embezzlement, or grand theft auto will present a problem for nonbelievers. That's not where we're most likely to cause others to stumble. In my experience, it's not the big things that cause another person to stumble, but the little things. I've had a few people in my life—more than I care to recall—who have said to me on occasion, "This particular thing you did really offended me." And almost without exception, it wasn't a big thing; it was little. It was "small" in the sense that I had forgotten all about it, but it was significant to that other person.

Let me challenge you to do something a little risky, something that might make you feel uncomfortable but is worth the effort. Approach some of the people in your life and say, "It occurs to me that I might have hurt your feelings or caused you grief by something I did in the past. If so, I would like to know about it. Have I ever offended you?" Then, just listen. Don't explain. Don't defend. Just listen and empathize with them.

Of course you have offended others. There's no question about that. By asking the question, you give people permission to address one or two particular incidents that continue to bother them.

A second area to consider: *things we can do, or should do, that we don't do*. When we forgive someone, we need to say something to close the issue. I heard one man say, "This is in the past; I will never bring it up again." That was marvelous. What a huge relief to hear those words!

When someone needs encouragement, we should be the first to

cheer them on. And when a complimentary thought pops into our minds, we have an opportunity to say it! Why keep to ourselves something that is affirming to others?

When given the opportunity to serve, we should jump in with enthusiasm, while setting aside any thoughts of compensation or gratitude or recognition or even a "thank you." Just serve.

When something good happens, we would do well to thank God audibly. Not with a big show, but with a simple "Thank you, Lord." Or perhaps an appreciative comment about His goodness in a particular situation. And, if the good we experience comes from another person, we *must* go out of our way to express our thanks. For example, at the restaurant, leave a generous tip.

Knowing Where You Are . . . Knowing Where You're Going
LUKE 17:20-37

NASB

20 Now having been questioned by the Pharisees as to when the kingdom of God was coming, He answered them and said, "The kingdom of God is not coming with ªsigns to be observed; 21 nor will they say, 'Look, here it is!' or, 'There it is!' For behold, the kingdom of God is ªin your midst."

22 And He said to the disciples, "The days will come when you will long to see one of the days of the Son of Man, and you will not see it. 23 They will say to you, 'Look there! Look here!' Do not go away, and do not run after them. 24 For just like the lightning, when it flashes out of one part ªof the sky, shines to the other part ªof the sky, so will the Son of Man be in His day. 25 But first He must suffer many things and be rejected by this generation. 26 And just as it happened in the days of Noah, so it will be also in the days of the Son of Man: 27 they were eating, they were drinking, they were marrying,

NLT

20 One day the Pharisees asked Jesus, "When will the Kingdom of God come?"

Jesus replied, "The Kingdom of God can't be detected by visible signs.* 21 You won't be able to say, 'Here it is!' or 'It's over there!' For the Kingdom of God is already among you.*"

22 Then he said to his disciples, "The time is coming when you will long to see the day when the Son of Man returns,* but you won't see it. 23 People will tell you, 'Look, there is the Son of Man,' or 'Here he is,' but don't go out and follow them. 24 For as the lightning flashes and lights up the sky from one end to the other, so it will be on the day* when the Son of Man comes. 25 But first the Son of Man must suffer terribly* and be rejected by this generation.

26 "When the Son of Man returns, it will be like it was in Noah's day. 27 In those days, the people enjoyed

NASB

they were being given in marriage, until the day that Noah entered the ark, and the flood came and destroyed them all. ²⁸ªIt was the same as happened in the days of Lot: they were eating, they were drinking, they were buying, they were selling, they were planting, they were building; ²⁹ but on the day that Lot went out from Sodom it rained fire and ªbrimstone from heaven and destroyed them all. ³⁰ It will be ªjust the same on the day that the Son of Man is revealed. ³¹ On that day, the one who is on the housetop and whose goods are in the house must not go down to take them out; and likewise the one who is in the field must not turn back. ³² Remember Lot's wife. ³³ Whoever seeks to keep his ªlife will lose it, and whoever loses *his life* will preserve it. ³⁴ I tell you, on that night there will be two in one bed; one will be taken and the other will be left. ³⁵ There will be two women grinding at the same place; one will be taken and the other will be left. ³⁶ [ªTwo men will be in the field; one will be taken and the other will be left."] ³⁷ And answering they said to Him, "Where, Lord?" And He said to them, "Where the body *is*, there also the ªvultures will be gathered."

17:20 ªLit *observation* 17:21 ªOr *within you*
17:24 ªLit *under heaven* 17:28 ªLit *In the same way as* 17:29 ªI.e. burning sulfur 17:30 ªLit *according to the same things* 17:33 ªOr *soul*
17:36 ªEarly mss do not contain this v
17:37 ªOr *eagles*

NLT

banquets and parties and weddings right up to the time Noah entered his boat and the flood came and destroyed them all.

²⁸ "And the world will be as it was in the days of Lot. People went about their daily business—eating and drinking, buying and selling, farming and building—²⁹ until the morning Lot left Sodom. Then fire and burning sulfur rained down from heaven and destroyed them all. ³⁰ Yes, it will be 'business as usual' right up to the day when the Son of Man is revealed. ³¹ On that day a person out on the deck of a roof must not go down into the house to pack. A person out in the field must not return home. ³² Remember what happened to Lot's wife! ³³ If you cling to your life, you will lose it, and if you let your life go, you will save it. ³⁴ That night two people will be asleep in one bed; one will be taken, the other left. ³⁵ Two women will be grinding flour together at the mill; one will be taken, the other left.*"

³⁷ "Where will this happen, Lord?"* the disciples asked.

Jesus replied, "Just as the gathering of vultures shows there is a carcass nearby, so these signs indicate that the end is near."*

17:20 Or *by your speculations.* 17:21 Or *is within you,* or *is in your grasp.* 17:22 Or *long for even one day with the Son of Man.* "Son of Man" is a title Jesus used for himself. 17:24 Some manuscripts do not include *on the day.* 17:25 Or *suffer many things.* 17:35 Some manuscripts add verse 36, *Two men will be working in the field; one will be taken, the other left.* Compare Matt 24:40. 17:37a Greek *"Where, Lord?"*
17:37b Greek *"Wherever the carcass is, the vultures gather."*

From the earliest days of His ministry, Jesus proclaimed the coming of God's kingdom, always in reference to Himself and usually in the present tense (4:17-21; 6:20; 9:27; 10:9; 11:20). Yet He also spoke of the kingdom as a future event, closely associated with the end of days (11:2; 13:28). At still other times, He spoke of the kingdom's establishment not as an event but as a process (13:18-21). Everyone, including the Pharisees, wanted to know when the kingdom of God would finally overthrow the dominion of evil. After all, if anyone should know the plans for the kingdom, it would be its King.

The truth Jesus had to tell was neither easy to explain nor pleasant to hear. Like a five-year-old asking where babies come from, the people of His generation didn't have the ability to understand the complex issues involved—at least not yet. Therefore, Jesus answered their questions in a way that prepared them for the future without overwhelming their limited ability to comprehend. With the cross still before Him, the Messiah unveiled the future for followers and enemies alike.

— 17:20-21 —

Luke presents the Lord's view of the kingdom of God in two parts. In the first part, Jesus briefly answered the Pharisees' question about the timing of the kingdom. Their curiosity may have been genuine, but Luke insinuates a lack of sincerity. The Lord offered only a cursory reply. Note its relative length compared to the teaching He gave His followers.

Jesus didn't answer the Pharisees' question—at least not directly. He merely demonstrated that the nature of the kingdom of God shares this in common with all kingdoms: A kingdom is never far from its king. In fact, a kingdom *is* its king. In Luke's narration of the event, Jesus pointed to Himself as He said, in effect, "The kingdom is right here!"

He didn't reveal any more details about the kingdom because they were not relevant. People who reject the King need to know nothing more about His government.

— 17:22-24 —

In the second part, when instructing His followers, Jesus explained all that He could—as much as they could hear. He began by gently removing their flawed expectations.

First, the kingdom will not come right away. From the standpoint of His earthly ministry looking forward, there would come a time when the followers of the Messiah would long for the kingdom but would not see it. By calling the kingdom "the days of the Son of Man" (see Isa. 13:9; Joel 1:15; 2:1, 31; 3:14; Zeph. 1:14-16; Mal. 4:1, 5), Jesus reaffirmed His earlier statement that the kingdom and its King are one and the same. In this way, He essentially told them that both will disappear for a time.

Furthermore, during the absence of the King, people will claim the kingdom has come in one form or another, but they will be wrong.

When the kingdom returns—in the person of its King—there will be no mistaking it. The image of lightning flashing across the sky illustrates both dramatic suddenness and broad visibility. Lightning also carries strong supernatural connotations.

Theologians debate which event Jesus had in mind when describing this obvious, highly visible inauguration of His kingdom. Did He mean His resurrection, His ascension, the sending of the Holy Spirit, or His return in power (the Second Coming)? The general character of the Lord's description in the following verses leans heavily toward the last option: the consummate manifestation of the King and the establishment of the kingdom of God on earth.

— 17:25-27 —

After removing the faulty expectations of His followers, Jesus revealed some difficult truths about how the kingdom would be established on earth. Before "the days of the Son of Man," the King must suffer and be rejected by "this generation" (*genea* [1074]), a reference to the nation of Israel (see Luke 7:31; 11:29-32, 50-51; 21:32). He predicted a time of uncertainty following His suffering and rejection, a time in which evil becomes complacent in its apparent victory (cf. 11:21-23). Jesus illustrated the attitudes of nonbelievers during this time using two familiar stories from the Old Testament.

The first recalls Noah's generation, people who carried on with normal life even as Noah built the ark. The expression "eating, drinking, marrying, and giving in marriage" doesn't describe specific sins; it merely depicts a society living blissfully in the moment and planning for the future. Of course, from the standpoint of history, we know they had no future, which is precisely the point. They watched as Noah labored on his ark for 120 years, they lived as though the world would always be as it was, and then they perished in the Flood.

— 17:28-29 —

The second story from history recalls the days of Lot. Even as Lot's uncle, Abraham, interceded on behalf of Sodom and Gomorrah, pleading for divine mercy on their behalf (Gen. 18:22-33), the doomed inhabitants lived as if everything were normal. The Lord commanded Lot to take his family away from the notoriously sinful cities, warning that none of the family should look back while escaping the destruction (Gen. 19:17). Soon afterward, fire and molten sulfur rained down on the cities, reducing the entire valley to nothing. Unfortunately, Lot's wife disobeyed the Lord's warning; she cast a longing look over her shoulder and suddenly turned to a pillar of salt (Gen. 19:26).

— 17:30-33 —

In Luke 17:30, the Greek sentence reads, literally, "According to the same things, it will be on the day the Son of Man is made manifest." In a generalized sense, this most likely refers to the main point of both illustrations: People will continue to live in blissful ignorance, rejecting the testimonies of godly men and women until their world undergoes a cataclysmic change. Some expositors downplay the "cataclysmic change" parts of these illustrations, but we dare not set them aside or minimize their seriousness.

The Lord carried the illustrations forward and graphically applied them to the future day of His manifestation. The images of the "one on the housetop" and the "one who is in the field" convey the ideas of making haste and remembering priorities. In the same spirit, we might say, "When the house is on fire, don't try to save the coin collection; escape with your life!" Lot's wife looked back, mourning the life she had left, and her desire to carry her old life with her became the means of her death.

Jesus applied the illustrations in a familiar way. One can cling to only one kind of "life." The life of this world, defined by the pursuit of "wealth" (16:13), will result in eternal, spiritual death. Life in the kingdom demands putting to death any desire for "wealth." We must not become like Lot's wife when it comes to preserving our earthly comforts. We must move toward the kingdom with haste, as though the world were on fire. It soon will be.

— 17:34-36 —

Jesus concluded with a haunting, foreboding image consisting of two or three vignettes.[38] In each, the scene is the same. Two exist together for a time and then something occurs to separate them. One is "taken," the other left behind. The verb translated "taken" is not "raptured" but *paralambanō* [3880], which means "to take along" or "to bring along with" (cf. 9:10, 28).

Paul revealed more about this event when believers in Thessalonica began to wonder if the kingdom had come and they were left behind. He reassured them that no genuine citizen of the kingdom would miss the coming of the King. He will appear in the sky, accompanied by the blast of a trumpet and the shout of an angel—as obvious and unmistakable as lightning. "The dead in Christ will rise first. Then we who are alive and remain will be caught up together with them in the clouds to meet the Lord in the air, and so we shall always be with the Lord" (1 Thes. 4:16-17). The unsuspecting men and women who carried out their lives without regard for the kingdom of God will remain.

If the illustrations of Noah and Lot are any indication, the one "left" is abandoned to judgment and condemnation; the other is "taken" to safety.

— 17:37 —

Expositors differ on the nature of the disciples' question. The apostles asked, simply, "Where, Lord?" The lack of any clarifying phrase strongly suggests we look at what was just said to figure out what the disciples meant. Because Jesus ended with "the other will be left," it makes the most sense that the disciples' question, "Where, Lord," is essentially asking, "Where is the one left for judgment?"

Jesus replied with what may have been an idiom or even an allusion to Job 39:30. A good paraphrase would be, "If you want to find a dead body, look for the circling of vultures." His cryptic answer pointed to the earth as the place of death, as evidenced by the carrion birds of evil. Evil and death are always found in the same places. In the eschatological sense (referring to the end times, after His return in power and judgment of unbelievers), His statement will have a literal fulfillment (Rev. 19:21).

• • •

While Jesus always spoke prophetically—that is, forthtelling the Word of God—He rarely foretold future events. And like all revelation of future history, it is tantalizingly detailed, yet frustratingly vague. After Jesus died, rose again, ascended to heaven, and sent the Holy Spirit, His followers understood much more; and, therefore, so do we. Still, much remains a mystery.

While His discourse on future events fails to satisfy our every curiosity, it is enough—more than enough—if we take time to absorb the information He did provide instead of lament the gaps that only the future can fill. After all, prophecy was not given so that we will know all the details related to the future; it was given so that we will know how to obey when the time is right. Like a road map, prophecy tells you where you are, where you are going, and how to get there alive.

You have the map; now drive carefully!

APPLICATION: LUKE 17:20-37

Strength for Today, Advice for Tomorrow

When present circumstances are difficult, the future can seem downright terrifying. Jesus understood this as well as anyone, so He gave special attention to helping His followers make sense of their circumstances. He gave them valuable perspective on the present, and He provided just enough information about the future to help them live joyfully.

Based on the Lord's discourse about the future of the kingdom and His followers' place in it, let me offer three perspectives regarding the future. While these anticipate the coming kingdom, each has value for today.

First, *be willing to submit your vision of the future to the Lord's, even if His will is a mystery.*

The disciples expected a certain kind of future, along with a certain kind of messiah to lead them there. They envisioned Jesus outwitting His enemies to claim the throne of Israel. They imagined Him leading the nation to independence from Rome. They saw a miraculous Jewish renaissance and the expansion of the Messiah's world empire. But Jesus had a different agenda for the kingdom, one His followers would struggle to understand.

Die? On a cross? How will *that* rebuild a nation?

God has ordained a future for Israel and all of humanity that is far greater than anyone in the first century could have imagined. In fact, two thousand years of reflection on the Lord's redemptive plan has done only a little to expand our appreciation for its greatness. But soon enough, we will understand.

On an individual level, God has plans for you, too. How quickly you can accept His agenda for your life depends on how quickly you're ready to abandon your own.

Second, *don't let present circumstances cloud your vision of the future.*

Wall Street investment firms continually warn customers, "Past returns are not an indication of future performance." That's bad news in a good market, but great news when the economy slumps. And the same goes for circumstances. When things are going well in life, we are foolish to think that good times never end. And when struggling to overcome difficulties, we naturally wonder if we'll ever see blue sky again.

It's helpful to remember that, though circumstances change, God and His Word never change. This may sound trite, but trust me, you need the mind-stabilizing effects of Scripture in both good times and bad. Scripture will give you wisdom to prepare for downturns and hope to survive misfortune. You need the perspective of the Bible.

Third, *remember that this world is not your home.*

On a larger scale, never forget that the present world order will give way to a completely different future. A cataclysmic reordering of the world is imminent; we have been forewarned. Remember Noah. Expect the days of the Son of Man. Keep your eyes on the horizon of world events and prepare accordingly.

And don't forget Lot's wife. No thing is worth turning back for.

You Want to Be Godly? Start Here!
LUKE 18:1-17

NASB

¹ Now He was telling them a parable to show that at all times they ought to pray and not to lose heart, ² saying, "In a certain city there was a judge who did not fear God and did not respect man. ³ There was a widow in that city, and she kept coming to him, saying, 'ᵃGive me legal protection from my opponent.' ⁴ For a while he was unwilling; but afterward he said to himself, 'Even though I do not fear God nor respect man, ⁵ yet because this widow bothers me, I will ᵃgive her legal protection, otherwise by continually coming she will ᵇwear me out.'" ⁶ And the Lord said, "Hear what the unrighteous judge said; ⁷ now, will not God bring about justice for His elect who cry to Him day and night, ᵃand will He delay long over them? ⁸ I tell you that He will bring about justice for them quickly. However, when the Son of Man comes, will He find ᵃfaith on the earth?"

⁹ And He also told this parable to

NLT

¹ One day Jesus told his disciples a story to show that they should always pray and never give up. ² "There was a judge in a certain city," he said, "who neither feared God nor cared about people. ³ A widow of that city came to him repeatedly, saying, 'Give me justice in this dispute with my enemy.' ⁴ The judge ignored her for a while, but finally he said to himself, 'I don't fear God or care about people, ⁵ but this woman is driving me crazy. I'm going to see that she gets justice, because she is wearing me out with her constant requests!'"

⁶ Then the Lord said, "Learn a lesson from this unjust judge. ⁷ Even he rendered a just decision in the end. So don't you think God will surely give justice to his chosen people who cry out to him day and night? Will he keep putting them off? ⁸ I tell you, he will grant justice to them quickly! But when the Son of Man* returns, how many will he find on the earth who have faith?"

⁹ Then Jesus told this story to some

some people who trusted in themselves that they were righteous, and viewed others with contempt: ¹⁰ "Two men went up into the temple to pray, one a Pharisee and the other a tax collector. ¹¹ The Pharisee stood and was praying this to himself: 'God, I thank You that I am not like other people: swindlers, unjust, adulterers, or even like this tax collector. ¹² I fast twice a week; I pay tithes of all that I get.' ¹³ But the tax collector, standing some distance away, was even unwilling to lift up his eyes to heaven, but was beating his breast, saying, 'God, be ªmerciful to me, the sinner!' ¹⁴ I tell you, this man went to his house justified rather than the other; for everyone who exalts himself will be humbled, but he who humbles himself will be exalted."

¹⁵ And they were bringing even their babies to Him so that He would touch them, but when the disciples saw it, they *began* rebuking them. ¹⁶ But Jesus called for them, saying, "Permit the children to come to Me, and do not hinder them, for the kingdom of God belongs to such as these. ¹⁷ Truly I say to you, whoever does not receive the kingdom of God like a child will not enter it *at all.*"

18:3 ªLit *Do me justice* **18:5** ªLit *do her justice* ᵇLit *hit me under the eye* **18:7** ªOr *and yet He is very patient toward them* **18:8** ªLit *the faith* **18:13** ªOr *propitious*

who had great confidence in their own righteousness and scorned everyone else: ¹⁰ "Two men went to the Temple to pray. One was a Pharisee, and the other was a despised tax collector. ¹¹ The Pharisee stood by himself and prayed this prayer*: 'I thank you, God, that I am not like other people—cheaters, sinners, adulterers. I'm certainly not like that tax collector! ¹² I fast twice a week, and I give you a tenth of my income.'

¹³ "But the tax collector stood at a distance and dared not even lift his eyes to heaven as he prayed. Instead, he beat his chest in sorrow, saying, 'O God, be merciful to me, for I am a sinner.' ¹⁴ I tell you, this sinner, not the Pharisee, returned home justified before God. For those who exalt themselves will be humbled, and those who humble themselves will be exalted."

¹⁵ One day some parents brought their little children to Jesus so he could touch and bless them. But when the disciples saw this, they scolded the parents for bothering him.

¹⁶ Then Jesus called for the children and said to the disciples, "Let the children come to me. Don't stop them! For the Kingdom of God belongs to those who are like these children. ¹⁷ I tell you the truth, anyone who doesn't receive the Kingdom of God like a child will never enter it."

18:8 "Son of Man" is a title Jesus used for himself. **18:11** Some manuscripts read *stood and prayed this prayer to himself.*

Prayer is a mysterious thing—at least with respect to the God of Scripture. Pagan prayer, on the other hand, makes perfect sense. In false religions, prayer is merely part of a transaction, a process in which petitioners attempt to bend the will of the deity to give them what they want. Therefore, pagan prayers always involve bargaining (promising to do this or that in exchange for a positive answer), bribing (making large donations to gain a favorable hearing), begging (making oneself pitiful enough to warrant kindness), and justification (proving oneself worthy of divine favor). That's what makes pagan prayer uncomplicated—arduous and painstaking, yet straightforward—because it reduces the deity to the level of a vending machine. Insert enough money, perform the correct button-pushing ritual, and out pops the fulfillment of your request. The deity might require some additional shaking, but that's just part of the process.

Prayer before God, however, is exactly the opposite. The God of the Bible cannot be bribed or manipulated. He needs nothing, so we have nothing to offer that might convince Him to do what we want. And He knows our hearts, so there's no use trying to inform Him or appear worthy of favor. Furthermore, He's completely sovereign, so He will not abandon His agenda to serve ours. Therefore, prayer before God is not an exercise in manipulation, but a necessary part of a relationship. He is a relational Being who desires personal interaction. Unlike pagan prayer, which is simple yet demanding, prayer with God is complex yet effortless—complex because He is a personality, not a vending machine, and effortless because He welcomes us into His presence.

Jesus knew His followers would face difficult and uncertain days. His march to the cross and His agonizing death in Jerusalem would carry them to their lowest emotional depths, leaving them feeling God-forsaken and confused. Even after His triumphant resurrection, His people would still face difficulties and disappointments. After all, living in the dominion of evil as citizens of God's kingdom would not be easy. Therefore, Jesus wanted to encourage them to pray, even when it seemed like God wasn't listening. Jesus encouraged His followers to:

Pray with persistence. (18:1-8)
Pray with humility. (18:9-17)

— 18:1-2 —

Pray with persistence. This is another instance of teaching by negative example. Jesus frequently used ungodly human behavior to show the superiority of God. Earlier, Jesus made the point that earthly fathers love their children and desire to give them nice things (11:10-13); so, how much more would the Lord, who is perfect in love, desire to give us what we need? Using the same logic, Jesus told the story of an unrighteous judge.

In ancient times, people took their disputes to a respected elder in the community or even a council of elders, whose word carried weight. According to Jewish Law and tradition, certain wise, devout men were designated by the temple to act as arbiters in their particular regions, settling minor disputes according to the Law (see Exod. 18:19-22; Deut. 1:13, 15; 2 Chr. 19:5-10). They were to be "able men who fear God, men of truth, those who hate dishonest gain" (Exod. 18:21).

This man took the job of judge, yet served only his own interests; he didn't honor God's values in his deliberations, nor did he care for the needs of people.

— 18:3-5 —

The Old Testament Scriptures commanded that all people, not only judges, care for the rights and welfare of the helpless, especially widows and orphans (Exod. 22:22-24; Pss. 68:5; 146:9; Isa. 1:17; Jer. 7:6-7). Yet this man wouldn't rule in the woman's favor or protect the woman from her opponent's attempt to defraud her. The story reflected a common scenario in which unscrupulous people trumped up debts against a widow in order to place a lien against her property. Without the aid of a husband or children to help her raise crops or produce income, she was helpless. Her only hope: legal protection.

The Lord characterized the judge as having no regard for God or people, implying he favored the widow's opponent because it was politically, socially, and financially advantageous to turn a blind eye to injustice. Were it not for sheer exasperation, he would have ignored justice. The descriptive Greek idiom translated "wear me out" literally means "give me a black eye" (cf. 1 Cor. 9:27). It was sometimes used figuratively to mean "to defame" or "to castigate." It has the idea of pummeling someone in the boxing ring of public opinion.[39] Her persistence triggered the judge's desire to serve himself, and he became her advocate to preserve his own reputation.

— 18:6-7 —

Jesus applied the parable predictably. If the unrighteous judge will dispense justice in response to the desperate woman's persistent petitioning, how much more can we count on God, who is perfectly righteous, to do what is right on behalf of "His elect"?

The expression "His elect" is a crucial qualification. The term translated "elect" means "chosen," and it is a highly significant (and controversial) concept in Christian theology (see Matt. 24:22; Rom. 8:33; Col. 3:12; 2 Tim. 2:10; Titus 1:1). Throughout the Old Testament, God is depicted as choosing certain people for special blessing and/or salvation, and His choice was *always* an expression of His grace, apart from any merit in the persons He selected.

Yet, God is very rarely portrayed as selecting individuals in Old Testament times; His election almost always involved groups. In this case, the Greek term is plural—"elect ones" (Luke 18:7). The qualification "elect ones" limits this application to believers. Furthermore, the granting of justice is to the collection of believers, not merely to one individual. While individuals are important to God, in this lesson, the expression of prayer is corporate.

Note also the content of the petition in both the parable and in the application. It is for justice. Jesus didn't suggest that persistent repetition of one's selfish desire for one thing or another would eventually wear down God's resolve. The topic is justice, and God is by nature just. Therefore, we do not have to bend God's will to ours; we can expect justice because it is something both God and His elect long to see. If we do not see justice quickly, we can be sure it is not because God doesn't want His people to receive fair treatment; we can safely assume that other, unseen factors are at work. Often, "justice rolls down" slowly (Amos 5:24). His ways are not our ways (Isa. 55:8).

— 18:8 —

The Lord's concluding statement bears two important implications. First, expect delayed justice, but count on seeing righteousness prevail in the end. The promise to dispense justice "quickly" should be interpreted "as quickly as possible." The literal translation is "in haste."

Second, "His elect" bear some responsibility during the Messiah's absence; they have a duty to perform. Having encouraged His followers to persistently pray for justice on earth (Luke 11:2; 18:7), His rhetorical question points toward faith—not merely trust in His work on earth or His ability to save us from sin, but belief in His imminent return. He called His followers to pray persistently and with confident expectation of fulfillment.

— 18:9 —

Pray with humility. Luke transitions to another parable of Jesus with an explanation about His present audience. He doesn't single them out as Pharisees in particular, but his lengthy description appears to fit them. Furthermore, Jesus featured a Pharisee in His story. It's reasonable to conclude, therefore, that His listeners admired the Pharisees and, being like them, thought themselves righteous. They placed confidence in their own ability to earn God's favor through good deeds and religious devotion. Moreover, they viewed God's relationship with humanity as a moral high-jump contest in which the best performers were saved and underachievers were judged.

— 18:10-12 —

Jesus compared the prayers of two men. The Pharisees ranked among the highest esteemed Jews in terms of religious effort, while tax collectors, as traitors to their people, were considered worse than Gentiles or even Samaritans. A Jew of Jews stood in close proximity to a Roman collaborator as both appealed to God.

The Lord described the prayer of the Pharisee in terms we would find comical today. The arrogance and self-righteousness almost make a caricature of the man, except it was quite accurate! In his book *The Life and Times of Jesus the Messiah*, Alfred Edersheim includes this actual prayer from rabbinic literature:

> I thank Thee, O Lord my God, that Thou hast put my part with those who sit in the Academy, and not with those who sit at the corners [money-changers and traders]. For, I rise early and they rise early: I rise early to the words of the Law, and they to vain things. I labour and they labour: I labour and receive a reward, they labour and receive no reward. I run and they run: I run to the life of the world to come, and they to the pit of destruction.'[40]

The Pharisee cleverly couched praise for himself in the form of thanks to God! If he asked for anything, he expected the Lord to grant him favor because he had earned it. He personified arrogance even in his prayers.

— 18:13-14 —

By complete contrast, the tax collector stood "some distance away," probably along the outer perimeter of the Court of Israel, within sight of the Pharisee (18:11). His "standing away" conveys his sense of unworthiness to approach God, whose presence was represented by the altar complex at the center of the court. The act of beating one's breast accompanies mourning (see comments on 8:52-53); in this case, mourning for the death of his own righteousness and for deserving God's judgment for sin. And rather than present himself as worthy before God, the man openly acknowledged his guilt.

The Greek term rendered "be merciful" in Luke 18:13 is the same word that is used in the Septuagint—the Greek translation of the Hebrew Scriptures—to translate the Hebrew word *kippur* [H3722], as in

Yom Kippur or Day of Atonement. The mercy he requests is atoning, propitiating grace. There's no long, drawn-out process, no great promises to do this or stop doing that, no impressive words, no profound statements of faith. The humble man simply asks for God to cover his sins with atoning blood.

Jesus applied the parable with special focus on the tax collector's humility in contrast to the Pharisee's pride. Both men left the temple for home, but only one arrived "justified" (*dikaioō* [1344]), which describes the legal status of a defendant before a judge—a legal standing that ultimately determines that person's future. If a person is considered "just," they will not receive punishment. If, on the other hand, a person is considered "unjust," they face fines, imprisonment, or worse. In human courts, one must prove one's innocence in order to be declared just by the judge; but in God's courtroom, one may emerge justified only by grace.

Jesus juxtaposed two terms: "exalt" and "humble." "Exalt" is a common figurative use of the verb *hypsoō* [5312], which also means "to lift up." "Humble" is a translation of the verb *tapeinoō* [5013], which also means "to make low" or "to make small or insignificant." Jesus spoke figuratively to describe two attitudes leading to very different outcomes. Therefore, context must help define what Jesus meant with each notion.

In the first line of the couplet, "exalt" describes the Pharisee's attempt to justify himself, to prove himself righteous before God. Because everyone stands irrefutably guilty before our Creator and Judge, this can lead only to being "made low," a grossly understated description of condemnation to hell.

In the second line, "humble" describes an attitude expressed physically by bowing the head, kneeling down, or even prostrating oneself. Humility does not lead one to feel inferior or to doubt one's own worth. Self-loathing is not the path to humility. Thinking too little of oneself is actually a subtle form of pride. On the contrary, humility is seeing oneself as God does. The tax collector gave himself the one-word label that all people deserve to wear: "sinner."

Humility before God prompts Him to "lift up" the repentant sinner—not only to a place of undeserved honor, but all the way to heaven!

— 18:15-17 —

After presenting two complementary parables teaching persistence and humility in prayer, Luke describes an encounter that illustrates both persistence and humility. What believers are expected to do in prayer is pictured through the actions of those who were bringing their "babies" (the Greek term for infants or toddlers) to be "touched." This refers to the tradition of an elder placing his hand on the head of a person to pronounce a blessing (Gen. 48:14-15; Mark 10:16)—menial work for an important rabbi. What's more, the verb translated "were bringing" shows this to be an ongoing process, describing either repeated or continual action, perhaps involving a long line of people seeking a blessing from Jesus. That takes persistence! The disciples may have intended to rescue the Lord from the monotonous task by rebuking the parents. The term for "rebuked" means "to blame" or "to express strong disapproval."

Jesus turned the rebuke around to fall upon the disciples. He swung the verbal sword both ways, saying, "Permit . . . and don't hinder!" Throughout ancient history—primarily in Gentile, pagan societies—children represented helplessness and, to a certain degree, worthlessness. In the most pragmatic terms, children consume resources and provide very little to the community in the form of work. Hebrew ethics took a higher view, of course, regarding children as a long-term blessing to build one's legacy.

To Jesus, children were not the least valuable in kingdom society; on the contrary, they represented the ideal citizen: guileless, helpless, quick to believe, unself-conscious, and without worry over questions of acceptability. He never considered children a nuisance; He welcomed them with enthusiasm. (Children don't run toward frowning, crotchety adults.) And the Father is no different. He throws open the doors of heaven to childlike faith, and He delights to welcome the prayers of His children. What a picture of humility!

APPLICATION: LUKE 18:1-17

Baby Steps toward Godliness

Most Christians I know have the same objective in life: to be godly. The more serious a person is about their faith, the greater the desire to be a godly man or woman. Even though that is such a clear and desirable objective, how few of us ever feel we achieve it! Perhaps we do not grow in godliness because we don't know how to begin.

Like any worthwhile pursuit, godliness begins with prayer. When teaching His followers how to pray, the Lord didn't give them words to memorize or even a formula to follow. He gave them a few guidelines and then modeled prayer for them (11:1-4). He also provided positive and negative examples in these two parables.

Taking these examples as a starting point, consider three suggestions to help you with the first steps in your journey toward godliness.

Stop fretting and complaining; take your worries to God.

God gave us prayer as an antidote to worry and stress. Set aside special times to pray, even if it's no more than five or ten minutes. And then keep a running dialogue with God throughout your day. Redirect all of your worrying energy by channeling your stress into prayer. Turn complaints into a steady stream of petitions to God.

As I say that, be prepared for a certain level of frustration. He probably will not answer your requests like you might hope. He is creative, endlessly resourceful, sovereign, and stubbornly interested in your spiritual growth. You will not receive all that you ask for, but you will develop spiritually and you will grow in wisdom. And, as that happens, you will suffer less anxiety and enjoy greater godliness.

Stop impressing others with your piety and start asking for mercy.

When someone wants to be known as a godly person, they can face failure in two respects: either no spiritual growth occurs, or no one is impressed.

Prayer begins with humility—not self-abusing thoughts, but realistic acceptance of who we are before God. While deeply flawed and thoroughly broken, we are nonetheless His priceless treasures. Prayers become most effective when we begin with humility. And if we want the Lord to fix the world's problems, let Him begin with us.

Stop thinking of children as being in the way; think of them as models of the way.

Jesus was the great protector of children. He always had a soft place in His heart for them, but there's another reason He gave them so much attention. He admired children as the greatest among His followers. For a child, the world is big and dangerous, while he or she is small and helpless. Children see the world as it is, which helps them see God as He is: bigger than any danger they will ever face. And because He loves them, He will care for them in every circumstance.

Let your prayers begin with this image of God and expect big changes, beginning with yourself.

Rich Man, Poor Man, Son of Man . . . Me
LUKE 18:18–19:10

NASB

[18] A ruler questioned Him, saying, "Good Teacher, what shall I do to inherit eternal life?" [19] And Jesus said to him, "Why do you call Me good? No one is good except God alone. [20] You know the commandments, 'Do not commit adultery, Do not murder, Do not steal, Do not bear false witness, Honor your father and mother.'" [21] And he said, "All these things I have kept from *my* youth." [22] When Jesus heard *this,* He said to him, "One thing you still lack; sell all that you possess and distribute it to the poor, and you shall have treasure in heaven; and come, follow Me." [23] But when he had heard these things, he became very sad, for he was extremely rich. [24] And Jesus looked at him and said, "How hard it is for those who are wealthy to enter the kingdom of God! [25] For it is easier for a camel to ᵃgo through the eye of a needle than for a rich man to enter the kingdom of God." [26] They who heard it said, "Then who can be saved?" [27] But He said, "The things that are impossible with people are possible with God."

[28] Peter said, "Behold, we have left ᵃour own *homes* and followed You." [29] And He said to them, "Truly I say to you, there is no one who has left house or wife or brothers or parents or children, for the sake of the kingdom of God, [30] who will not receive many times as much at this time and in the age to come, eternal life."

NLT

[18] Once a religious leader asked Jesus this question: "Good Teacher, what should I do to inherit eternal life?"

[19] "Why do you call me good?" Jesus asked him. "Only God is truly good. [20] But to answer your question, you know the commandments: 'You must not commit adultery. You must not murder. You must not steal. You must not testify falsely. Honor your father and mother.'*"

[21] The man replied, "I've obeyed all these commandments since I was young."

[22] When Jesus heard his answer, he said, "There is still one thing you haven't done. Sell all your possessions and give the money to the poor, and you will have treasure in heaven. Then come, follow me."

[23] But when the man heard this he became very sad, for he was very rich.

[24] When Jesus saw this,* he said, "How hard it is for the rich to enter the Kingdom of God! [25] In fact, it is easier for a camel to go through the eye of a needle than for a rich person to enter the Kingdom of God!"

[26] Those who heard this said, "Then who in the world can be saved?"

[27] He replied, "What is impossible for people is possible with God."

[28] Peter said, "We've left our homes to follow you."

[29] "Yes," Jesus replied, "and I assure you that everyone who has given up house or wife or brothers or parents or children, for the sake of the Kingdom of God, [30] will be repaid many times over in this life, and will have eternal life in the world to come."

NASB

31 Then He took the twelve aside and said to them, "Behold, we are going up to Jerusalem, and all things which are written through the prophets about the Son of Man will be accomplished. 32 For He will be ᵃhanded over to the Gentiles, and will be mocked and mistreated and spit upon, 33 and after they have scourged Him, they will kill Him; and the third day He will rise again." 34 But the disciples understood none of these things, and *the meaning of* this statement was hidden from them, and they did not comprehend the things that were said.

35 As ᵃJesus was approaching Jericho, a blind man was sitting by the road begging. 36 Now hearing a crowd going by, he *began* to inquire what this was. 37 They told him that Jesus of Nazareth was passing by. 38 And he called out, saying, "Jesus, Son of David, have mercy on me!" 39 Those who led the way were sternly telling him to be quiet; but he kept crying out all the more, "Son of David, have mercy on me!" 40 And Jesus stopped and commanded that he be brought to Him; and when he came near, He questioned him, 41 "What do you want Me to do for you?" And he said, "Lord, *I want* to regain my sight!" 42 And Jesus said to him, "ᵃReceive your sight; your faith has ᵇmade you well." 43 Immediately he regained his sight and *began* following Him, glorifying God; and when all the people saw it, they gave praise to God.

19:1 He entered Jericho and was passing through. 2 And there was a man called by the name of Zaccheus; he was a chief tax collector and he was rich. 3 Zaccheus was trying to see who Jesus was, and was unable because of the crowd, for he was small in stature. 4 So he ran on ahead and climbed up into a ᵃsycamore tree in order to see Him, for He was about to pass through that way. 5 When Jesus

NLT

31 Taking the twelve disciples aside, Jesus said, "Listen, we're going up to Jerusalem, where all the predictions of the prophets concerning the Son of Man will come true. 32 He will be handed over to the Romans,* and he will be mocked, treated shamefully, and spit upon. 33 They will flog him with a whip and kill him, but on the third day he will rise again."

34 But they didn't understand any of this. The significance of his words was hidden from them, and they failed to grasp what he was talking about.

35 As Jesus approached Jericho, a blind beggar was sitting beside the road. 36 When he heard the noise of a crowd going past, he asked what was happening. 37 They told him that Jesus the Nazarene* was going by. 38 So he began shouting, "Jesus, Son of David, have mercy on me!"

39 "Be quiet!" the people in front yelled at him.

But he only shouted louder, "Son of David, have mercy on me!"

40 When Jesus heard him, he stopped and ordered that the man be brought to him. As the man came near, Jesus asked him, 41 "What do you want me to do for you?"

"Lord," he said, "I want to see!"

42 And Jesus said, "All right, receive your sight! Your faith has healed you." 43 Instantly the man could see, and he followed Jesus, praising God. And all who saw it praised God, too.

19:1 Jesus entered Jericho and made his way through the town. 2 There was a man there named Zacchaeus. He was the chief tax collector in the region, and he had become very rich. 3 He tried to get a look at Jesus, but he was too short to see over the crowd. 4 So he ran ahead and climbed a sycamore-fig tree beside the road, for Jesus was going to pass that way. 5 When Jesus came by, he looked came to the place, He looked up and said to him, "Zaccheus, hurry and come down, for today I must stay at your house." [6] And he hurried and came down and received Him [a]gladly. [7] When they saw it, they all *began* to grumble, saying, "He has gone [a]to be the guest of a man who is a sinner." [8] Zaccheus stopped and said to the Lord, "Behold, Lord, half of my possessions I [a]will give to the poor, and if I have defrauded anyone of anything, I [a]will give back four times as much." [9] And Jesus said to him, "Today salvation has come to this house, because he, too, is a son of Abraham. [10] For the Son of Man has come to seek and to save that which was lost."

18:25 [a]Lit *enter*   18:28 [a]Lit *our own things*
18:32 [a]Or *betrayed*   18:35 [a]Lit *He*   18:42 [a]Lit *Regain your sight*   [b]Lit *saved you*   19:4 [a]I.e. fig-mulberry   19:6 [a]Lit *rejoicing*   19:7 [a]Or *to find lodging*   19:8 [a]Lit *am giving*

up at Zacchaeus and called him by name. "Zacchaeus!" he said. "Quick, come down! I must be a guest in your home today."

[6] Zacchaeus quickly climbed down and took Jesus to his house in great excitement and joy. [7] But the people were displeased. "He has gone to be the guest of a notorious sinner," they grumbled.

[8] Meanwhile, Zacchaeus stood before the Lord and said, "I will give half my wealth to the poor, Lord, and if I have cheated people on their taxes, I will give them back four times as much!"

[9] Jesus responded, "Salvation has come to this home today, for this man has shown himself to be a true son of Abraham. [10] For the Son of Man* came to seek and save those who are lost."

18:20 Exod 20:12-16; Deut 5:16-20.   18:24 Some manuscripts read *When Jesus saw how sad the man was.*   18:32 Greek *the Gentiles.*   18:37 Or *Jesus of Nazareth.*   19:10 "Son of Man" is a title Jesus used for himself.

Any study of the life of Jesus reveals Him as a master communicator. He didn't merely talk; He connected. He didn't ask aimless or random questions; He pierced through pretense to expose the real issues of the heart, often without others realizing what was happening. But Jesus never used His skills to humiliate or demean others; He used truth like a scalpel, never a dagger. He interacted with others to educate and then to liberate. He sought out sinners—not to condemn, but to redeem.

As the journey section of Luke's narrative (9:51–19:27) approaches its climactic destination, Jesus encounters three remarkable men: a rich, young ruler; a poor, blind beggar; and a tax collector on the verge of repentance. The Lord undoubtedly met many other remarkable people on this leg of His journey, but Luke chose these for a specific purpose. All three stories have something to do with wealth and its influence on a person's ability to enter the kingdom of God. Like the last turn before the final stretch in a race, this crucial theme in Luke's narrative will propel us toward the finish line.

— 18:18-20 —

The Lord's first encounter involves a man Luke calls "a ruler," a term the writer used earlier to describe a leading official in the synagogue (8:41) and also uses to describe leaders among the Pharisees (14:1; 23:13, 35; 24:20). According to Matthew, the ruler was a young man (Matt. 19:22) and therefore probably not a member of the Jewish ruling body, the Sanhedrin. Most likely, his community regarded him as a wealthy, up-and-coming elder.

According to Mark, the man ran up to Jesus and kneeled before Him prior to asking his question (Mark 10:17). Unlike the jaded religious leaders the Lord had encountered so many times before, this ruler approached Jesus in all sincerity. In addition, he addressed Jesus as "Good Teacher," something no other person had done.

Before the Lord answered the man's question, He challenged the young ruler's choice of terms, for two reasons. First, Jesus gave no quarter to flattery; He didn't have an ego to stroke. Second, the man's concept of "good" didn't amount to much, as the story will soon reveal. Therefore, his compliment didn't mean very much. Jesus realized that if they were going to talk about eternal life, He must redefine "good" for the man. The moral worth of a person must be measured against a proper example of goodness. God is the only valid benchmark, and He revealed His holy character through the Mosaic Law.

Jesus helped the man not only to adjust his "goodness scale" to match God's, but He also answered his question. To gain entrance to the kingdom of God, one must obey the Law of Moses with sinless perfection. Jesus then rattled off a partial list of commandments, more than enough to indict most people:

7. Do not commit adultery. (Exod. 20:14)
6. Do not murder. (Exod. 20:13)
8. Do not steal. (Exod. 20:15)
9. Do not bear false witness. (Exod. 20:16)
5. Honor your father and mother. (Exod. 20:12)

While Jesus didn't present these five of the Ten Commandments in any particular order, it's worth noting that He quoted only those regulating human relationships. He deliberately omitted God's prohibition of coveting, and He skipped over the first four regarding our relationship with God Himself:

1. You shall have no other gods before Me. (Exod. 20:3)
2. You shall not make for yourself an idol. (Exod. 20:4)

3. You shall not take the name of the Lord your God in vain [that is, misuse My name]. (Exod. 20:7)
4. Remember the Sabbath day, to keep it holy. (Exod. 20:8)

— 18:21-23 —

The young man may have been sincere, but his arrogance ran high. By his own estimation, he was good and deserved to take his place in the Messiah's kingdom, affirming his obedience to all five commandments throughout his life. And, by the standards established by the Pharisees, he probably did! But because no one can obey the Law of God perfectly, the religious leaders modified the Law with their own rules and traditions, thereby lowering the standard in order to call themselves "good." In other words, if you can't jump high enough to clear the moral high bar, set it lower. (See comments on Luke 16:18.)

Jesus could have sifted through the man's past to prove him wrong, but He took a different approach. Instead, He cut straight to the heart of the issue: the first four commandments. Rather than delve into the past, Jesus issued a challenge for the future that exposed his sinfulness.

Earlier, Jesus stated that true disciples must make the kingdom of God their number one priority over family, wealth, possessions, and even their own lives (14:26-27; 16:13). This was not a new requirement of the kingdom. When God brought the Hebrew people out of Egypt to establish them in the Promised Land, intending to make of them His kingdom on earth, the first four commandments set the standard. The first rule of citizenship: God first.

Jesus simply applied the first four commandments to the young man's situation in life. He said, in so many words, "Put God first by sacrificing your worldly treasure."

At first, it might seem Jesus had responded to the man's salvation question with a works answer. In all other instances, Jesus forgave sins on the basis of faith alone; but in this case, He called for the man to do an extraordinary good deed. That's because genuine belief always changes a person's behavior. People act on what they believe to be true and they cling to what they treasure. By commanding the young man to relinquish his wealth, Jesus exposed the man's lack of trust in God's provision and laid bare his true priority. When given the choice between his money and his God, the young man chose money.

— 18:24-27 —

Perceiving the rich man's sorrow, Jesus exposed the distracting, deluding effects of material wealth. His analogy compares wealthy people to camels and the gate of God's kingdom to the eye of a needle. Jesus used this bit of hyperbole to stress the idea of human impossibility, which prompted those overhearing the conversation to ask an astute question. They didn't ask, "Then how can rich people be saved?" They correctly understood that all people struggle with the young man's issue; everyone treasures possessions too much. Even poor people do so—sometimes more than others! Their question made a great point: If utter devotion to God is the standard of salvation, then no one qualifies.

Jesus acknowledged the *human* impossibility of salvation to underscore the need for God to do what people cannot. We cannot be good enough. We can only trust God to do something on our behalf deep within our hearts.

— 18:28-30 —

During the exchange, Peter began to wonder if his personal sacrifice was enough. He had left a lucrative fishing enterprise, abandoned his wealth, sacrificed his future, even left his wife in the care of others to devote himself exclusively to the Messiah and His mission. In a very literal way, Peter had done what Jesus required of the young ruler, but he needed reassurance.

Jesus affirmed Peter's choice, downplaying what they had given up while calling attention to what genuine followers of the Messiah stood to gain—not only on earth, but also in the next life. Theirs was a wise investment that will pay eternal dividends.

— 18:31-34 —

Without retracting anything He had said in public about the rewards associated with the kingdom of God, Jesus wanted to prepare His leadership trainees, "the Twelve." They would indeed receive far more in the kingdom of God than they had sacrificed; however, the road to glory always runs through the valley of suffering. Jesus again clarified the mission. His purpose for marching to Jerusalem was not to take it by storm but to fulfill "all the things that are written through the prophets." Not only would He fulfill these Old Testament messianic predictions—particularly those concerning the Suffering Servant predicted and portrayed by the prophet Isaiah (Isa. 42:1-9; 49:1-13; 50:1-11; 52:13–53:12)—the Son of God also came to satisfy the requirements of the Law, whereas Israel had failed. He would uphold Israel's part of God's conditional covenant in order to receive its blessings (Deut. 28). The Messiah would fulfill all of the Old Testament, not only its prophetic sections.

Jesus warned that success in His mission would look like failure by human standards. Nevertheless, He promised to rise from the dead.

Luke reflects on the perspective of the Twelve, describing their inability to understand. Despite His explicit and detailed prediction of events to come, the meaning of Jesus' warning "was hidden from them." The passive voice hints at divine activity, subtly suggesting that God prevented them from understanding until later. At the same time, it can be said that the future differed so dramatically from their expectations that they chose to remain in denial (see commentary at 9:43b-45). Furthermore, because the Holy Spirit had not yet come, they did not have the eyes to see.

— 18:35 —

Luke's abrupt transition to another scene is deliberate. Another encounter along the Lord's route to Jerusalem offers a dramatic contrast to His dialogue with the rich, young ruler. On the road leading into Jericho, He passed by a blind beggar. The city of Jericho was the last stop before an arduous 2,950-foot (900-meter) climb in less than 20 miles (32 kilometers) to reach Jerusalem, and almost every Jewish pilgrim traveling from Galilee used this route. So, in the weeks prior to Passover, the beggar had access to tens of thousands of Jews walking up to the temple.

On the outside, the blind beggar could not have been more different from the rich, young ruler. Whereas the ruler had both health and wealth in abundance, the blind man had neither. The predominant theology of the day interpreted the rich man's good fortune as evidence of God smiling on his good character. The same theology regarded the blind man's affliction and poverty as God's chastisement for sin (cf. John 9:1-2). But the contrast is only external. On the inside, the two men suffered from the same, universal disease of sin, and both faced the prospect of eternal death for their guilt.

— 18:36-38 —

The blind man heard the crowd passing by, a crowd which would not have been remarkable by itself. Pilgrims typically banded together for the sake of safety, especially as they prepared for the bandit-infested road from Jericho to Jerusalem. Large groups passed the beggar every day. But this crowd seemed different. This group traveled with the Messiah to Jerusalem, excited to see what He would do to establish the kingdom of God on earth. This group was a messianic procession, and the man with no sight could feel their energy.

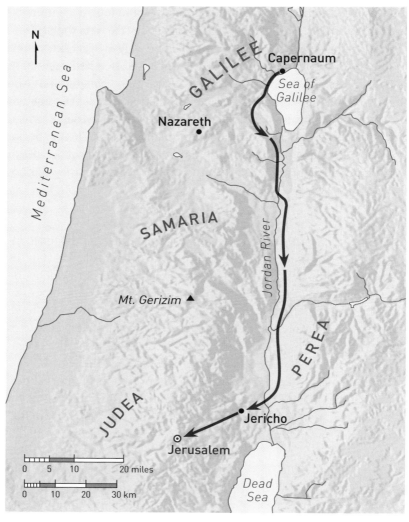

Jews from Galilee traveled this route—avoiding the unclean Samaritans—to Jerusalem to celebrate the Passover.

When he heard the name "Jesus of Nazareth" he immediately called Him by His messianic title: "Son of David," heir to the throne of Israel. The town name "Nazareth" most likely derives from the Hebrew term *netzer* [H5342], meaning "branch" or "shoot," which forms a wordplay in Isaiah 11:1, speaking of the coming messianic king:

> Then a shoot will spring from the stem of Jesse,
> And a branch from his roots will bear fruit.
> The Spirit of the LORD will rest on Him,

The spirit of wisdom and understanding,
The spirit of counsel and strength,
The spirit of knowledge and the fear of the LORD.
And He will delight in the fear of the LORD,
And He will not judge by what His eyes see,
Nor make a decision by what His ears hear;
But with righteousness He will judge the poor,
And decide with fairness for the afflicted of the earth.
    (Isa. 11:1-4)

The blind man called upon Israel's future King to have mercy—that is, deep-felt compassion. This was common vocabulary among beggars making an emotional appeal for money.

— 18:39-42 —

Apparently, the members of the Messiah's procession took the man's cry for mercy as an appeal for money—a reasonable assumption, all things considered. Despite their attempts to rebuke the blind beggar, he shrieked all the more. The first term translated "called out" (Luke 18:38) is *boaō* [994], which means "to shout" or "to cry out" (cf. 9:38; 18:7). The second (18:39) is *krazō* [2896] (cf. 9:39), defined by one lexicon as "to make a vehement outcry, cry out, scream, shriek." It could refer to one uttering loud cries without words capable of being understood— particularly of mentally disturbed persons, epileptics, or the evil spirits living in them.[41] The man's desperate need overwhelmed any sense of pride and any measure of restraint. With his only hope about to pass him by, he made a spectacle of himself.

It worked. Jesus heard maniacal shrieking in the distance and commanded his assistants to bring the beggar to Him. He could have walked to the man Himself, but perhaps Jesus wanted to use this opportunity to instruct His followers. By commanding them to bring the man, He gently rebuked their attempt to silence the needy (cf. 18:16-17).

Jesus asked the man a straightforward question: "What do you want Me to do for you?" His response would reveal his heart. Would he ask for money? If so, the blind man saw Jesus as nothing more than a man of earthly wealth, and he wanted nothing more than the ability to make his present condition a little more comfortable.

The blind man's response revealed something different. He called Jesus "Lord"—*kyrie* (pronounced kyr-ee-yay)—a common enough title for important men; but when combined with his request for sight, it takes on heightened meaning. He believed in the supernatural power of Jesus to do what only God can do, and he asked the Lord to meet his most pressing need: to gain his sight.

Luke's choice of Greek word for "receive sight," *anablepō* [308], is a possible double entendre. It can mean "to gain sight," either for the first time or after losing the ability to see. However, New Testament writers use the term just as often to mean "to look up" (see 9:16; 19:5; 21:1). In response, Jesus commended the man's faith, to which He attributes the man's healing. Moreover, the phrase rendered "has made you well" is literally "has saved (*sōzō* [4982]) you," another double entendre.

In other words, throughout the entire episode, there's more than meets the eye for those who have eyes to see! The man's physical blindness reflected his spiritual condition, which makes Luke's concluding statement even more intriguing.

— 18:43 —

As we have seen, Luke uses the word *parachrēma* [3916], "immediately," throughout his narrative to highlight the dramatic and instantaneous results of the Lord's divine power (4:39; 5:25; 8:44, 47, 55; 13:13). The man immediately "regained his sight" or "looked up"—either rendering fits the context—and began following Jesus. This prompted the crowd, which earlier had rebuked the man, to praise God for the miracle and the addition of a new citizen of God's kingdom.

Meanwhile—let us not forget—the rich ruler sat in his palace, counting his coins, contemplating the kingdom of God.

— 19:1 —

Again, with barely a transition, Luke carries the narrative forward from the outskirts of Jericho to its center. When his narrative lacks transition, it usually points to a unifying theme. The rich, young ruler was blind, as it were, to his own sinfulness and need for a savior (18:18-25). And when confronted with his sin of covetousness, he refused to repent or ask for deliverance. Because he loved his wealth more than he loved God, he gave tacit allegiance to the dominion of evil rather than enter the kingdom of God. His love of wealth made salvation impossible for him.

Then Jesus heard the desperate, shrieking anguish of a penniless man all too aware of his own need, both physically and spiritually (18:35-43). He asked the Messiah for the ability to see, and Jesus restored his physical sight and gave him spiritual sight for the first time.

Soon, Jesus would encounter another wealthy man.

— 19:2 —

The first-century Jewish historian Josephus described Jericho as "the most fruitful country of Judea, which bears a vast number of palm trees, besides the balsam tree, whose sprouts they cut with sharp stones, and at the incisions they gather the juice, which drops down like tears."[42] Josephus continued, "This country withal produces honey from bees: it also bears that balsam which is the most precious of all the fruits in that place, cypress trees also, and those that bear myrobalanum; so that he who should pronounce this place to be divine would not be mistaken, wherein is such plenty of trees produced as are very rare, and of the most excellent sort."[43]

Jericho's temperate climate made it an ideal retreat for royals, who built enormous palaces, and it was complete with swimming pools, gardens, bathhouses, a hippodrome, and a theater. The city also sat on one of the busiest trade routes in the ancient world, with formalized connections to important coastal cities in northern Israel and to Egypt in the south. Wherever you find vast amounts of wealth and large numbers of politicians, you inevitably find a funnel for taxes.

A man in Jericho by the name of Zaccheus, as a *chief* tax collector, was one of a handful of men who managed this tax funnel. This not only gave him immense power over the daily lives of ordinary citizens, but it also gave him direct access to the powerful. He undoubtedly dined with royalty and counseled with Roman dignitaries on a regular basis, and he enjoyed a lifestyle few could imagine. To say that Zaccheus was rich is an understatement. He was unbelievably rich. But as a tax collector—a Roman collaborator against his own people— he abused the power of his office to exact higher taxes than were due and then bankrolled the surplus. So, while eminently wealthy, he was despised, enormously hated.

Ironically, the name Zaccheus is the Greek form of a Hebrew term that means "innocent." He was anything but!

— 19:3-4 —

The Lord's entourage probably contained many thousands of people by this time, so the commotion would have been considerable, not unlike an unorganized parade. Luke states that Zaccheus wanted to "see who Jesus was," implying he had heard rumors and wanted more information. But he didn't approach Jesus as a dignitary. Surely as one of the most important men in the city, he could have tried to arrange an official meeting. Instead, he tried to catch a glimpse as Jesus was passing by, and because of his small physical stature and the size of the crowd, he ran ahead and climbed one of the many trees lining the route.

To put this in perspective, this would be like the mayor of Las Vegas climbing a tree along the parade route of an arriving religious figure. This illustrates a complete disregard for his own dignity for the sake of finding out more about Jesus.

— 19:5-7 —

While Zaccheus took extraordinary initiative to understand more about Jesus, he didn't initiate contact. Jesus did, calling him by name and then stating, "It is necessary for me to stay in your house" (literally rendered).

In Western culture, it's considered poor etiquette to invite oneself to another's home for room and board, but Jesus honored the diminutive sinner immensely. Ancient Near Eastern culture counted it a privilege to provide shelter, food, protection, and comfort to travelers, especially persons of high social rank. Everyone with a home in Jericho hoped to host the Messiah on His journey. Surprisingly, He gave that distinction to the city's most notorious sinner. Zaccheus responded immediately. And then he received Jesus as his guest "gladly," literally "with rejoicing."

Again, to put this into perspective, Jesus' staying in the home of Zaccheus was like accepting the hospitality of Al Capone, affording the criminal a tacit endorsement by His very presence. If calling Zaccheus "rich" was an understatement, so was calling him a sinner! This turn of events must have shocked the citizens of Jericho.

— 19:8-10 —

Jesus apparently went to the home of Zaccheus, although Luke's narrative remains vague. The verb rendered "stopped" actually means "to stand." The witnesses spoke of Jesus dining with Zaccheus in the past tense,[44] not the future tense. What's more, Jesus referred to "this house," strongly suggesting His presence there. Therefore, I see good evidence for a space of time between 19:6 and 19:7, compressed by Luke to support his point.

At some point during the meal, perhaps after hearing Jesus teach or after seeing the response of his other guests, Zaccheus stood up from his reclining position to make an important announcement. Standing taller than ever before in his life, the city's most public sinner repented, promising to give half of everything he owned to the poor—a vast sum of money. He also pledged to repay anyone he had defrauded four times what he had taken. Surely, mouths dropped open.

The Greeks had an interesting way of expressing conditional statements ("if . . . then" statements). A number of types of conditions were used in Greek sentences, one of which is called the "first class condition," where the statement is assumed as true. Luke used the first class condition when recording the open confession of Zaccheus. We could translate his words, "In every instance in which I have defrauded anyone." Because his crimes were financial, he undoubtedly had detailed records of each sin. Without hesitation, the notorious tax collector promised to make things right.

In response, Jesus declared that "salvation" had come to the house and affirmed Zaccheus as "a son of Abraham." Earlier, John called all Jews—and the religious leaders in particular—to repent, saying, "Bear fruits in keeping with repentance, and do not begin to say to yourselves, 'We have Abraham for our father,' for I say to you that from these stones God is able to raise up children to Abraham" (3:8). The repentant sinner not only renounced his citizenship in the dominion of evil—both literally and figuratively—he did what the rich, young ruler refused to do. Zaccheus showed outward evidence of his inward change. His heart regretted stealing the money. He had it in his power to reverse the misfortune he had caused . . . and that is exactly what he promised to do.

Jesus, pointing to Zaccheus, restated His purpose in coming to earth: "to seek and to save that which was lost" (cf. 15:6-7, 9-10, 24).

• • •

Three distinct personalities encountered Jesus near Jericho. A rich, young ruler's money and privileged status blinded him to his spiritual need. He simply loved his money more than he loved God. A penniless blind man had nothing to shield his eyes from his need of a Savior. Even in his blindness, he saw more clearly than his wealthy counterpart. He responded to the Messiah in faith and received his sight. And Zaccheus proves that camels can indeed pass through the eye of a needle—"The things that are impossible with people are possible with God" (18:27). Despite his immense wealth, impressive power, and sordid past, Zaccheus compared everything he had gained to the kingdom of God and came to an easy decision. He cast it all aside for the sake of becoming a follower of Jesus.

APPLICATION: LUKE 18:18–19:10

Listening and Lessons

Regardless of your walk in life—whether a rich, young ruler or a poor, blind man or a person with everything—if you don't have Jesus Christ, there's something missing. But once you have accepted His free gift of eternal life and you have received God's forgiveness, there's more! These three scenes in Luke 18–19 illustrate three important lessons.

The first lesson: *When we don't know what we want but we know something's missing, let God educate.* The rich, young ruler wasn't willing to be educated by the Savior. He had his mind made up. He wasn't about to release the things that he had set his heart on. He wasn't open to further information. You may find yourself misled by information given you from some other source. Let God educate. You may discover you have believed in something that really is not the Father's will and you've set your heart on it. It's a dream not yet realized. But as time passes, you don't quite know what you want; you just know something's missing. Let Him reveal it to you. Let Him set it before you. Let Him show you His plan.

The second lesson: *When we do know what we need but we can't change our situation, let God liberate.* He's good at that, you know. Some long-standing addiction you've not been able to break—let Him liberate. Some emotional scar or wound—let Him liberate. Often, it will not happen immediately but through a process of time. And it will likely be painful. Still, let Him liberate! Trust Him to bring you out of the bondage and into the light of a whole new beginning.

I have read and heard stories from I don't know how many people who have addressed very painful and embarrassing addictions in their life. And they all said something like, "I will never forget the time when I finally laid down my arms, my defensiveness, my denial, and I looked, as it were; I looked the Lord straight in the eye and said something as basic as, 'Liberate me. Come to my rescue. I can't stop this. I can't seem to get past where I'm stuck.'"

The third lesson: *When we can't understand what is happening but we realize it's out of our control, let God be God.* It may happen between you and your mate. It may occur in relation to your job. It may happen between you and a very close friend. It may happen between you and one of your children or one of your parents. It may occur between you and your pastor. It may occur between you and your partner at work. God has a plan that supersedes, that transcends our wishes. His plan is full of the unexpected—remember that. Never forget that. His plan is grander than our plan.

Making Sense with Your Dollars
LUKE 19:11-27

NASB

¹¹ While they were listening to these things, Jesus went on to tell a parable, because He was near Jerusalem, and they supposed that the kingdom of God was going to appear immediately. ¹² So He said, "A nobleman went to a distant country to receive a kingdom for himself, and *then* return. ¹³ And he called ten of his slaves, and gave them ten ªminas and said to them, 'Do business *with this* ᵇuntil I come *back*.' ¹⁴ But his citizens hated him and sent ªa delegation after him, saying, 'We do not want this man to reign over us.' ¹⁵ When he returned, after receiving the kingdom, he ordered that these slaves, to whom he had given the money, be called to him so that he might know what business they had done. ¹⁶ The first appeared, saying, 'ªMaster, your ᵇmina has made ten minas more.' ¹⁷ And he said to him, 'Well done, good slave, because you have been faithful in a very little thing, you are to be in authority over ten cities.' ¹⁸ The second came, saying, 'Your ªmina, ᵇmaster, has made five minas.' ¹⁹ And he said to him also, 'And you are to be over five cities.' ²⁰ Another came, saying, 'Master, here is your mina, which I kept put away in a handkerchief; ²¹ for I was afraid of you, because you are an

NLT

¹¹ The crowd was listening to everything Jesus said. And because he was nearing Jerusalem, he told them a story to correct the impression that the Kingdom of God would begin right away. ¹² He said, "A nobleman was called away to a distant empire to be crowned king and then return. ¹³ Before he left, he called together ten of his servants and divided among them ten pounds of silver,* saying, 'Invest this for me while I am gone.' ¹⁴ But his people hated him and sent a delegation after him to say, 'We do not want him to be our king.'

¹⁵ "After he was crowned king, he returned and called in the servants to whom he had given the money. He wanted to find out what their profits were. ¹⁶ The first servant reported, 'Master, I invested your money and made ten times the original amount!' ¹⁷ "'Well done!' the king exclaimed. 'You are a good servant. You have been faithful with the little I entrusted to you, so you will be governor of ten cities as your reward.' ¹⁸ "The next servant reported, 'Master, I invested your money and made five times the original amount.' ¹⁹ "'Well done!' the king said. 'You will be governor over five cities.' ²⁰ "But the third servant brought back only the original amount of money and said, 'Master, I hid your money and kept it safe. ²¹ I was afraid because you are a hard man to deal

487

NASB

exacting man; you take up what you did not lay down and reap what you did not sow.' ²²He said to him, '*By your own words I will judge you, you worthless slave. Did you know that I am an exacting man, taking up what I did not lay down and reaping what I did not sow? ²³Then why did you not put my money in the bank, and having come, I would have collected it with interest?' ²⁴Then he said to the bystanders, 'Take the mina away from him and give it to the one who has the ten minas.' ²⁵And they said to him, 'Master, he has ten minas *already.' ²⁶I tell you that to everyone who has, more shall be given, but from the one who does not have, even what he does have shall be taken away. ²⁷But these enemies of mine, who did not want me to reign over them, bring them here and slay them in my presence."

19:13 ªA mina is equal to about 100 days' wages
ᵇLit *while I am coming* 19:14 ªOr *an embassy*
19:16 ªLit *Lord* ᵇV 13, note 1 19:18 ªV 13, note 1
ᵇLit *lord* 19:22 ªLit *Out of your own mouth*

NLT

with, taking what isn't yours and harvesting crops you didn't plant.'

²²"You wicked servant!' the king roared. 'Your own words condemn you. If you knew that I'm a hard man who takes what isn't mine and harvests crops I didn't plant, ²³why didn't you deposit my money in the bank? At least I could have gotten some interest on it.'

²⁴"Then, turning to the others standing nearby, the king ordered, 'Take the money from this servant, and give it to the one who has ten pounds.'

²⁵"But, master,' they said, 'he already has ten pounds!'

²⁶"Yes,' the king replied, 'and to those who use well what they are given, even more will be given. But from those who do nothing, even what little they have will be taken away. ²⁷And as for these enemies of mine who didn't want me to be their king—bring them in and execute them right here in front of me.'"

19:13 Greek *ten minas*; one mina was worth about three months' wages.

What we need most cannot be purchased with money. Money can buy a bed, but not sleep. Money can buy food, but not an appetite. Money can buy books, but not intelligence. Money can buy pleasures, but not peace. Money can buy companionship, but not friendship. Money can buy a crucifix, but not a Savior. Money can buy a Bible, but not a place in heaven.

I doubt many would disagree with any of that, yet the pursuit of wealth and possessions continues to dominate our priorities and compel our obedience, despite the Lord's promise to supply all our needs. He has freed us from the tyranny of survival so that we may invest our resources in the kingdom of God, but we do not trust Him—and our bank statements prove it. A quick review of the average Christian's expenditures would probably trigger a panic attack, because spending reveals our priorities; and—truth be told—our priorities often do not fall in line with the Lord's.

As Jesus turned His thoughts to the final leg of His journey to

Jerusalem, He prepared His followers for what they were about to witness. Their Messiah would soon sacrifice *everything* this world values for the sake of God's kingdom. The kingdom would not be fully realized immediately, and they, too, would be called upon to invest their all. Those following Him would soon discover that their dreams of earthly prosperity would not come true. If they were to continue as followers, they would have to adjust their view of temporal wealth to match their King's.

— 19:11 —

The setting for this episode in Luke's narrative is the city of Jericho at a banquet in the home of Zaccheus. The tax collector had just made the stunning announcement that he had repented of his sin, and as restitution, he promised to give half of his considerable wealth to the poor and then repay those he had defrauded four times above what he had taken. It was political, social, and financial suicide. There would be little, if anything, left of his estate. He also risked losing the respect and confidence of his Roman colleagues. If he were a follower of Jesus, no one holding power in Jerusalem would call him friend.

Jesus responded to Zaccheus with heaven's affirmation: "Salvation has come to this house." The tax collector's giant leap from the highest social strata in the dominion of evil to the lowest gave the man of short stature an exalted status in the kingdom of God. Though the Lord's followers "were listening to these things," they did not understand them. Nor would they, until much later. Jesus came to establish a different kind of kingdom. They expected that He would raise an army, overthrow Rome, conquer the world, and usher Israel into a new golden age of power and prosperity. He will do that eventually, but not "immediately." The true Messiah—as opposed to the messiah of selfish expectations—came with a different kind of agenda. To help His disciples shift their earthbound perspective to see the world through His eyes, Jesus told a parable.

— 19:12-14 —

A "man of noble birth" (literally rendered) prepared for a journey to a foreign land, where he was to "receive a kingdom for himself." The nobleman in the story represents Jesus, and His death is the journey. The parable clearly illustrates that the kingdom of God will not be set up in Jerusalem right away; a journey was required, during which He would receive authority to rule the kingdom. This was very common in ancient politics. In fact, Herod the Great traveled to Rome around 40 BC to be elected "King of the Jews" by the Senate, but he assumed power only after three years of fighting with the help of the Romans. Herod's son Archelaus also traveled to Rome in AD 4 to receive the assent of Augustus but was opposed by his brother Antipas and a delegation of Pharisees.

Before leaving, the nobleman charged ten slaves with the responsibility to "do business"—that is, invest a sum of money during his absence. Each received a *mina*, which equaled one hundred *drachmas*. A common laborer earned one *drachma* for a day's work, so a *mina* represented one hundred days' wages. In other words, the nobleman gave each slave roughly one-third of a year's salary to invest on his behalf.

The ten slaves represent the Lord's followers. Note the master in the story didn't leave one servant in charge as a chief administrator; he distributed responsibility evenly among the servants. And while each received a large sum, none thought of the money as a gift. The slaves didn't own the money; they merely held it in trust for their master.

The "citizens" most likely represent the ruling authorities in Jerusalem. Jesus may have drawn inspiration for this detail from the accession of Archelaus, who was opposed by virtually every faction in Israel.

— 19:15-19 —

Upon his return, the master called in the slaves for an accounting. The story began with his having authority over the slaves, and that doesn't change. His authority over the kingdom, however, begins while he is away. As it turns out, the master didn't conduct the exercise to make himself richer; ten *minas* was nothing compared to the holdings of an entire kingdom. He used investment as a test of fitness to rule cities. How the slaves managed the money entrusted to them revealed their trustworthiness and gauged their prudence. And each slave was made a vice-regent over territories in proportion to their success with the money.

— 19:20-23 —

The third slave's failure to multiply the money entrusted to him reveals his lack of wisdom at best and his insolence at worst. Perhaps he didn't expect the master to return and thus didn't feel any obligation to obey.

His reason for sitting on his *mina*, however, causes the greatest concern. His rationale reveals an intense mistrust, even calling into question his master's kindness and integrity. The term rendered "exacting" literally means "dry." It can also mean "rigid" or "strict," describing a person who is severe with himself and unyielding with others. In addition to attacking his master's personal style, the slave accused his master of placing him in a no-win scenario. He said, in effect, "If I make money, you will take it; if I lose money, you'll punish me. Therefore, I played it safe so you can do neither."

His impudence earned him a severe rebuke and a challenge to his sincerity. His rationale would make more sense if he had simply deposited the money in a bank to draw interest. Drawing interest required no work from him and ran no risk of failure; therefore, he must have had another reason for sitting on the money.

— 19:24-26 —

By transferring the unfaithful slave's *mina* to the care of the most successful slave, the master proves that he cares less about fairness than faithfulness. Be that as it may, the master *was* fair. None of the slaves ended up with less than when they started out. Even the worthless slave ended where he began; he started with nothing and he ended with nothing. In truth, none of the slaves were at risk of personal loss, and they had been given every opportunity to gain personally by acting as faithful stewards.

— 19:27 —

Only one group suffered loss in the parable. The citizens who rejected the master's authority and actively worked against him became the object of his wrath. While the unfaithful slave received no reward, he remained a citizen of the master's kingdom. He suffered disgrace, but his life was never in danger. Not so for the rebels. The master's order to slay the rebels in his presence foreshadows the final judgment in which Israel's political and religious leaders will suffer eternal death for their opposition of the Messiah.

APPLICATION: LUKE 19:11-27

Investing Now for Then

By the end of Jesus' parable, He had established two clear facts. These facts present us with important principles that require personal reflection and practical responses.

First, *the kingdom—with all its power, peace, and prosperity—will indeed fully come in due time, but not right away.* Before God restores the nation of Israel, He will first banish their rebellion and redeem their hearts. In a similar manner, between Christ's first and second coming, God is at work in us, His people, to banish our rebellion and redeem our hearts. Like ancient Israel, we can become hardened to His plan and impatient toward His timing. Over time, we can begin to lose confidence in Christ's coming and even become like the scoffer who says, "Where is the promise of His coming? For ever since the fathers fell asleep, all continues just as it was from the beginning of creation" (2 Pet. 3:4). Instead of folding our arms and tapping our foot, let's use the time He's graciously given us to get right with Him and to lead others into a right relationship with the coming King.

Second, *everything we have in our possession belongs to God.* He owns it all. We have been entrusted with twenty-four hours in each day, a measure of personal capabilities, and a sum of wealth. It may be a million *minas* or it might be a tiny *drachma.* Whatever we've been given is His. And that doesn't just apply to money. He has entrusted us with gifts, opportunities, relationships, abilities, experiences, training, skills, and other things we like to call "mine." All of these are investments given for the purpose of yielding heavenly fruit in our earthly realm. The time He's given us between the first and second coming of Christ gives us each an opportunity to put this spiritual capital to use.

The Master has gone to receive authority to rule the earth and will return in power. He expects us to invest well rather than sit on our *minas.* These facts should shape our minute-by-minute decisions as we passionately seek to invest in the coming kingdom.

CONQUERING AND COMMISSIONING (LUKE 19:28–24:53)

Jesus had a long climb ahead of Him. The 3,000-foot ascent from Jericho to Jerusalem didn't present the hardest challenge; the distance could be traveled in less than a day, and He had made the 17-mile jaunt no fewer than three times a year since the age of twelve. He had also visited Judea many other times for the sake of ministry. But this trip differed from all the others. He did not come to worship, but to die; He did not enter Jerusalem as a visitor, but as its King.

Some time earlier, Jesus had "determined to go to Jerusalem" (Luke 9:51). There, He would lay legitimate claim to David's throne as the long-awaited Messiah; and as the Lord's anointed, He would confront the corruption in the Lord's temple—a move that would call the whole nation to repentance, beginning with its leaders. But He didn't entertain any fantasies. Although He would present Himself as the Messiah in good faith, He had long ago accepted the inevitable outcome. The prophets had predicted the Messiah's arrival in Jerusalem as well as His rejection. According to Isaiah, the mighty King would suffer unspeakable agony (Isa. 42:1-4; 49:1-6; 50:4-9). He would be exalted and then humiliated (Isa. 52:13-15), rejected as king (Isa. 53:1-3), scourged and pierced (Isa. 53:4-6), led to slaughter like a sacrificial lamb (Isa. 53:7-9), offered to God as an atoning sacrifice and then raised to life again (Isa. 53:10-12). The result would overturn the very foundations of the evil world system; it would prove to be a fatal wound that will doom Satan himself in the coming age when Christ's return establishes the millennial kingdom on earth. But in the meantime, the Messiah's rejection by Israel and God's planned postponement of the earthly kingdom would appear to many to be an unanticipated failure.

Since His decision to head for Jerusalem, Jesus had crisscrossed Galilee and penetrated deep into Samaria, proclaiming the kingdom of God in every synagogue that welcomed Him. All along the way, He gathered followers by the thousands, so that by the time He reached Jericho, a massive entourage of cheering disciples went before Him.

KEY TERMS IN LUKE 19:28–24:53

paradidōmi (παραδίδωμι) [3860] "hand over," "surrender," "transfer possession"

Based on the verb meaning "to give," this term carries the idea of surrendering possession of something to the control of another. Based on the context, some translators will render the term "betray," but the Greek word itself does not suggest whether the motivation is good or evil. We see it used extensively in the passion narrative, in which Jesus is "given over" to the authorities (Luke 20:20; 22:4, 21). Earlier, Jesus prepared His followers, telling them that He will be "given over" (9:44); and he indicated that they, too, will be "given over" to the authorities (21:16).

paschō (πάσχω) [3958] "to suffer," "to rescue," "to recover," "to preserve one's well-being"

This word can have the general sense of experiencing something, whether good or bad. But in practice, it almost always appears in the negative: experiencing something unpleasant. In Luke's narrative, the word often appears in an absolute sense, meaning it doesn't directly state what is causing the suffering. Its most frequent context in Luke, however, is the death of the Messiah. Interestingly, the Greek word for "Passover" is *pascha*, although there is no linguistic connection. Rather, *pascha* is transliterated from Aramaic. While the similarity in sound is merely coincidence, Luke makes use of it in a wordplay (22:15).[1]

proseuchomai (προσεύχομαι) [4336] "to pray," "to ask for," "to call upon God"

This term is the most common for the spiritual discipline of prayer, denoting, in general, the act of calling upon God, including the presentation of needs. Luke uses it nineteen times in his Gospel and sixteen times in Acts.

genea (γενεά) [1074] "race," "kind," "generation," "people of a certain type"

In a very broad use of the word, it simply means "people sharing the traits of a certain type," in which the shared trait may be specified. In Luke, the term gradually takes on the specific, technical meaning "people who think and act according to the present world system" as opposed to acting in line with the ethics and values of the kingdom of God. Therefore, "this generation" will pass away when the kingdom of God finally displaces the old, fallen, sin-corrupted creation.

Despite His many warnings, they expected the city would be His before the end of Passover. They still had not understood. Indeed, He *would* ultimately triumph; but not in the manner they expected. Even His closest disciples would need further explanation after His resurrection

(Luke 24:13-35; Acts 1:6-8). Patiently loving these disciples and burdened for the fate of the sin-ridden world, Jesus marched relentlessly toward His destiny.

The Messiah Confronts Jerusalem
LUKE 19:28-48

NASB

28 After He had said these things, He was going on ahead, going up to Jerusalem.

29 When He approached Bethphage and Bethany, near the ᵃmount that is called Olivet, He sent two of the disciples, 30 saying, "Go into the village ahead of *you;* there, as you enter, you will find a colt tied on which no one yet has ever sat; untie it and bring it *here.* 31 If anyone asks you, 'Why are you untying it?' you shall say, 'The Lord has need of it.'" 32 So those who were sent away and found it just as He had told them. 33 As they were untying the colt, its ᵃowners said to them, "Why are you untying the colt?" 34 They said, "The Lord has need of it." 35 They brought it to Jesus, and they threw their coats on the colt and put Jesus *on it.* 36 As He was going, they were spreading their coats on the road. 37 As soon as He was approaching, near the descent of the Mount of Olives, the whole crowd of the disciples began to praise God ᵃjoyfully with a loud voice for all the ᵇmiracles which they had seen, 38 shouting:

"BLESSED IS THE KING WHO
   COMES IN THE NAME OF THE
   LORD;
Peace in heaven and glory in the
   highest!"

39 Some of the Pharisees ᵃin the crowd said to Him, "Teacher, rebuke Your disciples." 40 But Jesus answered, "I

NLT

28 After telling this story, Jesus went on toward Jerusalem, walking ahead of his disciples. 29 As he came to the towns of Bethphage and Bethany on the Mount of Olives, he sent two disciples ahead. 30 "Go into that village over there," he told them. "As you enter it, you will see a young donkey tied there that no one has ever ridden. Untie it and bring it here. 31 If anyone asks, 'Why are you untying that colt?' just say, 'The Lord needs it.'"

32 So they went and found the colt, just as Jesus had said. 33 And sure enough, as they were untying it, the owners asked them, "Why are you untying that colt?"

34 And the disciples simply replied, "The Lord needs it." 35 So they brought the colt to Jesus and threw their garments over it for him to ride on.

36 As he rode along, the crowds spread out their garments on the road ahead of him. 37 When he reached the place where the road started down the Mount of Olives, all of his followers began to shout and sing as they walked along, praising God for all the wonderful miracles they had seen.

38 "Blessings on the King who comes
   in the name of the LORD!
Peace in heaven, and glory in
   highest heaven!"*

39 But some of the Pharisees among the crowd said, "Teacher, rebuke your followers for saying things like that!"

40 He replied, "If they kept quiet,

NASB

tell you, if these become silent, the stones will cry out!"

⁴¹When He approached *Jerusalem*, He saw the city and wept over it, ⁴²saying, "If you had known in this day, even you, the things which make for peace! But now they have been hidden from your eyes. ⁴³For the days will come upon you ªwhen your enemies will throw up a ᵇbarricade against you, and surround you and hem you in on every side, ⁴⁴and they will level you to the ground and your children within you, and they will not leave in you one stone upon another, because you did not recognize the time of your visitation."

⁴⁵Jesus entered the temple and began to drive out those who were selling, ⁴⁶saying to them, "It is written, 'AND MY HOUSE SHALL BE A HOUSE OF PRAYER,' but you have made it a ROBBERS' ªDEN."

⁴⁷And He was teaching daily in the temple; but the chief priests and the scribes and the leading men among the people were trying to destroy Him, ⁴⁸and they could not find ªanything that they might do, for all the people were hanging on to ᵇevery word He said.

19:29 ªOr *hill...Olive Grove;* Mount of Olives **19:33** ªLit *lords* **19:37** ªLit *rejoicing* ᵇOr *works of power* **19:39** ªLit *from* **19:43** ªLit *and* ᵇI.e. a dirt wall or mound for siege purposes **19:46** ªLit *cave* **19:48** ªLit *what they would do* ᵇLit *Him, listening*

NLT

the stones along the road would burst into cheers!"

⁴¹But as he came closer to Jerusalem and saw the city ahead, he began to weep. ⁴²"How I wish today that you of all people would understand the way to peace. But now it is too late, and peace is hidden from your eyes. ⁴³Before long your enemies will build ramparts against your walls and encircle you and close in on you from every side. ⁴⁴They will crush you into the ground, and your children with you. Your enemies will not leave a single stone in place, because you did not recognize it when God visited you.*"

⁴⁵Then Jesus entered the Temple and began to drive out the people selling animals for sacrifices. ⁴⁶He said to them, "The Scriptures declare, 'My Temple will be a house of prayer,' but you have turned it into a den of thieves."*

⁴⁷After that, he taught daily in the Temple, but the leading priests, the teachers of religious law, and the other leaders of the people began planning how to kill him. ⁴⁸But they could think of nothing, because all the people hung on every word he said.

19:38 Pss 118:26; 148:1. **19:44** Greek *did not recognize the time of your visitation,* a reference to the Messiah's coming. **19:46** Isa 56:7; Jer 7:11.

By the time Jesus set out to lay kingly claim to Jerusalem as the Messiah, the capital city had served as a seat of pagan corruption for centuries. After Jerusalem fell to Babylon in 586 BC, the city remained the property of one world empire or another for more than four hundred years, until the Seleucid king Antiochus IV Epiphanes pushed Gentile occupation too far. In 175 BC, he banned all Jewish sacrifices in the temple and outlawed all Jewish rituals and festivals everywhere else in Israel. He then required all Jews to worship Greek deities and killed any priest who refused to conduct pagan sacrifices.

Then, in 167 BC, a priest named Mattathias, serving in the rural town of Modein, refused to compromise even when threatened with death. When one of his neighbors stepped forward to sacrifice to another god, the priest drew his sword, killed the man, and then killed the general who ordered the sacrifice. His uncompromising dedication sparked what is now known as the Maccabean Revolt.

About a year into the revolution, the courageous priest called his sons around his deathbed and charged them:

> Arrogance and scorn have now become strong; it is a time of ruin and furious anger. Now, my children, show zeal for the law, and give your lives for the covenant of our ancestors. . . . And so observe, from generation to generation, that none of those who put their trust in [the Lord] will lack strength. Do not fear the words of sinners, for their splendor will turn into dung and worms. Today they will be exalted, but tomorrow they will not be found, because they will have returned to the dust, and their plans will have perished. My children, be courageous and grow strong in the law, for by it you will gain honor. (1 Macc. 2:49-50, 61-64, NRSV)

After the old man's death, his son Judas Maccabeus (also known as Judah "the Hammer") led Israel to several victories over the Seleucid armies and retook control of Jerusalem. When the priests entered the temple to restore the sacrifices and to light the lampstand (Exod. 27:20-21; Lev. 24:2), they found that all of the sacred oil had been defiled except for one container—enough for one day. But in faith, they lit the lamp as the Lord had commanded . . . and it burned for eight days! This gave enough time for the priests to prepare more oil for the temple. Jews celebrate this miracle with the Feast of Dedication, also known as the Feast of Lights, or Hanukkah.

After Judah "the Hammer" died in battle, his brother Jonathan led the nation. But he deviated from the devotion of his father, Mattathias. Rather than trust God to help him keep the Seleucids out of Jerusalem, he accepted a treaty in which he declared allegiance to an invading Seleucid general in exchange for confirmation as high priest. Thus, he was not selected by the established Jewish process, but rather was appointed by Gentile authority. This proved to be a crucial turning point in Israel's history. In past years, the selection process may have been political—perhaps even corrupt—but for the first time in the history of God's temple, a religious leader assumed the role of high priest on the authority of a Gentile ruler rather than by divine authority.

After Jonathan's death, his brother Simon took his place. And, like his brother, Simon ruled as high priest by order of the Seleucid king. Soon afterward, the Jewish aristocracy and priests made Simon their king in all but name "until a trustworthy prophet should arise" (1 Macc. 14:41, NRSV). To safeguard his hold on power, Simon betrayed his Seleucid benefactor by seeking the protection of Rome in 139 BC. This, of course, opened the door to increasing Roman control. Consequently, by the first century AD, a Roman procurator occupied the king's palace, and Caesar's puppet priests ruled the sanctuary of the Almighty.

From their lofty positions of military and political might, the rulers of Jerusalem felt secure. As long as they kept a lid on popular unrest, what could go wrong? Meanwhile, as the once-holy city prepared for the great Feast of Passover, a thirty-something-year-old rabbi from Galilee set out from Jericho, accompanied by several thousand followers.

Jesus and his disciples traveled from Jericho to Jerusalem. As they approached Bethphage, Bethany, and the Mount of Olives, Jesus sent his disciples ahead to secure the donkey colt that he would ride into Jerusalem.

— 19:28-34 —

After a sumptuous banquet, the remarkable conversion of Zaccheus, a final lesson on the use of money in the kingdom, and perhaps a good night's rest, Jesus and His followers began their ascent from Jericho to Jerusalem, a 17-mile hike nearly 3,000 feet uphill.

We know from the Gospel of John that Jesus stayed with his friends Lazarus, Martha, and Mary, who lived in Bethany. This small town lay on the eastern slope of the Mount of Olives (see Zech. 14:4), about 2 miles (3.2 kilometers) from Jerusalem. As he approached, he sent two of his disciples on an errand. They were to obtain a colt He may have prearranged to use. Some suggest Jesus utilized an ancient custom called "angaria," in which certain citizens were required to keep an animal ready for use by government couriers. It's far more likely the owners expected Jesus to borrow the animal.

— 19:35-40 —

Jesus could have walked to Jerusalem as He had countless times before. He mounted the animal because this trip down the Mount of Olives, across the Kidron Valley, and into Jerusalem was different. This "triumphal entry" of Jesus to the capital of the Hebrews marked a change in His relationship to the ancient seat of Hebrew power and religion. He no longer visited as a worshiper; He claimed the city as King and the temple as God's ultimate High Priest.

Unlike a conquering warrior king, however, He entered the city on a symbol of peace. He rode on a humble donkey in fulfillment of a well-known messianic prophecy:

> Rejoice greatly, O daughter Zion!
> Shout in triumph, O daughter Jerusalem!
> Behold, your king is coming to you;
> He is just and endowed with salvation,
> Humble, and mounted on a donkey,
> Even on a colt, the foal of a donkey. (Zech. 9:9)

The Messiah's followers—the thousands who followed Him from Galilee and many others living in Judea—lined the road leading into the city with palm branches and clothes, shouting "Hosanna!" which means "Save us!" Their praise drew inspiration from a messianic psalm (Ps. 118:26). Meanwhile, the Pharisees stood back, outraged by the blatant celebration of Jesus as the Messiah. They commanded Jesus to silence what they considered sacrilege. By calling Him "Teacher" they suggest He take responsibility for His followers' proper instruction, which would include their not calling Him "Messiah."

The Lord's response not only affirms the "sacrilege" of His followers, but it also raises the stakes. He replied, in so many words, "If I silence the people, My other created things will take up their praise." Of course, Jesus knew this would prompt the religious leaders to push back. The time had come to confront their corruption in His official capacity as their King.

— 19:41-44 —

While the people cheered, Jesus wept over the city with audible sobbing (*klaiō* [2799]). Grief overwhelmed the Lord as He bewailed the future of Jerusalem. Throughout the ages, prophets begged the rulers of Jerusalem to trust in the Lord for the city's protection rather than in treaties, alliances, compromises, or submission to pagan rulers (Deut. 23:6;

Ezra 9:12; Isa. 30:1-3; 31:1; Jer. 43:5-7; Amos 5:4-8). Soon they would reject the Lord's Christ, bringing severe condemnation upon themselves. If only they had abandoned their dreams of political power and humbled themselves before the mighty hand of God! If only Jerusalem had accepted the way of Christ instead of resisting it by saying, "We do not want this man to reign over us"! (See Luke 19:14.)

Jesus prophesied the city's doom. The details of the Lord's prophecy were not intended to specify the exact methods of the invasion, but they describe siege warfare in general. He also used hyperbole—"they will not leave in you one stone upon another"—to convey the idea of severe, total destruction. Neither should be taken literally.

In AD 70, Titus did indeed construct barricades and siege ramps in order to sack the city.[2] While the Romans kept some towers and parts of the wall intact for their own use, Josephus writes, "But for all the rest of the wall, it was so thoroughly laid even with the ground by those that dug it up to the foundation, that there was left nothing to make those that came thither believe it had ever been inhabited."[3] Besides the destruction, the killing bordered on extermination. Then, in AD 135, Hadrian brought a crushing and final end to the nation of Israel, even attempting to eradicate Judaism and permanently erase their very existence from history, changing the name of the region to Syria Palaestina. The nation was doomed to such obliteration because the majority of its citizens rejected the Lord's sovereign claim (see 19:14).

— 19:45-46 —

In His first official act after the crowd asserted his Messiahship, Jesus challenged what was going on at the temple. On several occasions, He had spoken against the corruption taking place in the outer courts. This was the result of the influence of Annas, who had ruled as Israel's high priest for almost ten years, only to be deposed (see commentary at 3:1-2). By then, however, Annas had established an extensive, organized crime network in the temple, not unlike a quasi-religious "mafia."

Annas retreated from public view but continued to control every Jewish political office in Jerusalem, including that of high priest. After his removal from office, no fewer than five sons and a grandson succeeded him; and at the time of Jesus, his son-in-law Caiaphas ran the temple.

The temple corruption kept money flowing into the family's pockets and funded their hold on power. The chief priests refused to accept any currency except shekels minted in Israel. Money changers within the temple precincts gladly exchanged any currency for Jewish shek-els at an inflated rate and then pocketed the difference. Furthermore, since the Law of Moses stated that any animal offered to God had to be flawless—only the best would do—the men running the temple would inspect the animals brought for sacrifice. One can imagine how a cor-rupt priesthood would find a way to play the system: arbitrarily reject otherwise fine animals in order to supply a suitable replacement in exchange . . . for a fee!

The time for weeping had ended for Jesus. He drove the crooked merchants out of the temple, quoting Isaiah 56:7 and Jeremiah 7:11, calling them "robbers." The Greek term (*lēstēs* [3027]) is the same word used in the Good Samaritan story to refer to the men who ambushed the traveler, beat him mercilessly, stripped him of every possession, and then left him for dead (Luke 10:30).

— 19:47-48 —

Luke concludes the episode with a summary statement that leads di-rectly into the next several scenes. After cleansing the temple, Jesus continued to teach, which disturbed the "chief priests" and "leading men among the people." For most of His ministry, Jesus clashed with the Pharisees, who were middle-class experts in the Law. Now He had upset the Sadducees, who were ruling-class aristocrats. These men pos-sessed political power through their ties with Rome, unlike the Phari-sees who enjoyed the support of the common people. His continued presence in the temple gave them opportunity to challenge His author-ity and to attack His teaching.

Initially, the Jewish leaders hoped to discredit Jesus, effectively nul-lifying His influence among the people (see 11:53-54). But His reasoning left them no place for criticism. Moreover, the crowds listening to Him grew more loyal, preventing the leaders from doing anything to Jesus without incurring public wrath.

• • •

While Jesus entered the temple with divine authority and a large group of supporters, He did not come to take it by force—at least not yet. He came in peace to confront His covenant people, giving them ample opportunity to humble themselves, confess their wrongdoing, repent of their rebellion, seek God's forgiveness, receive His grace, and thereby enter His kingdom as true citizens. From this point forward, all the way to the cross, Jesus used every means at His disposal to convince the nation—from its leaders down to its commoners—to embrace their

King and be saved. But in order for that to happen, they would have to sacrifice everything they valued. If the rich, young ruler struggled with that decision, the nation's wealthiest and most powerful stood very little chance at all.

APPLICATION: LUKE 19:28-48
Courage and Faithfulness

As I consider these three scenes—the Triumphal Entry, the Lord's weeping over the city, and His angry cleansing of the temple—I see two qualities worth emulating, especially as the world becomes more corrupt with the steady approach of the end times.

The first quality is *courage*, which can be demonstrated as effectively in our anger as in our compassion. There are times when sitting idly by and shrugging helplessly at evil can be the most cowardly thing one can do. When done correctly, expressing anger can be the most spiritually productive response to wrongdoing.

Now, I know it's risky to make that statement without surrounding it with conditions and explanations, because it could be misused very easily. I don't suggest hot-tempered and out-of-control anger, which is destructive, potentially abusive, and always counterproductive; rage doesn't encourage others to behave righteously.

There is, however, a time and place for sanctified hostility. There are appropriate times for the Christian to say with fists clenched, "That is enough! That is wrong! And here are the Scriptures to prove it. I will not sit idly by and let it go."

The second quality is *faithfulness*. Faithfulness is revealed as much in ending well as in continuing strong. What a model Jesus provided for all of us! He entered Jerusalem knowing His destiny would put Him under the lictor's scourge and on a criminal's cross. Still, He wept over Jerusalem like a grieving parent of a convicted felon. He confronted the Pharisees' hypocrisy and called out the Sadducees' corruption, knowing where it would lead.

Courage and faithfulness—what a model Jesus provided! May God give us increasing measures of both!

Fighting Fire with Fire
LUKE 20:1-47

¹On one of the days while He was teaching the people in the temple and preaching the gospel, the chief priests and the scribes with the elders confronted *Him,* ²and they spoke, saying to Him, "Tell us by what authority You are doing these things, or who is the one who gave You this authority?" ³Jesus answered and said to them, "I will also ask you a ªquestion, and you tell Me: ⁴Was the baptism of John from heaven or from men?" ⁵They reasoned among themselves, saying, "If we say, 'From heaven,' He will say, 'Why did you not believe him?' ⁶But if we say, 'From men,' all the people will stone us to death, for they are convinced that John was a prophet." ⁷So they answered that they did not know where *it came* from. ⁸And Jesus said to them, "Nor ªwill I tell you by what authority I do these things."

⁹And He began to tell the people this parable: "A man planted a vineyard and rented it out to ªvine-growers, and went on a journey for a long time. ¹⁰At the *harvest* time he sent a slave to the vine-growers, so that they would give him *some* of the produce of the vineyard; but the vine-growers beat him and sent him away empty-handed. ¹¹And he proceeded to send another slave; and they beat him also and treated him shamefully and sent him away empty-handed. ¹²And he proceeded to send a third; and this one also they wounded and cast out. ¹³The ªowner of the vineyard said, 'What shall I do? I will send my beloved son; perhaps they will respect him.' ¹⁴But when the vine-growers saw him, they reasoned with one another, saying, 'This is the heir; let us kill him so that the inheritance

¹One day as Jesus was teaching the people and preaching the Good News in the Temple, the leading priests, the teachers of religious law, and the elders came up to him. ²They demanded, "By what authority are you doing all these things? Who gave you the right?"

³"Let me ask you a question first," he replied. ⁴"Did John's authority to baptize come from heaven, or was it merely human?"

⁵They talked it over among themselves. "If we say it was from heaven, he will ask why we didn't believe John. ⁶But if we say it was merely human, the people will stone us because they are convinced John was a prophet." ⁷So they finally replied that they didn't know.

⁸And Jesus responded, "Then I won't tell you by what authority I do these things."

⁹Now Jesus turned to the people again and told them this story: "A man planted a vineyard, leased it to tenant farmers, and moved to another country to live for several years. ¹⁰At the time of the grape harvest, he sent one of his servants to collect his share of the crop. But the farmers attacked the servant, beat him up, and sent him back empty-handed. ¹¹So the owner sent another servant, but they also insulted him, beat him up, and sent him away empty-handed. ¹²A third man was sent, and they wounded him and chased him away.

¹³"'What will I do?' the owner asked himself. 'I know! I'll send my cherished son. Surely they will respect him.'

¹⁴"But when the tenant farmers saw his son, they said to each other, 'Here comes the heir to this estate. Let's kill him and get the estate for

NASB

will be ours.' ¹⁵So they threw him out of the vineyard and killed him. What, then, will the ᵃowner of the vineyard do to them? ¹⁶He will come and destroy these vine-growers and will give the vineyard to others." When they heard it, they said, "May it never be!" ¹⁷But ᵃJesus looked at them and said, "What then is this that is written:

'THE STONE WHICH THE BUILDERS REJECTED,
THIS BECAME THE CHIEF CORNER *stone*'?

¹⁸Everyone who falls on that stone will be broken to pieces; but on whomever it falls, it will scatter him like dust."

¹⁹The scribes and the chief priests tried to lay hands on Him that very hour, and they feared the people; for they understood that He spoke this parable against them. ²⁰So they watched Him, and sent spies who ᵃpretended to be righteous, in order that they might ᵇcatch Him in some statement, so that they *could* deliver Him to the rule and the authority of the governor. ²¹They questioned Him, saying, "Teacher, we know that You speak and teach correctly, and You ᵃare not partial to any, but teach the way of God in truth. ²²Is it ᵃlawful for us to pay taxes to Caesar, or not?" ²³But He detected their trickery and said to them, ²⁴"Show Me a ᵃdenarius. Whose ᵇlikeness and inscription does it have?" They said, "Caesar's." ²⁵And He said to them, "Then render to Caesar the things that are Caesar's, and to God the things that are God's." ²⁶And they were unable to ᵃcatch Him in a

NLT

ourselves!' ¹⁵So they dragged him out of the vineyard and murdered him.

"What do you suppose the owner of the vineyard will do to them?" Jesus asked. ¹⁶"I'll tell you—he will come and kill those farmers and lease the vineyard to others."

"How terrible that such a thing should ever happen," his listeners protested.

¹⁷Jesus looked at them and said, "Then what does this Scripture mean?

'The stone that the builders rejected
  has now become the cornerstone.'*

¹⁸Everyone who stumbles over that stone will be broken to pieces, and it will crush anyone it falls on."

¹⁹The teachers of religious law and the leading priests wanted to arrest Jesus immediately because they realized he was telling the story against them—they were the wicked farmers. But they were afraid of the people's reaction.

²⁰Watching for their opportunity, the leaders sent spies pretending to be honest men. They tried to get Jesus to say something that could be reported to the Roman governor so he would arrest Jesus. ²¹"Teacher," they said, "we know that you speak and teach what is right and are not influenced by what others think. You teach the way of God truthfully. ²²Now tell us—is it right for us to pay taxes to Caesar or not?"

²³He saw through their trickery and said, ²⁴"Show me a Roman coin.* Whose picture and title are stamped on it?"

"Caesar's," they replied.

²⁵"Well then," he said, "give to Caesar what belongs to Caesar, and give to God what belongs to God."

²⁶So they failed to trap him by

saying in the presence of the people; and being amazed at His answer, they became silent.

27 Now there came to Him some of the Sadducees (who say that there is no resurrection), 28 and they questioned Him, saying, "Teacher, Moses wrote for us that IF A MAN'S BROTHER DIES, having a wife, AND HE IS CHILDLESS, HIS BROTHER SHOULD ᵃMARRY THE WIFE AND RAISE UP CHILDREN TO HIS BROTHER. 29 Now there were seven brothers; and the first took a wife and died childless; 30 and the second 31 and the third ᵃmarried her; and in the same way ᵇall seven ᶜdied, leaving no children. 32 Finally the woman died also. 33 In the resurrection therefore, which one's wife will she be? For ᵃall seven ᵇhad married her."

34 Jesus said to them, "The sons of this age marry and are given in marriage, 35 but those who are considered worthy to attain to that age and the resurrection from the dead, neither marry nor are given in marriage; 36 for they cannot even die anymore, because they are like angels, and are sons of God, being sons of the resurrection. 37 But that the dead are raised, even Moses showed, in the *passage about the burning* bush, where he calls the Lord THE GOD OF ABRAHAM, AND THE GOD OF ISAAC, AND THE GOD OF JACOB. 38 Now He is not the God of the dead but of the living; for all live to Him." 39 Some of the scribes answered and said, "Teacher, You have spoken well." 40 For they did not have courage to question Him any longer about anything.

41 Then He said to them, "How *is it that* they say ᵃthe Christ is David's

what he said in front of the people. Instead, they were amazed by his answer, and they became silent.

27 Then Jesus was approached by some Sadducees—religious leaders who say there is no resurrection from the dead. 28 They posed this question: "Teacher, Moses gave us a law that if a man dies, leaving a wife but no children, his brother should marry the widow and have a child who will carry on the brother's name.* 29 Well, suppose there were seven brothers. The oldest one married and then died without children. 30 So the second brother married the widow, but he also died. 31 Then the third brother married her. This continued with all seven of them, who died without children. 32 Finally, the woman also died. 33 So tell us, whose wife will she be in the resurrection? For all seven were married to her!"

34 Jesus replied, "Marriage is for people here on earth. 35 But in the age to come, those worthy of being raised from the dead will neither marry nor be given in marriage. 36 And they will never die again. In this respect they will be like angels. They are children of God and children of the resurrection.

37 "But now, as to whether the dead will be raised—even Moses proved this when he wrote about the burning bush. Long after Abraham, Isaac, and Jacob had died, he referred to the Lord* as 'the God of Abraham, the God of Isaac, and the God of Jacob.'* 38 So he is the God of the living, not the dead, for they are all alive to him."

39 "Well said, Teacher!" remarked some of the teachers of religious law who were standing there. 40 And then no one dared to ask him any more questions.

41 Then Jesus presented them with a question. "Why is it," he asked, "that the Messiah is said to be the

NASB

son? ⁴²For David himself says in the book of Psalms,

'THE LORD SAID TO MY LORD,
"SIT AT MY RIGHT HAND,
⁴³ UNTIL I MAKE YOUR ENEMIES A
　　　FOOTSTOOL FOR YOUR FEET."'

⁴⁴Therefore David calls Him 'Lord,' and how is He his son?"

⁴⁵And while all the people were listening, He said to the disciples, ⁴⁶"Beware of the scribes, who like to walk around in long robes, and love respectful greetings in the market places, and chief seats in the synagogues and places of honor at banquets, ⁴⁷who devour widows' houses, and for appearance's sake offer long prayers. These will receive greater condemnation."

20:3 ªLit *word*   20:8 ªLit *do I tell*   20:9 ªOr *tenant farmers*, also vv 10, 14, 16   20:13 ªLit *lord*   20:15 ªLit *lord*   20:17 ªLit *He*   20:20 ªLit *falsely represented themselves* ᵇLit *take hold of His word*   20:21 ªLit *do not receive a face*   20:22 ªOr *permissible*   20:24 ªThe denarius was a day's wages ᵇLit *image*   20:26 ªLit *catch His statement*   20:28 ªLit *take*   20:31 ªLit *took* ᵇLit *the seven also* ᶜLit *left no children, and died*   20:33 ªLit *the* ᵇLit *had her as wife*   20:41 ªI.e. the Messiah

NLT

son of David? ⁴²For David himself wrote in the book of Psalms:

'The LORD said to my Lord,
Sit in the place of honor at my
　　right hand
⁴³ until I humble your enemies,
　　making them a footstool under
　　your feet.'*

⁴⁴Since David called the Messiah 'Lord,' how can the Messiah be his son?"

⁴⁵Then, with the crowds listening, he turned to his disciples and said, ⁴⁶"Beware of these teachers of religious law! For they like to parade around in flowing robes and love to receive respectful greetings as they walk in the marketplaces. And how they love the seats of honor in the synagogues and the head table at banquets. ⁴⁷Yet they shamelessly cheat widows out of their property and then pretend to be pious by making long prayers in public. Because of this, they will be severely punished."

20:17 Ps 118:22.   20:24 Greek *a denarius*.   20:28 See Deut 25:5-6.   20:37a Greek *when he wrote about the bush. He referred to the Lord*.   20:37b Exod 3:6.   20:42-43 Ps 110:1.

We live in a time when many people have an inordinate need to be liked. Winning a popularity contest can be more desirable than standing for what is right. For some, applause is addictive. They want compliments, not confrontation—and certainly not criticism. They would prefer to be liked by the majority than to be respected by the discerning truth-seekers.

When I find myself weakening at this point, I remind myself of the words of Jesus: "Woe to you when all men speak well of you, for their fathers used to treat the false prophets in the same way" (6:26). The New Living Translation reads, "What sorrow awaits you who are praised by the crowds, for their ancestors also praised false prophets." The Phillips paraphrase renders this verse thus, "How miserable for you when everybody says nice things about you; for that is exactly how their fathers treated the false prophets." And *The Message* paraphrases the Lord's warning very well: "There's trouble ahead when you live only for the approval of others, saying what flatters them, doing what indulges them. Popularity contests are not truth contests—look how many scoundrel preachers were approved by your ancestors! Your task is to be true, not popular."

Jesus' point was simple: Anyone who desires public applause at any cost is headed for trouble. Unfortunately, so are those who stand for what is right! Anyone who has taken an unpopular stand for truth has suffered the backlash of their peers. Instead of affirmation, we receive criticism. Instead of encouragement, we get questions about our motives. Instead of seeking to understand, others assume the worst. All of this makes for a strange trade-off. Instead of being surrounded by support, truth-tellers suddenly find themselves the objects of scorn, criticism, resentment, even deliberate misunderstanding.

Soon after expelling the corrupt merchants from the temple, Jesus began teaching in the temple, drawing large crowds. The temple rulers responded to his challenge to their authority by challenging Jesus in return. Luke describes four specific confrontations:

The question of Jesus' authority to cleanse the temple and to teach (20:1-8)

The Lord's indictment of the temple rulers (20:9-18)

The question of civil authority in the kingdom of God (20:19-26)

The difference between the kingdom of God and the present world (20:27-47)

— 20:1-2 —

The question of Jesus' authority to cleanse the temple and to teach (20:1-8). Luke mentions three groups of men: chief priests, scribes, and elders—the constituent members of the Sanhedrin.[4] This governing body of seventy Jewish statesmen was, for Israel, the equivalent of a parliament and supreme court. A presiding elder called the *Nasi* worked closely with the high priest to set the council's agenda, which included making laws, setting the official Jewish ritual calendar, deciding national policy, regulating the temple, and ruling on serious court cases. According to Jewish tradition, the *Nasi* during this time was Gamaliel, the grandson of the great rabbi Hillel and teacher of a young Pharisee named Saul of Tarsus (Acts 22:3).

Jesus had predicted that such men would reject Him (Luke 9:22). The term used by Luke in this earlier prediction means "rejected after investigation." This is that investigation. They clearly understood the stakes. Jesus was exercising authority over the temple, acting like He literally owned the place. In response, the leaders demanded to see His credentials. Their question, literally rendered, is "Tell us by what kind of authority You do these things, or who is the one giving you this authority?" They said, in effect, "We operate under the authority of the high priest, who has the backing of Rome and every political official in Israel. From whom do You derive power?"

Of course, only two answers existed: human authority and divine authority. If He said, "I have been empowered by . . ." and then named His backers, He would have set the stage for a political showdown. They undoubtedly presumed He laid claim to the temple on the basis of a populist movement—tens of thousands of Jews itching for a revolution to bring about change. They would have accused Him of sedition against Rome and proceeded with a plan to undo Him.

If, on the other hand, He claimed divine authority, they would have drawn Him into a game of religious "King of the Hill," comparing and contrasting qualifications, most likely based on their traditional theology of the "divine right of priests." Their reasoning would look something like this: "God is sovereign over everything. We have authority over the temple; therefore, God must approve. You don't suppose God has lost control of His temple, do you?"

If the temple rulers couldn't destroy or discredit Jesus, perhaps they could draw Him into a stalemate, which, of course, would leave them in power.

— 20:3-4 —

Jesus recognized the religious authorities were fishing for something to attack. By design, they placed Him in a position in which He stood nothing to gain and much to lose by answering directly. Therefore, Jesus needed to respond wisely, giving them nothing to use against Him. He did this by employing a classic rabbinic debate strategy: the counter question. He asked them to state from their official position as religious leaders—*ex cathedra*, as it were—the nature of John the Baptizer's authority, whether it was human or divine.

He reversed their positions, placing *them* in a no-win scenario. John had been immensely popular among Jews. He called them to a baptism of repentance, pointing them toward uncompromising devotion to God. He spoke with a voice of authority that the general population regarded as authentically prophetic and unquestionably inspired by God. He stood against the open corruption of Agrippa and was beheaded for it. He also declared Jesus as the Messiah.

With all of those facts in mind, consider the religious leaders' deliberations as Luke records them in 20:5-6.

— 20:5-6 —

"If we say, 'From heaven,' He will say, 'Why did you not believe him?'"

The temple rulers owed their positions to the political clout of Israel's aristocracy—including men like Agrippa—and were backed by a network of "Herodians," wealthy Jews who derived their power from the king, who in turn answered to Caesar. The temple rulers also served at the pleasure of the Roman procurator, who appointed the high priest and maintained tight control over every other political office. To say, "From heaven," put them on the wrong side of the man who had murdered John the Baptizer. In addition, because John named Jesus as the Messiah, they would have had to agree that Jesus ruled the temple by divine authority.

"But if we say, 'From men,' all the people will stone us to death."

Stoning was the penalty for false prophecy (Deut. 13:1-11). By extension, prophesying against a true prophet amounted to false prophecy. Jesus had already stated His position: "I say to you, among those born of women there is no one greater than John" (Luke 7:28). Meanwhile, the Pharisees and lawyers had already demonstrated their opposition to John (7:30). Surrounded by a multitude of Jesus' supporters, the temple officials risked losing credibility that they might never regain.

— 20:7-8 —

The officials shrewdly assessed their position and, realizing they had nothing to gain and everything to lose by answering, decided on a tactical retreat. Jesus allowed them to back away. The stalemate left Him with the upper hand. Nevertheless, He concluded with a statement designed to rebuke their cowardice and defy their presumed authority over Him.

— 20:9 —

The Lord's indictment of the temple rulers (20:9-18). With barely a breath taken between sentences, and before the leaders could retreat, Jesus began a parable.

Most of the images in Jesus' teaching drew upon the common experiences of Jews living in the first century: shepherd and sheep, sower and seed, wine and wineskins, master and servants. But no metaphor touched the Hebrew soul like the picture of the vinedresser and his vineyard. This image poignantly illustrated God's special care for the nation of Israel (Ps. 80:8-16; Isa. 5:1-7).

In the Lord's parable, the owner of the vineyard (God) left the vineyard (Israel) in the care of tenant farmers (the religious leaders).

— 20:10-13 —

In time, following the requisite waiting period (Lev. 19:23-25), the owner sends a servant to conduct an accounting and to collect what belongs to him. These servants, of course, represent the prophets of old, who came one after another, many of them facing persecution and even martyrdom. After three servants return to the owner with nothing but injuries to show for their errands, he sends his son, hoping for a different response. The son is "beloved," a fact that will intensify the owner's response later. The verb rendered "respect" (*entrepō* [1788]) means "to cause to turn (in shame)" or "to show deference in recognition of higher status."[5]

Obviously, the son in the Lord's parable represents Himself.

— 20:14-16 —

The tenant farmers hatch a plan when they see the son appear on the horizon. Unfortunately for them, their plan makes no sense. They foolishly think that murdering the son positions them to inherit the owner's estate! Or, they presume that no court would intervene, thus counting on lawlessness to work on their behalf.

At this point in the story, the temple rulers undoubtedly knew which part they played. If they couldn't discredit Jesus in public, they would dispose of Him privately, using violence if necessary. Consequently, the parable not only convicted His enemies, but it also warned them to reconsider.

At the end of His story, Jesus engaged the audience with a question and answer, which invited them to see the situation from the owner's perspective. He asked, in essence, "If you were the owner/father, what would *you* do to those murderers?" The answer, of course, was obvious: severe judgment. He will "destroy" them. By application, this destruction refers to eternal condemnation.

The other part of the judgment states that he will "give the vineyard to others." While cryptic at the time, history suggests the "others" are the church. Regardless, the idea of God's vineyard being given to "others" was unthinkable. The phrase "May it never be!" is an emotionally-charged interjection of shock and dismay. "God forbid!" "Perish the thought!" "This must never happen!"

— 20:17-18 —

Jesus followed their reaction "May it never be!" (Luke 20:16) with a solemn prediction from the Old Testament—a psalm which celebrates the Lord's saving grace, foreshadowing the reign of the Messiah when He takes His place of authority over the earth:

> The stone which the builders rejected
> Has become the chief corner stone.
> This is the LORD's doing;
> It is marvelous in our eyes.
> This is the day which the LORD has made;
> Let us rejoice and be glad in it. (Ps. 118:22-24)

This psalm illustrates the idea of vindication. What had been rejected as worthless ultimately became the most important stone in a building. When constructing a foundation, the cornerstone becomes the reference by which every part of the building is measured.

Jesus then extended the metaphor beyond the mere embarrassment of failing to appreciate something of such great value. This stone plays a passive role, and then an active role, in the utter destruction of those who reject it.

— 20:19-20 —

The question of civil authority in the kingdom of God (20:19-26). The religious leaders, of course, knew what Jesus was saying and against whom. Most everyone did. Attacking Him openly and overtly didn't work, so they took their campaign underground, working in secret through covert agents. They hoped to find something to put Jesus at odds with the Romans. Luke's phrasing is significant: "so that they would have an excuse to hand Him over to the ruling authority and judicial power of the governor [Procurator Pontius Pilate]" (my contextualized rendering). This reveals their perspective of the world, which sacrifices all for the sake of earthly authority and leaves no place in their thinking for divine authority.

— 20:21-22 —

The religious leaders formulated an insidious question designed to alienate Jesus from important political factions in the temple as well as to lay the groundwork for a case before Pilate. They approached Him in apparent deference to His authority as a teacher of the Law. Ironically, however, their flattery was the only truth they spoke. Indeed, Jesus did speak and teach correctly; He was not partial to any faction; and He did teach the way of God in truth. They had never spoken truer words!

The spies chose their words carefully. The phrase rendered "Is it lawful" is better translated "Is it permitted." The question assumes a common understanding of the governing rules. Without stating so specifically, the spies' question could be interpreted as either "Is it permissible [under the Law of Moses]?" or "Is it permissible [according to ethics]?"

Both the spies and Jesus knew that the Law of Moses says nothing about paying tribute to a foreign power ruling over Israel. God never intended Israel to be anything but free! He established His covenant people in the Promised Land to be subject to Him alone. Therefore, tradition had to speak; and this was a topic of intense debate between the Pharisees, who resented Gentile interference, and the Sadducees, who depended upon Roman might to secure their positions. A "yes" put Jesus on the side of the Sadducees, which would make the Messiah complicit in foreign domination. A "no" made the Messiah an enemy of Rome, tantamount to encouraging His followers to withhold taxes.

— 20:24-26 —

On a philosophical level, how Jesus answers their question reveals his perspective of God's kingdom and how it relates to the temporal governments of earth. The Sadducees were clear that they had no problem paying the tax as a means to an end. Their history shows them trying to establish God's kingdom through clever diplomacy and strategic alliances with Gentiles—at least that was their rationalization. Pharisees and zealots opposed Rome at every turn and did all they could to distance Israel from Gentiles. Yet they hypocritically served money—even loved money—in actual practice.

Both parties—the Sadducees and the Pharisees—assumed correctly that the kingdom of God will eventually displace the kingdoms of earth. They differed in how they saw that kingdom being established.

Jesus knew their intentions, but He didn't merely sidestep their clumsy trap; He took the opportunity to instruct His disciples at the same time. Citizens of God's kingdom will have to live under the authority of earthly governments for an indeterminate time—two millennia so far! He thus answered the additional question, "How shall citizens of God's kingdom live under the rule of pagan authorities until Christ returns?"

Jesus had the spies produce a specific kind of coin, a *denarius*, which bore the image of Tiberius and the inscription "TI CAESAR DIVI AVG F AVGVSTVS," or "Tiberius Caesar, Augustus, son of Divine Augustus." His response acknowledges that we live under the authority of earthly governments but that they exist within the sovereign plan of God. Sometimes the values of the two conflict, but not always. God does not ask us to choose between Rome and Israel, but between wealth and righteousness. Until Christ returns, we need money, but we must not serve it. We obey governments, but we do not serve them when their law conflicts with God's.

Governmental authority is instituted by God. Romans 13 makes that clear. We have a duty to respect government officials. And even though our ultimate citizenship is in heaven, making us strangers and pilgrims on this earth, that does not mean that we should ignore our earthly responsibilities or avoid paying what is due.

The Lord's reply left His enemies speechless. They were "amazed" and likely made a hasty retreat back to the war room.

Classical Numismatic Group, Inc.

When Jesus is questioned about taxes in Luke 20:20-26, He is handed a Roman coin. It was likely a coin that looked like this one that bears an image of Tiberius Caesar, who was the emperor of Rome during Jesus' ministry.

— 20:27 —

The difference between the kingdom of God and the present world (20:27-47). An unknown period of time passed, but it could not have been more than a few days. Jesus continued daily lessons in the temple, undaunted by the repeated attempts of His enemies to trap Him with His own words. On this occasion, a group of Sadducees approached Jesus with another riddle—this one more elaborate than the others.

Three beliefs distinguished the Sadducees from their political rivals, the Pharisees. First, the Sadducees believed inspiration stopped with the Pentateuch, the first five books of the Old Testament. They held a lower view of the rest of the Old Testament—the books of

THE SADDUCEES

LUKE 20:27

The Sadducees were a peculiar faction of Jews. Conservative by Jewish standards—some would say conveniently so—they accepted no teaching or tradition beyond what could be found in the Pentateuch, the first five books of the Old Testament and the only Scripture to have come from the hand of Moses.[6] Based on their reading of these Scriptures, they did not believe in life after death or resurrection or angels or spirits.

The deists of the 1800s, who were vehemently skeptical of anything supernatural and were fatalistic to the core, resembled the Sadducees. They believed God to be ineffably remote, leaving each person free to craft their own fate with no prospect of eternal reward or punishment. The Sadducees believed that punishment for sin was the duty of men and that such punishment should be both merciless and severe.[7] They believed each person had free will; therefore, each is responsible for the events of their life, including sickness, poverty, misfortune, and even manner of death. The Jewish historian Josephus described them as contentious with everyone, including their own, even thinking it "an instance of virtue to dispute with those teachers of philosophy whom they frequent."[8] Sadducees delighted in word games and crafted ludicrous scenarios to demonstrate the absurdity of any teaching that transcended experience in the here and now. We see this kind of scenario presented to Jesus in Luke 20:27-33.

history, wisdom, and prophecy—and completely ignored the Pharisees' traditions.

Second, the Sadducees didn't believe in an afterlife or a resurrection or a final judgment. They believed that nothingness followed this life, so God punishes the wicked and rewards the righteous now, not later.

Third, the Sadducees believed in a distant, hands-off God who did not interact or interfere in human events.

— 20:28-33 —

The Sadducees devised a riddle with the intention to characterize the Lord's theology as absurd. It involved the Jewish custom of levirate marriage. If a man died, leaving his wife without children, an eligible brother was to marry her, father children with her, and raise them to assume the dead man's name and carry on his legacy (Deut. 25:5-6). Because this had been commanded in the Pentateuch, the Sadducees accepted the custom as divinely ordained.

With this practice as the basis of the riddle, the Sadducees told the unlikely tale of one brother after another dying without producing any heirs. The poor widow became the wife of all seven men in turn until she also died. When all are raised again, presumably to live in the kingdom of God, the question of her marriage would have to be settled—to whom would she be married? In their minds, this conundrum proved the absurdity of the doctrine of resurrection. Certainly, God would not have been so shortsighted; therefore, the doctrine must be false.

— 20:34-36 —

Jesus answered the complicated question in two stages. First, life in the kingdom of God will be fundamentally different from our present existence (Luke 20:34-36). Then, only after presuming the reality of the resurrection, He demonstrated from the Pentateuch that Moses did, indeed, affirm life after death (20:37-38).

The Sadducees assumed that if an afterlife exists, it closely resembles life as we live it now. Jesus clarified that in the next life, everything is different. Marriage is an earthly institution—good for its time and purpose—but has no place in heaven. The vow "till death do us part" has no meaning there. Death is also confined to earth; people in heaven don't die. Moreover, the whole concept of family changes, and marriage will be rendered unnecessary. In comparing the citizens of heaven to angels, Jesus touched on another doctrine the Sadducees rejected: the existence of angels.

In the course of answering their question—at least in this stage of His reply—Jesus clarified that not all will enjoy a resurrection to live in the kingdom of God. Only those considered worthy will have that privilege.

— 20:37-38 —

Jesus spoke of the resurrection as a fact in the first stage of His answer. Still, He took the opportunity to show the reasonableness of the doctrine. While the Sadducees spoke of the resurrection only in hypothetical terms, He demonstrated from the Pentateuch that Moses assumed a resurrection in his writings. To prove His point, Jesus quoted Exodus 3:6, in which God spoke from the burning bush: "I am the God of your father, the God of Abraham, the God of Isaac, and the God of Jacob." God used the present tense, not the past tense, indicating that He is still the God of these patriarchs.

— 20:39-40 —

While the Sadducees led the attack in this instance, the audience included scribes, who—almost without exception—were Pharisees. Naturally, as strong advocates of the resurrection, they liked what Jesus had to say. Sadducees and Pharisees agreed on very little except their hatred for Jesus; but on this day, their collusion weakened, if only a little.

Luke states that "they"—that is, the scribes, Pharisees, chief priests, and Sadducees—abandoned their futile attempts to outwit Jesus in debate. Soon they would switch to deadlier tactics; but before the dialogue closed, Jesus took time to address their need for salvation. He had entered the temple to claim the institution as His own; now He presented Himself to the men as their Messiah.

— 20:41-44 —

While His enemies stood in silence, unable to offer any rebuttal, Jesus asked a riddle of His own. Drawing inferences from Psalm 110:1, He asked, "If the Messiah is a descendant of David, why does David call him 'Lord'?"

For the sake of clarity, the solution can be expressed as a syllogism:

The Messiah is a descendant of David.
David called his descendant, the Messiah, "My Lord."
David also called God "The LORD."
Therefore, David saw the Messiah as equal with God.

Luke doesn't record the response of the Lord's enemies. He doesn't even reveal whether they understood His point. Most likely they did. After His messianic entry into Jerusalem, His claiming authority over the temple, and His many allusions to the kingdom of God, it was clear that Jesus claimed to be the Messiah. His rhetorical question then pushed the religious leaders to make a final connection. If Jesus is the Messiah, and the Messiah is equal with God, then He was God in their midst.

Later, during his trial, it was a similar allusion to Psalm 110:1 that led to a charge of blasphemy (Luke 22:67-71; cf. Mark 14:61-64). Ironically, they could not trap Jesus with lies; they could convict Him only with the truth.

— 20:45-47 —

With the scribes, Pharisees, chief priests, and Sadducees still shuffling uncomfortably, Jesus addressed His followers, perhaps pointing at the assembled religious leaders. He singled out the scribes for redress—the scribes craved the applause of humans above all else—although much of his indictment applied to the whole group.

"Long robes" were the functional equivalent of an expensive, hand-tailored, silk suit. "Respectful greetings" describes public recognition of their exalted status. "Chief seats" are those in the synagogue that are up front, facing the congregation, where a leader can receive the greatest visibility (see Luke 11:43). "Places of honor" go to people of the highest social rank (see 14:7-8).

None of these things are, of course, wrong in their own right. As with money, the object is not as important as the motivation. The scribes delighted in these petty perks because they loved approval.

To illustrate their hypocrisy, Jesus highlighted two activities that sit on opposite poles of the moral spectrum. To "devour widows' houses" is to take advantage of the helpless. The prophet Isaiah condemned such religious leaders in his day, writing,

> Woe to those who enact evil statutes
> And to those who constantly record unjust decisions,
> So as to deprive the needy of justice
> And rob the poor of My people of their rights,
> So that widows may be their spoil
> And that they may plunder the orphans. (Isa. 10:1-2)

There may have been many ways a religious official could defraud widows, but the Lord may have had the scribes' judicial role in mind (see Luke 18:2-5). Regardless, these same corrupt men who preyed on the helpless also made long prayers, not to seek God's favor, but to win human admiration. While some sin out of ignorance, others have intimate knowledge of God's Word yet violate His statutes without a second thought. These will suffer the worst torment of all.

When Jesus entered the temple, He did His best to teach divine truth and to reconcile all of His listeners to their God. But He never entertained any illusions about success. He understood the dark power that veiled men's eyes and kept the temple leaders blinded to the light of God's Word. While He strongly desired to be received as their Messiah, their Ultimate High Priest, Jesus never regarded His path to the cross as anything but the successful unfolding of a plan. He had said early in His ministry, "Do not think that I came to bring peace on the earth; I did not come to bring peace, but a sword" (Matt. 10:34). The sword of which He spoke is the sharpest of all implements of conflict—He wielded the sword of truth. The sword of truth has but one target: the heart. And when the heart of a hypocrite is pierced, it bleeds resentment and, ultimately, hatred. As a result, those who hold the sword of truth will find themselves hunted by evil.

APPLICATION: LUKE 20:1-47

Enduring Lessons for Truth Tellers

Few weapons against evil can rival the sword of truth. Though readily available to anyone brave enough to hold it, few will. And it's little wonder. The privilege of wielding so powerful a tool comes at great cost—misunderstandings, false accusations, broken relationships, loneliness, frustration. Furthermore, standing for what's right frequently involves terrifying bouts with self-doubt and even self-recrimination. Sometimes the choice to take truth by the handle results in glorious victory, but more often the counterstrike of evil comes with startling ferocity and lasting devastation.

For those who are called to grip the sword of truth, I offer four lessons from the example of Jesus.

First, *knowing your mission will help you stay focused on the goal.* Jesus clearly understood the reason for His coming to earth and never allowed popularity, success, opposition, threats, or even dissention within His ranks to distract Him. He remained steadfastly focused on that mission, though not without due care for those around Him. He worked hard to make the truth plain. He often repeated the invitation to embrace the truth. But He never allowed the failure of others to pull Him off course.

Second, *encountering evil requires confrontation.* Few people enjoy confrontation, but standing for the truth against evil will inevitably require it. And sometimes what must be said will be difficult to say as well as difficult for others to hear. Only rarely—perhaps once in a lifetime—will confrontation require the kind of severe rebuke Jesus brought against the Pharisees. The greater the evil, the stronger the confrontation must be. In general, I advise kindness unless a kind approach is irresponsible, but I never advise kindness at the expense of plain talk.

Be prepared to state the truth plainly.

Third, *boldness in the course of a noble fight is worth the risk.* Standing for truth requires boldness. Some will be offended by it, and you can expect to be criticized for style when the opposition can find no fault with content. Furthermore, boldness may require strong action to accompany strong speech. You may have to quit a job, end a relationship, confront a powerful opponent, cope with a fear, deal with threats, perhaps even face certain defeat. Don't back down. If you stand on truth, you'll never regret being bold. But you will regret your timidity.

Fourth, *truth telling offers no guarantee of victory.* We live in a world that does not operate according to God's rules. The present world system punishes good deeds and rewards those who choose evil. In the words of James Russell Lowell, "Truth forever on the scaffold; wrong forever on the throne."[9] And, unfortunately, truth tellers often find themselves on the receiving end of the most outrageous abuse imaginable. So be realistic. Take courage. Your stand on truth will not likely be vindicated any time soon or even in your lifetime. To finish Lowell's line: "Yet that scaffold sways the future, and, behind the dim unknown, standeth God within the shadow, keeping watch above his own."[10]

A two-fisted grip on the sword of truth, while sacrificial, does offer great reward. Truth grants freedom from guilt and shame. Truth breeds contentment, instills confidence, stimulates creativity, fosters intimacy, encourages further honesty, inspires courage, and sets people free. But, most importantly, it puts us on God's side of the issue. We have His promise that He will amply reward any sacrifice that truth demands—if not in this life, then certainly in the next.[11]

Lifting the Prophetic Veil
LUKE 21:1-38

NASB

¹And He looked up and saw the rich putting their gifts into the treasury. ²And He saw a poor widow putting ᵃin two ᵇsmall copper coins. ³And He said, "Truly I say to you, this poor widow put in more than all *of them;* ⁴for they all out of their ᵃsurplus put into the ᵇoffering; but she out of her poverty put in all ᶜthat she had to live on."

NLT

¹While Jesus was in the Temple, he watched the rich people dropping their gifts in the collection box. ²Then a poor widow came by and dropped in two small coins.*

³"I tell you the truth," Jesus said, "this poor widow has given more than all the rest of them. ⁴For they have given a tiny part of their surplus, but she, poor as she is, has given everything she has."

NASB

⁵ And while some were talking about the temple, that it was adorned with beautiful stones and votive gifts, He said, ⁶ "As for these things which you are looking at, the days will come in which there will not be left one stone upon another which will not be torn down."

⁷ They questioned Him, saying, "Teacher, when therefore will these things happen? And what *will be* the ªsign when these things are about to take place?" ⁸ And He said, "See to it that you are not misled; for many will come in My name, saying, 'I am *He*,' and, 'The time is near.' Do not go after them. ⁹ When you hear of wars and disturbances, do not be terrified; for these things must take place first, but the end *does* not *follow* immediately."

¹⁰ Then He continued by saying to them, "Nation will rise against nation and kingdom against kingdom, ¹¹ and there will be great earthquakes, and in various places plagues and famines; and there will be terrors and great ªsigns from heaven.

¹² "But before all these things, they will lay their hands on you and will persecute you, delivering you to the synagogues and prisons, ªbringing you before kings and governors for My name's sake. ¹³ It will lead to ªan opportunity for your testimony. ¹⁴ So make up your minds not to prepare beforehand to defend yourselves; ¹⁵ for I will give you ªutterance and wisdom which none of your opponents will be able to resist or refute. ¹⁶ But you will be betrayed even by parents and brothers and relatives and friends, and they will put *some* of you to death, ¹⁷ and you will be hated by all because of My name. ¹⁸ Yet not a hair of your head will perish. ¹⁹ By your endurance you will gain your ªlives.

²⁰ "But when you see Jerusalem

NLT

⁵ Some of his disciples began talking about the majestic stonework of the Temple and the memorial decorations on the walls. But Jesus said, ⁶ "The time is coming when all these things will be completely demolished. Not one stone will be left on top of another!"

⁷ "Teacher," they asked, "when will all this happen? What sign will show us that these things are about to take place?"

⁸ He replied, "Don't let anyone mislead you, for many will come in my name, claiming, 'I am the Messiah,'* and saying, 'The time has come!' But don't believe them. ⁹ And when you hear of wars and insurrections, don't panic. Yes, these things must take place first, but the end won't follow immediately." ¹⁰ Then he added, "Nation will go to war against nation, and kingdom against kingdom. ¹¹ There will be great earthquakes, and there will be famines and plagues in many lands, and there will be terrifying things and great miraculous signs from heaven.

¹² "But before all this occurs, there will be a time of great persecution. You will be dragged into synagogues and prisons, and you will stand trial before kings and governors because you are my followers. ¹³ But this will be your opportunity to tell them about me.* ¹⁴ So don't worry in advance about how to answer the charges against you, ¹⁵ for I will give you the right words and such wisdom that none of your opponents will be able to reply or refute you! ¹⁶ Even those closest to you—your parents, brothers, relatives, and friends—will betray you. They will even kill some of you. ¹⁷ And everyone will hate you because you are my followers.* ¹⁸ But not a hair of your head will perish! ¹⁹ By standing firm, you will win your souls.

²⁰ "And when you see Jerusalem

surrounded by armies, then [a]recognize that her desolation is near. 21 Then those who are in Judea must flee to the mountains, and those who are in the midst of [a]the city must leave, and those who are in the country must not enter [a]the city; 22 because these are days of vengeance, so that all things which are written will be fulfilled. 23 Woe to those who are pregnant and to those who are nursing babies in those days; for there will be great distress upon the [a]land and wrath to this people; 24 and they will fall by the edge of the sword, and will be led captive into all the nations; and Jerusalem will be trampled under foot by the Gentiles until the times of the Gentiles are fulfilled.

25 "There will be [a]signs in sun and moon and stars, and on the earth dismay among nations, in perplexity at the roaring of the sea and the waves, 26 men fainting from fear and the expectation of the things which are coming upon the [a]world; for the powers of [b]the heavens will be shaken. 27 Then they will see THE SON OF MAN COMING IN A CLOUD with power and great glory. 28 But when these things begin to take place, straighten up and lift up your heads, because your redemption is drawing near."

29 Then He told them a parable: "Behold the fig tree and all the trees; 30 as soon as they put forth *leaves*, you see it and know for yourselves that summer is now near. 31 So you also, when you see these things happening, [a]recognize that the kingdom of God is near. 32 Truly I say to you, this [a]generation will not pass away until all things take place. 33 Heaven and earth will pass away, but My words will not pass away.

34 "Be on guard, so that your hearts will not be weighted down with dissipation and drunkenness and the worries of life, and that day will not

surrounded by armies, then you will know that the time of its destruction has arrived. 21 Then those in Judea must flee to the hills. Those in Jerusalem must get out, and those out in the country should not return to the city. 22 For those will be days of God's vengeance, and the prophetic words of the Scriptures will be fulfilled. 23 How terrible it will be for pregnant women and for nursing mothers in those days. For there will be disaster in the land and great anger against this people. 24 They will be killed by the sword or sent away as captives to all the nations of the world. And Jerusalem will be trampled down by the Gentiles until the period of the Gentiles comes to an end.

25 "And there will be strange signs in the sun, moon, and stars. And here on earth the nations will be in turmoil, perplexed by the roaring seas and strange tides. 26 People will be terrified at what they see coming upon the earth, for the powers in the heavens will be shaken. 27 Then everyone will see the Son of Man★ coming on a cloud with power and great glory.★ 28 So when all these things begin to happen, stand and look up, for your salvation is near!"

29 Then he gave them this illustration: "Notice the fig tree, or any other tree. 30 When the leaves come out, you know without being told that summer is near. 31 In the same way, when you see all these things taking place, you can know that the Kingdom of God is near. 32 I tell you the truth, this generation will not pass from the scene until all these things have taken place. 33 Heaven and earth will disappear, but my words will never disappear.

34 "Watch out! Don't let your hearts be dulled by carousing and drunkenness, and by the worries of this life. Don't let that day catch you unaware,

come on you suddenly like a trap; 35for it will come upon all those who dwell on the face of all the earth. 36But keep on the alert at all times, praying that you may have strength to escape all these things that are about to take place, and to stand before the Son of Man."

37 Now ªduring the day He was teaching in the temple, but ᵇat evening He would go out and spend the night on ᶜthe mount that is called ᵈOlivet. 38 And all the people would get up early in the morning *to come* to Him in the temple to listen to Him.

21:2 ªLit *there* ᵇGr *lepta* 21:4 ªOr *abundance* ᵇLit *gifts* ᶜLit *the living that she had* 21:7 ªOr *attesting miracle* 21:11 ªOr *attesting miracles* 21:12 ªLit *being brought* 21:13 ªLit *a testimony for you* 21:15 ªLit *a mouth* 21:19 ªLit *souls* 21:20 ªLit *know* 21:21 ªLit *her* 21:23 ªOr *earth* 21:25 ªOr *attesting miracles* 21:26 ªLit *inhabited earth* ᵇOr *heaven* 21:31 ªLit *know* 21:32 ªOr *race* 21:37 ªLit *days* ᵇLit *nights* ᶜOr *the hill* ᵈOr *Olive Grove*

35like a trap. For that day will come upon everyone living on the earth. 36Keep alert at all times. And pray that you might be strong enough to escape these coming horrors and stand before the Son of Man."

37 Every day Jesus went to the Temple to teach, and each evening he returned to spend the night on the Mount of Olives. 38The crowds gathered at the Temple early each morning to hear him.

21:2 Greek *two lepta* [the smallest of Jewish coins]. 21:8 Greek *claiming, 'I am.'* 21:13 Or *This will be your testimony against them.* 21:17 Greek *on account of my name.* 21:27a "Son of Man" is a title Jesus used for himself. 21:27b See Dan 7:13.

If you had only two months to live, would it make much difference in how you spent your remaining days? Undoubtedly, that tragic news would make all the difference in the world.

Let me push this to an even greater extreme. If you had only two *weeks* to live, how would that affect your perspective on values and priorities? Clearly, everything would change. The value of something would be far more important than its cost. Time would become the most treasured commodity, more precious than all the gold in the world. Temporal matters would fade into the background as eternal matters loomed large.

When Jesus entered Jerusalem to the cheers of thronging followers, He had no more than one week to live. After His final theological confrontation with the temple leaders, He had perhaps no more than two or three days. In the final hours of life, Jesus continued to teach in the temple while His enemies plotted His destruction. In the quiet before the storm, Jesus spent every spare moment in His father's house, praying, observing, and reflecting.

Luke chose to highlight two themes from the Lord's last days before the Passover celebration. First, Jesus reflected on the issue of values— what the kingdom of God considers precious as compared with the dominion of evil. Second, he spoke of the future of humanity—what will occur once He wins the decisive battle in the war against Satan.

As we examine these events, keep three words in the forefront of your mind: "Time is short."

— 21:1-2 —

Luke's focus on the widow ties this incident to the Lord's rebuke of the scribes, "who devour widows' houses, and for appearance's sake offer long prayers" (20:47). Jesus sat in the Court of Women, where thirteen, horn-shaped receptacles collected the freewill offerings of worshipers (see Deut. 16:10-11). In contrast to the scribes' ostentatious, false piety, the woman's humble gift barely tips the scales in the market. While most worshipers contributed silver coins worth a day's wages each, the woman deposited two *lepta*. Each *lepton* is worth around one-hundredth of a denarius, or one-hundredth of a day's wage for a common laborer.

— 21:3-4 —

The rich may be far more impressive. They may contribute larger amounts. They may cause heads to turn with their giant gifts. I am always grateful to large donors for the tangible impact they have in ministry—usually contributing to more than one cause. The point of the Lord's comment is not to disparage large donors but to honor those who have but a small amount to offer. While the widow gave less in terms of precious metal, she gave out of her need, not her surplus. What the wealthy gave was impressive, but what she gave hurt. As a result, she modeled total commitment, what the Lord wants more than anything.

Sacrifice requires trust in the Lord's provision, and it can come only from a grateful heart. In the kingdom of God, the value of a gift is not measured in terms of how much is given, but by how much is left over. When rich people give sacrificially, God—who owns everything—doesn't treasure the gift nearly as much as the heart of the giver.

— 21:5-6 —

As Jesus and a group of followers continued to congregate in the temple, watching worshipers come and go, someone who was admiring the grandeur of the enormous complex commented on the "beautiful stones" and "votive gifts." According to Josephus, Herod the Great quarried massive marble stones and polished them to a mirror finish; "some of them were forty-five cubits in length, five in height, and six in breadth."[12] In modern units, these blocks measured 67.5 feet (20.6 meters) long, 7.5 feet (2.3 meters) high, and 9 feet (2.7 meters) thick.

The description "votive gifts" refers to ornate accoutrements, such as gold-plated doors, giant lighting fixtures, exquisite tapestries, and finely-crafted artwork.

Jesus probably appreciated the beauty and expense of the temple building, and He gratefully remembered the sacrificial giving that made it all possible—the greed and hypocrisy of some notwithstanding. But He hastened to point out that nothing in the temple was permanent. The votive gifts could be plundered. The massive stones that appeared so immovable could be toppled. In fact, Jesus lamented the coming destruction of the temple, which would occur in the near future. The leaders had failed to heed His warning, which doomed their precious building (Luke 19:43-44).

— 21:7 —

At the time of the Lord's prophecy, Jerusalem was a simmering cauldron of political unrest. The Sadducees placated Rome and the Pharisees managed the populace—the two parties locked in a political tug-of-war that somehow maintained a precarious national balance. Meanwhile, every few years at Passover, "messiahs" came out of nowhere to rally gullible followers in a bid for revolution.

Things were reasonably stable for the moment, but the Lord's followers didn't doubt His prophecy. Their questions didn't merely satisfy their curiosity; they had practical reasons to know when the destruction would transpire. Whatever forces could dismantle the temple so completely would undoubtedly cause destruction throughout Israel. Knowing either the date or the precipitating events would give them ample warning to find safety.

Jesus took the opportunity to answer their question concerning the temple, but he also wanted to set the record straight. As bad as the temple destruction would be, it would be a relatively minor event compared to the end of days. One might avoid the former, but no one will escape the latter.

— 21:8-11 —

What follows is a summary of future history, including a brief reference to end-time calamities. After the summary, Jesus will discuss the stages in detail.

Jesus acknowledged the inevitability of false alarms before the "terrors and great signs from heaven" (21:11). So-called messiahs will continue to emerge, wars will be fought, and unrest will ebb and flow like always. These events are part of the normal chaos associated with the dominion of evil; they do not necessarily signal the beginning of end-time events. And, unfortunately, Christians will not be immune. Believers will not only suffer misfortune like everyone else, but they will also become targets of persecution—even martyrdom.

Still, "the end does not follow immediately." Nations will go to war, disasters will strike, diseases will afflict, and then, eventually, an accelerated number of supernatural events will occur (cf. Isa. 13:10, 13; 34:4; Jer. 30:4-7; Ezek. 14:21; 32:7-8; Dan. 9:26-27; Amos 8:9; Hag. 2:6). The phrase "terrors and great signs" uses apocalyptic language, strongly suggesting metaphysical disasters, not merely more of what we experience now.

— 21:12-19 —

"These things" most likely refers to the "terrors and great signs" of the end times. Before these things occur, while nations battle and disasters strike and diseases afflict, Christians will not remain immune. Citizens of the kingdom—living in enemy territory, as it were—will suffer the world's chaos along with everyone else.

Jesus regarded this as a necessary part of His plan of redemption. Just as He suffered, His followers will suffer. The sentence in Luke 21:13 reads, literally, "It will turn out to you for a witness." Like He promised earlier (12:11-12), God will give His people the right words at the right time, leaving the dominion of evil just as dumbstruck as the Lord's enemies in the temple.

The promises of 21:18-19 must be taken together. Clearly, persecution includes injury to the body, and martyrdom involves physical death. Jesus promises that the gain of eternal life will vindicate the loss of physical life. "Perish" is a translation of the same Greek word rendered "lose" in the paradoxical statement, "Whoever seeks to keep his life will lose it, and whoever loses his life will preserve it" (17:33). That Greek word (*apollymi* [622]) carries the idea of "utter loss" or "coming to ruin." In both instances, the Lord compared the value of this temporal life to our eternal existence after death and placed far greater importance on the latter. To "perish" in the temporal realm is nothing compared to "perishing" in the eternal realm, which is nothing less than damnation.

Jesus used this hyperbole to elevate the enduring worth of eternal life as compared to the loss of fleeting, temporal life on earth.

— 21:20-24 —

Luke views the prediction of 21:20-24 through a lens different from that of his counterparts Matthew and Mark. For Luke, this prediction has both a near-term fulfillment and a long-term fulfillment, which is not unusual in prophetic speech. The near-term fulfillment serves two purposes: to validate the authenticity of the long-term fulfillment and to illustrate in some small way the ultimate fulfillment in the distant future.

For example, take the prophecy of Isaiah concerning the birth of the Messiah. Around 734 BC, God gave King Ahaz a sign to reassure him that, despite his lack of trust, the kingdom of Judah would not fall to its enemies. Isaiah said,

> Therefore the Lord Himself will give you a sign: Behold, a virgin will be with child and bear a son, and she will call His name Immanuel. He will eat curds and honey at the time He knows enough to refuse evil and choose good. For before the boy will know enough to refuse evil and choose good, the land whose two kings you dread will be forsaken. (Isa. 7:14-16)

In the near-term, a young maiden had relations with her husband and gave birth to a son. Matthew, however, writing more than seven centuries later about the birth of the Messiah, saw a long-term, ultimate fulfillment of this prophecy: the conception of Jesus by a literal virgin.

The key to understanding Luke's perspective can be found in Luke 21:24. The fall of Jerusalem precedes an era Jesus called "the times of the Gentiles" (cf. Rom 11:25). In Matthew and Mark, however, the sack of Jerusalem *follows* the famous eschatological event called "the abomination of desolation" described in Daniel 9:27; 11:31; and 12:11, and is thus considered an event still future for Jesus and for us today.

So, which destruction of Jerusalem does Jesus mean? The AD 70 decimation or the destruction associated with the Great Tribulation (Dan. 9:27; 11:31; 12:11) at the end of days?

The answer is both. Luke sees the former; Matthew and Mark see the latter. Taken together, we have a composite view of the near-term and long-term events. In Luke, an era known as "the times of the Gentiles" follows the first destruction of Jerusalem.

— 21:25-28 —

Beginning with the fall of Jerusalem in AD 70, a new era would begin. The "times of the Gentiles" (still future in this discourse) will be a time of great oppression for the Jews, a time when the Gentiles are given authority over them. It will continue for an undetermined number of years, until God steps in and says, in effect, "That's enough!"

Once "the times of the Gentiles are fulfilled," the end-time cataclysms begin. Armies will again invade Jerusalem and a wholly different decimation will begin (Rev. 11:2). These events will differ in severity and in type from those described in Luke 21:8-11 and 21:12-19. The disasters will be supernatural, directed by God for the sake of warning the wicked and calling them to repentance. Then, the Messiah will return in power (Dan. 7:13; Luke 17:24; Rev. 1:7) to displace the dominion of evil and establish the kingdom of God on earth.

— 21:29-31 —

Jesus followed His discourse on future events with a parable to help His followers learn how to interpret and apply prophetic revelation. He pointed to a fig tree, an extremely common sight around Jerusalem. Fig trees—and all trees—behave in predictable ways that can give insight into other natural phenomena, *if* one knows how to read the signals. In the case of the fig tree, which loses all its leaves during the winter, the first sprigs of green are hard to miss. And it doesn't take a meteorological or horticultural expert to know that spring has arrived and summer is not far away.

Like a fig tree, prophecy can reliably point to future events. The symbols are clear; interpretation isn't difficult. Most anyone with common sense can read them so long as one takes time to observe. The events described by Jesus are like the leaves of the fig tree coming to life after winter; the kingdom of God should not come as a shock to anyone with eyes to see.

— 21:32-33 —

The Lord's disciples may not have understood His next comment at the time, but they certainly did later. They had not yet reconciled themselves to the idea of His suffering and dying, so the rest of redemptive history would not have crossed their minds. We, of course, have the clarity of hindsight to interpret His meaning.

The phrase "this generation" (*genea* [1074]) is difficult because the actual identity of "this" is not obvious. One thing is certain: He didn't mean the generation of the disciples. The simplest, most straightforward solution is to look for an antecedent. "This generation" refers to the people who see the first signs of green on the fig tree, the people who see the beginning of the end. That generation will not pass away before the King returns in power and the kingdom of God replaces the present world order. It will not be a long, drawn out process. Like Noah's flood and Lot's escape from Sodom, the end-time events will commence suddenly and transpire quickly.

— 21:34-36 —

Jesus encouraged His followers—in that generation and in all generations to follow—to be in a continuous state of alertness (see Luke 12:35-40). This doesn't mean we are to sell all our possessions and sit on a hill looking with anticipation into the sky. On the contrary, like faithful household stewards, we have business to attend to (12:35-38). We maintain readiness by fulfilling our responsibilities, not allowing ourselves to become passive by idle complacency or distracted by meaningless activity. Then, when the Master returns, we don't have to scramble at the last minute to get our lives in order. And, in the meantime, our diligence will prepare us to endure the difficulties of persecution and even martyrdom.

— 21:37-38 —

Luke quickly turns from the Lord's clash with the temple leaders and His lifting the prophetic veil on the future to final preparations for Passover. In the days leading up to the Feast, Jesus continued to teach in the temple each day and then would retreat to a private location on the Mount of Olives each evening. He may have stayed in Bethany with His friend Lazarus (see John 12:1). During the day, the large crowds in the temple protected Him from arrest; His private location kept Him safe from kidnapping or execution in the evenings.

The day of preparation approached. Soon, households all around Jerusalem would be preparing their Passover lambs for sacrifice. And so it was for the Lamb of God.

APPLICATION: LUKE 21:1-38

In the Meantime, before the End Time

While we must carry on in the "here and now," I don't consider only living in the "sweet by and by" an entirely good thing. Throughout history, extremists have taken the Lord's command for readiness to ridiculous lengths, setting dates and leading scores of families to hilltops on the supposed morning of Christ's return. Others have taken His command to mean we must always live like we're "just a-passin' through" in the words of that old gospel song. For them, life is just a mud pit on the way to heaven, something to get through as quickly as possible without getting anything on your clothes.

Jesus didn't view our time on earth that way. It is to be enjoyed, but not abused; treasured, but not clenched. We have many opportunities to engage fully during our lives. Readiness, then, has a specific meaning when anticipating something that may or may not come in our lifetimes. Jesus gave us two commands in Luke 21:34-36, one negative and one positive.

First, *be on guard*, avoiding behavior that neglects His return. Look again at how He put it:

> "Be on guard, so that your hearts will not be weighted down with dissipation and drunkenness and the worries of life, and that day will not come on you suddenly like a trap; for it will come upon all those who dwell on the face of all the earth." (21:34-35)

Take a look at how you spend your days. Review the things that you spend your time and money maintaining. Do your priorities, in effect, neglect that He is your King who will reign, literally, as King of kings? Regardless of your theology or what you say you believe, do your actions suggest you're living in denial of Jesus' literal return? What we do reveals what we *really* believe—whether we do or do not expect His imminent return. Be on guard. Avoid behavior that forgets His return.

Second, *keep on the alert*, anticipating the One who will indeed return. Jesus put it this way:

> "But keep on the alert at all times, praying that you may have strength to escape all these things that are about to take place, and to stand before the Son of Man." (21:36)

This describes faithfulness that glorifies God in daily life. As you examine your daily routine—your schedule, your bank account, your priorities—would you feel affirmed or apologetic if the Lord were to ask for an accounting today? Sins aside, generally speaking, do your activities anticipate that His return could occur at any moment?

Don't put life on hold. Be on guard against behaviors that ignore His return, and instead choose to engage in activities He would find pleasing if He were to catch you in the act.

Strong Leadership in
Stormy Times
LUKE 22:1-30

NASB

¹Now the Feast of Unleavened Bread, which is called the Passover, was approaching. ²The chief priests and the scribes were seeking how they might put Him to death; for they were afraid of the people.

³And Satan entered into Judas who was called Iscariot, ªbelonging to the number of the twelve. ⁴And he went away and discussed with the chief priests and officers how he might betray Him to them. ⁵They were glad and agreed to give him money. ⁶So he consented, and *began* seeking a good opportunity to betray Him to them ªapart from the crowd.

⁷Then came the *first* day of Unleavened Bread on which the Passover *lamb* had to be sacrificed. ⁸And Jesus sent Peter and John, saying, "Go and prepare the Passover for us, so that we may eat it." ⁹They said to Him, "Where do You want us to prepare it?" ¹⁰And He said to them, "When you have entered the city, a man will meet you carrying a pitcher of water; follow him into the house that he enters. ¹¹And you shall say to the owner of the house, 'The Teacher says to you, "Where is the guest room in which I may eat the Passover with My disciples?"' ¹²And he will show you a large, furnished upper room; prepare it there." ¹³And they left and found *everything* just as He had told them; and they prepared the Passover.

¹⁴When the hour had come, He reclined *at the table,* and the apostles with Him. ¹⁵And He said to them, "I have earnestly desired to eat this Passover with you before I suffer;

NLT

¹The Festival of Unleavened Bread, which is also called Passover, was approaching. ²The leading priests and teachers of religious law were plotting how to kill Jesus, but they were afraid of the people's reaction.

³Then Satan entered into Judas Iscariot, who was one of the twelve disciples, ⁴and he went to the leading priests and captains of the Temple guard to discuss the best way to betray Jesus to them. ⁵They were delighted, and they promised to give him money. ⁶So he agreed and began looking for an opportunity to betray Jesus so they could arrest him when the crowds weren't around.

⁷Now the Festival of Unleavened Bread arrived, when the Passover lamb is sacrificed. ⁸Jesus sent Peter and John ahead and said, "Go and prepare the Passover meal, so we can eat it together."

⁹"Where do you want us to prepare it?" they asked him.

¹⁰He replied, "As soon as you enter Jerusalem, a man carrying a pitcher of water will meet you. Follow him. At the house he enters, ¹¹say to the owner, 'The Teacher asks: Where is the guest room where I can eat the Passover meal with my disciples?' ¹²He will take you upstairs to a large room that is already set up. That is where you should prepare our meal." ¹³They went off to the city and found everything just as Jesus had said, and they prepared the Passover meal there.

¹⁴When the time came, Jesus and the apostles sat down together at the table.* ¹⁵Jesus said, "I have been very eager to eat this Passover meal with you before my suffering begins.

¹⁶for I say to you, I shall never again eat it until it is fulfilled in the kingdom of God." ¹⁷And when He had taken a cup *and* given thanks, He said, "Take this and share it among yourselves; ¹⁸for I say to you, I will not drink of the fruit of the vine from now on until the kingdom of God comes." ¹⁹And when He had taken *some* bread *and* given thanks, He broke it and gave it to them, saying, "This is My body which is given for you; do this in remembrance of Me." ²⁰And in the same way *He took* the cup after they had eaten, saying, "This cup which is poured out for you is the new covenant in My blood. ²¹But behold, the hand of the one betraying Me is with ᵃMine on the table. ²²For indeed, the Son of Man is going as it has been determined; but woe to that man by whom He is betrayed!" ²³And they began to discuss among themselves which one of them it might be who was going to do this thing.

²⁴And there arose also a dispute among them *as to* which one of them was regarded to be greatest. ²⁵And He said to them, "The kings of the Gentiles lord it over them; and those who have authority over them are called 'Benefactors.' ²⁶But *it is* not this way with you, but the one who is the greatest among you must become like the youngest, and the leader like the servant. ²⁷For who is greater, the one who reclines *at the table* or the one who serves? Is it not the one who reclines *at the table?* But I am among you as the one who serves.

²⁸"You are those who have stood by Me in My trials; ²⁹and just as My Father has granted Me a kingdom, I grant you ³⁰that you may eat and drink at My table in My kingdom,

¹⁶For I tell you now that I won't eat this meal again until its meaning is fulfilled in the Kingdom of God."

¹⁷Then he took a cup of wine and gave thanks to God for it. Then he said, "Take this and share it among yourselves. ¹⁸For I will not drink wine again until the Kingdom of God has come."

¹⁹He took some bread and gave thanks to God for it. Then he broke it in pieces and gave it to the disciples, saying, "This is my body, which is given for you. Do this in remembrance of me."

²⁰After supper he took another cup of wine and said, "This cup is the new covenant between God and his people—an agreement confirmed with my blood, which is poured out as a sacrifice for you.*

²¹"But here at this table, sitting among us as a friend, is the man who will betray me. ²²For it has been determined that the Son of Man* must die. But what sorrow awaits the one who betrays him." ²³The disciples began to ask each other which of them would ever do such a thing.

²⁴Then they began to argue among themselves about who would be the greatest among them. ²⁵Jesus told them, "In this world the kings and great men lord it over their people, yet they are called 'friends of the people.' ²⁶But among you it will be different. Those who are the greatest among you should take the lowest rank, and the leader should be like a servant. ²⁷Who is more important, the one who sits at the table or the one who serves? The one who sits at the table, of course. But not here! For I am among you as one who serves.

²⁸"You have stayed with me in my time of trial. ²⁹And just as my Father has granted me a Kingdom, I now grant you the right ³⁰to eat and drink at my table in my Kingdom.

NASB	NLT
and you will sit on thrones judging the twelve tribes of Israel.	And you will sit on thrones, judging the twelve tribes of Israel.
22:3 ªLit *being of* **22:6** ªOr *without a disturbance* **22:21** ªLit *Me*	**22:14** Or *reclined together.* **22:19-20** Some manuscripts do not include 22:19b-20, *which is given for you . . . which is poured out as a sacrifice for you.* **22:22** "Son of Man" is a title Jesus used for himself.

Hard times call for strong hearts. Leading others through those hard times calls for even greater strength within. People who succeed in that difficult task emerge as memorable leaders who accomplish great things.

As my mind skims notable low points in history, I recall Winston Churchill summoning his country's courage to stand against Hitler while the rest of Europe crumbled. I think of Abraham Lincoln shouldering the burden of holding a nation together without tolerating slavery. And I admire George Washington, who led inferior, ill-equipped troops in what may have appeared to be a lost cause against the greatest world power of the time.

Those are notable examples of stronghearted leadership; but my mind's eye cannot look away from Martin Luther, who, when not quite forty years old, was called to stand before the most powerful religious authorities in the Western world, compelled to renounce his teaching or face excommunication. After a long night of agonizing deliberation, he faced his inquisitors and said, "Unless I am convinced by Scriptures and plain reason—I do not accept the authority of pope and council, for they have contradicted each other—my conscience is captive to the Word of God. I cannot and will not recant anything, for to go against conscience is neither right nor safe. Here I stand. I can do no other. God help me. Amen."[13]

I can only hope that if confronted with the choice between standing upon truth and enduring an agonizing execution, I would have the courage to stand firm.

Fifteen centuries before Luther took his stand, Jesus of Nazareth peered into the inky-black abyss of evil and contemplated His destiny. As the Passover Feast approached, darkness enveloped Jerusalem; and soon, He would walk into it. In a little more than twenty-four hours, He would stand before the rulers of the temple, compelled to renounce His messianic claims or face scourging and the cross. More than that, during His agonizing execution, He would suffer the wrath of God for the sins of all humanity. With all of that before Him, Jesus gathered His inner circle of intimate followers for a final evening together. Despite the immense personal pressures, He still found the strength to lead His disciples.

— 22:1-2 —

The Feasts of Passover and Unleavened Bread were close at hand. The two feasts are celebrated simultaneously, so many call the combined feasts by one name, using "Passover" and "Unleavened Bread" interchangeably.

As pilgrims looked forward to the Passover celebration, the chief priests and scribes met to discuss the problem of Jesus (cf. 20:1, 19). Normally, their rivalry kept them at odds, but with the entire population of Israel beginning to side with Jesus against the temple, they agreed: Jesus must die.

The Jewish Calendar and Festival Cycle

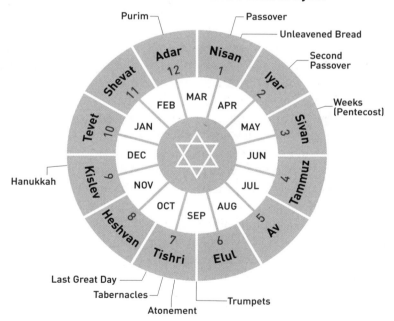

— 22:3-6 —

During the day, Jesus taught in the temple, surrounded by many thousands of witnesses; so they couldn't seize Him in public. Each night, He left for an undisclosed location somewhere east of the city, so ambushing Him in private proved impossible. They needed help from the inside.

In John's Gospel, we see Judas's long, slow, deliberate slide into evil; but Luke offers no background, no explanation, no rationale. Those didn't matter. Luke summarizes the reason Judas betrayed the Lord in three words: Satan entered him (22:3). Possession had been a recurring theme throughout Luke's portrayal of Jesus' ministry (4:33; 8:2, 27; 9:38-39, 49; 10:17; 11:14; 13:32)—and always with Him victorious. But now, it struck close to home. One of His beloved Twelve. And this was no mere demon; this was Satan himself. Notably, this is Satan's first appearance in the narrative since his temptation of Jesus in the wilderness (4:1-13).

In the cosmic war between the kingdom of God and the dominion of evil, Judas defected—*for money*. From that moment on, the quintessential traitor started looking for an opportunity to betray Jesus.

— 22:7-12 —

Luke sets the time as "the first day of Unleavened Bread." The fourteenth day of the Jewish lunar month of Nisan is a day of preparation for the Feast. But preparations always began well in advance. For weeks, Jews from all over Israel and across the empire ascended to the Holy City to find lodging and to prepare for the most significant meal of the year. In keeping with Jewish Law, anyone renting a room for the Passover meal began purging the house of leaven (yeast) at least two full days beforehand. Furthermore, Passover lambs were to have been secured by the tenth day of the month (Exod. 12:3).

Peter and John were sent to locate a room and to begin setting everything in order for the actual meal. In addition to the lamb, which would be slain later that day, they needed bitter herbs, unleavened bread, and wine. To guide them to the specific room, Jesus gave instructions reminiscent of the obtaining of the colt a week earlier (Luke 19:30-31). Like before, this could have been an example of Jesus using His foreknowledge to guide the men to the right place; but more likely, He had secured the room sometime earlier. Either way, Jesus remained in control of every detail of His destiny.

In those days, houses were simple and rectangular in shape. For the sake of hospitality or to generate extra income, families added a second story with an external stairway by which guests could enter the upper quarters without disturbing anyone below.

— 22:13 —

Once Peter and John located the room, they arranged everything for the meal. By midday on the fourteenth, all work came to an end as a representative of each family carried their lamb to the temple. At about 3 p.m., a Levite blew the ram's horn, worshipers filled the temple court, and the massive gates closed behind them. Each representative then killed his own lamb, skinned it, and drained its blood into a basin.

While this mass killing of lambs is hard for the twenty-first-century reader to imagine, we must keep in mind that ancient people didn't have the luxury of packaged meat from the grocery store. They kept meat fresh by keeping it alive. Killing a lamb and preparing it for supper was as ordinary a task as driving to the supermarket is for us.

For Passover, the lamb was killed in the temple to consecrate it as a substitute. Worshipers drained the animal's blood into a basin held by a priest who then splashed it against the base of the altar to signify atonement for sin. The fat and kidneys were burned on the altar as a part of the "peace offering," reaffirming good relations between God and the worshiper's family.

After the sacrifice, each household representative took the lamb home before sunset and roasted the meat. In keeping with God's instructions to Moses, the disciples smeared some of the blood on the doorposts and lintel of the main entrance.

— 22:14-16 —

The Jewish day begins sometime between the moment the sun disappears behind the horizon and the appearance of three medium-sized stars in the night sky. Therefore, "the hour" was a relative time at which the disciples began the Passover meal.

We have no detailed records of the rituals observed at this meal during the first century. The elaborate order of singing, recitation, and blessings and the specific arrangement of food now associated with the "Seder" reflect the Passover tradition from centuries later; however, those customs undoubtedly grew out of rudimentary traditions, some of which are preserved in the Mishnah. Passages such as Exodus 12:1–13:16 and Deuteronomy 16:1-8 contain the commands that shaped the proceedings of the feast, and Psalms 113–118 have long been associated with the Passover celebration. Conservatively, we can surmise that Jesus would have settled into the honored place reserved for Him and then lit a ceremonial lamp to signify the end of work and the beginning of celebration. He would have filled the first ceremonial cup of wine and held it up for the *kiddush* (meaning "sanctification"), which included a recitation and blessing.

Before His prayer, however, Jesus made an announcement, the first of two. Jesus was well aware of His imminent suffering (*paschō* [3958]); so, He first announced that He would not celebrate the Passover meal again "until it is fulfilled in the kingdom of God." "It" must refer to the redemption of Israel celebrated by the Passover meal. The blood of a sacrificial lamb had secured their safety from the angel of death. While profoundly important in Hebrew history, the redemption of Israel in the Exodus pales in comparison to their redemption from sin and their establishment in the kingdom of God.

— 22:17-18 —

When the time came for the first cup, Jesus held it up during a prayer of thanks to the Father for His faithfulness to Israel in the Exodus. But, instead of drinking, He passed the cup to His disciples. He then made His second announcement: He would no longer drink wine until His mission was complete. Jewish men sometimes took a vow, called the "nazirite vow," promising to abstain from all grape products and to refrain from cutting their hair until completing a consecrated task (Num. 6:1-21). Jesus may have been implying that He was taking such a vow to complete His God-ordained task.

— 22:19-20 —

During the ritual meal, Jesus recast some of the more important images, giving them new meaning. Customarily, the head of the household would have announced that the unleavened bread represented "the bread of affliction." Jesus, however, identified the bread as a symbol of His body broken on behalf of His followers. The command "Do this in remembrance of Me" is a perpetual command, not unlike the Lord's order for the Israelites to observe the Passover. This command is the basis of Christian Communion, a memorial meal to honor Christ's atoning sacrifice on behalf of sinners.

Luke mentions only two of the four ceremonial cups that are shared at Passover. This was most likely the third, which follows the meal, sometimes called the "cup of blessing" and, on rare occasions, the "cup of redemption." Jesus gave it new significance. In Hebrew history, God sealed covenants with the blood of a sacrifice (see. Exod. 24:8; Lev. 17:11-14); so here, Jesus used the wine to represent the blood He would soon shed on behalf of His followers. Drinking the wine at this Passover supper looked forward to that sealing of the "new covenant" (Jer. 31:31-34). Today, it commemorates that past event.

— 22:21-23 —

Throughout the evening, as Jesus solemnly celebrated God's faithfulness to Israel and prepared His disciples to receive a miraculous new covenant, Satan sat nearby in the presence of Judas Iscariot. Judas had followed Jesus for more than three years as a trusted member of the Twelve. The time had come for him to carry out his sinister mission. So, Jesus announced that one among them would betray Him. His declaration that the hand of the betrayer was with His on the table is simply an expression to say, "One of you dining with Me will betray Me." It highlights the duplicity, almost as much as identifying Jesus to the enemy with a kiss.

No one suspected Judas. His pious, loyal outward demeanor did not match the corruption of his heart. Luke doesn't state when Judas left on his evil mission. According to the other Gospel accounts, it was soon after the Lord's announcement. Still, no one made the connection.

— 22:24 —

Soon after the Lord's somber discussion about His suffering, His atoning death on behalf of His followers, the institution of the new covenant—which every Jew identified with the Messiah's kingdom of God—and the betrayal that will set everything in motion, the remaining eleven apostles began arguing over rank. It was not their first argument of this sort (see Luke 9:46). They compared their relative worth and jockeyed for position in the Messiah's future court. Who will be prime minister? Who will be secretary of war? Who will preside over the parliament? Who will rule which cities?

— 22:25-27 —

Jesus interrupted their argument to correct their view of the coming kingdom, which operates according to completely different rules from the present world order, the dominion of evil. One cannot simply observe how government works here and apply it to the new kingdom. Moreover, He had to address their selfish concerns about authority, rank, greatness, position, titles, entitlements, privilege, and all the perks of holding government office in the ancient world.

How sad and alone Jesus must have felt at that moment, having just unveiled the coming of God's kingdom and the terrible price He must pay to be its King!

The King of all creation reflected on the way the kings of earth rule their subjects. He highlighted the irony of their "lording over" others and then giving themselves the title "benefactor" or "servant of the people." In the kingdom of God, "rulers" truly are servants. Rather than taking the positions of highest honor, rulers take the jobs no one else wants. He then used Himself as the prime example of this kind of leadership. Memorably, John's Gospel describes the Lord's model of servant leadership in His washing of the disciples' feet.

— 22:28-30 —

The Lord's next statement strongly suggests Judas had left the upper room by this time. He commended the remaining eleven for their faithful devotion to Him, even affirming their belief that each will rule with great power in the coming kingdom. They will, indeed, sit on thrones to rule the nation of Israel as vice-regents of the Messiah. But their manner of rule will not resemble the kings of earth. What He did not say, but we would later see, was that the coming of the Holy Spirit would change everything. Rulers in the new kingdom, under the new covenant, will have new hearts upon which God will have written His Law.

Soon, Jesus would step out of the comfort of the Passover meal and into the darkness that had fallen over Jerusalem. Yet, even as He faced His darkest hours on earth, the Messiah led His men.

APPLICATION: LUKE 22:1-30

When the Going Gets Tough, the Toughest Become Leaders

As the evening drew to a close and the disciples lingered over the remaining morsels of the paschal meal, a storm gathered overhead. Evil men with evil in their hearts converged on a secret location in Jerusalem to plot the arrest of the Messiah. The Lord, of course, knew this night would be His last. Yet, He didn't focus on His own need for comfort or reassurance; instead, He prepared His men for the confusion of the next twenty-four hours. Here was Jesus, the stronghearted leader, who, by not only standing tall in hard times but also leading others to do the same, showed Himself even stronger. He stayed focused regardless of the pressure. He kept dreaming of better times without denying the harshness of reality around Him. The best stronghearted leaders are those who model servant-hearted humility.

The person who realizes that their calling is more than business and provision recognizes when their family needs them, thinking something like, "My spouse deserves my complete attention right now; I need to serve my family."

The person who stays home and invests their life in their family full-time understands this—being stronghearted as they defend their home to preserve purity and godliness, all the while faithfully serving in humility in ways no one knows.

And so it is—or should be—among church leaders and in Christian organizations, where stronghearted servant leaders commit themselves to the well-being of those they lead, even when life has become personally challenging.

And so it must be where you live and work. Regardless of the situation of your home or place of business, you can be that stronghearted leader when times get tough. You have the strength within you because you have a stronghearted Savior within you. So, get on your knees and lead!

The Darkest of All Nights
LUKE 22:31-65

NASB

31 "Simon, Simon, behold, Satan has ademanded *permission* to sift you like wheat; 32 but I have prayed for you, that your faith may not fail; and you, when once you have turned again, strengthen your brothers." 33 But he said to Him, "Lord, with You I am ready to go both to prison and to death!" 34 And He said, "I say to you, Peter, the rooster will not crow today until you have denied three times that you know Me."

35 And He said to them, "When I sent you out without money belt and bag and sandals, you did not lack anything, did you?" They said, "*No*, nothing." 36 And He said to them, "But now, awhoever has a money

NLT

31 "Simon, Simon, Satan has asked to sift each of you like wheat. 32 But I have pleaded in prayer for you, Simon, that your faith should not fail. So when you have repented and turned to me again, strengthen your brothers."

33 Peter said, "Lord, I am ready to go to prison with you, and even to die with you."

34 But Jesus said, "Peter, let me tell you something. Before the rooster crows tomorrow morning, you will deny three times that you even know me."

35 Then Jesus asked them, "When I sent you out to preach the Good News and you did not have money, a traveler's bag, or an extra pair of sandals, did you need anything?"

"No," they replied.

36 "But now," he said, "take your

NASB

belt is to take it along, likewise also a bag, and ªwhoever has no sword is to sell his ᵇcoat and buy one. ³⁷For I tell you that this which is written must be fulfilled in Me, 'AND HE WAS NUMBERED WITH TRANSGRESSORS'; for that which refers to Me has *its* ªfulfillment." ³⁸They said, "Lord, look, here are two swords." And He said to them, "It is enough."

³⁹And He came out and proceeded as was His custom to the Mount of Olives; and the disciples also followed Him. ⁴⁰When He arrived at the place, He said to them, "Pray that you may not enter into temptation." ⁴¹And He withdrew from them about a stone's throw, and He knelt down and *began* to pray, ⁴²saying, "Father, if You are willing, remove this cup from Me; yet not My will, but Yours be done." ⁴³ªNow an angel from heaven appeared to Him, strengthening Him. ⁴⁴And being in agony He was praying very fervently; and His sweat became like drops of blood, falling down upon the ground. ⁴⁵When He rose from prayer, He came to the disciples and found them sleeping from sorrow, ⁴⁶and said to them, "Why are you sleeping? Get up and pray that you may not enter into temptation."

⁴⁷While He was still speaking, behold, a crowd *came,* and the one called Judas, one of the twelve, was preceding them; and he approached Jesus to kiss Him. ⁴⁸But Jesus said to him, "Judas, are you betraying the Son of Man with a kiss?" ⁴⁹When those who were around Him saw what was going to happen, they said, "Lord, shall we strike with the sword?" ⁵⁰And one of them struck the slave of the high priest and cut off his right ear. ⁵¹But Jesus answered and said, "ªStop! No more of this." And He touched his ear and healed him. ⁵²Then Jesus said to the chief priests and officers of the temple and elders

NLT

money and a traveler's bag. And if you don't have a sword, sell your cloak and buy one! ³⁷For the time has come for this prophecy about me to be fulfilled: 'He was counted among the rebels.'* Yes, everything written about me by the prophets will come true."

³⁸"Look, Lord," they replied, "we have two swords among us."

"That's enough," he said.

³⁹Then, accompanied by the disciples, Jesus left the upstairs room and went as usual to the Mount of Olives. ⁴⁰There he told them, "Pray that you will not give in to temptation."

⁴¹He walked away, about a stone's throw, and knelt down and prayed, ⁴²"Father, if you are willing, please take this cup of suffering away from me. Yet I want your will to be done, not mine." ⁴³Then an angel from heaven appeared and strengthened him. ⁴⁴He prayed more fervently, and he was in such agony of spirit that his sweat fell to the ground like great drops of blood.*

⁴⁵At last he stood up again and returned to the disciples, only to find them asleep, exhausted from grief. ⁴⁶"Why are you sleeping?" he asked them. "Get up and pray, so that you will not give in to temptation."

⁴⁷But even as Jesus said this, a crowd approached, led by Judas, one of the twelve disciples. Judas walked over to Jesus to greet him with a kiss. ⁴⁸But Jesus said, "Judas, would you betray the Son of Man with a kiss?"

⁴⁹When the other disciples saw what was about to happen, they exclaimed, "Lord, should we fight? We brought the swords!" ⁵⁰And one of them struck at the high priest's slave, slashing off his right ear.

⁵¹But Jesus said, "No more of this." And he touched the man's ear and healed him.

⁵²Then Jesus spoke to the leading priests, the captains of the Temple

who had come against Him, "Have you come out with swords and clubs as you would against a robber? 53 While I was with you daily in the temple, you did not lay hands on Me; but ªthis hour and the power of darkness are yours."

54 Having arrested Him, they led Him *away* and brought Him to the house of the high priest; but Peter was following at a distance. 55 After they had kindled a fire in the middle of the courtyard and had sat down together, Peter was sitting among them. 56 And a servant-girl, seeing him as he sat in the firelight and looking intently at him, said, "This man was with Him too." 57 But he denied *it,* saying, "Woman, I do not know Him." 58 A little later, another saw him and said, "You are *one* of them too!" But Peter said, "Man, I am not!" 59 After about an hour had passed, another man *began* to insist, saying, "Certainly this man also was with Him, for he is a Galilean too." 60 But Peter said, "Man, I do not know what you are talking about." Immediately, while he was still speaking, a rooster crowed. 61 The Lord turned and looked at Peter. And Peter remembered the word of the Lord, how He had told him, "Before a rooster crows today, you will deny Me three times." 62 And he went out and wept bitterly.

63 Now the men who were holding ªJesus in custody were mocking Him and beating Him, 64 and they blindfolded Him and were asking Him, saying, "Prophesy, who is the one who hit You?" 65 And they were saying many other things against Him, blaspheming.

22:31 ªOr *obtained by asking* 22:36 ªLit *he who* ᵇOr *outer garment* 22:37 ªLit *end* 22:43 ªMost early mss do not contain vv 43 and 44 22:51 ªOr `` `Let Me at least do this," and He touched* 22:53 ªLit *this is your hour and power of darkness* 22:63 ªLit *Him*

guard, and the elders who had come for him. "Am I some dangerous revolutionary," he asked, "that you come with swords and clubs to arrest me? 53 Why didn't you arrest me in the Temple? I was there every day. But this is your moment, the time when the power of darkness reigns."

54 So they arrested him and led him to the high priest's home. And Peter followed at a distance. 55 The guards lit a fire in the middle of the courtyard and sat around it, and Peter joined them there. 56 A servant girl noticed him in the firelight and began staring at him. Finally she said, "This man was one of Jesus' followers!"

57 But Peter denied it. "Woman," he said, "I don't even know him!"

58 After a while someone else looked at him and said, "You must be one of them!"

"No, man, I'm not!" Peter retorted.

59 About an hour later someone else insisted, "This must be one of them, because he is a Galilean, too."

60 But Peter said, "Man, I don't know what you are talking about." And immediately, while he was still speaking, the rooster crowed.

61 At that moment the Lord turned and looked at Peter. Suddenly, the Lord's words flashed through Peter's mind: "Before the rooster crows tomorrow morning, you will deny three times that you even know me." 62 And Peter left the courtyard, weeping bitterly.

63 The guards in charge of Jesus began mocking and beating him. 64 They blindfolded him and said, "Prophesy to us! Who hit you that time?" 65 And they hurled all sorts of terrible insults at him.

22:37 Isa 53:12. 22:43-44 Verses 43 and 44 are not included in the most ancient manuscripts.

I once heard the father of a teenager discussing the possibility of extending his curfew. Naturally, Dad didn't like the idea. He said in a matter-of-fact tone, "Son, nothing good happens out there after midnight." It was hard to argue with his logic. Certainly, good people *can* accomplish good things after sundown; but darkness is the traditional domain of evil, where idleness finds trouble and bad intentions become bold.

As Jesus and His disciples enjoyed their Passover celebration together, evil made use of the darkness. Just across the Kidron Valley, in the cloisters of Israel's religious elite, the Lord's conspirators finally found the opportunity they had been seeking. Judas arrived with a specific plan to seize his Master—away from potential witnesses, when all of Jerusalem was sleeping.

Even in the intimate warmth of the upper room, Satan wheedled his way into the disciples' midst, using their pride to divide their unity and seeking to undo their future leader, Peter. When Jesus left the city to find strength from His Father in the garden of Gethsemane, He would find Satan slithering among the trees. And later, as the city slumbered unaware, illegal nighttime trials would charge the only righteous man ever born of a woman and label Him guilty.

For all who loved the light, this was going to be the longest, darkest night of all.

— 22:31-32 —

The Passover meal had been eaten, the symbols of the new covenant given, the plan of redemption set in motion; and with Judas scurrying to the temple, nothing stood between Jesus and the cross. He had said and done everything He could. Those who had eyes to see and ears to hear had been reached. The forces of evil would now push the Lord toward His redemptive destiny—just as God had intended from the beginning.

The disciples, unaware of the cosmic import of that night, bickered like children. While their Master entered the longest night of His life, they tried to settle the matter of who would sit where in the new government. In the middle of the Messiah's rebuke and reassurance, He held the gaze of the future lead apostle. His double vocative "Simon, Simon" (cf. 8:24; 10:41; 13:34) expressed the gravity of the disciple's immediate future. The warning "Satan has demanded permission to sift you like wheat" uses a verb meaning "to ask for and receive." The image recalls Satan's requests to afflict Job for the sake of proving him unworthy (Job 1:7-12; 2:1-6). Satan didn't have only Peter in mind, however. The

Lord's warning "sift you like wheat" uses the plural pronoun "you." The devil would attack the whole group by attacking Peter, their future front man.

Jesus saw Peter's inevitable failure, but still encouraged him. He said, in effect, "After you have failed, remember that your faith need not fail; I command that when you recover from your stumble, you become a stronger leader than you are now." The pronouns are singular in the Lord's affirmation.

— 22:33-34 —

I have noticed that those who protest the loudest in a particular area often are the very ones who fall in that area. Peter's expression of un-qualified devotion echoes the Lord's earlier calls to discipleship (Luke 9:23-24; 14:26), but Peter's spontaneous pledge of allegiance was shot through with overconfidence. Thinking like a warrior or a violent revo-lutionary, Peter vowed to remain true to his King to the bitter end. But he was mistaken. Jesus patiently and kindly predicted the details of Peter's soon-to-be failure.

Of course, Peter will not fail alone. Luke's narrative describes three failures:

Unreliable disciples (22:39-46)
Deceitful Judas (22:47-53)
Cowardly Peter (22:54-62)

— 22:35-38 —

A quick change of subject rescues Peter from further self-recriminations. Any more protest would simply add to his humiliation later.

Jesus reminded the disciples of their earlier missions, which they completed without first acquiring provisions, such as food, money, and extra clothes (9:3; 10:4). The conditions have changed. The con-trastive force of the conjunction "but" (22:36) is strong. They would now conduct ministry without His physical presence in the world. He counseled them to obtain money, travel provisions, extra clothes, and a sword.

Some see the Lord's reference to a sword as symbolic or metaphori-cal, perhaps illustrating their need to be armed for spiritual warfare. But this doesn't fit with the other provisions, which also would have to be metaphorical in some way. And without some frame of reference, they could mean anything. Therefore, it makes better sense to see the sword as literal, although not for the sake of violence. Carrying a sword on the highway was very common, standard equipment for travelers wanting to ward off robbers.

Jesus advocated peace. He called His disciples to refrain from taking revenge and to love enemies in return for their hatred. But He wasn't naïve. He recognized the world to be a dangerous place, especially for those aligning themselves against the dominion of evil to become agents of the kingdom. Consequently, He encouraged self-defense in the face of mortal danger such as robbery (see 10:30).

Jesus, in alluding to a prophecy (Isa. 53:12), implied that because the world has declared the Son of God a "transgressor," the disciples would face similar treatment. The same powers that convict Jesus will also declare the disciples enemies of the state, simply because they associated with Him.

The disciples heard the Lord's discourse as literal and produced two swords. Jesus' response, "It is enough," is best interpreted "Enough of this talk." They would understand His meaning later.

— 22:39-42 —

The Lord's discourse in the upper room ended with a short journey to a familiar retreat on the Mount of Olives, just across the Kidron Valley, perhaps on the western slope overlooking Jerusalem. Luke doesn't name the place, but from the other Gospel accounts, we know He used a private garden called Gethsemane. The phrase "as was His custom" explains how Judas and the temple officials were able to trap Jesus; as a disciple, Judas had been to the place many times and probably learned of Jesus' plan to go there after the Passover meal.

Soon after entering the olive grove, Jesus asked His disciples to pray while He sought comfort from His Father. Luke doesn't mention Satan specifically, but the allusions are clear. He told His men to pray (*proseuchomai* [4336]) specifically for deliverance from temptation, no doubt to counter Satan's "sifting" (Luke 22:31). His urging them to be on guard against temptation suggests He had begun to feel its tugging Himself. At the beginning of His ministry, Satan had tempted Jesus to abandon the mission or to take shortcuts to glory. Here in the garden, Jesus struggled with the desire to avoid the ordeal before Him, referred to as "this cup" (22:42).

We can only try to imagine the agony of this moment. In those terrible hours, Jesus had to choose between obedience and self-preservation, the same choice all people face—usually before sinning. Because of His human nature, Jesus could be genuinely tempted. Because of His

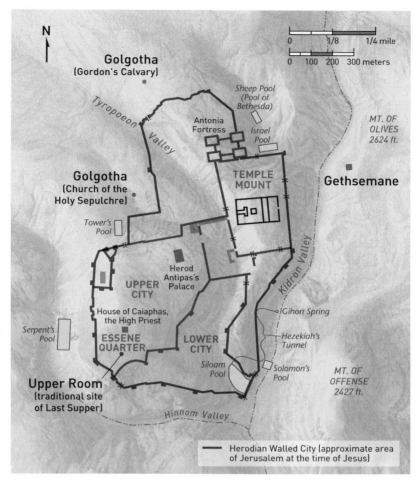

After supper, Jesus and his disciples walked across town, past the Temple Mount, to Gethsemane on the Mount of Olives.

divine nature, He would be victorious. However, we should not forget that though His victory was sure, His suffering was real.

— 22:43-46 —

Each of the synoptic Gospels emphasizes the enormous emotional strain felt by Jesus during His temptation. According to Matthew, Jesus prayed at least three hours (Matt. 26:37-46), and Matthew describes His mental state as "deeply grieved, to the point of death." Mark's account presents a similar portrayal of Jesus' distress and agony (Mark 14:32-42).

Luke describes the Lord's emotional agony in both supernatural and natural terms. Jesus required angelic assistance to bolster His strength for the excruciating experience before Him (Luke 22:43). And he used terms a physician would appreciate: "His sweat became like drops of blood, falling down upon the ground" (22:44). Some have interpreted this literally to mean He bled through His pores, but Luke seems to intend only to draw a comparison ("*like* drops of blood"). Jesus sweat so profusely that the water poured off His body as though He were bleeding; the size of the sweat drops falling resembled thick drops of blood.

Jesus emerged from the garden to find the disciples sleeping instead of praying as He had requested. According to Matthew and Mark, Jesus found them dozing no fewer than three times. Luke mentions only the final conversation, highlighting again the problem of temptation.

— 22:47-51 —

Luke uses the word "crowd" to describe the people arriving to arrest Jesus. Throughout his narrative, Luke used this term in a mostly positive sense in reference to those following Jesus. And by the end of the "journey section," the "crowd" accompanied Jesus to Jerusalem and gave Him a king's welcome, shouting, "Blessed is the King who comes in the name of the LORD" (19:38). The reference here is an early indication the "crowd" would turn against Jesus. While Jesus prayed and the men dozed, a small army had encircled the garden. Judas emerged from the darkness, walking deliberately toward Jesus, intending to give Him the customary greeting of Near Eastern cultures: a kiss—perhaps one on each cheek as is done today. Regardless, Judas's greeting was not genuine.

Having positively identified Jesus, the betrayer stood aside for the troops to move in. Some of the disciples drew their swords; we know they had at least two (22:38). In the short skirmish, one lopped off the ear of one poor man. Before things could get further out of hand, Jesus put a stop to the fighting and healed the severed ear (22:51).

— 22:52-53 —

The coalition surrounding Jesus included the chief priests, temple guards, and elders—the senior leadership of the Temple. Jesus' question to them demonstrates the absurdity and injustice of the situation. The arresting force arrived ready to hunt down a "robber." This term generally described two kinds of outlaws. The first was an armed bandit; these often formed gangs for the purpose of overpowering travelers—even armed ones—for their money and possessions. The second was an insurrectionist; these used robbery to fund their causes and would ruthlessly murder their enemies. The first-century historian Josephus

Trial	Officiating Authority	Scripture	Accusations	Legality	Type	Result
			THE TRIALS OF JESUS			
1	Annas, former high priest from AD 6–15	John 18:12-23	No specific charges brought.	Illegal: • No jurisdiction • Held at night • No charges • No witnesses • Abused during trial	Jewish and Religious	Found "guilty" of irreverence and sent to Caiaphas.
2	Caiaphas, high priest from AD 18–36, and the Sanhedrin	Matthew 26:57-68 Mark 14:53-65 John 18:24	Claimed to be the Messiah, the Son of God, which they deemed blasphemy.	Illegal: • Held at night • False witnesses • No formal charge • Abused during trial	Jewish and Religious	Declared "guilty" of blasphemy and held for sentencing until morning.
3	Sanhedrin	Mark 15:1 Luke 22:66-71	As a continuation of the earlier trial before the Sanhedrin, the charges remained the same.	Illegal: • Accusation changed • No witnesses • Improper vote	Jewish and Religious	Sentenced to be turned over to Romans for execution.
4	Pilate, governor of Judea from AD 26–36	Matthew 27:11-14 Mark 15:2-5 Luke 23:1-7 John 18:28-38	Charged with treason and sedition against Rome.	Illegal: • Found "not guilty," yet kept in custody • No defense representation • Abused during trial	Roman and Civil	Declared "not guilty" and pawned off on Herod Antipas to find a loophole.
5	Herod Antipas, governor of Galilee from 4 BC–AD 39	Luke 23:8-12	No specific charges brought. Questioned at length by Herod.	Illegal: • No jurisdiction • No specific charges • Abused during trial	Roman and Civil	Mistreated, mocked, falsely accused, and returned to Pilate without a decision made.
6	Pilate	Matthew 27:15-26 Mark 15:6-15 Luke 23:13-25 John 18:39–19:16	As a continuation of the earlier trial before Pilate, the charges remained the same.	Illegal: • Declared "not guilty," yet condemned.	Roman and Civil	Declared "not guilty" but sentenced to be crucified to mollify the angry mob. Simultaneously, a man guilty of murder, treason, and sedition was released.

described one particularly insidious faction of "robbers" known as the Sicarii:

> There sprang up another sort of robbers in Jerusalem, which were called Sicarii, who slew men in the daytime, and in the midst of the city; this they did chiefly at the festivals, when they mingled themselves among the multitude, and concealed daggers under their garments, with which they stabbed those that were their enemies; and when any fell down dead, the murderers became a part of those that had indignation against them; by which means they appeared persons of such reputation, that they could by no means be discovered.[14]

Jesus also objected to their using the cover of night and His private location to arrest Him. If their charges were legitimate, they should have had no problem seizing Him in public on any given day He taught in the temple. His phrasing is significant: "The power of darkness" has double meaning, referring to the secrecy of their nighttime arrest and their service to the forces of evil.

— 22:54-55 —

Jesus endured no fewer than six trials after His arrest (see chart, "The Trials of Jesus," page 547). Luke compresses the events of the first and second trials. Combining the information from all four Gospels, we discover that Jesus first appeared before Annas, the Godfather-like power behind the office of high priest. Then he was sent to Caiaphas, the son-in-law of Annas, who held the office at that time.

While the Gospel of John details the events of the trial, Luke focuses on the courtyard, where Peter warmed himself by a fire with a group of servants and soldiers.

— 22:56-62 —

The fulfillment of the Lord's predictions concerning Peter's denial began with the accusation of a servant girl in the courtyard of Annas's home. The second denial occurred soon after when a man recognized Peter as one of the Twelve. The third came in response to another man's insistence. By this time, Jesus had been taken from Annas to Caiaphas for the second trial.

As that trial came to a close, two events combined to convict Peter of his sin: A rooster crowed, and then Peter's eyes met his Master's. The term rendered "looked" is *emblepō* [1689], meaning "to look at something directly and therefore intently."[15] This was a lingering stare—an eloquent, albeit silent, rebuke that penetrated Peter like a dagger to the heart. The phrase "wept bitterly" is doubly intensive. The verb "wept" by itself describes the mournful cry of those grieving a death; the adverb "bitterly" further intensifies the sense of anguish. His remorse knew no bounds.

— 22:63-65 —

Luke offers only a couple of brief comments about the proceedings of the first two trials. For him, the details were not as important as the treatment Jesus received, which established the guilt of the religious leaders and denounced the trials as a sham. In truth, the first two trials before Annas and Caiaphas had two objectives. The first objective was to craft a credible case against Jesus, a clear violation of Sanhedrin rules:

> In property cases they begin [argument] with the case either for acquittal or for conviction, while in capital cases they begin only with the case for acquittal, and not with the case for conviction. In capital cases all argue for acquittal, but all do not argue for conviction.[16]

Their second objective: Intimidate Jesus or otherwise break down His will so that He would voluntarily recant His messianic claims. A humiliated Jesus, reading a retraction in the temple, would serve their cause better than a potential martyred hero. Their intimidation, mocking, beating, humiliation, taunting, and blasphemy failed, however. Jesus stood firmly on the truth of His identity and continued to endure His long, dark night.

When it became clear that Jesus wouldn't renounce His messianic claims, the temple authorities disbanded for the night. As the sun rose the next morning, they would convene at least a quorum of the council in its official chambers.

APPLICATION: LUKE 22:31-65

Thank God for the Grace of God

Two thousand years and several thousand miles removed from Jerusalem during the Lord's long, dark night, it is easy to blame Peter for his disloyalty. Of course, the other apostles didn't fare much better; they ran for cover when the authority of Israel came crashing down on Jesus. From the standpoint of history, it's easy to forget these two things:

First, *no matter how confident we may feel about ourselves, we are all human.*

No one is more than that. I don't care what your IQ is. I don't care what your training has been. I do not care how well read or widely traveled you have been; you are human, finite, vacillating, hot-and-cold, on-and-off, up-and-down, obedient and rebellious, and easily misled into believing that you are stronger than you actually are.

I have stood before couples and their God to perform wedding ceremonies in which bride and groom uttered sacred vows in the company of their family and friends. And I have counseled my share of divorced individuals, struggling to overcome the heartache of broken vows. They are human. Though at one time they made strong promises before God that only death would separate them, they are disobedient. Interestingly, both are living and going on with their lives, despite their broken promise.

Before we come down on these couples with too much condemnation, let me ask: Who among us has not made significant promises to God in a great emotional moment only to break those solemn vows under the pressure of temptation?

Second, *no matter how devoted we may be to Christ, we will all fail.*

We will fail in one way or another. Peter has no lonely corner on disloyalty or denial. His is not the last account of people who thought themselves stronger than they really were.

Let's look back now at the three scenes discussed in this section and contemplate what we can learn from them. In the first scene, we find the disciples unfaithful and falling asleep rather than praying with their Lord. My comment here is that *everyone must endure a Gethsemane.* You may have only one in your lifetime; while you may not have many, you will have at least one. It is a lonely but necessary time. It is a place of agonizing suffering into which others will not enter with you. Now hear this: It is in the Gethsemane experiences that we learn submission to Christ alone. It is there we discover *God's* faithfulness, in spite of the unfaithfulness of others—or of ourselves. He is touched by your struggle. Your Lord understands. He's been there.

The second scene is Judas's betrayal. As I said earlier, everyone will experience at least one betrayal. It is bitter and disillusioning. A close friend. A once-trusted colleague. A long-standing partner in business, in ministry, or in marriage. A once-enjoyable relationship you thought would go on forever. In Jesus' case, a disciple becomes a deceiver. When we encounter betrayal, we learn a heartbreaking reality. What a change takes place in our lives when we discover that, realistically, others will fail us! We also discover that God never fails, and as a result, we mature and become better for the experience.

The third scene involves Peter and his tragic denial. It is both humiliating and heartbreaking. After such an experience we feel horrible. We feel humiliated. We weep. We later look into the face of the one we let down, and that glance melts us. Nothing but time can bring healing.

F. B. Meyer writes, "This is the bitterest of all—to know that suffering need not have been; that it is the harvest of one's own sowing; that the vulture which feeds on the vitals is a nestling of one's own rearing. Ah me! This is pain!"[17]

Our Gethsemane teaches us submission. Betrayal teaches us realism. The journey that Peter took, a journey of failure, teaches us humility. I don't think Peter ever again made a sweeping promise like the one he had made here to his Lord. Jesus' glance leveled him, but all for the sake of humility. What a leader of the church he became!

The Day the Sun Refused to Shine
LUKE 22:66–23:46

NASB

66 When it was day, the ªCouncil of elders of the people assembled, both chief priests and scribes, and they led Him away to their council *chamber,* saying, 67 "If You are the ªChrist, tell us." But He said to them, "If I tell you, you will not believe; 68 and if I ask a question, you will not answer. 69 But from now on THE SON OF MAN WILL BE SEATED AT THE RIGHT HAND of the power OF GOD." 70 And they all said, "Are You the Son of God, then?" And He said to them, "ªYes, I am." 71 Then they said, "What further need do we have of testimony? For we have heard it ourselves from His own mouth."

NLT

66 At daybreak all the elders of the people assembled, including the leading priests and the teachers of religious law. Jesus was led before this high council,* 67 and they said, "Tell us, are you the Messiah?"

But he replied, "If I tell you, you won't believe me. 68 And if I ask you a question, you won't answer. 69 But from now on the Son of Man will be seated in the place of power at God's right hand.*"

70 They all shouted, "So, are you claiming to be the Son of God?"

And he replied, "You say that I am."

71 "Why do we need other witnesses?" they said. "We ourselves heard him say it."

NASB

23:1 Then the whole body of them got up and brought Him before Pilate. 2 And they began to accuse Him, saying, "We found this man misleading our nation and forbidding to pay taxes to Caesar, and saying that He Himself is aChrist, a King." 3 So Pilate asked Him, saying, "Are You the King of the Jews?" And He answered him and said, "*It is as* you say." 4 Then Pilate said to the chief priests and the crowds, "I find no guilt in this man." 5 But they kept on insisting, saying, "He stirs up the people, teaching all over Judea, starting from Galilee even as far as this place."

6 When Pilate heard it, he asked whether the man was a Galilean. 7 And when he learned that He belonged to Herod's jurisdiction, he sent Him to Herod, who himself also was in Jerusalem aat that time.

8 Now Herod was very glad when he saw Jesus; for he had wanted to see Him for a long time, because he had been hearing about Him and was hoping to see some asign performed by Him. 9 And he questioned Him aat some length; but He answered him nothing. 10 And the chief priests and the scribes were standing there, accusing Him vehemently. 11 And Herod with his soldiers, after treating Him with contempt and mocking Him, dressed Him in a gorgeous robe and sent Him back to Pilate. 12 Now Herod and Pilate became friends with one another that very day; for before they had been enemies with each other.

13 Pilate summoned the chief priests and the rulers and the people, 14 and said to them, "You brought this man to me as one who incites the people to rebellion, and behold, having examined Him before you, I have found no guilt in this man regarding the charges which you make against Him. 15 No, nor has Herod, for he sent Him back to us; and behold, nothing deserving death has been

NLT

23:1 Then the entire council took Jesus to Pilate, the Roman governor. 2 They began to state their case: "This man has been leading our people astray by telling them not to pay their taxes to the Roman government and by claiming he is the Messiah, a king."

3 So Pilate asked him, "Are you the king of the Jews?"

Jesus replied, "You have said it."

4 Pilate turned to the leading priests and to the crowd and said, "I find nothing wrong with this man!"

5 Then they became insistent. "But he is causing riots by his teaching wherever he goes—all over Judea, from Galilee to Jerusalem!"

6 "Oh, is he a Galilean?" Pilate asked. 7 When they said that he was, Pilate sent him to Herod Antipas, because Galilee was under Herod's jurisdiction, and Herod happened to be in Jerusalem at the time.

8 Herod was delighted at the opportunity to see Jesus, because he had heard about him and had been hoping for a long time to see him perform a miracle. 9 He asked Jesus question after question, but Jesus refused to answer. 10 Meanwhile, the leading priests and the teachers of religious law stood there shouting their accusations. 11 Then Herod and his soldiers began mocking and ridiculing Jesus. Finally, they put a royal robe on him and sent him back to Pilate. 12 (Herod and Pilate, who had been enemies before, became friends that day.)

13 Then Pilate called together the leading priests and other religious leaders, along with the people, 14 and he announced his verdict. "You brought this man to me, accusing him of leading a revolt. I have examined him thoroughly on this point in your presence and find him innocent. 15 Herod came to the same conclusion and sent him back to us. Nothing this man has done calls for

done by Him. ¹⁶Therefore I will punish Him and release Him." ¹⁷[ᵃNow he was obliged to release to them at the feast one prisoner.]

¹⁸But they cried out all together, saying, "Away with this man, and release for us Barabbas!" ¹⁹(He was one who had been thrown into prison for an insurrection made in the city, and for murder.) ²⁰Pilate, wanting to release Jesus, addressed them again, ²¹but they kept on calling out, saying, "Crucify, crucify Him!" ²²And he said to them the third time, "Why, what evil has this man done? I have found in Him no guilt *demanding* death; therefore I will punish Him and release Him." ²³But they were insistent, with loud voices asking that He be crucified. And their voices *began* to prevail. ²⁴And Pilate pronounced sentence that their demand be granted. ²⁵And he released the man they were asking for who had been thrown into prison for insurrection and murder, but he delivered Jesus to their will.

²⁶When they led Him away, they seized a man, Simon of Cyrene, coming in from the country, and placed on him the cross to carry behind Jesus.

²⁷And following Him was a large crowd of the people, and of women who were ᵃmourning and lamenting Him. ²⁸But Jesus turning to them said, "Daughters of Jerusalem, stop weeping for Me, but weep for yourselves and for your children. ²⁹For behold, the days are coming when they will say, 'Blessed are the barren, and the wombs that never bore, and the breasts that never nursed.' ³⁰Then they will begin TO SAY TO THE MOUNTAINS, 'FALL ON US,' AND TO THE HILLS, 'COVER US.' ³¹For if they do these things ᵃwhen the tree is green, what will happen ᵇwhen it is dry?"

³²Two others also, who were criminals, were being led away to be put to death with Him.

the death penalty. ¹⁶So I will have him flogged, and then I will release him."*

¹⁸Then a mighty roar rose from the crowd, and with one voice they shouted, "Kill him, and release Barabbas to us!" ¹⁹(Barabbas was in prison for taking part in an insurrection in Jerusalem against the government, and for murder.) ²⁰Pilate argued with them, because he wanted to release Jesus. ²¹But they kept shouting, "Crucify him! Crucify him!"

²²For the third time he demanded, "Why? What crime has he committed? I have found no reason to sentence him to death. So I will have him flogged, and then I will release him."

²³But the mob shouted louder and louder, demanding that Jesus be crucified, and their voices prevailed. ²⁴So Pilate sentenced Jesus to die as they demanded. ²⁵As they had requested, he released Barabbas, the man in prison for insurrection and murder. But he turned Jesus over to them to do as they wished.

²⁶As they led Jesus away, a man named Simon, who was from Cyrene,* happened to be coming in from the countryside. The soldiers seized him and put the cross on him and made him carry it behind Jesus. ²⁷A large crowd trailed behind, including many grief-stricken women. ²⁸But Jesus turned and said to them, "Daughters of Jerusalem, don't weep for me, but weep for yourselves and for your children. ²⁹For the days are coming when they will say, 'Fortunate indeed are the women who are childless, the wombs that have not borne a child and the breasts that have never nursed.' ³⁰People will beg the mountains, 'Fall on us,' and plead with the hills, 'Bury us.'* ³¹For if these things are done when the tree is green, what will happen when it is dry?*"

³²Two others, both criminals, were led out to be executed with him.

NASB

33 When they came to the place called ªThe Skull, there they crucified Him and the criminals, one on the right and the other on the left. 34ªBut Jesus was saying, "Father, forgive them; for they do not know what they are doing." And they cast lots, dividing up His garments among themselves. 35 And the people stood by, looking on. And even the rulers were sneering at Him, saying, "He saved others; let Him save Himself if this is the ªChrist of God, His Chosen One." 36 The soldiers also mocked Him, coming up to Him, offering Him sour wine, 37 and saying, "If You are the King of the Jews, save Yourself!" 38 Now there was also an inscription above Him, "THIS IS THE KING OF THE JEWS."

39 One of the criminals who were hanged *there* was ªhurling abuse at Him, saying, "Are You not the ᵇChrist? Save Yourself and us!" 40 But the other answered, and rebuking him said, "Do you not even fear God, since you are under the same sentence of condemnation? 41 And we indeed *are suffering* justly, for we are receiving ªwhat we deserve for our deeds; but this man has done nothing wrong." 42 And he was saying, "Jesus, remember me when You come ªin Your kingdom!" 43 And He said to him, "Truly I say to you, today you shall be with Me in Paradise."

44 It was now about ªthe sixth hour, and darkness ᵇfell over the whole land until ᶜthe ninth hour, 45ªbecause the sun was obscured; and the veil of the temple was torn ᵇin two. 46 And Jesus, crying out with a loud voice, said, "Father, INTO YOUR HANDS I COMMIT MY SPIRIT." Having said this, He breathed His last.

22:66 ªOr *Sanhedrin* 22:67 ªI.e. Messiah
22:70 ªLit *You say that I am* 23:2 ªI.e. Messiah
23:7 ªLit *in these days* 23:8 ªOr *attesting
miracle* 23:9 ªLit *in many words* 23:17 ªEarly
mss do not contain this v 23:27 ªLit *beating
the breast* 23:31 ªLit *in the green tree* ᵇLit *in*

NLT

33 When they came to a place called The Skull,* they nailed him to the cross. And the criminals were also crucified—one on his right and one on his left.

34 Jesus said, "Father, forgive them, for they don't know what they are doing."* And the soldiers gambled for his clothes by throwing dice.*

35 The crowd watched and the leaders scoffed. "He saved others," they said, "let him save himself if he is really God's Messiah, the Chosen One." 36 The soldiers mocked him, too, by offering him a drink of sour wine. 37 They called out to him, "If you are the King of the Jews, save yourself!" 38 A sign was fastened above him with these words: "This is the King of the Jews."

39 One of the criminals hanging beside him scoffed, "So you're the Messiah, are you? Prove it by saving yourself—and us, too, while you're at it!"

40 But the other criminal protested, "Don't you fear God even when you have been sentenced to die? 41 We deserve to die for our crimes, but this man hasn't done anything wrong." 42 Then he said, "Jesus, remember me when you come into your Kingdom." 43 And Jesus replied, "I assure you, today you will be with me in paradise."

44 By this time it was about noon, and darkness fell across the whole land until three o'clock. 45 The light from the sun was gone. And suddenly, the curtain in the sanctuary of the Temple was torn down the middle. 46 Then Jesus shouted, "Father, I entrust my spirit into your hands!"* And with those words he breathed his last.

22:66 Greek *before their Sanhedrin*. 22:69 See
Ps 110:1. 23:16 Some manuscripts add verse 17,
*Now it was necessary for him to release one
prisoner to them during the Passover celebration.*
Compare Matt 27:15; Mark 15:6; John 18:39.
23:26 *Cyrene* was a city in northern Africa.

The Sanhedrin was the supreme governing body of Israel, limited only by the authority of Rome, which typically gave local leaders wide latitude. In most regions, the emperor posted a governor, supplied him with troops, and charged him with two responsibilities: maintain order and keep the tax revenues flowing. To do that, a wise governor cooperated with indigenous authorities when he could and had people executed only when he must.

Traditionally, governors in Israel allowed the Sanhedrin to run the nation. This council of seventy elder statesmen and religious experts created laws and other rules of conduct. They managed the day-to-day operation of the temple. They also ruled on significant civil cases, major criminal cases, and charges of egregious religious misconduct. The council heard capital cases but was not permitted to carry out a death sentence. For that, they had to convince the local governor it was in the best interest of Rome to execute that individual.

After Jesus' nighttime arrest, He was taken to the home of Annas, the Godfather figure of Jerusalem, and then to Caiaphas, Annas's puppet high priest. These were not trials in the strictest sense, as the council failed to abide by its own jurisprudence. (See chart, "The Mistrials of Jesus," pages 556–557.) The hearing was held in secret, at night, and in the high priest's palace instead of the council's meeting hall. Furthermore, no advocate for the accused had been provided, the council argued for conviction—not acquittal—the accused was compelled to testify against Himself, and the proceedings were conducted during a feast.

All the Judean heads of state convened to compel a confession or retraction from the Lord rather than hear evidence and then render a ruling. His judicial fate had been decided long before He arrived. But, to maintain at least the appearance of propriety, the council disbanded. According to their strict rules, the members were to withhold judgment until morning. In the meantime, they were to meet in pairs, share a sparse meal, and discuss the case exhaustively in preparation for a final ruling the following day.

As morning dawned, the ruling council of elders called an emergency meeting—at least from the perspective of the trusting public.

THE MISTRIALS OF JESUS

	Rule	Primary Source
#1	No trials were to occur during the night hours (before the morning sacrifice).	Mishnah: Sanhedrin 4:1
#2	Trials were not to occur on the eve of a Sabbath or during feasts.	Mishnah: Sanhedrin 4:1
#3	All trials were to be public; secret trials were forbidden.	Mishnah: Sanhedrin 1:6
#4	All trials were to be held in the Hall of Judgment in the temple area.	Mishnah: Sanhedrin 11:2
#5	Capital cases required a minimum of twenty-three judges.	Mishnah: Sanhedrin 4:1
#6	An accused person could not testify against himself.	Mishnah: Sanhedrin 3:3-4
#7	Someone was required to speak on behalf of the accused.	
#8	Conviction required the testimony of two or three witnesses to be in perfect alignment.	Deuteronomy 17:6-7; 19:15-20
#9	Witnesses for the prosecution were to be examined and cross-examined extensively.	Mishnah: Sanhedrin 4:1
#10	Capital cases were to follow a strict order, beginning with arguments by the defense, then arguments for conviction.	Mishnah: Sanhedrin 4:1
#11	All Sanhedrin judges could argue for aquittal, but not all could argue for conviction.	Mishnah: Sanhedrin 4:1
#12	The high priest should not participate in the questioning.	
#13	Each witness in a capital case was to be examined individually, not in the presence of other witnesses.	Mishnah: Sanhedrin 3:6
#14	The testimony of two witnesses found to be in contradiction rendered both invalid.	Mishnah: Sanhedrin 5:2
#15	Voting for conviction and sentencing in a capital case was to be conducted individually, beginning with the youngest, so younger members would not be influenced by the voting of the elder members.	Mishnah: Sanhedrin 4:2
#16	Verdicts in capital cases were to be handed down only during daylight hours.	Mishnah: Sanhedrin 4:1
#17	The members of the Sanhedrin were to meet in pairs all night, discuss the case, and reconvene for the purpose of confirming the final verdict and imposing sentence.	Mishnah: Sanhedrin 4:1
#18	Sentencing in a capital case was not to occur until the following day.	Mishnah: Sanhedrin 4:1

Secondary Source	Actual Practice
Laurna L. Berg, "The Illegalities of Jesus' Religious and Civil Trials," (*Bibliotheca Sacra,* Vol. 161, No. 643, July–September, 2004), 330–342.	Jesus was taken to Annas, Caiaphas, and the Sanhedrin at night.
Ibid.	The trials occurred at night during the Passover celebration.
Ibid.	Jesus was taken before the Sanhedrin at night for questioning and was immediately delared "guilty." Only His official sentencing took place during the day.
Ibid.	Jesus was first taken to Annas, then Caiaphas, before He was put before the Sanhedrin.
Ibid.	We don't know how many judges were present. The trials took place at night during a feast.
Ibid.	The Sanhedrin convicted Jesus on His own words and did not see the need for witnesses.
Darrell L. Bock, "Jesus v. Sanhedrin: Why Jesus 'lost' his trial," (*Christianity Today,* Vol. 42, No. 4, April 6, 1998), 49.	No one spoke for Jesus, and when He objected to the illegality of the proceeding, He was struck in the face.
	The prosecution sought witnesses against Jesus, but their testimony conflicted.
	Witnesses were sought against Jesus for the purpose of conviction, not to aquit Him or even find the truth.
Berg, "Illegalities."	No one spoke in Jesus' defense, neither before the accusations nor after.
Ibid.	The chief priests and the council sought witnesses against Jesus.
Bock, "Jesus v. Sanhedrin."	Both Annas and Caiaphas interrogated Jesus directly, asking questions designed to incriminate Him.
Berg, "Illegalities."	We don't know how many witnesses were brought to testify at any given time.
Ibid.	The prosecution sought witnesses against Jesus, but their testimony conflicted.
Ibid.	The members of the Sanhedrin voted simultaneously and nearly rioted.
Ibid.	The Sanhedrin convicted Jesus and condemned Him right away, then reconvened the next day to give the appearance of order.
	We see only a rush to judgment and no indication that the judges met for any reason, least of all to find Jesus "not guilty."
Ibid.	The Sanhedrin convicted Jesus and condemned Him right away, then reconvened the next day to give the appearance of order.

Sanhedrin Hall

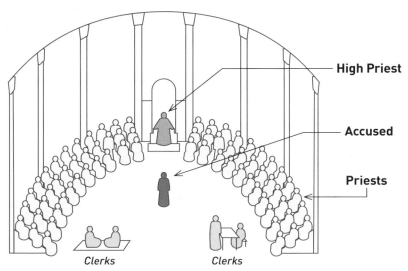

At the east end of the Royal Portico in the temple, seventy-one elders sat in semicircular rows around an area resembling a threshing floor. The Sanhedrin officially met here to set national and religious policy and to rule on civil and criminal cases. All of their deliberations and decisions were open to the public.

In truth, their attempts to control Jesus had failed, forcing their only remaining option: to prove Jesus guilty of sedition and then convince Pilate to execute Him. To keep Jesus from becoming a martyred hero and, consequently, the nucleus of a rebellion, the Sanhedrin also needed to gain popular support for His conviction. The other Gospel accounts emphasize the council's case for blasphemy; Luke's narrative highlights their case for sedition.

With the specific charge determined and the verdict already decided, the high priest summoned the council to the official place of judgment, a semicircular hall at the east end of the Royal Portico of the temple, designed to resemble a threshing floor.[18] In ancient times, farmers used a communal threshing floor to separate wheat from chaff. In time, it became the most logical place for the community to separate truth from fiction on all matters of justice. (See diagram, "Sanhedrin Hall.") For first-century Israel, this hall was Capitol Hill. It was the Kremlin. It was the seat of supreme power in Israel's national life. But in this case, it would not be a place of justice, for the spiritual darkness of Satan's evil dominion exercised a stronger grip here than in Galilee. This was the place from which religious hypocrisy flowed, and where the nation bred rebellion against God—Jerusalem, where the Messiah should have His throne.

— 22:66-69 —

Finally in the light of day, finally in the proper venue, and finally before the eyes of the public, the third "trial" began. Still, the council violated its own rules of jurisprudence. The jury became the defendant's accusers. No one advocated for the accused. The officials tried a capital case during the Feast of Unleavened Bread. They compelled the accused to testify against Himself and used His statements to convict Him without corroborating evidence. They put on a trial for show, merely presenting before the public what they had already rehearsed in private.

Luke briefly summarized the council's dual case against Jesus. If they could attach to Him the label "Christ" or "Messiah," then Pilate undoubtedly would see the wisdom of executing Jesus as a source of political unrest in Judea. If they could get Jesus to admit His claims to deity, then they might make the case for blasphemy before the general population. And by the end of His appearance in the hall of the Sanhedrin (also known as the "Chamber of Hewn Stone"), Jesus admitted to both charges. He is, indeed, the Christ, the King of the Jews. And He is, indeed, deity in human flesh.

Jesus refused to answer the question about His being the Messiah to avoid supporting their motive. He did, indeed, claim the right of kingship, but He would not verify their implication that He intended to lead an insurrection against Rome. Nevertheless, He stated the truth plainly, calling Himself "Son of Man" as He alluded to a well-known messianic psalm: "The LORD says to my Lord: 'Sit at My right hand until I make Your enemies a footstool for Your feet'" (Ps 110:1).

Jesus intended this allusion in the cosmic, end-time sense predicted by Daniel in the Old Testament:

> And behold, with the clouds of heaven
> One like a Son of Man was coming,
> And He came up to the Ancient of Days
> And was presented before Him.
> And to Him was given dominion,
> Glory and a kingdom,
> That all the peoples, nations and men of every language
> Might serve Him.
> His dominion is an everlasting dominion
> Which will not pass away;
> And His kingdom is one
> Which will not be destroyed. (Dan. 7:13-14)

The council fully understood Jesus' meaning but rejected the personal and national implications of His claim. Instead, they pulled from it what they needed to get Him killed. Actually, the Lord's words pronounced judgment upon *them*. Their condemnation of Jesus in this earthly kingdom would become the means of His exaltation in the kingdom of God, where He would become King and they His footstool.

— 22:70-71 —

Until this point in Luke's narrative, only supernatural beings ascribed to Jesus the title "Son of God": the angel before Mary (Luke 1:35), Satan in the wilderness temptations (4:3, 9), and the many demons Jesus exorcised in His ministry (4:41). The council correctly inferred from Jesus' claim that He would be seated at God's right hand that He claimed equality with God. In Hebrew vernacular, to be the "son" of someone was to share their defining qualities and to inherit their place of position. When asked directly, Jesus said, literally, "You say that I am" (22:70).

Again, Jesus didn't shy away from the truth. He merely affirmed the facts of His identity without supporting the council's unrighteous efforts. In other words, He wanted the truth to stand on its own while making it clear that the religious leaders were entirely responsible for their decision to kill their King. Jesus didn't bring this on Himself. He didn't encourage or aid His own martyrdom. The enemies of God's kingdom acted of their own volition to call God's Christ a liar.

By the end of the third trial, after fishing for a suitable charge that would both convince Pilate to execute Jesus and appease the restless Hebrew masses, the religious leaders had what they felt they needed. But this was an all-or-nothing decision. Hypothetically, if they failed to convince Pilate, Jesus would have emerged the political victor, having won the support of Rome against them. If they succeeded in killing Jesus, however, His very death would vindicate their claim that He was a false messiah—or so they thought!

— 23:1-2 —

The Jewish Feast of Unleavened Bread brought tens of thousands of Jews into Jerusalem. Pilate normally resided in Caesarea, but with the city population nearly ten times its normal level and with the need to preserve law and order, he took up residence in the Praetorium in Jerusalem. This could have been either a residence within the Fortress of Antonia adjacent to the temple or, more likely, the palace once inhabited by Herod the Great.

Todd Bolen/Bibleplaces.com.

After Herod Archelaus was deposed and banished to Gaul, the family palace became the official residence of the Roman procurator, which, at the time of Jesus' trials, was Pilate. To avoid ritual defilement during the Passover feast, the religious leaders refused to enter Pilate's house. He most likely heard their complaints in the courtyard bounded by the three towers behind the palace at the top right of the photo.

The Jewish leaders recognized that Rome cared only about Rome, so they concentrated on three charges that portrayed Jesus a threat to the state. The first charge, "misleading our nation," gave His threat national scope—He was no petty rabble-rouser; He could cause real trouble nationwide. The second charge, "forbidding to pay taxes to Caesar," affected the bottom line of Pilate's duty in Judea. Earlier, they put the question of taxes before Jesus but failed to get the seditious statements they hoped to use (20:22-26). But no matter. They simply lied. However, on the third count, "saying that He Himself is Christ," they had Him. To emphasize the implications to Rome, they added, "a King!"

— 23:3-4 —

Pilate apparently didn't care about the first two charges. Let the people be misled, so long as they shut up and pay their taxes. And let the people begrudge paying taxes; who doesn't? Roman troops will offer all the encouragement they need. Therefore, the procurator probed the only relevant matter in their complaint. He turned to the accused and asked a straightforward question: "Are You the King of the Jews?" Pilate didn't care about the religious title "Christ." Instead, he assessed the prisoner's threat to the stability of Judea.

Literally rendered, Luke quotes Jesus: "You are saying."

His reply is notoriously difficult to interpret, partly because it was idiomatic. In terms of defense, Jesus didn't back away from the truth of His claim to the throne of Israel, but He refused to convict Himself of a crime. He was King, but not in the normal human sense of the word (see John 18:33-38); and He didn't plan to lead an insurrection, which would have been an expected element in the claim to be king. Moreover, the burden of proof lay with his accusers, and they had offered no evidence to support their indictment. Again, let it be said that Jesus contributed nothing to the injustice done to Him.

Pilate turned to the religious leaders and said, in effect, "You have failed to prove your case; I find Him 'not guilty.'"

— 23:5-7 —

The angry rulers pressed their case, desperate for conviction. The political damage was too great if Jesus won. They emphasized His national influence, hoping the potential threat of insurrection was worth the trouble of killing just one, solitary man. Pilate didn't find their appeal convincing, but he did hear a possible way out for himself: "Galilee." Jesus was from Galilee, the official jurisdiction of Herod Antipas, who had killed the popular John the Baptizer.

Not far away from the Praetorium, Herod Antipas, the tetrarch of Galilee, had taken up residence for the Jewish Passover Feast. The Jewish aristocracy recognized him as a leader, and Jesus was a citizen of his realm. It was a perfect way for Pilate to rid himself of a political no-win scenario. The move did pose a risk for the governor, however. He and Antipas had clashed before, with Rome siding against Pilate. Furthermore, Pilate's only political advocate in Rome had been executed for treason against Tiberius, so Pilate would not likely survive another political loss.

— 23:8 —

Herod Antipas was the son of Herod the Great and, like his father, he ruled with notorious cruelty. Earlier, Luke stated, "[Herod] kept trying to see Him" (Luke 9:9), but he had not yet been able to do so.

In a gesture not unlike a practical joke, Pilate gave Herod this opportunity. Luke describes the primary reason Herod wanted to meet Jesus: "to see some sign performed by Him." The Greek term translated "sign"

HEROD ANTIPAS

LUKE 23:7

Herod Antipas, a son of Herod the Great, had inherited many of his father's qualities, including a love for large-scale building projects and a cruel disregard for his subjects. (See map, "Israel after Herod the Great," page 82.) Along with an impressive list of buildings and cities to his credit, Antipas continued the Herodian immorality befitting the family name.[19] His forebearers had converted to Judaism and claimed Jewish heritage to legitimize their claims to the throne, and he sided with Jewish leaders in Rome to secure their support.[20] But he behaved more like a Roman than like the people he ruled. For example, he built a magnificent city on the western shore of the Sea of Galilee in honor of Tiberius and made it his capital. In the process of construction, he destroyed a cemetery, leading Jews to consider the entire Greek-inspired city unclean.[21] As a result, Antipas had difficulty getting people to live there, so in order to attract citizens, he offered free real estate and tax exemptions to the first voluntary citizens.

Antipas became more infamous for his family affairs. He drove his prior wife into exile in order to marry his sister-in-law and niece, Herodias. By marrying his brother's wife, he not only violated an important marriage treaty, causing political unrest, but he also violated Jewish Law (Lev. 18:16; 20:21), drawing public scorn from John the Baptizer. Were it not for John's immense popularity—and Herod's sometimes positive feelings about John's teachings—he would have been executed immediately (Matt. 14:5; Mark 6:20). As it happened, he kept John in prison for two years until "the daughter of Herodias danced before [Herod and his guests] and pleased Herod, so much that he promised with an oath to give her whatever she asked" (Matt. 14:6-7). At her mother's insistence, she asked for the Baptizer's head on a platter, which Herod promptly delivered.

Throughout his thirty-five-year reign, Antipas cleverly balanced his Roman allegiance with the appearance of loyalty to his people. During several clashes with Pilate, he advocated for the Jewish leaders, successfully gaining support from Rome. Ironically, through the events surrounding Jesus' condemnation, the relationship between Antipas and Pilate improved (Luke 23:12). Not only did the sentence given to Jesus appease the riotous religious authorities, it also cemented local political partnerships.

Eventually, however, Antipas's political calculations failed, and in AD 39, Caligula banished him to present-day France.

refers to a miraculous wonder. Not only would Herod finally get to see Jesus and perhaps witness a magic show, but he would also have the opportunity to judge "the King of the Jews."

— 23:9-12 —

If Antipas wanted a show, he was disappointed. Jesus recognized a basic fact of life: Words are wasted on people who have no desire for truth. Herod questioned Jesus, but He remained stock-still and completely silent. Perhaps Herod cajoled Him for a miracle; if so, He refused. Herod and his soldiers made a game of humiliating Jesus, but He gave them no satisfaction. Eventually, Antipas grew bored with Jesus and threw Pilate's problem back in his face. He did, however, acknowledge the procurator's joke by returning Jesus to him wearing a royal robe from his own wardrobe.

While the problem returned to Pilate, the two men shared a laugh, and Pilate gained an important ally.

— 23:13-16 —

Pilate probably looked up from the breakfast table to see a gaunt silhouette at his gate. His political no-win scenario had returned.

He summoned Jesus' original accusers to reveal his judgment and explain his actions. The religious leaders had failed to prove their case, and Antipas concurred, so they would find no support from him. But, in an effort to appease the angry mob, Pilate offered to "punish" Jesus before releasing Him. The term for "punish" can mean "to teach a lesson" or "to punish for the purpose of improved behavior."[22]

— 23:17 —

The lack of early manuscript evidence attesting to this verse's authenticity, its insertion in two different locations in later copies, and its distinct wording all argue against the notion that Luke originally included this detail. It is, nevertheless, a helpful detail. While not a widespread custom by any means, Pilate either honored the custom of his predecessor or made this his habit in Israel to win back Jewish favor after behaving so cruelly early on.

— 23:18-19 —

Not far from the Praetorium judgment seat, a man named Barabbas awaited execution. His name was nonsensical, meaning "son of a father," probably similar to the name "John Doe" today. He had been convicted of insurrection and murder. He was most likely a member of the notorious Sicarii, the kind of criminal Romans delighted to execute using the most agonizing means possible. He faced death on a cross. Certainly, if forced to choose between an innocent man and one proven guilty of numerous crimes against Rome, they wouldn't urge the release of a proven enemy of the state. Releasing Barabbas would put them on the opposite side of the issue from Caesar.

It was, perhaps, a bluff. Pilate would not likely risk releasing a convicted insurrectionist and murderer. Yet, he underestimated their hatred for Jesus and the desperation of their position. If they lost this case, their entire scheme would backfire, discrediting them and vindicating Jesus. So, without hesitation, they demanded the release of Barabbas. Bluff or not, they had no choice.

— 23:20-25 —

Pilate's strategy failed. Not only did he fail to solve the problem of Jesus, but he also added another problem. Now he was duty bound to release Barabbas, thus risking the wrath of Tiberius!

He tried two more times to argue for the release of Jesus, even promising to "teach Him a lesson" or "punish Him" (23:22), but the religious leaders would not relent. Finally, he decided the life of one man was not worth risking his career. He had a new friend in Antipas, and he would gain the favor of the foremost leaders of Israel by killing their enemy. With a wave of his hand and the stroke of a pen, he condemned Jesus to take Barabbas's place on the cross.

— 23:26 —

History has no shortage of cruel ways to kill a person. Sadists and sociopaths have occupied positions of power since the beginning of civilization, and they have devised hundreds of ways to execute their enemies—most of them designed to bring death as slowly and as painfully as possible. But none exceeds crucifixion in terms of suffering and humiliation. The ancient orator Cicero described crucifixion as "the worst extreme of the tortures inflicted upon slaves."[23] While the Romans didn't invent crucifixion, it became for them the standard means of execution, which they transformed into a macabre art. Death on a cross brought together four qualities the Romans prized most in an execution: unrelenting agony, protracted death, public spectacle, and utter humiliation.

Perhaps because everyone reading his account knew the practice all too well, Luke spent little time describing its details. Instead, he focused on the cosmic implications of humans putting to death the Son of God. The phrase "when they led Him away" skips over several hours of cruelty the Lord endured. Everyone in the first century knew that people condemned to the cross endured a beating with a *flagrum* beforehand, a punishment known as "the halfway death." A *flagrum* was a whip with long, leather tails, often with small weights or bits of sheep bone braided into the straps in order to inflict maximum damage. After the lictor completed his cruel task, the executioner stripped his prisoner naked, and the prisoner was then forced to carry the implement of their own demise to the place of execution. They hung a *titulus* around the neck of the condemned, a crude sign bearing the prisoner's name and a list of their crimes. The execution detail would attach the sign to the cross above their head to let everyone know why they had been condemned.

Luke's detail that the soldiers compelled a random stranger to carry Jesus' cross told the first century reader that Jesus barely survived the flogging.

— 23:27-31 —

The Lord's death processional followed a well-traveled path from the Fortress of Antonia to a place outside the city reserved for execution. A large crowd of Jesus' followers "mourned and lamented." More specifically, they "beat their breast" (*koptō* [2875]) and "sang a dirge" (*thrēneō* [2354]), which people customarily did during a funeral procession from the home of the deceased to the burial cave.

Jesus addressed the mourners, specifically the women, telling them to weep for themselves rather than for Him. While He went to the place of execution, He was not only a martyr but also a judge. He would rise again, but Jerusalem—that is, the official leaders and the majority of its inhabitants—would suffer unspeakable agony for its crime against God (cf. 21:20-24). His allusion to Hosea 10:8 recalls a lament associated with God's judgment for Israel's idolatry.

His concluding image of green wood versus dry wood is likely a comparison between Himself and Israel. Green, sap-filled wood doesn't catch fire nearly as quickly as dead, dry wood. The judgment falling upon Him—as horrific as it was—cannot compare to the condemning fire coming to those who conspired against the Christ.

— 23:32-34 —

Three men were crucified that dark day. Jesus bore the cross intended for Barabbas. The other two criminals—called by Luke "evildoers" (*kakourgos* [2557])—may have been the freed man's accomplices. The executioners led the men to a place the locals had nicknamed "The Skull"—we know it in English as "Calvary."

The soldiers laid the cross-beam on the ground and attached it to the top of the post. Each condemned man was placed on top of the wood with arms outstretched and feet pressed flat against the face of the upright beam. A sharp spike was driven through each wrist near the base of the palm, and another through the crossed feet. The soldiers then tilted the cross up and dropped it into a hole.

While the executioners carried out their gruesome duty, Jesus interceded for them before His Father. The imperfect tense of the verb "was saying" (23:34) suggests He prayed throughout the process. Then, in fulfillment of the remarkable Psalm 22, the soldiers gambled to see who kept which items of His clothing (cf. Ps. 22:18).

Cross

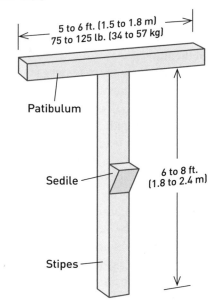

5 to 6 ft. (1.5 to 1.8 m)

75 to 125 lb. (34 to 57 kg)

Patibulum

Sedile

6 to 8 ft. (1.8 to 2.4 m)

Stipes

The Romans wasted nothing during the execution, including wood and nails. Everything would be used again. Therefore, the *patibulum* (crossbeam) was attached to the top of the *stipes* (vertical member) with a mortise and tenon joint, which allowed them to dismantle the cross for the next victim more easily. Sometimes, to delay death and to prolong the victim's agony, the executioner attached a *sedile* (seat) between the victim's legs.

— 23:35-38 —

The Romans used crucifixion as a form of execution to heighten the shame of the condemned. Citizens were encouraged to taunt such condemned criminals, which many did on this day. "Rulers" (members of the Sanhedrin) "sneered" (the same term translated "scoffed" in Luke 16:14). In their minds, the very fact that Jesus hung on a cross proved He was not the Messiah, a perspective they hoped to impress upon the multitudes who had followed Jesus. Their derision publicly justified the unscrupulous means by which they crucified the man that so many had expected to become king.

Obviously, the soldiers found their logic credible. They joined the cruel chorus of taunts while, ironically, offering kindness in the form of "sour wine." Soldiers and laborers enjoyed this refreshing mixture of water and dry wine along with meals and as an aid to reduce fever.

The *titulus* above Jesus' head announced His "crime," a taunt from Pilate for the religious leaders who had cornered him: "This is the King of the Jews" (see John 19:19-22).

Luke strings these images together to underscore the apparent contradiction of the Messiah falling prey to the enemies of God and then succumbing to death. In the popular mind, this should not have been possible. After all, how can a dead savior save his people? How can a dead messiah lead his nation to greatness? How can the kingdom of God come to earth if its king lies cold in a grave?

— 23:39-43 —

Luke highlights one individual who didn't accept the conventional wisdom that the Savior's death disproved His messianic identity. While one crucified "evildoer" joined the growing chorus of taunts, the other "rebuked" his associate. The term "rebuke" is a favorite of Luke's, used throughout the narrative as a response to various forms of evil, such as demons (4:35, 41; 9:42), misbehaving natural elements (8:24), physical ailments (4:39), sinning brothers (17:3), and judgmental disciples (9:55). This man admitted his own guilt and affirmed the innocence of Jesus.

In a remarkable expression of faith, the criminal accepted the absurd notion that death on a cross didn't preclude Jesus from becoming the King of God's kingdom. Furthermore, knowing he himself would soon die, he asked to become a citizen of that kingdom.

Jesus welcomed the criminal's faith and promised him a place in "Paradise." The Greek term (*paradeisos* [3857]) was borrowed from Persian and appears throughout the Septuagint (the Greek translation of the Old Testament) as "garden." This offers a tantalizing hint that believers go to a place of delight after death and exist there until the end of days and the consummation of God's kingdom on earth.

— 23:44-46 —

For Luke, the story of Jesus transcended the physical universe. The Savior's becoming flesh and moving about in the tangible world affected the whole universe, seen and unseen, physical and spiritual. Everything He did had cosmic, metaphysical implications. His ministry began in Judea with a personal confrontation with Satan, after which He battled the forces of evil in their various forms: demons, disasters, disease, and death. He journeyed from Galilee to Jerusalem, where evil men held the Lord's temple captive and corrupted His Word, and the conflict with spiritual darkness intensified. The dominion of evil presumed to destroy "the Christ of God" (9:20), but what Satan intended for evil, God used for good, even as He poured out His wrath upon the Savior hanging on the cross.

At the "sixth hour" (or noon by our method of timekeeping), darkness draped the region as Jesus suffered condemnation for the myriad sins of innumerable people through countless generations, ever since Adam's first transgression. In the Old Testament, darkness was used as a metaphor to describe the coming judgment of God (Joel 2:10; 2:30-31; Amos 8:9; Zeph. 1:15); here, for three hours, it became a physical reality as something prevented the sun's light from reaching the ground. The phrase "the sun was obscured" could literally be rendered "the sun failed." The eerie darkness was palpable.

As Jesus became the atoning sacrifice for the sins of the world, the "veil of the temple was torn in two." This thick veil shielded the "holy of holies," where the light of God's presence once appeared in a cloud over the cover of the ark of the covenant (Exod. 25:21-22; Lev. 16:2). In this symbolic act, which Luke vaguely attributes to God, the barrier between God and humanity was forever removed.

His work completed, His sacrifice made, Jesus shouted a prayer of faith in God taken from Psalm 31. While it expressed the Son's trust in the Father, it was also an invitation for people to follow His example: "Into Your hand I commit my spirit; You have ransomed me, O LORD, God of truth" (Ps. 31:5). As Jesus breathed His last, Satan's doom was secured.

APPLICATION: LUKE 22:66–23:46

Your One and Only Response

Such an extreme price for our salvation calls for extreme obedience out of gratitude to God.

Some people today continue to play the religious part. Perhaps you are one of them. You have played church most of your life. Jesus is a name you've heard since you were born. You saw pictures of Him in Sunday school. You learned stories about Him and about the cross as you grew up. You can't imagine life without the church and Jesus. But as a result, the edge has been taken off of your faith. Being overexposed, your faith has been dulled by indifference. Whatever your denominational background, when you come to a scene like this, as narrated by Luke, it becomes clear what it took to make the payment, the ransom for sins. And this is just the physical part of it. We can't fathom what it meant for Jesus to have the Father's back turned on Him. When you come to a point like this, recognizing the extreme price that was paid for our salvation, you may realize that such an act calls for extreme obedience. This obedience is not simply a nice option. We *must* obey. And it is a commitment for life, this following Christ.

I urge you, don't underestimate the gift of eternal life. Although it cost you and me nothing, it cost Him everything—untold suffering in that span of time when the sins of the world were poured out on Him.

If you genuinely understand what the Lord has done for you, then you have but one response, and it must be obedience.

The Day the Son Came Out Again
LUKE 23:47–24:12

NASB

47 Now when the centurion saw what had happened, he *began* praising God, saying, "Certainly this man was ªinnocent." 48 And all the crowds who came together for this spectacle, when they observed what had happened, *began* to return, ªbeating their breasts. 49 And all His acquaintances and the women who accompanied Him from Galilee were standing at a distance, seeing these things.

50 And a man named Joseph, who was a member of the Council, a good and righteous man 51 (he had not consented to their plan and action), *a man* from Arimathea, a city of the Jews, who was waiting for the kingdom of God; 52 this man went to Pilate and asked for the body of Jesus. 53 And he took it down and wrapped it in a linen cloth, and laid Him in

NLT

47 When the Roman officer* overseeing the execution saw what had happened, he worshiped God and said, "Surely this man was innocent.*" 48 And when all the crowd that came to see the crucifixion saw what had happened, they went home in deep sorrow.* 49 But Jesus' friends, including the women who had followed him from Galilee, stood at a distance watching.

50 Now there was a good and righteous man named Joseph. He was a member of the Jewish high council, 51 but he had not agreed with the decision and actions of the other religious leaders. He was from the town of Arimathea in Judea, and he was waiting for the Kingdom of God to come. 52 He went to Pilate and asked for Jesus' body. 53 Then he took the body down from the cross and

a tomb cut into the rock, where no one had ever lain. ⁵⁴It was the ^apreparation day, and the Sabbath was about to ^bbegin. ⁵⁵Now the women who had come with Him out of Galilee followed, and saw the tomb and how His body was laid. ⁵⁶Then they returned and prepared spices and perfumes.

And on the Sabbath they rested according to the commandment.

^{24:1}But on the first day of the week, at early dawn, they came to the tomb bringing the spices which they had prepared. ²And they found the stone rolled away from the tomb, ³but when they entered, they did not find the body of the Lord Jesus. ⁴While they were perplexed about this, behold, two men suddenly stood near them in dazzling clothing; ⁵and as *the women* were terrified and bowed their faces to the ground, *the men* said to them, "Why do you seek the living One among the dead? ⁶He is not here, but He has ^arisen. Remember how He spoke to you while He was still in Galilee, ⁷saying that the Son of Man must be delivered into the hands of sinful men, and be crucified, and the third day rise again." ⁸And they remembered His words, ⁹and returned from the tomb and reported all these things to the eleven and to all the rest. ¹⁰Now they were Mary Magdalene and Joanna and Mary the *mother* of James; also the other women with them were telling these things to the apostles. ¹¹But these words appeared ^ato them as nonsense, and they would not believe them. ¹²But Peter got up and ran to the tomb; stooping and looking in, he saw the linen wrappings

wrapped it in a long sheet of linen cloth and laid it in a new tomb that had been carved out of rock. ⁵⁴This was done late on Friday afternoon, the day of preparation,* as the Sabbath was about to begin.

⁵⁵As his body was taken away, the women from Galilee followed and saw the tomb where his body was placed. ⁵⁶Then they went home and prepared spices and ointments to anoint his body. But by the time they were finished the Sabbath had begun, so they rested as required by the law.

^{24:1}But very early on Sunday morning* the women went to the tomb, taking the spices they had prepared. ²They found that the stone had been rolled away from the entrance. ³So they went in, but they didn't find the body of the Lord Jesus. ⁴As they stood there puzzled, two men suddenly appeared to them, clothed in dazzling robes.

⁵The women were terrified and bowed with their faces to the ground. Then the men asked, "Why are you looking among the dead for someone who is alive? ⁶He isn't here! He is risen from the dead! Remember what he told you back in Galilee, ⁷that the Son of Man* must be betrayed into the hands of sinful men and be crucified, and that he would rise again on the third day."

⁸Then they remembered that he had said this. ⁹So they rushed back from the tomb to tell his eleven disciples—and everyone else—what had happened. ¹⁰It was Mary Magdalene, Joanna, Mary the mother of James, and several other women who told the apostles what had happened. ¹¹But the story sounded like nonsense to the men, so they didn't believe it. ¹²However, Peter jumped up and ran to the tomb to look. Stooping, he peered in and saw the

NASB

ªonly; and he went away to his home, marveling at what had happened.

23:47 ªLit *righteous*   23:48 ªI.e. as a traditional sign of mourning or contrition   23:54 ªI.e. preparation for the Sabbath   ᵇLit *dawn*   24:6 ªOr *been raised*   24:11 ªLit *in their sight*   24:12 ªOr *by themselves*

empty linen wrappings; then he went home again, wondering what had happened.

23:47a Greek *the centurion.*   23:47b Or *righteous.*
23:48 Greek *went home beating their breasts.*
23:54 Greek *It was the day of preparation.*
24:1 Greek *But on the first day of the week, very early in the morning.*   24:7 "Son of Man" is a title Jesus used for himself.

NLT

I looked up "death" in the dictionary. Here is what I found:

death \'deth\ *noun*

1   a: a permanent cessation of all vital functions: the end of life[24]

In the case of Jesus, that definition is wrong on two points. First, it was not a *permanent* cessation of anything. Second, it was not the *end* of life—not by a long shot! His physical life came to an end, but He didn't cease to exist. Jesus would later rise from the grave—not just His spirit, but His body, too. He was miraculously raised to a new kind of life with a new kind of body.

But I get ahead of myself.

Jesus died. He was human in every respect; so, when subjected to the cruelty of the cross, He died just like any other human would die. But the man who died on "Skull Hill" as the sun failed and darkness shrouded the land and the temple veil was torn—this man was no mere mortal. He was the Son of the Living God, bearing the sins of all humanity. What His followers didn't see—though Jesus had made this abundantly clear many times—was that the Son of God had laid the axe at the root of evil (see Luke 3:9).

Still, from the limited perspective of everyone who knew Jesus, death was the end. And no one was the wiser.

— 23:47-49 —

Seconds after Jesus breathed His last, a centurion—a Gentile—"began praising God." The Greek verb is *doxazō* [1392], which means "to influence one's opinion about another so as to enhance the latter's reputation."[25] He declared Jesus "innocent" or "righteous," using the judicial term *dikaios* [1342], thereby adding his own declaration to a string of others (23:4, 14-15, 22, 41). The secular Greek idea of a "righteous" person is a man or woman who fulfills the requirements of civic duty, someone who is a virtuous citizen. And in the strict legal sense, which the centurion undoubtedly intended, it refers to the status of one not guilty of a crime and, therefore, not deserving punishment. In declaring "not guilty" the man he had just put to death, the centurion repented of his sin.

Many in the gathered crowd may have shared that sentiment with the centurion, having witnessed the supernatural phenomena surrounding the Savior's death, and they began to mourn. The statement that the Lord's followers "were standing at a distance" may indicate that the people beating their breasts in grief had not been believers before, although this is not to suggest that every observer repented or that everyone grieved. Certainly the Lord's most dedicated enemies breathed a sigh of relief, glad to see their rival dead.

— 23:50-52 —

At least two members of the Sanhedrin did not partake in the conspiracy against Jesus. Luke doesn't mention Nicodemus (see John 19:39), only Joseph of Arimathea. According to Sanhedrin rules, only twenty-three of the seventy members were needed to try a capital case, so there's a good chance neither man knew what had happened until after the trial. It's also possible they didn't *want* to know anything. As John's Gospel states, "Many even of the rulers believed in Him, but because of the Pharisees they were not confessing Him, for fear that they would be put out of the synagogue; for they loved the approval of men rather than the approval of God" (John 12:42-43). Regardless, Luke describes Joseph as good and righteous (*dikaios*), a man anticipating the kingdom of God (cf. Luke 2:25, 38).

If Joseph had been a cowardly follower before the Lord's death, he found his courage afterward. Like a lot of people, he had a change of heart as a result of the ordeal. He asked Pilate for the body so he could bury it.

— 23:53-54 —

Jesus died on a Friday afternoon. Jews referred to the day before a Sabbath as the "day of preparation." No work could be done on the Sabbath, so anything that was needed on Saturday had to be prepared on Friday before sundown. With nightfall approaching, Joseph and those helping him found themselves pressed for time between two Old Testament commandments. They were influenced by Deuteronomy 21:22-23, which required the body of someone who had been hanged (which included crucifixion) to be buried that same day, but they were also bound by the requirement to stop all work for the Sabbath. They had just enough time to hurriedly wrap His body in linen, apply at least some of the spices, and place Him inside the burial cave. An enormous stone covered the entrance to keep grave robbers out and the odors of decomposition in.

Luke doesn't mention anyone but Joseph and the women, but others must have been on hand to help. Those familiar with burial practices in those days assume that a team of men rolled the large, heavy stone in place. (For additional details regarding the burial, see the other Gospel accounts.)

— 23:55-56 —

"The women" refers to the women who followed Jesus and cared for His needs as well as the needs of the Twelve (Luke 8:2-3; 23:49). Normally, they would have taken great care to wrap the body of Jesus from head to toe in long strips of linen, which had been soaked in a mixture of spiced resin. In total, seventy-five to one hundred pounds of heavily scented spices were applied to offset the smell of decomposition. But with little time to work, they did all they could and planned to return after the Sabbath.

While everyone in Jerusalem rested, the followers of Jesus mourned—many of them alone, all of them disillusioned. They undoubtedly wondered, *What went wrong? What do we do now?*

— 24:1 —

The graveyard near Jerusalem became a bustling place early Sunday morning! The combined Gospel accounts reveal that several women came to the garden to complete the burial process. They probably arranged to meet at the same time, but arrived separately. While John's narrative follows only Mary Magdalene, the synoptic Gospels—Matthew, Mark, and Luke—trace the steps of the other women as well. Luke names only two: Joanna and Mary, the mother of James (24:10).

— 24:2-3 —

Burial caves were designed for security. No one wanted the remains of their loved one disturbed by grave robbers or wild animals. So they covered the entrance with a large, circular stone, sometimes weighing a ton or more. The giant disk rolled in a groove carved into the ground, so when released, the enormous stone wheel naturally rolled into place over the grave opening. To gain access, several strong men used levers to roll the massive disk away from the opening and then wedge it into place.

This tomb, hewn from a cave near Jerusalem, with a large cylindrical stone at the entrance, is similar to the one where Jesus would have been laid.

When the women arrived, the stone had been rolled away and the grave stood open. Upon entering, the women found no body inside. According to John's Gospel, Mary Magdalene left immediately to find the apostles (John 20:1-2). Perhaps the other women remained behind.

— 24:4-7 —

The women were "perplexed"—they could think of no credible way to explain the mystery of Jesus' missing body. People stole valuables placed on or around dead bodies, but they didn't steal bodies. The stone had been rolled away, so animals could not have been the culprits. They stood dumbstruck, staring blankly until two "men" appeared. Luke doesn't call them angels (until later in Luke 24:23), but his description is clear enough. They wore "dazzling" clothes, using the same adjective as in 17:24 when depicting a flash of lightning. Furthermore, Luke's description of the angels' appearance and the women's reaction recalls the angelic announcement to the shepherds at the beginning of the narrative (cf. 2:9).

The angels' rhetorical question suggests the women should have known better than to look for Jesus in the tomb, or at least should not be so perplexed. The declaration "He has risen" is a passive verb (i.e., "He has been raised"). Most likely it's a divine passive, implying that God has done the raising. They went on to remind the women of the Lord's many predictions of His suffering, death, and resurrection

(9:22, 44; 17:25; 18:31-33; 22:15-16). Everything that occurred had not only been predicted, *it was necessary*.

— 24:8-11 —

The women connected what they saw with what they remembered, and the realization struck like a thunderbolt. Jesus was alive! And they couldn't wait to tell the apostles and His other followers.

The women reported the news to the disciples, sharing about the empty tomb and the angels who appeared to them. But no one took the women seriously. The Greek word translated "nonsense" (24:11; *lēros* [3026]) was also used in a medical context of the feverish ramblings of a delirious patient.[26] The disciples dismissed the women's story as insane babbling prompted by hysterical wishful thinking.

— 24:12 —

According to John's Gospel, both Peter and John heard the news from Mary Magdalene, who had not yet seen the angels or the risen Lord. From her perspective, someone had removed the body. Luke's account focuses on Peter's experience.

Immediately, Peter ran to the tomb to investigate. When he arrived, he was "stooping and looking in." Luke uses a single term for this action (*parakuptō* [3879]), which expresses two primary ideas: first, "to bend over for the purpose of looking, with focus on satisfying one's curiosity" and, second, "to try to find out something intellectually."[27] Peter not only observed the scene, but he also studied it for clues, trying to comprehend what might have happened.

Based on his study of the four Gospel accounts, the history and customs of first-century burials, and the language used by the New Testament witnesses, Merrill Tenney concludes, "The wrappings were in position where the body had lain, and the head cloth was where the head had been, separated from the others by the distance from the armpits to neck. The shape of the body was still apparent in them, but the flesh and bone had disappeared."[28] If so, the strange appearance of hollow linen wrappings still in the shape of a body suggested it had vanished from within, leaving a sort of undisturbed cocoon shell.

Peter left the tomb "marveling" (*thaumazō* [2296]), but not necessarily convinced of the Resurrection. John's account agrees with Luke's; John believed, but Peter remained neutral. While the other disciples dismissed the women's report outright, Peter at least considered their claims reasonable given the evidence he had seen and the Lord's predictions throughout His ministry.

The expression "he went away to his home" could be rendered, literally, "he went away to his own" or "he went away to himself." "To himself/to his own" is a prepositional phrase that could be associated either with the preceding verb "went away," as in the NASB and NLT texts, or with the subsequent participle, which would result in "marveling to himself" (cf. NIV). Most translators, however, favor a connection with the preceding verb (cf. John 20:10). This same idiom appears in the Greek translation of the Old Testament in Numbers 24:25 to translate the Hebrew phrase meaning "went on his way."

Peter departed the tomb, most likely for his place of lodging, not his family home in Galilee. He would go there soon, but not right away. He undoubtedly remained in the city, at least until the convocation of the Feast of Unleavened Bread.

• • •

With all due respect to the venerable *Merriam-Webster's Collegiate Dictionary*, death need not be defined as "a permanent cessation of all vital functions," and it is most certainly not "the end of life." At least, not anymore. The resurrection of Jesus Christ is a historical fact that has far-reaching implications. He did not merely emerge from the tomb, resuscitated to exist a few more years. He was resurrected to a new kind of life, one that transcends the frail, fleeting existence we now endure. While these bodies get sick and suffer injury, He will never feel pain again. While our present relationships are doomed to end through betrayal, distance, or death, He will never feel abandonment or rejection again. While seasons of joy must eventually yield to sorrow, He will always know joy.

Because Jesus was raised, we now have hope of that kind of life through Him. The dominion of evil has been vanquished, its power to harm us limited to the realm of space and time. If we trust in Him, we will be like Him. While evil may kill the body, we will be raised to receive eternal life in His kingdom.

APPLICATION: LUKE 23:47–24:12
What the Resurrection Means

He's been raised! We celebrate it every Easter. It is the Christian's cornerstone of hope. Because He is raised, we also shall be raised. Because He is raised, sin can be forgiven. Because Christ is raised, death is not the final conqueror. Because He is raised, Satan's doom is sealed and sure. Nobody knows it more than Satan, who now lives on borrowed time and works overtime to destroy what he can. The grim reaper comes to call over a hundred thousand times a day around the world but never wins the ultimate victory. Resurrection is the Lord's ultimate answer to the problem of evil. There will be a day when bodies like yours and mine, even though dead and decaying, will be brought up out of the grave and joined to their souls; and we shall forever be with our Lord, never again to suffer pain or sorrow or disease or death. What a wonderful hope!

We witnessed in this passage the reaction to the death of Jesus by a seasoned soldier, a righteous member of the Sanhedrin, and a mixed group gathered at the cross. We also observed the initial response to the empty tomb by a small group of women and by the eleven apostles, who initially disbelieved but later carried the message into the streets of Jerusalem and out into Judea, Samaria, and around the world.

Never, ever forget that the story of the gospel that you share with another is not complete if you leave out the fact of the Resurrection. Jesus not only died for our sins, but He rose for our justification. As one of my mentors, S. Lewis Johnson, used to say, "The Resurrection was God's 'Amen' to Jesus' 'It is finished.'"

The Master Says Farewell to His Friends
LUKE 24:13-53

NASB

13 And behold, two of them were going that very day to a village named Emmaus, which was ªabout

NLT

13 That same day two of Jesus' followers were walking to the village of Emmaus, seven miles* from Jerusalem.

seven miles from Jerusalem. ¹⁴And they were talking with each other about all these things which had taken place. ¹⁵While they were talking and discussing, Jesus Himself approached and *began* traveling with them. ¹⁶But their eyes were prevented from recognizing Him. ¹⁷And He said to them, "What are these words that you are exchanging with one another as you are walking?" And they stood still, looking sad. ¹⁸One *of them,* named Cleopas, answered and said to Him, "Are You ªthe only one visiting Jerusalem and unaware of the things which have happened here in these days?" ¹⁹And He said to them, "What things?" And they said to Him, "The things about Jesus the Nazarene, who was a prophet mighty in deed and word in the sight of God and all the people, ²⁰and how the chief priests and our rulers delivered Him to the sentence of death, and crucified Him. ²¹But we were hoping that it was He who was going to redeem Israel. Indeed, besides all this, it is the third day since these things happened. ²²But also some women among us amazed us. When they were at the tomb early in the morning, ²³and did not find His body, they came, saying that they had also seen a vision of angels who said that He was alive. ²⁴Some of those who were with us went to the tomb and found it just exactly as the women also had said; but Him they did not see." ²⁵And He said to them, "O foolish men and slow of heart to believe in all that the prophets have spoken! ²⁶Was it not necessary for the ªChrist to suffer these things and to enter into His glory?" ²⁷Then beginning ªwith Moses and ªwith all the prophets, He explained to

¹⁴As they walked along they were talking about everything that had happened. ¹⁵As they talked and discussed these things, Jesus himself suddenly came and began walking with them. ¹⁶But God kept them from recognizing him.

¹⁷He asked them, "What are you discussing so intently as you walk along?"

They stopped short, sadness written across their faces. ¹⁸Then one of them, Cleopas, replied, "You must be the only person in Jerusalem who hasn't heard about all the things that have happened there the last few days."

¹⁹"What things?" Jesus asked.

"The things that happened to Jesus, the man from Nazareth," they said. "He was a prophet who did powerful miracles, and he was a mighty teacher in the eyes of God and all the people. ²⁰But our leading priests and other religious leaders handed him over to be condemned to death, and they crucified him. ²¹We had hoped he was the Messiah who had come to rescue Israel. This all happened three days ago.

²²"Then some women from our group of his followers were at his tomb early this morning, and they came back with an amazing report. ²³They said his body was missing, and they had seen angels who told them Jesus is alive! ²⁴Some of our men ran out to see, and sure enough, his body was gone, just as the women had said."

²⁵Then Jesus said to them, "You foolish people! You find it so hard to believe all that the prophets wrote in the Scriptures. ²⁶Wasn't it clearly predicted that the Messiah would have to suffer all these things before entering his glory?" ²⁷Then Jesus took them through the writings of Moses and all the prophets,

NASB

them the things concerning Himself in all the Scriptures.

²⁸ And they approached the village where they were going, and He acted as though He were going farther. ²⁹ But they urged Him, saying, "Stay with us, for it is *getting* toward evening, and the day ᵃis now nearly over." So He went in to stay with them. ³⁰ When He had reclined *at the table* with them, He took the bread and blessed *it,* and breaking *it,* He *began* giving *it* to them. ³¹ Then their eyes were opened and they recognized Him; and He vanished from ᵃtheir sight. ³² They said to one another, "ᵃWere not our hearts burning within us while He was speaking to us on the road, while He was ᵇexplaining the Scriptures to us?" ³³ And they got up that very hour and returned to Jerusalem, and found gathered together the eleven and those who were with them, ³⁴ saying, "The Lord has really risen and has appeared to Simon." ³⁵ They *began* to relate ᵃtheir experiences on the road and how He was recognized by them in the breaking of the bread.

³⁶ While they were telling these things, He Himself stood in their midst and said to them, "Peace be to you." ³⁷ But they were startled and frightened and thought that they were seeing a spirit. ³⁸ And He said to them, "Why are you troubled, and why do doubts arise in your ᵃhearts? ³⁹ See My hands and My feet, that it is I Myself; touch Me and see, for a spirit does not have flesh and bones as you see that I have." ⁴⁰ And when He had said this, He showed them His hands and His feet. ⁴¹ While they still ᵃcould not believe *it* because of their joy and amazement, He said to them, "Have you anything here to eat?" ⁴² They gave Him a piece of a broiled fish; ⁴³ and He took it and ate *it* before them.

NLT

explaining from all the Scriptures the things concerning himself.

²⁸ By this time they were nearing Emmaus and the end of their journey. Jesus acted as if he were going on, ²⁹ but they begged him, "Stay the night with us, since it is getting late." So he went home with them. ³⁰ As they sat down to eat,* he took the bread and blessed it. Then he broke it and gave it to them. ³¹ Suddenly, their eyes were opened, and they recognized him. And at that moment he disappeared!

³² They said to each other, "Didn't our hearts burn within us as he talked with us on the road and explained the Scriptures to us?" ³³ And within the hour they were on their way back to Jerusalem. There they found the eleven disciples and the others who had gathered with them, ³⁴ who said, "The Lord has really risen! He appeared to Peter.*"

³⁵ Then the two from Emmaus told their story of how Jesus had appeared to them as they were walking along the road, and how they had recognized him as he was breaking the bread. ³⁶ And just as they were telling about it, Jesus himself was suddenly standing there among them. "Peace be with you," he said. ³⁷ But the whole group was startled and frightened, thinking they were seeing a ghost!

³⁸ "Why are you frightened?" he asked. "Why are your hearts filled with doubt? ³⁹ Look at my hands. Look at my feet. You can see that it's really me. Touch me and make sure that I am not a ghost, because ghosts don't have bodies, as you see that I do." ⁴⁰ As he spoke, he showed them his hands and his feet.

⁴¹ Still they stood there in disbelief, filled with joy and wonder. Then he asked them, "Do you have anything here to eat?" ⁴² They gave him a piece of broiled fish, ⁴³ and he ate it as they watched.

44Now He said to them, "These are My words which I spoke to you while I was still with you, that all things which are written about Me in the Law of Moses and the Prophets and the Psalms must be fulfilled." 45Then He opened their ªminds to understand the Scriptures, 46and He said to them, "Thus it is written, that the ªChrist would suffer and rise again from the dead the third day, 47and that repentance ªfor forgiveness of sins would be proclaimed ᵇin His name to all the nations, beginning from Jerusalem. 48You are witnesses of these things. 49And behold, I am sending forth the promise of My Father upon you; but you are to stay in the city until you are clothed with power from on high."

50And He led them out as far as Bethany, and He lifted up His hands and blessed them. 51While He was blessing them, He parted from them and was carried up into heaven. 52And they, after worshiping Him, returned to Jerusalem with great joy, 53and were continually in the temple ªpraising God.

24:13 ªLit *60 stadia;* one stadion was about 600 ft   24:18 ªOr *visiting Jerusalem alone*   24:26 ªI.e. Messiah   24:27 ªLit *from*   24:29 ªLit *has now declined*   24:31 ªLit *them*   24:32 ªLit *Was not our heart*   ᵇLit *opening*   24:35 ªLit *the things*   24:38 ªLit *heart*   24:41 ªLit *were disbelieving*   24:45 ªLit *mind*   24:46 ªI.e. Messiah   24:47 ªLater mss read *and forgiveness*   ᵇOr *on the basis of*   24:53 ªLit *blessing*

44Then he said, "When I was with you before, I told you that everything written about me in the law of Moses and the prophets and in the Psalms must be fulfilled." 45Then he opened their minds to understand the Scriptures. 46And he said, "Yes, it was written long ago that the Messiah would suffer and die and rise from the dead on the third day. 47It was also written that this message would be proclaimed in the authority of his name to all the nations,* beginning in Jerusalem: 'There is forgiveness of sins for all who repent.' 48You are witnesses of all these things.

49"And now I will send the Holy Spirit, just as my Father promised. But stay here in the city until the Holy Spirit comes and fills you with power from heaven."

50Then Jesus led them to Bethany, and lifting his hands to heaven, he blessed them. 51While he was blessing them, he left them and was taken up to heaven. 52So they worshiped him and then returned to Jerusalem filled with great joy. 53And they spent all of their time in the Temple, praising God.

24:13 Greek *60 stadia* [11.1 kilometers].
24:30 Or *As they reclined.*   24:34 Greek *Simon.*
24:47 Or *all peoples.*

A little more than a week earlier, the followers of the Messiah had welcomed their King to Jerusalem. They covered His path with their cloaks and with cut palm branches; they cheered, praised God, and shouted, "Save us! Save us!" A substantial number of people joined His march from Galilee to Jerusalem, fully expecting Him to redeem Israel (cf. Luke 1:68; 2:25, 38; 23:51) and restore the nation to righteousness, prosperity, freedom, and power. He would throw off Roman tyranny, place the temple into godly hands, restore the rule of God's Law, and finally establish Israel as the light of the world (Isa. 42:6; 49:6; 60:1-3).

Jesus was their Messiah. He had promised abundant life. But when a king dies, his reign ends. As the sky darkened over Jerusalem the day before the Sabbath, their King hung cold and lifeless on a Roman cross between two condemned criminals. Meanwhile, His enemies preened themselves in the temple market for further business, and politicians resumed their daily trade, exchanging truth for power. Everything returned to "business as usual" in the temple; but for the followers of Jesus, the Passover celebration marked the death of a long-awaited dream.

On Sunday morning, disillusioned citizens of God's kingdom wondered what to do next. The Twelve had scattered at Jesus' arrest and were now gathered in a large home somewhere in the city, huddled behind locked doors for fear of the religious leaders (Luke 24:33; John 20:19). Before the day ended, however, the darkness of their despair would dawn with joy. And by the light of the following morning, their confusion had turned to rejoicing. Luke records their experience with a great deal of interest.

— 24:13 —

The identification "two of them" refers to two followers of Jesus. Perhaps deciding to leave their idealistic dreams in Jerusalem and return to their home, the pair of disciples quietly set out for Emmaus. The exact location is unknown today, but Luke sets the distance at 60 *stadia*. If one *stadion* measured roughly 600 feet (183 meters), then the town lay less than 7 miles (11 kilometers) away from Jerusalem.

Luke later names one of the disciples as Cleopas (Luke 24:18), whom some have suggested is the same as Clopas, the husband of a follower named Mary (John 19:25). This is unlikely, however. Although sounding similar, the names differ in origin, owing their difference to more than a mere spelling variation. Cleopas is a shortened version of the Greek name Cleopatros, while Clopas derives from Hebrew.

— 24:14-16 —

Luke describes their discussion using the verb *syzēteō* [4802], which carries the notion of bantering ideas back and forth. They undoubtedly did so with great emotion as the two sought answers to the questions "What happened?" and "Where did it all go wrong?" This conversation took place as the two walked along the road. Somewhere along the way, Jesus drew near and kept pace without identifying Himself. We read that the disciples' eyes "were prevented from recognizing Him."

The situation is similar to that relayed in Luke 9:45 (see comments there), and Luke deliberately leaves vague the reason for their inability. The verb "prevented" is passive, suggesting a divine passive, which implies that the action of the verb is completed by God. In another sense, which is just as likely, the passive tense could simply describe the disciples' personal inability. If God didn't restrict their vision, then something about *them* prevented their recognizing Jesus.

— 24:17-18 —

Jesus joined the discussion with a polite question: "What are these matters you are discussing?" Luke uses the term *antiballo* [474], a verb which means "to throw back and forth." The confused followers had been debating the possible reasons their expectations of the Messiah had come to such a disillusioning end.

Luke employs a narrative device called "literary irony," in which the reader has knowledge about the story that the characters do not have. Irony jumps off the page as one of the Emmaus-bound disciples chided Jesus: "Are You the only one . . . unaware of the things which have happened?" If the story were later read aloud in churches in the first century, listeners may have burst into laughter. If anyone understood what had happened, it was Jesus. The two disciples, however, were clueless!

— 24:19-24 —

Like a wise counselor, Jesus prompted Cleopas and the other disciple to explain their thoughts in order to get their problem out into the open. The grieving disciples summarized the Lord's ministry accurately enough (24:19-20) but failed to understand His mission. From their perspective, the notion "redeem Israel" included the expectation that Jesus would behave like a typical earthly king, delivering earthly, tangible, temporal blessings—only more righteously than any before Him. A king who was crucified could not establish this kind of kingdom— hence, their disillusionment. Their noble expectations for a social, political, and economic messiah had failed to materialize.

Hope is like a windowpane. It's clear enough, but if your focus is off, you can see only what's behind you. The men's faulty perspective prevented them from seeing what stood right in front of them—literally and figuratively. They were as blind to the facts of the Resurrection as they were to the face of Jesus. And what follows is an almost comical inability to assemble the clues and arrive at the obvious conclusion.

The two recounted the major facts of the day. They said, in so many words, "The women found the tomb empty, angels said the tomb was

583

empty because Jesus is alive, and some other people verified that the tomb is empty. But we can't figure out what happened."

— 24:25-27 —

The challenge for Jesus became clear: Adjust the disciples' perspective to help them see the true Messiah, His actual mission, and the real kingdom of God. He began with a rebuke and a rhetorical question. Both responses chastised the men for ignoring the clues in the prophecies, all of which pointed to the necessity of the Christ suffering and dying to redeem His people. Indeed, Jesus had called attention to this necessity several times in His ministry (9:22; 13:33; 17:25; 22:37).

The Jews of Jesus' day found prophecies concerning the Messiah very perplexing, as they seemed to present a dual image of the Christ. This future king was to suffer and die to save His people, yet He was to reign over a worldwide kingdom that would have no end. How could a dead king rule a kingdom? Some Jewish teachers have tried to solve the logical problem by suggesting the Messiah is really two individuals, one who dies as the "suffering servant" and the other who reigns as supreme king.[29]

Jesus reviewed the Hebrew Scriptures, starting with the beginning and working His way through the prophets. The reference to "Moses" points to his writings, the first five books of the Bible. Without directly identifying himself, he pointed to those portions of Scripture that referred to himself, specifically demonstrating the necessity of the sacrifice for becoming the kind of King that Cleopas and the other disciple hoped to serve. This could be accomplished if the "suffering servant" (see Isaiah 52:13–53:12) rose from the dead to rule as King.

— 24:28-31 —

In keeping with ancient Near Eastern rules of hospitality, the disciples then invited the "stranger" to stay the night. Jesus accepted their offer, yet maintained His cover in order to complete the lesson He had begun.

Luke doesn't explain how the breaking of bread opened the disciples' eyes. They may have seen the nail prints on His hands. Perhaps they had witnessed the feeding of the multitude in the wilderness and saw something familiar in the way He broke the matzo. All we can know for certain is that the eyes of the two disciples were suddenly able to see everything clearly—literally and figuratively—for the first time.

The statement "their eyes were opened and they recognized Him" could be better rendered in its context as "their eyes were *completely* opened and they came to *fully comprehend* Him." This action was more than a mere recognition of His features. They instantly connected all the dots. They came to recognize Jesus in all His significance as the Messiah, the Suffering Servant, the Son of God, and their risen Lord. Then, once their eyes were open, He suddenly vanished.

The irony is worth noting. These disciples had been staring into the face of the risen Jesus for hours, yet they did not see him until they buried their faulty expectations. A careful review of the Scriptures gave them a divine perspective on what they once saw as dismal circumstances. Then, once their eyes were opened to the divine perspective, Jesus became invisible to their physical eyes.

— 24:32-35 —

In a less literal way, such ironic experiences still happen today. Some of our Lord's best visits are those that we do not expect. And they often come at the lowest times: when a mate has walked away, when a loved one has died, when we're released from work, when the lessons of life seem unintelligible, when a sudden twist sends life in a different direction, when a good-bye takes a friend far away. Those are the times God Himself seems far away, when in fact, He's closer than ever—and we're closer to learning something important about Him.

Initially, these two disciples saw the trials, crucifixion, and burial of Jesus as the end of their hopes; and they were heading away from Jerusalem. By the end of their time with Jesus, they saw the same events as the fulfillment of God's prophetic promise, and now they were headed back to Jerusalem. The pair had left Jerusalem disbelieving the account of the Resurrection; they returned to Jerusalem when they had a story of their own to tell. By the time they arrived, Jesus had appeared to Peter.

— 24:36-43 —

Somewhere in Jerusalem, while the rest of the city continued to celebrate the Feast of Unleavened Bread and otherwise carried on with life as usual, a collection of Jesus' closest followers were assembled behind closed doors, most likely in the house of a wealthy believer. Later, as told in volume two of Luke's narrative (The Acts of the Apostles), the Lord's followers would gather in homes to sing, celebrate, share Communion, read Scripture, and encourage one another.

As the Lord's people huddled together for encouragement and safety, hope began to displace fear. Each told what he or she had experienced, and the community grew stronger. Then suddenly, they became aware of Jesus standing among them. In a reversal of what occurred at Luke 24:31, He joined the disciples without entering the room by normal means and comforted them with a greeting of "peace"—*shalom*.

The startled fear experienced by the group reinforced the supernatural nature of Jesus' sudden presence in the room. While the apostles had seen at least three people raised from the dead (7:14-16; 8:54-56; John 11:43-45), this was different. The people Jesus had brought back from beyond did not pass through walls or cross great distances in an instant. Keep in mind that in Jewish folklore, spirits visited the living only with bad intentions. To allay their fears about His being "a spirit"—presumably an evil one—Jesus offered tangible proof of His literal, bodily resurrection. His body bore visual evidence of His thirty-plus years on earth. He had flesh and bone that could be handled—real and tactile, not virtual and ethereal. And to settle any remaining doubts, He ate something in front of them!

While His body differed from the destructible flesh and bone of His earthly existence, He possessed a body nonetheless.

— 24:44-49 —

In His last appearance in Luke's narrative, Jesus showed His disciples how His earthly ministry and suffering had been predicted in the Hebrew Scriptures—"the Law of Moses and the Prophets and the Psalms" (Luke 24:44). The discourse as described here takes less than a minute to read, so Luke obviously condensed His message. Jesus undoubtedly spent several hours with His followers, calming their fears, answering their questions, comforting their sorrow, forgiving their sins, solidifying their faith, and preparing them for kingdom building without His physical presence.

His commissioning modeled the kind of preaching His followers were to emulate. He demonstrated from the Scriptures that the plan of God had *always* been to send His Son, who would suffer on behalf of His people and conquer death on the third day. The call of God had *always* been to repent of sin, receive His forgiveness, and trust that His grace is sufficient to save. The city of Jerusalem had *always* been the Lord's intended "light on a hill" (cf. Ps. 43:3; Matt. 5:14) and would finally become the starting point of world evangelism (cf. Isa. 43:10; 44:8; Acts 1:8), under the guidance of Jesus, the incorruptible King.

Jesus assured His followers they had a message the world needs to hear (Luke 24:47). But even the apostles did not yet possess the power necessary to take the torch and run with it. The Lord's proclamation is densely packed with meaningful terms and expressions. The term for "witnesses" is *martys* [3144], from which we derive the English term "martyr." The "promise of My Father" (24:49) refers to the Holy Spirit, by whom they would soon be "clothed with power," a word picture taken from the commissioning ceremony of a government official. The qualification "from on high," of course, declares the source of their commissioning and power: God Himself.

This remarkable passage foreshadows many of the key themes and events in the Acts of the Apostles. Geographically, the two volumes form a reflection of each other as they express these themes. In the Gospel of Luke, Jesus journeys from Galilee to Jerusalem and into the temple. Following the Gospel's account of Jesus' ascension from the Mount of Olives, adjacent to the temple, Acts recounts His ascension—with attention to different details—and traces the growth of the church beginning with the coming of the Holy Spirit in Jerusalem (Acts 2). Acts then traces the proclamation of the gospel message, beginning in Jerusalem and emanating through Judea to Samaria, Galilee, and beyond.

John MacArthur succinctly demonstrates the overlap between the closing of Luke's first volume and the opening of his second volume, Acts, noting these similarities:

- Christ's suffering and resurrection (Luke 24:46; Acts 1:3);
- the message of repentance and remission of sins (Luke 24:47; Acts 2:38);
- the disciples as His witnesses (Luke 24:48; Acts 1:8);
- the Promise of the Father (Luke 24:49; Acts 1:4);
- tarrying in Jerusalem (Luke 24:49; Acts 1:4);
- the beginning of gospel outreach [in Jerusalem] (Luke 24:47; Acts 1:8);
- power from on high (Luke 24:49; Acts 1:8);
- Christ's ascension (Luke 24:51; Acts 1:9-11);
- the disciples' return to Jerusalem (Luke 24:52; Acts 1:12);
- and their meeting in the temple (Luke 24:53; Acts 2:46).[30]

— 24:50-53 —

After comforting and commissioning His apostles, Jesus led them out of hiding into the light of day. They walked together through the streets of Jerusalem, across the Kidron Valley, and up the western slope of the Mount of Olives, over the ridge to the eastern side. This is a deeply meaningful location in Hebrew history and end-time literature. When the light of God's presence departed the forsaken temple, never to be seen there again, "the glory of the Lord went up from the midst of the city and stood over the mountain which is east of the city" (Ezek. 11:23). The prophet Zechariah saw the Messiah come in power to this location:

> In that day His feet will stand on the Mount of Olives, which is in front of Jerusalem on the east; and the Mount of Olives will be split in its middle from east to west by a very large valley, so that half of the mountain will move toward the north and the other half toward the south. (Zech. 14:4)

At this prophetically crucial location, Jesus turned to face His followers, lifted His hands for a benediction, blessed them, and ascended to heaven while they watched. The followers of Jesus worshiped, shared the joy of His victory over the dominion of evil, and then returned to Jerusalem as He had instructed.

Luke's concluding summary statement describes the believers' action with an imperfect participle construction, showing ongoing action: The followers of Jesus "were continually in the temple praising God" (Luke 24:53). The corruption of the temple establishment would not be able to squelch the truth of the Resurrection. As the Holy Spirit fell like lightning on the followers of Christ, the light of the gospel would emanate from God's holy hill against the crippled forces of darkness that continued (and still continue) to act in this world.

APPLICATION: LUKE 24:13-53

What the Ascension Means

As we wrap up our reflections on the Gospel of Luke, let me repeat part of its last two verses: "They returned to Jerusalem with great joy, and were continually in the temple praising God" (24:52-53). This isn't a description of a body of defeated, broken people, huddling in despair and wallowing in regret. They've seen the resurrected Christ! They've watched His ascension into heaven!

They knew that this wasn't an abandonment. From His exalted position at the right hand of the Father, He would send His Spirit. And through the ever-present, indwelling Spirit, Christ's presence would be mediated to His people. Christ said, "I will not leave you as orphans; I will come to you" (John 14:18). So, the Ascension means not only that

Christ has been exalted on high, but also that He is able to draw near to us in an intimate fellowship through the Spirit. Let's consider both of these aspects of the Ascension.

First, *the ascended Lord draws near.* He comes alongside us by the power of the Spirit. Though He is always present with us, sometimes we experience this closeness more than other times. I don't want to get overly mystical, but sometimes it's obvious. He answers a prayer in an unexpected way, reminds us of His provision, or makes clear His protection of us. Of course, in our case, no sound fills the room, no sudden burst from heaven. But we "sense" His active presence in our lives. He's there with us, just as He is at the right hand of the Father. Do you remember a time in your past when you have experienced that? Perhaps when things seemed very bleak and very difficult? When you had more questions than answers? When your losses seemed to outnumber your gains? When it was night and seemed like dawn would never come again? And then He came alongside you? Because of His ascension, our hearts are calmed. Our panic subsides. Our fears are relieved. He draws near to us in our lowly state.

Second, *the ascended Lord is seated on high.* He is "far above all rule and authority and power and dominion, and every name that is named" (Eph. 1:21). He is our great High Priest, "able also to save forever those who draw near to God through Him, since He always lives to make intercession for them" (Heb. 7:25). What an awesome Savior we have, who is seated above anything or anyone who could ever do us harm! How glorious a High Priest who serves as our eternal mediator before the throne of God! And because of His love, God has also "raised us up with Him and seated us with Him in the heavenly places in Christ Jesus" (Eph. 2:6). We can "draw near with confidence to the throne of grace, so that we may receive mercy and find grace to help in time of need" (Heb. 4:16). Because of His ascension, our hearts are calmed. Our panic subsides. Our fears are relieved. We draw near to Him in His high position.

ENDNOTES

INTRODUCTION

1. See Charles R. Swindoll, *Swindoll's Living Insights New Testament Commentary*, vol. 6, *Romans* (Carol Stream, IL: Tyndale House, 2015), 375.
2. W. M. Ramsay, *Luke the Physician and Other Studies in the History of Religion* (London: Hodder & Stoughton, 1908), 35–36.
3. Everett Ferguson, *Backgrounds of Early Christianity*, 2nd ed. (Grand Rapids: Eerdmans, 1993), 101–102.
4. Darrell L. Bock, *Luke 1:1–9:50*, Baker Exegetical Commentary on the New Testament (Grand Rapids: Baker, 1994), 9.
5. Interestingly, Luke chose a similar structure for volume two of his history (Acts), which shows the gospel flowing out of Jerusalem, through Samaria and Galilee, and to the farthest reaches of the earth (see Acts 1:8).

LUKE'S PREFACE (LUKE 1:1-4)

1. John W. Gardner, *Excellence: Can We Be Equal and Excellent Too?*, rev. ed. (New York: W. W. Norton & Company, 1995), 102.
2. Mitchell Landsberg, "Claremont Seminary Reaches Beyond Christianity," *The Los Angeles Times*, June 9, 2010.
3. Martin Luther, quoted in Ewald M. Plass, ed., *What Luther Says: An Anthology*, vol. 3 (St. Louis: Concordia, 1959), 1392.
4. Luke most likely used Mark's Gospel as one of his sources.
5. The Holy Spirit prompted Luke to write, superintended the work, spurred him to excellence, and kept him from error. This is not typical of every Christian's efforts.

ANNOUNCED AND APPEARING (LUKE 1:5-4:13)

1. Gerhard Kittel and Gerhard Friedrich, eds., *Theological Dictionary of the New Testament: Abridged in One Volume*, trans. Geoffrey W. Bromiley (Grand Rapids: Eerdmans, 1995), 316.
2. Macrobius, *The Saturnalia*, trans. Percival Vaughan Davies (New York: Columbia University Press, 1969), 171.
3. Flavius Josephus, *Wars of the Jews* 1.6.2, in *The Works of Josephus: Complete and Unabridged*, trans. William Whiston (Peabody, MA: Hendrickson, 1996); cf. Flavius Josephus, *Antiquities of the Jews* 14.1.3, in *The Works of Josephus: Complete and Unabridged*, trans. William Whiston (Peabody, MA: Hendrickson, 1996).
4. Gerhard Kittel and Gerhard Friedrich, eds., *Theological Dictionary of the New Testament*, vol. 3, ed. and trans. Geoffrey W. Bromiley (Grand Rapids: Eerdmans, 1973), 262.
5. Excerpted from Charles R. Swindoll, *A Bethlehem Christmas: Celebrating the Joyful Season* (Nashville: Thomas Nelson, 2007), 15–19.
6. Mishnah *Tamid* 7:2, in Jacob Neusner, trans., *The Mishnah: A New Translation* (New Haven, CT: Yale University Press, 1988), 871.

7 Bock, *Luke 1:1–9:50*, 95.
8 John Paul II, *L'Osservatore Romano*, English edition, April 16, 1997, 7.
9 Gerhard Kittel and Gerhard Friedrich, eds., *Theological Dictionary of the New Testament*, vol. 5, ed. and trans. Geoffrey W. Bromiley, (Grand Rapids: Eerdmans, 1973), 828.
10 Adapted from Swindoll, *Bethlehem Christmas*, 168–170.
11 Helen H. Lemmel, "Turn Your Eyes Upon Jesus" (Singspiration, 1922 [Renewal, 1950]).
12 Bock, *Luke 1:1–9:50*, 905.
13 Gerhard Kittel and Gerhard Friedrich, eds., *Theological Dictionary of the New Testament*, vol. 6, ed. and trans. Geoffrey W. Bromiley (Grand Rapids: Eerdmans, 1973), 491.
14 W. Dittenberger, *Sylloge inscriptionum Graecarum* (Leipzig, 1915–24), cited by I. Howard Marshall, *The Gospel of Luke: A Commentary on the Greek Text*, The New International Greek Testament Commentary (Exeter, UK: Paternoster Press, 1978), 109.
15 Tom Constable, *Tom Constable's Expository Notes on the Bible* (Galaxie Software, 2003), Luke 2:10.
16 Stonemasons and bricklayers measure their work against a single cornerstone. Every aspect of the building must be plumb, level, and square in relation to the cornerstone.
17 Josephus, *Wars of the Jews* 2.89.
18 See Bruce B. Barton, Mark Fackler, Linda K. Taylor, and David R. Veerman, *Matthew*, Life Application Bible Commentary, ed. Grant Osborne and Philip Comfort (Carol Stream, IL: Tyndale House, 1996), 35.
19 Mishnah *Pirqe Abot* 5:21 A.
20 Mishnah *Nidda* 5:6 D-E.
21 Kittel and Friedrich, *Theological Dictionary of the New Testament: Abridged*, 219.
22 Mishnah *Pirqe Abot* 5:21 A.
23 Kittel and Friedrich, *Theological Dictionary of the New Testament: Abridged*, 939.
24 Steven Curtis Chapman, "This Baby" (Sparrow Records, 1995).
25 Geoffrey W. Bromiley, ed., *International Standard Bible Encyclopedia* (Grand Rapids: Eerdmans, 1979), 1:128.
26 See Everett Ferguson, *Baptism in the Early Church: History, Theology, and Liturgy in the First Five Centuries* (Grand Rapids: Eerdmans, 2009), 33. There is some dispute about whether the rabbinical sources describing "proselyte baptism" reflect a later post-Christian development or a practice that was current at the time of Christ and the founding of the church. For a discussion, see ibid., 76–82.
27 Mishnah *Pirqe Abot* 5:21 A.
28 Dietrich Bonhoeffer, *Creation and Fall: Temptation* (New York: Touchstone, 1997), 132.
29 Josephus, *Antiquities* 15.11.5.
30 Martin Luther, quoted in Ewald M. Plass, ed., *What Luther Says: An Anthology*, vol. 1 (St. Louis: Concordia: 1959), 395.

MINISTERING AND SERVING (LUKE 4:14–9:50)

1 C. H. Spurgeon, *Lectures to My Students: A Selection from Addresses Delivered to the Students of the Pastors' College, Metropolitan Tabernacle*, vol. 1 (London, 1875), 173.
2 Flavius Josephus, *The Life of Flavius Josephus*, trans. William Whiston, *The Works of Josephus: Complete and Unabridged* (Peabody: Hendrickson, 1996), 87.
3 Josephus, *Wars of the Jews* 3.2.

4   A "lectionary" divides Scripture into sections to be read in church on certain dates.

5   Alfred Edersheim, *Sketches of Jewish Social Life in the Days of Christ* (Bellingham, WA: Logos Research Systems, 2003), 277–278; see also Mishnah *Megillah* 4:1-2.

6   Bock, *Luke 1:1–9:50*, 404.

7   Frederick W. Seward, *Seward at Washington as Senator and Secretary of State* (New York: Derby and Miller, 1891), 197.

8   Walter Liefeld, "Luke" in *The Expositor's Bible Commentary*, ed. Frank. E. Gaebelein, vol. 8 (Grand Rapids: Zondervan, 1984), 871.

9   Dietrich Bonhoeffer, quoted in Eric Metaxas, *Bonhoeffer: Pastor, Martyr, Prophet, Spy: A Righteous Gentile vs. The Third Reich* (Nashville: Thomas Nelson, 2010), 321.

10 Marshall, *Gospel of Luke*, 208.

11 V. George Shillington, *An Introduction to the Study of Luke-Acts*, T & T Clark Approaches to Biblical Studies (London: T & T Clark, 2007), 136.

12 C. S. Lewis, *Mere Christianity*, rev. ed. (New York: Macmillan, 1965), 40.

13 Brennan Manning, *Abba's Child: The Cry of the Heart for Intimate Belonging* (Colorado Springs: NavPress, 2002), 80.

14 William Barclay, *The Gospel of Luke* (Louisville, KY: Westminster Press, 2001), 81.

15 John F. Walvoord and Roy B. Zuck, eds., *The Bible Knowledge Commentary: An Exposition of the Scriptures by Dallas Seminary Faculty*, vol. 2 (Wheaton, IL: Victor, 1983), 45.

16 Geoffrey W. Bromiley, ed., *The International Standard Bible Encyclopedia*, vol. 4, rev. ed. (Grand Rapids: Eerdmans, 1988), 251.

17 William P. Barker, *Twelve Who Were Chosen: The Disciples of Jesus* (New York: Revel, 1957), 121.

18 Walvoord and Zuck, *Bible Knowledge Commentary*, vol. 2, 220.

19 Walter Bauer et al., *A Greek-English Lexicon of the New Testament and Other Early Christian Literature*, 3rd ed. (Chicago: University of Chicago Press, 2000), 510.

20 Ibid., 256.

21 Center for Disease Control and Prevention, "Twenty Leading Causes of Death Highlighting Suicide Among Persons Ages 10 Years and Older, United States, 2006."

22 Thornton Wilder, *Theophilus North* (New York: HarperCollins, 2003), 291–292.

23 John J. Rousseau and Rami Arav, *Jesus and His World: An Archaeological and Cultural Dictionary* (Minneapolis: Fortress, 1995), 213.

24 See description of ancient Jewish burial preparation and funerals in S. Safrai, "Home and Family," in S. Safrai and M. Stern, eds., *The Jewish People in the First Century: Historical Geography, Political History, Social, Cultural, and Religious Life and Institutions*, vol. 2 (Philadelphia: Fortress, 1987), 776–780.

25 Bock, *Luke 1:1–9:50*, 652.

26 Blaise Pascal, "Thoughts," trans. W. F. Trotter, *The Harvard Classics*, vol. 48, ed. Charles L. Eliot (New York: P. F. Collier & Sons, 1910), 97.

27 Alfred Tennyson, *In Memoriam* (Charleston, SC: BiblioBazaar, 2008), 143.

28 Pascal, "Thoughts," 97.

29 Gladys M. Hunt, "That's No Generation Gap!" *Eternity* (October 1969), 15.

30 Bock, *Luke 1:1–9:50*, 695.

31 See Martin Luther, *Hausz-Postill* (Lüneburg: Johann und Heinrich Stern, 1638), 182.

32 Gerald L. Mattingly, "Plow, Plowshare," in David Noel Freedman and Allen C. Myers, eds., *Eerdmans Dictionary of the Bible* (Grand Rapids: Eerdmans, 2000), 1064–1065.

33 The middle voice with this verb is rare in the New Testament, used elsewhere only in Luke 2:37 and 1 Timothy 4:1. In both cases, the context clearly indicates a choice to withdraw from something.

34 Robert L. Thomas, *Revelation 8–22: An Exegetical Commentary* (Chicago: Moody, 1995), 440.

35 Pliny, *Natural History* 16.74.

36 See Bock, *Luke 1:1–9:50*, 774. See also A. T. Robertson (*Word Pictures of the New Testament*, vol. 1, *The Gospel According to Matthew, The Gospel According to Mark*, rev. and updated ed., ed. Wesley J. Perschbacher [Grand Rapids: Kregel, 2004], 223), who suggests that, at the time of Augustus, "a full Roman legion had 6,100 foot soldiers and 726 horse soldiers."

37 Mishnah *Nidda* 5:6; 6:11.

38 Esther Juhasz, "Tzitzit," in Raphael Patai and Haya Bar-Tizhak, eds., *Encyclopedia of Jewish Folklore and Traditions*, vols. 1–2 (New York: Routledge, 2015), 548.

39 Kittel and Friedrich, *Theological Dictionary of the New Testament: Abridged*, 219.

40 Ibid., 838.

41 Bock, *Luke 1:1–9:50*, 817.

42 Josephus, *Antiquities* 18.28.

43 Bauer et al., *Greek-English Lexicon*, 36.

44 Metonymy is a figure of speech in which the expression symbolizes something closely associated with it. For example, "the White House" is often used as a metonym for the President of the United States: "The White House expressed concern for the economy in a speech to the nation."

45 According to a 2006 interview with Gagarin's close friend, Colonel Valentin Petrov, the words were not actually spoken by the cosmonaut but were attributed to him after a statement by Nikita Khrushchev in the Central Committee of the CPSU. While promoting the state's official atheist policy, the Premier said (according to Petrov), "Why should you clutch at God? Here is Gagarin who flew to space but saw no God there." (See *Interfax*, "I am proud to be accused of having introduced Yury Gagarin to Orthodoxy" [April 12, 2006].) At the time, the Central Committee wanted the quote attributed to Gagarin, and he was not in a position to object!

INSTRUCTING AND SUBMITTING (LUKE 9:51–19:27)

1 J. Goetzmann, "Conversion, Penitence, Repentance, Proselyte," in *The New International Dictionary of New Testament Theology*, ed. Colin Brown (Grand Rapids: Zondervan, 1986), 1:357.

2 Josephus, *Antiquities* 13.254–256.

3 Martin Luther, *Commentary on Peter & Jude*, trans. and ed. John Nichols Lenker (Grand Rapids: Kregel, 1990), 207.

4 H. Norman Schwarzkopf, *It Doesn't Take a Hero: The Autobiography* (New York: Bantam, 1992), 200.

5 2 Enoch 29:4-5. Translation taken from Robert Henry Charles, ed., *Pseudepigrapha of the Old Testament*, vol. 2 (Bellingham, WA: Logos Research Systems, 2004), 446.

6 *The Testament of Solomon* 114. Translation taken from F. C. Conybeare, "The Testament of Solomon," *The Jewish Quarterly Review* 11.41 (1898): 40.

7 David Maraniss, *When Pride Still Mattered: A Life of Vince Lombardi* (New York: Touchstone, 1999), 274.

8 Bauer et al., *Greek-English Lexicon*, 804.

9 Darrell L. Bock, *Luke 9:51–24:53*, Baker Exegetical Commentary on the New Testament (Grand Rapids: Baker, 1998), 1056.

10 Imperative verbs express a command; indicative verbs state a fact or describe a reality.

11 The verb for "seek" is generally used in the context of seeking God Himself, not merely for what one wants from Him (see Exod. 33:7; Deut. 4:29; Ps. 105:4; Isa. 55:6; 65:1).

[12] Helmut Thielecke, *Encounter with Spurgeon*, trans. John W. Doberstein (Philadelphia: Fortress, 1963), 14.

[13] Quoted in "I Made Mistakes," interview with Richard Dortch, *Christianity Today*, March 18, 1988, 46–47.

[14] John Piper, *Brothers, We Are Not Professionals: A Plea to Pastors for Radical Ministry* (Nashville, TN: B & H Publishing Group, 2002).

[15] Max Lucado, *UpWords* (San Antonio, TX: UpWords Radio Ministry, May 1993), 2.

[16] Alfred Edersheim, *The Life and Times of Jesus the Messiah*, vol. 2 (London: Longmans, Green, and Co., 1883), 11.

[17] Marshall, *Gospel of Luke*, 499.

[18] Kittel and Friedrich, *Theological Dictionary of the New Testament: Abridged*, 1236.

[19] G. K. Beale and D. A. Carson, eds., *Commentary on the New Testament Use of the Old Testament* (Grand Rapids: Baker, 2007), 327.

[20] William Hendriksen and Simon J. Kistemaker, *Exposition of the Gospel According to Matthew*, New Testament Commentary (Grand Rapids: Baker, 1982), 529.

[21] Paul Tsongas on *NewsHour*, Public Broadcasting Station, April 10, 1991.

[22] Quoted by Anna Quindlen, *A Short Guide to a Happy Life* (New York: Random House, 2000), 4–7.

[23] Neusner, *Mishnah*, 806–807.

[24] Liefeld, "Luke," 961.

[25] Arthur Somers Roche, quoted in Bob Phillips, *Phillips' Book of Great Thoughts and Funny Sayings: A Stupendous Collection of Quotes, Quips, Epigrams, Witticisms, and Humorous Comments. For Personal Enjoyment and Ready Reference* (Carol Stream, IL: Tyndale House, 1993), 21.

[26] Charles H. Spurgeon, *Faith's Checkbook* (New Kensington, PA: Whitaker House, 1992), 307.

[27] Stephanie Ambrose May, quoted by Peggy and Clayton Bell in "A Look at Grief," *Leadership* 1, no. 4 (1980), 40–51.

[28] Bromiley, *International Standard Bible Encyclopedia*, 4:544.

[29] See Niels Jørgen Cappelørn, "The Restrospective Understanding of Søren Kierkegaard's Total Production," in Daniel W. Conway and K. E. Gover, eds., *Søren Kierkegaard: Critical Assessments of Leading Philosophers*, vol. 1, *Authorship and Authenticity: Kierkegaard and Pseudonyms* (New York: Routledge, 2002), 21.

[30] *Merriam-Webster's Collegiate Dictionary*, 10th ed. (Springfield, MA: Merriam-Webster, 1996), s.v. "hate."

[31] Constable, *Tom Constable's Expository Notes*, Luke 14:34.

[32] Keith Miller and Bruce Larson, *The Edge of Adventure* (Dallas: Word, 1977), 189.

[33] In the first two stories, Jesus conceded the perspective of prideful humanity. In truth, as every true disciple eventually learns, *all* have gone astray! (See Isa. 53:6.) He saved this crucial correction for His third story.

[34] C. S. Lewis, *The Problem of Pain* (New York: HarperCollins, 1996), 93–94.

[35] Kenneth E. Bailey, *The Cross and the Prodigal: Luke 15 through the Eyes of Middle Eastern Peasants*, rev. and exp. ed. (Downers Grove: InterVarsity, 2005), 71.

[36] Mishnah *Gittin* 9:10 A-F.

[37] Bauer et al., *Greek-English Lexicon*, 879.

[38] Many of the earliest manuscripts do not have verse 36, suggesting that later copyists assimilated Matthew 24:40. With or without the third vignette, the illustration is the same. Nothing about the meaning is affected either way.

[39] Matthew E. Carlton, *The Translator's Reference Translation of the Gospel of Luke* (Dallas: SIL International, 2008), 342.

[40] Talmudic Tractate, *Berakhoth* 28b, quoted in Edersheim, *Life and Times*, 291.

[41] Bauer et al., *Greek-English Lexicon*, 563.

[42] Josephus, *Wars of the Jews* 1.138.

⁴³ Ibid., 4.469.

⁴⁴ The verb tense is aorist to be precise. The aorist tense describes the action of a verb in summary fashion, without specifying when the action takes place. The "mood" of the verb and the context determine when the action is completed. The indicative mood together with the aorist tense usually points to a past event.

CONQUERING AND COMMISSIONING (LUKE 19:28–24:53)

¹ Bock, *Luke 9:51–24:53*, 1698.

² Josephus, *Wars of the Jews* 5.465–470.

³ Ibid., 7.1.3.

⁴ While chief priests, scribes, and elders performed distinct functions, they nevertheless overlapped. For example, a chief priest could be a scribe, and a man of any occupation could bear the title of "elder."

⁵ Bauer et al., *Greek-English Lexicon*, 341.

⁶ Psalm 90 is taken from Deuteronomy 32–33.

⁷ Josephus, *Wars of the Jews* 2.164–166.

⁸ Josephus, *Antiquities* 18.16.

⁹ James Russell Lowell, "The Present Crisis," in James Russell Lowell, *The Poetical Works of James Russell Lowell in Five Volumes*, vol. 1, *Earlier Poems, The Vision of Sir Launfal*, The Complete Writings of James Russell Lowell, vol. 9 (New York: Houghton Mifflin, 1904), 188.

¹⁰ Ibid.

¹¹ Adapted from Charles R. Swindoll, *Jesus: The Greatest Life of All* (Nashville: Thomas Nelson, 2008), 169–170.

¹² Josephus, *Wars of the Jews* 5.224.

¹³ Martin Luther, quoted in Roland H. Bainton, *Here I Stand: A Life of Martin Luther* (New York: Penquin, 1995), 146.

¹⁴ Josephus, *Wars of the Jews* 2.254–255.

¹⁵ Bauer et al., *Greek-English Lexicon*, 321.

¹⁶ Mishnah *Sanhedrin* 4.1E, 4.1H.

¹⁷ F. B. Meyer, *Christ in Isaiah* (Fort Washington, PA: Christian Literature Crusade, [n.d.]), 9.

¹⁸ Mishnah *Sanhedrin* 11:2.

¹⁹ Morten Hørning Jensen, *Herod Antipas in Galilee*, 2nd ed., *Wissenschaftliche Untersuchungen zum Neuen Testament* 2. Reihe (Tübingen: Mohr Siebeck, 2010), 240.

²⁰ In truth, as a son of Herod the Great, Antipas was Idumean. Idumeans were Edomites, a people descended not from Jacob, but from Esau, who had sold his birthright as the oldest son in the line of God's covenant people (Gen. 25:29-34). The Edomite nation had been a sworn enemy of Israel since the Exodus (Num. 20:14-21).

²¹ Jerusalem Talmud, *Shevi'it* 9:1.

²² Johannes P. Louw and Eugene Albert Nida, *Greek-English Lexicon of the New Testament: Based on Semantic Domains*, vol. 1, 2nd ed. (New York: United Bible Societies, 1996), 489.

²³ Cicero, *The Verrine Orations*, vol. 2, trans. L. H. G. Greenwood (Cambridge: Harvard University Press, 1976), 655.

²⁴ *Merriam-Webster's Collegiate Dictionary*, 11th ed. (Springfield, MA: Merriam-Webster, 2003), s.v. "death."

²⁵ Bauer et al., *Greek-English Lexicon*, 258.

²⁶ Bock, *Luke 9:51–24:53*, 1898.

²⁷ Bauer et al., *Greek-English Lexicon*, 767.

²⁸ Merrill C. Tenney, *The Reality of the Resurrection* (New York: Harper & Row, 1963), 119.

[29] Joseph Klausner, *The Messianic Idea in Israel: From Its Beginning to the Completion of the Mishnah*, trans. W.F. Stinespring (New York: Macmillan, 1955), 11.

[30] John MacArthur, *The MacArthur Study Bible* (Nashville: Word, 1997), 1534.